Life and Fate

Vasily Grossman was born in 1905 in the Ukrainian town of Berdichev, the home of one of the largest Jewish communities in Eastern Europe. In 1933 he published his first novel, *Gluchkauf*. This, and his second novel, *Stepan Kolchagin*, were typical of the official Soviet literature of the time.

During World War II Grossman worked for the army newspaper *Red Star*, reporting on the defence of Stalingrad and the fall of Berlin. An eye-witness of the consequences of the Holocaust, he published the first journalist's account of a German death-camp in any language. In 1952 he published a novel about Stalingrad, *For a Just Cause*.

In 1960 Grossman completed *Life and Fate* and submitted it to an official literary journal. A year later two KGB officers arrived at his home with orders to confiscate not only the manuscript but even sheets of used carbon paper and typewriter ribbons. Grossman was told that there was no question of the novel being published for another two hundred years. Somehow, however, a copy of the manuscript found its way into the hands of Vladimir Voinovich, a leading dissident, who brought it on microfilm to the West.

Vasily Grossman died in September 1964, having completed a short novel, *Everything Flows*, that he had begun in 1955.

'As a piece of literature, *Life and Fate* is the most important work to have come out of the Soviet Union so far.' Kyril FitzLyon/*The Literary Review*

'This extraordinary novel . . . remains as remarkable a document of the conflicts of daily working lives under political and moral stress as we are likely to be given.' Elaine Feinstein/*TLS*

'The richest and most vivid account to be found of what the Second World War meant to the Soviet Union . . . I shall never forget this utterly convincing and startingly vivid picture of the semi-barbaric life of soldiers and workers among the rubble and the wrecked machines . . . No more powerful war novel has come from any country for many years past.' H. T. Willetts/*The Times*

'The humanity and grace with which Grossman reconstructs the tragic death of 350,000 people at Stalingrad recalls Tolstoy; the great sadness with which Grossman imbues discussions of solidarity, friendship, dignity recalls Dostoevsky; the gentleness and sensitivity with which Grossman eulogizes the simple life recalls Chekhov.' *Il Giorno*

'A historical fresco, a monumental work, *the* great Russian novel of the twentieth century.' *Le Monde*

'The novel is visually brilliant . . . some truly Tolstoyan moments' Norman Shrapnel/*The Guardian*

'Passages of such strength that one will remember them for ever . . . superb documentary reporting' Penelope Lively/*The Sunday Telegraph*

Vasily Grossman

Life and Fate

Translated by
Robert Chandler

FLAMINGO

Published by Fontana Paperbacks

First published in Great Britain
by Collins Harvill 1985

This Flamingo edition first published
in 1986 by Fontana Paperbacks,
8 Grafton Street, London W1X 3LA

Flamingo is an imprint of
Fontana Paperbacks, part of
the Collins Publishing Group

Made and printed in Great Britain by
William Collins Sons & Co. Ltd, Glasgow

CONTENTS

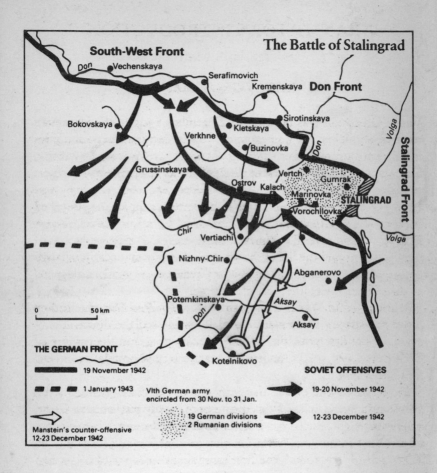

The Battle of Stalingrad

South-West Front

Don — Vechenskaya
Serafimovich
Kremenskaya — **Don Front**
Sirotinskaya
Bokovskaya
Kletskaya
Verkhne
Buzinovka
Grussinskaya
Vertch.
Ostrov — Kalach
Gumrak
Marinovka — **STALINGRAD**
Vorochilovka
Chir
Vertiachi
Nizhny-Chir
Abganerovo
Potemkinskaya
Aksay
Don
Aksay
Kotelnikovo

Volga
Stalingrad Front
Volga

THE GERMAN FRONT

	19 November 1942

| — — — | 1 January 1943 |

Vlth German army
encircled from 30 Nov. to 31 Jan.

⟶ Manstein's counter-offensive
12-23 December 1942

19 German divisions
2 Rumanian divisions

0   50 km

SOVIET OFFENSIVES

| ➤ | 19-20 November 1942 |

| ➤ | 12-23 December 1942 |

TRANSLATOR'S INTRODUCTION

VASILY GROSSMAN

Vasily Grossman was born on 12 December 1905 in the Ukrainian town of Berdichev, the home of one of the largest Jewish communities in Eastern Europe. After studying chemistry at Moscow University, Grossman worked in a mine in the Donbass as an engineer and expert on safety precautions. In 1933 he moved to Moscow, where he was 'discovered' by Maxim Gorky; with the latter's support, he published his first novel, *Glückhauf*. It was followed by a long novel, *Stepan Kolchagin*, and several volumes of short stories, mostly evocations of the Civil War and the life of the workers. Despite an occasional vivid detail or slightly risky piece of philosophizing, these works are typical of the official Soviet literature of the time.

During World War II Grossman worked for *Red Star*, the leading army newspaper. Grossman personally witnessed the disastrous retreats of the first year, the defence of Stalingrad and the capture of Berlin. As a war correspondent, he was second in popularity only to Ilya Ehrenburg.

He was also one of the first witnesses of the consequences of the Holocaust. His articles on this theme were mostly published in *Unity*, a newspaper produced for international distribution by the Jewish anti-Fascist committee. In the Russian journal *Znamya* he published 'The Hell of Treblinka', the first journalistic account of a German death-camp in any language. Together with Ilya Ehrenburg, Grossman was on the editorial committee of the *Black Book*, a massive anthology – yet to be printed in the Soviet Union – of documents relating to the Holocaust.

It was this collective tragedy – together with the death, at the hands of the Germans, of his own mother – that led Grossman to become conscious of his Jewish roots. His mother, a schoolteacher, had stayed behind in Berdichev in order to look after a sick niece. She apparently continued working even after the Jews had been confined to the ghetto. Her fate is evoked with extraordinary eloquence and power in one of the most moving passages of *Life and Fate*.

As the Cold War began in the autumn of 1946, Grossman was viciously attacked by several of the most authoritative Soviet literary critics. The occasion was the publication of his play, *If You Believe the Pythagoreans*. Ideologically unorthodox views put in the mouth of an extremely negative character were taken as an expression of Grossman's own beliefs. However orthodox these were at that time, his naturally philosophical cast of mind was a danger to him; it was hazardous to present unorthodox views in any guise – even if one then went on to refute them.

In 1943 Grossman had begun work on an epic novel about Stalingrad. In 1952 it was published in instalments in *Novy Mir* under the title *For a Just Cause*. Grossman enjoyed the full support of both Tvardovsky, the editor of *Novy Mir*, and Fadeev, the General Secretary of the Writers' Union. The initial reviews were highly favourable.

In February 1953, however, as a new series of purges, directed particularly at Jews, gathered momentum, Grossman was again attacked, possibly at the instigation of Stalin himself. During the following months he was repeatedly and hysterically denounced as a Jewish nationalist, a reactionary idealist alienated from Soviet society; Fadeev himself took part in these attacks. Grossman was saved from almost certain arrest not by his own 'letter of repentance', but by the change in the political climate following Stalin's death in March 1953. In 1954 *For a Just Cause* was republished in book form, once again with Fadeev's seal of approval.

The remaining years of the fifties were a time of public success for Grossman. *For a Just Cause*, acclaimed as a Soviet *War and Peace*, was republished several times, together with collections of his stories and articles written during the thirties and forties. In 1955 Grossman was awarded the important decoration 'The Banner of Labour'. Meanwhile he was writing his two great works, *Life and Fate* and *Everything Flows*.

*

8

Grossman completed *Life and Fate* in 1960. Originally intended as a sequel to *For a Just Cause*, in the event it was written in an entirely different spirit and can best be seen as a separate novel that happens to portray many of the same characters. *For a Just Cause* has pretensions towards the epic quality of Tolstoy, but is deadened by its ideological conformity; *Life and Fate* is the true *War and Peace* of this century, the most complete portrait of Stalinist Russia we have or are ever likely to have. The power of the other great dissident writers – Pasternak, Nadezhda Mandelstam, Solzhenitsyn – derives from their position as outsiders in Soviet society; Grossman's power derives from his extraordinarily intimate knowledge of every level of Soviet society.

Grossman delivered the manuscript to the editors of the journal *Znamya*. One can speculate on his reasons for doing this; it is possible that he seriously imagined the novel to be publishable – this was, after all, the height of Khruschev's 'thaw'. In any case, the editors wasted no time in handing over the manuscript to the Cultural Section of the Central Committee. A year later it was returned to Grossman with a brief note to the effect that the novel was anti-Soviet. In February 1961 two KGB officers came to his home with orders to confiscate the manuscript. They took away every scrap of paper they could lay their hands on, even sheets of used carbon paper and typewriter ribbons; Grossman told them the whereabouts of any remaining copies or fragments.

It is worth noting that the only other book to have merited such serious attention from the Soviet authorities is *The Gulag Archipelago*, a work of history rather than imaginative literature. Pasternak, for example, made no attempt to conceal the existence of *Doctor Zhivago*. He gave copies to friends and editors and even trusted the manuscript to the Soviet postal service. The attacks on Pasternak were unleashed not by the discovery of the novel's existence, but by its eventual publication abroad.

Grossman wrote to the Politburo to request the return of his manuscript. In response, Suslov, the principal Party ideologist, told him that there could be no question of *Life and Fate* being published for another two hundred years. Many people have commented on the extraordinary presumption of this remark; the emigré writer Vladimir Voinovich, on the other hand, has said that what he finds most striking is Suslov's unquestioning recognition of the novel's lasting importance.

The fate of the manuscript during the next twenty years is uncertain. There are reports that Grossman wanted to do further work on the novel, and that he complained bitterly to a friend that the absence of even a rough version was unbearable. It appears that the KGB did indeed confiscate every copy of the manuscript. Nevertheless, as Simon Markish has said in *Le Cas Grossman* (Julliard/L'Age d'Homme, 1983): 'We know now from a reliable source that one of the principal dissidents of the mid-seventies – who wishes not to divulge his name in view of possible harmful repercussions on other people – somehow obtained a copy of the manuscript, copied it and had the microfilm smuggled abroad.'

And, in a speech made at the Frankfurt Book Fair in 1984, Vladimir Voinovich admitted that it was he who had brought the microfilm to the West.

Little is known about Grossman's last years. He died of cancer on 14 September 1964. It appears he was deeply depressed, that he suffered great physical pain, and that he lived in a state of poverty and isolation. Worst of all, he had no assurance that his masterpiece would ever see the light of day. One of his few friends of the time reports him lamenting the confiscation of the manuscript and saying: 'They strangled me in a doorway.'

He did, however, continue writing until the end of his life. In the first place he completed the short novel *Everything Flows* which he had begun in 1955.* This part novel, part meditation on the fate of Russia contains a brief study of the camps (a *Gulag Archipelago* in miniature), some of the most eloquent and moving pages ever written on the fate of the Russian peasantry, and Grossman's reflections on Lenin and Russian history. Grossman was the first Soviet writer to argue Lenin's responsibility for the evils of Soviet society; other writers had laid the blame only on Stalin.

During his last years Grossman also wrote several short stories that have yet to be published either in the Soviet Union or in the West, and 'Peace Be with You', an account of a journey to Armenia. This fine

* Published in English translation in 1972 as *Forever Flowing*.

essay, Grossman's literary testament, has been published in the Soviet Union, though only in a censored version.

There are a large number of important 'Soviet' writers who were brought up as members of the pre-Revolutionary intelligentsia: Pasternak, Bulgakov, Mandelstam, Akhmatova. . . . Grossman, however, is a Soviet writer in a deeper sense; he will be remembered as both the first and the greatest of the dissidents of the post-Stalin era, the generation of dissidents who emerged from within Soviet Russia and who are themselves products of Soviet Russia.

LIFE AND FATE

The structure of *Life and Fate* is similar to that of *War and Peace*: the life of a whole society is evoked by means of a large number of different sub-plots centred around one family. Alexandra Vladimirovna is an old woman whose spiritual roots are in the Populist traditions of the pre-Revolutionary intelligentsia; it is her children, together with their own families, who are the central figures in the novel. Two sub-plots, set in a Russian labour-camp and a Physics Institute, revolve around the former and present husbands of Lyudmila Nikolaevna, Alexandra Vladimirovna's elder daughter. Two more sub-plots trace the careers of Commissar Krymov and Colonel Novikov, the ex-husband and the present fiancé of Lyudmila's sister Yevgenia: Krymov, an Old Bolshevik, ends up in the Lubyanka; Novikov, after commanding a tank corps that plays a crucial role at Stalingrad, also falls foul of the authorities. Other sub-plots concern friends and relatives of the family working at the Stalingrad power station, serving at the Front, attempting to organize rebellions in a German concentration camp, and being transported by cattle-truck to the gas chambers. . . .

Like *War and Peace*, *Life and Fate* contains many of the author's own reflections on history and philosophy. It is perhaps these reflections, even more than the devastatingly accurate portrayal of Stalinist Russia, that appalled the authorities. No other writer has so convincingly established the identity of Nazism and Soviet Communism. The parallels between the two systems are drawn repeatedly: between the career of a typical German Party functionary and that of a typical

Russian Party functionary, between the thoughts of a German dissident and those of a Russian dissident, between a German concentration camp and a Russian concentration camp.

The real battle portrayed in the novel is not the clash between the Third Reich and Stalin's Russia, but the clash between Freedom and Totalitarianism. At Stalingrad the Russian people believed they were fighting against Totalitarianism in the name of Freedom; the freedom they won, however, lasted only as long as the final outcome of the war remained undecided. Grossman movingly describes the development of a genuine spirit of camaraderie and egalitarianism among the defenders of Stalingrad; he also shows how this spirit was stamped out by Party functionaries who saw it as a greater danger than the Germans themselves.

'The clash between Freedom and Totalitarianism', however, is too grand and abstract a phrase. Grossman sees no value in fighting for freedom unless one can do so in a spirit of humility, a spirit of love and kindness. The battle Grossman portrays is the battle we must fight each day in order to preserve our humanity, the battle against the power of ideology, against the power of the State, against all the forces that combine to destroy the possibility of kindness and compassion between individuals.

The victors in this battle are not the Soviet military commanders, not General Chuykov who finally crosses to the East bank, after his heroic defence of Stalingrad has culminated in the German surrender, only in order to attend a banquet celebrating the 25th anniversary of the founding of the Soviet Secret Police. The true victors are the Russian peasant woman who takes pity on a wounded German soldier while his comrades are shooting her friends and relatives, the woman who sacrifices her own career and happiness in order to send a food-parcel to the Lubyanka – everyone whose actions, however historically insignificant, are motivated by the spirit of senseless, irrational kindness. It is these spontaneous, dangerous acts of kindness that Grossman sees as the truest expression of human freedom.

In *Le Cas Grossman*, Simon Markish quotes an anonymous Russian friend's opinion of *Life and Fate*: 'Yes, all this is noble, elevated, morally irreproachable, but I don't need a follower of Leo Tolstoy.'

The novel is indeed a remarkably old-fashioned one. It could, paradoxically, be described as the greatest work of fiction to have been written according to the Soviet doctrine of Socialist Realism. Even its faults are typical of Socialist Realism: an occasional tendency towards sententious philosophizing, a certain long-windedness and lack of sparkle.

Grossman has succeeded in achieving what every other Socialist Realist has merely pretended to do: he has portrayed the life, not of a few individuals, but of an entire age. All the characters endure fates that are typical of their generation. Each character, however vividly realized, is somehow typical of a particular group or class: Krymov and Mostovskoy the Old Bolsheviks, Getmanov the successful Stalinist functionary, Novikov the honourable and talented officer whose talents were never acknowledged before the war, Shtrum the Jewish intellectual. There is nothing eccentric about the novel, either stylistically or in the action and characterization. Probably no great novel of the last sixty years is so untouched by the influence of Modernism.

Grossman reached adolescence only after the Revolution and he had little contact, even through reading, with the West. Unlike Solzhenitsyn with his idealization of nineteenth-century Russia, he never tried to break free of his age. His power as a writer is that of an insider, that of a man who speaks from within Soviet society and in its own language. It is perhaps only through writing in its own style that one can portray an entire age; it would surely be impossible to portray the world of Jane Austen in the language of Joyce, or the world of Beowulf in the language of Jane Austen. It is interesting to note that Ilya Ehrenburg, many of whose books are modernist in technique, chose to write his novel about Stalinism, *The Thaw*, in the same slightly ponderous style, the style that is so characteristic of Socialist Realism.

THE HISTORICAL BACKGROUND

From January 1941 Stalin had received repeated warnings of Hitler's intentions, both through his own intelligence network and through those of Britain and the United States. He chose to ignore these warnings, to do everything in his power to appease Hitler, to avoid scrupulously any action that might be construed as provocation.

Possibly he was playing for time, aware that the Soviet Union was unprepared for war, both militarily and industrially; more likely he was simply burying his head in the sand, expecting his own wishes automatically to take on the status of objective reality. In any case, he clung desperately to the Nazi-Soviet pact. As a result the Soviet armed forces were taken largely unawares by the German offensive of 22 June 1941.

During the ensuing months the Soviet forces were thrown into headlong retreat. Armies that attempted to hold their ground were for the most part encircled. By late October the Germans had taken nearly three million prisoners, had isolated Leningrad, and had breached the outer defence line of Moscow itself. Meanwhile more than 1500 factories, not to mention entire universities and scientific institutes, had been evacuated by rail to the Urals, Siberia, the Volga and Central Asia.

The first important Soviet success was Zhukov's defence of Moscow in December 1941. This gave an important boost to national morale, destroying the myth of German invincibility. The Soviet counter-offensive of early 1942, however, was largely unsuccessful; throughout the rest of 1942 the Germans continued to hold their ground in the north and centre, while sweeping through the Ukraine towards the Volga and the oil-fields of the Caucasus. By September 1942 they were laying siege to Stalingrad, the key industrial and communications centre on the Volga. It is at this point that *For a Just Cause* ends, and *Life and Fate* begins.

From an historical point of view, *Life and Fate* is on the whole accurate; Grossman's observations as a journalist have clearly been supplemented by a vast amount of detailed historical research. Like Tolstoy, he includes in the novel a number of historical figures: Hitler and Stalin make brief appearances – as do Paulus, Eichmann, several important German officers, and most of the senior Russian officers at Stalingrad. Several of the minor characters are also based on real figures: Naum Rosenberg, for example, the Jewish accountant, was derived by Grossman from his researches for the *Black Book*.

The Jewish nuclear physicist Viktor Shtrum, perhaps the most important character in the novel, is a portrait of the author himself: his mother's death, his growing consciousness of his Jewish roots, his increasingly hostile attitude to Stalin, his agony over whether to write a letter of repentance – all these reflect the various stages of Grossman's own development. In other, more superficial respects, Shtrum is based on Lev Davidovich Landau, a brilliant physicist, not a Party member, who was dismissed from his work during the anti-Jewish campaigns of the early fifties, only to be reinstated by P. L. Kapitsa, an ex-student of Rutherford's and one of the most important Soviet physicists of the time. Kapitsa himself, at least in his eventual refusal to work on the development of the atom bomb, is clearly a model for Chepyzhin in *Life and Fate*.

The novel does contain one important departure from historical truth, though only in regard to chronology: Grossman considerably telescopes the rise of official anti-Semitism in the Soviet Union. Symbolically, Grossman is justified in linking the Stalingrad victory to the rise of Russian chauvinism; in reality it developed more slowly, reaching its peak in the late 1940s and early 1950s. The campaign against Einstein, for example, began only in the late forties, not – as in the novel – in 1942.

THE TEXT AND THE TRANSLATION

The Russian text of *Life and Fate*, first published in Lausanne in 1980, is based on the collation of two incomplete microfilms. For the main part, the two microfilms complemented one another; gaps and obscurities in one could be filled in from the other. Nevertheless, there are still passages where the published text breaks off in mid-chapter or mid-sentence. No attempt has been made to conceal these hiatuses; they are indicated in this translation by a bracketed ellipsis: [. . . .]

I have also chosen to omit or abridge some of the more sententious philosophical passages. Grossman's style is occasionally repetitive; I hope that my abridgments allow the power of his thought to stand out with greater clarity. In justification of such high-handedness, I can only plead that the manuscript was never finally prepared for publication by Grossman himself, and there is evidence he himself wished to carry out further revision. The omissions amount to approximately six pages in the Russian text.

A translation of this length must always, to some degree, be a collective task. I offer my sincere thanks to the large number of people who have helped in their various ways: Igor Golomstok for first bringing the novel to my attention and suggesting I attempt a translation; George Theiner and Hugh Lunghi for publishing extracts from my translation in their admirable magazine *Index on Censorship*; Mark Bonham Carter, Carol O'Brien and Dan Franklin for their patience, understanding and extraordinarily conscientious editing; James Greene, David Black, Barbara Hart and Dinny Thorold for their criticisms of sections of the manuscript; Robin Leanse for his versions of the poems in Chapters 70 and 72 of Part I, which I have adopted with only slight alterations; Christine and Benito Difazio for providing me with a home while I completed the translation; Elizabeth Grimwade for retyping a number of chapters; Christopher Donnelly of the Soviet Studies Unit at Sandhurst, and Brigadier B. C. Elgood for their help with military terminology. Above all, I must thank Harry Willetts of St Antony's, Oxford, for checking the entire manuscript against the Russian; with his encyclopedic knowledge of both Soviet history and contemporary Russian idiom he has saved me from more blunders than I care to admit.

I wish to dedicate this translation to the memory of four people I would very much like to have read this book: my father Colonel R. E. Chandler; my ex-wife's father, the Russian-Jewish theoretical physicist Grigory Lazarev; Colonel G. H. Nash, a friend and expert on Soviet military history; and my former teacher, Gordon Pirie, who disapproved of dedications.

ROBERT CHANDLER
March 1985

PART ONE

———◆———

1

There was a low mist. You could see the glare of headlamps reflected on the high-voltage cables beside the road.

It hadn't rained, but the ground was still wet with dew; the traffic-lights cast blurred red spots on the asphalt. You could sense the breath of the camp from miles away. Roads, railway tracks and cables all gradually converged on it. This was a world of straight lines: a grid of rectangles and parallelograms imposed on the autumn sky, on the mist and on the earth itself.

Distant sirens gave faint, long-drawn-out wails.

The road drew alongside the railway line. For a while the column of trucks carrying paper sacks of cement moved at the same speed as an endless train of freight wagons. The truck-drivers in their military greatcoats never once looked at the wagons or at the pale blurred faces inside them.

Then the fence of the camp appeared out of the mist: endless lines of wire strung between reinforced-concrete posts. The wooden barrack-huts stretched out in long broad streets. Their very uniformity was an expression of the inhuman character of this vast camp.

Among a million Russian huts you will never find even two that are exactly the same. Everything that lives is unique. It is unimaginable that two people, or two briar-roses, should be identical. . . If you attempt to erase the peculiarities and individuality of life by violence, then life itself must suffocate.

The grey-haired engine-driver watched casually yet attentively. Concrete posts, revolving searchlights on high masts, and glass-domed towers flashed by. In the domes stood guards with mounted machine-guns. The driver winked at his mate and the locomotive gave a warning hoot. A brilliantly lit cabin passed by, then a queue of cars beside a striped level-crossing barrier and a red traffic signal.

From the distance came the hoot of an approaching train. The driver turned to his mate. 'That's Zucker. I can tell by the whistle. He's already unloaded. Now he's taking the empty wagons back to Munich.'

There was a deafening roar as the two trains met. The air was torn apart, patches of grey flashed past between the wagons – and then the torn shreds of space and grey autumn light were woven together into a seamless cloth.

The driver's mate took out a pocket-mirror and looked at his smudged cheek. With a gesture, the driver asked if he could borrow it himself.

'Honestly, comrade Apfel,' said the mate excitedly, 'if it wasn't for all this disinfecting the wagons, we'd be back home by supper-time. As it is, we'll be out till four in the morning. As though they couldn't be disinfected back at the junction!'

The old driver had heard this complaint many times before. 'Give a good long hoot,' he said. 'We're to be put straight through to the main unloading area.'

2

In the German camp, for the first time since the Second Congress of the Comintern, Mikhail Sidorovich Mostovskoy had the chance to make use of his knowledge of foreign languages. Before the war, in Leningrad, there had been few opportunities to speak to foreigners. Now he remembered his years of exile in London and Switzerland, years when he and his fellow-revolutionaries had talked, quarrelled and sung in nearly all the languages of Europe.

Gardi, the Italian priest who was Mostovskoy's neighbour on the bedboards, had said that there were fifty-six different nationalities in the camp. The tens of thousands of prisoners shared the same fate, the same pallor, the same clothes, the same shuffling gait, and the same soup made from swedes mixed with the ersatz sago known by the Russians as 'fish-eyes'.

The camp authorities distinguished the prisoners by number and by the colour of the stripe sewn onto their jackets: red for politicals, black for saboteurs, green for thieves and murderers.

People unable to understand one another in the confusion of tongues were bound by a shared fate. Specialists in molecular physics or ancient manuscripts lay on the bedboards beside Italian peasants and Croat shepherds who were unable to sign their names. A man who used to order breakfast from his cook, worrying his housekeeper with his bad appetite, walked to work beside a man who had lived all his life on a diet of salt-cod. Their wooden soles made the same clatter on the ground, and they looked round with the same anxiety to see if the *Kossträger* were coming round with their rations.

The very differences in the lives of these prisoners gave rise to a certain similarity. Whether their vision of the past was a small garden beside a dusty Italian road, the sullen boom of the North Sea, or an orange paper lantern in a house for senior personnel on the outskirts of Bobruysk – all these prisoners, without exception, had enjoyed a wonderful past.

The more difficult a man's life had been before the camp, the more furiously he lied. This lie had no practical purpose; it served simply to glorify freedom. How could a man be unhappy outside the camp?

Before the war this camp had been known as a camp for political criminals. National Socialism had created a new type of political criminal: criminals who had not committed a crime. Many of the prisoners had been sent here merely for telling political anecdotes or for criticizing the Hitler regime in conversation with friends. The charge against them was not that they actually had distributed political leaflets or joined underground parties, but that one day they might.

The detainment of prisoners-of-war in a concentration camp for political prisoners was another innovation of Fascism. Here, as well as English and American pilots shot down over Germany, were officers and commissars of the Red Army. The latter were of especial interest to the Gestapo and were constantly being pressured to give information, to collaborate, to sign every conceivable sort of document.

There were 'saboteurs' in the camp: men who had left their work at military factories or construction sites without permission. Sending idle workers to concentration camps was another innovation of National Socialism.

There were people with lilac stripes on their jackets: émigrés from

21

Fascist Germany. This too was an innovation of National Socialism: anyone who had left Germany, however patriotically he had behaved abroad, was a political enemy.

The people with green stripes on their jackets, the thieves and burglars, were a privileged caste: the authorities relied on them to supervise the politicals. Giving common criminals power over political prisoners was yet another innovation of National Socialism.

There were people whose past history was so peculiar that no appropriate colour of stripe had been found for them. But the Italian snake-charmer, the Persian who had come from Tehran to study German painting and the Chinese student of physics all found National Socialism ready to offer them a board to lie on, a bowl of watery soup and twelve hours a day of work on the marshland.

Day and night trainloads of men continued to arrive at the death camps and concentration camps. The air was full of the rumble of wheels, the whistling of locomotives and the thud of hundreds of thousands of prisoners marching to work, each with a five-figure number sewn onto his clothes. These camps – with their streets and squares, their hospitals and flea markets, their crematoria and their stadiums – were the expanding cities of a new Europe.

How naïve, how kindly and patriarchal the old prisons huddled on the outskirts of towns now appeared – beside these camp-cities, beside the awful crimson-black glow that hung over the gas ovens!

You might well think that the management of such a vast number of prisoners would have required an equally vast army of guards and supervisors. In fact, whole weeks would pass by without anyone in an SS uniform so much as appearing inside the barrack-huts. It was the prisoners themselves who policed the camp-cities. It was the prisoners themselves who supervised the internal routine, who made sure that the rotten, half-frozen potatoes ended up in their own saucepans while the good-quality ones were set aside for army supply-bases.

The prisoners themselves were the doctors and bacteriologists in the camp hospitals and laboratories, the caretakers who swept the camp pavements. They were even the engineers responsible for providing the camp with light and heat, for maintaining the motorized transport.

The 'kapos' – the fierce and vigilant camp police – wore a thick yellow band on their left sleeve. Together with the camp orderlies, block orderlies and hut orderlies, they controlled the hierarchy of camp life – from matters that concerned the camp as a whole to the personal affairs that were carried on at night on the bedboards. The prisoners played their part in the most confidential work of the camp: even the selection of prisoners to be sent to the death camps, even the interrogation of prisoners in the concrete boxes known as the 'dark-rooms'. It seemed as though the German authorities could disappear altogether – the prisoners would maintain the high-voltage current in the wires and go on with their work.

The kapos and block orderlies simply carried out the tasks assigned to them. Sometimes they gave a sigh of regret, sometimes they shed a few tears for the people they sent to the gas ovens. What they did not do, however, was include their own names on these lists.

What Mostovskoy found most sinister of all was that National Socialism seemed so at home in the camp: rather than peering haughtily at the common people through a monocle, it talked and joked in their own language. It was down-to-earth and plebeian. And it had an excellent knowledge of the mind, language and soul of those it deprived of freedom.

3

Mikhail Mostovskoy, Agrippina Petrovna, Sofya Levinton, and Semyonov had been captured by the Germans on the outskirts of Stalingrad one night in August. They had been taken straight to the headquarters of an infantry division.

Agrippina Petrovna had been released after interrogation. On the instructions of a military-police officer, the translator had provided her with a loaf of pea-flour bread and two thirty-rouble coins. Semyonov, an army driver, had been sent to join a column of prisoners being marched to a camp near the village of Vertyachiy. Mostovskoy and Sofya Levinton, an army doctor, had been driven to Army Group Headquarters.

That was the last time Mostovskoy had seen Sofya Levinton. She had been standing in the middle of a dusty yard; she had no forage cap and the insignia of rank had been ripped from her uniform. The look of sullen hatred on her face had filled Mostovskoy with admiration.

Mostovskoy had been interrogated three times. He had then been marched to the railway station where a train carrying supplies of corn was about to depart. Ten coaches had been set aside for young men and women being sent as forced labourers to Germany; Mostovskoy could hear the women screaming as the train moved off. He himself had been locked into a small service compartment. His guard was quite polite, but whenever Mostovskoy asked a question, his face took on the expression of a deaf-mute. At the same time, it was clear that all his attention was focused on Mostovskoy. He was like an experienced zoo-keeper watching a box that housed a wild animal being transported by rail.

When the train entered Poland, Mostovskoy had been joined by a Polish bishop – a tall handsome man with grey hair and full, boyish lips. Immediately, with a marked accent, he had started telling Mostovskoy about the current executions of the Polish clergy. Mostovskoy had begun to abuse Catholicism and the Pope, and the bishop had fallen silent. From then on he had answered Mostovskoy's questions brusquely and in Polish. A few hours later, at Poznan, he had been taken off the train.

Mostovskoy had been taken directly to the camp, without visiting Berlin . . . Now it seemed that he'd been here for years, in this block for prisoners of special interest to the Gestapo. They were better-fed here, but their good life was that of guinea-pigs in a laboratory.

The orderly would call a man to the door; a friend would offer him some tobacco in exchange for a ration of bread and the man would return to his place on the bedboards, grinning with satisfaction. The orderly would then call another man who was telling a story – and the friend he'd been talking to would never hear how the story ended. The following day a kapo would walk up to his place on the boards and tell the orderly to collect his belongings. Someone else would then beg Keyze, the hut orderly, for permission to occupy the now-empty place.

Mostovskoy had even got used to the conversation here – a terrible mixture of the lists for the death camps, the gas ovens and the camp football teams: 'The Marsh team's the best – the bog soldiers. And Sick-bay's not bad. The Kitchen team's got some fast forwards. The Poles have got no defence at all . . .' He had grown equally accustomed to the countless rumours that spread through the camp: either about the invention of some new weapon or about rifts between the National Socialist leaders. These rumours were invariably both comforting and false – the opium of the camps.

4

Snow fell early in the morning and lay there till noon. The Russians felt a joy that was steeped in sorrow. Russia herself was breathing over them, spreading a mother's shawl beneath their poor exhausted feet. The barracks, with their white roofs, looked like the huts in a Russian village.

The orderly, a Spanish soldier called Andrea, came up to Mostovskoy and addressed him in broken French. He said that a clerk he knew had seen Mostovskoy's name on a paper, but his boss had taken the paper away before he'd had time to read it.

'My fate hangs on that bit of paper,' thought Mostovskoy. He was glad to find this thought left him so calm.

'But it doesn't matter,' murmured Andrea. 'We'll still be able to find out.'

'From the commandant?' asked Gardi, his huge black eyes shining in the half-light. 'Or from SS officer Liss?'

Mostovskoy was amazed at the difference between Gardi by day and Gardi by night. During the day he talked about the soup and the new arrivals, drove bargains with his neighbours and recalled the piquant, garlic-flavoured dishes of his homeland. The Russian soldiers all knew his favourite saying: '*Tutti kaputi*', and would shout it out to him across the camp square, smiling as though they were saying something reassuring. They called him 'Papa padre', thinking that 'padre' was his first name.

One evening the Soviet officers and commissars in the special block had been laughing at Gardi, joking about whether or not he had observed his vow of chastity. Gardi had listened unsmilingly to the jumbled fragments of French, German and Russian. Then he had begun to speak himself, and Mostovskoy had translated. In the name of their ideals the Russian revolutionaries had gone to penal servitude and the scaffold; why then should they doubt that for a religious ideal a man might renounce intimacy with women? After all, it was hardly comparable to sacrificing one's life.

'Tell us another,' Brigade Commissar Osipov had muttered.

At night, while everyone was asleep, Gardi became another man. He would sit there and pray. It would seem then that all the suffering in this penal city could dissolve in the black velvet of his ecstatic, bulging eyes. The veins would stand out on his brown neck and his long, apathetic face would take on an expression of obstinate and sombre happiness. He would go on praying for a long time and Mostovskoy would fall asleep to the sound of his quick, low whispering. After an hour or two Mostovskoy usually woke up. By then Gardi would be sleeping his usual turbulent sleep. It was as though he were trying to reconcile his two different selves: he would snore, smack his lips, gnash his teeth, let out thunderous farts and then suddenly begin a wonderful prayer about the mercy of God the Father and the Virgin Mary.

Gardi often questioned Mostovskoy about Soviet Russia, never once reproaching him for his atheism. He would nod his head as he listened to the Old Bolshevik, as though approving the closing down of churches and monasteries and the nationalization of the huge estates that had belonged to the Synod. Finally Mostovskoy would ask irritably: '*Vous me comprenez?*'

With his usual smile, as though he were talking about ragout or tomato sauce, Gardi would say: '*Je comprends tout ce que vous dites, je ne comprends pas seulement pourquoi vous dites cela.*'

The other Russian prisoners-of-war in the special block were not exempt from work. It was only late in the evening or during the night that Mostovskoy was able to talk to them. The sole exceptions were Brigade Commissar Osipov and General Gudz.

Someone Mostovskoy did often talk to was Ikonnikov-Morzh, a strange man who could have been any age at all. He slept in the worst place in the whole hut: by the main door, where there was a freezing draught and where the huge latrine-pail or *parasha* had once stood. The other Russians referred to him as 'the old parachutist'. They looked on him as a holy fool and treated him with a mixture of disgust and pity.

He was endowed with the extraordinary powers of endurance characteristic of madmen and simpletons. He never once caught cold, even though he would go to bed without taking off his rain-soaked clothes. And surely only the voice of a madman could be so clear and ringing.

He had first introduced himself by walking up to Mostovskoy and staring silently into his face. 'What's the good news then?' Mostovskoy had asked. Then he had smiled mockingly as Ikonnikov said in his sing-song voice: 'Good? But what is good?'

These words took Mostovskoy back to his childhood, to the days when his elder brother would come home from the seminary and discuss questions of theology with their father. 'That really is a hoary old question,' he said. 'People have been puzzling over it ever since the Buddhists and the early Christians. And we Marxists have pondered it too.'

'And have you found any answer?' asked Ikonnikov in a voice that made Mostovskoy laugh.

'The Red Army are finding an answer right now,' said Mostovskoy. 'But there's something rather unctuous, if I may say so, in your tone of voice. You sound like a priest or a Tolstoyan.'

'That's hardly surprising,' said Ikonnikov. 'I used to be a Tolstoyan.'

'You don't say!' exclaimed Mostovskoy. The strange man had begun to interest him.

'Do you know something?' said Ikonnikov. 'I'm certain that the persecution of the Church by the Bolsheviks was beneficial to the Christian ideal. The Church was in a pitiful state before the Revolution.'

'You're a true dialectician!' said Mostovskoy. 'I too in my old age have been allowed to witness the miracle of the Gospel!'

'No,' replied Ikonnikov with a frown. 'For you, the end justifies the means – and the means you employ are inhuman. I'm no dialectician and you're not witnessing a miracle.'

'So what can I do for you?' snapped Mostovskoy.

'Don't make fun of me.' Ikonnikov was standing to attention and his mournful voice now sounded tragic. 'I didn't come over here just to make you laugh. On the fifteenth of September last year I watched twenty thousand Jews being executed – women, children and old men.

That day I understood that God could not allow such a thing and that therefore he did not exist. In the darkness of the present day I can see your power and the terrible evil it's fighting. . .'

'All right then,' said Mostovskoy, 'let's talk!'

Ikonnikov worked in the marshland not far from the camp. Huge concrete pipes were being laid – to channel the river and its streams, and so drain the low ground. The men sent to work here – for the most part those who had incurred the disapproval of the authorities – were called 'the bog soldiers'.

Ikonnikov had small hands with fine fingers and the fingernails of a child. He would return from work, soaked to the bone and smeared with clay, walk up to Mostovskoy's place on the boards and say: 'Can I sit with you for a moment?'

Without looking at Mostovskoy, he would sit down, smile and draw his hand across his forehead. He had a very strange forehead: it was quite small, bulging, and so bright that it seemed to exist independently of his dirty ears, his dark brown neck and his hands with their broken nails.

The other Soviet prisoners-of-war, men with straightforward personal histories, considered him dubious and untrustworthy.

Since the days of Peter the Great, generation after generation of his ancestors had been priests. It was only the last generation that had followed a different path: at their father's wish, Ikonnikov and his brothers had received a lay education. He had been a student at the Petersburg Institute of Technology. During the final year, however, he had been converted to the teachings of Tolstoy; he had left the Institute and become a people's teacher in a village to the north of Perm. After eight years he had gone to Odessa. There he had been taken on as an engine-room mechanic in a merchant ship and had travelled to India and Japan. He had lived for a while in Sydney. After the Revolution he had returned to Russia and joined a peasant commune. This was a long-cherished dream: he had believed that communist agricultural labour would bring about the Kingdom of Heaven on earth.

During the period of all-out collectivization he had seen special trains packed with the families of kulaks. He had seen exhausted men and women collapse in the snow, never to rise again. He had seen 'closed' villages where there wasn't a living soul in sight and where every door and window had been boarded up. He remembered one ragged peasant woman with an emaciated neck and swarthy hands. Her guards had been staring at her in horror: mad with hunger, she had just eaten her two children.

Without leaving the commune, he had begun preaching the Gospel and praying to God to take pity on the dying. In the end he was sent to prison. The horrors of these years had affected his reason; after a year's internment in the prison psychiatric hospital he had been released. He had then gone to Byelorussia to live with his elder brother, a professor of biology who had managed to find him a job in a technical library.

Then the war had begun and Byelorussia had been invaded. Ikonnikov had witnessed the torments undergone by the prisoners-of-war and the executions of Jews in the towns and shtetls.* He began to approach people, in a state of near-hysteria, begging them to give sanctuary to the Jews. He even tried to save the lives of Jewish women and children himself. Escaping the gallows by a miracle, he had ended up in the camp.

The ideas of this dirty, ragged old man were a strange hotchpotch. He professed a belief in an absurd theory of morality that – in his own words – 'transcended class'.

'Where acts of violence are committed,' he explained to Mostovskoy, 'sorrow reigns and blood must flow. I saw the sufferings of the peasantry with my own eyes – and yet collectivization was carried out in the name of Good. I don't believe in your "Good". I believe in human kindness.'

'So you want us to be horrified when Hitler and Himmler are strung up on the gallows in the name of Good? You can count me out!'

'You ask Hitler,' said Ikonnikov, 'and he'll tell you that even this camp was set up in the name of Good.'

During these arguments Mostovskoy felt like a man fighting off a jellyfish with a knife. The thrusts of his logic were powerless.

'The world has progressed no further,' repeated Ikonnikov, 'than the truth spoken by a sixth-century Christian: "Condemn the sin and forgive the sinner."'

---

* The Jews of the Russian Empire, who were forced to live in special zones of residence, lived in small towns, *shtetls*, where they made up the majority of the population.

There was another old Russian in the hut, a one-eyed man called Chernetsov. One of the guards had smashed his glass eye and the gaping red socket stood out against his pale face. When he was talking to someone, he covered it over with the palm of his hand.

A former Menshevik, he had escaped from Soviet Russia in 1921. For twenty years he had worked as a bank clerk in Paris. He had been sent to the camp after calling upon his fellow employees to disobey the orders of the new German administration.

Mostovskoy had as little to do with Chernetsov as possible. Chernetsov, for his part, was clearly deeply upset by the popularity of the Old Bolshevik. Somehow everyone in the hut was drawn to him; the Spanish soldier, the Belgian lawyer, the Norwegian owner of a stationery shop would all come to him with their questions.

One day, Major Yershov, who was something of a hero to the Russian prisoners-of-war, had been sitting beside Mostovskoy. He was leaning towards him, one hand on his shoulder, speaking quickly and excitedly. Mostovskoy had suddenly looked round and seen Chernetsov staring at them from his place in the far corner. The anguish in his seeing eye had seemed more terrible than the gaping bloodshot socket. 'Yes, I'm glad I'm not in your shoes,' Mostovskoy had said to himself.

It certainly wasn't mere chance that everyone was constantly asking after Major Yershov. 'Where's Yershov? You haven't seen Yershov, have you? Comrade Yershov! Major Yershov! Yershov said . . . Ask Yershov. . .' People from the other huts would come to see him; there was always a constant bustle around his place on the boards.

Mostovskoy had christened him 'The Master of Men's Minds'. The 1860s and 1880s had both had their 'masters of men's minds'. First there had been the Populists; then Mikhailovsky had come and gone. Now this Nazi concentration camp had its own 'master of men's minds'.

Whole decades had gone by since Mostovskoy had first been imprisoned in a Tsarist jail. That had been in another century.

There had been occasions in the last few years when Mostovskoy had taken offence at the lack of confidence in his practical abilities shown by some of the Party leaders. Now he again felt conscious of his own power; every day he saw how much weight his words carried with

General Gudz, with Brigade Commissar Osipov, with the sad and depressed Major Kirillov.

Before the war, he had consoled himself with the thought that his removal from posts of responsibility at least meant that he was less involved with matters that aroused his misgivings: Stalin's autocratic rule, the bloody trials of the Opposition, the lack of respect shown towards the Old Bolsheviks. The execution of Bukharin, whom he had known and loved, had upset him deeply. He had known, however, that if he opposed the Party in any one of these matters, he would turn out, against his will, to have opposed the very cause to which he had devoted his life: the cause of Lenin. At times he had been tormented by doubt. Was it just cowardice that stopped him from speaking out? There had been many terrible things at that time. Yes, he would have given anything to talk once again to his friend Lunacharsky – they had always understood one another so quickly, so easily.

In this terrible camp he had recovered his self-confidence, but there was one uneasy feeling that never left him. He was unable to recover his former sense of clarity and completeness, of being a friend among friends and a stranger among strangers.

An English officer had once suggested that in Russia the censorship of anti-Marxist views might stand in the way of his philosophical work. But this wasn't what troubled him.

'It might inconvenience other people,' he had replied. 'But it doesn't inconvenience a Marxist like myself.'

'It's precisely because you're an old Marxist that I asked the question,' the Englishman had retorted.

He had winced with pain, but had been able to come out with an answer.

Nor was it that he sometimes felt irritated with people as close to him as Osipov, Gudz and Yershov . . . No, what troubled Mostovskoy was that many things in his own soul were now foreign to him.

He could remember times when he had felt overjoyed at meeting an old friend – only to find that he was now a stranger. But what could he do now it was a part of himself that had become alien, that was out of place in the present day? He could hardly break with himself . . .

He often got annoyed with Ikonnikov. He would be rude and sarcastic. He would call him feeble-minded, a wet rag, a half-wit. But if they didn't meet for some time, he missed him.

Yes, this was the main difference between the present and the years he had spent in prison as a young man: in those days he had been able to understand and love everything about his friends and comrades, while the least word or thought of his enemies had seemed alien and monstrous; now, however, he would sometimes glimpse in the thoughts of an enemy what he had once found important himself, and discover something strangely alien in the thoughts of his friends.

'I must just be getting old!' he said to himself.

5

The American colonel had an individual cell in the special block. He was allowed to leave the hut during the evening and was given special meals. Rumour had it that the King of Sweden had intervened on his behalf, at the request of President Roosevelt himself.

This colonel had once given Major Nikonov a bar of chocolate when he was ill. He was very interested in the Russian prisoners-of-war and was always trying to start up conversations with them about German tactics and the causes of the disasters of 1941.

He would often talk to Yershov. Sometimes he looked into his bright, thoughtful eyes and forgot that he couldn't speak English. He found it hard to believe that a man with such an intelligent face could fail to understand him – especially when what they were saying was of such consuming interest.

'I can't believe it!' he would say. 'You really don't understand?'

And Yershov would answer in Russian: 'The old sergeant had a fine command of every kind of language – except foreign ones.'

Nevertheless, in a language composed of smiles, glances, slaps on the back and ten or fifteen words of atrociously mangled Russian, French, German and English, the Russians were able to discuss comradeship, solidarity, fellow-feeling, love of one's home, love of one's wife and children, with people from dozens of different countries.

Kamerad, gut, brot, suppe, kinder, zigarette, arbeit and another dozen words that had originated in the camps themselves, *Revier,*

*Blockälteste, Kapo, Vernichtungslager, Appell, Appellplatz, Waschraum, Flugpunkt, Lagerschütze,** were enough to express everything of real importance in the simple yet bewildering life of the prisoners.

There were also several Russian words – *rebyata, tabachok, tovarisch*** – that were also used by other nationalities. As for the word *dokhodyaga* – meaning a prisoner who was on his last legs – this had been accepted by all fifty-six nationalities.

[....]†

The Soviet prisoners-of-war were unable even to agree among themselves: some were ready to die rather than betray their country, while others considered joining up with Vlasov.†† The more they talked and argued, the less they understood each other. In the end they fell silent, full of mutual contempt and hatred.

And in this silence of the dumb and these speeches of the blind, in this medley of people bound together by the same grief, terror and hope, in this hatred and lack of understanding between men who spoke the same tongue, you could see much of the tragedy of the twentieth century.

6

The conversations of the Russian prisoners-of-war were particularly sad on the evening after the first snowfall. Even men as energetic and self-disciplined as Colonel Zlatokrylets and Brigade Commissar Osipov had fallen into a gloomy silence. Major Kirillov was sitting beside Mostovskoy; his shoulders were drooping and his head was nodding slowly up and down. The whole of his vast body seemed filled

---

* Comrade, good, bread, soup, children, cigarettes, work ... sickbay, block orderly, military police, extermination camp, roll-call, roll-call square, ablutions, flight point, camp guards.

** Lads, tobacco, comrade.

† Passage missing in the original text.

†† General A. A. Vlasov was a Red Army officer who, after being captured by the Germans in 1942, formed an army of Russian prisoners to fight against the Soviet Union.

with melancholy. As for his dark eyes, they were like the eyes of someone with terminal cancer. Looking into such eyes, even a man's nearest and dearest would hope that his sufferings would soon be over.

Pointing at Kirillov, the ubiquitous Kotikov whispered to Osipov: 'Either he's about to hang himself or he's going to join up with Vlasov.'

Mostovskoy rubbed the grey stubble on his cheeks and said: 'Listen, cossacks! Everything's fine! Can't you see that? Every day that the State created by Lenin continues to exist is a death-blow to Fascism. Fascism has no choice: it must either destroy us or perish. The hatred Fascism bears us is yet another proof – a far-reaching proof – of the justice of Lenin's cause. The more the Fascists hate us, the more certain we can be of our own rightness . . . And in the end we will defeat them.'

He turned to Kirillov.

'What's the matter with you? Don't you remember that story of Gorky's? How he was walking up and down the prison courtyard and a Georgian shouted out: "Hold your head up! You look like a bedraggled chicken!"'

Everyone burst out laughing.

'And he was quite right! We must hold our heads high! Just think – the Soviet State is defending the ideals of Communism! Do you think Hitler can get the better of that . . . ? Stalingrad is still holding out. It may have seemed before the war that we were going too far, that we had really tightened the screws . . . But now even a blind man can see that the end justifies the means.'

'We certainly did tighten the screws,' said Yershov. 'That's for sure.'

'We didn't tighten them enough,' said General Gudz. 'We should have gone further still. Then Hitler wouldn't have reached the Volga.'

'It's not for us to give lessons to Stalin,' said Osipov.

'True enough,' said Mostovskoy. 'And if we perish in prisons or damp mines, then that's that. We must just think of something else.'

'Such as?' asked Yershov loudly.

Everyone exchanged glances, looked away again and fell silent.

'Oh Kirillov! Kirillov!' said Yershov abruptly. 'The old man's quite right. We should rejoice that the Fascists hate us. We hate them and they hate us. Right? But just imagine being sent to a Russian camp! That really would be hard. But as for this . . . ! We're stout-hearted lads! We'll give the Germans a run for their money!'

7

General Chuykov, the commander of the 62nd Army,* had lost all contact with his troops. Most of the wireless sets had gone dead and the telephone cables had all been severed.

Sometimes it seemed as though the gently rippling Volga was something fixed and stable, and that the quaking earth was huddling against its still margins. From the left bank, hundreds of pieces of Soviet heavy artillery kept up a constant barrage. Round the German positions on the southern slopes of Mamayev Kurgan, the earth whirled into the air like smoke. These clouds of earth then passed through the sieve of gravity, the heavier lumps falling straight to the ground, the dust rising into the sky.

Several times during the day the soldiers had fought off attacks by German tanks and infantry. Their eyes were bloodshot and their ears deafened.

To the senior officers cut off from their troops the day seemed interminable. Chuykov, Krylov and Gurov had tried everything under the sun to fill in the time: they had invented work for themselves, written letters, argued about what the enemy might do next, drunk vodka with and without something to eat, and had listened in silence to the roar of the guns. An iron whirlwind howled over the bunker, slicing through anything living that raised its head above the earth's surface. The Army Headquarters was paralysed.

'Let's have a game of fool!' said Chuykov, pushing aside a large ashtray full of cigarette-ends.

Even Krylov, the chief of staff, had lost his composure. Drumming

* The Russian Army on the right, or west, bank of the Volga, in the city of Stalingrad itself.

his fingers on the table, he said: 'I can't imagine anything worse. We're just sitting here – waiting to be eaten!'

Chuykov dealt, announced, 'Hearts are trumps,' and then suddenly scattered the cards. 'I can't bear it!' he exclaimed. 'We're just sitting in our holes like rabbits.' He sat there in silence. His face was agonized and full of hatred.

As though predicting his own end, Gurov murmured thoughtfully: 'Another day like this and I'll have a heart attack!'

He suddenly burst out laughing and said: 'At the divisional command-post it's impossible even to go to the bog during the day. I heard that Lyudnikov's chief of staff once jumped down into the bunker and shouted out: "Hurrah! I've been for a shi . . . !" He looked round and there was the lady-doctor he was in love with.'

The German air-raids stopped at dusk. A man arriving in Stalingrad at night, deafened by the guns, might well imagine that some cruel fate had brought him there just as a major offensive was being launched. For the veterans, however, this was the time to shave, to wash clothes and write letters; for the turners, mechanics, solderers and watchmakers this was the time to repair clocks, cigarette-lighters, cigarette-holders, and the oil-lamps made from old shellcases with strips of greatcoat as wicks.

In the flickering light from the shell-bursts you could see the banks of the river, the oil-tanks and factory-chimneys, the ruins of the city itself. The view was sullen and sinister.

In the dark the signals centre came to life again. Typewriters clattered away as they copied dispatches, motors hummed, orders were tapped out in Morse code, telephonists exchanged messages as the command-posts of divisions, regiments, batteries and companies were once again connected up . . . Signals officers who had just arrived gave measured coughs as they waited to give their reports to the duty-officer.

Pozharsky, the elderly artillery commander; General Tkachenko, the sapper in charge of the dangerous river-crossing; Guryev, the newly-arrived commander of the Siberian division; and Lieutenant-Colonel Batyuk, the Stalingrad veteran whose division was disposed below Mamayev Kurgan, all hurried to report to Chuykov and Krylov. At the front line itself, letters folded into triangles were handed to postmen . . . And the dead were buried – to spend the first night of their eternal rest beside the dug-outs and trenches where their comrades were writing letters, shaving, eating bread, drinking tea and washing in improvised baths.

8

This was the beginning of the most difficult period for the defenders of Stalingrad. In the confusion of the street-fighting, of the different attacks and counter-attacks, of the struggle for the 'House of Specialists', for the mill, for the State Bank – and for each square, courtyard and cellar – the superiority of the German forces was indisputable.

The wedge the Germans had driven into the southern part of Stalingrad was widening every day. From positions beside the water, German machine-gunners were able to cover the left bank to the south of Krasnaya Sloboda. The staff officers responsible for plotting the position of the front line on the map saw how inexorably the blue markers moved forward from day to day, how the band separating the red line of the Soviet defences from the light blue of the Volga grew steadily thinner.

The initiative at this time belonged to the Germans. For all their fury, the Russian counter-attacks could do nothing to halt their remorseless advance. From dawn to dusk the sky was filled with the whine of German dive-bombers, pounding the earth with their high-explosive bombs. And hundreds of men lived day after day with the same terrible question: what will happen tomorrow – or next week – when the thin band of the Soviet defences is reduced to a thread, when this thread is snapped by the iron teeth of the German offensive?

9

Late that night, General Krylov lay down to sleep in the bunker. His temples throbbed and his throat burned: he had smoked dozens of cigarettes that day. He licked his dry palate and turned over to face the wall. As he lay there, half-asleep, he remembered the fighting in Odessa and Sebastopol: the shouts of the Rumanian infantry as they attacked; Sebastopol and its naval splendour; Odessa and its cobble-paved courtyards cloaked in ivy.

Once again he was back at the command-post in Sebastopol. General Petrov's pince-nez was gleaming through the mist. The gleam broke into a thousand splinters and he saw the sea. A grey cloud, the dust raised by shell-bursts on the cliffs, floated above the heads of the soldiers and sailors and stood over Sapun Mountain.

He could hear the waves lapping unconcernedly against the launch. Then a gruff voice from below: 'Jump!' He leaped into the deep – and landed on the hull of the submarine . . . He took his last look at Sebastopol, at the stars, at the fires on the shore.

The war kept its hold on him even while he was asleep . . . The submarine was taking him to Novorossiysk. His legs were numb, his chest and back were damp with sweat, the noise of the engines was beating against his temples. Then the engines cut out and the submarine settled quietly onto the sea-bed. The closeness inside was unbearable; the ceiling, criss-crossed by dotted lines of riveting, was crushing him . . .

Then he heard a roar and a splash. A depth-charge had exploded. The submarine lurched and he was thrown out of his bunk. He opened his eyes and found everything in flames. There was a stream of fire running towards the Volga past the open door of the bunker. He could hear shouting and the rattle of tommy-guns.

'Put this over your head! Quick!' shouted a soldier he had never seen before. He was thrusting an overcoat towards him.

Krylov pushed him aside. 'Where's Chuykov?' he shouted.

Suddenly he realized what had happened: the oil-tanks were on fire. Flaming oil was streaming past towards the Volga.

It seemed impossible to escape from the liquid fire. It leaped up, humming and crackling, from the streams of oil that were filling the hollows and craters and rushing down the communication trenches. Saturated with oil, even the clay and stone were beginning to smoke. The oil itself was gushing out in black glossy streams from tanks that had been riddled by incendiary bullets; it was as though sheets of flame and smoke had been sealed inside these tanks and were now slowly unrolling.

The life that had reigned hundreds of millions of years before, the terrible life of the primeval monsters, had broken out of its deep tombs; howling and roaring, stamping its huge feet, it was devouring everything round about. The fire rose thousands of feet, carrying with it clouds of vaporized oil that exploded into flame only high in the sky. The mass of flame was so vast that the surrounding whirlwind was unable to bring enough oxygen to the burning molecules of hydrocarbon; a black, swaying vault separated the starry sky of autumn from the burning earth. It was terrible to look up and see a black firmament streaming with oil.

The columns of flame and smoke looked at one moment like living beings seized by horror and fury, at another moment like quivering poplars and aspens. Like women with long, streaming hair, the black clouds and red flames joined together in a wild dance.

The blazing oil formed a thin film over the water, hissing, smoking and twisting as it was caught by the current.

It was surprising how quickly the soldiers managed to find a path to the bank. Some of them then made two or three journeys back to the flaming bunkers, helping the staff officers to the promontory where, between two streams of fire flowing into the Volga, a small group of men were standing in safety. They had already rescued Chuykov himself. They had carried Krylov – who had been considered lost – out of the flames. Blinking their scorched eyelashes, they forced their way back to the bunkers through the thickets of red dog-rose.

The staff officers of the 62nd Army stood until morning on this small promontory. Between shielding their faces from the scorching air and brushing off the sparks that fell on their clothes, they kept looking round at Chuykov. He had a soldier's greatcoat thrown over his shoulders and locks of hair were sticking out under his service cap. He looked calm and thoughtful.

Gurov looked round and said: 'It seems that even fire can't burn us.' He began fingering the hot buttons on his greatcoat.

'Hey! You there with a spade!' shouted the chief sapper, General Tkachenko. 'Dig a channel through here! Otherwise we'll have flames coming down on us from that mound!'

He turned to Krylov.

'Everything's back to front, comrade General. Fire flows like water and the Volga's burning. Thank God there's no wind to speak of. Otherwise we'd be roasted alive!'

Now and then a breeze did blow from the Volga and the great tent of flame swayed towards them.

A few men went right down to the river and splashed water over their boots; it evaporated immediately off the hot leather. Some men stared silently down at the ground. Some were continually looking over their shoulders. Some tried to crack jokes: 'You don't even need matches – you can just light up from the wind or the Volga.' Others kept feeling themselves, shaking their heads as they touched the hot metal clasps on their belts.

A few hand-grenades exploded inside the dug-outs of the headquarters battalion. Then there was a rattle of machine-gun fire. A German mortar bomb whistled through the flames to explode in the Volga. Through the smoke they glimpsed distant figures; they were probably trying to divert the flames. But everything vanished again in flames and smoke.

Peering into the flames, Krylov had room in his head for only one thought: whether or not the Germans would exploit the fire and launch an attack. The Germans didn't know the location of the Army command-post – a prisoner they'd taken yesterday had refused to believe it was still on the right bank . . . And this seemed to be merely a local operation . . . Yes, there was a chance of surviving till morning. As long as the wind didn't get up!

He looked at Chuykov who was standing beside him, gazing into the fire. His soot-covered face seemed to be made of incandescent copper. When he took off his cap and drew his hand through his hair, he looked like a village blacksmith; he was covered in sweat, and sparks were leaping over his head. He gazed up at the cupola of fire and then down at the Volga. The few spaces of darkness over the river were clearly outlined against the twisting and coiling flames. Krylov imagined that Chuykov was fretting over the same questions as he was: would the Germans launch a major offensive at night . . . ? Where should they relocate the command-post if they survived till morning . . . ?

Chuykov sensed Krylov's gaze and smiled. Tracing a wide circle in the air with one hand, he said: 'Quite a spectacle, isn't it? Damn it!'

The fire was clearly visible from the Headquarters of the Stalingrad Front on the left bank. The chief of staff, Lieutenant-General Zakharov, went straight to Yeremenko after receiving the first report. Yeremenko ordered him to go to the signals centre in person and get through to Chuykov. Breathing heavily, Zakharov hurried along. An orderly was lighting the way with a flashlight; now and then he would say, 'Careful, comrade General!' as he pushed aside the branches of apple trees that were hanging over the path. The distant glow lit up the tree-trunks and lay in rose-coloured stains over the earth. The surrounding silence, broken only by the low calls of the sentries, made this pale, mute fire seem still more threatening.

The duty-signaller, a young girl, told Zakharov that they had lost all contact with Chuykov – telephone, telegraph and radio . . .

'And with the divisions?' asked Zakharov quickly.

'We were in touch with Batyuk only a moment ago, comrade Lieutenant-General.'

'Get him for me at once!'

Zakharov was notorious for his quick temper; the girl was afraid even to look at him again. Then she suddenly handed him the receiver and said joyfully: 'Here, comrade General!'

On the other end of the line was Batyuk's chief of staff. Like the girl, he grew increasingly nervous as he heard Zakharov's heavy breathing and imperious voice.

'What's going on over there? Give me a report! Are you in contact with Chuykov?'

The chief of staff told Zakharov about the burning oil-tanks and the wave of flame that had swept down on the Army command-post. They had been unable to make contact with Chuykov, but it did seem that not everyone there had perished. Through the fire and smoke they could make out a group of people standing on the bank, but the river itself was on fire and there was no way of reaching them. Batyuk had set out with the headquarters company to draw off the fire and rescue the survivors.

When he finished his report, Zakharov said: 'Tell Chuykov . . . If he's alive, tell Chuykov . . .'

Surprised by the long pause, the young girl glanced timidly at Zakharov. He was wiping the tears from his eyes with a handkerchief.

That night, forty officers from Army HQ were burned to death in collapsed bunkers.

10

Krymov arrived in Stalingrad soon after the burning of the oil-tanks.

Chuykov had located his new command-post on the sloping banks of the river, in the area where one of Batyuk's infantry regiments was disposed. He visited the officer in command, Captain Mikhailov, and nodded with satisfaction as he inspected his spacious bunker with its many layers of beams. Seeing the dismay on the captain's freckled face, Chuykov said brightly: 'You've built yourself a bunker above your station, comrade Captain.'

The regimental staff collected their impedimenta, moved thirty or forty yards downstream and evicted the battalion commander from his quarters. The now homeless battalion commander decided to leave his company commanders in peace – their quarters were in any case extremely cramped – and ordered a new bunker to be constructed on the high plateau.

Engineering works were already in full swing when Krymov arrived at the command-post. The sappers were digging a whole network of communication trenches between the different sections – Political, Operations and Artillery. His conversation with Chuykov was twice interrupted as the latter went out to inspect the progress of this work.

There was probably nowhere in the world where the construction of living-quarters was taken more seriously than in Stalingrad. These bunkers were built neither for warmth, nor in order to impress posterity. It was the likelihood of greeting the next dawn and eating the next meal that depended on the solidity of the beams, the depth of the communication trenches, the nearness of the latrine and the effectiveness of the camouflage.

When you were talking about someone, you always mentioned the quality of his bunker: 'Batyuk's done some fine work on Mamayev Kurgan with his mortars. He's got a fine bunker by the way. A huge oak door just like the Senate. Yes, he's certainly got a head on his shoulders.' While of another man it might be said: 'Well, what do you know, he was forced to retreat during the night. He had no liaison with his units and he lost a key position . . . As for his command-post, it was visible from the air. And he had a cape by way of a door – to keep out the flies, I suppose. An empty-headed fellow – I heard his wife left him before the war.'

There were any number of stories in circulation that had to do with dug-outs and bunkers . . . The story of the conduit that housed Rodimtsev's command-post: water had suddenly gushed through and swept away all his files; wits had subsequently marked the confluence of Rodimtsev and the Volga on maps. The story of the destruction of Batyuk's famous door. And the story of how Zholudyev and his staff had been buried alive in their bunker at the Tractor Factory.

The river bank, packed tightly with bunkers, reminded Krymov of a vast warship. To port lay the Volga, to starboard a wall of enemy fire.

Krymov had been instructed by the Political Administration to sort out a quarrel between the commanding officer and the commissar* of an infantry regiment in Rodimtsev's division. He intended first to give a short lecture to the staff officers and then to sort out the quarrel.

An orderly from the Army Political Section led him to the mouth of the vast conduit that housed Rodimtsev's command-post. A sentry announced his arrival, and a gruff voice replied: 'Bring him in! The poor man's probably shitting in his pants by now.'

---

* A political officer was attached to each unit. The lowest rank was 'political instructor', the highest 'Member of the Military Soviet' for an Army or a Front. The intermediate ranks were 'battalion commissar', 'regimental commissar', etc. There was frequently friction between these political officers and the corresponding commanding officers.

Krymov walked in under the low ceiling. Conscious that everyone was watching, he introduced himself to Vavilov, the divisional commissar. He was a stout man in a soldier's jacket, sitting on top of an empty crate.

'Splendid!' said Vavilov. 'A lecture's just what we need. People have heard that Manuilsky and a few others have arrived on the left bank and aren't even coming over to Stalingrad.'

'I've also been instructed to sort out a quarrel between the commander of one of your infantry regiments and his commissar.'

'Yes, we did have some difficulties there,' said Vavilov. 'But yesterday they were settled: a one-ton bomb fell on the command-post. Eighteen men were killed, the commander and his commissar among them.

'They couldn't have been more different,' he went on confidingly, 'even in appearance. They were like chalk and cheese. The commander was a straightforward man, the son of a peasant, while the commissar had a ring on one finger and always wore gloves. And now they are lying side by side.'

In the manner of someone used to being in control, both of his own feelings and of other people's, he suddenly added in a quite different tone of voice:

'Once, when we were based near Kotluban, I had to drive a lecturer from Moscow to the front – Pavel Fyodorovich Yudin.* The Member of the Military Soviet had said it would be the end of me if he lost so much as a hair off his head. Now that really was hard work. We had to dive straight into the ditch if a plane came anywhere near. But comrade Yudin certainly knew how to take care of himself – I'll say that for him! He showed true initiative.'

The other listeners laughed. Krymov knew it was him they were making fun of.

As a rule, he was able to establish good relations with officers in the field, tolerable relations with staff officers, and only awkward, rather insincere relations with his fellow political-workers. It was the same now: he was irritated by this commissar. He'd only just been sent to the front and he put on the airs of a veteran. He probably hadn't even joined the Party till just before the war.

* P. F. Yudin was one of Stalin's favourite hack philosophers.

On the other hand, there was obviously something about Krymov that got under Vavilov's skin.

After the lecture, people began asking questions. Belsky, Rodimtsev's chief of staff, who was sitting beside the general, asked: 'When are the Allies going to open a second front, comrade lecturer?'

Vavilov, who had been stretched out on a narrow bunk fixed to the stone facing of the conduit, sat up, raked aside some straw with his fingers and said: 'Who cares about that? What I want to know is when our own Command intends to act.'

Krymov glanced at him in irritation. 'Since the commissar puts the question in that form, it seems more appropriate that the general should answer it.'

Everyone turned to Rodimtsev.

'A tall man can't even stand up in here,' he began. 'This is a dead end if ever there was one. You can't launch an offensive from out of a pipe. I'd be only too glad – but how can you effect a concentration of troops in a pipe?'

The telephone rang. Rodimtsev picked up the receiver.

Everyone's eyes were on him.

He put down the receiver, leant over towards Belsky and whispered a few words in his ear. The latter reached out for the receiver himself. Rodimtsev put his hand over it and said: 'Why bother? Can't you hear?'

Up above they could hear frequent bursts of machine-gun fire and the explosions of hand-grenades. The conduit amplified every sound. The gunfire was like the clatter of carts going over a bridge.

Rodimtsev said a few words to various staff officers and again picked up the impatient telephone-receiver. He caught Krymov's eye for a moment, smiled calmly and said: 'The weather's turned fine here on the Volga.'

The telephone was now ringing incessantly. Krymov had gathered what was happening from the conversations he had overheard. Colonel Borisov, the second-in-command, went up to the general and leaned over the crate where the plan of Stalingrad was spread out. With a sudden, dramatic gesture he drew a blue perpendicular through the red dots of the Soviet front line right up to the Volga, then looked pointedly at Rodimtsev. A man in a cape came in out of the darkness and Rodimtsev got up to meet him.

It was obvious enough where he had come from. He was shrouded in an incandescent cloud and his cape seemed to be crackling with electricity.

'Comrade General,' he said plaintively, 'the swine have forced me back. They've reached the ravine and they're almost at the Volga. I need reinforcements!'

'You must stop the enemy yourselves, at whatever cost,' said Rodimtsev. 'There are no reserves.'

'At whatever cost,' repeated the man in the cape. He clearly understood what this meant.

'Just here?' asked Krymov, pointing to a spot on the map.

Rodimtsev didn't get a chance to answer. From the mouth of the conduit came the sound of pistol-shots and the flashes of hand-grenades.

Rodimtsev blew a piercing blast on his whistle. Belsky ran towards him, shouting: 'Comrade General, the enemy have broken through to the command-post!'

Suddenly the respected general, the man who had coloured in troop dispositions on a map with almost theatrical calm, was no longer there. And the war in these overgrown ravines and ruined buildings was no longer a matter of chromium-plated steel, cathode lamps and radio sets. There was just a man with thin lips, shouting excitedly: 'Divisional staff! Check your personal weapons, take some grenades and follow me!'

Both his voice and eyes had the burning cold of alcohol. His strength no longer lay in his military experience or his knowledge of the map, but in his harsh, wild, impetuous soul.

A few minutes later, staff officers, clerks, signallers and telephonists were pushing and shoving each other as they streamed out of the conduit. Following the light-footed Rodimtsev, they ran towards the ravine. It was full of the sound of shots and explosions, of shouting and cursing.

Krymov was one of the first to reach the ravine. As he looked down, breathing heavily, his heart gave a shudder of mingled disgust, fear and hatred. Dim figures appeared out of the darkness, rifles flashed, red and green eyes gleamed momentarily, and the air was full of the whistle of iron. He seemed to be looking into a vast pit full of hundreds of poisonous snakes that were slithering

46

about in confusion, hissing and rustling through the dry grass.

With a feeling of revulsion and fury, Krymov began firing at the flashes below and the quick shadows creeping their way up the slope.

Thirty or forty yards away a group of Germans appeared on the crest. They were making for the mouth of the conduit. The rumble of exploding grenades shook both the air and the earth.

It was as though a huge black cauldron were boiling and Krymov were immersed, body and soul, in its gurgling, bubbling waters. He could no longer think or feel as he had ever thought or felt before. For a moment he seemed to be in control of the whirlpool that had seized hold of him; then a thick black pitch seemed to pour into his eyes and nostrils – there was no air left to breathe, no stars over his head, nothing but this darkness, this ravine and these strange creatures rustling through the dry grass.

And yet, in spite of the confusion around him, he retained a clear sense both of his own strength and of the strength of the men beside him; he felt an almost palpable sense of solidarity with them, and a sense of joy that Rodimtsev was somewhere nearby.

This strange clarity, which arose at a moment when it was impossible to tell whether a man three yards away was a friend or an enemy, was linked to an equally clear and inexplicable sense of the general course of the fighting, the sense that allows a soldier to judge the true correlation of forces in a battle and to predict its outcome.

11

The intuition of a deafened and isolated soldier often turns out to be nearer the truth than judgements delivered by staff officers as they study the map.

An extraordinary change takes place at the turning-point in a battle: a soldier looks round, after apparently gaining his objective, and suddenly finds he has lost sight of his comrades; while the enemy, who had seemed so weak, scattered and stupid, is now united and therefore invincible. A deep change in perception takes place at this mysterious turning-point: a gallant, intelligent 'We' becomes a frail, timid 'I', while the enemy changes from a hunted, isolated prey to a terrible, threatening 'Them'.

As he overcame the enemy resistance, the advancing soldier had perceived everything separately: a shell-burst here, a rattle of machine-gun fire there, an enemy soldier there, hiding behind that shelter and about to run . . . He can't not run – he's cut off from that isolated piece of artillery, that isolated machine-gun, that isolated soldier blazing away beside him. But I – I am we, I am the mass of infantry going into the attack, I am the supporting tanks and artillery, I am the flare lighting up our common cause. And then suddenly I am alone – and everything that was isolated and weak has fused into a solid roar of enemy rifle-fire, machine-gun fire and artillery fire. This united enemy is now invincible; the only safety lies in my flight, in hiding my head, in covering my shoulders, my forehead, my jaw . . .

Often, it is the understanding of this transition that gives warfare the right to be called an art. This alternating sense of singularity and plurality is a key not only to the success of night-attacks by companies and battalions, but to the military success and failure of entire armies and peoples.

One sense almost entirely lost during combat is that of time.

After dancing all night at a New Year's ball, a girl will be unable to say whether the time passed quickly or slowly. Similarly, a man who has done twenty-five years in the Schlüsselburg Prison will say: 'I seem to have been a whole eternity in this fortress, and at the same time I only seem to have been here a few weeks.'

The night at the ball is full of looks, smiles, caresses, snatches of music, each of which takes place so swiftly as to leave no sense of duration in the girl's consciousness. Taken together, however, these moments engender the sense of a long interval of time that contains all the joys of human existence.

For the prisoner it is the exact opposite: his twenty-five years are composed of discrete intervals of time – from morning roll-call to evening roll-call, from breakfast to lunchtime – each of which seems unbearably long. But the twilight monotony of the months and years engenders a sense that time itself has contracted, has shrunk. And all this gives rise to the same sense of simultaneous quickness and endlessness felt by the girl at the ball.

The distortion of the sense of time during combat is something still more complex. Here there is a distortion even in the individual, primary sensations. One second can stretch out for eternity, and long hours can crumple together.

The sense of duration is linked to such fleeting events as the whistle of shells and bombs, the flashes of shots and explosions. The sense of quickness, on the other hand, is linked to protracted events: crossing a ploughed field under fire, crawling from one shelter to another. And as for hand-to-hand fighting – that takes place quite outside time.

In this chaos of blinding light and blinding darkness, of shots, explosions and machine-gun fire, in this chaos that tore into shreds any sense of the passing of time, Krymov could see with absolute clarity that the German storming-party had been routed.

12

It was morning. The bodies of the dead were lying in the burnt grass. The river lapped heavily and joylessly against its banks. Looking at the ploughed-up earth and the empty shells of buildings, one wanted to weep.

A new day was beginning and the war was about to fill it to the brim with smoke, rubble, iron and bloodstained bandages. Every day was the same. There was nothing left in the world but this battered earth and this blazing sky.

Krymov, perched on a crate, his head propped against the stone facing of the conduit, was dozing. He could hear voices and the clinking of cups; the commissar and the chief of staff were exchanging a few sleepy words as they drank their tea. Apparently yesterday's prisoner was a sapper; his battalion had been flown in from Magdeburg only a few days ago. Krymov suddenly remembered a picture from a school textbook: two vast cart-horses, whipped on by drivers in pointed caps, were trying to separate two empty hemispheres containing a vacuum. This image made him feel as bored now as it had when he was a child.

'That's a good sign,' said Belsky. 'They're bringing up their reserves.'

'A very good sign,' said the commissar, 'especially with the divisional staff having to take part in a counter-attack.'

Then Krymov heard Rodimtsev's low voice:

> 'There'll be flowers, there'll be flowers,
> There'll be berries in the factories.'

The night attack had exhausted Krymov. He would have to turn his head to look at Rodimtsev – and he was too tired. 'This is what a well must feel like after being drained,' he thought to himself. He dozed off again; the low voices fused with the sounds of explosions and gunfire into a monotone hum.

Then something new entered Krymov's consciousness: he dreamed he was lying in a room with closed blinds, watching a patch of morning sunlight on the wallpaper. This patch crept to the edge of the mirror and then expanded into a rainbow. The boy's heart trembled; the man with greying temples, the man with a heavy pistol hanging at his waist, opened his eyes and looked round.

Someone was standing in the middle of the conduit, wearing an old tunic and a forage cap with the green star of the Front. His head cocked to one side, he was playing a fiddle.

Noticing that Krymov had just woken up, the commissar leant over towards him and said: 'That's our barber, Rubinchik – a re-eal expert!'

Now and then someone would interrupt the music with a jocular curse. People would shout, 'Beg leave to report!' – and speak to the chief of staff. A spoon would clink against a tin mug. Or someone would give a long yawn and begin to shake up his straw bedding.

The barber was anxious not to disturb the officers; he was ready to break off at any moment.

Krymov thought of Jan Kubelik with his silver hair and his black dinner-jacket. But how was it that the famous violinist now seemed overshadowed by a mere barber? Why should this simple tune played on a cheap fiddle seem to express the depths of the human soul more truly than Bach or Mozart?

For the thousandth time Krymov felt the pain of loneliness. Zhenya had left him . . .

Once again he thought how Zhenya's departure expressed the whole dynamic of his life. He remained, but there was nothing left of him; and she had gone. There were many harsh truths he had to admit to himself. Yes, he had been closing his eyes for too long . . .

Somehow the music seemed to have helped him to understand time. Time is a transparent medium. People and cities arise out of it, move through it and disappear back into it. It is time that brings them and time that takes them away.

But the understanding that had just come to Krymov was a very different one: the understanding that says, 'This is my time,' or, 'No, this is no longer our time.' Time flows into a man or State, makes its home there and then flows away; the man and the State remain, but their time has passed. Where has their time gone? The man still thinks, breathes and cries, but his time, the time that belonged to him and to him alone, has disappeared.

There is nothing more difficult than to be a stepson of the time; there is no heavier fate than to live in an age that is not your own. Stepsons of the time are easily recognized: in personnel departments, Party district committees, army political sections, editorial offices, on the street . . . Time loves only those it has given birth to itself: its own children, its own heroes, its own labourers. Never can it come to love the children of a past age, any more than a woman can love the heroes of a past age, or a stepmother love the children of another woman.

Such is time: everything passes, it alone remains; everything remains, it alone passes. And how swiftly and noiselessly it passes. Only yesterday you were sure of yourself, strong and cheerful, a son of the time. But now another time has come – and you don't even know it.

In yesterday's fighting, time had been torn to shreds; now it emerged again from the plywood fiddle belonging to Rubinchik the barber. This fiddle told some that their time had come and others that their time had passed.

'I'm finished,' Krymov said to himself. 'Finished!'

He looked at Commissar Vavilov's calm, good-natured face. He was sipping tea from a mug and very slowly chewing some bread and a piece of sausage. His inscrutable eyes were fixed on the patch of light at the mouth of the conduit.

Rodimtsev, his face clear and peaceful and his shoulders hunched against the cold, was gazing at the musician. A grey-haired, pock-marked colonel, the commander of the divisional artillery, seemed to be looking at a map spread out in front of him; there was a harsh frown on his face, and it was only his kind sad eyes that showed he was listening to the music, not studying the map at all. Belsky was hurriedly drawing up a report for Army Headquarters; he seemed quite absorbed in this, but he had his head bent to one side so as to hear better. Further away sat the signallers, telephonists and clerks; you could see the same expression of seriousness on their exhausted faces as on the face of a peasant chewing a piece of bread.

Suddenly Krymov remembered one summer night: the large, dark eyes of a Cossack girl and her hot whisper . . . Yes, in spite of everything, life was good.

The fiddler stopped and a quiet murmur became audible: the sound of the water flowing by under the wooden duckboards. It seemed to Krymov that his soul was indeed a well that had been dry and empty; but now it was gently filling with water.

Half an hour later the fiddler was shaving Krymov. With the exaggerated seriousness that often makes a customer laugh, he was asking whether the razor was too harsh and then stroking Krymov's cheekbones to see if they were cleanly shaven. The smell of eau-de-cologne and powder seemed heart-rendingly out of place in this sullen kingdom of earth and iron.

Narrowing his eyes, Rodimtsev looked Krymov over – he had by now been thoroughly sprinkled with powder and eau-de-cologne – and nodded with satisfaction. 'Well, you've certainly done a good job on our guest. Now you can give me the once-over.'

The fiddler's dark eyes filled with happiness. He inspected Rodimtsev's head, shook out his white napkin and said: 'Maybe we should just tidy up your sideburns a little, comrade General?'

13

After the fire, Lieutenant-General Yeremenko decided to cross to the right bank and visit Chuykov. This dangerous journey served no practical purpose, but there was a very real human and moral necessity for it; Yeremenko wasted three days waiting to cross the river.

The bright walls of his bunker in Krasniy Sad seemed very peaceful, the shade of the apple trees very pleasant. But the distant rumble of Stalingrad merged with the sound of the leaves and the sighing of the rushes and felt somehow strangely oppressive; Yeremenko always cursed and swore as he went for his morning walk.

Yeremenko informed Zakharov of his decision to visit Stalingrad and ordered him to take command during his absence. He joked with the waitress laying the table for breakfast, gave permission to his deputy chief of staff to fly to Saratov for two days, and acceded to a request from General Trufanov – the commander of one of the armies in the steppe – that he should bomb a powerful Rumanian artillery position: 'All right, all right, you can have your long-range bombers!'

Yeremenko's aides tried to guess the reason for his good mood. Good news from Chuykov? A telephone conversation with Moscow? A letter from home? But such matters seldom escaped their notice; in any case the news from Chuykov had been bad and there had been no call from Moscow.

After breakfast, Yeremenko put on a jacket and went out for a walk. Parkhomenko, one of the aides, followed ten yards behind. Yeremenko walked with his usual unhurried stride, stopping now and then to scratch his thigh and glance towards the Volga.

Yeremenko stopped by a group of middle-aged labourers digging a pit. The napes of their necks were tanned dark brown and their faces were sullen and gloomy. They worked on in silence, glancing irritably at the stout man in a green cap who was standing idly by the edge of the pit.

'Tell me now,' said Yeremenko. 'Which of you is the worst worker?'

This question seemed very opportune; the men were tired of wielding their spades. They all looked round at a man who was busy emptying his pocket, pouring out breadcrumbs and tobacco-dust into the palm of one hand.

'Maybe him,' said two of them, looking round at the others for their agreement.

The man in question gave a dignified sigh and looked meekly up at Yeremenko. Realizing that Yeremenko was asking questions purely for the sake of it, he didn't say anything.

'And which of you is the best worker?'

They all pointed at a man with grey, thinning hair.

'Troshnikov,' said one of them. 'He really does put his heart into it.'

'He's used to hard work – he just can't help it,' said some of the others. It was almost as though they were apologizing on his behalf.

Yeremenko fumbled in his trouser-pocket and took out a gold watch that gleamed in the sun. Bending down with considerable awkwardness, he held it out to Troshnikov. Troshnikov looked at him blankly.

'Go on!' said Yeremenko. 'That's your reward.' Still looking at Troshnikov, he said: 'Parkhomenko, write out a certificate for him!'

He walked on, leaving a buzz of excitement behind him. Everyone was laughing, gasping with amazement at the hard-working Troshnikov's amazing stroke of luck.

Yeremenko waited three days to cross the river. Communications with the right bank had almost been severed. Those launches that did get through to Chuykov were holed fifty to seventy times in only a few minutes. They arrived at the right bank with their decks covered in blood.

Yeremenko was irritable and quarrelsome. The officers in charge of the crossing came to be more afraid of his anger than of the German bombs and grenades. He seemed to think it was negligent majors and idle captains who were to blame for the excesses of the German mortars, cannons and aircraft.

One night Yeremenko left his bunker and stood on a sand-dune beside the water. What had once been a map spread flat on a table was now suddenly alive – thundering, smoking, and breathing out death.

He seemed to recognize the red dots of the front line, the thick arrows of Paulus's thrusts towards the Volga, the key defences, the concentrations of artillery that he himself had circled in coloured pencil. But looking at the map, he had felt he had the power to bend and shift the line of the front. He had been the master; the power to order the heavy artillery to open fire from the left bank was his . . . His feelings now were very different indeed. The glow of the fire, the slow thunder in the sky were awesome. And their power had nothing to do with him, in no way depended on him.

He heard a faint cry from the area of the factories, a cry that was almost drowned by the shell-bursts and gunfire: 'A-a-a-a-a-h!' There was something terrible, but also something sad and melancholy in this long cry uttered by the Russian infantry as they staged an attack. As it crossed the cold water, it lost its fervour. Instead of valour or gallantry, you could hear the sadness of a soul parting with everything that it loved, calling on its nearest and dearest to wake up, to lift their heads from their pillows and hear for the last time the voice of a father, a husband, a son or a brother . . .

Yeremenko felt the same sadness in his own heart. Suddenly he had been sucked in by the war he was used to directing from outside. There he was – a solitary soldier on the shifting sands, stunned by the fire and thunder, standing on the bank like tens of thousands of other soldiers. He knew now that this people's war was beyond his understanding and outside his power . . . This was perhaps the highest understanding of the war he was ever to reach.

Just before morning Yeremenko crossed to the right bank. Chuykov had been notified by telephone; he walked down to the water and watched the armoured launch as it sped across.

The gangplank bent under Yeremenko's weight as he got out. He stepped clumsily over the pebbles and went up to Chuykov.

'Greetings, comrade Chuykov!'

'Greetings, comrade Lieutenant-General!'

'I wanted to see how you're getting on over here. Well, you certainly don't seem to have got yourself burnt! You're still as shaggy as ever . . . And you haven't even grown thin – we must be feeding you all right after all!'

'Do you expect me to grow thin from sitting all day and night in a bunker?' asked Chuykov. Still offended at Yeremenko's greeting, he went on: 'But what am I doing – receiving a guest out here on the bank?'

Now it was Yeremenko's turn to feel angry. It was very galling indeed to be referred to as a guest in Stalingrad. When Chuykov invited him in, he said: 'It's all right. I'll stay out here in the fresh air.'

The right bank, lit up by flares, shell-bursts and burning buildings, seemed quite deserted. The light brightened and faded, flaring up for a few seconds at a time with blinding intensity. Yeremenko gazed at the slopes pitted with bunkers and communication trenches, at the heaps of stone by the water – massive shapes that loomed out of the darkness and quickly slipped back into it.

Just then a loudspeaker struck up from across the river. An immense voice began to sing:

> May noble fury boil up like waves!
> This is the people's war, a sacred war.

Since there were no human beings in sight, and since everything round about – the earth, the sky and the Volga – was lit up by flame, it seemed as though the war itself were singing this ponderous song.

Yeremenko was embarrassed by the interest he felt in the picture before him; it really was as though he was a guest come to see the master of Stalingrad. It angered him that Chuykov appeared to understand the anxiety that had led him to cross the Volga, to know how tormented he had felt as he paced about Krasniy Sad listening to the rustle of dry leaves.

He began questioning the master of this fiery hell about the disposition of his reserves, the co-ordination between the infantry and the artillery, and the build-up of German forces around the factories. Chuykov answered in the customary tone of an officer being questioned by a superior.

They fell silent for a moment. Chuykov wanted to say: 'This has been the greatest defensive action in history. But still, what about a counter-offensive?' But he didn't dare. Yeremenko would think that the defenders of Stalingrad lacked endurance, that they were begging for a burden to be lifted from their shoulders.

Suddenly Yeremenko asked: 'Your mother and father are from the country, aren't they? Somewhere round Tula?'

'That's right, comrade General.'

'Does the old man write to you?'

'Yes, he does. He's still working.'

They looked at one another. The lenses of Yeremenko's spectacles were pink from the glow of the fire.

Another moment and it seemed they might begin the one conversation that really mattered – about the meaning of Stalingrad. But Yeremenko just said: 'You probably want to ask the usual question an officer puts to his superior – about reinforcements and supplies of ammunition.'

The one conversation that could have had meaning failed to take place.

A sentry on the crest of the slope glanced down at them. Hearing the whistle of a shell, Chuykov looked up and said: 'I bet that sentry's wondering who on earth the two eccentrics by the river can be.'

Yeremenko sniffed and started to scratch his nose. The moment had come for him to leave. It was an unwritten law that a superior officer standing under enemy fire should only leave when his subordinate asked him to. But Yeremenko's indifference to danger was so complete and so unfeigned that this rule seemed irrelevant.

A mortar-bomb whistled past. He turned his head quickly and unthinkingly to follow its trajectory.

'Well, Chuykov, it's time I was off!'

Chuykov stood for a while on the bank and watched the launch disappear. The foam of the wake reminded him of a white handkerchief – as though a woman were waving goodbye to him.

For his part, Yeremenko stood on the deck and gazed at the left bank. It was undulating gently in the dim glow from Stalingrad, while the river itself was as still as stone. He paced irritably about; once again his mind was full of dozens of familiar thoughts and anxieties. There were new tasks before him. What mattered now were his instructions from the Stavka: to build up a concentration of armour in readiness for an attack on the enemy's left flank.* This was something he hadn't so much as mentioned to Chuykov.

Chuykov himself returned to his bunker. The soldier on sentry-duty, the duty-officer inside, Guryev's chief of staff – like everyone else who jumped up at the sound of Chuykov's heavy footsteps – could see that their commander was upset.

He was indeed – and not without reason. His troops were slowly melting away. In the alternation of attack and counter-attack, the Germans were slowly gaining precious metres of ground. And two full-strength infantry divisions had been brought up from the rear and disposed opposite the Tractor Factory; there they remained ominously inactive.

No, he certainly had not expressed all his fears and anxieties to Yeremenko . . . But neither of the two men quite understood why their meeting had been so unsatisfactory; that the main thing about it was not the practical part, but what they had both been unable to say.

* Based in the Kremlin, the Stavka was the Soviet equivalent of GHQ and was responsible for the strategic direction of the war.

14

One cold October morning, Major Byerozkin woke up, thought about his wife and daughter, about heavy machine-guns, and listened to the now familiar rumble of gunfire. Then he called his orderly, Glushkov, and told him to fetch some water.

'It's nice and cold, just as you like it,' said Glushkov, smiling at the thought of the pleasure Byerozkin always took in his morning wash.

'It's probably already been snowing in the Urals,' said Byerozkin. 'That's where my wife and daughter are. Do you know, I still haven't heard from them.'

'You will, comrade Major,' said Glushkov.

While Byerozkin was drying himself and putting on his shirt, Glushkov told him about the events of the small hours.

'A shell fell on the kitchen block and killed the storeman. The chief of staff of the second battalion went out to relieve himself and was caught in the shoulder by a splinter. And some sappers caught a five-kilo pike-perch that had been stunned by a bomb. I've seen it myself – they gave it as a present to Captain Movshovich. And the commissar's been round – he wants you to phone him when you wake up.'

'Very well,' said Byerozkin. He drank a cup of tea, ate some calf's-foot jelly, rang the chief of staff and the commissar to say he was going out to inspect his battalions, put on his jacket and walked to the door.

Glushkov shook out the towel and hung it up on a nail, felt the hand-grenade hanging from his belt, slapped his pocket to check his tobacco-pouch was in place, took a tommy-gun from the corner and followed the regimental commander outside.

Byerozkin screwed up his eyes as he came out into the light. He had been in Stalingrad for a month and the picture before him was by now familiar: clay scree and a brown slope dotted with the tarpaulin roofs of soldiers' dug-outs and the smoking chimneys of improvised stoves. Higher up he could see the dark silhouettes of factories whose roofs had fallen in.

On the left, towards the Volga, were the tall chimneys of the 'Red October' factory and some goods wagons that looked like a herd of animals huddled around the body of their dead leader – a locomotive that was lying on its side. Still further away one could see the skeletons of ruined buildings, with thousands of patches of open sky appearing through what had once been windows. Smoke was rising from the factory workshops, there were glimpses of flame, and the air was filled with a staccato banging. It was almost as though these factories were still working.

Byerozkin carefully looked over the 300 metre-wide sector – most of it the small houses of a workers' settlement – where his regiment was disposed. Some sixth sense enabled him to tell apart, in the chaos of ruined buildings and alleyways, the houses where his own soldiers were cooking their buckwheat *kasha* and those where the Germans were eating fatback bacon and drinking schnapps.

A mortar-bomb whistled through the air; Byerozkin bowed his head and cursed. There was the crash of an explosion and a cloud of smoke covered the entrance to a bunker on the opposite slope of the gully. Still in his braces, the chief signaller of the neighbouring division emerged from the bunker. He'd barely taken a step, however, when there was another whistle; he ducked back and closed the door as another mortar-bomb burst only ten metres away.

Lieutenant-Colonel Batyuk had been watching this episode from the doorway of his own bunker at the top of the gully. As the signaller had taken his first step, Batyuk had shouted out in his Ukrainian accent: 'Fire!' It was, in fact, just then that the obedient German had fired his mortar. Batyuk caught sight of Byerozkin and called out: 'Greetings, neighbour!'

This little walk of Byerozkin's was mortally dangerous. After they'd had a good sleep and some breakfast, the Germans kept an especially close eye on this path. Not sparing their ammunition, they took potshots at everyone who passed by. At a corner, Byerozkin stood for a while by a heap of rubble; looking across a deceptively silent empty space, he said: 'You go first, Glushkov.'

'What do you mean? There's sure to be a sniper.'

It was a superior's privilege to be the first to cross a dangerous spot; usually the Germans were too slow to open fire straight away.

Byerozkin glanced round at the houses occupied by the Germans, winked at Glushkov and ran. As he reached the embankment, there was a sharp crack just behind him; a German had fired an explosive bullet. Byerozkin stood there and lit up a cigarette . . . Then Glushkov ran across, taking long, quick strides. A burst of machine-gun fire kicked up the dirt under his feet; it was almost as though a flock of sparrows had suddenly shot up from the ground. Glushkov swayed, stumbled, fell, jumped up again and finally reached Byerozkin.

'He almost got me – the bastard!'

After he'd got his breath back, Glushkov explained: 'I thought he'd be annoyed at letting you through and that he'd break off for a cigarette. But he obviously doesn't smoke – the swine!' He fingered the torn flap of his jacket and began cursing again.

When they reached the command-post, Byerozkin asked: 'Are you wounded, comrade Glushkov?'

'It's all right. The bastard just chewed the heel off my boot, that's all.'

The cellar of a large grocery store housed the command-posts of both an infantry and a sapper battalion. On the table stood two tall lamps made from empty shellcases. The damp air was full of the smell of sauerkraut and apples. A placard nailed to the door read: 'Customer and shop-assistant, be polite to one another!'

The two battalion commanders, Podchufarov and Movshovich, were sitting at the table and eating breakfast. As he opened the door, Byerozkin heard Podchufarov's excited voice.

'If there's one thing I can't stand, it's watered-down booze. I'd rather do without altogether.'

Seeing Byerozkin, they both got up and stood to attention. At the same time, the chief of staff buried a quarter-litre bottle of vodka under some hand-grenades and the cook moved sideways to hide the famous pike-perch. Podchufarov's orderly jumped to his feet; he had been squatting down, about to put on the record 'Chinese Serenade'. He just had time to take off the record, but he left the gramophone humming idly away. He stood there, looking straight ahead with an open, soldierly gaze; when the accursed machine hummed particularly loudly, he caught an angry glance from Podchufarov out of the corner of his eye.

They were all well aware of the strange quirks of superior officers: how they seem to expect everyone in a battalion always to be fighting, peering at the enemy through binoculars, or puzzling over a map. But a man can't be shooting or on the phone to his superiors and subordinates twenty-four hours a day; he has to eat sometime.

Byerozkin looked askance at the murmuring gramophone and grinned.

'All right!' he said. 'Sit down, comrades, carry on!'

It was unclear whether these words were to be taken at their face value. Podchufarov looked both sad and repentant, while Movshovich – the commander of an independent sapper battalion and thus not directly subordinate to Byerozkin – merely looked sad.

In what struck them as a particularly unpleasant tone, Byerozkin said: 'So where's this five-kilo pike-perch, comrade Movshovich? The whole division's talking of nothing else.'

With the same sad look, Movshovich ordered: 'Cook, show him the fish please.'

The cook, the only man present to have been carrying out his duties, explained: 'The comrade captain wanted it stuffed in the Jewish manner. I've got some pepper and bay-leaves, but I haven't any white bread or horse-radish . . .'

'I see,' said Byerozkin. 'I once had one done like that in Bobruysk, at the house of one Sara Aronovna – though, to be quite frank, I didn't think much of it.'

Suddenly they all realized that it hadn't even occurred to Byerozkin to get angry. It was as though he knew that Podchufarov had fought off a German attack during the night; that he had been half-buried under falling earth during the small hours; that his orderly, the man responsible for the 'Chinese Serenade', had had to dig him out, shouting: 'Don't worry, comrade Captain, I'll get you out of there.' It was as though he knew that Movshovich and his sappers had crept along one particularly vulnerable street, scattering earth and crushed brick over a chessboard pattern of anti-tank mines.

They were all young and they were glad to be alive one more morning, to be able to lift up a tin mug and say, 'Your good health!', to be able to eat cabbage and smoke cigarettes . . . In any case, nothing had really happened – they had just stood up for a moment before a superior and then invited him to eat, watching with pleasure how he enjoyed his cabbage.

Byerozkin often compared the battle for Stalingrad with what he had been through during the previous year of the war. He knew it was only the peace and silence within him that enabled him to endure this stress. As for the soldiers, they were able to eat soup, repair their boots, carve spoons and discuss their wives and commanding officers at a time when it might well seem impossible to feel anything except fury, horror and exhaustion. Byerozkin knew very well that the man with no quiet at the bottom of his soul was unable to endure for long, however courageous he might be in combat. He thought of fear or cowardice, on the other hand, as something temporary, something that could be cured as easily as a cold.

But what cowardice and bravery really were, he was by no means certain. Once, at the beginning of the war, he had been reprimanded by a superior for his timidity: without authorization, he had withdrawn his regiment from under enemy fire. And not long before Stalingrad, he had once ordered a battalion commander to withdraw over the brow of a hill, so as not to expose his men unnecessarily to the fire of the German mortars.

'What's all this, comrade Byerozkin?' the divisional commander had reproached him. 'People always told me you were calm and courageous, not someone to lose his nerve easily.'

By way of answer, Byerozkin had merely let out a sigh; people must have been mistaken.

Podchufarov had red hair and clear blue eyes. It was only with difficulty that he could restrain his sudden, unexpected fits of anger that were usually followed by equally sudden bursts of laughter. Movshovich was very thin; he had a long, freckled face and streaks of grey in his dark hair. He answered Byerozkin's questions in a hoarse voice and then sketched out a new scheme for mining the areas most vulnerable to tank attacks.

'You can give me that sketch as a souvenir,' said Byerozkin, leaning over the table. 'I was sent for just now by the divisional commander,' he went on very quietly. 'According to our scouts, the Germans are withdrawing forces from the town itself and concentrating them against you. And there are a lot of tanks. Do you understand?'

He listened to a nearby explosion that shook the walls of the cellar and smiled.

'Things are very quiet here. In my own gully at least three people will have been round from Army HQ while I've been out. There are different inspection teams coming and going all day long.'

The building was shaken by yet another blow. Lumps of plaster rained down from the ceiling.

'Yes, that's true enough,' said Podchufarov. 'No one really bothers us here.'

'Right. And you don't know how lucky you are,' said Byerozkin.

He went on confidingly, genuinely forgetting – perhaps because he was so used to being a subordinate – that he himself was now the officer in command:

'You know what the brass hats are like? "Why don't you advance? Why didn't you take that height? Why so many losses? Why no losses? Why haven't you reported back yet? Why are you sleeping now? Why, why, why . . . ?"'

Byerozkin stood up. 'Let's go, comrade Podchufarov. I'd like to inspect your sector.'

There was something heart-rending about this little street in a workers' settlement, about the exposed inner walls hung with brightly-coloured wallpaper, about the flower and vegetable gardens that had been ploughed up by tanks, about the solitary dahlias that were still flowering.

'Do you know, comrade Podchufarov,' said Byerozkin suddenly, 'I still haven't heard from my wife. I only found out where she was on my way here – and now it's weeks since I heard from her. All I know is that she and our daughter were going to the Urals.'

'You'll hear from them soon, comrade Major.'

The wounded were lying in the basement of a two-storey house, waiting to be evacuated during the night. The windows had been blocked up with bricks. On the floor stood a mug and a bucket of water. A postcard of a nineteenth-century painting, 'The Major's Courtship', had been stuck up on the wall.

'This is the rear,' said Podchufarov. 'The front line's further on.'

'Let's have a look at it then,' said Byerozkin.

They walked through a lobby and into a room where the ceiling had fallen in. It was like walking out of a factory office straight onto the shop-floor. Empty cartridge-cases creaked underfoot and the air was full of the peppery smell of gunpowder. Some anti-tank mines had been stacked on top of a cream-coloured pram.

'The Germans captured that ruin over there last night,' said Podchufarov. 'It's a real shame. It's a splendid building with windows facing south-west. Now the whole of my left flank's exposed to enemy fire.'

A heavy machine-gun was installed in the narrow aperture of another bricked-up window. The gunner, a dusty, smoke-blackened bandage round his head, was inserting a new cartridge-belt. His number one, baring his white teeth, was chewing a piece of sausage, ready to return to work in half a minute's time.

The company commander came up, a lieutenant. He had a white aster poking out of the pocket of his tunic.

'A real young eagle!' said Byerozkin with a smile.

'It's lucky you've come round, comrade Major,' said the lieutenant to Podchufarov. 'It happened just like I said it would. Last night they made another attack on house 6/1. They began bang on nine o'clock.'

'The CO's present. Make your report to him.'

'I'm sorry, I didn't see you,' said the lieutenant, saluting quickly.

Six days before, the Germans had isolated several buildings in the sector and begun chewing them up with Teutonic thoroughness. The Soviet resistance had been snuffed out – together with the lives of the defenders. But there was one factory building with particularly deep cellars where the Russians were still holding out. Its strong walls stood up to direct hits, even though holes had been blasted in them by grenades and mortar-bombs. The Germans had tried to destroy the building from the air and torpedo-bombs had been dropped on it three times. One whole corner had collapsed. But beneath the ruins the cellar remained intact; the defenders had cleared away the debris, mounted machine-guns, mortars and a light cannon, and were still keeping the Germans at bay. The building was fortunately situated, with no hidden approaches.

The lieutenant made his report and said: 'We tried to get through at night, but it was no good. We had one man killed and two who returned wounded.'

'Get down!' screamed the soldier on watch. Several men dropped flat on the ground; the lieutenant, unable to finish what he was saying, threw up his arms as though he were about to make a dive, and flopped down.

The whine rose to a piercing howl and was followed by a series of thunderous explosions that shook the earth and filled the air with a suffocating stench. Something big and black crashed onto the floor, bounced, and rolled between Byerozkin's legs. At first he thought it was a log that had been thrown there by the force of the explosion; then he realized it was a live grenade. The tension of the next second was unbearable.

The grenade failed to explode. The shadow that had swallowed up the earth and sky, that had blotted out the past and cut short the future, faded away.

The lieutenant got back to his feet.

'Nasty little thing!' said a voice.

'Well, I really did think I'd bought it then!' said someone else with a laugh.

Byerozkin wiped the sweat off his brow, picked up the white aster, shook off the dust and stuck it back in the lieutenant's tunic. 'I suppose someone gave it to you as a present.' He then turned to Podchufarov and went on: 'So why do I say things are nice and quiet here? Because there are no senior officers coming and going. Senior officers always want something from you . . . You've got a good cook – you can hand him over to me! You've got a splendid barber, a splendid tailor – let me have them! . . . Yes, they're a bunch of extortioners . . . That's a fine dug-out – you can climb out of it right now! That is good sauerkraut – have it sent to me straight away!'

Then he suddenly asked the lieutenant: 'Why did you say two men returned without reaching the surrounded house?'

'They were wounded.'

'I see.'

'You were born lucky,' said Podchufarov as they left the building and made their way through the vegetable gardens. Yellow potato-tops stuck up between the trenches and dug-outs belonging to No. 2 Company.

'Who knows?' said Byerozkin, jumping down into a trench.

'The earth's better adapted to war than any of us,' said Podchufarov. 'She must be used to it.' Then, going back to the conversation begun by Byerozkin, he added: 'That's nothing! I've even heard of women being requisitioned by a senior officer.'

The trench resounded with noise: people shouting, the crackle of rifle-shots and short bursts from machine-guns and tommy-guns.

'The company commander's been killed. Political Officer Soshkin's taken command. This is his bunker right here.'

'I see,' said Byerozkin, glancing in through the half-open door.

Soshkin, a man with thick, black eyebrows and a red face, caught up with them by the machine-guns. Shouting out each word, he reported that his company was keeping the Germans under fire with the aim of hindering their preparations for an attack on house 6/1.

Byerozkin borrowed his binoculars and began scrutinizing the quick flashes of rifle-fire and the flames that flickered like tongues from the mouths of mortars.

'There's a sniper right there, third floor, second window along.'

He'd hardly finished his sentence when there was a flash from that very window. A bullet whistled past, embedding itself in the wall of the trench half-way between Byerozkin's head and Soshkin's.

'You were born lucky!' said Podchufarov.

'Who knows?' replied Byerozkin.

They walked up the trench till they came to a device the company had invented themselves: an anti-tank rifle fixed to a cart-wheel.

'Our very own ack-ack gun,' said a sergeant with anxious eyes and a face covered in dust and stubble.

'One tank, a hundred metres distant, by the house with the green roof,' shouted Byerozkin, imitating the voice of a gunnery instructor.

The sergeant turned the wheel and quickly lowered the anti-tank rifle's long muzzle towards the earth.

'One of Dyrkin's soldiers,' said Byerozkin, 'fitted a sniper's sights to an anti-tank rifle and knocked out three machine-guns in one day.'

The sergeant shrugged his shoulders. 'It's all right for Dyrkin. He's behind walls.'

They walked further along the trench. Byerozkin went back to the conversation he had started at the very beginning of their tour of inspection. 'I sent them a food parcel – a very good one. And, do you realize? My wife still hasn't written. I don't know if the parcel even reached them. Maybe they've fallen ill. Anything can happen when you're evacuated.'

Podchufarov suddenly remembered how, in the past, carpenters who'd gone to work for a while in Moscow would return home laden with presents for their women, old people and children. The warmth and security of life at home had always meant more to them than the bright lights and noisy crowds of the capital.

Half an hour later they were back at the battalion command-post. Instead of going down into the cellar, Byerozkin began to take his leave in the courtyard.

'Provide every possible support for house 6/1,' he said. 'But don't try to break through to them yourselves. We'll do that by night – at regimental strength.'

'And now . . . ,' he went on. 'First – I don't like the way you treat your wounded. You've got divans at the command-post and your wounded are just lying on the floor. Second – you haven't sent for fresh bread and your men are eating dry rusks. Third – your political instructor Soshkin was roaring drunk. And now . . .'

Podchufarov listened, astonished at how much his commanding officer had noticed. The second-in-command of a platoon had been wearing German trousers . . . the officer in command of No. 1 Company had been wearing two watches . . .

Byerozkin ended with a warning.

'The Germans are going to attack. Is that clear?'

He set off towards the factory. Glushkov, who had managed to nail his heel back on and stitch up the tear in his jacket, asked: 'Are we going home now?'

Instead of answering directly, Byerozkin turned to Podchufarov.

'Phone the regimental commissar. Tell him I'm on my way to Dyrkin's – in the factory, the third shop.'

He winked and added: 'And I want you to send me some sauer-kraut. After all, I am a senior officer myself.'

15

Again there was no letter from Tolya . . . In the morning Lyudmila Nikolaevna Shaposhnikova would see her mother and husband off to work, and her daughter Nadya off to school. Her mother, Alexandra Vladimirovna, worked as a laboratory chemist in the famous Kazan soap factory; she was always the first to leave. As she passed her son-in-law's room, she would repeat a joke she had heard from the workers at the factory: 'We, the owners, must be at work by six, our employees by nine.'

Next, Nadya would go to school – or rather, gallop to school. It was impossible to get her out of bed in time; she always jumped out of bed at the last minute, grabbed her stockings, jacket, textbooks and exercise-books, gulped down her tea, and rushed down the staircase, flinging on her coat and scarf as she went.

By the time her husband, Viktor Pavlovich Shtrum, sat down to breakfast, the teapot would already be quite cold; Lyudmila would have to heat it up again.

Alexandra Vladimirovna would get quite angry when Nadya said: 'If only we could escape from this terrible hole!' Nadya didn't know that Derzhavin had lived in Kazan, that Aksakov, Tolstoy, Lenin, Zinin and Lobachevsky had all lived here, that Maxim Gorky had once worked in a Kazan baker's.

'What terrible senile indifference!' Alexandra Vladimirovna would say. It was strange to hear such a reproach levelled by an old woman at an adolescent girl.

Lyudmila could see that her mother remained interested both in the people she met and in her work. As well as awe at her mother's strength of character, she felt almost shocked: how could she, at such a terrible time, be interested in the hydrogenization of fats, in the streets and museums of Kazan?

Once, when Viktor said something about Alexandra Vladimirovna's youthfulness, Lyudmila, unable to restrain herself, had replied: 'It's not youthfulness. It's just senile egoism.'

'Grandmother's not an egoist, she's a populist,' said Nadya, and added, 'Populists are good people, but not very intelligent.'

Nadya always expressed her opinions both categorically and – perhaps because she was always in such a hurry – extremely abruptly. 'Rubbish!' she would say, rolling the 'r'. She followed the reports of the Soviet Information Bureau, kept up with the course of the war, and butted in on conversations about politics. After her spell on a *kolkhoz** during the summer, Nadya had begun enlightening her mother as to the reasons for the low productivity of Soviet agriculture. Although she usually never mentioned her school marks to her mother, she did once blurt out: 'Just imagine – they only gave me four out of five for good conduct! The maths mistress sent me out of the class. As I left I shouted, "Goodbye!" in English. Everyone just collapsed!'

Like many children from well-off families that had not needed to think about food or money before the war, Nadya, after their evacuation to Kazan, was constantly discussing rations and weighing up the good and bad points of the various ration-centres. She knew the pros and cons of each kind of buckwheat, the advantages of oil over butter and of lump sugar over granulated.

'Do you know what,' she would say to her mother. 'From today I want you to give me tea with honey instead of with condensed milk. It's all the same to you and it will be more nutritious for me.'

Sometimes Nadya would grow sullen and gloomy. Then she would smile contemptuously and be extraordinarily rude. Once, in Lyudmila's presence, she called her father an idiot. She pronounced the word with such venom that Viktor was too taken aback to reply.

Sometimes her mother saw Nadya crying over a book: the girl considered herself an unfortunate, backward creature who was doomed to live a difficult, colourless life.

'No one wants to be friends with me, I'm too stupid and boring,' she once said when they were at table. 'No one will want to marry me. I'll study to be a pharmacist and then go and live in a village.'

---

* *Kolkhoz:* a collective farm.

'They don't have pharmacies in remote villages,' said Alexandra Vladimirovna.

'And you're being much too pessimistic about your marriage prospects,' said Shtrum. 'You've grown prettier during the last few months.'

'Shut up!' said Nadya, glaring at her father.

That night Lyudmila saw Nadya reading a book of poetry, her thin bare arm sticking out from under the bedclothes.

On another occasion Nadya came back from the university ration-centre and announced: 'People, myself included, are vile swine to take advantage of all this. And Papa's a swine to sell his talents for butter. Why should weak children and sick men and women have to starve just because they don't understand physics and can't fulfil work-plans three times over . . . ? Only the chosen can stuff themselves with butter.'

That evening she said defiantly: 'Mama, I want double helpings of honey and butter. I didn't have time to eat this morning.'

In many ways Nadya was just like her father. Lyudmila noticed that the traits in Nadya which Viktor found most irritating were those that he shared with her.

On one occasion, Nadya, imitating her father's way of speaking, said of Postoev: 'He's a rogue, a nonentity, a careerist!'

Viktor was indignant. 'How dare you, a half-educated schoolgirl, speak like that about an Academician?'

But Lyudmila could remember very well how when Viktor was a student, he had abused the various academic celebrities in almost the same words. As for Nadya, Lyudmila could see that she was far from happy; she was difficult to get on with and extremely lonely.

After Nadya's departure, it was Viktor's turn to have breakfast. He would squint at his book, swallow his food without chewing, make stupid, surprised faces, grope for his cup without taking his eyes off the book, and say: 'Can I have some more tea? And make it a bit hotter, if you can.' She knew all his gestures: how he would scratch his head, pout his lips, then make a wry face and start picking his teeth. At this point she would say: 'Vitya, for the love of God, when are you going to get your teeth seen to?' She knew very well that if he scratched his nose, pouted his lips and so on, it was not because his nose or lips were hurting, but because he was thinking about his work. She knew that if she were to say, 'Vitya, you're not even listening!', he would reply, still squinting at his book, 'I heard every word. I can even repeat what you said: "For the love of God, when are you going to get your teeth seen to?"' Then he would gulp down another mouthful of tea, look surprised and begin to frown; this meant that he agreed with what his colleague had written on some points, but not on others. After that he would sit quite still for a long time, nodding his head sadly and submissively, with the same look in his eyes as an old man suffering from a brain tumour. This meant that he was thinking about his dead mother.

And as he drank his tea, thought about his work, or gave a despairing sigh, Lyudmila would look at the eyes she had so often kissed, at the curly hair she had so often rumpled, at the lips that had kissed her, at the hands with small, delicate fingers whose nails she had so often cut, and say to herself: 'Goodness me! What a sloven you are!'

She knew everything about him: how he liked to read children's books in bed; his face when he went out to clean his teeth; his clear, almost tremulous voice, when, dressed in his best suit, he had read his paper on neutron radiation. She knew that he liked Ukrainian borsch with haricot beans; she knew how he gave a quiet groan as he turned over in his sleep. She knew how quickly he always wore out the heel of his left shoe and dirtied the sleeves of his shirt; she knew that he liked two pillows in bed; she knew his secret dread of walking across large squares; she knew the smell of his skin, the shape of the holes in his socks. She knew the tune he hummed when he was waiting for lunch; the shape of the nails on his big toes; the names his mother had called him by when he was two; his slow, shuffling gait; the names of the boys he'd had fights with in his last year at school. She knew how he loved teasing his family and friends. Even now, for all his depression, he kept making fun of the way her closest friend, Marya Ivanovna Sokolova, had once confused Balzac and Flaubert.

He was expert at baiting Lyudmila and always succeeded in making her angry. That time she had leapt earnestly to her friend's defence.

'You always make fun of the people I love. Masha doesn't need to read a lot. She has impeccable taste and a real feeling for a book.'

'Certainly,' he had replied. 'And she knows that *Max and Maurice* was written by Anatole France.'

She knew his love of music and his political opinions. She had seen him cry. She had once seen him so enraged that he had torn his shirt and then got his legs tangled up in his trousers; he had hopped towards her with his fists clenched. She had seen his uncompromising fearlessness; she had seen him inspired; she had seen him reciting poetry; she had seen him taking a laxative.

Outwardly nothing had changed, but she knew he was angry with her at present. She could tell this from the fact that he no longer talked to her about his work. He talked to her about their rations and the letters he got from friends. He talked about the Institute: about events in the laboratory; about the discussion of their work schedule. He would tell her stories about his colleagues: how Savostyanov had fallen asleep at work after a drinking-bout the previous night; how the laboratory assistants had been cooking potatoes in the boiler; how Markov was preparing a new series of experiments. But he no longer spoke to her about his real work, the work that went on in his head. Previously she had been his only confidant.

Once he had told her that if he read out his notes or talked about half-formed hypotheses to his friends – even his closest friends – he would feel bad about it the next day; his work would seem dead, and he would find it hard to return to it. She had been the only person to whom he had been able to reveal his doubts, to whom he had been able to read both his fragmentary jottings and his boldest, most fantastic theories. But now he no longer so much as mentioned his work to her.

Now he found relief from his depressions in making accusations against Lyudmila. He thought incessantly about his mother. And he thought about something he would never have thought about but for Fascism: the fact that he and his mother were Jews.

In his heart he reproached Lyudmila for her coldness towards his mother. Once he had even said: 'If you hadn't got on so badly with my mother, she'd have been living with us when we were in Moscow.'

She, for her part, kept going over Viktor's many acts of injustice towards her son Tolya. She resented the way he had always been conscious only of Tolya's faults. He had never let him get away with anything – though he had always been only too willing to pardon Nadya her rudeness, her laziness, her slovenliness and unwillingness to help in the house.

Viktor's mother, Anna Semyonovna, had indeed suffered a terrible fate. But how could he have expected her to get on with Anna Semyonovna when Anna Semyonovna didn't like Tolya? That had been enough to make her letters and her visits to Moscow quite unbearable. It had always been Nadya, Nadya, Nadya . . . Nadya's got Viktor's eyes . . . Nadya's absent-minded, Nadya's quick-witted, Nadya's very thoughtful. Anna Semyonovna's tenderness and love for her son had extended into a tenderness and love for her granddaughter. But as for Tolya – he didn't even hold his fork in the same way Viktor had done.

She had also begun to think more and more often of Tolya's father, her first husband. She wanted to look up his relatives and his elder sister. Yes, they would immediately recognize Tolya's eyes, Tolya's wide nose, Tolya's slightly deformed thumb as the very eyes, nose and thumb of Abarchuk.

She now no longer remembered any of Viktor's kindness towards Tolya. In the same way she no longer remembered any of Abarchuk's cruelty towards herself – even the fact that he had left her when Tolya was a new-born baby, forbidding her to give him his surname.

In the morning Lyudmila would be left alone in the house. She looked forward to that; her family only got in her way. Everything in the world, the war, the fate of her sisters, Viktor's work, Nadya's unhappiness, her mother's health, her own compassion for the wounded, her grief over the men who had died in German camps – everything sprang from the pain and anxiety she felt for her son.

The feelings of her mother, the feelings of Viktor and Nadya, seemed to her to have been smelted from a quite different ore. Their devotion to Tolya, their love for him, seemed shallow. For her, the whole world was contained in Tolya; for them, Tolya was just a part of the world.

The weeks passed and still there was no letter from Tolya.

Every day Soviet Information Bureau bulletins were broadcast over the radio; every day the newspapers were full of the war. The Soviet forces were in retreat. The artillery was often mentioned in these bulletins and reports. Tolya served in the artillery. There was still no letter from Tolya.

She felt there was only one person in the world who could understand her anguish: Marya Ivanovna Sokolova.

Usually Lyudmila didn't get on with the wives of the other

academics; their endless talk about clothes, domestic servants and their husbands' successes made her feel bored and irritated. But she had grown very attached to Marya Ivanovna – partly because her shy, gentle character was so unlike her own, partly because she was moved by her concern over Tolya.

Lyudmila felt she could speak more freely about Tolya to her than to her own husband and mother; and she always felt calmer for these conversations. Even though Marya Ivanovna came round almost every day, Lyudmila would still wait for her impatiently, watching through the window for her slim figure and kind face.

There was still no letter from Tolya.

16

Lyudmila, Nadya and Alexandra Vladimirovna were sitting in the kitchen. Now and then Nadya crumpled up pages of her exercise-book and threw them into the stove; for a moment the stove would be filled with flames. Alexandra Vladimirovna glanced at Lyudmila out of the corner of her eye and said: 'One of the laboratory assistants invited me home yesterday. They certainly do live in cramped conditions. And the hunger! The poverty! We live like Tsars in comparison . . . ! Some neighbours came round and we started to talk about what we'd loved most before the war. Someone said "veal". Someone else said "pickled cucumber soup". And then my friend's little girl said: "What I liked most of all was 'lights out' in the pioneer camp."'

Lyudmila looked at her in silence.

'Grandmama, you've already got millions of friends here!' said Nadya.

'And you haven't got any.'

'And what's wrong with that?' asked Lyudmila. 'It's better than Viktor. These days he spends all his time at Sokolov's. You should just see the rabble that gather there. I really don't understand how Viktor and Sokolov can sit there for hours on end. Don't they get tired of chewing the fat all night? And why don't they give a thought to Marya Ivanovna? She needs a bit of peace. With all of them around the poor

74

woman can't even sit down for a minute. And they smoke like chimneys!'

'I like that Tartar, Karimov,' said Alexandra Vladimirovna.

'A nasty piece of work.'

'Mama's just like me,' said Nadya. 'She doesn't like anyone apart from Marya Ivanovna.'

'You are a strange lot,' said Alexandra Vladimirovna. 'You've got your own little circle of fellow evacuees from Moscow. And everyone else, everyone you happen to meet in a train or in the theatre, is just a nobody. Your friends are the people who've built themselves dachas in the same place as you have . . . Your sister Zhenya's just the same. The signs by which you recognize one another are almost invisible: "She's a real nonentity. Do you know, she doesn't even like Blok! He doesn't like Picasso! She gave him a present of a vase made from cut glass. What taste!" But Viktor's a democrat. He doesn't care tuppence for such airs and graces.'

'You're talking nonsense,' said Lyudmila. 'Dachas have nothing to do with it. There are bourgeois philistines with or without dachas, and I prefer to avoid them.'

Lyudmila seemed to be getting annoyed with her mother more and more frequently these days.

She would give Viktor advice, tick Nadya off for something she had done wrong or let it pass, spoil her or refuse to spoil her – and be conscious throughout that her mother had her own opinions about everything that she did. She never expressed these opinions, but they made themselves felt. Sometimes Viktor would catch his mother-in-law's eye and they would exchange mocking looks – as though they'd already discussed all Lyudmila's strange quirks. And it didn't matter whether or not they really had; what mattered was that a new force had appeared in the family, a force whose mere presence was enough to change all the existing relationships.

Viktor had once said that if he were in Lyudmila's shoes, he'd let Alexandra Vladimirovna take charge of the house; then she wouldn't be conscious all the time that she was a guest. Lyudmila had thought this hypocritical. It even crossed her mind that by emphasizing the warmth of his feelings for her mother, he was trying to remind her of her own coldness towards Anna Semyonovna.

She would never have admitted it, but there had been times when she had even been jealous of his love for Nadya. Now, though, it was no longer just jealousy. How could she admit, even to herself, that her own homeless mother had become a burden and an irritation to her? And yet, at the same time, she was ready to give her last dress away to Alexandra Vladimirovna, to share her last crust of bread with her.

For her part, Alexandra Vladimirovna sometimes felt like bursting into tears for no reason. Or she wanted to die; or to spend the night on a colleague's floor; or to pack her bags and set out to find Vera, Seryozha and Stepan Fyodorovich in Stalingrad.

Alexandra Vladimirovna usually agreed with what Viktor did or said, while Lyudmila usually disagreed. Nadya had noticed this and would say to her father: 'Go and tell Grandmama that Mama's been nasty to you!'

Now Alexandra Vladimirovna said: 'You two are as gloomy as owls. But Viktor's normal.'

'Words, words . . . ,' said Lyudmila wrily. 'You and Viktor will be as glad as any of us when the time comes to go back to Moscow.'

'When you do go back, dearest,' said Alexandra Vladimirovna abruptly, 'I think it would be best if I don't come with you. There isn't really enough room for me in your Moscow flat. Is that all right? Either I'll get Zhenya to come and live here, or else I'll go and live with her in Kuibyshev.'

It was a difficult moment. Everything that had troubled both mother and daughter was now out in the open. Lyudmila, however, took offence — as though she herself were in no way to blame. Alexandra Vladimirovna saw the expression of hurt on her face and felt guilty.

Usually both mother and daughter were cruelly forthright. Now, though, they felt frightened and tried to draw back.

'"Truth is good, but love is better" — the title of a new play by Ostrovsky,' remarked Nadya.

Alexandra Vladimirovna looked with some hostility, even fear, at this schoolgirl who could work out things she hadn't yet worked out for herself.

Soon after this Viktor came back from work. He let himself in and appeared suddenly in the kitchen.

'What a pleasant surprise!' said Nadya. 'We thought you'd be all night at the Sokolovs'.'

'How really splendid to find you all sitting at home by the stove!' said Viktor.

'Wipe your nose!' said Lyudmila. 'And I don't understand. What's so splendid about it?'

Nadya giggled. Imitating her mother's tone of voice, she said: 'Go on then! Wipe your nose! Don't you understand plain Russian?'

'Nadya, Nadya!' cautioned her mother. The right to try and educate Viktor was something she reserved for herself.

'Yes, yes, there's a cold wind outside,' said Viktor.

He went through to his room. He left the door open and they could see him sitting there at his desk.

'Guess what Papa's doing?' said Nadya. 'He's writing on the cover of a book again.'

'Well, that's none of your business,' said Lyudmila. She turned to her mother. 'Why do you think he's so pleased to find us all sitting here? He's quite obsessive – if any of us aren't at home, he gets worried. Right now he's working out some problem and he's glad there won't be anything to distract him.'

'Sh!' said Alexandra Vladimirovna. 'We probably really do distract him.'

'On the contrary,' said Nadya. 'If you speak loudly, he doesn't pay any attention. But the minute you start whispering, he rushes in and says: "So what's all this whispering about then?"'

'Nadya, you sound like a guide at the zoo talking about the instincts of the different animals,' said Lyudmila.

They all looked at each other and began to laugh.

'Mama, how could you be so unkind to me?' said Lyudmila.

Alexandra Vladimirovna patted her on the head without saying a word.

Then they all had supper together. That evening the warm kitchen seemed to Viktor to be endowed with a peculiar charm.

Viktor's life still rested on the same foundation. Recently he had been constantly preoccupied by a possible explanation of the contradictory results of the experiments carried out in the laboratory; he was itching to pick up his pencil and return to work.

'What splendid buckwheat stew!' he said, tapping his spoon against his empty bowl.

'Is that a hint?' asked Lyudmila.

He passed his bowl to her. 'Lyuda, you remember Prout's hypothesis?'

Taken aback, Lyudmila paused, her spoon in the air.

'The one about the origin of the elements,' said Alexandra Vladimirovna.

'Ah yes,' said Lyudmila. 'Everything deriving from hydrogen. But what's that got to do with the stew?'

'The stew?' repeated Viktor in astonishment. 'Listen now: what happened with Prout is that he arrived at a correct hypothesis largely because of the gross errors that were current in the determination of the atomic weights. If the atomic weights had already been determined with the accuracy later achieved by Dumas and Stas, he'd never have dared hypothesize that they were multiples of hydrogen. What led him to the correct answer was his mistakes.'

'But what's all that got to do with the stew?' asked Nadya.

'The stew?' Finally he understood and said: 'It hasn't got anything to do with the stew. But it's hard to make sense of anything in the stew I'm in.'

'Is that from today's lecture?' asked Alexandra Vladimirovna.

'No, no, it's just something . . . It's neither here nor there . . . I don't give lectures anyway.'

He caught Lyudmila's eye and knew that she understood: once again he felt inspired by his work.

'So how are things?' he asked. 'Did Marya Ivanovna come round? Did she read you any of *Madame Bovary*, the famous novel by Balzac?'

'That's enough from you!' said Lyudmila.

That night she expected him to talk to her again about his work. But he didn't say anything, and she didn't ask.

17

How naïve Viktor found the ideas of the mid-nineteenth-century physicists, the opinions of Helmholtz who had reduced all the problems of physics to the study of the forces of attraction and repulsion – themselves dependent only on distance.

The soul of matter is a field of energy! A unity, both a wave of energy and a material particle . . . The particle nature of light . . . Is it a shower of bright drops or a wave that moves with the speed of lightning?

Quantum theory had replaced the laws governing individual physical entities with new laws: the laws of probability, the laws of a special statistics that rejected the concept of an individual entity and acknowledged only aggregates. The physicists of the preceding century reminded Viktor of men in suits, with starched collars and cuffs and dyed moustaches, crowded around a billiard table. Deepthinking, serious men, armed with rulers and chronometers, knitting their thick brows as they measured speeds and accelerations and determined the masses of the resilient spheres which filled a universe of green cloth.

But space – measured by metal rods and rulers – and time – measured by the most accurate of watches – had suddenly begun to bend, to stretch and flatten. Their stability had turned out not to be the foundation-stone of science, but the walls and bars of its prison. The Day of Judgement had come; thousand-year-old truths had been declared errors. Truth had been sleeping for centuries, as though in a cocoon, inside ancient prejudices, errors and inaccuracies.

The world was no longer Euclidian, its geometrical nature no longer composed of masses and their speeds.

Science was progressing with ever increasing impetuousness in a world liberated by Einstein from the fetters of absolute time and space.

Two currents, one moving outwards together with whole universes, the other seeking to penetrate the nucleus of the atom, flowed in different directions but never lost sight of each other – though one moved in a world of parsecs while the other was measured in millimicrons. The more deeply physicists penetrated the heart of the atom, the more clearly they were able to understand the laws governing the luminescence of stars. The red shift in the spectrums visible from distant galaxies gave birth to the notion of universes receding into infinite space. But if one preferred a finite, convex space, distorted by speeds and masses, then one could suppose that space itself was expanding, dragging the galaxies after it.

Viktor never doubted it: no one in the world could be happier than the scientist . . . There were times – on his way to the Institute in the morning, during his evening stroll, this very night – when he thought about his work and was seized by a feeling of compounded happiness, humility and ecstasy.

The energies that filled the universe with the quiet light of the stars were being released by the transformation of hydrogen into helium . . .

Two years before the outbreak of war two young Germans had split the nuclei of heavy atoms by bombarding them with neutrons; Soviet scientists, reaching similar conclusions by different paths in their own researches, suddenly experienced what the cavemen had felt, thousands of years before, as they lit the first bonfire . . .

Of course, physics was determining the course of the twentieth century . . . Just as Stalingrad was now determining the course of events on every front of the World War.

But immediately behind Viktor, right at his heels, followed doubt, suffering, lack of belief.

18

Vitya, I'm certain this letter will reach you, even though I'm now behind the German front line, behind the barbed wire of the Jewish ghetto. I won't receive your answer, though; I won't be here to receive it. I want you to know about my last days. Like that, it will be easier for me to die.

It's difficult, Vitya, ever really to understand people . . . The Germans entered the town on July 7th. The latest news was being broadcast on the radio in the park. I was on my way back from the surgery and I stopped to listen. It was a war-bulletin in Ukrainian. Then I heard distant shooting. Some people ran across the park. I set off home, all the time feeling surprised that I'd missed the air-raid warning. Suddenly I saw a tank and someone shouted: 'It's the Germans.'

'Don't spread panic!' I warned. I'd been the day before to ask the secretary of the town soviet when we'd be evacuated. 'There'll be time enough to talk about that,' he'd answered angrily. 'We haven't even drawn up the lists of evacuees yet.'

Well, it was indeed the Germans. All that night the neighbours were rushing round to each other's rooms – the only people who stayed calm were myself and the little children. I'd just accepted that the same would happen to me as to everyone else. To begin with I felt utter horror. I realized that I'd never see you again. I wanted desperately to look at you once more. I wanted to kiss your forehead and your eyes. Then I understood how fortunate I was that you were safe.

When it was nearly morning, I fell asleep. I woke up and felt a terrible sadness. I was in my own room and my own bed, but I felt as though I were in a foreign country, alone and lost.

That morning I was reminded of what I'd forgotten during the years of the Soviet regime – that I was a Jew. Some Germans drove past on a lorry, shouting out: *'Juden kaput!'*

I got a further reminder from some of my own neighbours. The caretaker's wife was standing beneath my window and saying to the woman next door: 'Well, that's the end of the Jews. Thank God for that!' What can have made her say that? Her son's married to a Jew. She used to go and visit him and then come back and tell me all about her grandchildren.

The woman next door, a widow with a six-year-old daughter – a girl called Alyonushka with wonderful blue eyes, I wrote to you about her once – came round and said to me: 'Anna Semyonovna, I'm moving into your room. Can you clear your things out by this evening?' 'Very well, I'll move into your room then.' 'No, you're moving into the little room behind the kitchen.'

I refused. There isn't even a stove there, or a window.

I went to the surgery. When I came back, I found the door of my room had been smashed in and all my things piled in the little room. My neighbour just said: 'I've kept the settee for myself. There's no room for it where you are now.'

It's extraordinary – she's been to technical school and her late husband was a wonderful man, very quiet, an accountant at Ukopspilk. 'You're outside the law!' she said, as though that were something very profitable for her. And then her little Alyonushka sat with me all evening while I told her fairy-tales. That was my house-warming party – the girl didn't want to go to bed and her mother had to carry her away in her arms. Then, Vityenka, they opened the surgery again. I and another Jewish doctor were both dismissed. I asked for the previous month's pay but the new director said: 'Stalin can pay you whatever

you earned under the Soviet regime. Write to him in Moscow.'
The assistant, Marusya, embraced me and keened quietly,
'Lord God, Lord God, what will become of you, what will
become of you all?' And Doctor Tkachev shook me by the
hand. I really don't know which is worse – gloating spite, or
these pitying glances like people cast at a mangy, half-dead cat.
No, I never thought I'd have to live through anything like this.

Many people have surprised me. And not only those who
are poor, uneducated, embittered. There's one old man, a
retired teacher, seventy-five years old, who always used to ask
after you and send you his greetings and say, 'He's the pride of
our town.' During these accursed days he's just passed me by
without a word, looking in the other direction. And I've heard
that at a meeting called by the commandant, he said: 'Now the
air feels clean at last. It no longer smells of garlic.' Why, why? –
words like that are a stain on him. Yes, and how terribly the
Jews were slandered at that meeting . . . But then of course,
Vityenka, not everyone attended. Many people refused. And
one thing – ever since the time of the Tsars I've associated
anti-Semitism with the jingoism of people from the Union of
Michael the Archangel. But now I've seen that the people who
shout most loudly about delivering Russia from the Jews are
the very ones who cringe like lackeys before the Germans,
ready to betray their country for thirty pieces of German silver.
And strange people from the outskirts of town seize our
rooms, our blankets, our clothes. It must have been people like
them who killed doctors at the time of the cholera riots. And
then there are people whose souls have just withered, people
who are ready to go along with anything evil – anything so as
not to be suspected of disagreeing with whoever's in power.

People I know are constantly coming round with bits of
news. Their eyes are mad and they seem quite delirious. A
strange expression has come into vogue: 'hiding away one
another's things.' People somehow think a neighbour's house
is going to be safer. The whole thing is like a children's game.

An announcement was soon made about the resettlement
of the Jews. We were each to be permitted to take 15 kilograms
of belongings. Little yellow notices were hung up on the walls
of houses: 'All occupants are required to move to the area of
the Old Town by not later than 6.00 p.m. on 15 July, 1941.
Anyone remaining will be shot.'

And so, Vityenka, I got ready. I took a pillow, some bedclothes, the cup you once gave me, a spoon, a knife and two forks. Do we really need so very much? I took a few medical instruments. I took your letters; the photographs of my late mother and Uncle David, and the one of you with your father; a volume of Pushkin; *Lettres de mon moulin*; the volume of Maupassant with *Une vie*; a small dictionary . . . I took some Chekhov – the volume with 'A Boring Story' and 'The Bishop' – and that was that, I'd filled my basket. How many letters I must have written to you under that roof, how many hours I must have cried at night – yes, now I can tell you just how lonely I've been.

I said goodbye to the house and garden. I sat for a few minutes under the tree. I said goodbye to the neighbours. Some people are very strange. Two women began arguing in front of me about which of them would have my chairs, and which my writing-desk. I said goodbye and they both began to cry. I asked the Basankos to tell you everything in more detail if you ever come and ask about me after the war. They promised. I was very moved by the mongrel, Tobik – she was particularly affectionate towards me that last evening.

If you do come, feed her in return for her kindness towards an old Yid.

When I'd got everything ready and was wondering how I'd be able to carry my basket to the Old Town, a patient of mine suddenly appeared, a gloomy and – so I had always thought – rather callous man called Shchukin. He picked up my belongings, gave me 300 roubles and said he'd come once a week to the fence and give me some bread. He works at the printing-house – they didn't want him at the front because of his eye trouble. He was a patient of mine before the war. If I'd been asked to list all the people I knew with pure, sensitive souls, I might have given dozens of names – but certainly not his. Do you know, Vityenka, after he came, I began to feel once more that I was a human being – it wasn't only the yard-dog that still treated me as though I were.

He told me that a new decree was being printed: Jews are to be forbidden to walk on the pavements; they are required to wear a yellow patch, a Star of David, on the chest; they no longer have the right to use public transport, baths, parks, or cinemas; they are forbidden to buy butter, eggs, milk, berries, white bread, meat, or any vegetable other than potatoes; they are only allowed to make purchases in the market after six o'clock, when the peasants are already on their way home. The Old Town will be fenced off with barbed wire and people will only be allowed out under escort – to carry out forced labour. If a Jew is discovered in a Russian home, the owner will be shot – just as if he were harbouring a partisan.

Shchukin's father-in-law, an old peasant, had travelled in from the nearby village of Chudnov. He had seen with his own eyes how all the Jews there were herded into the forest with their parcels and suitcases. All day long he heard shots and terrible screams; not one Jew returned. As for the Germans who'd commandeered his rooms, they didn't come back till late at night. They were quite drunk and they carried on drinking and singing till dawn, sharing out brooches, rings and bracelets right under the old man's nose. I don't know whether the soldiers just got out of hand or whether that's a foretaste of our common fate.

What a sad journey it was, my son, to the medieval ghetto. I was walking through the town where I have worked for the last twenty years. First we went down Svechnaya Street, which was quite deserted. Then we came out onto Nikolskaya Street and I caught sight of hundreds of people all on their way to this same accursed ghetto. The street was white with little parcels and pillows. There were invalids being led by the hand. Doctor Margulis's paralysed father was being carried on a blanket. One young man was carrying an old woman in his arms while his wife and children followed behind, loaded with parcels. Gordon, a fat breathless man who manages a grocery shop, was wearing a winter coat with a fur collar; sweat was pouring down his face. I was struck by one young man; he had no belongings and he was walking with his head high, a book held open before him, and a calm, proud face. But how crazy and horror-struck most of the people beside him looked!

We all walked down the roadway while everyone else stood on the pavement and watched.

At one moment I was walking beside the Margulises and I could hear sighs of compassion from the women on the pavement. But everyone just laughed at Gordon's winter coat – though, believe me, he looked more terrible than absurd. I saw many faces I knew. Some nodded goodbye, others looked away. I don't think any eyes in that crowd were indifferent; some were pitiless, some were inquisitive, and some were filled with tears.

I realized there were two different crowds: there were the Jews – the men in winter coats and hats, the women wearing thick dresses – and there were the people in summer clothes on the pavement. There you could see bright dresses, men in shirt-sleeves, embroidered Ukrainian blouses. It was as though even the sun no longer shone for the Jews on the street, as though they were walking through the cold frost of a December night.

We came to the gateway into the ghetto and I said goodbye to my companion. He pointed out where we were to meet at the fence.

Can you guess what I felt, Vityenka, once I was behind the barbed wire? I'd expected to feel horror. But just imagine – I actually felt relieved to be inside this cattle-pen. Don't think it's because I'm a born slave. No. No. It's because everyone around me shares my fate: now I no longer have to walk on the roadway like a horse, there are no more spiteful looks, and the people I know look me straight in the eye instead of trying to avoid me. Everyone in this cattle-pen bears the stamp branded on us by the Fascists and it no longer burns my soul so fiercely. Now I'm no longer a beast deprived of rights – simply an unfortunate human being. And that's easier to bear.

I've settled down, together with a colleague of mine, Doctor Sperling, in a small two-roomed house. The Sperlings have got two grown-up daughters and a twelve-year-old son, Yura. I gaze for hours at his thin little face and his big, sad eyes; twice I've called him Vitya by mistake and he's corrected me: 'I'm Yura, not Vitya.'

How different people are! Sperling, at fifty-eight years of age, is full of energy. He's already managed to get hold of mattresses, kerosene and a cart for carrying firewood. Last night he had a sack of flour and half a sack of haricot beans brought to the house. He's as pleased as punch at each little success of his. Yesterday he was hanging out the rugs. 'Don't worry, don't worry, we'll survive,' he repeated. 'The main thing is to get stocked up with food and firewood.'

He said we ought to start up a school in the ghetto. He even suggested I gave Yura French lessons in exchange for a bowl of soup. I agreed.

Sperling's fat wife, Fanny Borisovna, just sighs, 'Everything's ruined, we're all ruined.' At the same time she keeps a careful watch on her elder daughter, Lyuba — a kind, good-natured girl — in case she gives anyone a handful of beans or a slice of bread. The mother's favourite is the younger daughter, Alya. She's the devil incarnate — mean, domineering and suspicious — and she's always shouting at her father and sister. She came on a visit from Moscow before the war and got stuck here.

God, what poverty there is everywhere! If only the people who are always talking about how rich the Jews are, how they've always got something put by for hard times, could have a look at the Old Town now. Hard times have come indeed — there can be no harder. But the people who've been resettled with fifteen kilograms of baggage aren't the only inhabitants of the Old Town: there have always been craftsmen living here — together with old men, workers, hospital orderlies . . . What terrible crowded conditions they live in! And what food they eat! If you could only see these half-ruined shacks that have almost become part of the earth.

Vityenka, I've seen many bad people here, people who are greedy, dishonest, capable even of betrayal. We've got one terrible man, Epstein, who came here from some little town in Poland — he wears a band round his sleeve and helps the Germans with their interrogations and searches; he gets drunk with the Ukrainian policemen and they send him round to people's homes to extort vodka, money and food. I've seen him twice, a tall handsome man in a smart cream-coloured suit — even the yellow star sewn on his jacket looks like a chrysanthemum.

But what I really want to talk to you about is something quite different. I never used to feel I was a Jew: as a child my circle of friends were all Russian; my favourite poets were Pushkin and Nekrasov; the one play which reduced me to tears, together with the whole audience — a congress of village doctors — was Stanislavsky's production of *Uncle Vanya*. And once, Vityenka, when I was fourteen, our family was about to emigrate to South America and I said to my father: 'I'll never leave Russia — I'd rather drown myself.' And I didn't go.

But now, during these terrible days, my heart has become filled with a maternal tenderness towards the Jewish people. I never knew this love before. It reminds me of my love for you, my dearest son.

I visit the sick in their houses. Dozens of people are crowded into minute little rooms — half-blind old men, unweaned babies, pregnant women. I'm used to looking into people's eyes for symptoms of diseases — glaucoma, cataract. Now I can no longer look at people's eyes like that; what I see now is the reflection of the soul. A good soul, Vityenka! A sad, good-natured soul, defeated by violence, but at the same time triumphant over violence. A strong soul, Vitya!

If you could only see with what concern the old men and women keep asking after you. How sincerely people try to console me, people I've never complained to and whose situation is far more terrible than my own.

Sometimes I think that it's not so much me visiting the sick, as the other way round — that the people are a kind doctor who is healing my soul. And how touching it is when people hand me an onion, a slice of bread, or a handful of beans.

And believe me, Vityenka, that's not a matter of payment for my visit. Tears come to my eyes when some middle-aged workman shakes me by the hand, puts two or three potatoes in a little bag and says, 'There, Doctor, I beg you.' There's something about it which is pure, kind, fatherly — but I can't find the right words.

I don't want to console you by saying that things have been easy for me — no, it's surprising that my heart hasn't broken from grief. But please don't worry that I'm going hungry — I haven't once felt hungry. Nor have I felt lonely.

What can I say about people? They amaze me as much by their good qualities as by their bad qualities. They are all so different, even though they must undergo the same fate. But then if there's a downpour and most people try to hide, that doesn't mean that they're all the same. People even have their own particular ways of sheltering from rain.

Doctor Sperling is certain that the persecution of the Jews will only last as long as the war. There aren't many people like him, and I've noticed that the more optimistic people are, the more petty and egotistic they tend to be. If someone comes in when we're eating, Alya and Fanny Borisovna hide away the food as quick as they can.

The Sperlings treat me well – especially as I eat little and provide more than I consume. But I've decided to leave. I don't like them. I'm trying to find some little corner for myself. The more sorrow there is in a man, the less hope he has of survival – the better, the kinder, the more generous he becomes.

The poorest people, the tailors and tinsmiths, the ones without hope, are so much nobler, more generous and more intelligent than the people who've somehow managed to lay by a few provisions. The young schoolmistresses; Spilberg, the eccentric old teacher and chess-player; the timid women who work in the library; Reyvich, the engineer, who's more helpless than a child, yet dreams of arming the ghetto with hand-made grenades – what wonderful, impractical, dear, sad, good people they all are!

I've realized now that hope almost never goes together with reason. It's something quite irrational and instinctive.

People carry on, Vitya, as though their whole life lies ahead of them. It's impossible to say whether that's wise or foolish – it's just the way people are. I do the same myself. There are two women here from a shtetl and they tell the same story as my friend did. The Germans are killing all the Jews in the district, children and old men included. The Germans and Ukrainian police drive up and recruit a few dozen men for field-work. These men are set to dig ditches and two or three days later the Jewish population is marched to these ditches and shot. Jewish burial mounds are rising up in all the villages round about.

There's a girl from Poland next door. She says that there the killing goes on continually. The Jews are being massacred; there are only a few ghettoes – Warsaw, Lodz and Radom – where there are any left alive. When I thought about all this it seemed quite clear that we've been gathered here not to be preserved – like the bison in the Bialowiezska forest – but to be slaughtered. Our turn will come in a week or two, according to plan. But just imagine – I still go on seeing patients and saying, 'Now bathe your eye regularly with the lotion and it will be better in two or three weeks.' I'm taking care of one old man whose cataract it will be possible to remove in six months or a year.

I give Yura French lessons and get quite upset at his bad pronunciation.

Meanwhile the Germans burst into people's houses and steal; sentries amuse themselves by shooting children from behind the barbed wire; and more and more people confirm that any day now our fate will be decided.

That's how it is – life goes on. Not long ago we even had a wedding . . . And there are always dozens of rumours. First a neighbour declares that our troops have taken the offensive and the Germans are fleeing. Then there is a rumour that the Soviet government and Churchill have presented the Germans with an ultimatum – and that Hitler's ordered that no more Jews are to be killed. Then we are informed that Jews are to be exchanged for German prisoners-of-war.

It seems that nowhere is there so much hope as in the ghetto. The world is full of events and all these events have the same meaning and the same purpose – the salvation of the Jews. What a wealth of hope!

And the source of all these hopes is one and the same – the life-instinct itself, blindly rebelling against the terrible fact that we must all perish without trace. I look round myself and simply can't believe it: can we really, all of us, already be condemned, about to be executed? The hairdressers, the cobblers, the tailors, the doctors, the stove-repairers are still working. A little maternity home has even been opened – or rather, the semblance of one. People do their washing, linen dries on the line, meals are prepared, the children have been going to school since the first of September, the mothers question the teachers about their children's marks.

Old Spilberg is having some books bound. Alya Sperling does physical training every morning, puts her hair in paper-curlers every evening and quarrels with her father about two lengths of material that she wants for summer dresses.

And I'm busy myself from morning till night – visiting my patients, giving lessons, darning my clothes, doing my washing, preparing for winter, sewing a lining into my winter coat. I hear stories about the terrible punishments Jews have suffered: one woman I know, a lawyer's wife, bought a duck egg for her child and was beaten till she lost consciousness; a boy, the son of Sirota the chemist, was shot in the shoulder for crawling beneath the wire after a ball that had rolled away. And then rumours, rumours, rumours . . .

What I say now isn't a rumour, however. Today the Germans came and took eighty young men to work in the fields, supposedly to dig potatoes. Some people were glad, imagining the men would be able to bring a few potatoes home for their relatives. But I knew all too well what the Germans meant by potatoes.

Night is a special time in the ghetto, Vitya. You know, my dearest, how I always taught you to tell the truth – a son must always tell the truth to his mother. But then so must a mother tell the truth to her son. Don't imagine, Vityenka, that your mother's a strong woman. I'm weak. I'm afraid of pain and I'm terrified to sit down in the dentist's chair. As a child I was afraid of darkness and thunder. As an old woman I've been afraid of illness and loneliness; I've been afraid that if I fall ill, I won't be able to go back to work again; that I'll become a burden to you and that you'll make me feel it. I've been afraid of the war. Now, Vitya, I'm seized at night by a horror that makes my heart grow numb. I'm about to die. I want to call out to you for help.

When you were a child, you used to run to me for protection. Now, in moments of weakness, I want to hide my head on your knees; I want you to be strong and wise; I want you to protect and defend me. I'm not always strong in spirit, Vitya – I can be weak too. I often think about suicide, but something holds me back – some weakness, or strength, or irrational hope.

But enough of that. I have dreams every night. I often see my mother and talk to her. Last night I dreamed of Sasha Shaposhnikov during our years in Paris. But I haven't once dreamed of you – though I think of you often, even at moments of the most terrible distress. In the morning I wake up and look at the ceiling, then I remember that the Germans are on our land and that I'm a leper – and it's as though I haven't woken up at all, but have just fallen asleep and begun to dream.

A few minutes go by and I hear Alya quarrelling with Lyuba over whose turn it is to go to the well. Then I hear people talking about how, during the night, the Germans smashed in the skull of some old man on the next street.

A girl I knew came round, a student at the teachers'

training college for technical subjects, and called me out on a visit. She turned out to be hiding a lieutenant who'd been wounded in the shoulder and burnt in one eye. A sweet, haggard, young man with a thick Volga accent. He'd slipped through the wire at night and found shelter in the ghetto. His eye wasn't seriously injured at all and I was able to check the suppuration. He talked a lot about different battles and how our army had been put to flight. He quite depressed me. He wants to recuperate and then slip through the German front line. Several young men intend to go with him, one of them an ex-student of mine. Oh Vityenka, if only I could go with them too. It was such a joy to me to be able to help that young man – I felt as though I too were taking part in the war against Fascism.

People had brought him some bread, beans and potatoes, and one old woman had knitted him a pair of woollen socks.

The whole day has been full of drama. Yesterday Alya managed, through a Russian friend of hers, to get hold of the passport of a young Russian girl who'd died in hospital. Tonight she's going to leave. And we heard today, from a peasant we know who was driving past the ghetto fence, that the Jews who were sent to dig potatoes are digging deep ditches four versts from the town, near the airfield, on the road to Romanovka. Remember that name, Vitya – that's where you'll find the mass grave where your mother is buried.

Even Sperling understood. He's been pale all day, his lips are trembling and he keeps asking confusedly: 'Is there any hope that specialists will be spared?' In fact I have heard that in some places the best tailors, cobblers and doctors have been left alive.

All the same, this very evening, Sperling summoned the old man who repairs stoves and had a secret cupboard built into the wall for flour and salt. And Yura and I have been reading *Lettres de mon moulin*. Do you remember how we used to read out loud my favourite story, *'Les Vieux'*, how we'd look at each other and burst out laughing, how each of us would have tears in our eyes? And after that I set Yura his lessons for the day after tomorrow. But what an ache I felt as I looked at my student's sad little face, as I watched his fingers note down in his exercise-book the numbers of the paragraphs of grammar I had just set.

And what a lot of children like that there are! Children with wonderful eyes and dark curly hair – probably future scientists, physicists, professors of medicine, musicians, even poets . . .

I watch them running to school in the morning, with a quite unchildlike seriousness, and wide, tragic eyes. Though sometimes they do begin laughing and fighting and romping about; then, rather than feeling happier, I am seized with horror.

They say that children are our own future, but how can one say that of these children? They aren't going to become musicians, cobblers or tailors. Last night I saw very clearly how this whole noisy world of bearded, anxious fathers and querulous grandmothers who bake honey-cakes and goose-necks – this whole world of marriage customs, proverbial sayings and Sabbaths will disappear for ever under the earth. After the war life will begin to stir once again, but we won't be here, we will have vanished – just as the Aztecs once vanished.

The peasant who brought us the news about the mass graves said that his wife had been crying at night. She'd been lamenting: 'They sew, and they make shoes, and they curry leather, and they mend watches, and they sell medicines in the chemist's. What will we do when they've all been killed?'

And how clearly I saw someone walk past our ruined houses and say: 'Once some Jews used to live here. Do you remember? An old stove-repairer called Borukh. On Saturday evenings his old wife sat on the bench and the children played round about.' And someone else said: 'And there was a doctor who used to sit there, beneath that old pear-tree – I can't remember her surname but I once went to her to have my eyes treated. After she'd finished work she used to bring out a wickerwork chair and sit there with a book.' Yes, Vitya, that's how it will be.

As though some terrible breath has passed over people's faces and everyone knows that the end is approaching.

Vityenka, I want to tell you . . . no, it's not that.

Vityenka, I'm finishing this letter and taking it to the ghetto fence to hand to my friend. It's not easy to break off. It's my last conversation with you. Once I send it off, I will have left you for ever and you will never know of my last hours. This is our final parting. What can I say to you in farewell, in eternal farewell? These last days, as during my whole life, you have been my joy. I've remembered you at night, the clothes you wore as a boy, your first books. I've remembered your first letter, your first day at school. I've remembered everything, everything from the first days of your life to the last news that I heard from you, the telegram I received on the 30th of June. I've closed my eyes and imagined that you were shielding me, my dearest, from the horror that is approaching. And then I've remembered what is happening here and felt glad that you were apart from me – and that this terrible fate will pass you by!

Vitya, I've always been lonely. I've wept in anguish through lonely nights. My consolation was the thought of how I would tell you one day about my life. Tell you why your father and I separated, why I have lived on my own for so many years. And I've often thought how surprised my Vitya would be to learn how his mother made mistakes, raved, grew jealous, made others jealous, was just what young people always are. But my fate is to end my life alone, never having shared it with you. Sometimes I've thought that I ought not to live far away from you, that I love you too much, that love gives me the right to be with you in my old age. And at other times I've thought that I ought not to live together with you, that I love you too much.

Well, *enfin* . . . Always be happy with those you love, those around you, those who have become closer to you than your mother. Forgive me.

I can hear women weeping on the street, and policemen swearing; as I look at these pages, they seem to protect me from a terrible world that is filled with suffering.

How can I finish this letter? Where can I find the strength, my son? Are there words capable of expressing my love for you? I kiss you, your eyes, your forehead, your hair.

Remember that your mother's love is always with you, in grief and in happiness, no one has the strength to destroy it.

Vityenka . . . This is the last line of your mother's last letter to you. Live, live, live for ever . . . Mama.

19

Never, before the war, had Viktor thought about the fact that he was a Jew, that his mother was a Jew. Never had his mother spoken to him about it — neither during his childhood, nor during his years as a student. Never while he was at Moscow University had one student, professor or seminar-leader ever mentioned it.

Never before the war, either at the Institute or at the Academy of Sciences had he ever heard conversations about it.

Never had he felt a desire to speak about it to Nadya, to explain to her that her mother was Russian and her father Jewish.

The century of Einstein and Planck was also the century of Hitler. The Gestapo and the scientific renaissance were children of the same age. How humane the nineteenth century seemed, that century of naïve physics, when compared with the twentieth century, the century that had killed his mother. There is a terrible similarity between the principles of Fascism and those of contemporary physics.

Fascism has rejected the concept of a separate individuality, the concept of 'a man', and operates only with vast aggregates. Contemporary physics speaks of the greater or lesser probability of occurrences within this or that aggregate of individual particles. And are not the terrible mechanics of Fascism founded on the principle of quantum politics, of political probability?

Fascism arrived at the idea of the liquidation of entire strata of the population, of entire nations and races, on the grounds that there was a greater probability of overt or covert opposition among these groupings than among others: the mechanics of probabilities and of human aggregates.

But no! No! And again no! Fascism will perish for the very reason that it has applied to man the laws applicable to atoms and cobble-stones!

Man and Fascism cannot co-exist. If Fascism conquers, man will cease to exist and there will remain only man-like creatures that have undergone an internal transformation. But if man, man who is endowed with reason and kindness, should conquer, then Fascism must perish, and those who have submitted to it will once again become people.

Was not this an admission on his part of the truth of what Chepyzhin had once said? That discussion now seemed infinitely far away, as though decades had passed since that summer evening in Moscow.

It seemed to have been another man – not Viktor at all – who had walked through Trubnaya Square, arguing heatedly and self-confidently.

Mother . . . Marusya . . . Tolya . . .

There were moments when science seemed like a delusion that prevented one from seeing the madness and cruelty of life. It might be that science was not a chance companion, but an ally of this terrible century. How lonely he felt. There was no one he could share his thoughts with. Chepyzhin was far away. Postoev found all this strange and uninteresting. Sokolov had a tendency towards mysticism, towards some strange religious submissiveness before the injustice and cruelty of Caesar.

There were two outstanding scientists who worked in his laboratory – Markov, who carried out the experiments, and the brilliant, debauched Savostyanov. But they'd think he was a psychopath if he started talking like this.

Sometimes he took his mother's letter out of his desk and read it through again.

'Vitya, I'm certain this letter will reach you, even though I'm now behind the German front line, behind the barbed wire of the Jewish ghetto . . . Where can I find the strength, my son . . . ?'

And once more he felt a cold blade against his throat.

20

Lyudmila Nikolaevna took an official envelope out of the letter-box.

She rushed into her room; holding the envelope up to the light, she tore off one corner of the coarse paper.

For a moment she thought that photographs of Tolya would come pouring out of the envelope – of Tolya when he was tiny, still unable to hold up his head, lying naked on a pillow, pouting his lips and waving his little legs in the air like a bear-cub.

In some incomprehensible manner, hardly reading the words, but somehow absorbing, almost breathing in, line after line of the red handwriting of some uneducated clerk, she understood: he's alive, he's alive!

She read that Tolya was seriously wounded in the chest and in his side, that he had lost a lot of blood and was too weak to write to her himself, that he had had a fever for four weeks . . . But her eyes were clouded by tears of happiness – so great was the despair she had felt a moment before.

She went out onto the staircase, read the first lines of the letter and, her mind at rest, walked down to the woodshed. There, in the cold twilight, she read the middle and end of the letter and thought that this was Tolya's final farewell to her.

She began filling a sack with firewood. And – although the doctor in Moscow, at the University Clinic in Gagarin Alley, had ordered her not to lift more than three kilograms and to make only slow, smooth movements – Lyudmila Nikolaevna, grunting like a peasant and without a moment's hesitation, hoisted a sack of wet logs onto her shoulders and climbed straight to the third floor. The plates on the table clattered as she threw down the sack.

Lyudmila put on her coat, threw a scarf over her head and walked downstairs to the street.

People passing by turned round to look at her. She crossed the street; there was the harsh sound of a bell and the tram-driver shook her fist.

If she turned right, there was an alley which would take her to the factory where her mother worked.

If Tolya were to die, no one would ever tell his father . . . How would they know what camp to look for him in? Maybe he was already dead . . .

Lyudmila set off to the Institute to see Viktor. As she passed by the Sokolovs', she walked into the yard and knocked at the window. The curtain remained drawn. Marya Ivanovna was out.

'Viktor Pavlovich has just gone to his office,' said a voice. Lydumila said thank you without knowing who had just spoken to her – whether it was a man or a woman, whether it was someone she knew or someone she didn't know – and walked through to the laboratory hall. As usual, hardly anyone was actually working. The men always seemed to be chatting or reading and smoking, while the women were always knitting, boiling tea in chemical retorts, or removing their nail-varnish.

She was aware of everything, all kinds of trivia, even the paper with which an assistant was rolling himself a cigarette.

In Viktor's office she was given a noisy welcome. Sokolov rushed up to her, waving a large white envelope, and said: 'There's a ray of hope. We may be re-evacuated to Moscow, together with our families and all our gear and apparatus. Not bad, eh? Admittedly, the dates haven't been fixed yet. But still!'

His animated face and eyes were quite hateful. Surely Marya Ivanovna wouldn't have come running up to her like that? No, no. Marya Ivanovna would have understood straight away – she would have been able to read Lyudmila's face.

If she'd known she'd see so many happy faces, she'd never have come to see Viktor. He too would be bubbling with joy, and in the evening he would share this joy of his with Nadya – yes, now at last they would be leaving this hateful Kazan!

Would all the people in the world be worth the young blood that was the price of this joy?

She looked reproachfully at her husband. And Viktor's eyes looked with anxiety and understanding into hers, which were full of gloom.

When they were finally alone, he said he'd realized at once that something terrible had happened. He read through the letter and said: 'What can we do? Dear God, what can we do?'

Then he put on his coat and they walked out towards the exit.

'I won't be back today,' he said to Sokolov.

Sokolov was standing next to Dubyonkov, the recently appointed director of the personnel department, a tall round-headed man in a fashionable, broad-fitting jacket that was still too narrow for his wide shoulders.

Letting go of Lyudmila's hand for a moment, Viktor said to Dubyonkov in an undertone: 'We were going to start on the Moscow re-evacuation lists, but it will have to wait. I'll explain why afterwards.'

'Don't worry, Viktor Pavlovich,' said Dubyonkov in his bass voice. 'There's no hurry. They're just plans for the future. Anyway I can do all the basic work by myself.'

Sokolov waved and nodded his head. Viktor knew he had already guessed that another tragedy had befallen him.

There was a cold wind out on the street. It picked up the dust, whirled it about and suddenly scattered it, flinging it down like black chaff. There was an implacable severity in the frost, in the branches that tapped together like bones, in the icy blue of the tram-lines.

Viktor's wife turned her thin, cold face towards him. It had grown younger from suffering. She looked at him fixedly, entreatingly.

Once they had had a young cat. As she was giving birth to her first litter, there had been one kitten she hadn't been able to get out. As she was dying, she had crawled up to Viktor and cried, staring at him with wide, bright eyes. But who was there in this vast empty sky, on this pitiless, dusty earth – who was there to beg or entreat?

'There's the hospital where I used to work,' said Lyudmila.

'Lyuda,' said Viktor suddenly, 'Why don't you go in? They'll be able to locate the field hospital for you. Why didn't I think of that before?'

He watched Lyudmila climb up the steps and explain herself to the janitor.

Viktor walked round the corner and then paced back to the main entrance. People were rushing along with their string bags; inside them were glass jars full of grey potatoes or bits of macaroni in a grey soup.

'Vitya,' his wife called out. He could tell from her voice that she had regained her self-possession.

'So,' she said, 'he's in Saratov. The assistant medical director happens to have been there not long ago. He's written down the address for me.'

At once there was a mass of things to do and problems to sort out. She needed to know when the steamer left and how she could get a ticket; she'd need to pack some food and borrow some money; and somehow she'd have to get an official authorization . . .

Lyudmila Nikolaevna left with no food, none of her things, and almost no money; in the general confusion and bustle of embarkation she made her way onto the deck without a ticket.

All she took with her was the memory of parting with her husband, her mother and Nadya on a dark autumn evening. Black waves lapped noisily against the sides of the boat. A fierce wind blew from downstream, howling and flinging up spray from the river.

21

Dementiy Trifonovich Getmanov, the secretary of the *obkom*** of one of the German-occupied areas of the Ukraine, had been appointed commissar of a tank corps now being formed in the Urals.

Before setting out to join the corps, Getmanov flew in a Douglas to Ufa where his family had been evacuated.

His comrades in Ufa had looked after his family well; their living conditions turned out to be not bad at all. Getmanov's wife, Galina Terentyevna, had a poor metabolism and had always been remarkably stout; rather than growing thinner since being evacuated, she had put on still more weight. His two daughters and his youngest son, who had not yet begun school, all seemed in good health.

Getmanov was in Ufa for five days. Before his departure several of his closest friends came round to say goodbye: his wife's younger brother, Nikolay Terentyevich, who was the deputy office-manager of

---

* *Obkom:* the Party committee of an *oblast* or province.

the Ukrainian Council of People's Commissars; one of his old comrades, Mashuk from Kiev, an official in the State security organs; and his sister-in-law's husband, Sagaydak, an executive in the propaganda department of the Ukrainian Central Committee.

Sagaydak arrived after ten o'clock, when the children had already gone to bed and people were talking in undertones.

'How about a quick drink, comrades?' asked Getmanov. 'A drop of vodka from Moscow?'

Taken separately, each one of Getmanov's features was large: his shaggy, greying head, his broad forehead, his fleshy nose, the palms of his hands, his fingers, his shoulders, his thick powerful neck . . . But he himself, the combination of these parts, was quite small. Strangely, it was his small eyes that were the most attractive and memorable feature of his large face. They were narrow, almost invisible beneath his swollen eyelids. Even their colour was somehow uncertain – neither grey nor blue. But there was something very alive about them, something penetrating and shrewd.

Galina Terentyevna, rising effortlessly despite her corpulent body, left the room. The men fell silent, as often happens – both in a village hut and in the city – when vodka is about to appear. Soon Galina Terentyevna returned with a tray. It seemed surprising that her large hands should have been able, in such a short time, to set out so many plates and open so many tins of food.

Mashuk glanced round at the wide ottoman, the Ukrainian embroidery hanging on the walls, the hospitable array of tins and bottles.

'I can remember that ottoman from your flat, Galina Terentyevna,' he said. 'Let me congratulate you on getting it out. You've got a real talent for organization.'

'Hear, hear!' said Getmanov. 'And I wasn't even at home when we were evacuated. She did it all by herself!'

'I couldn't just give it away to the Germans,' said Galina. 'Anyway Dima's used to it. When he comes home, he sits straight down on it and starts going over his work.'

'You mean he comes home and goes straight to sleep on it,' said Sagaydak.

She went out to the kitchen again. Mashuk gave Getmanov a broad wink. 'I can see the woman already!' he said under his breath. 'Our

Dementiy Trifonovich isn't one to waste time. He'll soon be friends with some pretty young medical officer.'

'Yes, he's a passionate man,' agreed Sagaydak.

Getmanov brushed this aside. 'Come off it now. I'm an invalid.'

'Oh yes,' said Mashuk. 'And who used to come back to his tent at three in the morning in Kislovodsk?'

The guests all burst out laughing. Getmanov glanced quickly but intently at his wife's brother. Galina came back into the room. Seeing everyone in fits of laughter, she said: 'I only have to be out of the room for half a minute and you're all talking nonsense to my poor Dima!'

Getmanov filled the glasses with vodka. With great deliberation, the guests began choosing something to eat. Looking at the portrait of Stalin on the wall, Getmanov raised his glass and said: 'Well, comrades, let's drink first of all to our father. May he always remain in good health!'

He pronounced these words in a rather bluff, free-and-easy tone of voice. The implication was that they all understood Stalin's greatness very well, but were drinking to him now as a human being, someone they loved for his straightforwardness, modesty and sensitivity. And Stalin himself, looking up and down the table and then at the ample breasts of Galina Terentyevna, appeared to say: 'Very well, fellows, I'll just get my pipe going. Then I'll bring my chair up a bit closer.'

'That's right, may our father live for a long time! Where would we be without him?' said Nikolay Terentyevich.

Holding his glass to his lips, Getmanov looked round at Sagaydak, as though expecting him to say something. Sagaydak just looked at the portrait as if to say, 'What more needs to be said, Father? You already know everything.' He downed his vodka and the others followed suit.

Dementiy Trifonovich Getmanov had been born in Liven in the province of Voronezh, but had worked many years in the Ukraine and had long-standing ties with his Ukrainian comrades. His links with Kiev had been further consolidated by his marriage to Galina Terentyevna: her many relatives occupied conspicuous positions in the Party and Soviet apparatus in the Ukraine.

Getmanov's life had been relatively uneventful. He had not taken part in the Civil War. He had not been hunted by the police and had never been exiled to Siberia at the decree of a Tsarist court. At conferences and congresses he usually read his reports from a written text. Even though he had not written them himself, he read these reports well, expressively and without hesitation. Admittedly, they were by no means difficult to read – they were printed in large type, double-spaced, and with the name of Stalin always in red. As a young man, Getmanov had been intelligent and disciplined; he had intended to study at the Mechanical Institute but had been recruited for work in the security organs. Soon he had become the bodyguard of the secretary of the *kraykom*, the area Party committee. He was taken notice of and sent on courses for Party workers. Then he was accepted for work in the Party apparatus – first in the organizational and educational department of the *kraykom*, then in the personnel department of the Central Committee. After a year he became an assistant in the Senior Appointments Department. And in 1937 he became secretary of the *obkom*, the *oblast* Party committee – 'master of the *oblast*', as people said.

His word could decide the fate of a head of a university department, an engineer, a bank manager, a chairman of a trade union, a collective farm or a theatrical production.

The confidence of the Party! Getmanov knew the immense meaning of these words. His whole life – which contained no great books, famous discoveries or military victories – was one sustained, intense, unsleeping labour. The supreme meaning of this labour lay in the fact that it was done at the demand of the Party and for the sake of the Party. The supreme reward for this labour was to be granted the confidence of the Party.

Every decision he made had to be infused with the spirit of the Party and be conducive to its interests, whether the issue in question was the fate of a child being sent to a home, the reorganization of a university biology department, or the eviction from premises belonging to a library of a workers' co-operative producing articles made from plastic. The attitude of a Party leader to any matter, to any film, to any book, had to be infused with the spirit of the Party; however difficult it might be, he had to immediately renounce a favourite book or a customary way of behaviour if the interests of the Party should conflict with his personal sympathies. But Getmanov knew that there was a still higher form of Party spirit: a true Party leader simply didn't have personal likings or inclinations; he loved something only because, and only in so far as, it expressed the spirit of the Party.

The sacrifices made by Getmanov in the name of Party loyalty were sometimes cruel. In this world neighbours from the same village or teachers to whom one had been indebted since youth no longer existed; love or sympathy were no longer to be reckoned with. Nor could one be disturbed by such words as 'turned away from', 'failed to support', 'ruined', 'betrayed' . . . But true Party spirit showed itself when a sacrifice was not even necessary, when no personal feeling could survive for even a moment if it happened to clash with the spirit of the Party.

The labour of those who enjoy the confidence of the Party is imperceptible. But it is a vast labour – one must expend one's mind and soul generously, keeping nothing back. The power of a Party leader does not require the talent of a scientist or the gift of a writer. It is something higher than any talent or gift. Getmanov's guiding word was anxiously awaited by hundreds of singers, writers and scientific researchers – though Getmanov himself was not only unable to sing, play the piano or direct a theatrical production, but incapable even of truly understanding a work of science, poetry, music or painting . . . The power of his word lay in the fact that the Party had entrusted him with its own interests in the area of art and culture.

No thinker, no people's tribune could enjoy as much power as Getmanov – the secretary of the Party organization of an entire *oblast*.

Getmanov felt that the deepest meaning of the words 'the confidence of the Party' was expressed in the opinions, thoughts and feelings of Stalin. The essence of the Party line lay in Stalin's confidence in his comrades-in-arms, his marshals and people's commissars.

The guests talked mainly of Getmanov's new posting. They understood that Getmanov had expected something more important – people in his position would usually be appointed Members of the Military Soviet of an Army or Front.

Getmanov had indeed felt upset and alarmed at being appointed to a mere corps. He had made enquiries through one of his friends, a member of the organizational bureau of the Central Committee, as to whether there was any dissatisfaction with him in higher circles. It seemed there was nothing to worry about.

Getmanov had then begun to console himself by seeing the good sides of his appointment. Not everyone would be sent to a tank corps: it was, after all, the tank corps that were going to determine the outcome of the war, to play the crucial role in the decisive battles. Yes, they'd sooner appoint someone as a Member of the Military Soviet of some second-rate army in an area of secondary importance than as commissar to a tank corps. It was through this that the Party had expressed its confidence in him. Nevertheless he was upset – he would have liked very much, after putting on his uniform and looking in the mirror, to pronounce the words: 'Member of the Army Military Soviet, Brigade Commissar Getmanov.'

For some reason his most extreme irritation was aroused by the commanding officer of the corps, Colonel Novikov. He had yet to meet this colonel, but everything that he had found out so far was profoundly displeasing.

Getmanov's friends understood his mood; all their remarks about his new posting were very reassuring.

Sagaydak said that the corps would most likely be sent to Stalingrad; that comrade Stalin had known General Yeremenko, the commanding officer of the Stalingrad Front, since the Civil War, even before the First Cavalry Army; that Stalin often talked to him on the telephone and received him in his own house when he came to Moscow . . . Not long ago Yeremenko had been at comrade Stalin's dacha outside Moscow and Stalin's conversation with him had lasted for two hours. It would be good to fight under the command of a man who enjoyed the confidence of comrade Stalin to such a degree.

After that someone said that Nikita Khrushchev remembered Getmanov's work in the Ukraine, and that if he were lucky he might be sent to the Front where Nikita Khrushchev was on the Military Soviet.

'It's not just coincidence,' said Nikolay Terentyevich, 'that comrade Stalin should have sent Nikita Khrushchev to Stalingrad. It's the key Front – who else could he have sent?'

'And is it just chance that comrade Stalin should post my Dementiy Trifonovich to a tank corps?' Galina Terentyevna asked provocatively.

'Now come on!' said Getmanov. 'For me to be posted to a corps is like becoming secretary of a *raykom*. After being first secretary of an *obkom*, it's nothing to write home about.'

'Far from it!' said Sagaydak very seriously. 'Your appointment is an expression of the confidence of the Party. It's not just some out-of-the-way *raykom*, but the *raykom* of an industrial centre like

Magnitogorsk or Dneproderzhinsk. It's not just any old corps, but a tank corps.'

According to Mashuk, the commanding officer of this corps had only recently been appointed – he had never before commanded such a large unit. He had been told this by an official from the Special Section of the Front, who had been in Ufa not long before.

'There's one other thing he told me,' said Mashuk. He paused. '. . . But there's no need for me to tell you, Dementiy Trifonovich. You probably already know more about him than he does himself.'

Getmanov screwed up his narrow, shrewd, eyes. 'A lot more.'

Mashuk gave an almost imperceptible smile that was nevertheless noticed by everyone at the table. Although he was related twice over to the Getmanovs, although at family gatherings he always seemed a kind, modest fellow who was fond of a good joke, the Getmanovs always felt a certain tension as they listened to Mashuk's soft, insinuating voice and watched his calm eyes and long, pale face. Getmanov himself did not find this in the least surprising. He was well aware of the power behind Mashuk; he understood how much more Mashuk often knew about things than he did himself.

'Tell us about him,' said Sagaydak.

'He's just someone who's jumped up during the war,' Getmanov explained condescendingly. 'He didn't do anything much before.'

'He wasn't in the *nomenklatura*?'* asked Galina's brother with a smile.

'The *nomenklatura*!' Getmanov gave a disparaging wave of the hand. 'But he's a useful fellow. I've heard he's a good soldier. And his chief of staff is General Nyeudobnov. I met him at the eighteenth Party Congress. He's very competent.'

'Nyeudobnov, Illarion Innokyentyevich?' exclaimed Mashuk. 'Well, well. He was the first man I worked under. Then we went our different ways. And before the war I once met him in Lavrentiy Beria's reception room.'

'Different ways,' repeated Sagaydak with a smile. 'You should approach the matter dialectically – look for the identity and unity, not just the contrast.'

'Everything goes crazy during the war,' said Mashuk. 'Some

* *Nomenklatura*: the register kept by the Party organs of persons professionally and politically eligible for posts of responsibility.

colonel or other is the commanding officer of a corps and General Nyeudobnov is made his subordinate!'

'He's got no wartime experience,' said Getmanov. 'That does have to be taken into account.'

'I don't believe it! Nyeudobnov! Why, there was a time when one word from him could decide anything. A Party member since before the Revolution, with a vast experience of both public and military service! He was expected to go right to the top.'

The other guests all agreed with Mashuk. Condoling with Nyeudobnov was the easiest way for them to express their sympathy for Getmanov.

'Yes, the war's turned everything upside down,' said Galina's brother. 'I hope it comes to an end soon.'

Getmanov pointed towards Sagaydak. 'Did you ever meet Krymov, a Muscovite? He once gave a talk about international affairs to the lecture group of the Kiev Central Committee.'

'A few years before the war? A deviationist? Used to work in the Comintern?'

'Yes, that's right. Well, this corps-commander of mine intends to marry his ex-wife.'

For some reason this piece of news made everyone laugh, although no one present had met either Krymov's ex-wife or the corps-commander who intended to marry her.

'Yes, it wasn't for nothing that our friend received his first training in the security organs,' said Mashuk. 'Is there anything he doesn't know?'

'There are no flies on him,' said Galina's brother. 'That's for sure.'

'Of course. The High Command's got no time for scatterbrains.'

'Yes, our Getmanov's certainly no scatterbrain,' said Sagaydak.

In a serious, matter-of-fact tone, as though he were back in his office, Mashuk said: 'Yes, that Krymov . . . I remember him from his visit to Kiev – a dubious character. He's been mixed up for years with all kinds of Trotskyists and Bukharinites.'

He spoke straightforwardly and openly, seemingly as straightforwardly as the manager of a knitwear factory or a teacher at a technical institute might talk about their work. But they all understood that this openness and freedom were only apparent – he knew better than any of them what could, and what could not, be talked about. Getmanov, who also loved to shock people by his boldness and candour, was well aware of the depths concealed beneath the surface of this animated and spontaneous conversation.

Although normally very thoughtful and serious, Sagaydak now tried to restore to the conversation its earlier note of lightness. Turning to Getmanov he said: 'That's why his wife's left him – she thinks he's an unreliable element.'

'I hope you're right,' said Getmanov. 'But it seems to me that this corps-commander of mine is marrying an alien and unreliable element himself.'

'Well, let him!' said Galina Terentyevna. 'What strange things you worry about. What matters is whether or not they love each other.'

'Love, of course, is fundamental,' agreed Getmanov. 'Everyone knows that. But there are other matters that certain Soviet citizens tend to forget about.'

'Absolutely,' said Mashuk, 'and we should be aware of everything.'

'Right. And then people wonder why the Central Committee hasn't ratified a new appointment, why this and why that . . . But what have they done to deserve the confidence of the Party?'

'You are a strange lot!' interrupted Galina Terentyevna in a sing-song voice. 'Anyone would think you'd quite forgotten about the war. All you seem to worry about is the ex-husband of the future wife of some corps-commander. Who are you fighting against, Dima?'

She looked mockingly at the men. Her beautiful brown eyes were somehow similar to the narrow eyes of her husband – perhaps because they were equally penetrating.

'What are you saying?' Sagaydak replied mournfully. 'Our sons and brothers are setting out to the war from every corner of the country, from the last hut in a *kolkhoz* to the Kremlin itself. This war is a war for the Fatherland, a great war. Comrade Stalin's son, Vasiliy, is a fighter-pilot. Comrade Mikoyan's son's in the Air Force too. I've heard that Lavrentiy Beria has got a son at the front, but I'm not sure which service. I think Timur Frunze is a lieutenant in the infantry . . . And then what's her name – Dolores Ibarruri – her son was killed outside Stalingrad.'

'Comrade Stalin had two sons at the front,' said Nikolay Terentyevich. 'The younger one, Yakov, was in command of an artillery battery . . . No, Yakov's the elder brother. Poor man – he's been taken prisoner.'

He stopped short, sensing that he'd touched on a matter his senior comrades preferred not to talk about. To break the awkward silence, he announced in a carefree tone: 'By the way, I've heard the Germans have been dropping ridiculous propaganda leaflets. They're making out that Yakov Stalin has given them information of his own free will.'

The void surrounding Nikolay Terentyevich grew still more unpleasant. He had spoken about something that should never be mentioned, even in jest. To express indignation at lying rumours about Iosif Vissarionovich's relationship with his wife would be as serious a blunder as to spread the same rumours – any word at all about such matters was inadmissible.

Turning suddenly to his wife, Getmanov said: 'My heart lies where comrade Stalin has taken the battle into his own hands, and with such a firm grip that he really has put the wind up the Germans!'

Guiltily and apologetically, Galina's brother caught Getmanov's eye. But these people hadn't met together just to pounce on some conversational gaffe. They weren't petty-minded.

In a good-natured, comradely tone of voice, as though defending Nikolay Terentyevich from Getmanov, Sagaydak said: 'That's all very well, but we must all take care not to slip up in our own work.'

'And not to speak without thinking,' added Getmanov.

The explicitness of Getmanov's reproach was a sign that he would think no more of Nikolay Terentyevich's blunder. Sagaydak and Mashuk nodded approvingly.

Galina's brother understood that this stupid, trivial incident would be forgotten; he also understood that it would not be forgotten entirely. One day, during a meeting to discuss a nomination for some particularly responsible post, Getmanov, Sagaydak and Mashuk would all nod their heads at mention of Nikolay Terentyevich; at the same time, however, they would give the merest hint of a smile. In reply to a question posed by an observant comrade, they would say, 'Perhaps just a trifle indiscreet,' measuring this trifle on the tip of their little finger.

Deep down they all understood that the Germans were probably not lying so very blatantly. That was why Yakov was best not discussed.

Sagaydak had a particularly fine grasp of such matters. He had worked on a newspaper for a long time; first he had been responsible for the news pages, then for the agricultural section. After that he had worked for about two years as editor of one of the Kiev papers. He considered that the aim of his newspaper was to educate the reader – not indiscriminately to disseminate chaotic information about all kinds of probably fortuitous events. In his role as editor Sagaydak might consider it appropriate to pass over some event: a very bad harvest, an ideologically inconsistent poem, a formalist painting, an outbreak of foot-and-mouth disease, an earthquake, or the destruction of a battleship. He might prefer to close his eyes to a terrible fire in a mine or a tidal wave that had swept thousands of people off the face of the earth. In his view these events had no meaning and he saw no reason why he should bring them to the notice of readers, journalists and writers. Sometimes he would have to give his own explanation of an event; this was often boldly original and entirely contradictory to ordinary ways of thought. He himself felt that his power, his skill and experience as an editor were revealed by his ability to bring to the consciousness of his readers only those ideas that were necessary and of true educational benefit.

When flagrant excesses occurred during the period of out-and-out collectivization, Sagaydak – before the publication of Stalin's article 'Dizziness from Success'* – wrote that the reason for the famine of this period was that the kulaks were burying their grain and refusing to eat, that whole villages – little children, old people and all – were dying, simply to spite the State.

At the same time he included material about how the children in *kolkhoz* crèches were fed chicken broth, *pirozhki* and rissoles made from rice. In reality they were withering away, their bellies distended.

Then came the war, one of the most cruel and terrible wars that had befallen Russia during the thousand years of her history. The ordeals of the first weeks and months brought the true course of events into the open; the war was now the arbiter of all fates, even that of the Party. But, as soon as this terrible period came to an end, Korneychuk explained the reason for the military disasters in his play *The Front*:

* An article condemning certain 'excesses' committed during collectivization – published when the famine resulting from the initial disasters threatened to get out of hand.

incompetent generals had failed to carry out the orders of the infallible High Command . . .

Nikolay Terentyevich was not the only one to experience some unpleasant moments that evening. Mashuk had been leafing through the thick pages of a large leather-bound photograph album. He suddenly raised his eyebrows so expressively that everyone craned over to look. It was a photograph of Getmanov in the office he had before the war as secretary of the *obkom*; he was wearing a semi-military Party tunic and sitting at a writing-desk as vast as the steppes; above him hung a portrait of Stalin of such huge dimensions as could be found only in the office of the secretary of an *obkom*. Stalin's face in the portrait had been scrawled over in coloured pencil; a blue pointed beard had been added to his chin and light-blue ear-rings hung from his ears.

'What has the boy gone and done now!' exclaimed Getmanov, wringing his hands womanishly.

Galina Terentyevna fell into utter confusion; she kept looking round and repeating: 'But before he went to sleep last night, he said, "I love Uncle Stalin as much as my own papa."'

'It's just a child's prank,' said Sagaydak.

'It's not just a prank, it's malicious hooliganism,' said Getmanov with an angry sigh.

He looked searchingly at Mashuk. They were both thinking of an incident that had occurred before the war: a polytechnic student, the nephew of someone they knew from Kiev, had fired an air-rifle at Stalin's portrait in the student hostel.

They knew that this halfwit of a student had been playing the fool, that there was no political or terrorist motive behind his act. Their friend from Kiev, a splendid fellow, the director of the Machine and Tractor Station, had asked Getmanov to intervene on behalf of his nephew.

After a committee meeting Getmanov had mentioned this affair to Mashuk. Mashuk had replied: 'We're not children, Dementiy Trifonovich. Whether or not he's guilty is hardly the point. If I do get this case dropped, someone will inform Moscow – they might even tell Lavrentiy Beria himself – that Mashuk took a liberal attitude towards someone shooting at a portrait of the great Stalin. Today I'm here in this office – tomorrow I'll be dust in a labour-camp. Will *you* take the responsibility? They'll say the same thing: today the student's shooting at portraits, tomorrow he'll be shooting at Stalin himself; and as for Getmanov – either he likes the boy for some reason, or else there's something about the act that appeals to him. So? Is that what you want?'

A month or two later Getmanov had asked Mashuk: 'Tell me, what happened to that student with the air-rifle?'

Mashuk, looking at him very calmly, had replied: 'Don't trouble yourself about him. He turned out to be a scoundrel, the son of some kulak whore. He confessed everything during the investigation.'

Now, Getmanov stared at Mashuk and repeated: 'No, it's not just a prank.'

'Come on!' said Mashuk. 'The boy's only four. You have to make allowance for his age.'

With a warmth and sincerity that everyone could feel, Sagaydak said: 'Let me say it straight out: I just don't have the strength to be strict with children. I ought to, but I haven't the heart. All I care about is that they should be in good health . . .'

They all looked at Sagaydak with compassion. He was not a happy father. His eldest son, Vitaliy, had been a troublemaker even while he was in the ninth class. He had once been picked up by the police during some brawl in a restaurant. His father had had to phone the Deputy People's Commissar for Internal Affairs in order to hush up a scandal that turned out to involve the children of several prominent people – the daughter of a writer, the daughter of the People's Commissar for Agriculture and the sons of various generals and Academicians. During the war young Sagaydak had decided he wanted to join the army as a volunteer; his father had managed to fix a place for him on a two-year course in an artillery school. He had been expelled for indiscipline and sent straight to the front.

Now, for the past month, young Sagaydak had been doing a mortar course; to the joy of his parents, no awkward incidents had yet occurred; they hoped for the best, but remained anxious.

Sagaydak's second son, Igor, had caught polio when he was two and the after-effects of the illness had turned him into a cripple – his withered legs had no strength in them and he walked about on crutches. Poor Igor was unable to go to school and the teachers had to come to his home. He was a keen and hard-working pupil.

There wasn't a famous neuropathologist in the Ukraine, or even in Moscow, Leningrad or Tomsk, whom the Sagaydaks hadn't consulted about Igor. There was no new foreign medicine Sagaydak hadn't managed to procure through either an embassy or a trade delegation. He knew that he could be reproved for his excessive love, but he also knew that this was not a mortal sin. He himself, coming up against very strong paternal feelings in several *oblast* officials, had made allowances for the fact that people of the new type had a particularly deep love for their children. He knew that he too would be forgiven the folk-healer he had brought from Odessa by plane and the herbs from some Far-Eastern holy man that had been delivered to Kiev by special courier.

'Our leaders are very special people,' said Sagaydak. 'I'm not talking about comrade Stalin – that goes without saying – but about his close aides. They even place the Party above their feelings as parents.'

'Yes, but they know one can't expect that from everyone,' said Getmanov. He went on to talk about the severity one of the Secretaries of the Central Committee had shown to a son of his who had been fined.

The conversation about children continued in a different tone, intimately and without pretension. One might have thought that all the strength of these people, all their joy in life, depended on whether their Tanechkas and Vitaliks had good colour in their cheeks, whether their Vladimirs and Lyudmilas were getting good marks at school and successfully moving up from class to class.

Galina Terentyevna began talking about her daughters. 'Svetlana was very poorly until she was four. She had colitis the whole time – the poor girl was quite worn out. And do you know what cured it in the end – grated apple!'

Then Getmanov joined in. 'This morning before school she said to me, "In class they call me and Zoya the general's daughters." And then Zoya, the cheeky little thing, started laughing and said: "General's daughter – that's no great honour. We've got one girl in our class who's a marshal's daughter – that really is something!"'

'I know,' said Sagaydak gaily. 'One can't satisfy them. Igor said to me the other day, "Third secretary – that's no big deal."'

There were many amusing little stories Nikolay Terentyevich could have recounted, but it wasn't for him to bring up the intelligence of his own children when the conversation was about the intelligence of Igor Sagaydak and the Getmanovs' daughters.

'Our fathers were much rougher with their children,' Mashuk said thoughtfully.

'But they still loved them,' said Galina's brother.

'Yes, of course they did. But they beat them too. At least they did me.'

'I've just remembered how my father went off to the war in 1915,' said Getmanov. 'No joking – he became a non-commissioned officer and was twice awarded the Cross of St George. It was early in the morning and my mother got everything ready for him: she put a sweater, some foot-cloths, some hard-boiled eggs and some bread in a bag while my sister and I lay there in bed, watching him sitting at table for the last time. He filled the water bucket that stood by the door and chopped lots of wood. My mother remembered every moment.'

Then, glancing at his watch, he said: 'Oho!'

'So, tomorrow's the day,' said Sagaydak as he got up.

'The plane leaves at seven.'

'From the civil airport?' asked Mashuk.

Getmanov nodded.

'So much the better,' said Nikolay Terentyevich as he too stood up. 'It's fifteen kilometres to the military airport.'

'What can that matter to a soldier?' said Getmanov.

They began saying goodbye, laughing again, embracing and generally making a stir. When they all had their hats and coats on and were standing out in the corridor, Getmanov remarked: 'A soldier can harden himself to anything. He can warm himself with smoke and shave with an awl. But what a soldier can never get used to is living apart from his children.'

And it was clear from his expression and tone of voice, from the way his guests looked at him as they went out, that he meant this.

22

It was night. Getmanov was in uniform, sitting at his desk and writing. His wife was sitting beside him in her dressing-gown and watching. He folded up a letter and said: 'That's to the director of the regional health authority in case you need special treatment or you have to travel somewhere for a consultation. He'll make out a certificate and then your brother can fix you up with a travel permit.'

'Have you made out the warrant for obtaining rations?'

'There's no need to. Just ring the person responsible at the *obkom*. Or even better, ring Puzichenko himself – he'll make one out for you.'

He went through the little pile of letters, notes and warrants. 'Well, that seems like everything.'

They fell silent.

'I'm afraid for you, my love,' said Galina. 'You're going to the war.'

'You just take care of yourself and look after the children,' he replied, getting to his feet. 'Did you remember to put some cognac in my suitcase?'

'Yes, yes. Do you remember – two years ago, when you were about to fly to Kislovodsk? Early in the morning you were writing out warrants – just like today.'

'Now the Germans are in Kislovodsk,' said Getmanov.

He walked up and down the room and then stopped for a moment to listen. 'Are they asleep?'

'Of course.'

They went through to the children's room. It was strange how silently these huge figures moved in the semi-darkness. The heads of the sleeping children showed up dark against the white of the pillow-cases. Getmanov listened attentively to their breathing.

He held his hand to his chest, afraid that his booming heart-beats would disturb the children. He felt a piercing ache of tenderness, anxiety and pity for them. He desperately wanted to embrace his son and daughters and kiss their sleeping faces. He was overwhelmed by a helpless tenderness, an unreasoning love; he felt lost, weak and confused.

He wasn't in the least worried or frightened at the thought of the new job he was about to begin. He had taken on many new jobs, and had never had difficulty in finding the correct line to follow. He knew it would be the same in the tank corps.

But how could he reconcile his unshakeable, iron severity with this limitless tenderness and love?

He looked round at his wife. She was standing beside him, resting her cheek on her hand like a peasant. In the half-light her face seemed younger and thinner – just as it had been when they had gone to the sea on their honeymoon and stayed in a hostel right on the cliffs.

There was a discreet hoot beneath the window – the car from the *obkom*. Getmanov turned once more towards his children and spread out his hands – expressing through this gesture his impotence before a feeling he was unable to control.

In the corridor he said goodbye, kissed his wife for the last time and put on his fur coat and cap. Then he stood and waited while the driver carried out his cases.

'Well then,' he said – and suddenly stepped up to his wife, removed his cap and embraced her once more. And this second farewell – with the cold damp air off the streets slipping in through the half-open door and blending with the warmth of the house, with the rough, tanned hide of his coat touching the sweet-scented silk of her dressing-gown – this final farewell made them feel that their life, which had seemed one, had suddenly split apart. They felt desolate.

23

Yevgenia Nikolaevna Shaposhnikova, Lyudmila's younger sister, had moved to Kuibyshev. She was living with an old German woman, Jenny Genrikhovna, who years before had worked for the Shaposhnikov family as a governess.

Yevgenia found it strange, after Stalingrad, to be sharing a small, quiet room with an old woman who never ceased marvelling at how a little girl with plaits could have turned into a grown woman.

Jenny Genrikhovna's gloomy little cubby-hole had once been part of the servants' quarters of a spacious merchant's flat. Now each room was inhabited by a whole family and was divided up by screens, curtains, rugs and the backs of sofas into little nooks and corners – one for eating, one for sleeping, one for receiving guests, another for the nurse to give injections to a paralysed old man . . .

In the evening the kitchen fairly hummed with the voices of all the inmates.

Yevgenia Nikolaevna liked this kitchen with its sooty ceiling and the dark red flames of the oil-stoves. People in dressing-gowns, padded jackets and soldiers' tunics bustled about below clothes that had been hung up to dry. Knives gleamed. Clouds of steam rose from tubs and bowls full of washing. The ample stove was no longer in use; the Dutch tiles lining its sides seemed cold and white – like the snow-covered slopes of some long-extinct volcano.

The tenants of the flat included the family of a docker who was now at the front, a gynaecologist, an engineer from an armaments factory, a single mother who worked as a cashier in a store, the widow of a hairdresser who had been killed at the front, the manager of a post-office, and – in what had once been the large dining-room – the director of a surgery.

The flat was as extensive as a town; it even had room in it for its own madman, a quiet little old man with the eyes of a sweet, good-natured puppy.

They were all crowded together and at the same time very isolated. They were always taking offence at one another and then making peace, one moment concealing every detail of their lives, and the next generously and excitedly sharing everything that happened to them.

Yevgenia would have liked to draw this flat – not so much the objects and people themselves as the feelings they aroused in her.

There were many facets to these feelings. It seemed unlikely that even a great artist could give expression to them. They arose from the strange incongruity between the tremendous military strength of the Soviet State and this dark kitchen with its poverty, gossip and general pettiness; the incongruity between cold, hard steel and kitchen pots and pans full of potato peelings.

The expression of these feelings would break up every line, distort figures and take the form of some apparently meaningless coupling of fragmented images and patches of light.

Old Jenny Genrikhovna was a meek, timid, obliging creature. She wore a black dress with a white collar and, in spite of her constant hunger, her cheeks were always rosy.

Her head was full of memories of Lyudmila's pranks when she was still in the first form, of amusing phrases little Marusya had once come out with, of how two-year-old Dmitry had once come into the dining-room in his pinafore and shouted out: 'Munch-time, munch-time!'

Now Jenny Genrikhovna worked as a daily help in the home of a dentist, looking after her sick mother. Sometimes the dentist would travel round the region for five or six days. Then Jenny would spend the night in her house to look after the old woman; she had recently had a stroke and was barely able to walk.

Jenny lacked any sense of property – she was constantly apologizing to Yevgenia and asking her permission to open the small upper window in order to let in her elderly tabby cat. Her main interests and worries were centred around this cat and how to protect it from her neighbours.

One of these neighbours, an engineer called Dragin, who was in charge of a workshop at his factory, looked with cruel mockery at her wrinkled face, her girlishly slim, emaciated waist and her pince-nez. His plebeian soul was indignant that the old woman should remain devoted to her memories of the past; indignant that she should continue, an idiotically blissful smile on her face, to tell stories about taking her pre-revolutionary charges out in the pram, or accompanying 'Madame' to Venice, Paris or Vienna. Many of the 'little ones' she had cared for had fought with Denikin or Wrangel during the Civil War and had been killed by the Red Army. The old woman, however, remained interested only in how they had once languished in bed with scarlet fever, diphtheria or colitis.

'I've never met anyone so gentle and so forgiving,' Yevgenia told Dragin. 'Believe me, she's a better person than any of the rest of us here in the flat.'

'Sweet little dicky bird!' said Dragin with a laugh. He looked her brazenly in the eye. 'You've sold yourself to the Germans, comrade Shaposhnikova – just for somewhere to live.'

Jenny Genrikhovna was evidently less fond of healthy children. She talked most often of all about the very sickliest of her charges, the son of a Jewish factory-owner. She still kept his exercise-books and drawings and would burst into tears each time she reached the point of describing the death of this quiet little boy.

It was many years since she had lived with the Shaposhnikovs, but she still remembered the names and nicknames of all the children. When she heard of Marusya's death she cried. She was always scrawling a letter to Alexandra Vladimirovna, but could never finish it.

She referred to caviare by its French rather than its Russian name and she told Yevgenia how her pre-revolutionary charges had breakfasted on a cup of strong broth and a slice of venison.

She fed her own rations to the cat, whom she called 'my dear, silver child.' The cat adored her; he was a rough and sullen beast, but would become suddenly animated and affectionate when he saw her.

Dragin kept asking her what she thought of Hitler. 'You must be happy now,' he would say. But the old woman shrewdly declared herself an anti-Fascist and called the Führer a cannibal.

She was utterly impractical; she was unable to cook or wash and when she went to the shop for some matches, the assistant always hurriedly tore off the coupon for her monthly allowance of sugar or meat.

Children nowadays were quite unlike her charges of that earlier period which she referred to as 'peacetime'. Everything was different, even the games. The 'peacetime' children had played with hoops; they had played diabolo with varnished sticks, and catch with a painted ball kept in a white string-bag; whereas today's children played volleyball, swam the crawl, and played ice-hockey during the winter in skiing trousers, shouting and whistling all the time.

These children knew more than Jenny Genrikhovna about alimony, abortions and dishonestly acquired ration-cards; about senior lieutenants and lieutenant-colonels who had presented other people's wives with the butter, lard and tinned foods they had brought back from the front.

Yevgenia liked to hear the old woman reminisce about the years of her childhood, about her father, and about her brother Dmitry whom Jenny Genrikhovna remembered particularly well; he had had both diphtheria and whooping cough.

Once Jenny Genrikhovna said: 'I can remember the last family I worked for in 1917. Monsieur was Deputy Minister of Finance. He walked up and down the dining-room saying, "Everything's ruined, estates are being burnt, factories have ground to a halt, the currency's collapsed, safes are being robbed." And then the whole family split up – the same as you. Monsieur, Madame and Mademoiselle went to Sweden; my own pupil joined up with General Kornilov as a volunteer; Madame wept and kept saying, "We spend day after day saying goodbye, the end is near." '

Yevgenia smiled sadly and didn't respond.

One evening a police inspector called and handed Jenny Genrikhovna a note. The old woman put on a hat with a white flower and asked Yevgenia to feed the cat; she said she was going first to the police station and then to work and that she'd be back the next day. When Yevgenia came back from work, she found the room in chaos. Her neighbours told her that Jenny Genrikhovna had been arrested.

Yevgenia set off to make inquiries. At the police station she was told that the old woman was being taken to the Far North with a trainload of Germans.

The next day the inspector and the house-manager came round to collect a sealed basket of old clothes and yellowed letters and photographs.

Yevgenia went to the NKVD to find out how to send the old woman a fur coat. The man behind the window asked: 'Are you a German yourself?'

'No, I'm Russian.'

'Go home then. Don't waste people's time by asking unnecessary questions.'

'I was just asking about winter clothes.'

'Don't you understand?' said the man in a terrifyingly quiet voice.

That evening she overheard people talking about her in the kitchen.

'All the same, I don't like the way she's behaved,' said one voice.

'I think she did well,' answered a second voice. 'First she got one foot in the door; then she informed the appropriate authorities and had the old woman taken away; and now she's got the room for herself.'

'It's more a cubby-hole than a room,' said a man's voice.

'She's no fool,' said a fourth voice. 'A man would do all right with her around.'

The cat came to a sad end. First people argued about what to do with him while he sat sleepily and dispiritedly in the kitchen. 'To hell with the damned German,' said the women. Dragin, of all people, said he was willing to provide a share of the cat's food. But without Jenny Genrikhovna the creature wasn't to survive long; he died after being scalded with boiling water by one of the women, perhaps accidentally, perhaps not.

24

Yevgenia enjoyed her solitary life in Kuibyshev.

Never had she felt such a sense of lightness and freedom – even though she still had no residence permit or ration-card and could only eat one meal a day with her coupons for the canteen. She would think all morning about the moment she would enter the canteen and be given her plate of soup.

She seldom thought of Novikov during this period. She thought more often of Krymov, almost constantly in fact – but with no real warmth.

Her memories of Novikov did not torment her; they just flared up and faded away. Once, though, far away down the street, she saw a tall soldier in a long greatcoat and thought it was Novikov. Her knees went weak and she found it hard to breathe; she felt quite disorientated by her sudden feeling of happiness. A moment later she realized her mistake and at once forgot her excitement. And then during the night she suddenly woke up and thought: 'But why doesn't he write? He knows the address.'

She lived alone, without Krymov or Novikov or any of her relatives. She sometimes thought – mistakenly – that this freedom and loneliness of hers was happiness.

Kuibyshev at this time was the location of many of the Moscow People's Commissariats, newspaper offices and other establishments. It was the temporary capital, and here had come much of the life of Moscow—diplomats, the Bolshoy ballet, famous writers, impresarios and foreign journalists.

All these thousands of people lived in cramped little rooms and hotels, and yet carried on with their usual activities. People's commissars and the heads of important enterprises planned the economy and gave orders to their subordinates; extraordinary and plenipotentiary ambassadors drove in luxurious cars to receptions with the architects of Soviet foreign policy; Ulanova, Lemeshev and Mikhailov delighted the audiences at the ballet and the opera; Mr Shapiro, the representative of the United Press Agency, asked the head of the Soviet Information Bureau, Solomon Abramovich Lozovsky, awkward questions at press conferences; writers wrote radio broadcasts or articles for national and foreign newspapers; journalists wrote up material gathered from hospitals into articles on the war.

But the everyday life of these people from Moscow was quite transformed. Lady Cripps, the wife of the extraordinary and plenipotentiary ambassador of Great Britain, ate supper in a hotel restaurant in exchange for a meal-coupon, wrapped up the left-over bread and sugar-lumps in newspaper and carried them up to her room; representatives of international news agencies pushed their way through the crowds of wounded at the market, discussed the quality of home-grown tobacco and rolled sample cigarettes – or else stood and waited, shifting their weight from foot to foot, in the long queue for the baths; writers famous for their hospitality discussed world politics and the fate of literature over a glass of home-distilled vodka and a ration of black bread.

Huge institutions were squeezed into cramped little buildings; the editors of the most important Soviet newspapers received visitors at tables where, after office hours, children prepared their lessons and women did their sewing. There was something strangely attractive in this coming together of the weighty apparatus of State with the bohemianism of the evacuation.

Yevgenia Nikolaevna had considerable difficulties over her residence permit. The head of the design office where she had got a job, Lieutenant-Colonel Rizin, a tall man with a soft voice, began complaining from the very first day about the responsibility he was assuming in taking on someone still without a permit. He gave Yevgenia a statement confirming her new post and sent her to the police station.

There a police officer took Yevgenia's passport and documents and told her to come back in three days' time.

When the day came, Yevgenia walked along the half-dark corridor. Everyone waiting their turn had that look on their faces peculiar to people who have come to a police station to enquire about passports and residence permits. She went up to the window. A woman's hand with dark red fingernails held out her passport and a calm voice announced: 'Your application has been refused.'

She took her place in the queue waiting to speak to the head of the passport section. The people in this queue talked in whispers; now and then they looked round as the secretaries with their thick lipstick, boots, and quilted jackets walked up and down the corridor. A man in a light overcoat and a cloth cap, the collar of his soldier's tunic just showing beneath his scarf, strolled down the corridor. His boots squeaked. He got out his key and opened the door – it was Grishin, the head of the passport section. Yevgenia soon noticed that, as they finally approached Grishin's door, people always looked round behind them, as though about to run away at the last moment.

While she waited in the queue, Yevgenia heard her fill of stories about people who had been refused residence permits: daughters who had wanted to live with their mothers, a paralysed woman who had wanted to live with her brother, another woman who had come to Kuibyshev to look after a war-invalid . . .

Yevgenia entered Grishin's office. Grishin motioned her to a chair, glanced at her papers and said: 'Your application has been refused. What can I do for you?'

'Comrade Grishin,' she said, her voice trembling, 'please understand: all this time I've been without a ration-card.'

He looked at her unblinkingly, an expression of absent-minded indifference on his broad young face.

'Just think, comrade Grishin,' she continued. 'There's a Shaposhnikov Street in Kuibyshev. It was named after my own father – he was one of the founders of the revolutionary movement in Samara. How can you refuse his daughter a residence permit?'

His calm eyes were watching her; he was listening.

'You need an official request on your behalf,' he said. 'Without that I can do nothing.'

'But I work in a military establishment,' said Yevgenia.

'That's not clear from your documents.'

'Does that help, then?'

'Possibly,' admitted Grishin reluctantly.

When she went in to work next morning, Yevgenia told Rizin that she had been refused a residence permit. Rizin shrugged his shoulders helplessly.

'How idiotic,' he murmured. 'Don't they realize that you are doing war-work? And that you've been an indispensable member of staff since the very beginning?'

'Exactly,' said Yevgenia. 'He said that I need an official document certifying that this office comes under the People's Commissariat for Defence Industry. Please write one out for me. I'll take it to the police station this evening.'

Later that morning Rizin came up to Yevgenia and explained apologetically: 'The police must first send a request. Without that I can't write such a document.'

She went to the police station in the evening and waited her turn in the queue. Hating herself for her ingratiating smile, she asked Grishin to send an official request to Rizin.

'I have no intention of sending any such request,' Grishin replied.

When Yevgenia told Rizin about Grishin's refusal, he sighed and said thoughtfully: 'I know, get him to ask me by telephone.'

The following evening, Yevgenia had arranged to meet Limonov, a man of letters from Moscow who had once known her father. She went to the police station straight after work and asked the people in the queue to let her see the head of the passport department 'just for a minute, to ask one question'. They all just shrugged their shoulders and looked in the other direction. Finally Yevgenia gave up and said angrily: 'Very well then, who's last?'

That day the police station was particularly depressing. A woman with varicose veins shouted, 'I beg you, I beg you!' and then fainted in Grishin's office. A man with only one arm swore obscenely at Grishin, and the next man also made a commotion; the people in the queue could hear him shouting: 'I won't leave this spot!' In fact he left very quickly. While all this noise was going on, Grishin himself couldn't be heard at all. He didn't once raise his voice; it was as though his visitors were shouting and making threats in an empty office.

She sat in the queue for an hour and a half. Grishin nodded to her to sit down. Once again hating herself for her ingratiating smile and hurried 'Thank you very much', Yevgenia asked him to telephone her boss. She said that Rizin had been uncertain whether he was permitted to give her the necessary document without first receiving a written request, but had finally agreed to write one out with the heading: 'In answer to your telephone inquiry of such and such a day of such and such a month.'

Yevgenia handed Grishin the note she had prepared in advance: in large, clear handwriting she had written Rizin's name, patronymic, telephone number, rank and office; in small handwriting, in brackets, she had written, 'Lunch-break: from 1 until 2.' Grishin, however, didn't so much as glance at this note.

'I have no intention of making any requests.'

'But why not?'

'It's not my responsibility.'

'Lieutenant-Colonel Rizin says that unless he receives a request, even an oral one, he is not permitted to make out the necessary document.'

'In that case he ought not to write one.'

'But what can I do then?'

'How do I know?'

It was his absolute calm that was so bewildering. If he had got angry, if he had shown irritation at her muddle-headedness, Yevgenia felt it would have been easier. But he just sat there in half-profile, unhurried, not batting an eyelid.

When men talked to Yevgenia, they usually noticed how beautiful she was – and she knew it. But Grishin looked at her just as he might look at a cripple or an old woman with watering eyes; once inside his office, she was no longer a human being, no longer an attractive young woman, but simply another petitioner.

Yevgenia was conscious of her own weakness and the sheer massiveness of Grishin's strength. She hurried down the street, nearly an hour late for her meeting with Limonov but not in the least looking forward to it. She could still smell the corridor of the police station; she could still see the faces of the people in the queue, the portrait of Stalin lit by a dim electric lamp, and Grishin beside it.

Limonov, a tall stout man with a large head and a ring of youthful curls surrounding his bald patch, greeted her joyfully.

'I was afraid you weren't going to come,' he said as he helped her off with her coat.

He began asking her about Alexandra Vladimirovna.

'To me, ever since I was a student, your mother has been the image of the courageous soul of Russian womanhood. I write about her in all my books – that is, not literally, but you know what I mean . . .'

Lowering his voice and looking round at the door, he asked: 'Have you heard anything about your brother Dmitry?'

Then their talk turned to painting, and they attacked Repin. Limonov began making an omelette on the electric cooker, saying he was the finest omelette-maker in the country and that the chef at the National restaurant in Moscow had been his pupil.

'How is it?' he asked anxiously as he served Yevgenia, and then added with a sigh: 'I can't deny it. I do like eating.'

How oppressed she was by her memories of the police station! In this room full of books and periodicals – where they were soon joined by two witty middle-aged men who were also both lovers of art – she could not get Grishin out of her mind.

But the word, the free, intelligent word has great power. There were moments when Yevgenia quite forgot about Grishin and the depressed-looking faces in the queue. Then there seemed to be nothing else in life but conversations about Rublev and Picasso, about the poetry of Akhmatova and Pasternak, about the plays of Bulgakov . . .

But when she walked out onto the street she at once forgot these intelligent conversations. Grishin . . . Grishin . . . No one in the flat had asked whether or not she had a residence permit; no one had demanded to see her passport and its registration stamp. But she had felt for several days that she was being watched by Glafira Dmitrievna, the senior tenant, a brisk, over-friendly woman with a long nose and an unbelievably insincere voice. Every time she met her and looked at her dark sullen eyes, Yevgenia felt frightened. She thought that in her absence Glafira Dmitrievna was stealing into her room with a duplicate key, searching through her papers, reading her letters and taking copies of her applications for registration.

In the corridor Yevgenia walked on tiptoe, and she always tried to open the door without making a noise. Any moment Glafira Dmitrievna might say: 'What do you think you're doing? Infringing the law! And I'm the one who'll have to answer for it!'

The next morning Yevgenia went into Rizin's office and told him about her latest failure at the passport bureau.

'Help me get a ticket for the steamer to Kazan. Otherwise I'll probably be sent to a peat-bog for infringement of passport regulations.'

She spoke angrily, sarcastically, not mentioning the necessary official document.

The tall handsome man with the quiet voice looked at her, ashamed of his timidity. She was aware of his tender, longing gaze, his insistent admiration of her shoulders, the nape of her neck, her legs. But the law governing the movements of incoming and outgoing papers was evidently something not to be trifled with.

That afternoon Rizin came up to Yevgenia and silently placed the longed-for document on her drawing paper. Equally silently, Yevgenia looked up at him, tears in her eyes.

'I made a request through the secret section,' said Rizin. 'I didn't think anything would come of it and then I suddenly received the director's approval.'

Her fellow-workers congratulated her, saying, 'Now at last your torments are over.' She went to the police station. People in the queue nodded at her – she'd already got to know some of them – and asked: 'How's it going?' Several voices said: 'Go to the front of the queue. You'll only be a minute – why should you have to wait two hours again?'

The office desk and safe, painted brown in a crude imitation wood design, no longer seemed quite so gloomy and official. Grishin watched as Yevgenia's quick fingers placed the necessary paper before him; he gave a barely perceptible, satisfied nod.

'Very well, leave your passport and papers and in three days you can collect the documents from the registry.'

His voice sounded the same as ever, but there seemed to be a friendly smile in his bright eyes.

As she walked home she thought that Grishin was a human being like anyone else – able to do something helpful, he had smiled. He wasn't really heartless at all. She felt quite uncomfortable at all the harsh things she had thought about him.

Three days later she went up to the window. A woman's hand with dark red fingernails handed back her passport with her papers folded carefully inside. Yevgenia read the neatly written statement: 'Residence permit refused on grounds of having no connection with the living space in question.'

'Son of a bitch!' said Yevgenia loudly. Unable to restrain herself, she continued: 'You've just been making fun of me, you bastard!' She was shouting, waving her unstamped passport in the air, turning to the people sitting in the queue, wanting their support but seeing them turn away from her. For a moment the spirit of insurrection, the spirit of fury and despair, flared up in her. Women had screamed like this in 1937 – as they waited for information about husbands, sons and brothers who had been sentenced, 'without right of correspondence',* to the dark halls of the Butyrka, to Matrosskaya Tishina, to Sokolniki.

A policeman standing in the corridor took Yevgenia by the elbow and pushed her towards the door.

'Let go! Leave me alone!' She pulled her arm free and pushed the policeman away.

'Cut it out, citizen!' he said warningly. 'You'll get ten years.' For a moment there seemed to be compassion and pity in the policeman's eyes.

Yevgenia walked quickly towards the exit. Out on the street, people jostled her – all of them registered, all of them with their ration-cards . . .

That night she dreamed of a fire: she was bending over a wounded man lying face down on the ground; she tried to drag him away and understood without seeing his face that it was Krymov. She woke up feeling exhausted and depressed.

'If only he'd come soon,' she thought, and then muttered: 'Help me, help me.'

It wasn't Krymov she wanted to see so desperately, but Novikov – the Novikov she had met that summer in Stalingrad.

This life without rights, without a residence permit, without a ration-card, this continual fear of the janitor, the house-manager and

* This was in fact a death-sentence.

127

Glafira Dmitrievna, had become quite unbearable. In the morning Yevgenia would steal into the kitchen when everyone was asleep and try to get washed before they woke up. When the other tenants did speak to her, her voice would become horribly ingratiating.

That afternoon Yevgenia wrote out a letter of resignation.

She had heard that after an application for residence had been refused, an inspector of police came round to collect a signed statement of one's undertaking to leave Kuibyshev within three days. In the text of this statement were the words: 'Those guilty of infringement of passport regulations are liable . . .' Yevgenia didn't want to be 'liable'. Now at last she was reconciled to leaving Kuibyshev. She felt calmer; she was no longer exhausted and frightened by the thought of Grishin, by the thought of Glafira Dmitrievna with her eyes like rotten olives. She had renounced lawlessness; she had submitted.

She had written out her resignation and was about to take it to Rizin, when she was called to the telephone. It was Limonov.

He asked her whether she was free the next evening: someone had arrived from Tashkent; he told very amusing stories about how things were there and had brought Limonov greetings from Aleksey Tolstoy. Once again Yevgenia felt the breath of another life.

Although she hadn't intended to, Yevgenia told Limonov about her attempts to obtain a residence permit.

He listened to her without interrupting and then said: 'What a story. It's really quite amusing. A father has a street named after him in Kuibyshev and his daughter is expelled, refused a residence permit. Very curious.'

He thought for a moment.

'Don't hand in your notice today, Yevgenia Nikolaevna. Tonight I'm going to a conference arranged by the secretary of the *obkom*. I'll talk to him about you.'

Yevgenia thanked him, thinking he would forget about her as soon as he put down the telephone. Still, she didn't hand in her notice and merely asked Rizin whether he would be able to get her a ticket, through the Military District HQ, for the steamer to Kazan.

'That's no problem,' said Rizin, spreading his hands helplessly. 'The police are impossible. But what can one do? Kuibyshev comes under special regulations – they have their instructions.'

Then he asked: 'Are you free this evening?'

'No,' answered Yevgenia angrily.

On the way home she thought that very soon she would see Viktor, Nadya and her mother and sister. Yes, life in Kazan would be easier than in Kuibyshev. She wondered why she had got so upset, shrinking with fear as she walked into the police station. They had rejected her application and to hell with it! And if Novikov wrote, she could ask her neighbours to forward the letter to Kazan.

The following morning she was called to the telephone as soon as she arrived at work. An obliging voice asked her to call at the passport bureau in order to collect her residence permit.

25

Yevgenia got to know one of the other tenants, Shargorodsky.

If Shargorodsky turned round abruptly, it looked as though his big, grey, alabaster head would come off his fine neck and fall to the ground with a crash. Yevgenia noticed that the pale skin on the old man's face was faintly tinged with blue. The combination of his blue skin and the light blue of his cool eyes intrigued her; the old man came from the highest ranks of the nobility and Yevgenia was amused at the thought that he would have to be drawn in blue.

Vladimir Andreyevich Shargorodsky's life had been still more difficult before the war. Now at least he had some kind of work. The Soviet Information Bureau had asked him to supply them with notes on Dmitry Donskoy, Suvorov and Ushakov,* on the traditions of the Russian officer class, on various nineteenth-century poets . . .

He informed Yevgenia that on his mother's side he was related to a very ancient princely house, one even older than the Romanovs. As a young man he had served in the provincial *zemstvo*** and had preached Voltaire and Chaadayev to the sons of landlords, to young priests and village schoolteachers.

He told Yevgenia about a remark made to him forty-four years before by the provincial marshal of the nobility:

* Donskoy, Suvorov and Ushakov are Russian military heroes.
** *Zemstvo:* a local government institution.

'You, a descendant of one of the oldest families of Russia, have set out to prove to the peasants that you are descended from a monkey. The peasants will just ask: "What about the Grand Dukes? The Tsarevich? The Tsaritsa? What about the Tsar himself . . . ?"'

Shargorodsky continued his subversive teaching and was finally exiled to Tashkent. A year later he was pardoned; he emigrated to Switzerland. There he met many of the revolutionary activists; Bolsheviks, Mensheviks, SRs and anarchists all knew the eccentric prince. He attended various gatherings and debates, was friendly with some of the revolutionaries but agreed with none of them. At that time he was a friend of the black-bearded Lipets, a student who was a member of the Jewish Bund.

Shortly before the First World War he returned to Russia and settled down on his estate, now and again publishing articles on historical and literary themes in the *Nizhnii Novgorod Listok*. He didn't concern himself with the actual management of the estate, leaving that entirely to his mother.

In the end he was the only landlord whose estate was left untouched by the peasants. The Committee of Poor Peasants even allocated him a cartload of firewood and forty cabbages. He sat in the one room of the house that was still heated and had its windows intact, reading and writing poetry. He read one of his poems to Yevgenia. It was entitled 'Russia':

> Insane carefreeness
> Wherever one looks.
> The plain. Infinity.
> The cawing of rooks.
>
> Riots. Fires. Secrecy.
> Obtuse indifference.
> A unique eccentricity.
> A terrible indifference.

He pronounced each word carefully, pausing for each punctuation mark and raising his long eyebrows – somehow without making his large forehead appear any smaller.

In 1926 Shargorodsky took it into his head to give lectures on the history of Russian literature; he attacked Demyan Byedniy* and praised Fet;** he took part in the then fashionable discussions about the beauty and truth of life; he declared himself an opponent of every State, declared Marxism a narrow creed, and spoke of the tragic fate of the Russian soul. In the end he talked and argued himself into another journey at government expense to Tashkent. There he stayed, marvelling at the power of geographical arguments in a theoretical discussion, until in late 1933 he received permission to move to Samara to live with his elder sister, Elena Andreevna. She died shortly before the war.

Shargorodsky never invited anyone into his room. Once, however, Yevgenia glanced into the Prince's chambers: piles of books and old newspapers towered up in the corners; ancient armchairs were heaped on top of each other almost to the ceiling; portraits in gilt frames covered the floor. A rumpled quilt whose stuffing was falling out lay on a sofa covered in red velvet.

Shargorodsky was a very gentle man, and quite helpless in any practical matter. He was the sort of man about whom people say, 'He's got the soul of a child,' or 'He's as kind as an angel.' And yet he could walk straight past a hungry child or a ragged old woman begging for crusts, feeling quite indifferent, still muttering his favourite lines of poetry.

As she listened to Shargorodsky, Yevgenia often thought of her ex-husband. There really was very little in common between this old admirer of Fet and Vladimir Solovyov, and Krymov the Comintern official.

She found it surprising that Krymov, who was just as much a Russian as old Shargorodsky, could be so indifferent to the charm of the Russian landscape and Russian folk-tale, to the poetry of Fet and Tyutchev. And everything in Russian life that Krymov had held dear since his youth, the names without which he could not even conceive of Russia, were a matter of indifference to Shargorodsky – or even aroused his antagonism.

To Shargorodsky Fet was a god. Above all he was a Russian god. Glinka's *Doubts* and the folk-tales about Finist the Bright Falcon

---

* Byedniy was a mediocre propagandist poet at the time of the Revolution.

** Fet was a lyric poet of the late nineteenth century, a precursor of the Symbolists.

were equally divine. Whereas Dante, much though he admired him, quite lacked the divine quality of Russian music and Russian poetry.

Krymov, on the other hand, made no distinction between Dobrolyubov and Lassalle, between Chernyshevsky and Engels.* For him Marx stood above all Russian geniuses and Beethoven's *Eroica* triumphed indisputably over all Russian music. Nekrasov, to him the world's supreme poet, was perhaps the only exception . . . Sometimes Yevgenia thought that Shargorodsky helped her to understand not only Krymov himself but also what had happened to their relationship.

Yevgenia liked talking to Shargorodsky. Their conversations usually began after some alarming news bulletin. Shargorodsky would then launch into a speech about the fate of Russia.

'The Russian aristocracy,' he would say, 'may stand guilty before Russia, Yevgenia Nikolaevna, but they did at least love her. We were pardoned nothing at the time of that first War: our fools, our blockheads, our sleepy gluttons, Rasputin, our irresponsibility and our avenues of lime-trees, the peasants' huts without chimneys and their bast shoes – everything was held against us. But my sister lost six sons in Galicia. My brother, a sick old man, was killed in battle in East Prussia. History hasn't taken that into account . . . It should.'

Often Yevgenia listened to his judgements on literature, judgements that were quite at odds with those of the present day. He ranked Fet above Pushkin and Tyutchev. No one in Russia can have known Fet like he did. Fet himself, by the end of his life, probably no longer remembered all that Shargorodsky knew about him.

Shargorodsky considered Lev Tolstoy to be too realistic. Though recognizing that there was poetry in his work, he didn't value him. He valued Turgenev but considered his talent too superficial. The Russian prose he loved most was that of Gogol and Leskov.

He considered Belinsky and Chernyshevsky to be the murderers of Russian poetry.

He once said to Yevgenia that, apart from Russian poetry, there

* Dobrolyubov (1836–61) and Chernyshevsky (1828–89) were among the ancestors of the Russian revolutionaries.

were three things in the world that he loved, all of them beginning with the letter 's' – sugar, sun and sleep.

'Will I really die without ever seeing even one of my poems in print?' he sometimes asked.

Once Yevgenia met Limonov on her way back from work. He was walking along the street in an unbuttoned winter overcoat. A bright checked scarf was dangling round his neck and he was leaning on a rather knotted stick. This massive man in an aristocratic beaver-fur hat stood out strangely in the Kuibyshev crowd.

Limonov walked Yevgenia home. She invited him in for some tea. He looked at her thoughtfully. 'Well yes, thank you. I suppose really you owe me some vodka for your residence permit.'

Breathing heavily, he began to climb the stairs. Then, as he walked into Yevgenia's little room he said: 'Hm, there isn't much space for my body. Perhaps there'll be lots of space for my thoughts.'

Suddenly, in a somewhat unnatural tone of voice, he began explaining to her his theory of love and sexual relationships.

'It's a vitamin deficiency,' he said, 'a spiritual vitamin deficiency! You know, the same terrible hunger that drives cows, bulls and deer when they need salt. What I myself lack, what those close to me lack, what my wife lacks, I search for in the object of my love. A man's wife is the cause of his vitamin deficiency! And a man craves in his beloved what for years, for decades, he has been unable to find in his wife. Do you understand?'

He took her by the hand and started to caress her palm. He moved on to her shoulders, her neck, and the back of her head.

'Do you understand?' he asked ingratiatingly. 'It's really very simple. A spiritual vitamin deficiency!'

Yevgenia watched with laughing, embarrassed eyes as a large white hand with polished fingernails moved from her shoulders down to her breast.

'Vitamin deficiencies can evidently be physical as well as spiritual,' said Yevgenia. 'No, you mustn't paw me, really you mustn't,' she scolded him, sounding like a primary school teacher.

He stared at her, dumbfounded. Instead of looking embarrassed, he began to laugh. Yevgenia laughed too.

They were drinking tea and talking about the artist Saryan when old Shargorodsky knocked at the door.

Limonov turned out to know Shargorodsky's name from someone's manuscript notes and from some letters in an archive. Shargorodsky had not read Limonov's books but likewise he had heard his name – it was mentioned in newspapers in lists of those writing on military-historical themes.

They began to talk, growing happy and excited as they discovered they shared a common language. Their conversation was full of names: Solovyov, Mereshkovsky, Rozanov, Hippius, Byeliy, Byerdyaev, Ustryalov, Balmont, Milyukov, Yevreinov, Remizov, Vyacheslav Ivanov.

It seemed to Yevgenia as though these two men had raised from the ocean-bed a whole sunken world of books, pictures, philosophical systems, theatrical productions . . .

Limonov suddenly gave voice to her thought.

'It's as though the two of us have raised Atlantis from under the sea.'

Shargorodsky nodded sadly. 'Yes, yes, but you're only an explorer of the Russian Atlantis; I'm one of its inhabitants, someone who sank with it to the bed of the ocean.'

'Well,' said Limonov. 'And now the war's raised you up.'

'Yes,' agreed Shargorodsky. 'The founders of the Comintern proved unable to think of anything better in the hour of war than the old phrase about "the sacred earth of Russia".' He smiled. 'Just wait. The war will end in victory and then the Internationalists will declare: "Mother Russia's equal to anyone in the world!"'

Yevgenia sensed that if these two were talking so animatedly and wittily, it was not only because they were glad to have met one another and to have found a topic so close to both their hearts. She realized that both these men – one of them very old and the other middle-aged – were conscious of her listening to them and that they were attracted to her. How strange it was. She was quite indifferent to all this, she even found it rather absurd – and yet it was very pleasing, not in the least a matter of indifference.

As she looked at them she thought: 'How can one ever understand oneself? Why does the past make me so sad? Why do I feel so sorry for Krymov? Why can't I stop thinking about him?'

Once she had felt alienated by Krymov's English and German comrades; but now, when Shargorodsky mocked the Comintern, she felt sad and angry . . . She couldn't make head or tail of it. Not even Limonov's theory of vitamin deficiencies was any help now. Nor was any other theory.

Then she had the idea that she must be worrying so much about Krymov only because she was longing for someone else – a man she hardly ever seemed to think about.

'Do I really love him?' she wondered, surprised.

26

During the night the sky over the Volga cleared. The hills floated slowly past beneath the stars, separated one from another by the pitch dark of the ravines.

Now and again a shooting-star flashed by and Lyudmila Nikolaevna silently prayed: 'Don't let Tolya die!'

That was her only wish: she asked Heaven for nothing else.

Once, when she was still a student in the Maths and Physics Faculty, she had been employed to do calculations at the Astronomical Institute. She had learned then that meteors came in showers, each meeting the earth in a different month. There were the Perseids, the Orionids, probably the Geminids, the Leonids. She no longer remembered which meteors reached the earth in October and November . . . But don't let Tolya die!

Viktor had reproached her for her unwillingness to help people and for her unkindness to his relatives. He believed that if Lyudmila had wanted it, his mother would have come to live with them instead of remaining in the Ukraine.

When Viktor's cousin had been released from camp and sent into exile, she hadn't wanted to let him stay the night, afraid that the house management committee would find out. She knew that her mother still remembered how Lyudmila had been staying at the seaside when her father died; instead of cutting short her holiday, she had arrived back in Moscow two days after the funeral.

Her mother sometimes talked to her about Dmitry, horrified at what had happened to him.

'He was honest as a boy and he remained honest all his life. And then suddenly − "espionage, plotting to murder Kaganovich and Voroshilov" . . . A wild, terrible lie. What's the point of it? Why should anyone want to destroy people who are sincere and honourable?' Once Lyudmila had told her: 'You can't vouch for Mitya entirely. Innocent people don't get arrested.'

She could still remember the look her mother had given her.

Another time she had said to her mother about Dmitry's wife: 'I never could stand the woman and I'm not going to change my mind now.'

'But just imagine!' her mother had protested. 'Being given a ten-year sentence for not denouncing your husband!'

And once she had brought home a stray puppy she'd found on the street. Viktor hadn't wanted to take it in and she'd shouted: 'You're a cruel man!'

'Lyuda,' he had answered, 'I don't want you to be young and beautiful. I only want one thing. I want you to be kind-hearted − and not just towards cats and dogs.'

She sat there on the deck, for once disliking herself instead of blaming everyone else, remembering all the harsh things that had ever been said to her . . . Once, when he was on the telephone, she'd heard her husband laugh and say: 'Now that we've got a kitten, I sometimes hear my wife sounding affectionate.'

Then there was the time when her mother had said to her: 'Lyuda, how can you refuse beggars? Just think: you've got enough to eat while someone else is hungry and begging . . .'

It wasn't that she was miserly: she loved having guests, and her dinners were famous amongst her friends.

No one saw her crying there in the darkness. Yes, yes, she was callous; she had forgotten everything she had ever learnt; she was useless; no one would ever find her attractive again; she had grown fat; she had grey hair and high blood pressure; her husband no longer loved her and thought she was heartless. But if only Tolya were still alive! She was ready to admit everything, to confess to all the faults her family accused her of − if only he were still alive!

Why did she keep remembering her first husband? Where was he? How could she find him? Why hadn't she written to his sister in

Rostov? She couldn't write now because of the Germans. She would have told him about Tolya.

The sound of the engine, the vibrating deck, the splash of water, the twinkling of the stars, all merged into one; Lyudmila dozed off.

It was nearly dawn. A thick mist swayed over the Volga and everything living seemed to have drowned.

Suddenly the sun rose – like a burst of hope. The dark autumn water mirrored the sky; it began to breathe and the sun seemed to cry out in the waves. The steep banks had been salted by the night's frost and the red-brown trees looked very gay. The wind rose, the mist vanished and the world grew cool and glass-like, piercingly transparent. There was no warmth in the sun, nor in the blue sky and water.

The earth was vast: even the vast forest had both a beginning and an end, but the earth just stretched on for ever . . . And grief was something equally vast, equally eternal.

On the boat were a number of passengers going to Kuibyshev. In the first-class cabins were important officials from the People's Commissariats, wearing long khaki overcoats and colonels' grey Astrakhan hats. The second-class cabins housed important wives and important mothers-in-law, also wearing uniforms appropriate to their rank – as though there were one for wives and another for mothers and mothers-in-law. The wives wore fur coats and white fur stoles; the mothers and mothers-in-law wore blue cloth coats with black Astrakhan collars and brown scarves. The children who were with them had bored, dissatisfied eyes.

Through the cabin-windows one could see their food-supplies. Lyudmila's experienced eye could easily distinguish the contents of the different bags: clarified butter and honey were sailing down the Volga in string-bags, in soldered tins and in big dark bottles with sealed necks. Now and then she overheard snatches of conversation between the passengers on the deck; she gathered that their main concern was the train leaving Kuibyshev for Moscow.

It seemed to Lyudmila that these women looked quite indifferently at the soldiers and subalterns sitting in the corridors – as though they themselves had no sons or brothers at the front. Instead of standing by the loudspeaker to listen to the morning news bulletin with the soldiers and crew, these women just screwed up their sleepy eyes and carried on with their own affairs.

Lyudmila heard from the sailors that the whole steamer had originally been assigned to the families of the officials returning via Kuibyshev to Moscow. Then the military authorities in Kazan had ordered an additional embarkation of both soldiers and civilians. The legitimate passengers had made a scene, refusing to let the soldiers on board and making telephone calls to a representative of the State Defence Committee.

It was very strange indeed to see these soldiers – bound for Stalingrad – looking awkward and uncomfortable because they had crowded the legitimate passengers.

Lyudmila found the calm eyes of these women unbearable. Grandmothers beckoned their grandchildren to them and, without even breaking off their conversation, stuffed biscuits into their mouths with practised movements. A squat old woman in a Siberian polecat coat emerged from a cabin in the bows to take two boys for a walk on the deck; the women all greeted her hurriedly and smiled, while an anxious, ingratiating expression appeared on the faces of their husbands.

If the radio were to announce the opening of a second front or the breaking of the blockade of Leningrad, not one of them would bat an eyelid. But if someone were to say that the first-class coach had been taken off the Moscow train, the events of the war would pale before the terrible passions aroused by the allocation of seats for the 'soft' and 'hard' coaches.

How extraordinary it all was! And yet Lyudmila herself, in her own fur stole and grey Astrakhan coat, was wearing the same uniform as these first- and second-class passengers. And she too, not long before, had been furiously indignant that Viktor had not been given a ticket for a 'soft' coach.

She told an artillery lieutenant that her son, a gunner lieutenant himself, was in the hospital at Saratov with severe wounds. She talked to a sick old woman about Marusya and Vera, and about her mother-in-law who had died in occupied territory. Her grief was the same grief that breathed on this deck, a grief that had always known the way from the military hospitals and graves of the front back to the huts of peasants, huts without numbers standing on patches of waste ground without a name.

She hadn't brought a mug or even any bread; she had thought she wouldn't want to eat or drink during the journey. On the steamer, however, she had felt desperately hungry all day and had realized that things were going to be difficult. And then, on the second day, the soldiers came to an arrangement with the stokers and cooked some millet soup in the engine-room; they called Lyudmila and poured some into a mess-tin for her.

She sat on an empty box, eating burning-hot soup from somebody else's tin and with somebody else's spoon.

'It's fine soup!' said one of the cooks. When Lyudmila didn't answer, he asked sharply: 'It is, isn't it? Isn't it good and rich?' There was an openness and simplicity of heart in this demand for praise, addressed to someone the man had himself just fed.

She helped another soldier to repair a spring in a defective rifle – something not even a sergeant-major with the Order of the Red Star had succeeded in doing.

Listening to an argument between some artillery lieutenants, Lyudmila took a pencil and helped them to work out a trigonometric formula. After that, a lieutenant who had previously addressed her as 'Citizen' suddenly asked her name and patronymic.

During the night Lyudmila walked up and down the deck. The river looked icy cold and there was a pitiless wind blowing from downstream out of the darkness. Up above shone the stars; there was neither comfort nor peace in the cruel sky, the sky of ice and fire, that arched over her unhappy head.

27

Before the steamer reached Kuibyshev, the captain received orders to continue to Saratov and take on board wounded from the hospitals there.

The cabin passengers got ready to disembark, carrying out their suitcases and packages and piling them on the deck.

The silhouettes of factories began to appear, together with small huts and houses with corrugated iron roofs. The sound of the steamer's wash seemed different. Even the hammering of the engine sounded somehow more anxious.

The vast bulk of the suburb of Samara rose up, grey, brown and black, with its gleaming panes of glass and wisps of smoke from factories and locomotives.

The passengers disembarking at Kuibyshev were waiting on one side of the deck. They didn't say goodbye or even give a nod to the people still on board. No friendships had been struck up on the journey.

A black limousine, a Zis-101, was waiting to pick up the old woman in the Siberian polecat coat and her two grandsons. A man with a yellow face, wearing a long general's overcoat, saluted the old woman and shook hands with the boys.

In the course of only a few minutes the passengers had vanished, together with their children, suitcases and packages. Only soldiers' greatcoats and padded jackets were left on the steamer. The passengers might never have existed.

Lyudmila imagined that she would now be able to breathe more freely, more easily, among people bound together by the same grief and the same labour.

28

Saratov greeted Lyudmila rudely and cruelly.

Right on the landing-stage she encountered a drunk in a soldier's greatcoat. He stumbled into her and began cursing.

Lyudmila started to climb the steep, cobbled slope and then stopped, breathing heavily, to look round. Down below, between the grey warehouses on the quay, she could see the white steamer. As though reading her mind, it gave a soft hoot: 'Go on then, go on!' She went on.

At the tram-stop some young women quietly shoved past anyone who happened to be old or weak. A blind man in a Red Army hat, obviously only recently released from hospital and still unable to cope alone, moved anxiously from one foot to the other, tapping his stick rapidly in front of him. With childish eagerness he grabbed at the sleeve of a middle-aged woman. She pulled her arm away from him and stepped aside, her hob-nailed boots ringing on the cobbles. Still clutching her sleeve, the blind man hurriedly explained: 'I'm just out of hospital. Will you help me on to the tram?'

The woman swore at him and pushed him away. He lost his balance and sat down on the pavement.

Lyudmila looked at the woman's face.

Where did this inhuman behaviour come from? What could have engendered it? The famine of 1921 that she had lived through as a child? The man-made famine of 1930? A life full to the brim with need?

The blind man froze for a moment and then jumped up, crying out in a bird-like voice. Probably he had just caught a glimpse of himself waving his stick senselessly in the air, his hat on one side. He beat the air with his stick, expressing through these circular movements his hatred for the merciless world of the sighted. People were jostling each other as they climbed into the tram-car – while he stood there, weeping and shouting. It was as though everyone Lyudmila had gathered together, with hope and love, into one great family of labour, need, grief and kindness, had conspired to behave inhumanly. It was as though they had made an agreement to refute the view that one can always be sure of finding kindness in the hearts of people with dirty clothes and grimy hands.

Something dark and agonizing touched Lyudmila, filling her with the cold and darkness of thousands of miles of desolate Russian steppe, with a feeling of helplessness amidst life's frozen wastes.

For a second time she asked the conductor where she should get off.

'I've already announced it,' the woman replied matter-of-factly. 'Have you gone deaf?'

The passengers standing in the aisle didn't respond when Lyudmila asked whether or not they were getting out. They just stood there as though turned to stone, reluctant to make any movement at all.

When she was a child, Lyudmila had gone to the preparatory, 'alphabet' class of the Saratov girls' high school. On winter mornings she had sat at table, her legs dangling, drinking her tea while her father spread some butter on a piece of warm, white bread . . . The lamp had been mirrored in the samovar's fat cheek and she hadn't wanted to leave her father's warm hand, the warm bread, the warmth of the samovar.

It seemed as though there had been no November wind in this city then – no hunger, no suicides, no children dying in hospital, only warmth, warmth, warmth.

Her elder sister Sonya, who had died of croup, was buried in the cemetery here. Alexandra Vladimirovna had named her Sonya in memory of Sofya Lvovna Pyerovskaya. She thought her grandfather was buried here too.

She walked up to a three-storey school-building. This was the hospital where Tolya was.

There was no sentry at the door, which seemed a good omen. She found herself in the stifling hospital atmosphere. It was so sticky and viscous that however chilled you were by the frost, you wanted to go back outside rather than stay and enjoy its warmth.

She went past the washrooms which still had notices saying 'Boys' and 'Girls'. She went down the corridor, past the smell of the kitchens, and came to a steamed-up window through which she could see a stack of rectangular coffins in the inner yard. Once again, as in her own entrance-hall with the still unopened letter, she thought: 'Oh God, what if I drop dead this moment!' But she strode on, along a strip of grey carpet, past some bedside tables with familiar house-plants – asparagus and philodendrons – till she came to a door where a hand-written sign saying 'Registry' hung next to the board saying 'Fourth Form'.

Lyudmila pulled open the door just as the sun broke through the clouds and struck the window-panes. Everything in the room began to shine.

A few minutes later a talkative clerk was looking through a long drawer of filing cards caught in the sunlight.

'So, so, Shaposhnikov A. Ah . . . Anatoly V . . . So . . . You're lucky you didn't meet the commandant still in your outdoor coat. He really would have given you what for . . . ! Now then . . . Shaposhnikov . . . Yes, that's him, that's right, Lieutenant.'

Lyudmila watched his fingers taking the card out of the long plywood drawer. It was as though she were standing before God; it was in his power to pronounce life or death, and he had paused for a moment to decide.

29

Lyudmila had arrived in Saratov a week after Tolya had been operated on for the third time. The operation had been performed by Dr Mayzel, an army surgeon. It had been protracted and complicated: Tolya had been under general anaesthetic for more than five hours and had had two intravenous injections of hexonal. This operation had never been carried out before in Saratov, neither by the doctors at the hospital nor the surgeons at the University clinic. It was known only from the literature: the Americans had included a detailed account of it in a 1941 army medical journal.

In view of the especial complexity of the operation Dr Mayzel had a long and frank discussion with the lieutenant after his routine X-ray examination. He explained the nature of the pathological processes that had been provoked by his grave wounds. At the same time he spoke very openly about the risks attendant upon the operation. The doctors he had consulted had not been unanimous in their decision: the old clinical physician Dr Rodionov had argued against it. Lieutenant Shaposhnikov asked Dr Mayzel two or three questions, thought about it for a moment and then gave his consent. Five days were then taken up with preparations for the operation.

The operation began at eleven o'clock in the morning and was not completed until nearly four in the afternoon. Dr Dimitruk, the director of the hospital, was present. According to the doctors who observed the operation, it was carried out brilliantly.

Without leaving the operating table, Mayzel solved several unexpected problems that were not envisaged in the published description.

The condition of the patient during the operation was satisfactory. His pulse was normal, with no prolapsus.

At about two o'clock, Dr Mayzel, who was overweight and far from young, felt ill and was forced to break off for several minutes. The therapist, Dr Klestova, gave him validol, after which he took no more breaks. Soon after the completion of the operation, however, when Lieutenant Shaposhnikov had been taken to intensive care, Dr Mayzel had a serious heart attack. Several injections of camphor and a dose of liquid nitro-glycerine were needed to bring to an end the spasms in the coronary arteries. The attack was obviously the result of the nervous excitement that had placed an excessive burden on an already weak heart.

Sister Terentyevna, who was on duty at Shaposhnikov's bedside, watched over his condition as instructed. Dr Klestova came into the intensive care unit and took his pulse. He was only semi-conscious, but his condition was satisfactory.

'Mayzel's given the lieutenant a new start in life and almost died himself,' said Dr Klestova to Sister Terentyevna, who answered: 'Oh, if only Lieutenant Tolya recovers!'

Shaposhnikov's breathing was almost inaudible. His face was still and his thin arms and neck were like those of a child. There was a barely perceptible shadow on his pale skin – a tan that still remained from exercises in the field and forced marches across the steppe. His condition was half-way between unconsciousness and sleep, a deep stupefaction caused by the remaining effects of the anaesthetic and his general exhaustion, both mental and physical.

The patient spoke occasionally, mumbling separate words and sometimes whole phrases. Once, Sister Terentyevna thought he said: 'It's a good thing you didn't see me like that.' After that he lay quite still, the corners of his mouth drooping. Unconscious as he was, it looked as though he was crying.

About eight o'clock in the evening the patient opened his eyes, and asked quite distinctly – Sister Terentyevna was astonished and delighted – for something to drink. She told him he was not allowed to drink and added that the operation had been a great success and that he would soon recover. She asked how he felt. He replied that his side and back hurt, but only a little.

She checked his pulse again and wiped his lips and forehead with a damp towel.

Just then an orderly, Medvedev, came into the ward and told Sister Terentyevna that the chief surgeon, Dr Platonov, wanted her on the telephone. She went to the room of the ward sister, picked up the receiver and informed Dr Platonov that the patient had woken up and that his condition was normal for someone who had undergone a serious operation.

Sister Terentyevna asked to be relieved: she had to go to the City War Commissariat to sort out a muddle that had arisen over the forwarding of an allowance made out to her by her husband. Dr Platonov promised to let her go, but told her to watch over Shaposhnikov until he himself came to examine him.

Sister Terentyevna went back to the ward. The patient was lying in the same position as when she had left, but his face no longer wore such a harsh expression of suffering. The corners of his mouth no longer hung down and his face seemed calm and smiling. Suffering had evidently made him appear older. Now that he was smiling, his face startled Sister Terentyevna; his thin cheeks, his pale, swollen lips, his high unwrinkled forehead seemed not those of an adult, or even an adolescent, but those of a child. Sister Terentyevna asked the patient how he was feeling. He didn't answer; he must have fallen asleep.

The expression on his face made Sister Terentyevna a little wary. She took Lieutenant Shaposhnikov by the hand. There was no pulse and his hand was barely warm. Its warmth was the lifeless, almost imperceptible warmth of a stove that had been lit on the previous day and had long since gone out.

Although Sister Terentyevna had lived all her life in the city, she fell to her knees and quietly, so as not to disturb the living, began to keen like a peasant.

'Our loved one, our flower, where have you gone to, where have you gone now you have left us?'

30

News of the arrival of Lieutenant Shaposhnikov's mother spread through the hospital. The hospital commissar, Battalion Commissar Shimansky, arranged to receive Lyudmila.

Shimansky, a handsome man with an accent that bore witness to his Polish origins, frowned and licked his moustache as he waited. He felt sad about the dead lieutenant and sorry for his mother; for that very reason, he felt angry with both of them. What would happen to his nerves if he had to give interviews to every dead lieutenant's mama?

Shimansky sat Lyudmila down and placed a carafe of water in front of her.

'No thank you,' she said. 'Not now.'

Lyudmila then listened to Shimansky's account of the consultation prior to the operation – the commissar didn't think it necessary to mention the one doctor who had spoken against it – of the difficulties of the operation itself, and its successful outcome. Shimansky added that the surgeons now considered this operation generally appropriate in cases of severe wounds such as those received by Lieutenant Shaposhnikov. He told her that Shaposhnikov's death had occurred as a result of cardiac arrest and that – as stated in the report of the anatomical pathologist, Junior Medical Officer Boldyrev – it had been beyond the power of the doctors to foresee or guard against such an event.

Shimansky went on to say that many hundreds of casualties passed through the hospital, but seldom had the staff taken anyone so much to their hearts as Lieutenant Shaposhnikov – an intelligent, well-educated and unassuming patient who had always scrupulously avoided making any unnecessary demands on them. Lastly he said that a mother should be proud to have brought up a son who had selflessly and honourably laid down his life for the Motherland. He then asked if Lyudmila had any requests.

Lyudmila apologized for taking up his time, took a sheet of paper from her handbag and began to read out her requests.

She asked to be shown her son's grave. Shimansky gave a silent nod of the head and made a note on his pad.

She asked if she could have a word with Dr Mayzel. Shimansky informed her that, on hearing of her arrival, Dr Mayzel had himself expressed a wish to speak with her.

She asked if she could meet Sister Terentyevna. Shimansky nodded and made a note.

She asked to be given her son's belongings. Shimansky made another note on his pad.

Finally she put two tins of sprats and a packet of sweets on the table and asked him to give the other patients the presents she had brought for her son.

Her large, light blue eyes suddenly met his own. He blinked involuntarily at their brilliance. Then he said that all her requests would be granted and asked her to return to the hospital at half-past nine the next morning.

Shimansky watched the door close behind her, looked at the presents she had left for the wounded, tried to find his pulse, gave up, and began to drink the water he had offered Lyudmila at the beginning of the interview.

31

Lyudmila seemed not to have a spare moment. That night she walked up and down the streets, sat on a park-bench, went to the station to get warm, and then walked up and down the deserted streets again with a quick, businesslike stride.

Shimansky carried out Lyudmila's requests to the letter.

At half-past-nine in the morning she saw Sister Terentyevna; she asked her to tell her everything she knew about Tolya. She then put on a white smock. Together with Terentyevna she went up to the first floor, walked down the corridor that led to the operating-theatre, stood by the door of the intensive care unit and looked at the solitary, now empty, bed. Sister Terentyevna stood beside her, dabbing her nose with her handkerchief. They went back down and Terentyevna said goodbye. Soon after that a stout man with grey hair came into the waiting-room. There were huge dark circles beneath his dark eyes. His starched, blindingly white smock seemed whiter still by comparison with his swarthy face and dark, staring eyes.

Dr Mayzel explained why Dr Rodionov had been against the operation. He seemed already to know everything Lyudmila wanted to ask him. He told her about his conversations with Lieutenant Tolya before the operation. Understanding Lyudmila's state of mind, he described the operation itself with brutal frankness.

Then he said that he had felt a fatherly tenderness towards Lieutenant Tolya. As he spoke, a high, plaintive note slipped into his bass voice. Lyudmila looked for the first time at his hands. They were peculiar; they seemed to live a quite separate life from the man with mournful eyes. His hands were severe and ponderous, the dark-skinned fingers large and strong.

Mayzel took his hands off the table. As though he had read Lyudmila's thoughts, he said: 'I did all I could. But, instead of saving him from death, my hands only brought his death closer.' He rested his huge hands on the table again.

Lyudmila could tell that every word he had said was true.

Everything he said, passionately though she had desired to hear it, had tortured and burnt her. But there was something else that had made the conversation difficult and painful: she sensed that the doctor had wanted this meeting not for her sake, but for his own. This made her feel a certain antagonism towards him.

As she said goodbye, she said she was certain he had done everything possible to save her son. He gave a deep sigh. She could see that her words had comforted him – and realized that it was because he felt he had a right to hear these words that he had wanted the meeting.

'And on top of everything else, they even expect me to comfort them!' she thought.

After the surgeon had left, Lyudmila spoke to the commandant, a man in a Caucasian fur-cap. He saluted and announced in a hoarse voice that the commissar had given orders that she was to be taken by car to the cemetery, but that the car would be ten minutes late since they were delivering a list of civilian employees to the central office. The lieutenant's personal belongings had already been packed; it would be easiest if she picked them up on her return from the cemetery.

All Lyudmila's requests were met with military precision and correctness. But she could feel that the commissar, the nurse and the commandant also wanted something from her, that they too wanted some word of consolation or forgiveness.

The commissar felt guilty because men were dying in his hospital. Until Lyudmila's visit this had never disturbed him: it was what was to be expected in a military hospital. The quality of the medical treatment had never been criticized by the authorities. What he had been reprimanded for was failing to organize enough political work or to provide adequate information about the morale of the wounded.

He hadn't fought hard enough against defeatism and against the

148

hostility of those socially backward patients opposed to collectivization. There had even been cases of military secrets being divulged. All this had led to a summons from the political division of the military district medical administration; he had been told that he would be sent to the front if the Special Section ever again informed them of ideological errors in the hospital.

Now, however, in front of the mother of the dead lieutenant, the commissar felt himself to blame for the fact that three patients had died the day before – while he himself had taken a shower, ordered his favourite dish of stewed sauerkraut from the cook and drunk a bottle of beer from the store in Saratov. And Sister Terentyevna felt guilty because her husband, a military engineer, served on the army staff and had never been to the front; while her son, who was a year older than Shaposhnikov, worked in the design office of an aviation factory. As for the commandant, a regular soldier, he was serving in a hospital back in the rear, sending home felt boots and good quality gabardine – while the uniform that had been passed on to the dead lieutenant's mother was made of the very cheapest material.

Even the thick-lipped sergeant-major with the fleshy ears, the man responsible for the burial of dead patients, felt guilty before the woman he was driving to the cemetery: the coffins were knocked together out of thin, poor-quality boards; the dead were laid out in their underclothes and buried in communal graves – extremely close together unless they were officers; the inscriptions over the graves were in an ugly script, on unpolished board and in paint that would not last. Of course, men who died in a field first-aid post were just heaped together in pits without individual coffins, and the inscriptions there were written in indelible pencil that would only last until it next rained. And men who died in combat, in forests, bogs, gullies and fields, often found no one at all to bury them – only wind, sand and snowstorms . . .

Nevertheless, the sergeant-major felt guilty about his poor-quality timber as the lieutenant's mother questioned him about the conduct of burials, asking how they dressed the corpses, whether they buried them together and whether a last word was spoken over the grave.

Another reason he felt awkward was that before the journey he had been to see a friend in the store; he had drunk a glass of diluted medical spirit and eaten some bread and onion. He was ashamed that his breath made the car stink of onions and alcohol – but he could hardly stop breathing.

He looked gloomily into the rectangular mirror in front of the driver: in it he could see the reflection of the man's bright, mocking eyes. 'Well, the sergeant-major's certainly had a good time,' they said mercilessly.

Everyone feels guilty before a mother who has lost her son in a war; throughout human history men have tried in vain to justify themselves.

32

The soldiers of a labour battalion, conscripts who were too old for active service, were unloading coffins from a truck. You could tell from their silence and lack of haste that they were used to this work. One man stood in the back of the truck and pushed a coffin to the rear; another man put his shoulder beneath it and took a few paces forward; a third walked silently up and took the other end of the coffin on his shoulder. Their boots squeaked on the frozen earth as they carried the coffins to the wide communal grave, laid them down beside it and returned to the truck. When the empty truck set off for the city, the soldiers sat down on the coffins and rolled cigarettes, using lots of paper and a very small amount of tobacco.

'There's not such a rush today,' said one of them, striking a light from a very good-quality steel: a thin cord of tinder running through a copper-casing where a flint had been set. The soldier pulled at the tinder and a puff of smoke rose into the air.

'The sergeant-major said there'd only be one lorry today,' said another soldier as he lit his cigarette, letting out clouds of smoke.

'In that case we can finish the grave.'

'That's right. It's best to do it straight away. Then he can come and check it against the list,' said a third soldier. He wasn't smoking; instead he took a piece of bread from his pocket, shook it, blew over it and began eating.

'Tell the sergeant-major to bring us a pickaxe. The earth's frozen solid almost quarter of the way down. Tomorrow we've got to do a new grave. We'll never be able to dig it just with spades.'

The soldier who had been striking a light clapped his hands, knocked the end of his cigarette out of a wooden holder and gently tapped the holder against the lid of the coffin.

All three fell silent, as though listening for something.

'Is it true we're being put on dry rations?' said the soldier eating the piece of bread. He spoke in a hushed voice so as not to disturb the men in the coffins with a conversation that didn't concern them.

The second of the two smokers blew his cigarette-end out of a long, smoke-blackened reed holder, held it up to the light and shook his head. Everything was quiet again . . .

'It's quite a good day, just a bit windy.'

'Listen. There's the truck. We'll be finished by lunchtime.'

'No. That's not our truck. It's a car.'

The sergeant-major got out of the car, followed by a woman in a shawl. They walked together towards the iron railings, to what had been the burial ground until they had run out of space the previous week.

'Thousands of people are being buried and no one attends the funerals,' said one of the soldiers. 'In peacetime it's the other way round: one coffin and a hundred people carrying flowers.'

'People mourn for them all the same,' said the soldier, tapping gently on the board with a thick oval fingernail, 'even if we don't see the tears . . . Look, the sergeant-major's coming back on his own.'

This time all three of them lit up. The sergeant-major walked up and said good-naturedly: 'So you're having another smoke, are you? How do you think we're going to get the work finished?'

They quietly let out three clouds of smoke. Then one of them, the owner of the steel, said: 'You only have to stop for a smoke and the truck arrives. Listen, I can tell by the sound of the engine.'

33

Lyudmila walked up to the small mound of earth. On a plywood board she read her son's name and rank.

She felt her hair stirring beneath her shawl. Someone was running their cold fingers through it.

On either side, stretching right up to the railings, were rows and rows of the same small grey mounds. There were no flowers on them, not even grass, just a single wooden stem shooting straight up from the grave. At the top of each stem was a plywood board with a man's name on it. There were hundreds of these boards. Their density and uniformity made them seem like a field of grain . . .

Now she had found Tolya at last. She had tried so many times to imagine where he was, what he was thinking about and what he was doing: leaning against the side of a trench and dozing; walking down a path; sipping tea, holding his mug in one hand and a piece of sugar in the other; or perhaps running across a field under fire . . . She had wanted to be there beside him. After all, he needed her: she would top up his mug of tea; she would say, 'Have another slice of bread'; she would take off his shoes and wash his chafed feet; she would wrap a scarf round his neck . . . But he had always eluded her. And now she had found him, he no longer needed her.

Further away she could see graves from before the Revolution with crosses made out of granite. The gravestones stood there like a crowd of unloved, unwanted old men. Some of them were lying on their sides, others leant helplessly against tree-trunks.

The sky seemed somehow airless – as though all the air had been pumped out and there was nothing but dry dust over her head. And the pump was continuing its work: together with the air, faith and hope had now disappeared; nothing was left but a small mound of grey, frozen earth.

Everything living – her mother, Nadya, Viktor's eyes, the bulletins about the course of the war – had ceased to exist.

Everything living had become inanimate. In the whole wide world only Tolya was still alive. But what silence there was all around him. Did he realize that she had come . . . ?

Lyudmila knelt down and, very gently, so as not to disturb her son, straightened the board with his name on it. He had always got angry with her when she straightened the collar of his jacket on their way to school.

'There. I'm here now. You must have thought Mama was never going to come.' She spoke in a half-whisper, afraid of being overheard.

Some trucks went past. The dust whirled about in the wind. Milkwomen with churns and people carrying sacks tramped by wearing soldiers' boots. Schoolchildren ran past in soldiers' winter caps.

But the day and all its movement seemed to Lyudmila just a misty vision.

What silence there was everywhere.

She was talking to her son, remembering every detail of his life; and these memories, which survived only in her consciousness, filled the world with the voice of a child, with his tears, with the rustle of the pages of a picture-book, the clinking of a teaspoon against the edge of a white plate, the humming of home-made radio sets, the squeak of skis, the creaking of rowlocks on the ponds near the dacha, the rustling of sweet-papers, with fleeting glimpses of a boy's face, shoulders and chest.

Animated by her despair, his tears, his moments of distress, his every act – good or bad – took on a distinct and palpable existence.

She seemed to be caught up, not by memories of the past, but by the anxieties of everyday life.

What did he think he was doing – reading all night long in such awful light? Did he want to have to wear spectacles at his age?

And now he was lying there in a coarse calico shirt, bare-footed. Why hadn't they given him any blankets? The earth was frozen solid and there was a sharp frost at night.

Blood began to pour from Lyudmila's nose. Her handkerchief was soon sodden and heavy. Her eyes blurred and she felt giddy; for a moment she thought she might faint. She screwed up her eyes. When she opened them again, the world brought to life by her suffering had vanished. There was nothing but grey dust whirling over the graves; one after another, they began to smoke.

The water of life, the water that had gushed over the ice and brought Tolya back from the darkness, had disappeared; the world created by the mother's despair, the world that for a moment had broken its fetters and become reality, was no more.

Her despair had raised the lieutenant from the grave, filling the void with new stars. For a few minutes he had been the only living person in the world; it was to him that everything else had owed its existence. But even the mother's tremendous strength was not enough to prevent the multitudes of people, the roads and cities, the seas, the earth itself, from swamping her dead Tolya.

Lyudmila dabbed at her eyes. They were quite dry, but the handkerchief was sodden. She realized that her face was smeared with sticky blood and sat there, hunched up, resigned, taking her first involuntary steps towards the realization that Tolya no longer existed.

The people in the hospital had been struck by her calm and the number of questions she had asked. They hadn't appreciated her inability to understand something quite obvious – that Tolya was no longer among the living. Her love was so strong that Tolya's death was unable to affect it: to her, he was still alive.

She was mad, but no one had noticed. Now, at last, she had found Tolya. Her joy was like that of a mother-cat when she finds her dead kitten and licks it all over.

A soul can live in torment for years and years, even decades, as it slowly, stone by stone, builds a mound over a grave; as it moves towards the apprehension of eternal loss and bows down before reality.

The soldiers finished their work and left; the sun had nearly gone down; the shadows of the plywood boards over the graves lengthened. Lyudmila was alone.

She ought to tell Tolya's relatives about his death. Above all, she must tell his father in the camp. His father. And what had Tolya been thinking about before the operation? Had they fed him with a spoon? Had he been able to sleep a little on his side? Or on his back? He liked water with lemon and sugar. How was he lying right now? Was he shaven or unshaven?

It must be the unbearable pain in her soul that was making everything darker and darker.

She suddenly felt that her grief would last for ever; Viktor would die, her daughter's grandchildren would die – and she would still be grieving.

When her anguish grew unbearable, the boundary between her inner world and the real world again dissolved; eternity retreated before her love.

Why should she give the news of Tolya's death to his father, to Viktor, to her other relatives? After all, she didn't yet know for sure. Perhaps it would be better to wait; things might turn out differently.

'Don't tell anyone,' she whispered. 'No one knows yet. It will be all right.'

Lyudmila covered Tolya's feet with the hem of her coat. She took off her shawl and laid it over her son's shoulders.

'Heavens! What are you doing? Why haven't they given you any blankets? You really must have something over your feet.'

She fell into delirium, talking to her son, scolding him for writing such short letters. Sometimes she woke up and adjusted the shawl; it had been blown aside by the wind.

How good that they were alone together, that there was no one to disturb them. No one had ever loved him. People had always said he was ugly: that he had swollen lips; that he was very strange; that he was ridiculously touchy and quick-tempered. No one had ever loved her either; the people close to her saw only her failings . . . My poor boy, my poor, timid, clumsy little son . . . He was the only person who loved her – and now he was alone with her in the cemetery at night; he would never leave her; he would still love her when she was a useless old woman who got in everyone's way . . . How ill adapted he was to life. He never asked for anything; he was always absurdly shy. The schoolmistress said he was the laughing-stock of the school; the boys all teased him till he was quite beside himself and began to cry like a little child. Tolya, Tolya, don't leave me alone.

Day dawned. An icy red glow flared up over the steppes east of the Volga. A truck rumbled down the road.

Her madness had passed. She was sitting beside her son's grave. His body was covered with earth. He was dead.

She could see her dirty fingers and a shawl of hers lying on the ground; her legs had grown numb: she could feel that her face was smeared with dirt. Her throat tickled.

But none of this mattered. And if someone had told her that the war was over or that her daughter had just died, if a glass of hot milk or a piece of warm bread had suddenly appeared beside her, she wouldn't have stirred; she wouldn't have stretched out her hands or made any movement. She was sitting there without thought, without anxiety. Nothing mattered to her; there was nothing she needed. All that existed was some agonizing force that was crushing her heart and pressing against her temples. A doctor in a white smock and some other people from the hospital were talking about Tolya; she could see their mouths open, but she couldn't hear what they said. A letter was lying on the ground. It had fallen out of her coat-pocket. It was the letter she had received from the hospital, but she didn't want to pick it up or shake the dust off it. She was no longer thinking about how, when he was two, Tolya had waddled clumsily after a grasshopper as it jumped from spot to spot; it didn't matter that she'd forgotten to ask whether he had lain on his side or on his back on the last day of his life. She could see the light of day; she was unable not to see it.

Suddenly she remembered Tolya's third birthday: in the evening they had had tea and pastries and Tolya had asked: 'Mummy, why's it dark when today's my birthday?'

She could see some trees, the polished gravestones shining in the sun and the board with her son's name. 'SHAPOSHN' was written in big letters, while 'IKOV' was written very small, each letter clinging to the one before. She had no thoughts and no will. She had nothing.

She got up, picked up the letter, flicked a lump of earth off her coat with numb fingers, wiped her shoes and shook her coat until it was white again. She put on her shawl, using the hem to wipe the dust off her eyebrows and clean the blood from her lips and chin. With even steps and without looking round, she began to walk towards the gates.

34

After her return to Kazan, Lyudmila began to lose weight; soon she began to look like photographs of herself as a student. She went to the store to collect the family's rations; she prepared meals; she stoked the stove; she cleaned the floors and did the washing. The autumn days seemed very long; she could find nothing to fill their emptiness.

On the day she got back she told her family all about her journey and her feelings of guilt towards everyone close to her. She described her visit to the hospital and unwrapped the parcel containing the bloodstained shreds of her son's uniform. Nadya cried; Alexandra Vladimirovna breathed heavily; Viktor's hands trembled so much he couldn't even pick up a glass of tea. Marya Ivanovna had rushed in to visit Lyudmila; she turned pale, her mouth fell open and a martyred expression appeared in her eyes. Lyudmila was the only person able to speak calmly, looking around her with her bright, wide-open, light blue eyes.

She had always been very argumentative, but now she no longer argued with anyone; in the past one had only had to direct someone to the station for Lyudmila to fly into a temper and excitedly start to prove that they should take a different street and quite another trolley-bus.

One day Viktor asked her: 'Lyudmila, who is it you talk to at night?'

'I don't know,' she answered. 'Perhaps I'm just dreaming.'

He didn't question her further, but he told Alexandra Vladimirovna that almost every night Lyudmila opened some suitcases, spread a blanket over the sofa in the corner and began talking in a quiet, anxious voice.

'I get the feeling that during the daytime she's with you and me and Nadya in a dream, while at night her voice comes alive again like it was before the war,' he said. 'I think she's ill. She's become someone else.'

'I don't know,' said Alexandra Vladimirovna. 'We're all of us suffering, each in our own way.'

Their conversation was cut short by a knock at the front door. Viktor got up to answer it, but Lyudmila called, 'I'll go,' from the kitchen.

No one could understand why, but they had all noticed that since her return from Saratov, Lyudmila had been checking the letter-box several times a day. And whenever there was a knock at the door, she rushed to answer it.

Viktor and Alexandra Vladimirovna looked at each other as they listened to Lyudmila's hurried steps – she was almost running.

Then they heard her say in an exasperated tone of voice: 'No, we haven't got anything today. And don't come so often. I gave you half a kilo of bread only the day before yesterday.'

35

Lieutenant Viktorov had been summoned to HQ to see Major Zakabluka, the commander of a fighter squadron that was being held in reserve. The duty-officer, Lieutenant Velikanov, said the major had flown off in a U-2 to the Air Army HQ near Kalinin and would return that evening. When Viktorov asked why he had been sent for, Velikanov winked and said that it might well have to do with the booze-up in the mess.

Viktorov glanced behind a curtain made out of a blanket and a tarpaulin sheet. He could hear the clatter of a typewriter. As soon as he caught sight of him, the chief clerk said: 'No, comrade Lieutenant, there aren't any letters for you.'

Lenochka, the civilian typist, glanced round at Viktorov. She then turned towards a mirror from a shot-down German plane – a present from the late Lieutenant Demidov – straightened her forage cap, moved the ruler lying on the documents she was copying, and started typing again.

This long-faced lieutenant bored Lenochka; he always asked the chief clerk the same gloomy question.

On his way back to the airfield, Viktorov turned off towards the edge of the forest.

The squadron had been in reserve for a month, replacing men and material.

The Northern countryside seemed very strange to Viktorov. The life of the forest and the young river that wound between the steep hills, the smell of mushrooms and mould, the rustling of the trees were all somehow disturbing.

When he was flying, the various smells seemed to reach right up to his cabin. From the forest and lakes came the breath of an old Russia Viktorov had previously only read about. Ancient tracks ran among these lakes and forests; houses and churches had been built from the tall, upright trees; the masts of sailing-boats had been hewn from them. The Grey Wolf had run through these forests. Alyonushka had stood and wept on the very bank along which Viktorov was now walking towards the mess. This vanished past seemed somehow simple-minded, youthful, naïve; not only the maidens in towers, but even the grey-bearded merchants, deacons and patriarchs seemed a thousand years younger than the worldly-wise young pilots who had come to this forest from a world of fast cars, machine-guns, diesel engines, radios and cinemas. The Volga itself – quick and slim, flowing between steep, many-coloured banks, through the green of the forest, through patterns of light blue and red – was a symbol of this vanished past.

How many of them there were – privates, sergeants and lieutenants – all travelling the same war-path. They all smoked countless cigarettes, tapped on tin bowls with tin spoons, played card-games in railway-carriages, treated themselves to ice-lollies in town, coughed as they downed their hundred-gram tots of vodka, wrote the same number of letters, shouted down field-telephones, fired light or heavy guns, yelled as they stepped on the accelerator of a T-34 tank . . .

The earth beneath Viktorov's boots was as squeaky and springy as an old mattress. The leaves on the surface were light, brittle and still separate from one another; under them lay leaves that had withered many years before and fused into a brown, crackling mass – the ashes of the life that had once burst into bud, rustled in the winds of a storm and gleamed in the sun after a shower. Rotten, almost weightless brushwood crumbled beneath his feet. A soft, gentle light fell on the forest-floor, diffused by a screen of foliage. The air itself was thick and congealed; a fighter-pilot, accustomed to a rushing wind, felt this very acutely. The living trees felt fresh and damp like cut timber. The smell of the dead trees and brushwood, however, was still stronger . . . From the pines rose a sharp note of turpentine, an octave higher. The aspen smelt sweet and sickly and the breath of the elder was bitter. The forest had its own life; it was as though he were entering an unfamiliar house where everything was different from outside. The smells were different, the light was filtered through drawn curtains, the sounds had a different resonance. All this made him feel strange and uncomfortable. It was as though he were at the bottom of a reservoir, looking up through a thick layer of water, as though the leaves were splashing about, as though the strands of gossamer clinging to the green star on his forage cap were algae suspended from the surface. It was as though the inert swarms of midges, the darting flies with their large heads, the blackcock squeezing through the branches, might flick their fins yet never be able to rise above the forest – just as a fish can never rise above the surface of the water; and if a magpie did happen to soar over the top of an aspen, then it immediately plunged down again into the branches – like a fish whose white belly gleamed for a moment in the sun before it flopped back into the water. And how very strange the moss seemed, covered in blue and green drops of dew that slowly faded away in the gloom of the forest-floor.

It was good to emerge from this silent semi-darkness into a bright glade. Suddenly everything was different: the earth was warm; the air was in movement; you could smell the junipers in the sun; there were large, wilting bluebells which looked as though they had been cast from mauve-coloured metal, and wild carnations on sticky, resinous stems. You felt suddenly carefree; the glade was like one happy day in a life of poverty. The lemon-coloured butterflies, the polished, blue-black beetles, the ants, the grass-snake rustling through the grass, seemed to be joining together in a common task. Birch-twigs, sprinkled with fine leaves, brushed against his face; a grasshopper jumped up and landed on him as though he were a tree-trunk; it clung to his belt, calmly tensing its green haunches as it sat there with its round, leathery eyes and sheep-like face. The last flowers of the wild strawberries. The heat of the sun on his metal buttons and belt-clasp . . . No U-88 or night-flying Heinkel could ever have flown over this glade.

36

At night Viktorov often remembered the months he had spent in the hospital at Stalingrad. But he no longer remembered how his night-shirt had been damp with sweat, how the brackish water had made him feel sick, how the thick, heavy smell had tormented him. Those days in hospital now seemed a time of happiness. Here in the forest, listening to the rustling of the trees, he thought: 'Did I really once hear her footsteps?'

Had it all really happened . . . ? She had taken him in her arms; she had stroked his hair; she had cried; and he had kissed her wet, salty eyes. In a Yak he could fly to Stalingrad in only a few hours; he could refuel in Ryazan – he had a friend there who was a controller. What did it matter if he then got shot for it?

He kept thinking of a story he had read in an old book: the Sheremetyev brothers, the rich sons of the field-marshal, gave their sixteen-year-old sister in marriage to Prince Dolgoruky. As far as Viktorov could remember, she only met him once before the wedding. The brothers gave the bride an enormous dowry – the silver alone took up three whole rooms. And then two days after the wedding Peter II was killed. Dolgoruky, who had been in attendance on him, was seized, taken to the far North and imprisoned in a wooden tower. The young wife could have had her marriage annulled – she had only lived with her husband for two days – but she refused to listen to anyone's advice. She set off after her husband and settled in a peasant hut in a remote forest. Every day for ten years she walked to the tower where Dolgoruky was imprisoned. One morning she found the window of the tower wide open and the door unlocked. The young princess ran down the street, falling on her knees before everyone she met – whether peasant or musketeer – begging them to tell her what had happened to her husband. She was told that Dolgoruky had been taken to Nizhny Novgorod. She made the long journey after him on foot, suffering great hardships. In Nizhny Novgorod she discovered that Dolgoruky had been executed and then quartered. The princess decided to enter a convent and travelled to the Pecherskaya Lavra in Kiev. On the day she was to take the veil she walked for a long time along the bank of the Dnieper. What she regretted was not her freedom but the obligation to take off her wedding-ring. She couldn't bring herself to part with it . . . Hour after hour she paced up and down the bank; as the sun was about to set, she took off the ring, threw it into the Dnieper and set off towards the convent gates.

The pilot, who had been brought up in an orphanage and who had once been a mechanic at the Stalingrad Power Station, couldn't stop thinking of Princess Dolgorukaya. He walked through the forest, imagining that he had died and been buried; that his plane had caught fire, nose-dived into the ground, grown rusty, disintegrated and been covered over by grass; and that now Vera Shaposhnikova was here, stopping, climbing down towards the Volga, looking into the water . . . And two hundred years ago it had been the young Dolgorukaya: she had come out into a clearing, made her way through the tall flax, and parted with her own hands these bushes laden with red berries. Viktorov felt a sensation of hopeless pain, of bitterness and sweetness.

A young, narrow-shouldered lieutenant was walking through the forest in a worn tunic. How many people there were like him — forgotten during unforgettable years.

37

Before he even got to the airfield, Viktorov knew that something had happened. Fuel-tankers were driving about the runway; technicians and mechanics were bustling around the fighter-planes covered in camouflage netting. The radio transmitter, normally silent, was chattering away.

'No doubt about it,' thought Viktorov, quickening his pace.

Everything was immediately confirmed when he met Solomatin, one of his fellow lieutenants, a man with pink scars on his cheeks.

'The order's come through. We're being taken out of reserve.'

'To the front?'

'Where do you think? Tashkent?' said Solomatin, striding off towards the village.

He looked very upset. He was seriously involved with his landlady and was obviously on his way to her now.

'Solomatin's decided to go halves. He's keeping the cow for himself and leaving the hut to the woman,' said a familiar voice at Viktorov's side. Lieutenant Yeromin, Viktorov's partner, fell in beside him.

'Where do you think they're sending us, Yeroma?'

'The North-Western Front may be about to advance. The divisional commander's just arrived in an R-5. I can ask a friend who's a Douglas pilot on the Air Force staff. He always knows everything.'

'Why bother? We'll be told soon enough.'

The flurry of excitement affected not only the pilots and ground staff, but the whole village. Junior Lieutenant Korol, the youngest pilot in the squadron, was walking down the street with some freshly washed and ironed linen; on top of it lay a honey-cake and a packet of dried berries. The other pilots often teased Korol, saying that his landladies, two elderly widows, were spoiling him with their honey-cakes. Whenever he'd been out on a mission, the two women – one tall and straight, the other hunch-backed – would come to meet him on his way back from the airfield. He would walk between them, looking like a spoiled and sullen little child; his comrades said he was flying in formation with a question mark and an exclamation mark.

Wing-Commander Vanya Martynov came out of his house, dressed in a greatcoat. He was carrying a suitcase in one hand and a dress forage cap in the other – he had left it out so it wouldn't get crumpled. The landlady's daughter, the red hair she had waved herself blowing in the wind, looked after him in a way that made their relationship only too plain.

A lame little boy told Viktorov that Political Instructor Golub and Lieutenant Vovka Skotnoy, with whom he shared his billet, had left with all their belongings. Viktorov had only moved in a few days before: until then he and Golub had been billeted with a dreadful landlady, a woman with a high forehead and protuberant yellow eyes. Looking into her eyes was enough to make you feel ill.

In order to get rid of her tenants, she used to fill the hut with smoke. Once she even sprinkled ash in their tea. Golub had tried to persuade Viktorov to report her to the commissar, but he couldn't bring himself to do so.

'Well, I hope the cholera gets her!' said Golub.

Their new billet had seemed like paradise. But they had not been allowed to stay there for long.

Soon Viktorov was carrying a kitbag and a battered suitcase past the tall grey huts that seemed almost two storeys high. The crippled boy hopped along at his side, taking aim at chickens and at planes circling over the forest with a German holster Viktorov had given him. He walked past the hut Yevdokiya Mikheevna had smoked him out of; he could see her expressionless face behind the dirty window-panes. No one ever talked to her when she stopped for a rest as she carried her two wooden buckets back from the well. She had no cows and no sheep; she didn't even have any house-martins in the eaves. Golub had asked questions about her, hoping to bring to light her kulak background, but she turned out to be from a very poor family. The women in the village said she had gone crazy after her husband's death: she had walked into a lake in cold autumn weather and sat there for days. But she had been taciturn even before that, even before her marriage.

There he was, walking through a village in the forest – and in a few hours he would have flown away for ever. The village, the forest, the elks who came into the vegetable gardens, the ferns, the yellow pools of resin, the cuckoos – all these would cease to exist for him. The old men and the little girls would disappear, as would the stories about collectivization, the stories of bears who had stolen punnets full of raspberries from the women, the stories of little boys who had stepped with bare heels on the heads of vipers ... This unfamiliar village would vanish – this village whose life revolved around the forest just as the workers' settlement where he had been born and raised revolved around the factory.

Then his fighter would land and a new airfield would come into being. Nearby they would find a new peasant village or workers' settlement – with its own old women and small girls, its own tears and jokes, its own cats with bald, scarred noses, its own good and bad landladies, its own stories about the past and about general collectivization. Here too the handsome Solomatin would put on his peaked service cap, walk down the street, sing to his guitar and drive some young girl out of her mind.

Major Zakabluka, with his bronzed face and a white, clean-shaven skull, read out their orders. His five Orders of the Red Star jingled as he swayed on his crooked legs. He told them that their route would be announced before take-off and that they were to sleep in their bunkers; anyone who absented himself from the airfield would be punished with the utmost severity.

'I don't want anyone nodding off when we're in the air,' he explained. 'Get some sleep before we set off.'

Then Berman, the commissar, stepped forward. He was generally considered too arrogant, though he could talk sensibly and eloquently about the finer points of flying. His unpopularity had increased after the Mukhin affair. Mukhin had been involved with Lida Voynovaya, a radio-operator. This love-affair had charmed everyone – whenever they had a spare moment, the two of them would be walking hand in hand along the banks of the river. Everything about the affair was so transparent that the men didn't even make jokes about it.

Then a rumour sprang up – apparently Lida had told a girl-friend and the girl-friend had passed it on to the squadron – that during one of their walks Mukhin had threatened Lida with a gun and raped her.

Berman was furious; he pursued the case with such furious energy that within ten days Mukhin had appeared before a tribunal and been sentenced to be shot.

Before the sentence was carried out, however, Major-General Alexeev, the Member of the Air Army Soviet, had flown in to ascertain the exact circumstances of Mukhin's crime. To his profound embarrassment, Lida knelt down before him and implored him to believe that the whole case against Mukhin was an absurd fabrication.

She then told him the full story. She and Mukhin had been kissing in a glade in the forest. She had dozed off and – as a jest – Mukhin had quietly placed his pistol between her knees and fired into the ground. She had woken up and screamed, and Mukhin had started kissing her again. She had told all this to her girl-friend – who had then circulated another, more sinister version. But only one thing in all this was true – and that was something exceptionally simple: her and Mukhin's love for one another.

Everything was finally resolved: Mukhin's sentence was rescinded and he was transferred to another squadron. But the whole affair made Berman very unpopular.

One day, in the mess, Solomatin remarked that a Russian would never have acted like that. Someone else, probably Molchanov, had answered that every nation had its villains.

'Take Korol,' said Vanya Skotnoy. 'He's a Jew – and he's a splendid person to have as a mate. It's good to know there's someone you can rely on at your tail.'

'Korol's not a Jew,' said Solomatin. 'He's one of us. In the air I trust him more than I trust myself. Once, over Rzhev, he shot down a Messerschmidt that was right on my tail. And I've twice let a damaged Fritz off the hook to get him out of trouble. And I forget everyone when I'm in combat – even my own mother'.

'I see,' said Viktorov. 'If you like a man, he can't be a Jew!'

Everyone laughed.

'It's all very well to laugh,' Solomatin replied, 'but Mukhin didn't think it was funny when Berman sentenced him to be shot.'

At this moment Korol came in. One of the pilots asked in a sympathetic tone of voice: 'Listen, Borya, are you a Jew?'

'Yes, I am,' answered Korol in some embarrassment.

'Are you sure?'

'Absolutely.'

'Are you circumcised, though?'

'To hell with you!' retorted Korol. Once again everyone laughed.

When they were on their way back to the village, Solomatin had come up to Viktorov and said: 'You're a fool to talk like that, you know. I used to work in a soap-works and the whole place was full of Jews. All the administrative staff were Jewish. I can tell you I had enough of those Samuel Abramoviches. They knew how to look after one another all right.'

'Why go on about it?' said Viktorov with a surprised shrug of the shoulders. 'Do you think I'm in league with them?'

Now it was Berman's turn to address the assembled pilots. He announced that this was the beginning of a new era for the fighter squadron: their time in the rear was over. Everyone knew this already, but they listened attentively in case he dropped any hint as to whether they would be kept on the North-Western Front and stationed near Rzhev, or whether they would be transferred to the South or the West.

'Now – first, a fighter pilot must know his machine, must know it well enough to be able to play with it; second, he must love it, love it as though it were his sister or mother; third, he must have courage – and courage means a cool head and a fiery heart; fourth, he must have the sense of comradeship that is instilled into us by the whole of Soviet life; fifth, he must be whole-hearted and selfless in combat. And success depends on each pair of aircraft working together. Follow the leading aircraft! A true pilot is always thinking – even when he's on the ground. He's always analysing the last combat, wondering if he made any mistakes.'

As they pretended to pay attention to Berman's homily, the pilots talked quietly among themselves.

'Perhaps we'll be assigned to escort the Douglases carrying provisions to Leningrad,' said Solomatin, who knew a young girl in Leningrad.

'Maybe we'll be stationed near Moscow,' said Molchanov, whose family lived on the outskirts.

'Or Stalingrad,' said Viktorov.

'I doubt it,' said Skotnoy. He didn't mind where they were sent; all his relatives were in occupied territory.

'What about you, Borya? I suppose you want to be off to Berdichev, your very own Jewish capital,' said Solomatin.

Korol's dark eyes went black with rage and he turned on Solomatin, cursing and swearing.

'Second Lieutenant Korol!' shouted Berman.

'Yes, comrade Commissar!'

'Silence!'

Major Zakabluka was renowned as a connoisseur of swear-words and would never have made an issue of anything like this himself. Every morning he would shout out to his orderly, 'Mazyukin . . . you damned motherfucker . . . ,' before concluding quietly, 'Will you hand me my towel?'

But knowing how captious Berman could be, Zakabluka was afraid of pardoning Korol then and there. Berman would report that Zakabluka had discredited the political leadership in front of the pilots. He had already reported that Zakabluka had set up his own private farm while he was in the rear, that he got drunk on vodka with his staff officers and that he was having an affair with Zhenya Bondarevaya, a livestock expert from the village.

So Zakabluka had no choice but to pursue the matter. In a stern, hoarse voice he barked: 'Stand up straight, Second Lieutenant Korol! Two paces forward! What's this slovenliness?'

He then took the matter a step further.

'Political Instructor Golub, explain to the commissar why Korol has just infringed discipline.'

'Beg to report, comrade Major. He quarrelled with Solomatin – I've no idea why.'

'Lieutenant Solomatin!'

'Yes, comrade Major.'

'Report to the commissar, not to me.'

'Beg to report, comrade Commissar.'

'Go ahead,' nodded Berman without so much as looking at Solomatin. He suspected that Major Zakabluka had his own reasons for what he was doing. Zakabluka was cunning, exceptionally so, both on the ground and in the air. Up in the air he was better than anyone at guessing an opponent's tactics, at outwitting his stratagems. And on the ground he was able to play a part when necessary, to act the simpleton and laugh ingratiatingly at some feeble joke made by a stupid superior. And he knew how to keep these wild young pilots under his thumb.

During their month in reserve, Zakabluka had displayed a considerable interest in farming, particularly poultry and livestock raising. He had also exploited the resources of the forest, making his own raspberry liqueur and preparing both pickled and dried mushrooms. His dinners were famous and other squadron commanders liked to drop by in their U-2s for a drink and a bite to eat. Zakabluka was very hospitable – but not without ulterior motives.

There was another side of his character which often complicated their relations: sly and calculating as he was, there were times when he would stop at nothing, when he would act so recklessly as to endanger his life.

'Arguing with one's superior officers is like pissing against the wind,' he would say – and then act quite senselessly, leaving Berman gasping in amazement.

When they were both in a good mood, they would wink at one another as they talked, patting each other on the back or the stomach.

'Yes, our commissar's certainly a sly old fellow,' Zakabluka would say.

'And our major's a true hero,' Berman would answer.

What Zakabluka most disliked in Berman was his unctuousness – and the diligence with which he reported every careless word anyone came out with. He made fun of Berman's weakness for pretty girls, the way he loved roast chicken – 'Give us a drumstick!' – but couldn't care less about vodka. He disapproved of the way he would turn a blind eye to other people's living conditions while knowing very well how to look after his own. At the same time he valued him for his intelligence and bravery – sometimes he seemed quite unaware of physical danger – and his readiness to take on his superiors for the good of the cause.

And now here they were – these two men who were about to lead a fighter squadron into action – glancing suspiciously at one another as they listened to Lieutenant Solomatin.

'Let me say straight out, comrade Commissar, that I am to blame for Korol's infringement of discipline. I was making fun of him. He put up with it for a while, but then he forgot himself.'

'Explain what it was that you said,' interrupted Zakabluka.

'We were trying to guess which front the Squadron would be transferred to. I said to Korol: "I suppose you want us to go to your own capital, Berdichev."'

The pilots all glanced at Berman.

'Which capital?' said Berman – and then understood.

Everyone could sense Berman's embarrassment. Zakabluka was very surprised – usually Berman was as sharp as a razor. But his next move was equally surprising.

'What's so terrible about that?' asked Berman. 'What if you, Korol, had said to Solomatin, who comes, as we know, from the village of Dorokhovo in the Novo-Ruzskiy district, that you presumed he wanted to fight above Dorokhovo? Would he have answered you with a punch in the face? I'm surprised to find the mentality of the shtetl in a member of the Komsomol.'*

Berman's words always had a strange, hypnotic effect on people. Everyone knew that Solomatin had deliberately offended Korol – and yet there was Berman confidently explaining that Korol had failed to overcome his nationalist prejudices and that his behaviour evinced a contempt for the friendship of peoples. And Korol should remember that it was the Fascists who exploited nationalist prejudices.

Everything Berman said was in itself quite fair and reasonable. The ideals he spoke about so excitedly were those of democracy and the Revolution. But Berman's strength at moments like this lay in the way he made use of an ideal rather than serving it, the way he subordinated it to his own – often questionable – needs of the moment.

'Do you understand, comrades?' he went on. 'Where there is no ideological clarity, there can be no discipline. That is the true explanation of Korol's behaviour.' He paused for a moment. 'Korol's disgraceful, anti-Soviet behaviour.'

By now, of course, it was quite impossible for Zakabluka to

* Komsomol: the Communist Youth League.

intervene: the incident had been transformed into a question of politics – and no officer dared interfere in political matters.

'And so, comrades,' said Berman, pausing again to give more weight to his final words, 'the responsibility for this incident lies with the immediate culprit, but it also lies with me, the squadron commissar, for failing to help Lieutenant Korol to grow out of his abominable nationalism. The whole affair is more serious than I at first realized. For that very reason I have decided not to punish Korol for his infringement of discipline. Instead I take upon myself the responsibility for re-educating him.'

Everyone settled down again in their chairs, sensing that the affair had now been resolved. Korol looked at Berman. Something in his look made Berman frown, twitch and turn away.

That evening Solomatin said to Viktorov: 'You see, Lenya, it's always like that. They stand up for each other all right – but on the sly. If it had been you or Vanya Skotnoy, you'd have ended up in a penal unit.'

38

That night, instead of going to sleep, the pilots were lying about on their bunks, smoking and chatting. Skotnoy, who had had a farewell ration of vodka at supper, began to sing:

> 'The plane's in a nose-dive –
> The earth's rushing to meet her.
> Don't cry for me, love;
> Forget me, my sweetest.'

In the end Velikanov couldn't keep his mouth shut. He blurted out that they were to be stationed near Stalingrad.

The moon rose over the forest; you could see its bright, restless light through the trees. Two kilometres away the village seemed silent and dark, as though covered in ashes. The pilots sitting by the entrance to the bunker gazed at the wonderful world of the earth. Viktorov looked at the faint shadows cast by the wings and tails of the planes out on the runway and joined in with Skotnoy:

'They'll drag out our bodies
From the twisted metal.
The hawks will escort us
On our last flight of all.'

The pilots lying on the bunks carried on talking. It was too dark to see, but they all knew each other's voices.

'Demidov was always volunteering for missions. He'd have wasted away if he hadn't been able to fly.'

'Remember that dogfight near Rzhev when we were escorting the Petlyakovs? Eight Messers went straight for him – and he fought them off for seventeen minutes.'

'He used to sing when we were in the air. I remember those songs of his every day. He even used to sing Vertinsky.'

'Yes, he was a cultured man – a Muscovite.'

'He certainly wasn't the kind of fellow to leave you in the lurch. He always kept an eye on anyone who was behind.'

'You hardly even knew him.'

'Nonsense! You get to know your mate from the way he flies. I knew him all right.'

Skotnoy came to the end of another verse. Everyone fell silent, expecting him to start up again. Instead he repeated a well-worn saying comparing the length of a fighter pilot's life to that of a child's shirt.

The conversation turned to the Germans.

'It's the same with them. You can tell at once whether someone's a real pilot, or whether he's just on the look-out for stragglers and greenhorns.'

'Their patrols don't stick together like we do.'

'I don't know about that.'

'They really sink their teeth into you if you're damaged. Otherwise they'd rather leave you alone.'

'One to one, I can always give them a good thrashing.'

'Don't take offence – but I wouldn't award medals just for shooting down a Junkers.'

'Why should I take offence? You can't take my medal away from me now.'

'I wonder what our squadron leader's going to do with his cow and his chickens. Is he going to put them in a Douglas and take them with him?'

'They've already had their throats cut. Now they're being cured.'

'Right now I'd be too shy to take a girl out to a club. I've forgotten what it's like.'

'Solomatin wouldn't be.'

'Are you jealous, Lenya?'

'Yes, but not concerning the girl in question.'

'I see. Faithful unto the grave.'

Their talk turned again to the combat over Rzhev, their last before being sent to the rear; seven of their fighters had encountered a large group of Junkers on a bombing raid, with an escort of Messerschmidts. Each pilot seemed to be blowing his own trumpet, but really they were talking about what they had achieved together.

'I could hardly make them out against the forest – but it was another matter once they began to climb. Ju-87s – I could tell at once by their yellow noses and their trailing undercarriage. "Well," I thought to myself, "things are going to get hot!"'

'For a moment I thought we were being fired on by our own anti-aircraft guns.'

'The sun certainly helped, I'll admit that. I dropped down on him with the sun right behind me. I was leading the left wing. And then my plane must have jumped a good thirty metres . . . I pulled back the stick – she was still listening . . . ! I opened fire on the Junkers. She was on fire. And then I saw a Messer banking towards me – like a long pike with a yellow head. But he was too late. And I could see his blue tracer bullets.'

'And I could see I was hitting the bull's-eye every time!'

'Now, now, let's not get carried away!'

'As a kid, I was always flying kites. My father used to thrash me for it. And when I was at the factory, I used to walk seven kilometres to the flying club after work. I was dead beat. But I didn't miss a single lesson.'

'Listen to me! He set me on fire – the oil-tank, the feed-pipes, even the fuselage itself. He even managed to smash the windshield and my goggles. There was glass everywhere, and tears in my eyes. Well, I dived beneath him and tore off my goggles. Solomatin covered me. I was on fire, but I didn't have time to feel frightened. Somehow I managed to land. The plane was in flames, my boots got burnt – but I was all right!'

'I could see my mate was almost down. I made two more turns. He dipped his wings at me to tell me to leave. Then I was on my own. I just gave a hand to anyone who needed it.'

'I was well and truly shot to pieces – as full of holes as an old grouse.'

'I went for that Messer twelve times. In the end I singed him. I could see him shaking his head and I knew that was my chance. I shot him down with my cannon at twenty-five metres.'

'They're not happy fighting in the horizontal. They're always more at home in the vertical.'

'Now that really is news!'

'Why do you say that?'

'Everyone knows that – even the girls in the village.'

After a moment of silence, a voice said: 'We'll be off at dawn – and Demidov will be left on his own.'

'Well, my friends, *you* can do as you please, but I'm off to the village.'

'A parting visit? Let's go then!'

Everything – the river, the fields, the forest – was so beautiful, so peaceful, that hatred, betrayal and old age seemed impossible; nothing could exist but love and happiness. The moon shone down through the grey mist that enveloped the earth. Few pilots spent the night in their bunkers. On the edge of the village you could glimpse white scarves and hear quiet laughter. Now and then a tree would shake, frightened by a bad dream; the water would mumble something and return to silence.

The bitter hour of parting had come. One pilot would forget his girl in a couple of days; another couple would be separated by death; another would be allowed to meet again.

The morning came. Motors roared, their wind flattened the grass and thousands of dew-drops trembled in the sun . . . One by one, the fighters took off, circled, waited for their comrades and settled into formation . . .

What had seemed so infinite during the night was now dissolving in the blue of the sky . . . Houses like little grey boxes, small rectangular gardens, slipped by under their wings . . . They could no longer see the

173

overgrown path, they could no longer see Demidov's grave . . . They were off! The forest slid past under their wings.

'Greetings, Vera!' said Viktorov.

39

The prisoners were woken by the orderlies at five in the morning. It was still pitch dark; the barrack-huts were lit by the merciless light that is common to prisons, railway stations and the waiting-rooms of city hospitals.

Thousands of men coughed and spat as they pulled on their padded trousers, wound their foot-cloths round their feet and had a good scratch. Sometimes the men on the upper tier of bedboards gave the men getting dressed down below a kick on the head; the latter just quietly pushed their feet out of the way.

There was something profoundly unnatural about the glaring electric light, the general bustle and the thick tobacco smoke. Hundreds of square miles of taiga lay frozen in icy silence – but the camp was crowded with people, full of noise, movement and light.

Snow had fallen during the first half of the night. Drifts had blocked the doors of the huts and covered the track to the mines . . .

Sirens began to howl in the mines; somewhere in the taiga the wolves howled out an accompaniment. The dogs were barking on the main square, the guards were shouting at one another and you could hear the tractors clearing the tracks outside.

In the light of the searchlights the dry snow seemed innocent and tender. Roll-call began on the main square, to the accompaniment of incessant barking; the voices of the guards sounded hoarse and irritated. Then a swollen river of people flowed out towards the mines. The snow creaked under thousands of leather and felt boots. The watch-tower stared after them with its single eye.

Throughout the North, sirens continued to howl. The same orchestra struck up over Krasnoyarsk, over the Autonomous Republic of Komi, over Sovietskaya Gavan, over the snows of Kolyma, the

Chukotsk tundra and the camps of Murmansk and Northern Kazakhstan . . .

To the accompaniment of the sirens or the blows of a crowbar against a metal rail, prisoners set off to mine the potassium of Solikamsk, the copper of Ridder and the shores of Lake Balkash, the nickel and lead of Kolyma and the coal of Kuznetsk and Sakhalin. They set off to build a railway line along the shore of the Arctic Ocean, to clear roads through the tundra of Kolyma, to fell trees in the forests of Siberia, Murmansk, Archangelsk and the Northern Urals . . .

Day began at the same hour of night, amid the same snow, in every one of the camps and sub-camps of the vast network of *Dalstroy*.*

40

During the night Abarchuk had a fit of despair. Not just the usual sullen despair of the camps, but something fierce and burning like malaria, something that made him scream out loud, fall off the bedboards and beat his fists against his skull.

In the morning, when the prisoners were reluctantly but hurriedly getting ready for work, Abarchuk's long-legged neighbour, Nyeumolimov, a gas foreman who had commanded a cavalry brigade during the Civil War, asked: 'What were you tossing about like that for during the night? Did you dream of a woman?'

'Don't you ever think of anything else?'

'I thought you were crying in your sleep. I wanted to wake you up,' said Monidze, another of Abarchuk's neighbours, who had once been on the Presidium of the Communist Youth International.

Another friend of Abarchuk's, Abrasha Rubin, a medical orderly, hadn't noticed anything. All he said, as they went outside into the dark and frost, was: 'Guess what? I dreamed Nikolay Ivanovich Bukharin had come to visit us at the Institute of Red Professors. He was very bright and lively. Yenchman's theory created a tremendous stir.'

Abarchuk worked in the tool store. While his assistant, Barkhatov,

* *Dalstroy*: the Far Eastern Construction Trust, i.e. the network of prison camps that covered thousands of miles of the far North-East of the Soviet Union.

a man who had once knifed a family of six during a robbery, was lighting the stove and stoking it with left-over cedar-logs, Abarchuk went through the tools in the drawers. The biting sharpness of the files and chisels, impregnated with the icy cold, seemed to embody the way he had felt during the night.

This day was exactly the same as every day that had gone before. The accountant had sent Abarchuk the requests from the distant sub-camps, already approved by the technical department. Now he had to get out the right tools and materials, pack them into boxes and draw up the accompanying documents. Some of the packages were incomplete; this necessitated the drawing up of special documents.

Barkhatov, as always, did nothing, and it was impossible to make him do anything. From the moment he arrived at the store, he concerned himself only with matters of nutrition; today he was boiling a small pot of cabbage and potato soup. A professor of Latin from the Kharkov Pharmaceutical Institute, now a messenger in the first section, rushed in for a moment to see him; with trembling red fingers he poured some dirty grains of millet onto the table. Barkhatov was evidently blackmailing him.

That afternoon Abarchuk was called to the accounts department; apparently his figures didn't tally. The deputy director shouted at him and threatened to report him to the director. Abarchuk felt sick. It was impossible for him to cope with the work by himself and he didn't dare complain about Barkhatov. He was tired, afraid of losing his job in the store, afraid of having to go out logging or being sent down the mines. His hair had already turned grey, he didn't have much strength left. Yes, that must be the reason for the despair he had felt during the night – his life had vanished beneath the ice of Siberia.

When he came back from the accounts department, he found Barkhatov asleep. His head was pillowed on a pair of felt boots he must have been given by one of the criminals. Beside it stood the empty cooking-pot; some of the millet was sticking to his cheek.

Abarchuk knew that Barkhatov sometimes stole tools from the store. He might, in fact, have bartered some for this very pair of felt boots. Once, Abarchuk had found three planes missing and had confronted his assistant.

'Stealing scarce metal during the War for the Fatherland! You should be ashamed of yourself!'

'Shut your mouth!' Barkhatov had retorted. 'Or else . . .'

Abarchuk did not dare wake Barkhatov directly; instead he coughed, banged the saws about and dropped a hammer on the floor. Barkhatov woke up. He gave Abarchuk a look of cool displeasure. After a while, he said very quietly: 'Someone from yesterday's transport told me that there are worse camps than these ones here in the lakes. The prisoners wear fetters and have their heads shaved. Surnames aren't used at all: they just have numbers sewn on their chest and their knees, and an ace of diamonds on their back.'

'Nonsense,' said Abarchuk.

'That's where you Fascist politicals should be sent,' Barkhatov continued thoughtfully. 'You first of all, you swine – so you can't wake me up.'

'Forgive me, citizen Barkhatov, for having disturbed your rest.' Although he was very frightened of Barkhatov, sometimes Abarchuk was unable to control his anger.

At the end of the shift, Nyeumolimov came in, black with coal-dust.

'Well,' asked Abarchuk, 'how's the work going? Are people entering into the spirit of competition?'

'Little by little. The coal's a military necessity – at least everyone understands that. Today the Culture and Education Section received some posters: "Let us help the Motherland with our shock labour!"'

Abarchuk sighed. 'You know what, someone ought to write a treatise on despair in the camps. There's a despair that crushes you, another that attacks you suddenly, another that stifles you and won't let you breathe. And then there's a special kind that doesn't do any of these things but somehow tears you to pieces from within – like a deep-sea creature brought suddenly up to the surface.'

Nyeumolimov smiled sadly. His rotten teeth were almost the same colour as the coal-dust on his face.

Barkhatov came up to them. Abarchuk looked round and complained: 'You walk so quietly you make me jump. All of a sudden I find you right beside me.'

A man of few smiles, Barkhatov said very seriously: 'You don't mind if I go to the food store?'

He left.

'During the night I remembered the son I had by my first wife,'

Abarchuk said to his friend. 'He's probably at the front now.'

He leant towards Nyeumolimov.

'I want the lad to grow up a good Communist. I was thinking to myself that if I met him, I'd say: "Remember, your father's fate doesn't matter. That's just a detail. But the cause of the Party is something holy! Something that conforms in the highest degree to the Law of the Epoch!"'

'Does he have your surname?'

'No,' answered Abarchuk. 'I was afraid he'd grow up to be a bourgeois.'

All through the previous evening and during the night he had thought of Lyudmila. He wanted to see her. He had been looking at pages torn from the Moscow papers, expecting all of a sudden to read: 'Lieutenant Anatoly Abarchuk'. He would know then that his son had wanted to bear his father's surname.

For the first time in his life he wanted someone to feel sorry for him. He imagined himself walking up to his son, gasping, hardly able to breathe, pointing to his throat and saying: 'I can't talk.'

Tolya would embrace him. Abarchuk would put his head on his son's chest and burst out crying, bitterly and unashamedly. They would stand like that for a long time, his son a head taller.

Tolya was probably thinking about him all the time. He would have searched out his old comrades and learned about the part his father had played in the battle for the Revolution. 'Daddy, Daddy,' he would say, 'your hair's turned quite white. How thin and lined your neck looks. You've been struggling all these years. You've been carrying on a great struggle, all on your own.'

For three days during the investigation he had been given salty food without water. He had been beaten . . . He had realized that it wasn't simply a matter of wanting him to sign confessions of sabotage and espionage or to make accusations against people. Most of all, they wanted him to doubt the justice of the cause to which he had devoted his life. During the investigation itself, he thought he must have fallen into the hands of a bunch of gangsters. He thought that if he could only obtain an interview with the head of the department, he would be able to have his thug of an investigator arrested.

But as time passed he realized it wasn't just a matter of there being a few sadists around.

He had learned the laws that applied on convict trains and in the holds of convict ships. He had seen criminals gambling away other people's belongings at card-games, even their lives. He had seen pitiable debauchery and betrayal. He had seen the criminal 'India',* bloody, hysterical and impossibly cruel. He had seen terrible battles between the 'bitches', who agreed to work, and the orthodox 'thieves', who refused to work.

He had repeated, 'You don't get arrested for nothing,' believing that only a tiny minority, himself among them, had been arrested by mistake. As for everyone else – they had deserved their sentences. The sword of justice was chastising the enemies of the Revolution.

He had seen servility, treachery, submissiveness, cruelty . . . And he had referred to all this as 'the birthmarks of capitalism', believing that these marks were borne by people of the past – White officers, kulaks, bourgeois nationalists . . .

His faith was unshakeable, his devotion to the Party infinite.

Just as he was about to leave, Nyeumolimov said: 'Oh, I forgot to say, someone was asking about you.'

'Who?'

'Someone from yesterday's transport. They were being assigned work. One of them asked about you. I said, "Yes, I do know him, I happen to have slept next to him for the last three years." He told me his surname, but it's gone clean out of my head.'

'What did he look like?'

'Well, rather shabby – and he had a scar on his temple.'

'Oh!' cried Abarchuk. 'You don't mean Magar?'

'Yes, that's right.'

'But he's my very oldest comrade, my teacher, the man who introduced me into the Party. What did he say? What did he ask about?'

'Just the usual question: the length of your sentence. I said you'd asked for five years and been given ten. I said you were beginning to cough and that you'd be released early.'

But Abarchuk was no longer listening.

'Magar, Magar . . . ,' he repeated. 'At one time he used to work in the Cheka. He was someone special, you know, very special. He'd give

* A barrack in a prison camp inhabited (solely or mainly) by professional criminals.

anything of his to a comrade. He'd take off his overcoat for you in the middle of winter, give you his last crust of bread. And he's intelligent, well-educated. And a true proletarian by birth, the son of a fisherman from Kerch.'

He glanced round and then bent towards Nyeumolimov.

'Do you remember? We used to say that the Communists in the camp should set up an organization to help the Party. Abrasha Rubin asked, "Who should we choose as secretary?" Well, he's the man.'

'I'll vote for you,' said Nyeumolimov. 'I don't know him. Anyway, how are you going to find him? Ten lorries have left for the sub-camps by now. He was probably in one of them.'

'Never mind. We'll find him. Magar . . . Well, well. And he asked after me?'

'I almost forgot why I came here,' said Nyeumolimov. 'Give me a clean sheet of paper. My memory's going.'

'For a letter?'

'No, for a statement to Marshal Budyonniy. I'm going to ask to be sent to the front.'

'Not a hope.'

'But Syoma remembers me!'

'They don't take politicals in the Army. What you can do is help increase our output of coal. The soldiers will thank you for that.'

'But I want to join up.'

'Budyonniy won't be able to help you. I wrote to Stalin myself.'

'What do you mean? Budyonniy not be able to help! You must be joking! Or do you grudge me the paper? I wouldn't ask, but I can't get any from the Culture and Education Section. I've used up my quota.'

'All right then, you can have one sheet,' said Abarchuk.

He had a small amount of paper that he didn't have to account for. In the Culture and Education Section paper was strictly rationed and you had to account for each sheet.

That evening everything was the same as usual in the hut.

The old guards officer, Tungusov, was recounting an endless romantic story: the criminals listened attentively, scratching themselves and nodding their heads in approval. The characters in this confused and elaborate yarn included Lawrence of Arabia and various ballerinas he had known; some of the incidents came from the life of the Three Musketeers and the voyage of Jules Verne's *Nautilus*.

'Wait a minute!' said one of the listeners. 'How was she able to cross the Persian frontier? You said yesterday she'd been poisoned by the cops.'

Tungusov paused, glanced meekly at his critic and announced brightly: 'It was only on the surface that Nadya's situation appeared hopeless. Life returned to her thanks to the efforts of a Tibetan doctor who poured several drops of a precious decoction – obtained from the blue herbs of the high mountains – through her half-open lips. By morning she was so far recovered that she was able to walk about her room without assistance. Her strength was returning.'

'Right then, carry on!' said his now satisfied listeners.

In the corner known as the '*kolkhoz* sector' everyone was laughing loudly as they listened to Gasyuchenko reciting obscene ditties in a sing-song voice. He was an old buffoon whom the Germans had appointed headman of his village.

A journalist from Moscow, a good-natured, shy, intelligent man with a hernia, was slowly chewing on a rusk of white bread – from a food parcel he had received from his wife the day before. His eyes were full of tears: the taste of the crunchy rusk evidently reminded him of his past life.

Nyeumolimov was engaged in an argument with a member of a tank-crew who had been sent to the camp for a particularly foul murder. The murderer was entertaining the listeners by making fun of the cavalry, while Nyeumolimov, pale with hatred, was shouting: 'Don't you know what we did with our swords in 1920!'

'Yes, you stabbed stolen chickens. One KV tank could have routed the whole of your First Cavalry Army. And you can hardly compare the Civil War with the War for the Fatherland.'

A young thief called Kolka Ugarov was pestering Abrasha Rubin, trying to persuade him to swap his boots for a pair of very worn slippers whose soles were coming off. Sensing trouble, Rubin yawned nervously and glanced round at his neighbours in the hope of finding support.

'Listen, Yid,' said Kolka, who looked like a wild, bright-eyed cat. 'Listen, you swine, you're beginning to get on my nerves.'

Then he asked: 'Why wouldn't you sign the form to release me from work?'

'I don't have the right. You're in excellent health.'

'Are you going to sign?'

'Kolya, my friend, I swear I'd be only too glad to, but I can't.'

'Are you going to sign?'

'Please understand. Surely you realize that if I could . . .'

'Very well then. That's that.'

'Wait a moment! Please understand.'

'I do understand. Soon you will too.'

Stedling, a Russified Swede supposed to have been a spy, looked up for a moment from the picture he was drawing on a piece of cardboard from the Culture and Education Section; he glanced at Kolka, then at Rubin, shook his head and returned to his picture. The picture was entitled 'Mother Taiga'. Stedling was not afraid of the criminals; for some reason they left him alone.

After Kolka had left, Stedling said to Rubin: 'You're behaving like a madman, Abram Yefimovich.'

The Byelorussian Konashevich was another man who wasn't afraid of the criminals. Before the war he had been an aircraft mechanic in the Far East and he had won the Pacific Fleet middleweight boxing championship. The criminals respected Konashevich, but he never intervened on behalf of anyone they were maltreating.

Abarchuk walked slowly down the narrow passageway between the two tiers of bedboards. His despair had returned. The far end of the long barrack-hut was thick with tobacco smoke. Abarchuk always imagined that when he reached that distant horizon he would see something new, but everything was always exactly the same: the hallway where the prisoners washed their foot-cloths in wooden troughs, the mops leaning against the wall, the painted buckets, the bedboards themselves, the mattresses stuffed with shavings that leaked out of the sacking, the even hum of conversation, and the drab, haggard faces of the zeks.

Most of the zeks were sitting down, waiting for lights-out and talking about soup, women, the dishonesty of the bread-cutter, the fate of their letters to Stalin and petitions to the Public Prosecutor, the new norms for cutting and trucking away the coal, how cold it was today, how cold it would be tomorrow . . .

Abarchuk walked slowly by, overhearing scraps of conversation as he passed. It seemed as though one and the same conversation had been going on for many years between thousands of men in transport-ships, trains and camps, the young talking about women and the old talking about food. It was somehow even worse when the old men talked greedily about women, and the young men talked about the delicious food in the free world outside.

Abarchuk quickened his pace as he passed Gasyuchenko. The old man – who was married, with children and grandchildren – was saying something truly awful.

If only the lights would go out, so he could lie down, bury his head in his jacket, see nothing, hear nothing . . .

Abarchuk looked at the door: any minute now Magar would come in. He would persuade Zarokov to put them side by side and when it was dark the two of them would be able to talk together, openly and sincerely – teacher and pupil, both of them members of the Party.

A feast was being held on the boards belonging to the masters of the hut – Zarokov, Barkhatov and Perekrest, the leader of the coal-team. Perekrest's lackey, an economist called Zhelyabov, had spread a towel over a bedside table and set out some bacon-fat, herrings and gingerbread – the tribute Perekrest had received from the members of his team.

Abarchuk felt his heart flutter as he walked past. They might call out to him and ask him to join them! He could do with something tasty to eat. Barkhatov was a real swine. He did just as he pleased in the storeroom: he pinched nails, he'd gone off with three planes, and Abarchuk had never said a word about it. He might at least call out: 'Hey, you! Why don't you come over here for a moment?'

Abarchuk knew – and he despised himself for it – that it wasn't just a matter of wanting something to eat. He was aware of one of those vile, petty desires born of the camps, the desire to hobnob with the strong, to chat with someone whom thousands of people lived in awe of.

Abarchuk cursed first himself and then Barkhatov.

They didn't call him, but they did call Nyeumolimov. The man who had once commanded a cavalry brigade, the holder of two Orders of the Red Flag, smiled as he walked over towards them. And twenty years before, he had led cavalry regiments into battle to fight for a world commune . . .

What could have made him talk to Nyeumolimov about Tolya, about everything he held most dear? But then he too had fought for Communism, he too had sent reports to Stalin from his office on a building site in the Kuzbass, and he too had anxiously hoped they would call his name as he walked past, looking down at the floor in pretended indifference.

He walked over towards Monidze's place. Monidze looked up from the socks he was darning and said: 'Guess what Perekrest said to me today? "Remember, my friend, I can smash your skull in – and when I tell the guards they'll thank me. You're the vilest of traitors."'

'There are worse things than that,' said Abrasha Rubin, who was sitting nearby.

'Yes,' agreed Abarchuk. 'Did you see how happy the commander of the cavalry brigade was when they called out his name?'

'I suppose you were disappointed not to be called yourself,' said Rubin.

'Look who's talking!' retorted Abarchuk, smarting at Rubin's perceptiveness.

'Me? It's not for me to feel disappointed,' Rubin murmured, his half-closed eyes making him look rather like a chicken. 'I'm one of the very lowest caste, the untouchables. Did you hear my conversation with Kolka just now?'

'You shouldn't say that kind of thing,' said Abarchuk dismissively, and walked on down the narrow passage between the boards. Once again he heard snatches of the same never-ending conversation.

'Borshch with pork every day, Sunday included.'

'What breasts! You wouldn't believe it.'

'I like things simple. *Kasha* and mutton. Who needs all these sauces of yours?'

He turned back and sat down by Monidze. Rubin was saying: 'I couldn't understand why he said, "You'll become a composer." It was a joke about informers. Do you see? Writing an opera – writing to the operations officer!'

Monidze carried on darning. 'To hell with him,' he said. 'Informing's the very last thing you should do.'

'What do you mean?' demanded Abarchuk. 'It's your duty as a Communist.'

'Ex-Communist,' replied Monidze. 'Like you.'

'I'm not an ex-Communist,' said Abarchuk. 'Nor are you.'

'Communism's got nothing to do with it,' said Rubin. 'I'm fed up with eating maize-slop three times a day. I can't even bear to look at the muck. That's one reason for informing. But then I don't want to be attacked during the night and found in the latrine next morning like Orlov – my head sticking through the hole. Did you hear my conversation with Kolka Ugarov just now?'

'Head down, feet up!' said Monidze and started laughing, evidently because there was nothing to laugh about.

'There's more to life than the instinct for self-preservation!' said Abarchuk, feeling an hysterical desire to hit Rubin. He jumped up and walked off down the hut.

Of course, he too was fed up with cornmeal soup. How many days now had he been trying to guess what they'd have for dinner on the anniversary of the October Revolution – vegetable ragout, sailor's macaroni, meat-and-potato pie?

And a lot depended on the operations officer – the ways of attaining high position were obscure and mysterious. He might end up working in the laboratory: he'd wear a white smock, the woman in charge would be a civilian worker and he would no longer be at the mercy of the criminals; or he might join the planning section or be put in charge of a mine . . . But all the same, Rubin was wrong. Rubin liked to degrade a man by ferreting out what was creeping up from his subconscious. Rubin was a saboteur.

Abarchuk had always been uncompromising with opportunists. He had hated all double-dealers and socially-alien elements.

His spiritual strength, his faith, had always lain in his right to make judgements. He had doubted his wife – and had separated from her. He hadn't trusted her to bring up his son a steadfast fighter – and had denied him the right to bear his surname. He had damned anyone who wavered; he had despised all grumblers and weak-minded sceptics. He had brought to trial some engineers in the Kuzbass who had been pining for their families in Moscow. He had condemned forty socially unreliable workers who had left the construction site for their villages. He had renounced his petty-bourgeois father.

It was sweet to be unshakeable. In passing judgement on people he had affirmed his own inner strength, his ideals, his purity. This was his consolation and his faith. He had never deviated from the directives of the Party. He had willingly renounced Party maximalism. For him, self-renunciation had been equivalent to self-affirmation. He had worn the same boots and the same soldier's tunic whether he was at work, at meetings of the Board of the People's Commissariat, or going for a walk along the quay at Yalta when he had been sent there to convalesce. He had wanted to become like Stalin.

And in losing his right to pass judgement, he lost himself. Rubin had sensed that. Almost every day he would allude to the weaknesses and cowardice, to all the petty desires that somehow stole into your soul in the camp.

The previous day he had said: 'Barkhatov supplies his young thugs with metal from the store, and our Robespierre doesn't say a word. As the song goes, even a chicken wants to stay alive.'

When Abarchuk was about to condemn someone and then felt he could equally well be condemned himself, he began to hesitate, to lose himself, to fall into despair.

Abarchuk stopped by the place where old Prince Dolgoruky was talking to Stepanov, a young professor at the Economics Institute. Stepanov behaved very arrogantly, refusing to get up when the camp authorities came into the hut and openly expressing anti-Soviet views. He was proud of the fact that, unlike the majority of the political prisoners, he was there for a reason: he had written an article entitled 'The State of Lenin and Stalin' and distributed it to his students. He had been denounced by either the third or fourth person who had read it.

Dolgoruky had returned to the Soviet Union from Sweden. Before that, he had lived for a long time in Paris and felt deeply homesick. He had been arrested a week after his return. In the camp he prayed, made friends with members of the different Christian sects and wrote mystical poems. At this moment he was reading one of them to Stepanov.

Abarchuk listened, leaning his shoulder against the post supporting the two tiers of boards. Dolgoruky's eyes were half-closed and his chapped lips were trembling as he recited.

> I feel that I have chosen everything –
> The time and place, the day I came into the world;
> I chose the strength to suffer fire, to fling

Myself into the water, to be hurled
Into the stench of flesh, smeared and profaned
With blood and pus, dabbed with these wads of filth
And fouled by the ten-horned beast – his belly's stealth
And blasphemies have left my soul unstained!
For I believe in justice from above,
The imponderable source of best and worst
That hears burned Russia speak in flames – and burst
Free in these words! Great lord of truth and love!
You carve in plenitudes of fire the life
Which craves abundance, craves your absolute –
Prune to fruition with your burning knife!
The tree submits! Now make my soul your fruit!

After he had finished, he sat for a moment with his eyes half-closed, his lips still moving.

'That's shit,' said Stepanov. 'Pure decadence!'

Dolgoruky gave a dismissive wave of his pale, anaemic hand.

'Look where all your Chernyshevskys and Herzens have got us! Don't you remember what Chaadayev wrote in his *Third Philosophical Letter*?'

'I detest you and your mystical obscurantism as much as I detest the organizers of this camp,' replied Stepanov in a schoolmasterly tone. 'Both they and you forget the third and most natural path for Russia: the path of democracy and freedom.'

Abarchuk had often argued with Stepanov, but just then he didn't feel like it; for once he didn't want to brand Stepanov as an enemy, an internal émigré. He went to the corner where the Baptists were praying and began listening to their muttering.

Suddenly the stentorian voice of hut-foreman Zarokov rang out: 'Everyone stand up!'

They all jumped up – someone in authority must have come into the hut. Abarchuk squinted round and saw Dolgoruky's long pale face. Yes, he was a goner. He was standing there at attention, still muttering away. Probably he was repeating the same poem. Stepanov was sitting; like the anarchist he was, he refused to submit to the sensible regulations of the camp.

'A search, there's going to be a search,' whispered the prisoners.

But no search took place. The two young escort-guards in their red and blue service caps just walked down between the bedboards, looking round at the prisoners.

As they passed Stepanov, one of them said: 'Still sitting there, professor? Afraid your arse will catch cold?'

Stepanov looked up – he had a wide snub-nosed face – and answered by rote in a loud parrot-like voice: 'Citizen guard, I request you to address me politely. I'm a political prisoner.'

That night there was an incident in the barrack-hut: Rubin was murdered.

The murderer had placed a large nail against his ear while he was asleep and driven it into his brain with one blow. Five people, Abarchuk among them, were summoned by the operations officer. What seemed to concern him was the provenance of the nail. This particular type of nail had only recently been delivered to the store; as yet there had been no requests for it from the production sections.

While they were washing, Barkhatov came and stood next to Abarchuk at the wooden trough. Licking the drops of water off his lips, his face still wet, he turned to Abarchuk and said very quietly: 'Listen, swine, nothing's going to happen to me if you squeal. But you'll really catch it! Yes, I'll fix you – and in a way that will make the whole camp shit themselves!'

He wiped himself dry, looked calmly into Abarchuk's eyes, saw what he was looking for and shook Abarchuk by the hand.

In the canteen Abarchuk gave Nyeumolimov his bowl of cornmeal soup.

His lips trembling, Nyeumolimov said: 'The swine! Our Abrasha! He was a real man!' and then pulled Abarchuk's bowl of soup towards him.

Abarchuk got up from the table without a word.

The crowd of people by the exit parted as Perekrest came in. He had to bend as he came through the doorway: camp ceilings were not designed for men of his height.

'Today's my birthday,' he said to Abarchuk. 'Come and join us. We've got some vodka.'

It was terrible. Dozens of people must have heard last night's murder, must even have seen the man walking up to Rubin's place. It would have been easy for one of them to jump up and raise the alarm. Together they could have dealt with the murderer in no time. They could have saved their comrade. But no one had looked up; no one had called out. A man had been slaughtered like a lamb. And everyone had just lain there, pretending to be asleep, burying their heads in their jackets, trying not to cough, trying not to hear the dying man writhing in agony.

How vile! What pathetic submissiveness!

But then he too had been awake, he too had kept silent, he too had buried his head in his jacket . . . Yes, there was a reason for this submissiveness – it was born of experience, of an understanding of the laws of the camp.

They could indeed have got up and stopped the murderer; but a man with a knife will always be stronger than a man without a knife. The strength of a group of prisoners is something ephemeral; but a knife is always a knife.

Abarchuk thought about the coming interrogation. It was all very well for the operations officer to ask for statements. He didn't have to sleep in the hut at night, he didn't have to wash in the hallway, leaving himself open to a blow from behind, he didn't have to walk down mine-shafts, he didn't have to go into the latrine where he might get jumped on and have a sack thrown over his head.

Yes, he had seen someone walk up to Rubin. He had heard Rubin wheezing, thrashing his arms and legs around in his death-agony.

The operations officer, Captain Mishanin, called Abarchuk into his office and closed the door. 'Sit down, prisoner.'

He put the usual initial questions, questions the political prisoners always answered quickly and precisely.

He then looked up with his tired eyes, and knowing very well that an experienced prisoner, afraid of the inevitable reprisals, would never say how the nail had come into the murderer's hands, stared at Abarchuk for a few seconds.

Abarchuk looked back at him. He scrutinized the captain's young face, looking at his hair and his eyebrows, and thought to himself that he could only be two or three years older than his own son.

The captain then asked the question which three prisoners had already refused to answer.

Abarchuk didn't say anything.

'Are you deaf or something?'

Abarchuk remained silent.

How he longed for the man to say to him, even if he weren't sincere, even if it were just a prescribed interrogation technique: 'Listen, comrade Abarchuk, you're a Communist. Today you're in the camp, but tomorrow we'll be paying our membership dues together. I need your help as a comrade, as a fellow Party member.'

Instead the captain said: 'So you've gone to sleep, have you? I'll wake you up.'

But it wasn't necessary. In a hoarse voice Abarchuk said: 'Barkhatov stole the nails from the storeroom. He also took three files. The murder was, in my opinion, committed by Nikolay Ugarov. I know that Barkhatov gave him the nails and that he threatened Rubin several times. Yesterday he swore he would kill him – Rubin had refused to put him on the sick-list.'

He took the cigarette that was offered him. 'I consider it my duty to the Party to inform you of this, comrade Operations Officer. Comrade Rubin was an old Party member.'

Captain Mishanin lit Abarchuk's cigarette, then took up his pen and began to write.

'You should know by now, prisoner,' he said gently, 'that you have no right to talk about Party membership. You are also forbidden to address me as "comrade". To you I am "citizen chief".'

'I apologize, citizen chief,' replied Abarchuk.

'It will be several days before I finish the inquiry,' said Mishanin. 'Then everything will be set straight. After that, well . . . We can have you transferred to another camp.'

'It's all right, citizen chief, I'm not afraid,' said Abarchuk.

He went back to the storeroom. He knew that Barkhatov wouldn't ask him any direct questions. Instead, he would watch him unrelentingly, squeezing out the truth from his movements, from his eyes, from the way he coughed . . .

He was happy. He had won a victory over himself.

He had won back the right to pass judgement. And when he thought about Rubin now, it was with regret that he'd never have the chance to say what he'd thought of him the other day.

Three days went by and there was still no sign of Magar. Abarchuk asked about him at the mines administration, but none of the clerks he knew could find his name on their lists.

That evening, just as Abarchuk had resigned himself to the fact that fate had kept them apart, a medical orderly called Trufelev came into the hut. Covered in snow and pulling splinters of ice from his eyelashes, he said to Abarchuk: 'Listen, we had a zek in the infirmary just now who wanted to see you. I'd better take you there straight away. Ask leave from the foreman. Otherwise . . . you know what our zeks are like. He might snuff it any moment – and it will be no good talking to him when he's in his wooden jacket.'

41

Trufelev led Abarchuk down the corridor of the infirmary. It had a foul smell of its own, quite distinct from that of the hut. They walked in semi-darkness past heaps of wooden stretchers and bundles of jackets waiting to be disinfected.

Magar was in the isolation ward, a cell with log walls containing two iron bedsteads standing side by side. This ward was usually kept for goners and people with infectious illnesses. The thin legs of the two bedsteads seemed to be made of wire, but they weren't in the least bent – no one of normal weight ever lay there.

'No, no, the bed on the right!' came a familiar voice. Abarchuk forgot about the camp and his white hair. It was as though he had found once again what he had lived for during so many years, what he would gladly have sacrificed his life for.

He stared into Magar's face. 'Greetings, greetings, greetings . . . ,' he said very slowly, almost ecstatically.

Afraid of being unable to contain his excitement, Magar spoke with deliberate casualness. 'Sit down then. You can sit on the bed opposite.'

Noticing the way Abarchuh looked at the bed, he added: 'Don't worry – you won't disturb him! No one will ever disturb him now.'

Abarchuk bent down to take a better look at his comrade's face, then glanced again at the corpse draped in blankets.

'How long ago?'

'It's two hours since he died. The orderlies won't touch him till the doctor comes. It's a good thing. If they put someone else there, we won't be able to talk.'

'True enough,' said Abarchuk.

Somehow he couldn't bring himself to ask the questions he so desperately wanted to: 'Were you sentenced along with Bubnov – or was it the Sokolnikov case? How many years did you get? Which isolation prison were you in – Vladimir or Suzdal? Were you sentenced by a Special Commission or a Military Board? Did you sign a confession?'

'Who was he?' he asked, indicating the draped body. 'What did he die of?'

'He was a kulak. He'd just had too much of the camp. He kept calling out for some Nastya or other. He wanted to go away somewhere . . .'

Gradually, in the half-light, he made out Magar's face. He would never have recognized him. It wasn't that he'd changed – it was that he was an old man who was about to die.

He could feel the corpse's hard, bony arm against his back. It was bent at the elbow. Sensing that Magar was looking at him, he thought: 'He's probably thinking the same thing – "Well, I'd never have recognized him."'

'I've just realized,' said Magar. 'He kept muttering something: "Wa . . . wa . . . wa . . . wa . . ." He wanted water. There's a glass right beside him. I could have carried out his last wish.'

'It seems as though he can interrupt us even now.'

'That's hardly surprising,' said Magar. Abarchuk could recognize the excitement in his voice. Magar had always begun serious conversations in this tone.

'It's not really him we're talking about,' Magar continued. 'We're talking about ourselves.'

'No!' said Abarchuk. 'No!'

He caught hold of Magar's hot hand, squeezed it, put his arms round his shoulders and then began to choke, sobbing silently and trembling.

'Thank you,' Magar murmured, 'my comrade, my friend.'

They both fell silent, breathing heavily. They were breathing in time with one another. To Abarchuk, it was not only their breathing that was united.

It was Magar who broke the silence.

'Listen now,' he said, sitting up in bed. 'Listen, my friend. This will be the last time I call you like this.'

'Don't talk like that,' said Abarchuk. 'You're going to live!'

'I'd sooner undergo torture, but I have to say this . . . You listen too,' he added, turning to the corpse. 'What I'm going to say has to do with you and your Nastya . . . This is my last duty as a revolutionary and I must fulfil it . . . You're someone very special, comrade Abarchuk. And we met at a very special time – our best time, I think . . . Let me begin now. First. We made a mistake. And this is what our mistake has led to. Look! You and I must ask this peasant to pardon us . . . Give me a fag. What am I saying? No repentance can expiate what we've done. I have to say this . . . Secondly. We didn't understand freedom. We crushed it. Even Marx didn't value it – it's the base, the meaning, the foundation that underlies all foundations. Without freedom there can be no proletarian revolution . . . Thirdly. We go through the camp, we go through the taiga, and yet our faith is stronger than anything. But this faith of ours is a weakness – a means of self-preservation. On the other side of the barbed wire, self-preservation tells people to change – unless they want to die or be sent to a camp. And so Communists have created idols, put on uniforms and epaulettes, begun preaching nationalism and attacking the working class. If necessary, they'll revive the Black Hundreds . . .* But here in the camp the same instinct tells people not to change, not to change during all the decades they spend here – unless they want to be buried straight away in a wooden jacket. It's the other side of the coin.'

'Stop!' screamed Abarchuk, raising his clenched fist to Magar's face. 'They've broken you. You weren't strong enough. What you're saying is all lies. You're raving.'

'I'm not. I wish I were. I'm calling you to follow me! Just as I called you twenty years ago. If we can't live the life of true revolutionaries, then the best we can do is die.'

* One of the ultra-reactionary and anti-Semitic organizations responsible for the pogroms at the beginning of the century.

'I've had enough! Stop!'

'Forgive me. I know. I'm like an old prostitute weeping over her lost virtue. But I'll say it again: remember! Forgive me, friend . . .'

'Forgive you! I wish one of us were lying here like this corpse, that we'd never lived to meet . . .'

Abarchuk was standing in the doorway when he finished.

'I'll come and see you again. I'll put you right. I'll be your teacher now.'

Next morning Abarchuk came across Trufelev outside in the compound. He was pulling a sledge with a churn of milk tied across it. It was odd, deep inside the Arctic Circle, to see someone with his face covered in sweat.

'Your friend won't be drinking any of this milk,' he said. 'He hanged himself during the night.'

It's always nice to pass on some surprising news. Trufelev gave Abarchuk a look of friendly triumph.

'Did he leave a note for me?' asked Abarchuk, gulping at the icy air. Magar must have left a note. What had happened yesterday was nothing. He hadn't been himself – something had come over him.

'What do you mean – a note? Anything you write goes straight to the operations officer.'

That night was the most painful Abarchuk had ever known. He lay there quite still, clenching his teeth, gazing with wide-open eyes at the hut wall and its dark smears of squashed bed-bugs. He turned then to his son, the son he had once denied the right to bear his surname, and called out: 'Now you're all I have left. You're my only hope. Do you understand, my friend? My teacher, Magar, wanted to strangle me, to strangle my mind and my will – and now he's hanged himself. Tolya, Tolya, you're all I have, all I have left in the world. Can you see me? Can you hear me? Will you ever know that during this long night your father never stooped, never wavered?'

And next to him, all around him, the camp slept, heavily, noisily and uglily; the thick, stifling air was full of snores, sleepy cries, protracted groans and the sound of teeth being ground together.

Suddenly Abarchuk sat up. He thought he had seen a shadow close by in the darkness.

42

In late summer 1942 Kleist's Army Group in the Caucasus seized the most important of the Soviet oilfields, near Maykop. German troops had reached Crete and North Cape, Northern Finland and the shores of the Channel. The desert fox, Marshal Erwin Rommel, was eighty kilometres from Alexandria. Chasseurs had hoisted the swastika over the peak of Mount Elbruz. Manstein had received orders to train giant cannons and *Nebelwerfer* rocket-launchers on Leningrad itself, the citadel of Bolshevism. The sceptical Mussolini was drawing up plans for his advance into Cairo and learning to ride an Arab stallion. Dietl was advancing over the snow in northern latitudes never before fought over by any European army. Paris, Vienna, Prague and Brussels had become provincial German cities.

The time had come for National Socialism to realize its cruellest designs against human life and freedom. It is a lie that it was the pressures of the war that forced the Fascist leaders to undertake these measures. On the contrary, danger and a lack of confidence in their own power were what most served to restrain and temper them.

If Fascism should ever be fully assured of its final triumph, the world will choke in blood. If the day ever dawns when Fascism is without armed enemies, then its executioners will know no restraint: the greatest enemy of Fascism is man.

In the autumn of 1942, during the apogee of National Socialism's military success, the government of the Reich announced a series of cruel and inhuman decrees: under one of these, that of 12 September, European Jewry was removed from the jurisdiction of the ordinary courts and transferred to that of the Gestapo.

Adolf Hitler and the Party leadership had decided upon the final destruction of the Jewish nation.

43

From time to time Sofya Osipovna Levinton remembered her old life: her five years at Zurich University, the summer holiday she had spent in Paris and Italy, the concerts she had been to at the Conservatory, the expeditions to the mountains of Central Asia, her thirty-two years as a doctor, her favourite dishes, the friends whose lives, with all their ups and downs, had been intertwined with her own, her frequent telephone calls, the odd phrases of Ukrainian she had always used, her games of cards, the belongings she had left in her room in Moscow.

She also remembered her time in Stalingrad – together with Alexandra Vladimirovna, Zhenya, Seryozha, Vera and Marusya. The closer people had been to her, the further away they now seemed.

Early one evening, while their train stood in a siding somewhere near Kiev, she was searching her collar for lice; two middle-aged women beside her were chattering away, very quietly, in Yiddish. She suddenly realized with absolute clarity that all this really was happening to her – to Sonechka, Sonka, Sofya, Major Sofya Osipovna Levinton of the Medical Service.

The most fundamental change in people at this time was a weakening of their sense of individual identity; their sense of fate grew correspondingly stronger.

'Who am I? In the end, who am I?' Sofya Osipovna wondered. 'The short, snotty little girl afraid of her father and grandmother? The stout, hot-tempered woman with tabs of rank on her collar? Or this mangy, lice-ridden creature?'

She had lost any hope of happiness, but many different dreams had appeared in its place: of killing lice . . . of reaching the chink in the wall and being able to breathe . . . of being able to urinate . . . of washing just one leg . . . And then there was thirst, a thirst that filled her whole body.

She had been thrown into the wagon. In the gloom, which had

seemed like complete darkness, she had heard the sound of quiet laughter.

'Is that a madman laughing?' she asked.

'No,' answered a man's voice. 'We're just telling jokes.'

Someone else said in a melancholy tone of voice: 'One more Jewess on our ill-fated train.'

Sofya Levinton stood by the door and answered people's questions, frowning as she tried to get used to the darkness. She felt suddenly overwhelmed, not only by the stench and the noise of people crying and groaning, but by the sound of words and intonations she had last heard in childhood.

She wanted to step further inside, but found this impossible. Feeling a thin little leg in short trousers, she said: 'Forgive me, son; did I hurt you?'

The boy didn't answer.

'Mother,' said Sofya into the darkness, 'perhaps you could move your dumb little boy. I can't stand here for ever.'

'You should have sent a telegram in advance,' said a hysterical voice from the corner. 'Then you could have reserved a room with a private bath.'

'Fool!'

A woman whose face she could now just make out, said: 'You can sit down beside me. There's plenty of room here.'

Sofya could feel her fingers trembling. Yes, this was a world she had known since childhood, the world of the shtetl – but very changed.

The cattle-wagon was full of workers from different co-operatives, girls at teacher-training college, teachers from a school for trade unionists; there was a radio technician, an engineer who worked at a canned-food factory, a livestock expert, and a girl who worked as a vet. Previously, such professions had been unheard of in the shtetl. But then Sofya herself was still the same small girl who had been afraid of her father and grandmother – she hadn't changed. Perhaps, at heart, this world remained equally unchanged. But what did it matter? Changed, or unchanged, the world of the shtetl was poised on the brink of the abyss.

'Today's Germans are just savages,' she heard a young woman say. 'They haven't even heard of Heinrich Heine.'

A man's voice from another corner said mockingly:

'What help's this Heine of yours been to us? The savages are rounding us up like cattle.'

People plied Sofya with questions about the position on the different fronts. Nothing she said was very encouraging and she was promptly told she had been misinformed; she realized that this wagon had its own strategy, a strategy founded on a passionate hunger to remain alive.

'Surely you must have heard that an ultimatum has been sent to Hitler demanding the immediate release of all Jews?'

Yes, of course. What saves people when their bovine melancholy, their mute fatalism yields to a piercing sense of horror – what saves people then is the opium of optimism.

They soon lost interest in Sofya. She was just one more prisoner – with no more idea of her destination than anyone else. No one asked her name and patronymic; no one remembered her surname. She realized with surprise that although the process of evolution had taken millions of years, these people had needed only a few days to revert to the state of cattle, dirty and unhappy, captive and nameless . . .

She was also surprised how upset everyone still got over trivia, how quick they were to quarrel with one another. One middle-aged woman turned to her and said: 'Look at that *grande dame* over there! She sits there beside that chink in the wall as though no one except her son has a right to any fresh air.'

The train stopped twice during the night. They listened to the squeaking boots of the guards, occasionally making out odd phrases of both German and Russian. The language of Goethe sounded quite appalling in the middle of the night at a Russian wayside halt, but the Russian spoken by the collaborators was still more sinister.

Like everyone else, Sofya began to suffer from hunger and thirst. Even her dreams had something pathetic about them; she dreamed of a squashed tin with a few drops of warm liquid at the very bottom. She scratched herself with the quick, jerky movements of a dog scratching itself for fleas.

Sofya now understood the difference between life and existence: her life had come to an end, but her existence could drag on indefinitely. And however wretched and miserable this existence was, the thought of violent death still filled her with horror.

It began to rain; a few drops came in through the barred window.

Sofya tore a strip from the hem of her shirt, made her way towards the wall and pushed the material through a small chink. She waited for it to absorb the rainwater, pulled it away and began to suck; it was cool and damp. Soon, the other people sitting by the wall were following her example. Sofya felt quite proud of herself; she was the one who had thought up a way of catching the rainwater.

The little boy she had bumped into during the night was still sitting nearby; he was watching everyone squeeze their shreds of material into the chinks. The dim light was enough for her to make out his thin face and sharp nose. He must have been about six years old. Sofya realized that he hadn't moved or said a word while she had been there; nor had anyone else said a word to him. She held out her wet rag and said: 'Here you are, son.'

He didn't answer.

'Go on. It's for you.'

Hesitantly, the boy stretched out his hand.

'What's your name?' she asked.

'David,' he answered quietly.

Sofya's neighbour, Musya Borisovna, told her that David was from Moscow. He had come to stay with his grandmother and been cut off by the outbreak of war. The grandmother had died in the ghetto and he had been left with another relative, Rebekka Bukhman; her husband had fallen ill and she wouldn't let the boy sit beside her in the wagon.

By evening Sofya had had her fill of conversations, stories and arguments; she was even talking and arguing herself. She often began with the words: 'Fellow Jews, what I think . . .'

Many of the people in the wagon were looking forward to the end of the journey; they thought they were being taken to camps where each person would be given work in his own field and the sick would receive special care. They talked about this incessantly. But, deep down, their souls were still gripped by a silent horror.

Sofya learned that there were many things in human beings that were far from human. She heard about a paralysed woman who had been frozen to death by her sister; she had been put in a tub and dragged out onto the street on a winter's night. She heard about mothers who had killed their own children; there was one in this very wagon. She heard about people who had lived in sewers for months on end, eating filth like rats, ready to endure anything if only they could stay alive.

The conditions the Jews lived in were terrible; and they were neither saints nor villains, they were human beings.

Sofya's pity for these people grew particularly intense when she looked at little David. Most of the time he just sat there without saying a word; sometimes he took a crumpled matchbox out of his pocket, looked inside, and hid it away again.

For several days now Sofya hadn't wanted to sleep. She sat there, wide awake, in the stinking darkness. 'I wonder where Zhenya Shaposhnikova is now,' she thought suddenly. As she listened to people's cries and mutterings, she realized that their heads were filled with painfully vivid images that no words could ever convey. How could these images be preserved, how could they be fixed – in case men remained alive on earth and wanted to find out what had happened?

'Golda! Golda!' cried a man's voice, racked with sobs.

44

. . . The brain of the forty-year-old accountant, Naum Rozenberg, was still engaged in its usual work. He was walking down the road and counting: 110 the day before yesterday, 61 yesterday, 612 during the five days before – altogether that made 783 . . . A pity he hadn't kept separate totals for men, women and children . . . Women burn more easily. An experienced *brenner* arranges the bodies so that the bony old men who make a lot of ash are lying next to the women. Any minute now they'd be ordered to turn off the road; these people – the people they'd been digging up from pits and dragging out with great hooks on the end of ropes – had received the same order only a year ago. An experienced *brenner* could look at a mound and immediately estimate how many bodies there were inside – 50, 100, 200, 600, 1000 . . . Scharführer Elf insisted that the bodies should be referred to as items – 100 items, 200 items – but Rozenberg called them people: a man who had been killed, a child who had been put to death, an old man who had been put to death. He used these words only to himself –

otherwise the Scharführer would have emptied nine grams of metal into him – but he continued obstinately muttering: 'So now you're coming out of the grave, old chap . . . There's no need to clutch your mother like that, my child, you won't be separated from her now . . .' 'What are you muttering about over there? Me? Nothing. You must have imagined it.' And he carried on muttering; that was his little struggle . . . The day before yesterday there had been a pit with only eight men in it. The Scharführer had spluttered: 'It's ridiculous; how can you have twenty *brenners* burning eight items?' The Scharführer was right, but what could you do if there were only two Jewish families in a whole village? Orders were orders – all graves were to be dug up and all bodies burnt . . . Now they had turned off the road, they were walking along the grass – and there, for the hundred and fifteenth time, was the grey mound of a grave in the middle of a clearing. Eight men dug; four men felled oak trees and sawed them into logs the length of a human body; two men split these logs with axes and wedges; two men went back to the road to fetch old dry planks, kindling and petrol cans; four prepared the bonfire site and dug a ditch for the ash-pit – yes, they'd have to work out which way the wind was blowing.

The smell of damp and mould immediately vanished; the guards began laughing, cursing and holding their noses; the Scharführer walked off to the edge of the clearing. The *brenners* threw down their spades, tied old rags round their mouths and noses and picked up their hooks again . . . 'Good day, grandad! So you're seeing the sun again! My! You are heavy . . . !' A mother who who had been killed with her three children – two boys, one of them already at school, and a girl born in 1939 who'd had rickets, but never mind, she's cured of that now . . . 'Don't clutch your mother like that, my child, she won't leave you now . . .' 'How many items?' shouted the Scharführer from the edge of the clearing. 'Nineteen,' – and then, very quietly, to himself – 'dead people.' Everyone cursed; they'd wasted half the day. But then last week they'd dug up a grave with two hundred young women in it. When they'd taken off the top layer of earth, a cloud of grey steam had risen from the grave. The guards had laughed: 'These women really are hot stuff!'

First they laid dry wood over the ventilation-ditches, then a layer of oak logs – they burned well – then women who'd been killed, then more wood, then men who'd been killed, then more wood, then the bits of human bodies that were left over, then a can of petrol, and then, right in the middle, an incendiary bomb. Then the Scharführer gave the order; the guards were already smiling as the *brenners* shouted out: 'It's alight!' Finally, the ash was shovelled back into the grave. And it was quiet again. It had been quiet before and it was quiet again.

Then they had been taken further into the forest. This time there was no mound in the middle of the green clearing and the Scharführer ordered them to dig a pit four metres long by three metres wide. They had understood at once: they had completed their task . . . 89 villages, 18 shtetl, 4 settlements, 2 district towns, 3 State farms – 2 arable and one dairy. Altogether that was 116 localities, 116 mounds they had dug . . . Rozenberg the accountant was still counting as he helped dig the pit for himself and the other *brenners:* 783 last week, and 4,826 during the thirty days before – that made 5,609 bodies they had cremated. He counted and counted and time slipped imperceptibly by; he was working out the average number of items – no, human bodies – in each grave: 5,809 divided by 116, the number of graves – that made 48.35 bodies in each communal grave, 48 in round numbers. If 20 *brenners* had been working for 37 days, then each *brenner* . . . 'Fall in!' shouted the chief guard. '*In die Grube marsch!*' bellowed the Scharführer.

But he didn't want to be buried. He started to run, he fell down, he started running again. He ran slowly – he didn't know how to – but they didn't get him. Now he was lying down on the grass, surrounded by the silence of the forest. He wasn't thinking about the sky above, nor was he thinking about Golda who had been killed in her sixth month of pregnancy; he was counting, trying to finish the calculations he had been doing in the pit: 20 *brenners*, 37 days . . . So, first, the total of *brenner* days; second, how much wood per man; third, how many hours each item took to burn, how many . . .

A week later he'd been caught by the police and taken to the ghetto.

And here he was in the cattle-wagon, still muttering away, counting, dividing, multiplying. The accounts for the year! He would have to hand them in to Bukhman, the chief accountant at the State Bank. And then suddenly, while he was dreaming, his tears had come gushing out, burning him, breaking through the crust that had formed over his brain and his heart.

'Golda! Golda!' he cried out.

45

The window of her room looked out onto the barbed-wire fence that surrounded the ghetto. Musya Borisovna the librarian woke up during the night, lifted the hem of the curtain and saw two soldiers dragging a machine-gun. There were blue patches on its polished body and the spectacles of the officer walking in front were glittering in the moonlight. She heard the quiet hum of motors. Cars and lorries with dimmed headlights were approaching the ghetto. The heavy, silvery dust swirled around their wheels; they were like gods floating through the clouds.

Musya Borisovna watched as sub-units of the SS and SD, detachments of Ukrainian police, auxiliary units and a column of cars belonging to the Gestapo drew up at the gates of the sleeping ghetto. In these few minutes of moonlight she took the measure of the history of our age.

The moonlight, the slow majestic movement of the armoured units, the powerful black trucks, the timid ticking of the pendulum clock on the wall, the stockings, bra and blouse that seemed to have frozen on the chair – everything most incongruous had fused together.

46

Natasha, the daughter of Karasik, an old doctor who had been arrested and executed in 1937, tried now and then to sing in the cattle-wagon. No one seemed to mind even when she began singing during the night.

She was very shy. She always looked down at the ground when she spoke and her voice was barely audible. She had never visited anyone except her close relatives and she was astonished at the boldness of girls who danced at parties.

She had not been included in the small number of craftsmen and doctors whose lives were considered useful enough to be preserved . . . A policeman had pushed her towards a dusty mound in the market-place where three drunken men were standing. She had known one of these men before the war: he had been in charge of some railway depot; now he was the Chief of Police. Before she had even understood that these three men were the arbiters of life and death, the policeman had given her another shove; she had joined the buzzing crowd of men, women and children who had been pronounced useless.

Then they had walked towards the airfield in the stifling heat of their last August day. As they walked past the dusty apple trees by the roadside, they had prayed, torn their clothes and uttered their last piercing cries. Natasha herself had remained quite silent.

She would never have thought that blood could be so strikingly red. When there was a momentary silence amid the shooting, scream-ing and groaning, she heard the murmur of flowing blood; it was like a stream, flowing over white bodies instead of white stones.

The quiet crackle of machine-gun fire and the gentle, exhausted face of the executioner – he had waited patiently as she walked timidly to the edge of the pit – had hardly seemed frightening at all . . . Later, during the night, she had wrung out her wet shirt and walked back to the town. The dead don't rise from the grave – so she must have been alive.

When she made her way back to the ghetto, through the small alleys and yards, she had found people dancing and singing on the main square. A band was playing a sad, dreamy waltz that had always been one of her favourites. Couples were whirling round in the wan light of the moon and the streetlamps; the shuffling of soldiers' boots and girls' shoes merged with the music. At that moment this young, drooping girl had felt joyful and self-assured. Quietly, under her breath, she began singing in anticipation of some future happiness. From time to time, when no one was watching, she had even tried to waltz.

47

David could only very dimly remember what had happened since the beginning of the war. There was one night, though, when a little of what he had just lived through came back to him,

It was dark and his grandmother was taking him to the Bukhmans. The sky was full of stars and the horizon was quite light, almost lemon-green. Burdock leaves brushed against his cheeks like cold, moist hands.

Everyone was sitting in a hiding-place in the attic, behind a false wall. In the sun the black sheets of corrugated-iron roofing gave off a fierce heat. Sometimes the smell of burning penetrated their hiding-place. The ghetto was on fire. During the day they had to lie absolutely still. The Bukhman's daughter, Svetlanochka, kept up a monotonous crying. Bukhman himself had a weak heart and in the daytime he looked as though he were dead. During the night he ate some food and quarrelled with his wife.

Suddenly they heard dogs barking. And words in a foreign language: '*Asta! Asta! Wo sind die Juden?*' There was a growing rumble over their heads: the Germans had climbed out of the dormer-window onto the roof.

Then the thundering in the black tin sky died down. Through the walls they heard quiet, sly blows – someone was testing for echoes.

The hiding-place became silent. It was a terrible silence, a silence of tensed shoulders and necks, of bared teeth, of eyes bulging out of their sockets.

Then little Svetlana began her wordless lament. Her cries broke off very abruptly. David looked round and met the frenzied eyes of her mother, Rebekka Bukhman.

Once or twice since then he had glimpsed those eyes . . . And the head of the little girl – thrown right back like the head of a rag-doll.

He could remember everything that had happened before the war.

Those memories came back to him all the time. He had become like an old man – living on his past, loving it and cherishing it.

48

On David's birthday, 12 December, his mother had bought him a picture book.

A small grey goat was standing in a clearing; the darkness of the forest seemed particularly sinister. Among the dark-brown tree-trunks, the toadstools and the fly-agarics, you could see the wolf's green eyes and his red jaw with its bared teeth.

Only David knew about the now inevitable murder. He banged his fist on the table, he screened the goat with the palm of his hand – but he knew there was no way he could save it.

During the night he shouted out: 'Mummy, Mummy, Mummy!'

His mother woke up. As she came towards him, she was like a white cloud in the darkness. He yawned blissfully, knowing that the strongest power in the whole world was now defending him from the darkness of the forest.

When he was older, it was the red dogs in *The Jungle Book* that most frightened him. One night his room had become filled with wild red beasts; he had made his way barefoot, past the sticking-out chest of drawers, to his mother's bed.

When he was feverish and delirious, he always had the same nightmare. He was lying on a sandy beach and tiny waves, no bigger than the smallest of little fingers, were tickling his body. Suddenly, on the horizon, appeared a blue mountain of water; it got bigger and bigger as it rushed silently towards him. David lay there on the warm sand; the dark blue mountain loomed over him. This was something even more terrible than the wolf and the red dogs.

In the morning his mother would leave for work. He would go down the back stairs and pour a cup of milk into an empty crab-meat can – this was for a thin stray cat with a pale nose, weepy eyes and a long fine tail. And then one day a woman who lived next door had said that some people had come in the early morning, put that disgusting animal in a box and taken it away to the Institute, thank God . . . !

'Where on earth is this Institute? How can you expect me to go there? It's quite impossible. You'll just have to forget that unfortunate cat,' his mother had said as she looked into his pleading eyes. 'How are you going to survive in the world? You mustn't let yourself be so vulnerable.'

His mother had wanted to send him to a children's summer-camp. He had cried and pleaded with her, throwing up his hands in despair and shouting: 'I promise I'll go to my grandmother's, but please not that camp!'

His mother had taken him to his grandmother's by train. On the way he refused to eat; the idea of eating a hard-boiled egg, of taking a meat-rissole from a piece of greasy paper, made him feel ashamed.

His mother stayed there with him for the first five days and then had to go back to work. He said goodbye to her without a single tear, but he put his arms round her neck and hugged her so fiercely that she said: 'You'll strangle me like that, you silly. There are lots and lots of cheap strawberries here, and in two months time I'll come back and fetch you.'

There was a bus-stop next to his grandmother's house. The bus went from the town to the tannery. The Ukrainian word for bus-stop was *zupynka*.

His late grandfather had been a member of the Jewish Bund; he had been very famous and had once lived in Paris. As a result, his grandmother was greatly respected – and frequently given the sack from her work.

He could hear radios blaring out through the open windows. 'Attention, attention, this is Radio Kiev speaking . . .'

In the daytime the street was quite deserted; it only came to life when the apprentices at the tannery came past, calling out across the street: 'Bella, did you pass? Yashka, come and help me go over Marxism again!'

In the evenings everyone came home – the tannery workers, the shop assistants, and Sorok, an electrician at the local radio-station. His grandmother worked for the trade-union committee at the surgery.

David never got bored, even when his grandmother was out.

Not far from the house was an old orchard that didn't belong to anyone. Chickens marked with paint wandered about between decrepit apple trees that no longer bore fruit; an elderly goat grazed quietly; ants appeared silently on the tall blades of grass. The town-dwellers – the blackbirds and sparrows – behaved with noisy self-assurance, while the birds from the fields outside, birds whose names David didn't know, were like timid village maidens.

He heard many words that were quite new to him: *gletchik . . . dikt . . . kalyuzha . . . ryazhenka . . . ryaska . . . puzhalo . . . lyadache . . . koshenya . . .** He could recognize in these words echoes and reflections of his own mother-tongue. He heard Yiddish. He felt quite astonished when his mother and grandmother began speaking it together; never before had he heard his mother speak a language he couldn't understand.

His grandmother took David to visit her niece, stout Rebekka Bukhman. David was struck by the number of white wicker blinds in her room. Edward Isaakovich Bukhman came in, wearing a soldier's tunic and a pair of boots. He was the head accountant at the State Bank.

'Chaim,' said Rebekka, 'this is our guest from Moscow, Raya's son.'

'Go on then,' she urged David. 'Say hello to Uncle Edward.'

'Uncle Edward, why does Aunt Rebekka call you Chaim?' David asked.

'That's a very difficult question,' said Edward Bukhman. 'Don't you know that in England all Chaims are called Edward?'

Then the cat began scratching at the door. Finally she managed to open it with her claws and everyone saw an anxious-looking little girl sitting on a pot in the middle of the room.

One Sunday David went with his grandmother to market. There were other women going in the same direction: old women in black dresses; peasant women in heavy boots; sullen, sleepy-looking women who worked as guards on the railways; haughty-looking women with red and blue handbags who were married to important local officials.

Jewish beggars kept shouting at them in rude, angry voices – people seemed to give alms out of fear rather than compassion. Big trucks from the collective farms drove along the cobbled roadway, carrying sacks of potatoes and wickerwork cages full of hens that

---

* Jug, plywood, puddle, sour milk, duckweed, scarecrow, lazy, kitten.

squawked at each pot-hole like a group of sickly old Jews. David saw a dead calf being dragged off a cart; its pale mouth was hanging half-open and the curly white hairs on its neck were stained with blood.

His grandmother bought a speckled hen; she carried it by its legs, which had been tied together with a white rag. David was walking beside her. He wanted to reach out and help the hen lift up its powerless head; he wondered how his grandmother could be so inhumanly cruel.

David remembered some incomprehensible words of his mother's: she had said that his grandfather's relatives were members of the intelligentsia, while his grandmother's relatives were all shopkeepers and tradesmen. That must be why his grandmother didn't feel sorry for the hen.

They went into a yard; an old man in a skull-cap came out to meet them. His grandmother said something in Yiddish. The old man picked the hen up in his hands and began mumbling; the hen cackled unsuspectingly. Then the old man did something very quick – something barely perceptible but obviously terrible – and threw the hen over his shoulder. It ran off, feebly flapping its wings. David saw that it had no head. The body was running all by itself. The old man had killed it. After a few steps it fell to the earth, scratching with its young, powerful claws, and died.

That night David felt as though the damp smell of dead cows and their slaughtered children had even got into his room.

Death, who had once lived in a fairy-tale forest where a fairy-tale wolf was creeping up on a fairy-tale goat, was no longer confined to the pages of a book. For the first time David felt very clearly that he himself was mortal, not just in a fairy-tale way, but in actual fact.

He understood that one day his mother would die. And it wasn't from the fairy-tale forest and the dim light of its fir-trees that Death would come for him and his mother – it would come from this very air, from these walls, from life itself, and there was no way they would be able to hide from it.

He sensed Death with a depth and clarity of which only small children or great philosophers are capable, philosophers who are themselves almost childlike in the power and simplicity of their thinking.

A calm warm smell came from the big wardrobe and the chairs whose worn seats had been replaced by plywood boards; it was the same smell that came from his grandmother's hair and dress. A warm, deceptively calm night surrounded him.

49

The living world was no longer confined to the pages of spelling books and the faces of toy bricks. David saw how much blue there was in the drake's dark wings and how much gay smiling mockery in the way he quacked. He climbed up the rough trunks of cherry trees and reached out to pick the white cherries that glowed among the leaves. He walked up to a calf that had been tethered on a patch of wasteland and offered him a sugar-lump; numb with happiness, he looked into the friendly eyes of this great baby.

Red-haired little Pynchik came up to David and said to him, rolling his r's splendidly: 'Let's have a scrrrap!'

There was little difference between the Jews and the Ukrainians who lived in the different houses that looked onto his grandmother's yard. Old Partynskaya called on his grandmother and said in her drawling voice: 'Guess what, Roza Nusinovna? Sonya's going to Kiev; she's made it up with her husband again.'

His grandmother threw up her hands and laughed.

'What a farce!'

David found he liked this world better than his own Kirov street – where an old woman called Drago-Dragon, with waved hair and a lot of rouge, went for walks with her poodle; where a Zis-101 limousine waited outside the front door every morning; where a woman with a pince-nez and a cigarette between her made-up lips stood over the communal gas-stove, furiously muttering, 'You Trotskyist, you've moved my coffee off the burner again!'

It had been night when he and his mother arrived at the station. In the moonlight they had walked down the cobbled street, past the white Catholic church – where a niche in the wall housed a rather thin, bowed Christ, about the height of a twelve-year-old, his head crowned with thorns – and past the teacher-training college where his mother had once studied.

A few days later, on Friday evening, David saw the old men walking to the synagogue through the clouds of golden dust kicked up by the barefooted footballers on the wasteland.

There was a heart-rending charm in this juxtaposition of white Ukrainian huts, squeaking well-handles and the ancient patterns on black-and-white prayer-shawls. Everything was jumbled together – *Kobzar*,* Pushkin and Tolstoy, physics textbooks, Lenin's *Left-Wing Communism, an Infantile Disorder* . . . And the sons of cobblers and tailors who had first come here at the time of the Civil War, teachers from the *raykom*, orators and troublemakers from the district trade-union soviets, truck-drivers, detectives, lecturers in Marxism . . .

It was at his grandmother's that David first learned that his mother was unhappy. Aunt Rachel – a stout woman whose cheeks were so red that she seemed to be always blushing – was the first person to tell him.

'Leaving such a wonderful woman as your mother! Well, he'll live to regret it!'

By the following day David knew that his father had left his mother for a Russian woman who was eight years his elder; that he earned two and a half thousand roubles a month in the Philarmonia Society; and that his mother refused to accept any alimony and lived on the three hundred and ten roubles a month she earned herself.

Once David showed his grandmother the cocoon he kept in a little matchbox.

'Ugh! What do you want that filth for? Throw it away!' she ordered.

Twice David went to the goods-yard and watched bulls, rams and pigs being loaded into the cattle-wagons. He heard one of the bulls bellowing loudly – complaining or asking for pity. The boy's soul was filled with horror, but the tired railway-workers in their torn, dirty jackets didn't so much as look round.

A week after David's arrival, Deborah, one of his grandmother's neighbours, gave birth to her first child. She was the wife of Lazar Yankelevich, a machinist in the agricultural-machinery factory. The previous year she had been to visit her sister in Kolyma and had been

---

* A collection of poems by the Ukrainian poet T. Chevtchenko.

struck by lightning during a storm. They had tried to give her artificial respiration, but finally gave up and buried her. She had lain there, as though dead, for two hours – and now she had given birth to a child. She had been sterile for fifteen years. His grandmother told David all this and then added: 'That's what they say – but she did have an operation last year.'

David and his grandmother went to call on Deborah.

'Well, Luzya! Well, Deba!' said David's grandmother, looking at the little creature in the washing-basket. There was something almost threatening in the way she pronounced these words, as though she were warning the father and mother never to be frivolous about the miracle that had just taken place.

There was an old woman called Sorgina who lived in a little house by the railway-line with her two sons; they were both deaf-mutes and both worked as hairdressers. All their neighbours were afraid of the family.

'Yes, yes, they're as quiet as mice till they get drunk,' old Partyn-skaya told David. 'But when they get drunk, they snatch up their knives and rush at one another, screaming and squealing like a pair of horses!'

Once David's grandmother sent him round to Musya Borisovna with a jar of sour cream. The librarian's room was tiny. There was a little cup on a table, some little books on a shelf fixed to the wall and a little photograph hanging over her bed. It was a photograph of David in swaddling clothes together with his mother. When David looked at the photograph Musya Borisovna blushed and said: 'Your mother and I shared the same desk at school.'

He read out the fable of the ant and the grasshopper and she, very quietly, read the poem 'Sasha Was Crying as They Cut Down the Forest'.

In the morning the whole yard was buzzing. Solomon Slepoy's fur coat had been stolen – it had been sewn up in moth-balls for the summer.

'God be praised!' said his grandmother. 'It's the least he deserves.'

David learned that Slepoy had been an informer and had betrayed lots of people at the time of the confiscation of foreign currency and gold coins. He had informed on people again in 1937. Two of the people he betrayed had been shot and one had died in a prison hospital.

Night and its strange noises, bird-song, innocent blood – everything was mixed together into a rich, seething stew. Decades later, David might have been able to understand it; but even at the time he was aware both of its horror and of its poignant charm.

50

Before slaughtering infected cattle, various preparatory measures have to be carried out: pits and trenches must be dug; the cattle must be transported to where they are to be slaughtered; instructions must be issued to qualified workers.

If the local population helps the authorities to convey the infected cattle to the slaughtering points and to catch beasts that have run away, they do this not out of hatred of cows and calves, but out of an instinct for self-preservation.

Similarly, when people are to be slaughtered en masse, the local population is not immediately gripped by a bloodthirsty hatred of the old men, women and children who are to be destroyed. It is necessary to prepare the population by means of a special campaign. And in this case it is not enough to rely merely on the instinct for self-preservation; it is necessary to stir up feelings of real hatred and revulsion.

It was in such an atmosphere that the Germans carried out the extermination of the Ukrainian and Byelorussian Jews. And at an earlier date, in the same regions, Stalin himself had mobilized the fury of the masses, whipping it up to the point of frenzy during the campaigns to liquidate the kulaks as a class and during the extermination of Trotskyist–Bukharinite degenerates and saboteurs.

Experience showed that such campaigns make the majority of the population obey every order of the authorities as though hypnotized. There is a particular minority which actively helps to create the atmosphere of these campaigns: ideological fanatics; people who take a bloodthirsty delight in the misfortunes of others; and people who want to settle personal scores, to steal a man's belongings or take over his flat or job. Most people, however, are horrified at mass murder, but they hide this not only from their families, but even from themselves. These are the people who filled the meeting-halls during the campaigns of destruction; however vast these halls or frequent these meetings, very few of them ever disturbed the quiet unanimity of the voting. Still fewer, of course, rather than turning away from the beseeching gaze of a dog suspected of rabies, dared to take the dog in and allow it to live in their houses. Nevertheless, this did happen.

The first half of the twentieth century may be seen as a time of great scientific discoveries, revolutions, immense social transformations and two World Wars. It will go down in history, however, as the time when – in accordance with philosophies of race and society – whole sections of the Jewish population were exterminated. Understandably, the present day remains discreetly silent about this.

One of the most astonishing human traits that came to light at this time was obedience. There were cases of huge queues being formed by people awaiting execution – and it was the victims themselves who regulated the movement of these queues. There were hot summer days when people had to wait from early morning until late at night; some mothers prudently provided themselves with bread and bottles of water for their children. Millions of innocent people, knowing that they would soon be arrested, said goodbye to their nearest and dearest in advance and prepared little bundles containing spare underwear and a towel. Millions of people lived in vast camps that had not only been built by prisoners but were even guarded by them.

And it wasn't merely tens of thousands, or hundreds of thousands, but hundreds of millions of people who were the obedient witnesses of this slaughter of the innocent. Nor were they merely obedient witnesses: when ordered to, they gave their support to this slaughter, voting in favour of it amid a hubbub of voices. There was something unexpected in the degree of their obedience.

There was, of course, resistance; there were acts of courage and determination on the part of those who had been condemned; there were uprisings; there were men who risked their own lives and the lives of their families in order to save the life of a stranger. But the obedience of the vast mass of people is undeniable.

What does this tell us? That a new trait has suddenly appeared in human nature? No, this obedience bears witness to a new force acting on human beings. The extreme violence of totalitarian social systems proved able to paralyse the human spirit throughout whole continents.

A man who has placed his soul in the service of Fascism declares an evil and dangerous slavery to be the only true good. Rather than overtly renouncing human feelings, he declares the crimes committed by Fascism to be the highest form of humanitarianism; he agrees to divide people up into the pure and worthy and the impure and unworthy.

The instinct for self-preservation is supported by the hypnotic power of world ideologies. These call people to carry out any sacrifice, to accept any means, in order to achieve the highest of ends: the future greatness of the motherland, world progress, the future happiness of mankind, of a nation, of a class.

One more force co-operated with the life-instinct and the power of great ideologies: terror at the limitless violence of a powerful State, terror at the way murder had become the basis of everyday life.

The violence of a totalitarian State is so great as to be no longer a means to an end; it becomes an object of mystical worship and adoration. How else can one explain the way certain intelligent, thinking Jews declared the slaughter of the Jews to be necessary for the happiness of mankind? That in view of this they were ready to take their own children to be executed — ready to carry out the sacrifice once demanded of Abraham? How else can one explain the case of a gifted, intelligent poet, himself a peasant by birth, who with sincere conviction wrote a long poem celebrating the terrible years of suffering undergone by the peasantry, years that had swallowed up his own father, an honest and simple-hearted labourer?

Another fact that allowed Fascism to gain power over men was their blindness. A man cannot believe that he is about to be destroyed. The optimism of people standing on the edge of the grave is astounding. The soil of hope — a hope that was senseless and sometimes dishonest and despicable — gave birth to a pathetic obedience that was often equally despicable.

The Warsaw Rising, the uprisings at Treblinka and Sobibor, the various mutinies of *brenners*, were all born of hopelessness. But then utter hopelessness engenders not only resistance and uprisings but also a yearning to be executed as quickly as possible.

People argued over their place in the queue beside the blood-filled ditch while a mad, almost exultant voice shouted out: 'Don't be afraid, Jews. It's nothing terrible. Five minutes and it will all be over.'

Everything gave rise to obedience – both hope and hopelessness.

It is important to consider what a man must have suffered and endured in order to feel glad at the thought of his impending execution. It is especially important to consider this if one is inclined to moralize, to reproach the victims for their lack of resistance in conditions of which one has little conception.

Having established man's readiness to obey when confronted with limitless violence, we must go on to draw one further conclusion that is of importance for an understanding of man and his future.

Does human nature undergo a true change in the cauldron of totalitarian violence? Does man lose his innate yearning for freedom? The fate of both man and the totalitarian State depends on the answer to this question. If human nature does change, then the eternal and world-wide triumph of the dictatorial State is assured; if his yearning for freedom remains constant, then the totalitarian State is doomed.

The great Rising in the Warsaw ghetto, the uprisings in Treblinka and Sobibor; the vast partisan movement that flared up in dozens of countries enslaved by Hitler; the uprisings in Berlin in 1953, in Hungary in 1956, and in the labour-camps of Siberia and the Far East after Stalin's death; the riots at this time in Poland, the number of factories that went on strike and the student protests that broke out in many cities against the suppression of freedom of thought; all these bear witness to the indestructibility of man's yearning for freedom. This yearning was suppressed but it continued to exist. Man's fate may make him a slave, but his nature remains unchanged.

Man's innate yearning for freedom can be suppressed but never destroyed. Totalitarianism cannot renounce violence. If it does, it perishes. Eternal, ceaseless violence, overt or covert, is the basis of totalitarianism. Man does not renounce freedom voluntarily. This conclusion holds out hope for our time, hope for the future.

51

An electronic machine can carry out mathematical calculations, remember historical facts, play chess and translate books from one language to another. It is able to solve mathematical problems more quickly than man and its memory is faultless. Is there any limit to progress, to its ability to create machines in the image and likeness of man? It seems that the answer is no.

It is not impossible to imagine the machine of future ages and millennia. It will be able to listen to music and appreciate art; it will even be able to compose melodies, paint pictures and write poems. Is there a limit to its perfection? Can it be compared to man? Will it surpass him?

Childhood memories . . . tears of happiness . . . the bitterness of parting . . . love of freedom . . . feelings of pity for a sick puppy . . . nervousness . . . a mother's tenderness . . . thoughts of death . . . sadness . . . friendship . . . love of the weak . . . sudden hope . . . a fortunate guess . . . melancholy . . . unreasoning joy . . . sudden embarrassment . . .

The machine will be able to recreate all of this! But the surface of the whole earth will be too small to accommodate this machine – this machine whose dimensions and weight will continually increase as it attempts to reproduce the peculiarities of mind and soul of an average, inconspicuous human being.

Fascism annihilated tens of millions of people.

52

Inside a large, bright, clean house in a village in the Urals surrounded by forest, Novikov, the commanding officer of the tank corps, and Getmanov, his commissar, finished reading the reports of their brigade commanders. They had just been ordered to prepare to leave for the front.

The present moment was a brief lull after the feverish activity of the previous few days.

As is always the case, Novikov and his subordinates felt they hadn't had enough time to complete their training programme. But now there was no more time to study optics, radio equipment, the principles of ballistics or the workings of motors and running parts. They had finished their exercises in the evaluation of targets, the determination of the correct moment to open fire, the observation of shell-bursts, the adjustment of aim and the substitution of targets. A new teacher — the war itself — would soon fill in the blanks and catch out anyone who had been left behind.

Getmanov stretched out his hand towards the small cupboard between the windows, tapped it with his finger and said: 'Come on, friend. Let's see you in the front line!'

Novikov opened the cupboard, took out a bottle of cognac and filled two large blueish glasses.

'Well then, who shall we drink to?' said the commissar thoughtfully.

Novikov knew who they were supposed to drink to, and why Getmanov had asked this question. After a moment's hesitation, he said: 'Comrade Commissar, let's drink to the men we're about to lead into battle. Here's hoping they don't shed too much blood!'

'That's right. Let's drink to the lads. They're the most precious capital of all.'

They clinked their glasses and drained them. With a haste he was unable to conceal, Novikov refilled the glasses and said: 'And here's to comrade Stalin. May we justify his faith in us!'

Novikov saw the hidden mockery in Getmanov's friendly, watchful eyes. Cursing himself, he thought: 'Damn it! I shouldn't have been in such a hurry.'

'Yes, let's drink to the old man,' Getmanov replied good-humouredly. 'Under his leadership we've marched to the banks of the Volga.'

Novikov stared at the commissar. But what could he hope to read in the slit eyes, bright but without kindness, of this intelligent forty-year-old man with his large smiling face and high cheekbones?

Suddenly Getmanov began to talk about their chief of staff, General Nyeudobnov.

'He's a fine fellow. A Bolshevik. A true Stalinist. A man with experience of leadership. And stamina. I remember him from 1937. Yezhov sent him to clean up the military district. Well, I wasn't exactly running a kindergarten myself at that time, but he really did do a thorough job. He was an axe – he had whole lists of men liquidated. Yes, he certainly merited Yezhov's trust – as much as Vasily Vasily-evich Ulrich.* We must ask him to join us now or he'll be offended.'

Getmanov's tone of voice made it seem as though he was condemning the struggle against the enemies of the people, a struggle in which – as Novikov knew – he had himself played an important role. Once again he looked at Getmanov and felt baffled.

'Yes,' he said slowly and reluctantly. 'Some people did go too far then.'

Getmanov made a gesture of despair. 'We received a bulletin from the General Staff today. It's quite appalling. The Germans have almost reached Mount Elbruz, and at Stalingrad they're forcing our troops into the river. And let me say this straight out: those lads are partly to blame for all this. They shot our own men, they destroyed our own cadres.'

Novikov felt a sudden surge of trust in Getmanov.

'Yes, comrade Commissar, many fine men were destroyed. Real damage was done to the Army then. Look at General Krivoruchko –

* Ulrich was President of the Military Collegium of the Supreme Court. He presided at several of the Great Purge Trials. N. I. Yezhov was People's Commissar for Internal Affairs, 1936–1938.

he lost an eye during interrogation. Though he did split open his interrogator's skull with an inkpot.'

Getmanov nodded in agreement. 'Lavrentiy Pavlovich Beria thinks very highly of Nyeudobnov. And Lavrentiy Pavlovich is an intelligent man: he never misjudges people.'

'Yes, yes,' thought Novikov resignedly. He didn't say anything.

For a moment they were both silent, listening to the low voices next door.

'Nonsense, those are our socks.'

'What do you mean, comrade Lieutenant? Have you gone blind or something? And don't you touch those – those are our collars.'

'Nonsense, comrade Political Instructor! Look! Can't you see?'

The two orderlies were sorting out Novikov's and Getmanov's laundry.

'I keep an eye on those devils the whole time,' said Getmanov. 'Once the two of us were on our way towards Fatov's battalion to watch their firing exercises. I crossed the river by some stepping-stones, while you jumped across and then stamped your feet to shake off the mud. I looked round and saw our two orderlies doing exactly the same thing: mine used the stepping-stones, while yours jumped across and stamped his feet.'

'Hey, you fire-eaters!' called Novikov. 'Try swearing a bit more quietly.' The two orderlies immediately fell silent.

General Nyeudobnov, a pale man with a high forehead and thick grey hair, came into the room. He looked at the bottle and glasses, put down his file on the table, and said to Novikov:

'Comrade Colonel, we need a new chief of staff for the second brigade. Mikhalev won't be back for six weeks; I just received a certificate from hospital.'

'And even then he'll be missing his guts and part of his stomach,' said Getmanov. He poured out some cognac and offered it to Nyeudobnov.

'Have a drink, comrade General, while your guts are still in one piece.'

Nyeudobnov raised his eyebrows and looked questioningly at Novikov.

'Please, comrade General, feel free!'

Novikov was annoyed by the way Getmanov always seemed to be

in control of every situation. At meetings he held forth at length about technical matters he knew nothing about. And, with the same assurance, he would invite people to lie down for a rest on someone else's bed, offer them someone else's cognac, or read through papers that had nothing to do with him.

'We could appoint Major Basangov temporarily,' said Novikov. 'He knows what's what. And he was taking part in tank-battles right at the beginning of the war, near Novograd-Volynsk. Does the commissar have any objections?'

'Of course not,' said Getmanov. 'It's not for me to object . . . There is one thing, though. The second-in-command of the second brigade is an Armenian; you want the chief of staff to be a Kalmyk – and we've already got some Lifshits as chief of staff of the third brigade. Couldn't we do without the Kalmyk?' He looked at Novikov, then at Nyeudobnov.

'That's how we all feel,' said Nyeudobnov. 'And on the face of it you're right. But then Marxism's taught us to look at things differently.'

'What matters is how well the comrade in question can fight the Germans,' said Novikov. 'That's what Marxism tells me. I'm really not interested in where his grandfather prayed – whether he went to church, to a mosque . . . ,' he paused for a moment to think, '. . . or to a synagogue. What matters in war is how well you can fight.'

'Quite right,' said Getmanov brightly. 'We're certainly not having synagogues and meeting-houses in our tank corps. We are, after all, defending Russia.'

A frown suddenly appeared on his face. 'Quite frankly,' he went on angrily, 'all this makes me want to vomit. In the name of the friendship of nations we keep sacrificing the Russians. A member of a national minority barely needs to know the alphabet to be appointed a people's commissar, while our Ivan, no matter if he's a genius, has to "yield place to the minorities". The great Russian people's becoming a national minority itself. I'm all for the friendship of nations, but not on these terms. I'm sick of it!'

Novikov thought for a moment, glanced at the papers on the table, then tapped a fingernail against his glass. 'So that's how it is. You think I discriminate against Russians out of a particular sympathy for Kalmyks?'

He turned to Nyeudobnov. 'Very well, I'm appointing Major Sazonov as temporary chief of staff of the second brigade.'

'A fine soldier,' said Getmanov quietly.

Yet again, Novikov, who had always been rude, harsh and high-handed with people, realized how uncertain of himself he felt with Getmanov. 'It doesn't matter,' he told himself. 'Politically, I'm illiterate. I'm just a proletarian who happens to know about war. My task is very simple – to smash the Germans.'

But however much he laughed at Getmanov's military ignorance, Novikov couldn't deny that he was afraid of him.

Getmanov was short and broad-shouldered. He had a large stomach and a large head with tousled hair. He was very active, quick to laugh, and he had a loud voice. He appeared inexhaustible. Despite the fact that he had never served at the front, people said of him: 'Yes, our commissar's a true soldier.' He enjoyed holding meetings and his speeches went down well with the troops: he made lots of jokes and spoke very simply, often quite coarsely.

He walked with a slight waddle and often made use of a stick. If an absent-minded soldier was slow in saluting him, he would stop in front of him, leaning on his famous stick, take off his cap, and make a deep bow – like some old man in a village.

He was quick-tempered and resented it if someone answered him back; if anyone did argue with him, he would at once start puffing and frowning. He once lost his temper and punched Captain Gubyonkov, the chief of staff of the heavy artillery regiment; the latter was rather obstinate and – in the words of his comrades – 'terribly high-principled'.

On this occasion, Getmanov's orderly had simply remarked: 'The swine – he really drove our commissar crazy.'

Getmanov felt no respect for people who had gone through the terrible first days of the war. He once remarked about Makarov, the commander of the First Brigade and a favourite of Novikov's, 'All that philosophy of 1941 – I'll shove it down his throat!' Novikov hadn't said anything, though he enjoyed talking to Makarov about that terrible but fascinating time.

On the surface, Getmanov, with his bold, sweeping judgements, seemed the very antithesis of Nyeudobnov. Nevertheless, there was something similar about them that brought them together.

Nyeudobnov's calm, deliberate manner of speaking, his blank, but expressive expression, were truly depressing. Getmanov, on the other hand, would laugh and say: 'We're in luck. The Fritzes have done more to put the peasants' backs up in one year than we Communists in twenty-five.' Or 'What can we do? The old boy really likes it when people call him a genius.' But this boldness of Getmanov's, far from being infectious, usually quite unnerved the man he was talking to.

Before the war, Getmanov had been in charge of an *oblast*. He had given speeches about the production of fire-bricks and the organization of scientific research at the Coal Institute, about the quality of bread from the municipal bakery, about the faults of a story entitled 'Blue Flames' that had been printed in the local almanac, about the reconstruction of the municipal garage, about inadequate storage facilities in the local warehouses, and about an epidemic of fowl-pest in the *kolkhozes*.

Now he spoke with the same authority about the quality of fuel and the rate of deterioration of engines, about tactics in battle, about the co-ordination of tanks, artillery and infantry if they broke through the enemy front, about medical assistance under fire, about radio codes, about the psychology of the soldier in combat, about the relations between one tank-crew and another, and between the individual members of each crew, about running repairs and major overhauls, and about the removal of damaged tanks from the battlefield.

Once, after a gunnery exercise, Novikov and Getmanov had stopped in front of the winning tank. As he answered their questions, the soldier in command had gently caressed the side of the tank. Getmanov had asked if he had found the exercise difficult.

'No, why should I? I love my tank very much. I came to the training school straight from my village. The moment I saw her, I fell in love. Impossibly in love.'

'So it was love at first sight, was it?' said Getmanov. He burst out laughing.

There was something condescending in Getmanov's laughter – as though he were criticizing this young man's ridiculous love for his tank. Novikov felt then that he himself could be equally ridiculous, that he could fall equally stupidly in love. But he said nothing of this to Getmanov. Getmanov had then become serious again.

'Good lad! Love for one's tank is a great strength,' he said sententiously. 'It's brought you success.'

'But what's there to love about it?' Novikov had asked ironically. 'It offers a magnificent target. Anyone can put it out of action. It makes an appalling din that gives its position away to the enemy and drives its crew round the bend. And it shakes you about so much you can hardly even observe, let alone take aim.'

Getmanov had looked at Novikov and smiled sardonically. Now, as he refilled the glasses, he looked at Novikov with that same smile and said: 'We'll be going through Kuibyshev. Our commanding officer will have a chance to see a friend or two there. Here's to your meeting!'

'That's all I needed,' thought Novikov. He was blushing like a schoolboy and he knew it.

Nyeudobnov had been abroad when the war began. It was only in early 1942, on his return to the People's Commissariat of Defence in Moscow, that he had first heard the air-raid warnings and seen the anti-tank defences beyond the Moscow river. Like Getmanov, he never asked Novikov direct questions about military matters, perhaps because he was ashamed of his own ignorance.

Novikov kept wondering how it was he had become a general. He began to study the pages of forms that made up Nyeudobnov's dossier; his life was reflected there like a birch tree in a lake.

Nyeudobnov was older than Novikov or Getmanov. He had been imprisoned in 1916 for belonging to a Bolshevik circle. After the Civil War he had been sent by the Party to work in the OGPU.* He had been posted to the frontier and then sent to the Military Academy where he had been secretary of the Party organization for his year . . . He had then worked in the military department of the Central Committee and in the central office of the People's Commissariat of Defence.

Before the war he had twice been sent abroad. He was on the *nomenklatura*. Before now, Novikov had never fully understood what this meant, just what special rights and privileges it entailed.

The period, usually a very lengthy one, between being recommended for promotion and having this confirmed had, in Nyeudobnov's case, always been reduced to a bare minimum. It was as if the

* Between 1923 and 1934 the Soviet security service was known as the OGPU (United State Political Administration).

People's Commissar for Defence had had no more urgent matters to attend to.

There was one strange thing, however, about the information contained in such dossiers: one moment they seemed to explain all the mysteries of a man's life, all his successes and failures – and then a moment later they seemed only to obscure matters, not to explain anything at all.

Since the beginning of the war, people's biographies, service records, confidential reports and diplomas of honour had come to be looked at differently . . . And so General Nyeudobnov had been subordinated to Colonel Novikov. He knew, though, that this was only a temporary abnormality, something that would be rectified as soon as the war was over.

Nyeudobnov had brought with him a hunting rifle that had made all the aficionados gasp with envy. Novikov had said that Nicholas II might have used one just like it. Nyeudobnov had been given it in 1938, together with a dacha and various other confiscated items: furniture, carpets, and some fine china.

Whether they were talking about the war, *kolkhozes*, a book by General Dragomir, the Chinese, the fine qualities of General Rokossovsky, the climate in Siberia, the quality of cloth used for military greatcoats, the superiority of blondes over brunettes, Nyeudobnov never ventured any opinion that was in the least original. It was hard to know whether this was a matter of reserve or simply a reflection of his true nature.

After supper he sometimes became more talkative and began telling stories about enemies of the people who had been unmasked in the most unlikely places – medical-instrument factories, workshops producing army boots, sweetshops, Pioneer* palaces, the stables of the Moscow Hippodrome, the Tretyakovsky Gallery . . .

He had an excellent memory and seemed to have studied the works of Lenin and Stalin in great detail. During an argument he would say: 'As early as the Seventeenth Congress, comrade Stalin said . . .' – and begin to quote.

'There are quotations and quotations,' Getmanov once said to him. 'All kinds of things have been said at one time or another. For

---

* The Communist children's organization.

instance: "We don't want other people's land and we won't yield an inch of our own." And where are the Germans now?'

Nyeudobnov had just shrugged his shoulders as though the Germans on the Volga were of no importance compared to the famous words he had quoted.

Suddenly everything vanished – tanks, service regulations, gunnery exercises, the forest, Getmanov, Nyeudobnov . . . Nothing was left but Zhenya. Zhenya! Was he really going to see her again?

53

Novikov had been surprised when Getmanov, having read a letter from home, had said: 'My wife says she feels sorry for us. I told her what our living conditions are like.' What Getmanov found arduous, Novikov regarded as uncomfortably luxurious.

For the first time he had been able to choose his own lodgings. Once, leaving to visit one of the brigades, he said he didn't like the sofa. On his return, he found it had already been exchanged for an armchair. His orderly, Vershkov, was waiting anxiously to see if he liked it.

The cook was always asking: 'Is the borshch all right, comrade Colonel?'

Ever since he was a child he had loved animals. Now he had a hedgehog that lived under his bed and pattered round the room at night. He also had a young chipmunk that ate nuts and lived in a special cage, decorated with an emblem of a tank, which had been presented to him by the maintenance workshop. The chipmunk had quickly got used to Novikov and now sometimes sat on his knee, looking up at him with childish trust and curiosity. Orlenev the cook, Kharitonov the driver, and Vershkov were all kind and attentive towards these animals.

All this was not without importance for Novikov. Once, before the war, he had brought a puppy into the officers' mess. It had taken a bite out of the slipper of the lady sitting next to him – a colonel – and made three puddles on the floor in half an hour. There had been such an outcry in the communal kitchen that he had had to part with the creature at once.

It was their last day – and it brought with it worries about fuel, about supplies for the journey and the best way to load the vehicles onto the tank-carriers.

He began to wonder about his future neighbours, the men whose artillery regiments and infantry battalions would also be setting out today. He began to wonder about the man before whom he himself would have to stand to attention and say: 'Comrade Colonel-General, allow me to report . . .'

It was their last day – and he hadn't managed to see his brother and niece. When he came to the Urals he had thought how near his brother would be, but in the end he hadn't had time for him.

He had already received reports that the tank-carriers were ready, that the brigades had set off, and that the hedgehog and chipmunk had been released into the forest.

It's hard to be the absolute master, to feel responsible for the last trifling detail. The tanks have already been loaded, but has everything been done correctly? Are they all in first gear, brakes firmly on, turrets pointing ahead, hatches battened down? Have wooden blocks been placed in position to stop the tanks shifting and unbalancing the wagons?

'How about a farewell game of cards?' asked Getmanov.

'All right,' said Nyeudobnov.

Novikov chose instead to go outside and be alone for a moment.

It was early in the evening, very quiet, and the air was extraordinarily transparent; even the smallest objects were clearly and distinctly visible. The smoke rose vertically from the chimneys. Logs crackled in the field-kitchens. A girl was embracing a dark-haired soldier in the middle of the street, her head on his chest, weeping. Boxes, suitcases and typewriters in black cases were being carried out of the buildings that had served as their HQ. Signallers were reeling in the thick black cables that stretched between corps headquarters and the headquarters of each brigade. A tank behind the barns backfired and let out puffs of exhaust smoke as it prepared to set off. Drivers were filling the petrol tanks of their new Ford trucks and removing the thick covers from their radiators. Meanwhile, the rest of the world was perfectly still.

Novikov stood on the porch and looked round; for a moment all his cares and anxieties fell away. Soon afterwards he set out in his jeep on the road to the station.

The tanks were coming out of the forest. The ground, already hardened by the first frosts, rang beneath the unaccustomed weight. The evening sun lit up the crowns of the distant firs where Karpov's brigade was slowly emerging. Makarov's brigade was passing through some young birch trees. The soldiers had decorated their tanks with branches; the pine-needles and birch-leaves seemed as much a part of the tanks as the armour-plating, the roar of the motors and the silvery click of their tracks.

When old soldiers see reserves being moved up to the front, they say, 'It looks like a wedding.'

Novikov pulled in to the side of the road and watched the tanks come past. What dramas had taken place here! What strange and ridiculous stories! What extraordinary incidents and emergencies had been reported to him . . . ! At breakfast one day a frog had been discovered in the soup . . . Sub-Lieutenant Rozhdestvensky, who had completed ten years of schooling, had accidentally wounded a comrade in the stomach while he was cleaning his rifle; he had then committed suicide . . . A soldier in the motorized infantry battalion had refused to take the oath, saying: 'I only swear oaths in church.'

Blue-grey smoke twined round the bushes by the side of the road. What diverse thoughts lay hidden beneath all these leather helmets! Some they all shared – love of one's country, the sorrow of war; others were extraordinarily varied.

My God . . . What a lot of them there were, all wearing black overalls with wide belts. They had been chosen for their broad shoulders and short stature – so they could climb through the hatches and move about inside the tanks. How similar the answers on their forms had been – to questions about their fathers and mothers, their date of birth, the number of years they had completed at school, their experience as tractor-drivers. The shiny green T-34s, hatches open, tarpaulins strapped to their armour-plating, seemed to blend into one.

One soldier was singing; another, his eyes half-closed, was full of dire forebodings; a third was thinking about home; a fourth was chewing some bread and sausage and thinking about the sausage; a fifth, his mouth wide open, was trying to identify a bird on a tree; a sixth was worrying about whether he'd offended his mate by swearing at him the previous night; a seventh, still furious, was dreaming of giving his enemy – the commander of the tank in front – a good punch on the jaw; an eighth was composing a farewell poem to the autumn forest; a ninth was thinking about a girl's breasts; a tenth was thinking about his dog – sensing that she was about to be abandoned among the bunkers, she had jumped up onto the armour-plating, pathetically wagging her tail in an attempt to win him over; an eleventh was thinking how good it would be to live alone in a hut in the forest, drinking spring-water, eating berries and going about barefoot; a twelfth was wondering whether to feign sickness and have a rest in hospital; a thirteenth was remembering a fairy-tale he had heard as a child; a fourteenth was remembering the last time he had talked to his girl – he felt glad that they had now separated for ever; a fifteenth was thinking about the future – after the war he would like to run a canteen.

'Yes,' thought Novikov, 'they're fine lads.'

They were looking at him. They thought he was inspecting their uniforms; that he was listening to the sound of the engines to check the competence of the drivers and mechanics; that he was checking whether the correct distance was being maintained between each tank and each section or whether there were any madmen trying to race one another. In fact he was just standing there, no different from them, full of the same thoughts – about his bottle of cognac that had been opened by Getmanov, about how difficult it was to get on with Nyeudobnov . . . He was thinking that he would never again go hunting in the Urals and what a pity it was that the last hunt had been a failure – just stupid anecdotes, too much vodka and the chatter of tommy-guns . . . He was thinking that soon he would see the woman he had been in love with for years . . . When he had heard, six years ago, that she had got married, he had written a brief note: 'I am taking indefinite leave. I return my revolver – number 10322.' That had been when he was serving in Nikolsk-Ussuriysk. But in the end he hadn't pulled the trigger . . .

There his men were: timid, gloomy, easily amused, thoughtful; womanizers, harmless egotists, idlers, misers, contemplatives, good sorts . . . There they all were – going into battle for a common, just cause. The simplicity of this truth makes it difficult to talk about; but it is often forgotten by people who should, instead, take it as their point of departure.

The thoughts of these men may have been trivial – an abandoned dog, a hut in a remote village, hatred for another soldier who's stolen your girl . . . But these trivialities are precisely what matter.

Human groupings have one main purpose: to assert everyone's right to be different, to be special, to think, feel and live in his or her own way. People join together in order to win or defend this right. But this is where a terrible, fateful error is born: the belief that these groupings in the name of a race, a God, a party or a State are the very purpose of life and not simply a means to an end. No! The only true and lasting meaning of the struggle for life lies in the individual, in his modest peculiarities and in his right to these peculiarities.

Novikov had the feeling that these men would succeed, that they would outwit and overcome the enemy. This vast reserve of intelligence, labour, bravery, calculation, skill and anger, of all the different endowments of these students, schoolboys, tractor-drivers, lathe-operators, teachers, electricians and bus-drivers – all this would flow into one, would coalesce. And once united, they were certain to conquer. They were too rich not to conquer.

If one failed, another would succeed; if it wasn't in the centre, it would be on a flank; if it wasn't in the first hour of battle, it would be in the second. These men would surpass the enemy in both strength and cunning; they would break him, destroy him . . . Victory depended on them alone. In the smoke and dust of battle they would turn, they would break through, they would strike a fraction of a second earlier than the enemy, a fraction of an inch more accurately, more crushingly . . .

Yes, they held the answer. These lads in their tanks, with their cannons and machine-guns, were the most precious resource of all.

But would they unite? Would the inner strength of all these men coalesce?

Novikov stood and watched. He felt a sense of mounting joy and confidence about Zhenya: 'She'll be mine! She'll be mine!'

54

What an extraordinary time this was! Krymov felt that history had left the pages of books and come to life.

Here, in Stalingrad, the glitter of sunlight on water, the colour of the sky and the clouds, struck him with a new intensity. It had been the same when he was a child: the patter of summer rain, a rainbow, his first glimpse of snow, had been enough to fill him with happiness. Now he had rediscovered this sense of wonder – something nearly all of us lose as we come to take the miracle of our lives for granted.

Everything Krymov had disliked in the life of these last years, everything he had found false, seemed absent from Stalingrad. 'Yes, this is how it was in Lenin's day!' he said to himself.

He felt that people were treating him differently, better than they had done before the war. It was the same now as when he had been encircled by the Germans: he no longer felt he was a stepson of the age. Recently, on the left bank, he had been preparing his talks and lectures with enthusiasm, quite reconciled to his new role.

Nevertheless, there were times when he did feel a sense of humiliation. Why hadn't he been allowed to continue as a fighting commissar? He had done his job well enough, better than many others . . .

There was something good about the relations between people here. There was a true sense of dignity and equality on this clay slope where so much blood had been spilt.

There was an almost universal interest in such matters as the structure of *kolkhozes* after the war, the future relations between the great peoples and their governments. The day-to-day life of these soldiers – their work with spades, with the kitchen-knives they used for cleaning potatoes and the cobblers' knives they used for mending boots – seemed to have a direct bearing on their life after the war, even on the lives of other nations and states.

Nearly everyone believed that good would triumph, that honest men, who hadn't hesitated to sacrifice their lives, would be able to build a good and just life. This faith was all the more touching in that these men thought that they themselves would be unlikely to survive until the end of the war; indeed, they felt astonished each evening to have survived one more day.

55

After his evening lecture, Krymov was taken to Batyuk's bunker. Lieutenant-Colonel Batyuk, a short man whose face expressed all the weariness of the war, was in command of the division disposed along the slopes of Mamayev Kurgan and alongside Banniy Ovrag.

Batyuk seemed glad of Krymov's visit. For supper there was meat in aspic and a hot pie. As he poured out some vodka for Krymov, Batyuk narrowed his eyes and said: 'I heard you were coming round giving lectures. I wondered who you'd visit first – me or Rodimtsev. In the end you went to Rodimtsev's.'

He smiled at Krymov and grunted. 'It's just like being in a village. As soon as things quieten down in the evening, we start phoning our neighbours. What did you have to eat? Has anyone been round? Are you going anywhere yourself? Did the high-ups say which of us has got the best bath-house? Has anyone been written about in the newspaper? Yes, they always write about Rodimtsev, never about us. To read the newspapers, you'd think he was defending Stalingrad all by himself.'

He gave his guest some more vodka, but himself just had some tea and a crust of bread. He seemed indifferent to the pleasures of the table.

Krymov realized that the deliberateness of Batyuk's movements and his slow Ukrainian manner of speech were misleading; in fact he was mulling over some very difficult problems. He was upset that Batyuk didn't ask a single question about his lecture. It was as though it bore no relation to any of Batyuk's real concerns.

Krymov was appalled by what Batyuk told him about the first hours of the war. During the mass retreat from the frontier, Batyuk led his own battalion west to hold a ford against the Germans. His superior officers, retreating along the same road, thought he was about to surrender to the Germans. There and then, after an interrogation consisting only of hysterical shouts and curses, it was decided to have Batyuk shot. At the last moment – he was already standing against a tree – he was rescued by his own soldiers.

'Yes, comrade Lieutenant-Colonel,' said Krymov. 'That's no joke.'

'I didn't quite die of a heart attack,' said Batyuk. 'But my heart hasn't been the same since – that's for sure!'

'Can you hear the firing over in the Market?' asked Krymov in a rather theatrical tone. 'Is Gorokhov up to something?'

Batyuk glanced at him.

'I know what Gorokhov's up to. He's playing cards.'

Krymov said he'd heard there was going to be a meeting of snipers at Batyuk's; he'd like to attend.

'Certainly,' said Batyuk. 'Why not?'

They began to talk about the Front. Batyuk said he was worried by the gradual build-up of German troops in the north of the sector; it was mostly taking place at night.

Finally the snipers assembled; Krymov realized who the pie was intended for. Men in padded jackets sat down one after another on benches beside the wall and round the table; they seemed shy and awkward, but at the same time conscious of their own worth. The new arrivals stacked their rifles and tommy-guns in the corner, trying to make as little noise as possible; they might have been workers putting down their axes and spades.

The famous Zaitsev looked somehow kind and gentle – just a good-natured country lad. But when he turned his head and frowned, Krymov glimpsed the true harshness of his features.

It reminded him of a moment at a conference before the war. Looking at an old friend seated beside him, he had suddenly seen his seemingly hard face in a different light. His eyes kept blinking, his mouth was half-open and he had a weak nose and chin. Altogether he seemed feeble and irresolute.

Next to Zaitsev were Bezdidko – a mortar man with narrow shoulders and brown, laughing eyes – and Suleiman Khalimov, a young Uzbek with the thick lips of a child. Then there was Matsegur, a crack-shot who kept having to wipe the sweat off his forehead; he looked like a quiet family-man – anything but a sniper. The other snipers – Shuklin, Tokarev, Manzhulya and Solodkiy – also looked like shy, diffident young lads.

Batyuk cocked his head to one side as he questioned them. He looked more like an inquisitive schoolboy than one of the canniest and most experienced officers in Stalingrad. Everyone's eyes lit up when he started talking, in Ukrainian, to Bezdidko; they were expecting some good jokes.

'Well, Bezdidko, how's it been?'

'Yesterday I gave the Fritzes a hard time, comrade Lieutenant-Colonel. You already know that. But today I only got five – and I wasted four bombs.'

'Well, you're not in the same class as Shuklin. He put fourteen tanks out of action with one gun.'

'Yes, and that gun was all that was left of his battery.'

'He blew up a German brothel yesterday,' said the handsome Bulatov, blushing.

'I just recorded it as an ordinary bunker.'

'Talking of bunkers,' said Batyuk, 'my door was smashed in yesterday by a mortar-bomb.' He turned to Bezdidko and said reproachfully: 'I thought that son of a bitch Bezdidko was aiming a bit wide.'

Manzhulya, a gun-layer who seemed even quieter than the rest, took a piece of pie and murmured: 'It's good pastry, comrade Lieutenant-Colonel.'

Batyuk tapped his glass with a rifle-cartridge.

'Well, comrades, let's get down to business.'

It was just another production conference – like those held in factories or village mills . . . Only the people here were not bakers, weavers or tailors, nor were they talking of threshing methods or bread.

Bulatov told them how he had seen a German walking down a path with his arm round a woman. He had made them drop to the ground, and then, before killing them, had let them get up three times, only to force them back to the ground by stirring up clouds of dust an inch or two from their feet.

'He was bending down towards her when I finished him off. They ended up stretched across the path like a cross.'

Bulatov's nonchalance made this story peculiarly horrible. It was quite unlike most soldiers' tales.

'Come on! That's enough of your bullshit, Bulatov!' Zaitsev interrupted.

'That takes my score to seventy-eight,' said Bulatov. 'And I'm not bullshitting. The commissar wouldn't allow me to lie. Here's his signature.'

Krymov wanted to join in the conversation; he wanted to say that among the Germans Bulatov had killed there might well have been workers, revolutionaries, internationalists. It was important to remember this or they'd become mere chauvinists . . . But he kept quiet. He knew that this kind of thinking was unhelpful, that it would serve only to demoralize the soldiers.

The blond Solodkiy said with a lisp that he'd killed eight Germans yesterday. He added: 'I come from a *kolkhoz* near Umansk. What the Fascists did in my village is unbelievable. And I haven't got off scot-free myself – I've been wounded three times. That's what's made me a sniper.'

After suggesting very earnestly that it was best to pick a spot along a path the Germans used to fetch water or to go to the kitchen, Tokarev said: 'I'm from Mozhaev. My wife's in occupied territory. I got a letter from her saying what they've been through. They killed my son because of the name I gave him – Vladimir Ilyich.'

'I never hurry,' said Khalimov excitedly. 'I shoot when my heart tells me. I come to the front – Sergeant Gurov my friend. He teach me Russian, I teach him Uzbek. Germans kill him, I kill twelve Germans. I take binoculars from officer and hang them round neck. I carry out your orders, comrade Political Instructor.'

There was something terrible about the reports of these snipers. Krymov had always scorned lily-livered intellectuals, people like Shtrum and Yevgenia Nikolaevna who had made such a to-do over the fate of the kulaks. Referring to 1937, he had told Yevgenia: 'There's nothing wrong with liquidating our enemies; what's terrible is when we shoot our own people.'

Now he felt like saying that he'd always, without the least hesitation, been ready to shoot White Guards, to exterminate Menshevik and SR scum, to liquidate the kulaks, that he had never felt the least pity for enemies of the Revolution, but that it was wrong to rejoice at the killing of German workers. There was something horrible about the way these soldiers talked – even though they knew very well what they were fighting for.

Zaitsev began to tell the story of his battle of wits with a German sniper at the foot of Mamayev Kurgan. It had lasted for days. The German knew Zaitsev was watching him and he himself was keeping watch on Zaitsev. They seemed well-matched; neither could catch the other out.

'He'd already picked off three of our men that day, but I just lay in my ditch. I didn't make a sound. Then he had one more go – his aim was perfect – another of our soldiers fell to the ground with his hands in the air. One of their soldiers went by with some papers. I just lay there and watched . . . I knew what he'd be thinking – that if I'd been around, I'd have picked off that soldier. And I knew he couldn't see the soldier he'd shot himself – he'd want to have a look. Neither of us moved. Then another German went by with a bucket – not a sound from my ditch. Another fifteen minutes and he started to get to his feet. He stood up. Then I stood up myself . . .'

Reliving what he'd been through, Zaitsev got up from the table. His face had now assumed the expression Krymov had earlier only glimpsed. Now he was no longer just a good-natured young lad – there was something leonine, something powerful and sinister in his flared nostrils, in his broad forehead, in the triumphant glare of his eyes.

'He realized who I was. And then I shot him.'

There was a moment of silence, probably the same silence that had followed Zaitsev's shot – you could almost hear the dead body falling to the ground. Batyuk suddenly turned to Krymov and asked: 'Well, do you find all this interesting?'

'It's great stuff,' said Krymov – and that was all he said.

Krymov stayed behind after the end of the meeting. Batyuk moved his lips as he counted out some drops for his heart into an empty glass; then he filled it with water. Yawning every now and then, he started to tell Krymov about everyday life in the division. Everything he said seemed to have some bearing on what had happened to him in the first hours of the war; it was as though all his thoughts had developed from that one point.

Ever since he had arrived in Stalingrad, Krymov had had a strange feeling. Sometimes it was as though he were in a kingdom where the

Party no longer existed; sometimes he felt he was breathing the ˌ the first days of the Revolution.

'Have you been a member of the Party for long, comrade Lieutenant-Colonel?' he asked Batyuk abruptly.

'Why do you ask, comrade Commissar? Do you think I'm deviating from the Party line?'

For a moment Krymov didn't answer. Then he said: 'I've always been considered quite a good orator, you know. I've spoken at large workers' meetings. But ever since I arrived here, I've felt that I'm following people rather than guiding them. It's very odd. Just now I wanted to say something to your snipers and then I thought they knew all they needed to know already. Actually, that wasn't the only reason I didn't say anything. We've been told to make the soldiers think of the Red Army as an army of vengeance. This isn't the moment for me to start talking about internationalism or class consciousness. What matters is to mobilize the fury of the masses against the enemy. I don't want to be like the idiot in the story who began reciting the funeral service at a wedding . . .'

He thought for a moment. 'Anyway, I'm used to it . . . The Party's mobilized the fury of the masses in order to destroy the enemy, to annihilate them. There's no place for Christian humanitarianism now. Our Soviet humanitarianism is something more stern . . . We certainly don't wear kid-gloves . . .' He paused again.

'Of course I'm not talking about incidents like when you were nearly shot. And in 1937 there were times when we shot our own people – yes, we're paying for that now. But now the Germans have attacked the homeland of workers and peasants. War's war! They deserve what they get.'

Krymov waited for a response from Batyuk, but it wasn't forthcoming – not because Batyuk was perplexed by what he had said, but because he had fallen asleep.

56

It was almost dark. Men in padded jackets were scurrying about between the furnaces of the 'Red October' steelworks. In the distance you could hear shooting and see brief flashes of light; the air was full of a kind of dusty mist.

Guryev, the divisional commander, had set up the regimental command-posts inside the furnaces. Krymov had the impression that the people inside these furnaces – furnaces that until recently had forged steel – must be very special, must themselves have hearts of steel.

You could hear the tramp of German boots; you could hear orders being shouted out; you could even hear quiet clicks as the Germans reloaded their tommy-guns.

As he climbed down, shoulders hunched, into the mouth of a furnace that was now the command-post of an infantry battalion, as his hands felt the warmth that still lingered in the fire-bricks, a sort of timidity suddenly came over Krymov; it was as though the secret of this extraordinary resistance was about to be revealed to him.

In the semi-darkness he made out a squatting figure with a broad face, and heard a welcoming voice.

'Here's a guest come to our palace! Welcome! Quick – some vodka and a hard-boiled egg for our visitor!'

A thought flashed through Krymov's brain: he would never be able to tell Yevgenia Nikolaevna how he had thought of her as he climbed into a dark, airless steel-furnace in Stalingrad. In the past he'd tried to forget her, to escape from her, but now he was reconciled to the way she followed him wherever he went. The witch – she'd even followed him into this furnace!

It was all as clear as daylight. Who needed stepsons of the time? Better to hide them away with the cripples and pensioners! Better to make them into soap! Her leaving him was just one more sign that his life was hopeless. Even here in Stalingrad they didn't want him as a combatant.

That evening, after his lecture, Krymov talked to General Guryev. Guryev had taken off his jacket and kept wiping the sweat off his red face. In the same harsh voice he offered Krymov vodka, shouted orders down the telephone to his battalion commanders, abused the cook for failing to grill the *shashlyks* correctly, and rang his neighbour, Batyuk, to ask if they were playing dominoes on Mamayev Kurgan.

'We've got some good men here,' said Guryev. 'They're a fine lot. Batyuk's certainly got a head on his shoulders. And General Zholudyev at the tractor factory's an old friend of mine. And then there's Colonel Gurtyev at "The Barricades" – only he's a monk, he never drinks vodka at all. That really is a mistake.'

Then he told Krymov about how no one else had so few men as he did – between six and eight in each company. And no one else was so cut off from the rear – when they sent him reinforcements, a third of them would arrive wounded. No one else, except perhaps Gorokhov, had to put up with that.

'Yesterday Chuykov summoned Shuba, my chief of staff. They had a disagreement over the exact position of the front line. Poor Colonel Shuba came back in a terrible state.'

He glanced at Krymov.

'Do you think Chuykov just swore at him?' He burst out laughing. 'No, he gets sworn at by me every day. He came back with his front teeth knocked out.'

'Yes,' said Krymov slowly. This 'yes' was an admission that the dignity of man didn't always hold sway on the slopes of Stalingrad.

Then Guryev held forth about how badly the war was reported in the newspapers.

'Those sons of bitches never see any action themselves. They just sit on the other side of the Volga and write their articles. If someone gives them a good dinner, then they write about him. They're certainly no Tolstoys. People have been reading *War and Peace* for a century and they'll go on reading it for another century. Why's that? Because Tolstoy's a soldier, because he took part in the war himself. That's how he knew who to write about.'

'Excuse me, comrade General,' said Krymov. 'Tolstoy didn't take part in the Patriotic War.'

'He didn't take part in it – what do you mean?'

'Just that,' said Krymov. 'He didn't take part in it. He hadn't even been born at the time of the war with Napoleon.'

'He hadn't been born?' said Guryev. 'What do you mean? How on earth?'

A furious argument then developed – the first to have followed any of Krymov's lectures. To his surprise, the general flatly refused to believe him.

57

The divisional commander asked Major Byerozkin about the position with regard to house 6/1. Should they withdraw?

Byerozkin advised against it – even though the building was indeed almost totally surrounded. It housed observation posts of great importance to the artillery on the left bank, and a sapper detachment able to prevent any further attacks by German tanks. The Germans were hardly likely to begin a major offensive without first liquidating this little pocket of resistance – their tactics were predictable enough. And with a minimum of support the building might be able to hold out for some time and disrupt the German strategy. Since the telephone cable had been cut repeatedly, and since signallers were only able to reach the building during a few hours in the middle of the night, it would be worth sending a radio-operator there.

The divisional commander agreed. During the night Political Instructor Soshkin managed to get through to house 6/1 with a group of soldiers. They brought with them several boxes of ammunition, hand-grenades, a radio set and a very young operator, a girl.

On his return the following morning, Soshkin said that the commander of the detachment holding the house had refused to write an official report. 'I haven't got time for any of that rubbish,' he had said. 'I give my reports to the Fritzes.'

'I can't make head or tail of what's going on there,' said Soshkin. 'They all seem terrified of this Grekov, but he just pretends to be one of the lads. They all go to sleep in a heap on the floor, Grekov included, and they call him Vanya. Forgive me for saying so, but it's more like some kind of Paris Commune than a military unit.'

Byerozkin shook his head. 'So he refused to write a report. Well, he is a one!'

Pivovarov, the battalion commissar, then came out with a speech about people behaving like partisans.

'What do you mean — "like partisans"?' said Byerozkin in a conciliatory tone. 'It's just independence, a show of initiative. I often dream of being surrounded myself — so I could forget all this paper-work.'

'That reminds me,' said Pivovarov. 'You'd better write a detailed report for the divisional commissar.'

The divisional commissar took a serious view of all this. He ordered Pivovarov to obtain detailed information about the situation in house 6/1 and to give Grekov a good talking-to then and there. At the same time he wrote reports to the Member of the Military Soviet and to the head of the Army Political Section, informing them of the alarming state of affairs, both morally and politically, in house 6/1.

At Army level, Soshkin's report was taken still more seriously. The divisional commissar received instructions to sort the matter out with the utmost urgency. The head of the Army Political Section also sent an urgent report to the head of the Political Section for the Front.

Katya Vengrova, the radio-operator, had arrived in house 6/1 during the night. In the morning she reported to Grekov, the 'house-manager'. As he listened, Grekov gazed into her eyes; they seemed confused, frightened, and at the same time mocking.

She was round-shouldered and she had a large mouth with pale, bloodless lips. Grekov paused for a moment when Katya asked if she could go. A number of different thoughts, all quite unrelated to the war, flashed through his head: 'By God, she's pretty . . . nice legs . . . she looks frightened . . . I guess she's mother's little girl . . . How old is she . . . ? Eighteen at the most . . . I just hope the lads don't all pounce on her . . .' His final thought was quite unrelated to those that had gone before: 'Can't you see who's boss here? Haven't I driven those Fritzes up the wall?'

'There isn't anywhere for you to go,' Grekov said at last. 'Just stay by your transmitter. We'll find you something to send soon enough.'

He tapped the transmitter and glanced up at the sky where German dive-bombers were whining and humming.

'Are you from Moscow?' he asked.

'Yes.'

'Sit down. We're quite without ceremony here. It's like being in the country.'

Katya stepped to one side; crumbled brick squeaked beneath her heels. She could see the sunlight glinting on the machine-gun barrels and on the dark metal of Grekov's German pistol. She sat down, looking at a pile of greatcoats beneath a ruined wall. For a moment she felt surprised that all this no longer surprised her. She knew that the machine-guns in the breach in the wall were Degterevs; that the captured Walther took eight bullets, that it was powerful but difficult to aim; that the greatcoats in the corner belonged to soldiers who had been killed and that the corpses hadn't been buried very deep – the general smell of burning blended with another smell that had already become all too familiar. And her wireless-set was just like the one she had worked with in Kotluban – the same dial on the receiver, the same switch. She remembered the times in the steppes when she had looked into the dusty glass of the ammeter and tidied her hair, smoothing it back under her cap.

No one spoke to her; it was as though she had nothing to do with the wild and terrible goings-on around her.

But when one grey-haired man started swearing – he seemed from the conversation to be a mortar man – Grekov chided: 'Softly now! That's no way to speak in front of our girl.'

Katya winced – not because of the old man's foul language, but because of the way Grekov had looked at her. Even though no one said anything to her, she knew that the atmosphere had changed since her arrival. She could feel the tension with her skin – a tension that didn't evaporate even when they heard the whine of dive-bombers, followed by explosions and a hail of broken brick.

By now Katya had grown used to falling bombs and the whistle of shrapnel, but she felt as confused as ever by the heavy male looks that bore down on her here.

The night before, the other girls had commiserated with her. 'It sounds quite terrifying there,' they had said.

A soldier had taken her to Regimental Headquarters. She had

sensed at once how close she was to the enemy, how fragile life had become. People themselves seemed suddenly fragile – here one minute, gone the next.

The officer in command had shaken his head sadly and said: 'How can they send children like you to the front?' And then: 'Don't be frightened, my dear. If anything's not as it should be, just inform me over the radio.'

He had said this in such a kind, fatherly voice that it was all she could do not to burst into tears.

She had then been taken to Battalion Headquarters. They had a gramophone there; the commander, a redhead, offered Katya a drink and invited her to dance to a record of 'The Chinese Serenade'.

The atmosphere there had been terrifying. Katya had felt that the commander was drinking not to enjoy himself, but simply to stifle some unbearable fear, to forget that his own life was now as fragile as glass.

And now here she was – sitting on a heap of bricks in house 6/1. For some reason she didn't feel any fear at all; instead, she thought of the wonderful, fairy-tale life she had enjoyed before the war.

The men in the surrounded building seemed extraordinarily strong and sure of themselves. This self-confidence was very reassuring – like that possessed by firemen, by tailors cutting some priceless cloth, by skilled workers in a metal-rolling mill, by old teachers expounding beside their blackboards, by eminent doctors.

Before the war Katya had always believed that her life was doomed to be unhappy. When she had seen friends of hers going anywhere by bus, she had thought them spendthrifts. As for people coming out of restaurants – however bad – they seemed like fabulous beings; sometimes she had followed a little group on their way home from some 'Daryal' or 'Terek' and tried to listen to their conversation. Returning home from school, she would announce solemnly: 'Guess what happened today! A girl gave me some fizzy water with syrup – real syrup that tasted of blackcurrants!'

To live on what remained – after the deduction of income tax, cultural tax and the State loan – of her mother's salary of 400 roubles had been far from easy. Instead of buying new clothes, they had always refashioned their old ones. The other tenants had paid Marusya, the caretaker's wife, to clean the communal areas, but they had done their share themselves; Katya herself had cleaned the floors and carried out the rubbish. They had bought milk at the State shop – the queues were enormous but it saved them six roubles a month; if there wasn't any milk in the State shop, then Katya's mother had gone to market late in the afternoon – the peasant women would be in a hurry to catch the evening train and would sell off their milk at almost the same price as in the State shop. They had never travelled by bus, and they only went by tram if they had to go a very long distance. Instead of going to the hairdresser's, Katya had always had her hair cut by her mother. They had done their own laundry and the light-bulb in their room was almost as dim as those in the communal areas. They had cooked for three days at a time. They had soup, and sometimes *kasha* with a little oil; once Katya had had three plates of soup one after the other and said: 'Well, today we've had a three-course meal.'

Her mother had never talked about how things had been while her father still lived with them; she herself couldn't remember. Once, Vera Dmitrievna, a friend of her mother's, had watched the two of them preparing a meal and said: 'Yes, we too had our hour of glory.' This had made her mother angry; she hadn't allowed Vera Dmitrievna to enlarge on how things had been during their hour of glory.

One day Katya had found a photograph of her father in a cupboard. It was the first time she had seen a photograph of him, but she knew immediately who it was. On the back was written: 'To Lida – I am from the tribe of Asra: when we love, we die in silence.'* She said nothing to her mother, but from then on, when she returned from school, she would often take the photograph out and gaze for a long time into her father's dark, melancholy eyes.

Once she had asked: 'Where's Papa now?'

Her mother had just said: 'I don't know.'

It was only when Katya left for the army that her mother at last told her about him; she learned that he had married again and that he had been arrested in 1937.

They had talked right through the night. Everything had been reversed: her mother, usually so reserved, had told her how she had been abandoned by her husband; she had talked about her feelings of jealousy, of humiliation and hurt, of love and pity. Katya had been

* A quotation from a poem by Heine.

quite astonished: the world of the human soul suddenly seemed so vast as to make even the raging war seen insignificant. In the morning they had said goodbye. Her mother had drawn her head towards her, but the pack on her shoulders had pulled her away. Katya had said: 'Mama, I'm from the tribe of Asra: when we love, we die in silence.'

Then her mother had gently pushed her away.

'Go on, Katya. It's time you left.'

And Katya had left – like millions of others, both young and old. She had left her mother's house, perhaps never to return, perhaps to return only as a different person, cut off for ever from her harsh and beloved childhood.

And now here she was, sitting next to Grekov, 'the house-manager', looking at his large head, at his frowning face and thick lips.

58

That first day, the telephone was still working; there was nothing for Katya to do. The feeling of being excluded from the life of the building became increasingly oppressive. Nevertheless, that day did much to prepare her for what lay in store.

She learned that the observation-post for the artillery on the left bank was situated in the ruins of the first floor. It was commanded by a lieutenant in a dirty tunic whose spectacles kept slipping down his snub nose.

The angry old man who swore a lot had been transferred from the militia; he was very proud indeed to be in command of a mortar team. The sappers were installed between a high wall and a heap of rubble; they were commanded by a stout man who groaned and grimaced when he walked, as though he was suffering from corns.

The single piece of artillery was in the charge of Kolomeitsev, a bald man in a sailor's tunic. Katya had heard Grekov shout: 'Kolomeitsev! Wake up! You've just slept through yet another golden opportunity!'

The infantry and the machine-guns were commanded by a second lieutenant with a blond beard. The beard made his face seem very young – though he no doubt imagined it made him look mature, perhaps in his thirties.

In the afternoon she was given something to eat – bread and mutton-sausage. Then she remembered she had a sweet in her tunic-pocket and slipped it quietly into her mouth. After that – in spite of the firing nearby – she felt like a nap. She soon fell asleep, still sucking her sweet; but even in her sleep she still felt a sense of anguish, of imminent disaster. Suddenly she heard a slow, drawling voice. Her eyes still closed, she listened to the words:

> 'Past sorrow is to me like wine,
> Stronger with every passing year.'*

In this stone well, lit by the amber evening light, a dirty young man with dishevelled hair was sitting reading out loud from a book. Five or six men were sprawled around him on piles of red bricks. Grekov was lying on his overcoat, resting his chin on his fists. One young man, probably a Georgian, listened with an air of suspicion. It was as though he were saying: 'Come on now – you won't get me to buy this rubbish.'

An explosion close by raised a cloud of dust. It was like something from a fairy-tale; the armed men, sitting on blood-coloured bricks and surrounded by this red mist, seemed to have sprung from the day of judgment recorded in the *Lay of Igor's Campaign*.** Suddenly Katya's heart stirred in an absurd expectation of some future happiness.

The following day, an event took place which appalled even these hardened soldiers.

The 'senior tenant' on the first floor, Lieutenant Batrakov, had under his command an observer, Bunchuk, and a plotter, Lampasov. Katya saw them all several times a day: sullen Lampasov, cunning yet simple-hearted Bunchuk and the strange lieutenant with glasses who was always smiling at his own thoughts. When it was quiet, she could even hear their voices through the hole in the ceiling.

Lampasov had reared chickens before the war; he loved telling Bunchuk about the intelligence and treacherous ways of his hens.

---

* From a short lyric of Pushkin's.
** An anonymous twelfth-century epic poem.

Peering through his telescope, Bunchuk would report in a sing-song voice: 'Yes, there's a column of vehicles coming from Kalach . . . a tank in the middle . . . Some more Fritzes on foot, a whole battalion . . . and then three field-kitchens just like yesterday . . . I can see smoke and some Fritzes with pans . . .' Some of his observations were of greater human than military interest: 'Now there's a German officer going for a walk with his dog . . . the dog's sniffing a post, it probably wants to pee . . . Yes, it must be a bitch . . . The officer's just standing there, he's having a scratch . . . Now I can see two girls chatting to some Fritzes . . . they're offering the girls cigarettes . . . One of them's lit up, the other's shaking her head . . . She must be saying: "I don't smoke".'

Suddenly, in the same sing-song voice, Bunchuk announced: 'The square's full of soldiers . . . and a band . . . there's a stage in the middle . . . no, a pile of wood . . .'

He fell silent. Then, in the same voice, now full of despair, he went on: 'Comrade Lieutenant, I can see a woman in a shift . . . she's being frog-marched . . . she's screaming . . . the band's struck up . . . they're tying the woman to a post . . . Comrade Lieutenant, there's a little boy with her . . . Ay . . . they're tying him up . . . Comrade Lieutenant, I can't bear to look . . . two Fritzes are emptying some cans of petrol . . .'

Batrakov hurriedly reported all this by telephone to the left bank. Then he grabbed the telescope himself.

'Ay, comrades, the band's playing and the whole square's full of smoke . . .'

'Fire!' he suddenly howled out in a terrible voice and turned in the direction of the left bank.

Not a sound from the left bank . . .

A few seconds passed, and then the place of execution was subjected to a concentrated barrage by the heavy artillery. The square was enveloped in dust and smoke.

Several hours later, they were informed by their scout, Klimov, that the Germans had been about to burn a gypsy woman and her son whom they suspected of being spies. The day before, Klimov had left some dirty washing with an old woman who lived in a cellar together with her granddaughter and a goat; he had promised to come back for it later when it was ready. Now he intended to ask this woman what had happened to the two gypsies – whether they had been burned to death on the pyre or killed by the Soviet shells.

Klimov crawled through the ruins along paths known to him alone – only to find that the old woman's dwelling had just been destroyed by a Russian bomb. There was nothing left of the old woman, her granddaughter or the goat – or of Klimov's pants and shirt. All he found among the splintered beams and lumps of plaster was a kitten, covered with dirt. It was in a pitiful state, neither complaining nor asking for anything, evidently believing that life was always just a matter of noise, fire and hunger.

Klimov had no idea what made him suddenly stuff the kitten into his pocket.

Katya was astonished by the relations between the inmates of house 6/1. Instead of standing to attention to give his report, Klimov simply sat down next to Grekov; they then talked together like two old friends. Klimov lit up from Grekov's cigarette.

When he had finished, Klimov went up to Katya. 'Yes, my girl,' he said, 'life on this earth can be terrible.'

Under his hard, penetrating stare, Katya blushed and gave a sigh. Klimov took the kitten out of his pocket and placed it on a brick beside her.

During the course of the day at least a dozen men came up to Katya and started to talk about cats; not one of them spoke about the gypsies, though they had all been deeply shocked. Some of them wanted a sentimental, heart-to-heart conversation – and spoke coarsely and mockingly; others just wanted to sleep with her – and spoke very solemnly, with cloying politeness.

The kitten trembled constantly, evidently in a state of shock.

'You should do away with it right now,' the old man in charge of the mortars said with a grimace – and then added: 'You must pick off the fleas.'

Another member of the mortar-crew, the handsome, swarthy Chentsov, also a former member of the militia, urged: 'Get rid of that vermin, my girl. Now, if it were a Siberian cat . . .'

The sullen Lyakhov, a sapper with thin lips and an unpleasant-looking face, was the only man to be genuinely concerned about the kitten and indifferent to the charms of the radio-operator.

'Once, when we were in the steppe,' he told her, 'something

suddenly hit me. I thought it must be a shell at the end of its trajectory. But guess what? It was a hare. He stayed with me till evening. Then things quietened down a bit and he left.

'Now, you may be a girl,' he went on, 'but at least you can understand: that's a 108 millimetre, that's the tune of a Vanyusha, that's a reconnaissance plane flying over the Volga ... But the poor stupid hare can't make out anything at all. He can't even tell the difference between a mortar and a howitzer. The Germans send up a flare and he just sits there and shakes – you can't explain anything to him. That's what makes me sorry for these dumb animals.'

Recognizing that he was in earnest, Katya responded in the same tone. 'I don't know ... Take dogs, for example – they can tell different planes apart. When we were stationed in the village, there was a mongrel called Kerzon. When our ILs flew over, he just lay there without even raising his head. But as soon as he heard the whine of a Junkers, he went straight to his hiding-place. He never once made a mistake.'

The air was rent by a piercing scream – a German Vanyusha. There was a metallic crash, a cloud of black smoke mixed with red dust, and a shower of rubble. A minute later, when the dust began to settle, Katya and Lyakhov resumed their conversation – for all the world as though it was two different people who had just fallen flat on their faces. The self-assurance of these soldiers seemed to have rubbed off on Katya. It was as though they were convinced that everything here, even the iron and stone, might be weak and fragile – but not they themselves.

A burst of machine-gun fire whistled over their heads, then another.

'This spring we were stationed near Sviatogorsk,' Lyakhov told her. 'Once there was a terrible whistling right over our heads, but we couldn't hear any shots. We didn't know what on earth was happening. It turned out to be the starlings imitating bullets ... The lieutenant had even put us on alert – they did it perfectly.'

'When I was at home,' said Katya, smiling, 'I imagined that war would be a matter of lost cats, children screaming and blazing buildings. That seems to be just how it is.'

The next man to approach her was the bearded Zubarev.

'Well,' he asked sympathetically, 'and how's our little man with the tail?'

He lifted up the scrap of cloth that had been laid over the kitten.

'Poor little thing. You do look weak!' As he said this, his eyes gleamed insolently.

That evening, after a brief skirmish, the Germans managed to advance a short distance along the flank of the building; now their machine-guns covered the path leading back to the Soviet lines. The telephone link with Battalion Headquarters was severed again. Grekov ordered a passage to be blasted to link up with a nearby tunnel.

'We'll use the dynamite,' said Antsiferov, the sergeant-major – a stout man with a mug of tea in one hand and a sugar-lump in the other.

The other inmates were sitting in a pit at the foot of the main wall and talking. As before, no one mentioned the two gypsies; nor did they seem worried at being encircled.

This calm seemed strange to Katya; nevertheless, she submitted to it herself. Even the dreaded word 'encirclement' no longer held any terrors for her. Nor was she frightened when a machine-gun opened up right next to them and Grekov shouted: 'Fire! *Fire*! Look – they've got right in!' Nor when Grekov ordered: 'Use whatever's to hand – knives, spades, grenades. You know your job. Kill the bastards – it doesn't matter how.'

During the few quiet moments, the men engaged in a long and detailed discussion of Katya's physical appearance. The short-sighted Batrakov, who had always seemed to live in another world, turned out to be surprisingly interested.

'All I care about are a woman's tits,' he said.

Kolomeitsev disagreed. He – in Zubarev's words – preferred to call a spade a spade.

'So have you talked to her about the cat, then?' asked Zubarev.

'Of course,' said Batrakov. 'Even old grey-beard here's had a chat with her about that.'

The old man in command of the mortars spat and drew his hand across his chest.

'Really! I ask you! Does she have what makes a woman a woman?'

He got particularly angry if anyone hinted that Grekov might have his eye on her.

'Well, of course! To us, even a Katya seems passable. In the country of the blind . . . She's got legs like a stork, no arse worth speaking of, and great cow-like eyes. Call that a woman?'

'You just like big tits,' Chentsov retorted. 'That's an outmoded, pre-revolutionary point of view.'

Kolomeitsev, a coarse, foul-mouthed man, whose large bald head concealed many surprising contradictions, said: 'She's not a bad girl, but I'm very particular. I like them small, preferably Armenian or Jewish, with large quick eyes and short hair.'

Zubarev looked thoughtfully at the dark sky criss-crossed by the beams of searchlights. 'Well, I wonder how it will work out in the end.'

'You mean who she'll end up with?' said Kolomeitsev. 'Grekov — that's obvious.'

'Far from it,' said Zubarev. 'It's not in the least obvious.' He picked up a piece of brick and hurled it against the wall.

The others laughed.

'I see! You're going to charm her with the down on your chin, are you?' said Batrakov.

'No,' said Kolomeitsev, 'he's going to sing. They're going to make a programme together: "Infantry at the microphone". He'll sing and she'll broadcast it into the ether. They'll make a fine pair!'

Zubarev looked round at the boy who'd been reading poetry the evening before. 'And how about you?'

'If he doesn't say anything, it's because he doesn't want to,' said the old grey-beard warningly. Then he turned to the boy and said in a fatherly way, as though he were rebuking his son for listening to the grown-ups: 'You'd do better to go down to the cellar and get some sleep while you can.'

'Antsiferov's down there right now with his dynamite,' said Batrakov.

Meanwhile Grekov was dictating to Katya. He informed Army Headquarters that the Germans were almost certainly preparing an offensive and that it would almost certainly be directed at the Tractor Factory. What he didn't say was that house 6/1 appeared to lie on the very axis of this offensive. But as he looked at Katya's thin little neck, at her lips, at her half-lowered eyelashes, he saw an all-too-vivid picture of a broken neck with pearly vertebrae poking out through lacerated skin, of two glassed-over, fish-like eyes, and of lips like grey, dusty rubber.

He was longing to seize hold of her, to feel her life and warmth while they were both alive, while this young being was still full of grace and charm. He thought it was just pity that made him want to embrace the girl – but does pity make your temples throb and your ears buzz?

Headquarters were slow to answer. Grekov stretched till every joint in his body began to crack, gave a loud sigh, thought, 'It's all right, we've got the night ahead of us,' and asked tenderly: 'How's Klimov's kitten getting on? Is he getting his strength back?'

'Far from it,' answered Katya.

She thought about the gypsies on the bonfire. Her hands were shaking. She glanced at Grekov to see if he'd noticed.

Yesterday she'd thought that no one in this building was ever going to talk to her; today the bearded second lieutenant, tommy-gun in hand, had rushed by as she was eating her *kasha* and called out as though they were old friends: 'Don't just pick at it, Katya!' He had gestured at her to show how she ought to plunge her spoon into the pot.

She had seen the boy who'd read the poem yesterday carrying some mortar-bombs on a tarpaulin. Later she had looked round and seen him standing by the water-boiler. Realizing he was watching her, she had looked away, but by then he had already turned away himself.

She already knew who would start showing her letters and photographs tomorrow, who would look at her in silence and sigh, who would bring her a present of half a flask of water and some rusks of white bread, who would say he didn't believe in women's love and would never fall in love again . . . As for the bearded second lieutenant, he would probably start pawing her.

Finally an answer came through from Headquarters. Katya started to repeat the message to Grekov.

'Your orders are to make a detailed report every day at twelve hundred hours precisely . . .'

Grekov suddenly knocked Katya's hand off the switch. She let out a cry.

He grinned and said: 'A fragment from a mortar-bomb has put the wireless-set out of action. Contact will be re-established when it suits Grekov.'

Katya gaped at him in astonishment.

'I'm sorry, Katyusha,' said Grekov and took her by the hand.

59

In the early morning Divisional Headquarters were informed by Byerozkin's regiment that the men in house 6/1 had excavated a passage into one of the concrete tunnels belonging to the Tractor Factory; some of them were now in the factory itself. A duty-officer at Divisional HQ informed Army HQ, where it was then reported to General Krylov himself. Krylov ordered one of the men to be brought to him for questioning. A signals officer was detailed to take a young boy, chosen by the duty-officer, to Army HQ. They walked down a ravine leading to the bank; on the way the boy kept turning round and anxiously asking questions.

'I must go back home. My instructions were to reconnoitre the tunnel – so we could evacuate the wounded.'

'Never mind,' said the officer. 'You're about to see someone a little senior to your own boss. You have to do as he says.'

On the way the boy told the officer how they had been in house 6/1 for over two weeks, how they'd lived for some time on a cache of potatoes they'd found in the cellar, how they'd drunk the water from the central heating system, and had given the Germans such a hard time that they'd sent an envoy with an offer of free passage to the factory. Naturally their commander – the boy referred to him as the 'house-manager' – had replied by ordering them all to open fire. When they reached the Volga, the boy lay down and began to drink; he then shook the drops from his jacket onto the palm of his hand and licked them off. It was as though he were starving and they were crumbs of bread. He explained that the water in the central heating system had been foul. To begin with, they had all had stomach-upsets, but then the house-manager had ordered them to boil the water and they had recovered.

They walked on in silence. The boy listened to the sound of the bombers and looked up at the night sky, now decorated by red and green flares and the curved trajectories of tracer-bullets and shells. He saw the glow of the guttering fires in the town, the white flame of the guns and the blue columns of water sent up by shells falling in the Volga. His pace gradually slackened, till finally the officer shouted: 'Come on now! Look lively!'

They made their way between the rocks on the bank; mortar-bombs whistled over their heads and they were constantly challenged by sentries. Then they climbed a little path that wound up the slope between the bunkers and trenches. Sometimes there were duck-boards underfoot, sometimes steps cut into the clay. Finally they reached the Headquarters of the 62nd Army. The officer straightened his belt and made his way down a communication trench towards some bunkers constructed from particularly solid logs.

The sentry went to call an aide; through a half-open door they glimpsed the soft light of an electric lamp under its shade. The aide shone his torch at them, asked the boy's name and told them to wait.

'But how am I going to get back home?' asked the boy.

'All roads lead to Kiev,' answered the aide. He then added sternly: 'Go on now – get inside! Otherwise you'll get yourself killed by a mortar-bomb and I'll have to answer for you to the general.'

The boy sat down in the warm, dark entranceway, leant against the wall and fell asleep.

In his dreams the terrible cries and screams of the last few days blurred together with the quiet, peaceful murmur of his own home – a home that no longer existed. Then someone shook him and he heard an angry voice:

'Shaposhnikov! You're wanted by the general! Look lively!'

60

Seryozha Shaposhnikov spent two days at Army HQ. He found it oppressive. People seemed to hang around all day doing nothing.

Somehow it reminded him of the time he had spent eight hours in Rostov with his grandmother, waiting for the train to Sochi – he laughed at the absurd idea of comparing house 6/1 to a holiday resort.

He kept begging the chief of staff to let him go, but the latter had had no definite instructions from the general. The general had already spoken to Shaposhnikov, but after two questions their conversation had been interrupted by a telephone call from his commanding officer. The chief of staff preferred not to let the boy go for the time being – the general might still remember him.

Every time the chief of staff came into the bunker, he felt Shaposhnikov looking at him. Sometimes he said: 'Don't worry, I haven't forgotten,' but at other times the boy's constant look of entreaty really got under his skin. 'Anyway,' he demanded, 'what are you complaining about? It's nice and warm here and you get lots of food. There'll be time enough to get yourself killed back at the front.'

When a man is plunged up to his neck into the cauldron of war, he is quite unable to look at his life and understand anything; he needs to take a step back. Then, like someone who has just reached the bank of a river, he can look round: was he really, only a moment ago, in the midst of those swirling waters?

Seryozha's old life in the militia regiment now seemed almost unbelievably peaceful: sentry-duty at night in the steppe, a distant glow in the sky, the soldiers' conversations . . .

Life in house 6/1 had blotted out everything that had gone before. Improbable though this life was, it now seemed the only reality; it was as if everything before was imaginary. Only now and then, at night, did he feel a sudden twinge, a sudden surge of love as he imagined Alexandra Vladimirovna's grey head or Aunt Zhenya's quick, mocking eyes.

During his first days in house 6/1 he had thought how strange and impossible it would be if people like Grekov, Kolomeitsev and Antsiferov were suddenly to appear at home . . . Now he sometimes thought how absurd his aunts, his cousin and Uncle Viktor would seem if they were suddenly to become part of his present life.

Heavens! If his grandmother could hear the way he swore now . . .

Grekov!

He wasn't sure whether these men had always been exceptional, or whether they had only become exceptional on arriving in house 6/1.

Grekov! What an extraordinary combination of strength, daring, authority and common sense. He remembered the price of children's shoes before the war; he knew the wages of a machinist or a cleaning lady, how much grain and money the peasants received for each unit of work on the collective farm where his uncle lived.

Sometimes he talked about how things had been in the army before the war: the purges, the constant examinations, the bribes you had to pay for an apartment. He talked about men who'd became generals in 1937 by writing dozens of statements and denunciations unmasking supposed enemies of the people.

Sometimes his strength seemed to lie in his mad bravery, in the gay desperation with which he would leap up from a breach in the wall, throw hand-grenades at the advancing Germans and shout: 'No you don't, you swine!' At other times it seemed to lie in his easy-going simplicity, in the way he could be friends with everyone in the house.

There was nothing exceptional about his life before the war: he had been a foreman, first in a mine, then on a building site, before becoming an infantry captain in a unit stationed on the outskirts of Minsk; he had studied both in the barracks and in the field and had gone to Minsk for further training; in the evening he had read a little, drunk vodka, gone to the cinema, played cards with his friends and quarrelled with his wife, who was jealous, not without reason, of a large number of the women and girls in the district. Grekov had revealed all this quite freely. And now – in Seryozha's eyes and in the eyes of many others – he had suddenly become a legendary warrior, a crusader for truth.

New people had entered Seryozha's life, taking the place even of his nearest and dearest.

Kolomeitsev had been in the Navy. He had served on various ships and had been sunk three times in the Baltic. For all his contempt for many highly-esteemed figures, Kolomeitsev always showed the greatest respect for scientists and writers. Seryozha found this very appealing. No military commander, whatever his rank, was of the least importance beside a bald Lobachevsky or an ailing Romain Rolland.

Kolomeitsev's views on literature were very different indeed from what Chentsov had said about instructive, patriotic literature. There was one writer, either an American or an Englishman, whom he particularly liked. Seryozha had never read this writer and Kolomeit-sev couldn't even remember his name; nevertheless, Kolomeitsev

praised him so enthusiasti...
that Seryozha was convince...

'What I like about him,' s...
teach me anything. A bloke g...
pissed, an old man loses his wi...
you laugh, you feel sorry, and in...
all about.'

Kolomeitsev was a friend of V...

One day, Klimov and Shapos...
German lines. They climbed over th...
up to a bomb-crater that sheltered a h...
artillery officer. Pressed flat against t...
Germans go about their tasks. One you... ...cket,
tucked a red checked handkerchief under ... ...gan shaving;
Seryozha could hear the scrape of the ra... ...ainst his wiry, dust-
covered stubble. Another German was eating something out of a small
flat tin; for a brief moment Seryozha saw his face take on a look of
concentrated, lasting pleasure. The officer was winding up his watch.
Seryozha felt like asking very quietly, so as not to frighten him: 'Hey!
What time is it?'

Klimov took the pin out of a grenade and dropped it into the crater.
Before the dust had settled, he threw another grenade after it and then
jumped in himself. The Germans were all dead; it was hard to believe
they could have been alive only a moment before. Sneezing at the dust
and gas, Klimov took what he needed – the breech-block from the
machine-gun, a pair of binoculars and the watch from the officer's still
warm wrist. Very carefully, so as not to get stained with blood, he
removed the soldiers' papers from the remains of their uniforms.

When they got back, Klimov handed over his prizes, described
what had happened, asked Seryozha to splash a little water over his
hands, then sat down next to Kolomeitsev, saying: 'Now we can have a
fag.'

Just then Perfilev rushed up. He had once described himself as 'a
peaceful inhabitant of Ryazan who likes fishing'.

'Hey, Klimov! Don't make yourself too comfortable!' he shouted.
'The house-manager's looking for you. You've got to go behind the
German lines again.'

'All right,' said Klimov guiltily. 'I'm coming.'

belongings – a tommy-gun and a
... He handled objects very carefully, as
...raid of hurting them. He never swore and
...ryone in the polite form of the second person.
...aptist, are you?' old Polyakov once asked this man
...a hundred and ten people.

... was by no means taciturn, however, and he particularly
...alking about his childhood. His father had worked at the Putilov
...ctory. He himself had been a skilled lathe-operator; before the war
he had taught apprentices. He made Seryozha laugh with a story of
how one of his apprentices had nearly choked to death on a screw; he
had gone quite blue before Klimov managed to remove the screw with
a pair of pliers.

Once Seryozha saw Klimov after he had drunk a captured bottle of
schnapps; then he had been quite terrifying – even Grekov had seemed
wary of him.

The untidiest man in the building was Lieutenant Batrakov. He
never cleaned his boots and one of the soles flapped on the ground –
people didn't have to look up to know when he was coming. On the
other hand he cleaned his glasses hundreds of times a day with a small
piece of chamois; apparently the lenses were the wrong strength – it
was as if they were blurred by dust and smoke. Klimov had brought
him several pairs of German spectacles but, though the frames were
good, the lenses were no better than his own.

Before the war Batrakov had taught mathematics at a technical
school; he was very arrogant and he talked about his ignorant students
with disdain. He had put Seryozha through a full-scale maths exam;
everyone had laughed at his failure and told him he would have to
retake the course.

Once, during an air-raid, when earth, stone and iron were being
smashed apart by sledge-hammer blows, Grekov saw Batrakov sitting
on top of what was left of a staircase, reading a book.

'No,' said Grekov, 'the Germans haven't got a hope. What can they
do against madmen like that?'

Far from terrifying the inmates of the building, the German attacks
only succeeded in arousing a certain condescending irony: 'Hm, the
Fritzes really are having a go at it today!' 'Look what those maniacs are
doing now!' 'The fool – where does he think he's dropping his bombs?'

Batrakov was a friend of Antsiferov, the commander of the sapper detachment, a man in his forties who loved talking about his various chronic illnesses. This was unusual at the front: when people were under fire, ulcers and sciaticas usually cleared up of their own accord.

Even in Stalingrad, however, Antsiferov continued to suffer from the numerous diseases that had attacked his enormous body; captured German medicines were of no help. He had a large, bald head, a full face, and his eyes were round. At times there was something quite bizarre about him – especially when he was sitting in the sinister light cast by the distant fires and drinking tea with his soldiers. He suffered from corns and he always felt hot; usually he took off both his shoes and his tunic. There he would sit – sipping hot tea from a cup decorated with tiny blue flowers, wiping his bald head with a huge handkerchief, smiling, sighing and blowing into his cup. The sullen Lyakhov, a bandage round his head, would constantly refill this cup with boiling water from a soot-encrusted kettle. Sometimes Antsiferov would climb up on a small mound of bricks, wheezing and groaning, to see what was happening in the world. Bare-foot, with no shirt, he might have been a peasant coming to the door of his hut during a downpour to keep an eye on his garden.

Before the war he had been a foreman on a building site. His experience of construction now proved useful for the opposite purpose: he was constantly mulling over the best way to destroy cellars, walls, even entire buildings.

Most of his discussions with Batrakov were about philosophical matters. He evidently needed to think over this shift from construction to destruction, to find meaning in it. Sometimes, however, they left the heights of philosophy (Does life have a meaning? Does Soviet power exist in other galaxies? In what way is Man intellectually superior to Woman?) to touch on more mundane matters.

Stalingrad had changed everything; now the muddle-headed Batrakov seemed a man of wisdom.

'You know, Vanya,' said Antsiferov. 'It's only through you that I've begun to understand anything. I used to think there was nothing more I needed to know about life: all I had to do was to get new tyres for one person's car, give another some vodka and something to eat, and slip a hundred roubles to a third . . .'

Batrakov seriously believed that it really was his muddle-headed philosophizing – rather than Stalingrad itself – that had led Antsiferov to see people in a different light.

'Yes, my friend', he said condescendingly. 'It's a real pity we didn't meet before the war.'

The infantry were quartered in the cellar. It was they who had to beat off the German attacks and, at Grekov's piercing call, launch counter-attacks themselves.

Their commander, Lieutenant Zubarev, had studied singing at the Conservatory before the war. Sometimes he crept up to the German lines at night and began singing 'Don't Wake Me, Breath of Spring', or one of Lensky's arias from *Eugene Onegin*.

If anyone asked why he risked his life to sing among heaps of rubble, he wouldn't answer. It may have been from a desire to prove – to himself, to his comrades and even to the enemy – that life's grace and charm can never be erased by the powers of destruction, even in a place that stank day and night of decaying corpses.

Seryozha could hardly believe he had lived all his life without knowing Grekov, Kolomeitsev, Polyakov, Klimov, Batrakov and the bearded Zubarev. He himself had been brought up among intellectuals; he could now see the truth of the faith his grandmother had repeatedly affirmed in simple working people. He was also able to see where his grandmother had gone wrong: in spite of everything, she had thought of the workers as simple.

The men in house 6/1 were far from simple. One statement of Grekov's had particularly impressed Seryozha:

'No one has the right to lead other people like sheep. That's something even Lenin failed to understand. The purpose of a revolution is to free people. But Lenin just said: "In the past you were led badly, I'm going to lead you well."'

Seryozha had never heard such forthright condemnations of the NKVD bosses who had destroyed tens of thousands of innocent people in 1937. Nor had he heard people talk with such pain of the sufferings undergone by the peasantry during collectivization. It was Grekov who raised these matters most frequently, but Kolomeitsev and Batrakov talked of them too.

Every moment Seryozha spent at Army HQ – away from house 6/1 – seemed interminably wearisome. There was something quite absurd in conversations about the duty-roster, about who had been called to see which commanding officer. Instead, he tried to imagine what Polyakov, Kolomeitsev and Grekov were up to now.

It was evening; things would be quietening down. Probably they were talking yet again about Katya.

Once Grekov had decided on something, neither the Buddha nor Chuykov would be able to stop him. Yes, that building housed a bunch of strong, remarkable, desperate men. Zubarev would probably be singing his arias again . . . And she would be sitting there helplessly, awaiting her fate.

'I'll kill them!' he thought, not knowing who he had in mind.

What chance did he have? He'd never kissed a girl in his life. And those devils were experienced; they'd find it easy enough to make a fool of her.

He looked at the door of the bunker. Why had he never thought before of simply getting up, just like that, and leaving?

Seryozha got up, opened the door, and left.

Just then the duty-officer at Army HQ was instructed over the phone to send the soldier from the encircled building to Vasiliev, the head of the Political Section, as quickly as possible.

If the story of Daphnis and Chloe still touches people's hearts, it is not simply because their love was born in the shade of vines and under a blue sky. That story is repeated everywhere – in a stuffy basement smelling of fried cod, in a concentration-camp bunker, to the click of an accountant's abacus, in the dust-laden air of a cotton mill.

And now the story was being played out again to the accompaniment of the howl of dive-bombers – in a building where people nourished their filthy sweat-encrusted bodies on rotten potatoes and water from an ancient boiler, where instead of honey and dream-filled silence there was only noise, stench and rubble.

61

Pavel Andreyevich Andreyev, an old man who worked as a guard in the Central Power Station, received a letter from his daughter-in-law in Leninsk; his wife, Varvara Alexandrovna, had died of pneumonia.

After receiving this news Andreyev became very depressed. He called very rarely on his friends the Spiridonovs and usually spent the evening sitting by the door of the workers' hostel, watching the flashes of gunfire and the play of searchlights against the clouds. If anyone tried to start a conversation with him, he just remained silent. Thinking that the old man was hard of hearing, the speaker would repeat the question more loudly. Andreyev would then say: 'I can hear you. I'm not deaf, you know.'

His whole life had been reflected in that of his wife; everything good or bad that had happened to him, all his feelings of joy and sadness, had importance only in so far as he was able to see them reflected in her soul.

During a particularly heavy raid, when bombs of several tons were exploding around him, Andreyev had looked at the waves of earth, dust and smoke filling the power station and thought: 'Well, I wonder what my old woman would say now! Take a look at that, Varvara!'

But she was no longer alive.

It was as though the buildings destroyed by bombs and shells, the central courtyard ploughed up by the war – full of mounds of earth, heaps of twisted metal, damp acrid smoke and the yellow reptilian flames of slowly-burning insulators – represented what was left to him of his own life.

Had he really once sat here in a room filled with light? Had he really eaten his breakfast here before going to work – with his wife standing next to him wondering whether to give him a second helping?

Yes, all that remained for him now was a solitary death . . .

He suddenly remembered her as she had been in her youth, with bright eyes and sunburnt arms.

Well, it wouldn't be long now . . .

One evening he went slowly down the creaking steps to the Spiridonovs' bunker. Stepan Fyodorovich looked at his face and said: 'You having a hard time, Pavel Andreyevich?'

'You're still young, Stepan Fyodorovich. You're not as strong as I am. You can still find a way of consoling yourself. But I'm strong; I can go all the way.'

Vera looked up from the saucepan she was washing, unable for a moment to understand what the old man meant. Andreyev, who had no wish for anyone's sympathy, tried to change the subject.

'It's time you left, Vera. There are no hospitals here – nothing but tanks and planes.'

Vera smiled and shrugged her shoulders.

'Even people who've never set eyes on her before say she should cross over to the left bank,' Stepan Fyodorovich said angrily. 'Yesterday the Member of the Military Soviet came to our bunker. He just looked at Vera without saying a word. But once we were outside and he was about to get into his car, he started cursing me. "And you call yourself her father! What do you think you're doing? If you like, we can have her taken across the Volga in an armoured launch." But what can I do? She just refuses to go.'

He spoke with the fluency of someone who has been arguing day in day out about the same thing. Andreyev didn't say anything; he was looking at an all-too-familiar darn on his sleeve that was now coming undone.

'As if she's going to get any letters from her Viktorov here!' Stepan Fyodorovich went on. 'There's no postal service. Think how long we've been here – we haven't heard from Zhenya or Lyudmila or even from Grandmother . . . We haven't the least idea what's happened to Tolya and Seryozha.'

'Pavel Andreyevich got a letter,' said Vera.

'Hardly a letter. Just a notification of death,' replied Stepan Fyodorovich. Shocked at his own words, he gestured impatiently at the walls of the bunker and the curtain that screened off Vera's bunk. 'And this is no place for a young woman – what with workers and military guards around day and night, all of them smoking like chimneys and shouting their heads off.'

'You might at least take pity on the child,' said Andreyev. 'It's not going to last long here.'

'And what if the Germans break through?' said Stepan Fyodorovich. 'What then?'

Vera didn't answer. She had convinced herself that one day she would glimpse Viktorov coming through the ruined gates of the power station. She would catch sight of him in the distance – in his flying suit and boots, his map-case at his side.

Sometimes she went out onto the road to see if he was coming. Soldiers going past in lorries would shout out: 'Come on, my beautiful. Who are you waiting for? Come and join us!'

For a moment she would recover her gaiety and shout back: 'Your lorry can't get through where I'm going.'

She would stare at Soviet fighters flying low overhead, feeling certain that any moment she would recognize Viktorov. Once a fighter dipped its wings in greeting. Vera cried out like a desperate bird, ran a few steps, stumbled, and fell to the ground; after that she had back-ache for several days.

At the end of October she saw a dogfight over the power station itself. It ended indecisively; the Russian planes flew up into the clouds and the Germans turned back to the West. Vera just stood there, gazing up into the empty sky. Her dilated eyes looked so full of tension that a technician going through the yard asked: 'Are you all right, comrade Spiridonova? You're not hurt?'

She was certain that it was here, in the power station, that she would meet Viktorov; she couldn't tell her father, however, or the angry Fates would prevent this meeting. Sometimes she felt so certain that she would jump up, bake some rye-and-potato pasties, sweep the floor, clean her dirty boots and tidy everything up . . . Sometimes, sitting with her father at table, she would listen for a moment and say: 'Just a second,' then throw her coat over her shoulders, climb up, and look round to see if there was a pilot in the yard, asking how to get to the Spiridonovs'.

Never, not even for one moment, did she think he might have forgotten her. She was sure that Viktorov thought about her day and night, just as she thought about him.

The power station was bombarded by heavy artillery almost every day. The Germans had found the range and their shells fell right inside the building; the ground was constantly shaken by the roar of explosions. Sometimes solitary bombers would fly over and drop their bombs. Low-flying Messerschmidts would strafe the station with their machine-guns. Occasionally German tanks appeared on the distant hills and you could hear the quick chatter of small-arms.

Stepan Fyodorovich, like the other workers, appeared quite accustomed to the bombs and shells, but they were all of them living on their last reserves of energy. Sometimes he felt overwhelmed by a sense of exhaustion; he just wanted to lie down, pull his jacket over his face and be still. Sometimes he got drunk. Sometimes he wanted to run to the Volga, cross over and make his way through the steppe without once looking back. He even felt ready to accept the shame of desertion – anything to escape the terrible whine of bombs and shells. Once he spoke to Moscow over the radio. The Deputy People's Commissar said: 'Comrade Spiridonov, greetings from Moscow to the heroic collective of which you are the leader!' This merely made Spiridonov feel embarrassed – it was hardly a matter of heroism. And then there were constant rumours that the Germans were preparing a massive raid on the power station, that they were determined to raze it to the ground with gigantic bombs. Rumours like that made his hands and feet go quite cold. All day long he would keep squinting up at the grey sky. At night he would suddenly jump out of bed, thinking he had heard the taut hum of the approaching German squadrons; his chest and his back would be covered in sweat.

He evidently wasn't the only person with frayed nerves. Chief Engineer Kamyshov once told him: 'I can't take any more. I keep imagining something terrible. Then I look at the road and think: "God, why don't I just scarper?"' And Nikolayev, the Party organizer, came round one night and said: 'Give me a drop of vodka, Stepan Fyodorovich. I've run out myself and I can't get to sleep without my anti-bomb medicine.' As he filled the glass, Stepan Fyodorovich said: 'You live and learn. I should have chosen a job with equipment that's easy to evacuate. But these turbines are nailed to the ground – and so are we. All the other factories were moved to Sverdlovsk months ago.'

'I just don't understand it,' Stepan Fyodorovich said to Vera one day. 'Everyone else keeps on at me to let them go. I've heard every excuse under the sun. And you still refuse, no matter what I say. If I had any choice in the matter, I'd be off right now!'

'I'm staying here because of you,' she answered bluntly. 'If it weren't for me, you'd be drinking like a fish.'

For all of this, Stepan Fyodorovich did more than sit there and tremble. There was also hard work, courage, laughter and the intoxicating sense of living out a merciless fate.

Vera was constantly tormented by anxiety about her child. She was afraid that it would be born sickly, that it would have been harmed by the life she led in this suffocating, smoke-filled cellar whose floor and walls were constantly shaken by explosions. She often felt sick and dizzy herself. What a sad, frightened baby it would be if its mother had had nothing to feed her eyes on but ruins, fire, tortured earth and a grey sky full of aeroplanes with black swastikas. Maybe it could hear the roar of explosions even now; maybe it cringed at the howl of the bombs, pulling its tiny head back into its contorted body.

But then there were the men – men in overcoats covered in oil and fastened at the waist with soldiers' canvas belts – who smiled and waved as they ran past, calling out: 'How are things, Vera? Vera, do you ever think of me?' Yes, she could sense a great tenderness around her. Maybe her little one would feel it, too; maybe he would grow up pure and kind-hearted.

Sometimes she looked inside the workshop used for repairing tanks. Viktorov had worked there once. She tried to guess which bench he had stood at. She tried to imagine him in his working clothes or his flying uniform, but she kept seeing him in a white hospital gown.

Everyone knew her there, the workers themselves and the soldiers from the tank corps. In fact, it was impossible to tell them apart – their caps were all crumpled, their jackets all covered in oil, their hands all black.

Vera could think of nothing but her fears for Viktorov and for the baby, whose existence she was now constantly aware of. The vague anxiety she felt about her grandmother, Aunt Zhenya, Seryozha and Tolya now took second place.

At night, though, she longed for her mother. She would call out to her, tell her her troubles and beg for help, whispering; 'Mama, dearest Mama, help me!'

She felt weak and helpless, a different person from the one who calmly told her father: 'There's nothing more to discuss. I'm staying here and that's that.'

62

While they were eating, Nadya said thoughtfully: 'Tolya preferred boiled potatoes to fried.'

'Tomorrow,' said Lyudmila, 'he'll be nineteen years and seven months old.'

That evening she remarked: 'How upset Marusya would have

been, if she'd known about the Fascist atrocities at Yasnaya Polyana.'

Soon Alexandra Vladimirovna came in from a meeting at the factory.

'What splendid weather, Vitya!' she said to Viktor as he helped her off with her coat. 'The air's dry and frosty. "Like vodka", as your mother used to say.'

'And if she liked the sauerkraut,' Viktor recalled, 'she used to say, "It's like grapes."'

Life went on like an iceberg floating through the sea: the underwater part, gliding through the cold and the darkness, supported the upper part, which reflected the waves, breathed, listened to the water splashing . . .

Young people in families they knew were accepted as research students, completed their dissertations, fell in love, married, but there was always an undertone of sorrow beneath the lively talk and the celebrations.

When Viktor heard that someone he knew had been killed at the front, it was as though some particle of life inside him had died, as though some colour had faded. Amid the hubbub of life, the dead man's voice still made itself heard.

The time Viktor was bound to, spiritually and intellectually, was a terrible one, one that spared neither women nor children. It had already killed two women in his own family – and one young man, a mere boy. Often Viktor thought of two lines of Mandelstam, which he had once heard from Madyarov, a historian who was a relative of Sokolov's:

> The wolfhound century leaps at my shoulders,
> But I am no wolf by blood.

But this time was his own time: he lived in it and would be bound to it even after his death.

Viktor's work was still going badly. His experiments, which he had begun long before the war, failed to yield the predicted results. There was something absurd and discouraging about the chaos of the data and the sheer obstinacy with which they contradicted the theory.

At first Viktor was convinced that the reason for these failures lay in his unsatisfactory working conditions and the lack of new apparatus. He was continually irritated with his laboratory assistants, thinking that they devoted too little energy to their work and were too easily distracted by trivia.

However, his troubles did not really stem from the fact that the bright, charming and talented Savostyanov was constantly scheming to obtain more ration-coupons for vodka; nor from the fact that the omniscient Markov gave lectures during working hours – or else spent his time explaining just what rations this or that Academician received and how this Academician's rations were shared out between his two previous wives and his present wife; nor from Anna Naumovna's habit of recounting all her dealings with her landlady in insufferable detail.

On the contrary – Savostyanov's mind was still clear and lively; Markov still delighted Viktor with his calm logic, the breadth of his knowledge and the artistry with which he set up the most sophisticated experiments: Anna Naumovna lived in a cold, dilapidated, little cubby-hole, but worked with a superhuman conscientiousness and dedication. And of course Viktor was still proud to have Sokolov as a collaborator.

Greater rigour in the execution of the experiments, stricter controls, the recalibration of the instruments – all these failed to introduce any clarity. Chaos had erupted into the study of the organic salts of heavy metals when exposed to fierce radiation.

Sometimes this particle of salt appeared to Viktor in the guise of an obscene, crazy dwarf – a red-faced dwarf with a hat over one ear, twisting and writhing indecently as he made obscene gestures at the stern countenance of the theory. The theory had been elaborated by physicists of international fame, its mathematics were flawless, and decades of experimental data from the most renowned laboratories of England and Germany fitted comfortably into its framework. Shortly before the war, an experiment had been set up in Cambridge with the aim of confirming, in certain extreme conditions, the behaviour of particles predicted by the theory. The success of this experiment was the theory's most brilliant triumph. To Viktor, it seemed as exalted and poetic as the experiment on relativity which confirmed the predicted deviation of a ray of light from a star passing through the sun's gravitational field. Any attack on this theory was quite unthinkable – it would be like a soldier trying to rip the gold braid off a field-marshal's shoulders.

Meanwhile, the dwarf carried on with his obscene foolery. Not long before Lyudmila had set off for Saratov, Viktor had thought that it might be possible to expand the framework of the theory – even though this necessitated two arbitrary hypotheses and considerable further complication of the mathematics.

The new equations related to the branch of mathematics which was Sokolov's particular speciality. Viktor wasn't sure of himself in this area and asked for Sokolov's help. Sokolov managed fairly quickly to extrapolate new equations for the expanded theory.

The matter now seemed settled – the experimental data no longer contradicted the theory. Delighted with this success, Viktor congratulated Sokolov. Sokolov in turn congratulated Viktor – but the anxiety and dissatisfaction still remained.

Viktor's depression soon returned. 'I've noticed, Pyotr Lavrentyevich,' he said to Sokolov, 'that I get into a bad mood whenever I see Lyudmila darning stockings in the evening. It reminds me of the two of us. What we've done is patch up the theory, and very clumsily at that, using different-coloured wools.'

He worried away at his doubts like someone scratching a scab. Fortunately he was incapable of deceiving himself, knowing instinctively that self-consolation could lead only to defeat.

The expansion of the theory had been quite valueless. Now the theory had been patched up, it had lost its inner harmony; the arbitrary hypotheses deprived it of any independent strength and vitality and the equations had become almost too cumbersome to work with. It had somehow become rigid, anaemic, almost talmudic. It was as though it no longer had any live muscle.

A new series of experiments carried out by the brilliant Markov then contradicted the new equations. To explain this contradiction, he would have to resort to yet another arbitrary hypothesis. Once again he would have to shore up the theory with splinters of wood and old matchsticks.

'It's a botched job,' he said to himself. Viktor knew all too well that he was following the wrong path.

A letter came from the Urals: the factory was busy with orders for military equipment and the work of casting and machining the apparatus ordered by Shtrum would have to be postponed for six to eight weeks.

This letter didn't upset Viktor. He no longer expected the arrival of the new apparatus to change anything. Now and again, however, he would be seized with a furious desire to get his hands on the apparatus as soon as possible – just to convince himself once and for all that the theory was hopelessly and irrevocably contradicted by the new data.

The failure of his work seemed to be linked with his personal sorrows. Everything had become grey and hopeless. For weeks on end he would feel depressed and irritable. At times like these he became uncharacteristically interested in the housekeeping, repeatedly interfering and expressing astonishment at how much Lyudmila spent.

He even took an interest in the quarrel between Lyudmila and their landlady. The landlady was demanding additional rent for the use of the woodshed.

'Well,' he would ask, 'how are the negotiations with Nina Matveevna?'

After hearing Lyudmila through, he would say: 'What a mean old bitch!'

Now he no longer thought about the link between science and people's lives, about whether science was a joy or a sorrow. Only a master, a conqueror, can think about such questions – and he was just a bungling apprentice.

He felt as though he'd never again be able to work as he had before. His talent for research had been crushed by his sorrows. He went through the names of great physicists, mathematicians and writers whose most important work had been accomplished in their youth and who had failed to achieve anything of note after the age of thirty-five or forty. They at least had something to be proud of – whereas he would live out his life without having accomplished anything at all worthy of memory. Evariste Galois, who had laid down the lines along which mathematics would develop for a whole century, had been killed at the age of twenty-one; Einstein had published 'On the Electrodynamics of Moving Bodies' at the age of twenty-six; Hertz had died before he was forty. What an abyss lay between these men and Shtrum!

Viktor told Sokolov that he'd like to suspend their laboratory work for a while. Sokolov, however, had high expectations of the new apparatus and thought they should continue. Viktor didn't even remember to tell him about the letter from the factory.

Lyudmila never once asked Viktor about his work, though he could see that she knew of his failure. She was indifferent to the most important thing in his life – but she had time for housework, for conversations with Marya Ivanovna, for her quarrels with the land-lady, for sewing a dress for Nadya, for meetings with Postoev's wife ... Viktor felt bitter and angry with Lyudmila, quite failing to understand her true state of mind.

Viktor thought that his wife had returned to her habitual way of life; in fact, she was able to carry out these tasks precisely because they were habitual and so placed no demands on her. She was able to cook noodle soup and talk about Nadya's boots simply because she had done this for years and years. Viktor failed to see that she was only going through the motions, not truly entering into her previous life. She was like someone deep in thought, who, quite without noticing them, skirts pot-holes and steps over puddles as he walks down a familiar road.

In order to talk to her husband about his work, she would have needed new strength, new spiritual resources. She didn't have this strength. Viktor, however, thought that she remained interested in everything except his work.

He was also hurt by the way Lyudmila kept on bringing up occasions when he had been unkind to Tolya. It was as though she were drawing up the accounts between Tolya and his stepfather – and the balance was not in Viktor's favour.

Once Lyudmila said to her mother:

'Poor boy! What a torment it was to him when he had spots all over his face. He even asked me to get some kind of cream from the beauty parlour. And Viktor just teased him.'

This was true. Viktor had liked teasing Tolya; when Tolya came home and said hello to his stepfather, Viktor used to look him up and down, shake his head and say thoughtfully: 'Well, brother, you have come out in stars!'

Recently Viktor had preferred not to stay at home in the evenings. Sometimes he went round to Postoev's to play chess or listen to music – Postoev's wife was quite a good pianist. Sometimes he called on Karimov, a new friend he had met here in Kazan. More often, though, he went to Sokolov's.

He liked the Sokolovs' little room; he liked the hospitable Marya

Ivanovna and her welcoming smile; above all, he enjoyed the conversations they had at table.

But, late at night, as he approached his front door, he was gripped by anguish — an anguish that had been lulled only for a moment.

63

Instead of going home from the Institute, Viktor went straight to his new friend, Karimov; he was to pick him up and go on to the Sokolovs'.

Karimov was an ugly man with a pock-marked face. His swarthy skin made his hair look still greyer, while his grey hair made his skin look still swarthier. He spoke Russian very correctly, and only the most attentive listener could detect his slight oddities of pronunciation and syntax.

Viktor had never heard his name before, but it appeared to be well-known even outside Kazan. Karimov had translated *The Divine Comedy* and *Gulliver's Travels* into Tartar; at present he was working on *The Iliad*.

At one time, before they had been introduced, they often used to run into one another at the University, in the small smoking-room on the way out of the reading-room. The librarian, a loquacious, slovenly old woman who used a lot of lipstick, had already told Viktor all about Karimov. He knew that Karimov had studied at the Sorbonne, that he had a dacha in the Crimea, and that he had formerly spent most of the year at the seaside. His wife and daughter had been caught in the Crimea by the war; Karimov had had no news of them since. The old woman had hinted that Karimov had been through eight years of great suffering, but Viktor had only looked at her blankly. It was clear that the old woman had also told Karimov all about Viktor. The two of them felt uneasy at knowing so much about each other without having been introduced; when they did meet, they tended to frown rather than smile. Finally, they bumped into each other one day in the library cloakroom, simultaneously burst out laughing and began to talk.

Viktor didn't know whether Karimov enjoyed his conversation; he only knew that he himself enjoyed talking when Karimov was listening. He knew from experience that a man who seems intelligent and witty at first often proves terribly boring to talk to.

There were people in whose presence Viktor found it hard to say even one word; his voice would go wooden and the conversation would become grey and colourless – as though they were both deaf-mutes. There were people in whose presence even one sincere word sounded false. And there were old friends in whose presence he felt peculiarly alone.

What was the reason for all this? Why is it that you occasionally meet someone – a travelling companion, a man sleeping next to you in a camp, someone who joins in a chance argument – in whose presence your inner world suddenly ceases to be mute and isolated?

Viktor and Karimov were walking side by side, talking away; Viktor realized that there were times now when he didn't think of his work for hours on end, especially during these evening talks at the Sokolovs'. He had never experienced this before; he normally thought about his work the whole time – in the tram, listening to music, eating, while he was drying his face after getting washed in the morning.

Yes, he must have got himself into a blind alley. Now he was unconsciously pushing away any thought of his work . . .

'How's your work gone today, Akhmet Usmanovich?' he asked.

'My mind's gone quite blank. All I can think of is my wife and daughter. Sometimes I think that everything's all right and that we will see each other again. And then I have a feeling that they're already dead.'

'I can understand,' said Viktor.

'I know,' said Karimov.

How strange it all was: here was someone Viktor had known for only a few weeks – and he could talk to him about what he couldn't even talk about with his wife or his daughter.

Almost every evening, people who would never have met in Moscow gathered together in the Sokolovs' small room.

Sokolov, though outstandingly talented, always spoke in a rather pedantic way. No one would have guessed from his smooth, polished speech that his father was a Volga fisherman. He was a kind, noble man, and yet there was something in his face that seemed sly and cruel.

There were other respects in which Sokolov differed from the

Volga fishermen: he never drank, he hated draughts, and he was terrified of infection – he was constantly washing his hands and he would cut the crust off a loaf of bread where he had touched it with his fingers.

Viktor was always amazed when he read Sokolov's work. How could a man think so boldly and elegantly, how could he elaborate and prove the most complex ideas with such concision – and then drone on so tediously over a cup of tea?

Viktor himself, like many people brought up in a cultured, bookish environment, enjoyed dropping phrases like 'a load of crap' or 'bullshit' into a conversation. In the presence of a venerable Academician, he would refer to a shrewish female lecturer as 'an old cow' or even 'a bitch'.

Before the war Sokolov had always refused to allow any discussion of politics. As soon as Viktor even mentioned politics, Sokolov had either fallen into a reserved silence or else changed the subject with studied deliberateness.

There was a strange streak of submissiveness in him, a passive acceptance of the terrible cruelties of collectivization and the year 1937. He seemed to accept the anger of the State as other people accept the anger of Nature or the anger of God. Viktor sometimes thought that Sokolov did believe in God, and that this faith showed itself in his work, in his personal relationships, and in his humble obedience before the mighty of this world.

[....]

Sokolov's brother-in-law, the historian Madyarov, spoke calmly and unhurriedly. He never openly defended Trotsky or the senior Red Army officers who had been shot as traitors to the Motherland; but it was clear from the admiration with which he spoke of Krivoruchko and Dubov, from the casual respect with which he mentioned the names of commissars and generals who had been liquidated in 1937, that he did not for one moment believe that Marshals Tukhachevsky, Blücher and Yegorov, or Muralov, the commander of the Moscow military district, or Generals Levandovsky, Gamarnik, Dybenko and Bubnov, or Unschlicht, or Trotsky's first deputy, Sklyansky, had ever really been enemies of the people and traitors to the Motherland.

No one had talked like this before the war. The might of the State had constructed a new past. It had made the Red cavalry charge a second time. It had dismissed the genuine heroes of long-past events and appointed new ones. The state had the power to replay events, to transform figures of granite and bronze, to alter speeches long since delivered, to change the faces in a news photograph.

A new history had been written. Even people who had lived through those years had now had to relive them, transformed from brave men to cowards, from revolutionaries to foreign agents.

Listening to Madyarov, however, it seemed clear that all this would give way to a more powerful logic – the logic of truth.

'All these men,' he said, 'would have been fighting against Fascism today. They'd have sacrificed their lives gladly. Why did they have to be killed?'

The landlord of the Sokolovs' flat was a chemical engineer from Kazan, Vladimir Romanovich Artelev. Artelev's wife worked late. Their two sons were at the front. He himself was in charge of a workshop at the chemical factory. He was badly dressed and he didn't even have a winter coat or fur hat. He had to wear a quilted jerkin under his raincoat, and he had a dirty, crumpled cap that he always pulled right down over his ears when he went out.

When Viktor saw him come in, blowing on his numb, red fingers, smiling shyly at the people round the table, he could hardly believe that this was the landlord; rather than the head of a large workshop at an important factory, he seemed like some beggarly neighbour coming to scrounge.

This evening, Artelev was hovering by the door, hollow-cheeked and unshaven, listening to Madyarov; he must have been afraid the floorboards would squeak if he walked right in. Marya Ivanovna whispered something in his ear on her way to the kitchen. He shook his head timidly, evidently saying he didn't want anything to eat.

'Yesterday,' said Madyarov, 'a colonel who's here for medical treatment was telling me he has to appear before a Party Commission for hitting a lieutenant in the face. That sort of thing never happened during the Civil War.'

'But you said yourself that Shchors had the members of a Revolutionary Military Commission whipped,' said Viktor.

'Yes,' said Madyarov, 'but that was a subordinate whipping his superiors. That's a little different.'

'It's the same story in industry,' said Artelev. 'Our director addresses everyone in the familiar form, but he'd take offence if you addressed him as "Comrade Shurev". No, it has to be "Leontiy Kuzmich". The other day in the workshop he got angry with one of the chemists, an old man. Shurev swore at him and said: "You do as I say – or I'll give you a boot up the arse that will send you flying onto the street." The old man is seventy-one years old.'

'And doesn't the trade union say anything?' asked Sokolov.

'What's the trade union got to do with it?' asked Madyarov. 'Their job is to exhort us to make sacrifices. You know: first we had to make preparations for the war; now it's "everything for the Front"; and after the war we'll be called upon to remedy the consequences of the war. They haven't got time to bother about some old man.'

'Maybe we should have some tea now?' Marya Ivanovna whispered to Sokolov.

'Yes, of course!' said Sokolov. 'Let's have some tea.'

'It's amazing how silently she moves!' thought Viktor, gazing absent-mindedly at Marya Ivanovna's thin shoulders as she glided out through the half-open door to the kitchen.

'Yes, comrades,' said Madyarov suddenly, 'can you imagine what it's like to have freedom of the press? One quiet morning after the war you open your newspaper, and instead of exultant editorials, instead of a letter addressed by some workers to the great Stalin, instead of articles about a brigade of steel-workers who have done an extra day's work in honour of the elections to the Supreme Soviet, instead of stories about workers in the United States who are beginning the New Year in a state of despondency, poverty and growing unemployment, guess what you find . . . ! Information! Can you imagine a newspaper like that? A newspaper that provides information!

'You begin reading: there's an article about the bad harvest in the region of Kursk, the inspector's report on conditions inside Butyrka Prison, a discussion about whether the White Sea canal is really necessary or not, an account of how a worker called Golopuzov has spoken out against the imposition of a new State loan.

'In short, you learn everything that's happened in the country: good and bad harvests; outbursts of civic enthusiasm and armed robberies; the opening of a new mine and an accident in another mine; a disagreement between Molotov and Malenkov; reports on the strike that has flared up in protest against a factory director who insulted a seventy-year-old chemical engineer. You read Churchill's and Blum's actual speeches instead of summaries of what they "alleged"; you read an account of a debate in the House of Commons; you learn how many people committed suicide in Moscow yesterday and how many were injured in traffic accidents. You learn why there's no buckwheat in Moscow instead of being told that the first strawberries have just been flown in from Tashkent. You find out the quantity of a *kolkhoz*-worker's daily ration of bread from the newspapers, not from the cleaning-lady whose niece from the country has just come to Moscow to buy some bread. Yes, and at the same time you continue to be a true Soviet citizen.

'You go into a bookshop and buy a book. You read historians, economists, philosophers and political correspondents from America, England and France. You can work out for yourself where these writers are mistaken – you're allowed out onto the street without your nanny.'

Just as Madyarov reached the end of his speech, Marya Ivanovna came in with a great pile of cups and saucers. And at the same moment, Sokolov banged on the table and said: 'That's enough! I absolutely insist that you bring this conversation to an end.'

Marya Ivanovna's mouth dropped open as she stared at her husband. The cups and saucers she was carrying began to tinkle; her hands were trembling.

'There we are,' said Viktor. 'Freedom of the press has been abolished by Pyotr Lavrentyevich. We didn't enjoy it for long. It's a good thing Marya Ivanovna wasn't exposed to such seditious talk.'

'Our system,' said Sokolov testily, 'has demonstrated its strength. The bourgeois democracies have already collapsed.'

'Yes,' said Viktor, 'but then in 1940 the degenerate bourgeois democracy of Finland came up against our centralism – and things didn't turn out too well for us. I'm no admirer of bourgeois democracy – but facts are facts. And what about that old chemist?'

Viktor looked round and saw Marya Ivanovna gazing at him very attentively.

'It wasn't Finland, but the Finnish winter,' said Sokolov.

'Come on, Petya!' said Madyarov.

'We could say,' Viktor went on, 'that during the war the Soviet State has demonstrated both its strengths and its weaknesses.'

277

'What weaknesses?' asked Sokolov.

'Well,' said Madyarov, 'for a start there are all the people who've been arrested when they could be fighting against the Germans. Why do you think we're fighting on the banks of the Volga?'

'What's that got to do with the system?'

'What on earth do you mean?' asked Viktor. 'I suppose you, Pyotr Lavrentyevich, think that the corporal's widow shot herself in 1937?'*

Once again Viktor felt Marya Ivanovna's attentive gaze. He thought to himself that he'd been behaving strangely in this argument: when Madyarov first began criticizing the State, he had argued against Madyarov; but when Sokolov attacked Madyarov, he had begun arguing against Sokolov.

Sokolov enjoyed the odd laugh at a stupid speech or an illiterate article, but his stance on any important issue was always steadfast and undeviating. Whereas Madyarov certainly made no secret of his views.

'You're attempting to explain our retreat in terms of the imperfections of the Soviet system,' pronounced Sokolov. 'But the blow struck against our country by the Germans was of such force that, in absorbing this blow, our State has demonstrated with absolute clarity not its weakness but its strength. What you see is the shadow cast by a giant, and you say: "Look, what a shadow!" You forget the giant himself. Our centralism is a social motor of truly immense power, capable of achieving miracles. It already has achieved miracles. And it will achieve more!'

'If you're no use to the State,' said Karimov, 'it will discard you; it will throw you out together with all your ideas, plans and achievements. But if your idea coincides with the interests of the State, then you'll be given a magic carpet.'

'That's true enough,' said Artelev. 'I was once posted for a month to a factory of special military importance. Stalin himself knew about each new workshop that opened – he was in telephone contact with the director . . . And what equipment! Raw materials, special components, spare parts – everything just appeared quite miraculously . . . And as for the living conditions! Bathrooms, cream brought to the door every morning! I've never known anything like it. And a superb

---

* An allusion to Gogol's play, *The Inspector*: the governor tries to make out that a widow, whom he has had whipped, has in fact whipped herself.

canteen. And above all, there was no bureaucracy. Everything could be organized without red tape.'

'Or rather,' added Karimov, 'the State bureaucracy, like the giant in a fairy-tale, was placed at the service of the people.'

'If such perfection has already been attained at factories of military importance,' said Sokolov, 'then it will clearly eventually be attained throughout the whole of industry.'

'No!' said Madyarov. 'There are two distinct principles. Stalin doesn't build what people need – he builds what the State needs. It's the State, not the people, that needs heavy industry. And as for the White Sea canal – that's no use to anyone. The needs of the State are one pole; people's needs are the other pole. These two poles are irreconcilable.'

'You're right,' said Artelev. 'And outside these special factories there's total chaos. People here in Kazan need a certain product, but according to the plan I have to deliver it to Chita – and from there it's sent back to Kazan. I need fitters, but haven't used up the funds allocated for children's nurseries – so what do I do? I put my fitters down in the books as child-minders. We're stifled by centralism! Some inventor suggested a method for producing fifteen hundred articles where we now produce two hundred. The director simply threw him out: the plan's calculated according to the total weight of what we produce – it's easier just to let things be. And if the whole factory comes to a standstill because of a shortage of some material that can be bought for thirty roubles, then he'll close the factory and lose two million roubles. He won't risk paying thirty roubles on the black market.'

Artelev looked round at his listeners and, as though afraid they wouldn't let him finish, went on hurriedly:

'A worker gets very little, but he does get paid according to his labour. Whereas an engineer gets almost nothing – you can earn five times as much selling fizzy water on the street. And the factory directors and commissariats just go on repeating: "The plan! The plan!" It doesn't matter if you're dying of hunger – you must fulfil the plan. We had a director called Shmatkov who was always shouting: "The factory's more important than your own mother. Even if you work yourself to death – you must fulfil the plan! And if you don't – I'll work you to death myself." And then one fine day we hear that

Shmatkov is being transferred to Voskresensk. "Afanasy Lukich," I asked him, "how can you leave us like this? We're behind with the plan!" He just said quite straightforwardly, "Well, we've got children living in Moscow and Voskresensk is much closer. And then we've been offered a good flat – with a garden. My wife's always getting ill and she needs some fresh air." I'm amazed the State can trust people like that, while workers – and famous scientists, if they're not Party members – have to beg for their bread.'

'It's quite simple really,' said Madyarov. 'These people have been entrusted with something far more important than factories and institutes. These people have been entrusted with the holy of holies, the heart, the life-force, of Soviet bureaucracy.'

'I can truly say,' Artelev continued, without acknowledging Madyarov's joke, 'that I love my workshop. And I work hard – I don't spare myself. But I lack the most important quality – I don't know how to work human beings to death. I can work myself to death, but not the workers.'

Everything Madyarov had said made sense; and yet, without understanding why, Viktor still felt a need to contradict him.

'There's something twisted in your reasoning,' he said. 'How can you deny that today the interests of the individual not only coincide with, but are one and the same as, the interests of the State? The State has built up the armaments industry. Surely each one of us needs the guns, tanks and aeroplanes with which our sons and brothers have been armed?'

'Absolutely!' said Sokolov.

64

Marya Ivanovna poured out the tea. The discussion turned to literature.

'Dostoyevsky's been forgotten,' said Madyarov. 'He never gets reprinted and the libraries try not to lend out his books.'

'Because he's a reactionary,' said Viktor.

'That's true,' said Sokolov. 'He shouldn't have written *The Devils*.'

'Are you sure, Pyotr Lavrentyevich, that he shouldn't have written *The Devils*?' enquired Viktor. 'Perhaps it's *The Diary of a Writer* he shouldn't have written?'

'You can't shave the edges off genius,' said Madyarov. 'Dostoyevsky simply doesn't fit into our ideology. Not like Mayakovsky – who Stalin called the finest and most talented of our poets . . . Mayakovsky is the personification of the State even in his emotionality. While Dostoyevsky, even in his cult of the State, is humanity itself.'

'If you're going to talk like that,' said Sokolov, 'there'll be no room in the official canon for any of the literature of the last century.'

'Far from it,' said Madyarov. 'What about Tolstoy? He made poetry out of the idea of a people's war. And the State has just proclaimed a people's war. Tolstoy's idea coincides with the interests of the State. And so – as Karimov would say – the magic carpet is whisked in. Now we have Tolstoy on the radio, we have literary evenings devoted to Tolstoy, his works are constantly being reprinted; he even gets quoted by our leaders.'

'Chekhov's done best of all. He was recognized both by the last epoch and by our own,' said Sokolov.

'You've hit the nail on the head!' exclaimed Madyarov, slapping his hand on the table. 'But if we do recognize Chekhov, it's because we don't understand him. The same as Zoshchenko, who is in some ways his disciple.'

'I don't understand,' objected Sokolov. 'Chekhov's a realist. It's the decadents that we criticize.'

'You don't understand?' asked Madyarov. 'Well then, I'll explain.'

'Don't you dare say anything against Chekhov!' said Marya Ivanovna. 'He's my favourite writer.'

'And you're quite right, my dear Masha,' said Madyarov. 'Now I suppose you, Pyotr Lavrentyevich, look to the decadents for an expression of humanity?'

Sokolov, by now quite angry, gave a dismissive wave of the hand. Madyarov paid no attention. He needed Sokolov to look to the decadents for humanity. Otherwise he couldn't finish his train of thought.

'Individualism is not the same as humanity,' he explained. 'Like everyone else, you confuse the two. You think the decadents are much criticized now? Nonsense! They're not subversive of the State, simply irrelevant to it. I am certain that there is no divide between Socialist Realism and the decadent movement. People have argued over the definition of Socialist Realism. It's a mirror: when the Party and the Government ask, "Mirror, mirror, on the wall, who's the fairest of them all?" it replies, "You – Party, You – Government, You – State, you're the fairest of them all!" While the decadents' answer to this question is, "Me, Me, Me, I'm the fairest of them all." Not so very different. Socialist Realism is the affirmation of the uniqueness and superiority of the State; the decadent movement is the affirmation of the uniqueness and superiority of the individual. The form may be different, but the essence is one and the same – ecstatic wonder at one's own superiority. The perfect State has no time for any others that differ from it. And the decadent personality is profoundly indifferent to all other personalities except two; with one of these it makes refined conversation, with the other it exchanges kisses and caresses. It may seem that the decadents with their individualism are fighting on behalf of man. Not a bit of it. The decadent are indifferent to man – and so is the State. Where's the divide?'

Sokolov was listening with his eyes half-closed. Sensing that Madyarov was about to infringe still more serious taboos, he interrupted:

'Excuse me, but what's all this got to do with Chekhov?'

'I'm just coming to that. Between him and the present day lies a veritable abyss. Chekhov took Russian democracy on his shoulders, the still unrealized Russian democracy. Chekhov's path is the path of Russia's freedom. We took a different path – as Lenin said. Just try and remember all Chekhov's different heroes! Probably only Balzac has ever brought such a mass of different people into the consciousness of society. No – not even Balzac. Just think! Doctors, engineers, lawyers, teachers, lecturers, landlords, shopkeepers, industrialists, nannies, lackeys, students, civil servants of every rank, cattle-dealers, tram-conductors, marriage-brokers, sextons, bishops, peasants, workers, cobblers, artists' models, horticulturalists, zoologists, innkeepers, gamekeepers, prostitutes, fishermen, lieutenants, corporals, artists, cooks, writers, janitors, nuns, soldiers, midwives, prisoners on the Sakhalin Islands . . .'

'That's enough!' Sokolov finally shouted out.

'Enough?' repeated Madyarov in a mock-threatening tone of voice. 'No, that isn't enough. Chekhov brought Russia into our consciousness in all its vastness – with people of every estate, every class, every age . . . More than that! It was as a democrat that he presented all these people – as a Russian democrat. He said – and no one had said this before, not even Tolstoy – that first and foremost we are all of us human beings. Do you understand? Human beings! He said something no one in Russia had ever said. He said that first of all we are human beings – and only secondly are we bishops, Russians, shopkeepers, Tartars, workers. Do you understand? Instead of saying that people are good or bad because they are bishops or workers, Tartars or Ukrainians, instead of this he said that people are equal because they are human beings. At one time people blinded by Party dogma saw Chekhov as a witness to the *fin de siècle*. No. Chekhov is the bearer of the greatest banner that has been raised in the thousand years of Russian history – the banner of a true, humane, Russian democracy, of Russian freedom, of the dignity of the Russian man. Our Russian humanism has always been cruel, intolerant, sectarian. From Avvakum to Lenin our conception of humanity and freedom has always been partisan and fanatical. It has always mercilessly sacrificed the individual to some abstract idea of humanity. Even Tolstoy, with his doctrine of non-resistance to Evil, is intolerant – and his point of departure is not man but God. He wants the idea of goodness to triumph. True believers always want to bring God to man by force; and in Russia they stop at nothing – even murder – to achieve this.

'Chekhov said: let's put God – and all these grand progressive ideas – to one side. Let's begin with man; let's be kind and attentive to the individual man – whether he's a bishop, a peasant, an industrial magnate, a convict in the Sakhalin Islands or a waiter in a restaurant. Let's begin with respect, compassion and love for the individual – or we'll never get anywhere. That's democracy, the still unrealized democracy of the Russian people.

'The Russians have seen everything during the last thousand years – grandeur and super-grandeur; but what they have never seen is democracy. Yes – and this is what separates Chekhov from the decadents. The State may sometimes express irritation with the decadents; it may box them on the ears or kick them up the arse. But it simply doesn't understand Chekhov – that's why it tolerates him.

There's still no place in our house for democracy – for a true humane democracy.'

It was obvious that Sokolov was very upset by Madyarov's boldness. Noticing this, and with a delight he couldn't quite understand, Viktor said: 'Well said! That's all very true and very intelligent. Only I beg you to be indulgent towards Scriabin. He may be a decadent, but I love him.'

Sokolov's wife offered Viktor a saucer of jam. He made a gesture of refusal. 'No thanks. Not for me.'

'It's blackcurrant,' replied Marya Ivanovna.

Viktor looked into her golden-brown eyes and said: 'Have I told you about my weakness, then?'

She smiled and nodded her head. Her teeth were uneven, and her lips thin and pale. When she smiled, her pallid, even slightly grey, face suddenly became quite charming.

'She's a splendid woman,' thought Viktor. 'If only her nose wasn't always so red.'

Karimov turned to Madyarov.

'Leonid Sergeich, how can you reconcile your earlier hymn to Dostoyevsky with this passionate speech in praise of Chekhov and his humanity? Dostoyevsky certainly doesn't consider everyone equal. Hitler called Tolstoy a degenerate, but they say he has a portrait of Dostoyevsky hanging in his office. I belong to a national minority myself. I'm a Tartar who was born in Russia and I cannot pardon a Russian writer his hatred of Poles and Yids. No – even if he is a genius. We had more than enough blood spilt in Tsarist Russia, more than enough of being spat at in the eye. More than enough pogroms. A great writer in this country has no right to persecute foreigners, to despise Poles and Tartars, Jews, Armenians and Chuvash.'

The grey-haired, dark-eyed Tartar smiled haughtily and angrily – like a true Mongol. Still addressing Madyarov, he continued:

'Perhaps you've read Tolstoy's *Hadji Mourat*? Perhaps you've read *The Cossacks*? Perhaps you've read the story "A Prisoner in the Caucasus"? They were written by a Russian count. While Dostoyevsky was a Lithuanian. As long as the Tartars remain in existence, they will pray to Allah on behalf of Tolstoy.'

Viktor looked at Karimov, thinking: 'Well, well. So that's how you feel, is it?'

'Akhmet Usmanovich,' said Sokolov, 'I profoundly respect your love for your people. But allow me to be proud of my nationality too. Allow me to love Tolstoy — and not only because of what he wrote about the Tartars. We Russians, for some reason, are never allowed to be proud of our own people. And if we show such pride, we're immediately taken for members of the Black Hundreds.'

Karimov got to his feet, his face covered in pearls of sweat.

'Let me tell you the truth. Why should I lie when I know the truth? Anyone who remembers how the pride of our race, every cultural figure of any importance, was exterminated way back in the twenties — anyone with a mind can see why *The Diary of a Writer* must be banned!'

'We suffered too,' said Artelev.

'It wasn't just people who were destroyed — it was a whole culture. Today's intelligentsia are savages by comparison.'

'Yes,' said Madyarov with heavy irony. 'But the Tartars might not have stopped at culture. They might have wanted Tartar home-rule and a Tartar foreign policy. And that's not on . . .'

'But you've got your own State now,' said Sokolov. 'You've got your own Institutes, your own schools, your own operas, your own books. You've got newspapers in Tartar. You owe all that to the Revolution.'

'Yes, a State opera and a comic-opera State. But it's Moscow that collects our harvest and Moscow that sends us to prison.'

'Would it be any better if you were jailed by a Tartar?' asked Madyarov.

'What if people weren't jailed at all?' asked Marya Ivanovna.

'Mashenka!' said Madyarov, 'what will you want next?' He looked at his watch and said: 'Hm, it's getting on.'

'Stay for the night, Lenechka,' Marya Ivanovna said hurriedly. 'I can make up the camp-bed.'

Madyarov had once told Marya Ivanovna that he felt particularly lonely late at night, when he came back to a dark empty room with no one waiting for him.

'Well,' he said, 'I won't say no. Is that all right by you, Pyotr Lavrentyevich?'

'Of course.'

'Said the master of the house without the least enthusiasm,' Madyarov added with a smile.

Everyone got up from the table and began saying goodbye. Sokolov accompanied his guests to the door. Marya Ivanovna lowered her voice and said to Madyarov: 'It is good that Pyotr Lavrentyevich no longer shrinks from these conversations. In Moscow he clammed up at the merest hint of anything political.'

She pronounced her husband's name and patronymic with particular tenderness and respect. At night she often copied out his work by hand; she kept all his notebooks and even pasted his casual jottings onto cards. She thought of him as a great man – and at the same time as her helpless child.

'I like Shtrum,' said Madyarov. 'I can't understand why people say he's disagreeable.' He smiled and added: 'I noticed he pronounced all his speeches in your presence, Mashenka. While you were busy in the kitchen, he spared us his eloquence.'

Marya Ivanovna had turned towards the door. She seemed not to have heard Madyarov. But then she asked: 'What do you mean, Lenya? He pays no more attention to me than to an insect. Petya considers him unkind, arrogant and too ready to mock people. That's why he's not popular and why some of the physicists are even afraid of him. But I don't agree. I think he's very kind.'

'That's the last thing I'd say of him,' said Madyarov. 'He disagrees with everyone and heaps sarcasm on them. But he's got a free mind; he hasn't been indoctrinated.'

'No, he *is* kind. And vulnerable.'

'But you have to admit,' said Madyarov, 'that our Petya doesn't let slip a careless word even now.'

Just then Sokolov came into the room. He overheard Madyarov.

'I'd like to ask you, Leonid Sergeyevich, first not to give me advice, and secondly never again to start conversations of that nature in my presence.'

'I don't need your advice, for that matter,' replied Madyarov. 'And just as you answer for your words, I'll answer for mine.'

Sokolov looked as if he wanted to say something very stinging. Instead, he left the room.

'Well, perhaps I'd better go home after all,' said Madyarov.

'You'll make me very upset,' said Marya Ivanovna. 'And you know how kind he is. It will torment him all night.'

She went on to explain that Pyotr Lavrentyevich had a very sensitive soul, that he had suffered a lot, that he had been interrogated very harshly in 1937 and as a result had had to spend four months in a clinic for nervous disorders.

Madyarov nodded his head. 'All right, Masha. I give in.'

Then, in a sudden fury, he added: 'That's all very well, but your Petya wasn't the only one to be interrogated. Have you forgotten the eleven months I spent in the Lubyanka? And how during all that time Pyotr only once telephoned my wife Klava – his own sister . . . ? Have you forgotten how he forbade you to telephone her? All that hurt Klava very deeply. Yes, your Petya may be a great physicist, but he's got the soul of a lackey.'

Marya Ivanovna buried her face in her hands and remained silent. Then she said very quietly: 'No one, no one will ever understand how deeply this pains me.'

No one else understood how appalled her husband had been by the savagery of general collectivization and the events of 1937. She alone understood his spiritual purity. But then she alone knew how servile he was in the face of power.

That was why he was so capricious at home, such a petty tyrant. That was why Masha had to clean his shoes for him, why she had to fan him in hot weather with her headscarf, why she had to keep the mosquitoes off with a branch when they went for walks near their dacha.

Once, during his last year at university, Viktor had thrown a copy of *Pravda* on to the floor and said to a fellow student: 'It's so deadly boring. How can anyone ever read it?'

Immediately afterwards he had felt terrified. He had picked up the newspaper, smoothed its pages and smiled weakly. Even now, years later, the memory of that pitiful, hang-dog smile was enough to make him break out into a sweat.

A few days later, Viktor had held out another issue of *Pravda* to that same friend and said animatedly: 'Grishka, have a look at the leading article. It's a good stuff.'

His friend had taken the newspaper from him and said pityingly:

'Vitya's frightened, is he? Do you think I'm going to denounce you?'

Viktor had then taken a vow either to remain silent and not express dangerous thoughts or else to say what he thought without funking it. He had not kept this vow. He had often flared up and thrown caution to the wind – only to suddenly take fright and attempt to snuff out the flame he himself had lit.

In 1938, after the trial of Bukharin, he had said to Krymov:

'Say what you like, but I've met Bukharin. I've talked to him twice. I remember his kind, intelligent smile. And he's certainly got a head on his shoulders. My impression is that he's someone of great charm and absolute purity.'

Krymov had looked at him morosely. Thrown into confusion, Viktor had muttered: 'But then who knows? Espionage. Working as an agent of the Okhrana.* There's nothing charming or pure about that. It's just despicable!'

Krymov's next words left Viktor even more confused.

'Since we're relatives,' he said sullenly, 'let me say one thing to you: I am quite unable, and always shall be unable, to associate the name of Bukharin with the Okhrana.'

'My God, I can't believe all this horror!' Viktor had burst out with sudden fury. 'These trials are a nightmare. But why do they confess? Why do they all confess?'

Krymov had said nothing more. He had obviously said too much already . . .

What a wonderful power and clarity there is in speaking one's mind. What a terrible price people paid for a few bold words.

How often Viktor had lain awake listening to the cars on the street! Sometimes Lyudmila had gone barefoot to the window and parted the curtains. She had stayed there for a while and watched; then, thinking that Viktor was asleep, she had gone silently back to bed and lain down. In the morning she had asked: 'Did you sleep well?'

'All right, thank you. And you?'

'It felt very stuffy. I had to go to the window for some fresh air.'

'Yes.'

How can one ever describe those nights and that extraordinary sense of both doom and innocence?

* The Tsarist Secret Police.

'Remember, Viktor, every word reaches them. You're destroying yourself, together with me and the children.'

And another time:

'I can't tell you everything. But for the love of God, don't say a word to anyone. Viktor, we live in a terrible age – you've no idea just how terrible. Remember, Viktor, not a word to anyone.'

Sometimes Viktor glimpsed the opaque, sad eyes of someone he had known since childhood. He had been frightened not by what his old friend said, but by what he didn't say. And of course he had been much too frightened to ask directly: 'Are you an agent? Do you get called in for questioning?'

He remembered looking at his assistant's face after making a thoughtless joke about Stalin's having formulated the laws of gravity long before Newton.

'You didn't say anything, and I didn't hear anything,' this young assistant had said gaily.

Why, why, why all these jokes? It was mad to make such jokes – like banging a flask of nitroglycerine with a hammer.

What power and clarity lies in the word! In the unfettered, carefree word! The word that is still spoken in spite of all one's fears.

Was Viktor aware of the hidden tragedy in these conversations? Everyone who took part in them hated German Fascism and was terrified of it . . . But why did they only speak their minds at a time when Russia had been driven back to the Volga, at a time when terrible military defeats held out the threat of slavery?

Viktor walked silently beside Karimov.

'There's something very surprising,' he suddenly said, 'about novels portraying the foreign intelligentsia. I've just been reading Hemingway. When his characters have a serious conversation, they are always drinking. Cocktails, whisky, rum, cognac, more cocktails, more cognac, still more different brands of whisky. Whereas the Russian intelligentsia has always had its important discussions over a glass of tea. The members of "People's Will", the Populists, the Social Democrats all came together over glasses of weak tea. Lenin and his friends even planned the Revolution over a glass of weak tea. Though apparently Stalin prefers cognac.'

'Yes, yes,' said Karimov, 'you're quite right. And the conversation we had today was over a glass of tea.'

'Absolutely. And isn't Madyarov intelligent? Isn't he bold? I'm really not used to anyone speaking the way he does. It excites me.'

Karimov took Viktor by the arm.

'Viktor Pavlovich, have you noticed that the most innocent remark of Madyarov's somehow sounds like a generalization? I find that worrying. And he was arrested for several months in 1937 and then released. At a time when no one was released. There must be a reason. Do you follow me?'

'Yes,' Viktor answered slowly, 'I do. How could I not understand you? You think he's an informer.'

They parted at the next corner. Viktor walked back towards his house.

'To hell with it all!' he said to himself. 'At least we've talked like human beings for once. Without fear and hypocrisy. Saying whatever we felt about whatever we liked. Paris is worth a mass . . .'

How good that there still were people like Madyarov, people who hadn't lost their independence. Yes. Karimov's warning didn't strike the usual chill into Viktor's heart.

Viktor realized that he had once again forgotten to tell Sokolov about the letter from the Urals.

He walked on down the dark, empty street. Suddenly an idea came to him. Immediately, with his whole being, he knew it was true. He had glimpsed a new and improbable explanation for the atomic phenomena that up until now had seemed so hopelessly inexplicable; abysses had suddenly changed into bridges. What clarity and simplicity! This idea was astonishingly graceful and beautiful. It seemed to have given birth to itself – like a white water-lily appearing out of the calm darkness of a lake. He gasped, revelling in its beauty . . .

And how strange, he thought suddenly, that this idea should have come to him when his mind was far away from anything to do with science, when the discussions that so excited him were those of free men, when his words and the words of his friends had been determined only by freedom, by bitter freedom.

65

The Kalmyk steppe seems sad and lifeless when you see it for the first time, when you come to it full of preoccupations, when you watch absent-mindedly as the low hills slowly emerge from the horizon and slowly sink back into it . . . Lieutenant-Colonel Darensky had the feeling it was the very same wind-swept hillock that kept appearing in front of him, the very same curve that his car kept following . . . The horsemen too seemed identical – even though some were beardless and others grey-haired, even though some were on dun ponies, others on black . . .

The jeep passed through hamlets and villages, past small houses with tiny windows that sheltered a jungle of geraniums; it looked as though you had only to break the glass for the life-giving air to drain away into the surrounding emptiness, for the thick green of the geraniums to wither and die. The jeep drove past circular yurts with clay-smeared walls, through tall, grey feather-grass, through prickly camel-grass, past white splashes of salt, past the little clouds of dust kicked up by flocks of sheep, past small fires that gave off no smoke and danced in the wind . . .

To someone travelling by jeep, on tyres filled with the smoky air of the city, everything here blurs into a uniform grey . . . This Kalmyk steppe, which stretches, gradually changing to desert, right to the mouth of the Volga and the shores of the Caspian, has one strange characteristic: the earth and the sky above have reflected one another for so long that they have finally become undistinguishable, like a husband and wife who have spent their whole lives together. It's impossible to tell whether dusty, aluminium-grey feather-grass has begun to grow on the dull, lustreless blue of the sky, or whether the steppe itself has become impregnated with the sky's blue; earth and sky have blurred together, dusty and ageless. In the same way, the thick opaque water of Lakes Dats and Barmantsak looks like a sheet of salt, while the salt flats look like lakes . . .

And in November and December – before the first snows – it's impossible to tell whether the earth has been dried and hardened by the sun or by frost.

All this may account for the number of mirages here: the boundary between air and earth, between water and salt, has been erased. The mind of a thirsty traveller can transform this world with ease: the scorching air becomes elegant, blueish stone; the lifeless earth is filled with the gentle murmur of streams; palm trees stretch out to the horizon and the terrible sun blends with the clouds of dust to form the golden cupolas of temples and palaces . . . In a moment of exhaustion, a man can transform this sky and this earth into the world of his dreams.

But there is another, unexpected side to the steppe. It is also a noble, ancient world; a world where there are no screaming colours or harsh lines, but only a sober grey-blue melancholy that can rival the colours of a Russian forest in autumn; a world whose soft undulating hills capture the heart more surely than the peaks of the Caucasus; a world whose small, dark, ancient lakes seem to express the very essence of water more truly than seas or oceans.

Everything passes; but there is no forgetting this huge, cast-iron sun shining through the evening mist, this bitter wind laden with the scent of wormwood . . .

And the steppe has its own riches. In spring the young tulip-filled steppe is an ocean of colours. The camel-grass is still green; its harsh spines are still soft and tender . . .

The steppe has one other unchanging characteristic: day and night, summer and winter, in foul weather or fine weather, it speaks of freedom. If someone has lost his freedom, the steppe will remind him of it . . .

Darensky got out of his car and looked at a horseman on top of a small hill. Dressed in a long robe tied by a piece of string, he was sitting on his shaggy pony and surveying the steppe. He was very old; his face looked as hard as stone.

Darensky called out to the man and then walked up to him, holding out his cigarette-case. The old man turned in his saddle; his movement somehow combined the agility of youth with the thoughtful caution of age. He looked in turn at the hand holding out the cigarettes, at Darensky's face, at the pistol hanging by his side, at the three bars indicating his rank, and at his smart boots. Then he took a cigarette and rolled it between his fine, brown, childlike fingers.

The old man's hard, high-cheekboned face suddenly changed; two kind intelligent eyes looked out from between his wrinkles. There was something very splendid about these old brown eyes, about their look of trust blended with wary scrutiny; for no apparent reason Darensky suddenly felt happy and at ease. The pony, who had pricked up his ears suspiciously at Darensky's approach, inquisitively pointed first one ear, then the other, and then smiled at him with his beautiful eyes and his two rows of large teeth.

'Thank you,' said the old man in a thin voice, putting his hand on Darensky's shoulder. 'I had two sons in a cavalry division. The first one' – he raised his hand a little above the pony's head – 'was killed by the Germans. The second one' – he lowered his hand a little below the pony's head – 'is a machine-gunner: he's got three medals. How about you? Is your father still alive?'

'My mother's alive, but my father's dead.'

'Ay! that's bad!' said the old man, shaking his head. Darensky had the feeling that he wasn't just being polite, that he felt genuinely sad to learn of the death of the father of the Russian lieutenant-colonel who had offered him a cigarette.

The old man gave a sudden cry, waved his hand in the air and galloped down the hill with extraordinary grace and speed. What was he thinking as he galloped through the steppe? Of his sons? Of the father of the Russian lieutenant-colonel whose jeep needed mending?

Darensky watched. One word pounded like blood at his temples: 'Freedom . . . freedom . . . freedom . . .'

Yes, he was envious of the old Kalmyk.

66

Darensky had been sent from Front Headquarters on a lengthy mission to the army deployed on the extreme left of the flank. These missions were particularly unpopular among the staff officers, on account of the lack of water and housing, the poor supplies, the vast distances and the vile roads. The High Command had little precise information about these troops, lost as they were in the sands between the shores of the Caspian and the Kalmyk steppe; Darensky had a lot of tasks to carry out.

After travelling hundreds of miles through the steppe, he felt overwhelmed by melancholy and boredom. Here no one even dreamed of an offensive; there was something hopeless about the situation of these troops who had been driven back almost to the end of the world . . .

The continual tension of life at Front HQ, the rumours of an impending offensive, the movements of the reserves, the codes and telegrams, the never-ending work of the Signals-Section, the roar of the columns of tanks and vehicles coming in from the North – had all this really just been an illusion?

As Darensky listened to the gloomy conversations of the officers, as he collated and checked data about the state of the equipment, inspected artillery regiments and batteries, noticed the sullenness on the faces of the men and the laziness of their movements, he slowly gave in to the monotonous gloom around him. Russia seemed like a wounded animal that had been driven back into the sand-dunes, into steppes fit only for camels; there she was, lying on the harsh earth, impotent, unable ever to rise again.

Darensky arrived at Army Headquarters. A plump-faced, balding young man, wearing a tunic without any insignia of rank, was playing cards with two women in uniform, both of them lieutenants. Instead of breaking off as the lieutenant-colonel entered the room, they looked at him absent-mindedly and went on with their game.

'Why not play a trump? Or a jack?'

Darensky waited for the end of the hand before asking, 'Are these the commander's quarters?'

'He's gone to the right flank. He won't be back till evening,' said one of the young women. She looked Darensky up and down. 'Are you from Front HQ, comrade Lieutenant-Colonel?'

'That's right,' said Darensky. With a barely perceptible wink, he asked: 'Excuse me, but could I see the Member of the Military Soviet?'

'He's with the commander. He won't be back till evening either,' said the second woman. 'Are you on the artillery staff?'

'That's right.'

Though she was clearly very much the older of the two, Darensky found the first woman extremely attractive. She was the kind of woman who can look very beautiful and yet – seen from the wrong angle – appear suddenly faded, middle-aged and dull. She had a fine straight nose and blue eyes that were lacking in warmth; you could tell she knew both her own value and that of other people.

Her face looked very young, not a year over twenty-five. But as soon as she frowned or looked thoughtful, you could see the wrinkles at the corners of her lips and the loose skin at her throat; then she looked at least forty-five. But her legs – in elegant, tailored boots – were quite splendid.

All these details, which take some time to recount, were taken in at once by Darensky's experienced eye.

The second woman was young, but already stout. Taken individually, none of her features was particularly beautiful: her hair lacked body, her face was very broad, and her eyes were an indeterminate colour. But she was young and feminine. Yes, sitting next to her, even a blind man would be conscious of her femininity.

These details, too, were noted by Darensky in less than a second. More than that – in this fraction of a second he was somehow able to weigh up the merits of the two women and make the choice, a choice quite without practical consequences, that nearly all men make in such a situation. Though he had a lot of questions on his mind – Where would he find the commanding officer? Would he be able to obtain the necessary information from him? Where could he eat and sleep? Would it be a long and difficult journey to the division on the extreme left? – Darensky still had time to say to himself: 'Yes, that's the one I'd choose!' It was merely a passing thought; and yet, instead of going straight to the chief of staff, he stayed behind for a game of cards.

He ended up partnering the woman with the blue eyes. During the game he learnt several things: his partner was called Alla Sergeyevna; the other woman worked in the first-aid post; the young man, Volodya, was a cook in the Military Soviet canteen and appeared to be a relative of someone high up.

From the very start, Darensky sensed Alla Sergeyevna's power; it was obvious from the way people addressed her when they came into the room. The commanding officer was clearly her husband – not just her lover, as he had first thought.

At first he couldn't understand why Volodya was so familiar with her. Then it suddenly dawned on him that Volodya must be the brother of the commander's first wife. What was still unclear was whether the commander's first wife was still alive; and if so, whether they had got a divorce.

The younger woman, Claudia, was equally clearly *not* the wife of the Member of the Military Soviet. There was an occasional note of arrogance and condescension in the way Alla Sergeyevna talked to her: 'Yes, we may be playing cards together, we may call each other '*ty*', but that's simply because of the war.'

Claudia in turn had a certain sense of her own superiority over Alla Sergeyevna. Darensky understood this as: 'All right, I may not be lawfully married, but at least I'm faithful to my Member of the Military Soviet. So you watch it! You may be properly married, but there are one or two things I could say about you.'

Volodya made no attempt to hide how strongly he was attracted to Claudia. He seemed to be saying: 'My love is hopeless. How can a mere cook hope to rival the Member of the Military Soviet? But even if I am only a cook, I love you with a pure love and you know it. All I ask is to be able to look into your pretty little eyes. As for what your Member of the Military Soviet loves you for, that doesn't matter to me.'

Darensky played very badly and Alla Sergeyevna took him under her wing. She liked this lean, elegant colonel. He said, 'I thank you,' and mumbled, 'Forgive me' if their hands touched during the deal; he looked pained when Volodya wiped his nose on his fingers and his fingers on his handkerchief; he smiled politely at other people's jokes and was extremely witty himself.

After one of his jokes she said: 'You're very witty, but it took me a moment to get the point. I'm losing my mind out here in the steppes.'

She said this very quietly, as if to let him know, or rather feel, how easily a conversation could develop between the two of them, a conversation that would send shivers up their spines, a conversation of the only kind that matters between a man and a woman.

Darensky continued to make mistakes and she continued to correct him; at the same time they began to play another game in which Darensky made no mistakes. Nothing had been said between them except, 'No, don't hang on to your low spades' or 'Go on, go on, there's no need to save your trumps'; but she already knew and appreciated all his charms – his strength and his gentleness, his discretion and his audacity, his shyness . . . Alla Sergeyevna sensed these qualities both because of her own perceptiveness and because Darensky knew how to display them. She for her part was able to show him that she understood the way he watched her smile, the way he watched her gesture with her hands or shrug her shoulders, the way he looked at her breasts under her elegant gabardine tunic, at her legs, at her carefully manicured nails. And he could tell that her voice was just a little more melodic than usual, that her smile lingered a little longer than usual – so that he could appreciate the beauty of her voice, her white teeth and the dimples in her cheeks . . .

Darensky was quite shaken by his sudden feeling of excitement. It was something he never got used to; it was always as though he was experiencing it for the first time. His considerable experience of women had never degenerated into mere habit; his experience was one thing, his joy and excitement quite another. It was this that made him a true lover of women.

It somehow came about that he had to stay the night at Army Headquarters.

The following morning he called on the chief of staff, a taciturn colonel who didn't ask a single question about Stalingrad itself or the position of the various fronts. By the end of their conversation Darensky had come to the conclusion that this colonel would be of no help at all; he asked him to stamp his documents and then went out to inspect the troops himself.

As he got into his jeep he felt a strange lightness and emptiness in his arms and legs, a total lack of thought or desire; he felt at once sated and drained. Everything round about seemed insipid and empty: the sky, the feather-grass and the hills that only yesterday had seemed so beautiful. He didn't want to talk or joke with his driver. Even his thoughts about his friends and relatives, about his beloved mother, were somehow cold and lifeless. His thoughts about this war in the desert, at the furthest limits of Russian territory, were equally lacking in passion.

Every now and then he spat, shook his head and muttered with a kind of obtuse surprise: 'What a woman . . .'

He thought remorsefully that this kind of affair always came to a bad end. He remembered something he had read, either in Kuprin or in some foreign novel, about love being like a lump of coal: hot, it burns you; cold, it makes you dirty. He wanted to cry, or rather to have a good moan, to find someone he could tell his troubles to. It wasn't his own choice, it was the will of Fate. This was the only kind of love he knew . . . Then he fell asleep. When he woke up, he thought suddenly: 'Well, if I don't get myself killed, I'll certainly drop in on Allochka on the way back.'

67

On his way back from work, Major Yershov stopped by Mostovskoy's place on the bedboards.

'One of the Americans heard the radio today: our resistance at Stalingrad has really upset the German strategy.'

Then he frowned and added: 'And there was a report from Moscow — something about the liquidation of the Comintern.'

'You must be crazy,' said Mostovskoy, looking into Yershov's intelligent eyes, eyes that were like the cool, turbid waters of spring.

'Maybe the American got it mixed up,' said Yershov, scratching his head. 'Maybe the Comintern's been expanded.'

During his life Mostovskoy had known several people who were like a diaphragm that resonated to the thoughts, ideals and passions of a whole society. Not one important event ever seemed to pass them by. Yershov was such a person; he was a mouthpiece for the thoughts and aspirations of the whole camp. But a rumour about the liquidation of the Comintern didn't hold the least interest for this master of men's minds.

Brigade Commissar Osipov, who had been responsible for the political education of a large military unit, was equally indifferent.

'General Gudz said that it was because of your internationalist propaganda that all this funk first set in. We should have brought people up in the spirit of patriotism, the spirit of Russia.'

'You mean God, the Tsar and the Fatherland?' said Mostovskoy mockingly.

'Nonsense,' said Osipov with a nervous yawn. 'Anyway, who cares about orthodoxy? What matters, dear comrade, is that the Germans are skinning us alive.'

The Spanish soldier known to the Russians as Andryushka, who slept on the third tier of boards, wrote 'Stalingrad' on a scrap of wood and gazed at the word during the night. In the morning he turned it over in case the kapos caught sight of it as they came by on their rounds.

'If I wasn't sent out to work, I used to lie on the boards all day long,' Major Kirillov told Mostovskoy. 'But now I wash my shirt and I chew splinters of pine-wood against scurvy.'

The SS officers, known as 'the happy lads' because of the way they sang on their way to work, now picked on the Russians with even more cruelty than usual.

There were invisible links between the barrack-huts and the city on the Volga. But no one was interested in the Comintern.

It was around then that the émigré Chernetsov approached Mostovskoy for the first time. Covering up his empty eye-socket with the palm of his hand, he began talking about the broadcast the American had heard. Mostovskoy was pleased; he needed to talk about this very badly.

'The sources aren't very reliable,' he said. 'It's probably just a rumour.'

Chernetsov raised his eyebrows. It looked grotesque – an eyebrow raised in neurotic bewilderment over an empty socket.

'What do you mean?' he asked. 'It makes perfect sense. Our masters the Bolsheviks set up the Third International, and our masters the Bolsheviks developed the theory of so-called Socialism in One Country. That theory's a contradiction in terms – like fried ice. Georgiy Plekhanov wrote in one of his last articles: "Socialism either exists as an international, world-wide system, or not at all."'

'So-called Socialism?' repeated Mostovskoy.

'That's right, "so-called". Soviet Socialism.'

Chernetsov smiled and saw Mostovskoy smile back. They recognized their past in these jibes, in this mockery and hatred.

The sharp blade of their youthful enmity flashed out anew, as though cutting through whole decades; this meeting in a concentration camp reminded them not only of years of hatred, but also of their youth.

This man, for all his hostility, knew and loved what Mostovskoy had known and loved in his youth. It was Chernetsov – not Osipov or Yershov – who remembered the First Party Congress and names that everyone else had long ago forgotten. They talked excitedly about the relations between Marx and Bakunin, about what Lenin and Plekhanov had said about the hard-liners and the softs on the editorial staff of *Iskra* . . . How warmly Engels had welcomed the young Russian Social Democrats who had come to visit him when he was a blind old man! What a pain Lyubochka Axelrod had been in Zurich!

Evidently sharing the same feelings as Mostovskoy, the one-eyed Menshevik grinned and said: 'Touching accounts have been written of meetings between old friends. What about meetings between old enemies, between tired, grey-haired old dogs like you and me?'

Mostovskoy glimpsed a tear on Chernetsov's cheek. They both knew that they would die soon. The events of their lives would be levelled over; their enmity, their convictions, their mistakes, would all be buried beneath the sand.

'Yes,' said Mostovskoy. 'If you fight against someone all your days, he becomes a part of your life.'

'How strange to meet in this wolf-pit,' said Chernetsov. Then, apropos of nothing at all, he murmured: 'What wonderful words: "wheat", "corn", "April showers".'

'This camp's a terrible place,' said Mostovskoy. He laughed. 'Anything else seems good in comparison – even meeting a Menshevik.'

Chernetsov nodded sadly. 'Yes, things are hard for you.'

'Hitlerism!' said Mostovskoy. 'I never imagined there could be such a hell.'

'Don't try and fool me,' said Chernetsov. 'There's not much you don't know about terror!'

The melancholy warmth of only a moment before might never have existed. They began to argue furiously and without mercy.

The terrible thing about Chernetsov's slander was that it contained an element of truth. What he did was to extrapolate general laws from occasional mistakes and incidental cruelties.

'Of course it suits you to think that some people went too far in 1937,' he said to Mostovskoy, 'that the success of collectivization went to people's heads, that your great and beloved leader is perhaps just a little cruel and megalomaniac. But the truth of the matter is very different: it's precisely Stalin's monstrous inhumanity that makes him Lenin's successor. As you love to repeat – Stalin is the Lenin of today. You still think that the workers' lack of rights and the poverty in the villages are something temporary, just growing pains. But you're the true kulaks, you're the true monopolists – the wheat you buy from a peasant for five kopecks a kilo and sell back to him for a rouble a kilo is the foundation-stone of your whole socialist edifice.'

'So even you, an émigré and a Menshevik, admit that Stalin is the Lenin of today,' retorted Mostovskoy. 'It's true: we are the heirs to all the generations of Russian revolutionaries from Pugachev to Razin. The heir to Razin, Dobrolyubov and Herzen is Stalin, not you renegade Mensheviks!'

'Fine heirs you make!' said Chernetsov. 'Do you realize the meaning of the elections for the Constituent Assembly? After a thousand years of slavery! During an entire millennium Russia has been free for little more than six months. Your Lenin didn't inherit Russian freedom – he destroyed it. When I think of the trials of 1937, I remember a very different legacy. Do you remember the secret-police chief Colonel Sudeykin? He and Degaev hoped to terrify the Tsar by inventing conspiracies, and then seize power themselves. And you think of Stalin as the heir to Herzen?'

'You must be mad,' said Mostovskoy. 'Are you serious about Sudeykin? And what about the great social revolution, the expropriation of the expropriators, the factories seized from the capitalists, the land seized from the gentry? Has all that passed you by? Whose legacy is that? Sudeykin's? And the way the workers and peasants have entered every sphere of social activity? Do you call that a legacy from Sudeykin? I almost pity you.'

'I know, I know,' said Chernetsov. 'One can't argue with facts. But one can explain them. Your Marshals and writers, your doctors of science, your people's commissars are servants not of the proletariat, but of the State. And as for the people who work in the fields and on the shop-floors! I don't think even you would have the nerve to call them masters. Fine masters they make!'

301

He leaned towards Mostovskoy.

'Incidentally, there's only one of you I really respect – and that's Stalin. He's a real man! The rest of you are just cissies. He understands the true basis of Socialism in One Country: iron terror, labour camps and medieval witch-trials!'

'I've heard all this shit before,' said Mostovskoy. 'But I must say, there is something particularly nasty about your way of putting things. Only a man who's lived in your home since he was a child and then been thrown out onto the street can be that despicable. And do you realize what that man is? A lackey!'

He stared hard at Chernetsov.

'Still, I'd wanted to talk about what brought us together in 1898, not what separated us in 1903.'

'So that's what you wanted, is it? A cosy little chat about the days before the lackey was sent packing?'

At that Mostovskoy really did get angry.

'Yes, that's just it! A runaway lackey. A lackey who's been thrown out onto the street! Wearing kid gloves. We don't wear gloves – we've got nothing to hide. We plunge our hands into dirt and blood. We came to the workers' movement without Plekhanov's kid gloves. What use have those gloves been to you, anyway? Thirty pieces of silver for some articles in the *Socialist Messenger*? While the whole camp – the English, the French, the Poles, the Norwegians and the Dutch – believes in us . . . ! The salvation of the world lies in our hands! In the power of the Red Army! The army of freedom!'

'And is that how it's always been?' interrupted Chernetsov. 'What about the pact with Hitler and the invasion of Poland in 1939? And the way your tanks crushed Latvia, Lithuania and Estonia? And the invasion of Finland? Your army and Stalin have taken back everything that was given to the small nations by the Revolution. And what about the suppression of the peasant rebellions in Central Asia? And Kronstadt? Was that in the name of freedom and democracy?'

Mostovskoy held his hand up to Chernetsov's face.

'I've already told you – we don't wear kid gloves.'

Chernetsov nodded.

'Do you remember Strelnikov, the political-police chief? He didn't wear kid gloves either. He had revolutionaries beaten up till they were half-dead and then wrote out false confessions . . . What was the purpose of 1937? You say you were preparing to fight Hitler. Was your teacher Marx or Strelnikov?'

'None of your filth surprises me,' said Mostovskoy. 'It's what I've come to expect. But you know what does surprise me? Why should the Nazis put you in a camp? They hate us frenziedly. That's clear enough. But why should Hitler imprison you and your friends?'

Once again, as at the very beginning of the conversation, Chernetsov smiled.

'Well,' he said, 'they haven't let me go yet. Maybe you should get up a petition for my release.'

Mostovskoy was in no mood for joking.

'No, you shouldn't be in one of Hitler's camps – not with the hatred you bear us. Nor should this character.' He pointed at Ikonnikov who was making his way towards them.

Ikonnikov's hands and face were smeared with clay. He held out some dirty sheets of paper covered in writing and said: 'Have a look through this. Tomorrow I might be dead.'

'All right. But why've you decided to leave us so suddenly?'

'Do you know what I've just heard? The foundations we've been digging are for gas ovens. Today we began pouring the concrete.'

'Yes,' said Chernetsov, 'there were rumours about that when we were laying the railway-tracks.'

He looked round. Mostovskoy thought Chernetsov must be wondering whether the men coming in from work had noticed how straightforwardly and naturally he was talking to an Old Bolshevik. He probably felt proud to be seen like this by the Italians, Norwegians, Spanish and English – and, above all, by the Russian prisoners-of-war.

'But how can people carry on working?' asked Ikonnikov. 'How can we help to prepare such a horror?'

Chernetsov shrugged his shoulders. 'Do you think we're in England or something? Even if eight thousand people refused to work, it wouldn't change anything. They'd be dead in less than an hour.'

'No,' said Ikonnikov. 'I can't. I just can't do it.'

'Then that's the end of you,' said Mostovskoy.

'He's right,' said Chernetsov. 'This comrade knows very well what it means to attempt to instigate a strike in a country where there's no democracy.'

His argument with Mostovskoy had upset him. Here, in the Nazi camp, the phrases he had repeated so often in his Paris apartment sounded absurd; they rang false even in his ears. The other prisoners were always repeating the word 'Stalingrad'. Like it or not, the fate of the world hung on that city.

A young Englishman had made a victory sign and said: 'I'm praying for you all. Stalingrad's halted the avalanche.' Words like these made Chernetsov feel happy and excited.

He turned to Mostovskoy.

'Heine said that only a fool reveals his weaknesses to an enemy. Very well, maybe I am a fool, but you're right – I do understand the meaning of the struggle being fought by your army. That's a bitter admission for a Russian socialist. It's hard to both rejoice and suffer, to hate you but feel pride in your achievements.'

He looked at Mostovskoy. For a moment it seemed as though even his good eye had filled with blood.

'But do you really not understand, even here, that man cannot live without freedom and democracy?'

'Come on now!' said Mostovskoy sternly. 'That's enough of your hysterics.'

He looked round. Chernetsov thought Mostovskoy must be wondering whether the men coming in from work had noticed how straightforwardly and naturally he was talking to a Menshevik, an émigré. He probably felt ashamed to be seen like this by the foreigners – and above all by the other Russians.

Chernetsov's blood-filled socket stared blindly at Mostovskoy.

Ikonnikov reached up and grasped the bare foot of the priest sitting on the second tier of boards.

'*Que dois-je faire, mio padre? Nous travaillons dans una Vernichtungslager.*'

Ikonnikov looked round at the three men with his coal-black eyes.

'*Tout le monde travaille là-bas. Et moi je travaille là-bas. Nous sommes des esclaves,*' he said slowly. '*Dieu nous pardonnera.*'

'*C'est son métier,*' added Mostovskoy.

'*Mais ce n'est pas votre métier,*' said Gardi reproachfully.

'Yes, that's what you said, Mikhail Sidorovich,' said Ikonnikov, speaking so quickly he almost tripped up over his own words, 'but I'm not asking for absolution. It's wrong to make out that only the people in power are guilty, that you yourself are only an innocent slave. I'm helping to build an extermination camp; I'm responsible before the people who are to be gassed. But I'm free. I can say "No!" What power can stop me if I have the strength not to be afraid of extinction? I will say "No!" *Je dirai non, mio padre, je dirai non!*'

Gardi placed his hands on Ikonnikov's grey head.

'*Donnez-moi votre main,*' he said.

'Now the shepherd's going to admonish the lost sheep for his pride,' said Chernetsov.

Mostovskoy nodded.

But, rather than admonishing Ikonnikov, Gardi lifted his dirty hand to his lips and kissed it.

68

The following day Chernetsov was talking to one of his few acquaintances among the Soviet Russians, a soldier called Pavlyukov who worked as a medical orderly in the infirmary. Pavlyukov was complaining about having to leave his present job to join the digging gangs.

'It's the Party members,' he said. 'They've got everything sewn up. They hate me because I bribed the right people and got myself a good job. But they know how to look after themselves, all right – they always end up working in the kitchens, washrooms and stores. Do you remember what it was like before the war, grandad? Well, it's the same here. They even get their men in the kitchen to give them the biggest portions of food. An Old Bolshevik gets looked after as if he were in a health-resort, but the rest of us are no better than dogs. They just look straight through you even when you're starving to death. Is that fair? After all, we've had to endure Soviet power too.'

Chernetsov admitted it was twenty years since he had last lived in Russia. He knew that the words 'émigré' and 'abroad' immediately made Soviet Russians keep their distance. But Pavlyukov didn't react at all.

They sat down on a pile of planks. Pavlyukov, who seemed a real son of the people with his wide nose and forehead, looked at the sentry pacing about his concrete tower and said: 'I've got no choice. I'll have to join up with Vlasov. Otherwise it'll be the end of me.'

'Is that your only reason?' asked Chernetsov. 'Is it just a matter of survival?'

'I'm certainly not a kulak,' said Pavlyukov, 'and I've never had to slave away in the camps felling trees, but I've got my own grudges against the Communists. "No, you mustn't sow that . . . No, you mustn't marry her . . . No, that's not your job . . ." You end up turning into a parrot. Ever since I was a child, I'd wanted to open a shop of my own – somewhere a man could buy whatever he wanted. With its own little restaurant. "There, you've finished your shopping – now treat yourself to a beer, to some vodka, to some roast meat!" I'd have served country dishes. And my prices would have been really cheap. Baked potatoes! Fat bacon with garlic! Sauerkraut! And you know what I'd have given people to go with their drinks? Marrow-bones! I'd have kept them simmering away in the pot. "There, you've paid for your vodka – now have some black bread and some bone-marrow!" And I'd have had leather chairs so there wouldn't be any lice. "You just sit down and be quiet – we'll look after you!" Well, if I'd come out with any of that, I'd have been sent straight off to Siberia. But I really don't see what harm it could have done anyone. And I'd only have charged half the price of the State shops.'

Pavlyukov cast a sidelong glance at Chernetsov.

'Forty men from our barracks have already signed up.'

'Why?'

'For a bowl of soup. And a warm greatcoat. And because they don't want to be worked to death.'

'Any other reasons?'

'Some of them have ideological reasons.'

'What exactly?'

'Oh, various ones. The people killed in the camps. The poverty in the villages. They just can't stand Communism.'

'No,' said Chernetsov, 'that's not right. It's despicable.'

The Soviet citizen looked at the émigré with half-mocking, half-bewildered curiosity.

'It's just not right,' repeated Chernetsov. 'It's dishonourable. This is no time to settle scores. And it's the wrong way to go about it. You're not being fair to yourself or to your country.'

He stood up and rubbed his buttocks.

'No one could accuse me of sympathy for the Bolsheviks,' he said. 'But believe me – now's not the time to settle accounts. Don't do it. Don't join Vlasov!' In his excitement he had begun to stammer. 'Listen to me, comrade,' he repeated, 'don't do it!'

Pronouncing the word 'comrade' took him back to the days of his youth. 'Oh God,' he muttered, 'oh God, could I ever . . . ?'

. . . The train drew away from the platform. The air was thick with dust and carried a variety of disparate smells – lilac, fumes from the kitchen of the station restaurant, smoke from the locomotives, the smell that comes from rubbish-dumps in the spring.

The lantern drew slowly further away. In the end it was just a still point among the red and green lights.

The student stood for a while on the platform and then went out through the gate beside the station. As she said goodbye, the woman had flung her arms round his neck and kissed his hair and forehead, overwhelmed – like he was – by a sudden surge of emotion . . . He walked away from the station. His head span and a new happiness welled up inside him; it was as though something were beginning that would eventually fill his whole life.

He remembered that evening when he finally left Russia. He remembered it as he lay in hospital after the operation to remove his eye. He remembered it as he walked through the cool, dark entrance to the bank where he worked.

The poet Khodasevich, who had also left Russia for Paris, had written about just this:

> A pilgrim walks away in the mist:
> It's you who comes into my mind.
> On a fume-filled street a car drives past:
> It's you who comes into my mind.
> I see the lamps come on at six,
> But have only you in my mind.
> I travel west – your image picks
> Its endless way through my mind.

He wanted to go back to Mostovskoy and ask:

'You didn't ever know a Natasha Zadonskaya, did you? Is she still alive? And did you really walk over the same earth as her for all those decades?'

69

Keyze, a burglar from Hamburg who wore yellow leggings and a cream-coloured check jacket with outside pockets, was in a good mood at roll-call that evening. Mispronouncing the words, he sang quietly: '*Kali zavtra voyna, yesli zavtra v pokhod . . .*'

There was a good-humoured expression on his yellow, wrinkled face. He clapped the other prisoners on the back with a puffy, hairless, snow-white hand whose fingers were strong enough to strangle a horse. He didn't think twice about killing; it was no more difficult than pulling out his knife in jest. He was always rather excited after he had killed someone, like a kitten that has been playing with a may-bug.

Most of the murders he committed were on the instructions of Sturmführer Drottenhahr, the director of the medical section of the eastern block. The most difficult part was carrying the corpses to the crematorium, but Keyze didn't have to do this himself and no one would have dared ask him. Nor were people allowed to get so weak they had to be taken to the place of execution on stretchers; Drottenhahr knew his job.

Keyze never made rude remarks or hurried the people who were to be operated on; he never pushed them or hit them. Although he had climbed the two concrete steps more than four hundred times, he felt a real interest in his victims – an interest aroused by the mixture of horror, impatience, submissiveness and passionate curiosity with which they looked at their executioner.

Keyze could never understand why the very mundaneness of his job so appealed to him. There was nothing special about the special cell; it was just a stool, a grey stone floor, a drain, a tap, a hosepipe, and a writing desk with a notebook on it.

The operation itself was equally mundane. If he had to shoot someone, Keyze called it 'emptying a coffee-bean into someone's head'; if he had to give someone an injection of carbolic acid, he called it 'a small dose of elixir'.

The whole mystery of human life seemed to lie in the coffee-bean or the elixir. Really this mystery was astonishingly simple.

Keyze's brown eyes simply weren't those of a human being; they seemed to be made of plastic or some yellowish-brown resin. When they took on an expression of merriment, they inspired terror – probably the same terror a fish feels when it swims up to a snag half-covered in sand and suddenly discovers that the dark mass has eyes, teeth and tentacles.

Keyze was well aware of his own superiority over the artists, revolutionaries, scholars, generals and members of religious sects in the barrack-huts. It wasn't just a matter of the coffee-bean or the elixir; it was an innate feeling of superiority that brought him real joy.

Nor was it a matter of his huge physical strength, his ability to brush obstacles aside, to knock people off their feet or smash through steel with his bare hands. No, what he admired in himself were the complex enigmas of his own soul. There was something very special in his anger, something in the play of his moods that transcended logic. On one occasion a group of Russian prisoners picked out by the Gestapo was being taken to the special barracks; Keyze had asked them to sing some of their favourite songs.

Four Russians with swollen hands and sepulchral expressions struck up 'Where Are You Now, My Suliko?' Keyze listened sorrowfully, glancing now and again at the man with high cheekbones who was standing furthest away. He respectfully refrained from interrupting, but at the end of the song he told this man that since he hadn't sung with the group he must now sing a solo. He looked at the dirty collar of his tunic and the remnants of his torn-off major's tabs and said: '*Verstehen Sie, Herr Major*? Do you understand, swine?'

The man nodded. Keyze picked him up by the collar and gave him a little shake; he might have been shaking an alarm-clock that had gone wrong. The newly-arrived prisoner punched Keyze on the cheekbone and cursed him.

Everyone thought that would be the end of the prisoner. But instead of killing Major Yershov there and then, Keyze simply led him to a place in the corner, beside the window. It had been lying unoccupied, waiting for the appearance of a prisoner Keyze took a liking to. Later that day Keyze brought Yershov a hard-boiled goose-egg and said with a laugh: '*Ihre Stimme wird schön!*'*

From then on Yershov remained a favourite of Keyze's. The other people in the barracks also treated him with respect; his unbending severity was tempered with gentleness and gaiety.

Brigade Commissar Osipov, one of the men who had sung 'Suliko', was furious with Yershov after the incident with Keyze. 'A very tricky customer indeed!' he said of him. Mostovskoy, on the other hand, soon christened him 'the Master of Men's Minds'.

Another man to dislike Yershov was Kotikov, a silent fellow who seemed to know everything about everyone. Kotikov was colourless; everything about him – his eyes, his lips, even his voice – was colourless. The lack of colour was so pronounced that it became a colour in its own right.

Keyze's gaiety during roll-call that evening made the prisoners tense and frightened. They were always expecting something bad to happen; day and night their anxious premonitions waxed and waned.

Towards the end of roll-call eight kapos came into the special barracks. They wore ridiculous, clown-like peaked caps and a bright yellow band on their sleeves. You could tell from their faces that they didn't fill their mess-tins from the general cauldron.

The man in command, König, was tall, fair-haired and handsome. He was dressed in a steel-coloured greatcoat with torn-off stripes; beneath it you could glimpse a pair of brilliantly polished boots that seemed almost white. A former SS officer, he had lost his commission and been imprisoned for various criminal offences. He was now head of the camp police.

'*Mütze ab!*' he shouted.**

The search began. With the trained, habitual movements of factory workers, the kapos tapped tables for hollow spaces, shook out rags, checked the seams of people's clothes and looked inside saucepans . . . Sometimes, as a joke, they kneed a prisoner in the buttocks and said: 'Your good health!'

Now and again they turned to König with something they had found: a note, a razor-blade, a pad of paper. With a wave of his glove,

* 'This will make your voice beautiful!'
** 'Caps off!'

König let them know whether or not it was of interest. Meanwhile the prisoners remained standing in ranks.

Mostovskoy and Yershov were standing next to each other, glancing at König and Keyze. The faces of the two Germans looked as though they had been cast from metal.

Mostovskoy swayed on his feet; he felt dizzy. He pointed at Keyze and said: 'A fine individual!'

'A truly splendid Aryan,' replied Yershov. Not wishing to be overheard by Chernetsov, he whispered: 'But some of our lads aren't much better.'

Keen to join in the conversation he couldn't hear, Chernetsov said: 'Every people has a sacred right to its own heroes, saints and villains.'

Mostovskoy turned towards Yershov, but what he said was also addressed to Chernetsov: 'Of course we've got our share of scoundrels too, but still, there's something unique about a German murderer.'

The search came to an end and the command was given to go to bed. The prisoners began to climb up onto the boards.

Mostovskoy lay down and stretched out his legs. Then he realized he hadn't yet checked to see if his belongings were all in place. He sat up with a wheeze and began to go through them. At first he thought he must have lost his scarf or his gingham foot-cloths. In the end he found them, but his feeling of anxiety remained.

Yershov came over and said in an undertone: 'Kapo Nedzelsky's been gossiping. He say's our block's being split up. A few of us are being kept for further interrogation; the rest are being sent to general camps.'

'What does it matter?' asked Mostovskoy.

Yershov sat down.

'Mikhail Sidorovich!' he said in a very clear whisper.

Mostovskoy raised himself up on one elbow and looked at him.

'I've been thinking about something important, Mikhail Sidorovich. I need to talk to you. If we're going to die, I think we should do it in style.'

Yershov went on in a whisper. As he listened, Mostovskoy grew more and more excited. It was as though some magical wind was blowing on him.

'Time is precious,' said Yershov. 'If the Germans ever take Stalingrad, then everyone will just sink back into apathy. You only have to look at someone like Kotikov to see that.'

Yershov's plan was to form a military alliance of prisoners-of-war. He went through this plan point by point, as though he were reading from notes.

'. . . The imposition of discipline and solidarity on all Soviet citizens in the camp. The expulsion of traitors. Sabotage. The setting-up of action committees among the Polish, French, Yugoslav and Czech prisoners . . .'

He glanced up at the dim light and said: 'There are some of our own men in the munitions factory. They trust me. We can start hoarding arms. Then we can widen our horizons. Three-men cells. An alliance with the German underground. The use of terror against traitors. Our final goal – a general uprising, a united free Europe.'

'A united free Europe! Oh Yershov, Yershov . . .'

'I'm not just talking. I mean business.'

'Well then,' said Mostovskoy, 'you can count on me.' He shook his head and repeated, 'A free Europe . . . Now we've even got our own section of the Communist International here in the camp . . . With two members, one of them not even a Communist.'

'With your knowledge of English, French and German we'll be able to make thousands of contacts,' said Yershov. 'What price your Comintern now? "Prisoners of the world unite!"'

Looking at Yershov, Mostovskoy pronounced a phrase he thought he had forgotten long ago: 'The Will of the People!' He felt quite surprised at himself.

'We'll have to talk to Osipov and Colonel Zlatokrylets,' Yershov went on. 'Osipov's an important figure. But he doesn't like me – you must talk to him yourself. And I'll talk to the Colonel today. That makes four of us.'

70

Day and night Yershov mulled over his plans for an underground movement embracing the whole of Germany. He worked out a system of communications between the various organizations and learned the name of each different camp together with its railway station. He would have to devise a secret code. And the organizers would need to be able to move freely from camp to camp – he would have to find a way of getting the clerks to include their names in the transport-lists.

His soul was inspired by a great vision. The work of thousands of underground agitators and heroic saboteurs would culminate in an armed take-over of the camps. The men involved in the uprising would need to capture the camp anti-aircraft guns and convert them to weapons that could be used against tanks and infantry. He would have to pick out the prisoners who had experience of anti-aircraft guns and form them into gun-crews.

Major Yershov knew what camp life was like; he was aware of the power of fear, bribery and the desire for a full stomach. He had seen how many people had exchanged honest soldiers' tunics for the epaulettes and light-blue overcoats of Vlasov's volunteers. He had seen apathy, betrayal and grovelling obsequiousness. He had seen people's horror at the horrors inflicted on them. He had seen them petrified with fear before the officers of the dreaded SS.

Yes, ambitious though he was, he was no mere dreamer. During the black days of the German blitzkrieg he had been able to rally men whose stomachs were distended with hunger; his boldness and enthusiasm had been a source of encouragement to all his comrades. He was a man whose contempt for violence was passionate and unextinguishable.

Everyone could feel the bright warmth that emanated from Yershov. It was the same simple, necessary warmth that comes from a birch log in a Russian stove. It was this good-hearted warmth – not just the power of his intellect and his fearlessness – that had made him the acknowledged leader of the Soviet officers in the camp.

He had long known that Mostovskoy was the first person he would reveal his plans to . . . Now, more than ever before in the thirty-three years of his life, he had a sense of his own strength. Here he was, lying on the bedboards and gazing up at the rough planks of the ceiling. He felt as though he were looking up at the lid of a coffin, his heart still beating . . .

His life before the war had been difficult. His father, a peasant in the *oblast* of Voronezh, had been dispossessed in 1930 after being denounced as a kulak. At that time Yershov had been doing his military service.

He had refused to break with his father. He was turned down by the Military Academy – even though he had passed the entrance exams with the grade 'excellent'. After graduating from military school with considerable difficulty, he was posted to a district recruiting office. Meanwhile his father and the rest of his family had been deported to the Northern Urals. Yershov applied for leave and set off to visit them. From Sverdlovsk he travelled two hundred kilometres on the narrow-gauge railway. On either side of the line were vast expanses of bog and forest, together with stacks of dressed timber, barbed wire, barrack-huts, dug-outs and tall watch-towers that looked like toadstools on giant legs. The train was delayed twice – a posse of guards was searching for an escaped prisoner. During the night they waited in a passing-loop for a train coming from the opposite direction. Yershov was unable to sleep for the whistles of sentries and the barking of OGPU dogs – close to the station was a large camp.

It took Yershov over two days to reach the end of the line. He had a lieutenant's tabs on his collar and his documents were in order; nevertheless, each time they were checked, he expected to be packed off to a camp with the words: 'Come on, get your things together.' It was as though even the air in this region had barbed wire round it.

He travelled the next seventy kilometres in the back of a lorry; once again there were bogs on either side of the road. The lorry belonged to the OGPU farm where Yershov's father was working. It was jammed with deported workers being sent to fell trees. Yershov questioned them, but they were afraid of his uniform and answered only in monosyllables.

Towards evening the lorry reached a small village squeezed in between the edge of the forest and the edge of the bog. Yershov was to remember the gentle calm of that sunset in the Northern wastes. In the evening light the huts looked quite black, as though they had been boiled in pitch.

When he entered the dug-out, bringing with him the evening light, he was met by the smell of poverty, by miserable food, miserable clothes and miserable bedding, by a warm, suffocating dampness that was filled with smoke.

Then his father emerged from the darkness. The expression on his thin face, in his handsome eyes, was indescribable.

He flung his thin arms around his son's neck. There was such pain in this plea for help, such trust, that Yershov could find only one response: he burst into tears.

Soon afterwards they visited three graves. Yershov's mother had died during the first winter, his elder sister Anyuta during the second winter, and Marusya during the third.

Here, in this world of camps, the cemeteries and villages merged together. The same moss grew on the walls of wooden huts, on the sides of dug-outs, on the grave-mounds and on the tussocks in the bogs. Yershov's mother and sisters would remain for ever beneath this sky – through dry winter frosts, through wet autumns when the soil of the cemetery swells as the dark bog encroaches.

Father and son stood there in silence, side by side. Then the father glanced up at his son and spread his hands helplessly as though to say: 'May I be pardoned by both the living and the dead. I failed to save the people I loved.'

That night his father told his story. He spoke calmly and quietly. What he described could only be spoken about quietly; it could never be conveyed by tears or screams.

On a small box covered with newspaper stood some food and a half-litre of vodka Yershov had brought as a present. The old man talked while his son sat beside him and listened. He talked about hunger, about people from the village who'd died, about old women who had gone mad, about children whose bodies had grown lighter than a chicken or a balalaika.

He described their fifty-day journey, in winter, in a cattle-wagon with a leaking roof; day after day, the dead had travelled on alongside the living. They had continued the journey on foot, the women carrying their children in their arms. Yershov's mother had been delirious with fever. They had been taken to the middle of the forest where there wasn't a single hut or dug-out; in the depths of winter they had begun a new life, building camp-fires, making beds out of spruce-branches, melting snow in saucepans, burying their dead . . .

'The will of Stalin,' he said without the least trace of anger or resentment. He spoke as simple people speak about a force of destiny, a force that knows no weakness or hesitation.

Yershov returned from leave and sent a petition to Kalinin, begging him to act with supreme, unprecedented mercy, to pardon an innocent old man and allow him to come and live with his son. Before his letter even reached Moscow, Yershov was summoned before the authorities; he had been denounced for making his journey to the Urals.

After being discharged from the army, he went to work on a building-site. He wanted to save some money and then join his father. Very soon, however, he received a letter from the Urals informing him of his father's death.

On the second day of the war, Lieutenant Yershov was called up.

During the battle for Roslavl his battalion commander was killed; Yershov took command. He rallied his men, launched a counter-attack, won back the ford and secured the withdrawal of the heavy artillery belonging to the General Staff reserves.

The greater the burden, the stronger his shoulders became. He didn't know his own strength. Submissiveness just wasn't a part of his nature. The stronger the force against him, the more furious his determination to fight.

Sometimes he wondered why it was he felt such hatred for the Vlasovites. What Vlasov said in his appeals to the prisoners was exactly what he had heard from his father. He knew it was true. But he also knew that on the tongues of the Germans and Vlasovites this truth turned into a lie.

He was certain that he was not only fighting the Germans, but fighting for a free Russia: certain that a victory over Hitler would be a victory over the death camps where his father, his mother and his sisters had perished.

Now that his background was no longer relevant, Yershov had proved himself a true leader, a force to be reckoned with; this realization was at once pleasant and bitter. High rank, decorations, the Special Section, personnel departments, examination boards, telephone calls from the *raykom*, the opinion of the deputy chief of the Political Section – none of this meant anything any more.

Mostovskoy once told him: 'In the words of Heinrich Heine, "we're all of us naked beneath our clothes." But while one man looks miserable and anaemic when he takes off his uniform, another man is disfigured by tight clothing – you only see his true strength when he's naked.'

His dreams had become a concrete task. He was constantly going over everything he knew about people, weighing up their good and bad points, wondering whom he should recruit, whom he should entrust with what position. Who should he include in his underground staff? There were five names that came to mind. Petty human weaknesses and eccentricities suddenly took on a new importance; trivial matters were no longer trivial.

General Gudz had the authority of his rank, but he was weak-willed, cowardly and obviously uneducated; he must have needed a good staff and an intelligent second-in-command. He took it for granted, never showing the least gratitude, that the other officers should do him favours and give him presents of food. He seemed to remember his cook more often than his wife and daughters. He was always talking about hunting, about ducks and geese; all he appeared to remember about the years he had served in the Caucasus was the wild goats and boar he had hunted. From the look of him he had drunk a lot. And he boasted. He often talked about the defeats of 1941: everyone else, including his neighbours on either side, had made countless mistakes – while he himself had always been right. But he never blamed the top brass for the disasters of that year . . . He had seen a lot of service. Yes, and he knew how to get on with the right people . . . If it had been up to him, Yershov wouldn't have trusted Gudz with a regiment, let alone a whole corps.

Brigade Commissar Osipov, on the other hand, was a very intelligent man. One moment he would crack a joke about how they had expected an easy war on the enemy's territory; an hour later he would be giving a sermon to someone who had shown signs of faint-heartedness, ticking him off with stony severity. And the next day he would be announcing in his lisping voice: 'Yes, comrades, we fly higher than anyone else, further than anyone else and quicker than anyone else. Just look how far we've managed to fly.'

He spoke very lucidly about the defeats of the first months of the war, but with no more regret than a chess-player who has lost a piece. He talked freely and easily to people, but with a bluff comradeliness that seemed affected and false. What he enjoyed most was talking to Kotikov . . . Why was it he was so interested in Kotikov?

Osipov had vast experience; he knew people. This was very important for Yershov's underground staff, even essential. But it might also turn out to be a hindrance.

Osipov liked to tell amusing anecdotes about important military figures, referring to them familiarly as Semyon Budyonniy, Andryusha Yeremenko . . .

Once he told Yershov: 'Tukhachevsky, Yegorov and Blücher were no more guilty than you or me.'

Kirillov, however, had told Yershov that in 1937, when Osipov had been Deputy Director of the Military Academy, he had mercilessly denounced dozens of men as enemies of the people.

He was terrified of being ill, constantly prodding himself or sticking out his tongue and squinting at it in case it was furred over. But he clearly wasn't afraid of death.

Colonel Zlatokrylets was very gloomy, but a straightforward man and a real soldier. He blamed the High Command for 1941. Everyone could sense his strength as a commanding officer. He was equally strong physically. He had a powerful voice, the kind of voice one needs to rally fugitives or lead an attack. And he swore a lot.

He found it easier to give orders than explanations. But he was a true comrade, someone who would give a soldier soup from his own mess-tin.

No, there were certainly no flies on Zlatokrylets. He was a man Yershov could work with. Even if he was coarse and boorish.

As for Kirillov, he was intelligent, but somehow very weak. He noticed every trifle; his tired, half-closed eyes saw everything. He was cold, misanthropic, but surprisingly ready to forgive weakness and cowardice. He wasn't afraid of death; indeed, there were times when it seemed to attract him.

His view of the retreat was more intelligent than that of any of the other officers. Not a Party member himself, he had once said: 'I don't believe the Communists can make people better. It just doesn't happen. Look at history.'

Although he appeared to feel indifferent about everything, one night he'd just lain there and cried. Yershov had asked what was the matter. After a long time he had replied very quietly: 'I'm sad about Russia.' On another occasion he had said: 'One thing I do miss is music.' And yesterday he'd come up with a crazy grin on his face and

318

said: 'Listen, Yershov, I'm going to read you a poem.' Yershov hadn't liked it, but the words had lodged themselves in his memory.

> No need, comrade, in this unceasing pain
> Of yours to call for help. Strange, but it's you
> I call to help me, to warm my hands again.
> Yes, on your still warm blood I'll warm mine too . . .
> So do not worry, do not weep or bleed!
> Nothing can harm you now that you are dead.
> Can you help me? There's one thing I still need –
> Your boots . . . There are still battles ahead.

Had he really written that himself?

No, he certainly didn't want Kirillov. How could he lead others if it was all he could do to keep going himself?

But as for Mostovskoy! He was astonishingly well-educated and he had an iron will. People said he'd been like granite under interrogation. Still, there was no one Yershov couldn't find fault with. The other day he'd said to Mostovskoy: 'Why do you waste so much time gossiping with riff-raff, Mikhail Sidorovich? Why bother with that gloomy Ikonnikov-Morzh and that one-eyed scoundrel of an émigré?'

'Are you afraid I'll waver in my convictions?' asked Mostovskoy teasingly. 'Do you think I'll become an evangelist or a Menshevik?'

'Who knows?' said Yershov. 'If you don't want to smell, you shouldn't touch shit. That Ikonnikov of yours was in our camps once. Now the Germans are dragging him off for interrogation. He'll sell himself, he'll sell you and he'll sell whoever's close to you . . .'

No one was ideal. Yershov simply had to weigh up everyone's strengths and weaknesses. That was easy enough. But it was only from a man's spirit that you could judge his suitability. And this could be guessed at, but never measured. He had begun with Mostovskoy.

71

Breathing heavily, Major-General Gudz was making his way towards Mostovskoy. He shuffled along, wheezing and sticking out his lower lip; brown folds of loose skin rippled over his cheeks and neck. At one time he had been impressively stout, and these sounds and movements were all that remained; now they seemed quite bizarre.

'My dear grandfather,' he said to Mostovskoy. 'I'm a mere milksop. I've no more right to criticize you than a major has to criticize a colonel-general. But still, let me be quite frank with you: fraternizing with Yershov is a mistake. He's politically dubious and he has no military understanding whatsoever. He likes giving advice to colonels, but he has the mentality of a lieutenant. You should be on your guard with him.'

'You're talking nonsense, your excellency,' said Mostovskoy.

'What do you expect?' wheezed Gudz. 'Of course I'm talking nonsense. But yesterday I was informed that twelve men from the general barracks have enrolled in this accursed Russian Liberation Army. Do you realize how many of them were kulaks? What I'm saying isn't just a personal opinion. I was instructed to say this by a man of considerable political experience.'

'You don't happen to mean Osipov, do you?'

'And what if I do? A theoretician like you will never be able to understand the swine we have to deal with here.'

'What a strange conversation this is,' said Mostovskoy. 'Sometimes I begin to think there's nothing left of people except political vigilance. Who'd have thought we'd end up like this?'

Gudz listened to the wheezing and bubbling of his bronchitis and said: 'I'll never live to see freedom. No.' There was something terrible about the sadness in his voice.

Watching him walk away, Mostovskoy suddenly slapped himself on the knee. Ikonnikov's papers had disappeared – that was why he had felt so anxious after last night's search.

'God knows what that devil's gone and written. Maybe Yershov's right and he is a provocateur. He probably planted the papers on me on purpose.'

He went over to Ikonnikov's place. He wasn't there and his neighbours had no idea what had happened to him. Yes, damn it – he should never have spoken to that holy fool, that seeker after God.

And as for Chernetsov – what if they had always done nothing but argue? What difference did that make? What was the use of such arguments? And Chernetsov had been there when Ikonnikov handed over the papers . . . There was a witness as well as an informer.

'You're a bloody fool – hobnobbing with scum and then throwing your life away when you're needed to fight for the Revolution,' he said bitterly to himself.

In the washroom he bumped into Osipov. Under a dim electric light he was washing his foot-cloths in a tin trough.

'I'm glad you're here,' said Mostovskoy. 'I want to talk to you.'

Osipov nodded, looked round and wiped his hands on his sides. The two of them sat down on the cement ledge by the wall.

'Just what I thought. The rascal certainly gets around,' said Osipov when Mostovskoy began to talk about Yershov's plans.

'Comrade Mostovskoy,' he said, stroking Mostovskoy's hand with his damp palm, 'I'm amazed at your decisiveness. You're one of Lenin's Bolsheviks. Age doesn't exist for you. You're an example to us all.'

He lowered his voice.

'Comrade Mostovskoy, we've already set up a military organiz-ation. We'd decided not to tell you about it prematurely so as not to risk your life. But there's no such thing as old age for a comrade of Lenin's. Still, there's one thing I must say: Yershov is not to be trusted. You must look at it objectively. He's a kulak. The repressions have soured him. All the same, we're realists – and we know that for the time being we can't get on without him. He's won himself a cheap popularity. You know better than I how the Party has always made use of people like that for its own ends. But you ought to be aware of our opinion of him: we trust him only so far, and only for the time being . . .'

'Comrade Osipov, you can trust Yershov all the way. I'm sure of him.'

They could hear the water dripping onto the cement floor.

'Listen, comrade Mostovskoy,' said Osipov slowly. 'There can be no secrets from you. We have one comrade who was sent here by Moscow. I can tell you his name: Kotikov. What I've been saying is his view of Yershov, not just my own. For us Communists Kotikov's directives are law – orders given to us by the Party, orders given to us, in exceptional circumstances, by Stalin himself. But we can work with this godson of yours, this "master of men's minds" as you've chris-tened him. We've already decided that. What matters is to be realistic, to think dialectically. But you know that better than anyone.'

Mostovskoy remained silent. Osipov embraced him and kissed him three times on the lips. There were tears in his eyes.

'It's as though I were kissing my own father,' he said. 'And I want to make the sign of the cross over you, just like my mother used to do over me.'

Slowly the feeling that had tortured Mostovskoy, the sense of life's impossible complexity, was melting away. Once again, as in his youth, the world seemed clear and simple, neatly divided into friends and enemies.

That night the SS came to the special barracks and took off six men, Mikhail Sidorovich Mostovskoy among them.

PART TWO

1

When people in the rear see fresh troops being moved up to the Front, they feel a sense of joyful expectation: these gun batteries, these freshly-painted tanks seem to be the ones destined to strike the decisive blow, the blow that will bring about a quick end to the war.

Men who have been held in reserve for a long time feel a special tension as they board the trains that will take them to the front line. Young officers dream of special orders from Stalin in sealed envelopes . . . More experienced men, of course, don't dream of anything of the sort: they just drink hot water, soften up their dried fish by banging it against a table or the sole of a boot, and discuss the private life of the major or the opportunities for barter at the next junction.

They already know only too well what happens when a train unloads at a station in the middle of nowhere, a place apparently known only to the German dive-bombers . . . How the new recruits slowly lose their high spirits; how, after the monotony of the journey, you can no longer even lie down for an hour; how for days on end you don't get a chance to eat or drink; how your temples seem to be about to burst from the incessant roar of overheated motors; how your hands barely have the strength to move the gears and levers. As for the commander – he's had more than enough of coded messages, more than enough of being cursed and sworn at over the radio. His superiors just want to plug a gap in the line – they don't care how well the men did in their firing exercises. 'Forward! Forward!' That's the only word the commander ever hears. And he does press forward – at breakneck speed. And then sometimes the unit gets flung into action before he's even had time to reconnoitre the area; an irritable, exhausted voice simply orders: 'Counter-attack at once! Along those heights! We've got no one there and the enemy's pushing hard. It's a mess.'

Then, in the ears of the drivers and mechanics, of the radio-operators and gun-layers, the roar of the long march blurs into the whistle of German shells, the crash of exploding mortar-bombs.

This is when the madness of war becomes most obvious . . . An hour later there is nothing to show for all your work except some broken-down, burning tanks with twisted guns and torn tracks. Where are the hard months of training now? What has become of the patient, diligent work of the mechanics and electricians?

And the superior officer draws up a standard report to cover up the useless waste of this fresh unit, this unit he flung into action with such thoughtless haste: 'The action of the forces newly arrived from the rear temporarily checked the enemy advance and made possible a regrouping of the forces under my command.'

If only he hadn't just shouted, 'Forward! Forward!' – if only he had just allowed them time to reconnoitre the area and not blunder straight into a minefield! Even if the tanks hadn't achieved anything decisive, at least they'd have given the Germans a run for their money.

Novikov's tank corps was on its way to the Front. The naïve young soldiers, men who had not yet received their baptism of fire, believed they were the ones who would take part in the decisive operation. The older men just laughed; Makarov, the commanding officer of the 3rd Brigade, and Fatov, the best of the battalion commanders, had seen all this too many times before.

The sceptics and pessimists had gained their knowledge and understanding through bitter experience; they had paid for it with blood and suffering. In this they were superior to the greenhorns. Nevertheless, they were wrong: Novikov's tank corps was indeed destined to play a decisive role in an operation that was to determine both the outcome of the war and the subsequent fate of hundreds of millions of people.

2

Novikov had been ordered to contact Lieutenant-General Ryutin on arrival in Kuibyshev, in order to answer several questions of interest to the *Stavka*. He had expected to be met at the station, but the commandant, a major with a wild and yet very sleepy look in his eyes, said that no one had asked for him. It turned out to be impossible even to telephone the general; his number was secret.

In the end Novikov set off on foot. In the station square he felt the usual timidity of a field officer in the unfamiliar surroundings of a city. His sense of his own importance suddenly crumbled: here there were no orderlies holding out telephone receivers, no drivers rushing to start up his car.

Instead, people were rushing along the cobbled street to join a newly formed queue at the door of a store. 'Who's last . . . ? Then I'm after you.' To these people with their clanking milk-cans this queue was evidently the most important thing in the world. Novikov felt particularly irritated by the soldiers and officers; nearly all of them were carrying bundles and suitcases. 'The swine – the whole lot of them should be put straight on a train for the Front!' he said to himself.

Could he really be about to see her? Today? 'Zhenya! Hello!'

His interview with General Ryutin was extremely brief. They had barely started when the general received a telephone call from the General Staff – he was to fly to Moscow immediately.

Ryutin apologized to Novikov and then made a call on the local exchange.

'Everything's been changed, Masha. I'm flying by Douglas at dawn tomorrow. Tell Anna Aristarkhovna. We won't be able to bring any potatoes – they're still at the State farm.'

His pale face took on a look of suffering and disgust. Then, evidently interrupting a flood of complaints, he snapped, 'So you want me to inform the General Staff that I'm unable to leave until the tailor's finished my wife's coat?' and hung up.

'Comrade Colonel,' he said to Novikov, 'give me your opinion of the suspension of these tanks. Do they answer to the requirements we originally laid down?'

Novikov found this conversation wearisome. During his months in command he had learned to evaluate people very quickly. He had learned to weigh up the importance of all the inspectors, instructors, heads of commissions and other representatives who had come to see him. He understood very well the importance of such simple phrases as 'Comrade Malenkov told me to inform you . . .' And he knew that there were generals covered in medals, full of bustle and eloquence, who were powerless even to obtain a ton of fuel-oil, appoint a storekeeper or fire a clerk.

Ryutin's position wasn't on the top level of the pyramid of State; he was merely a statistician, a provider of information. During their conversation Novikov looked repeatedly at his watch.

The general closed his large notebook.

'I'm sorry, comrade Colonel. I'm afraid I have to leave you. I'm flying at dawn tomorrow. I don't know what to do. Perhaps you should come to Moscow yourself?'

'Yes, comrade Lieutenant-General. Together with all the tanks under my command,' said Novikov coldly.

They said goodbye. Ryutin asked him to give his regards to General Nyeudobnov; they had once served together. As Novikov walked down the strip of green carpet leading towards the door of the large office, he heard Ryutin back on the telephone:

'Get me the director of *kolkhoz* number one.'

'Poor man,' thought Novikov. 'He's got to rescue his potatoes.'

He left the building and set out for Yevgenia Nikolaevna's. In Stalingrad he had visited her on a stifling summer night; he had come straight from the steppe, covered in the smoke and dust of the retreat. There seemed to be an abyss between the man he had been then and the man he was now. And yet here he was, the same person, about to visit her once again.

'You'll be mine!' he said to himself. 'You'll be mine!'

3

It was an old two-storey house, one of those obstinate buildings that never quite keep up with the seasons; it felt cool and damp in summer, but its thick walls retained a close, dusty heat during the autumn frosts.

He rang; the door opened and he felt the closeness inside. Then, in a corridor littered with trunks and broken baskets, he caught sight of Yevgenia Nikolaevna. He saw her, but he didn't see her black dress or the white scarf round her head, he didn't even see her eyes and face, her hands and her shoulders. It was as though he saw her not with his eyes but with his heart. She gave a cry of surprise, but she didn't step back as people often do at some unexpected sight.

He greeted her and she answered. He walked towards her, his eyes closed. He felt happy; at the same time he felt ready to die then and there. He sensed the warmth of her body.

He realized that this previously unknown feeling of happiness had no need of eyes, thoughts or words.

She asked him about something or other and he answered. As he followed her down the dark corridor, he clung to her hand like a little boy afraid of being lost in a crowd.

'What a wide corridor,' he thought. 'Big enough for a tank.'

They went into a room with a window looking out onto the blank wall of the house next door. There were two beds, one on each side – one with a grey blanket and a flat crumpled pillow, the other with fluffed-up pillows and a bedspread of white lace. Above this second bed hung Easter and New Year cards with pictures of men in dinner-jackets and chickens hatching out of eggs.

The table was cluttered with sheets of rolled-up drawing-paper; in one corner stood a bottle of oil, a chunk of bread and half of a tired-looking onion.

'Zhenya,' he said.

There was a strange look in her usually alert, mocking eyes.

'You've come a long way,' she said. 'You must be hungry.'

She seemed to want to destroy something new that had arisen between them, something it was already too late to destroy. Novikov had become somehow different – a man with absolute power over hundreds of men and machines, a man with the pleading eyes of an unhappy schoolboy. This incongruity confused her: she wanted just to look down on him, to pity him, to forget his strength. Her happiness had seemed to lie in her freedom; and yet even though this freedom was now slipping away from her, she still felt happy.

'Do you still not understand?' said Novikov abruptly.

Once again he stopped listening to what either of them was saying. Once again he felt a sense of happiness well up inside him, together with the somehow connected feeling of being ready to die then and there. She put her arms round his neck. Her hair flowed across his forehead and cheeks like a stream of warm water; through it he could glimpse her eyes.

Her whispering voice blotted out the war, drowned the roar of tanks.

In the evening they ate some bread and drank some hot water. Yevgenia said: 'Our commander's forgotten the taste of black bread.'

She brought in a saucepan of buckwheat *kasha* she had left outside the window. The frost had turned the grains blue and violet. In the warmth of the room they began to sweat.

'It's like lilac,' said Yevgenia.

Novikov tried some lilac and thought, 'How awful!'

'Our commanding officer's even forgotten the taste of buckwheat,' said Yevgenia.

'Yes,' thought Novikov. 'It's a good thing I didn't take Getmanov's advice and bring her a parcel of food.'

'At the beginning of the war I was with a fighter squadron near Brest,' he told her. 'The pilots all rushed back to the airfield and I heard a Polish woman shout out: "Who's that?" A little boy answered: "A Russian soldier." At that moment I felt very acutely: "I'm Russian, yes I'm Russian!" Of course I've always known very well that I'm not a Turk, but at that moment it was as though my whole soul was singing: "I'm Russian, I'm Russian!" Of course we were brought up in a different spirit before the war . . . And today, the happiest day of my life, it's just the same – Russian grief, Russian happiness . . . Well, I just wanted to say that . . . What is it?' he asked suddenly.

In her mind's eye Yevgenia had glimpsed Krymov and his dishevelled hair. God, had they really separated for ever? It was when she was happiest that she found this thought most unbearable.

For a moment she felt she was about to reconcile this present time, the words of the man now kissing her, with that time in the past; that she was about to understand the secret currents of her life, about to glimpse what always remains hidden – those depths of the heart where one's fate is decided.

'This room,' she said, 'belongs to a German. She took me in. This angelic little bed belongs to her. In all my life, I've never met anyone more innocent and more helpless . . . It sounds strange to say this while we're at war, but I'm sure there's no kinder person in the whole city. Isn't that strange?'

'Will she be back soon?'

'No, the war's already over for her. She's been deported.'

'Thank God for that.'

She wanted to tell him how sorry she felt for Krymov. He had no one to write to, no one to go home to, nothing but hopeless gloom and loneliness. She also wanted to tell him everything about Limonov and Shargorodsky. She wanted to tell him about the notebook where Jenny Genrikhovna had written down all the funny remarks she and the other children had come out with; if he wanted to, he could read it right now – it was there on the table. And she wanted to tell him the story of her residence permit and the head of the passport office. But she still felt shy; she didn't trust him enough. Would he really want to know all this?

How strange . . . It was as though she were reliving her break with Krymov. Deep down she had always thought she could make things up, that she could bring back the past. This had consoled her. But now she was being carried away by a new force; she felt frightened and tormented. Was what had happened final, irrevocable? Poor, poor Nikolay Grigorevich! What had he done to deserve all this?

'What's going to become of us all?' she asked.

'You're going to become Yevgenia Nikolaevna Novikova,' he answered.

She looked him in the face and laughed.

'But you're a stranger. You're a stranger to me. Who are you?'

'That I can't tell you. But you're Novikova, Yevgenia Niko-laevna.'

Now she was no longer somewhere up above, looking down on her life. She poured some more hot water into his cup and asked: 'More bread?'

'If anything happens to Krymov,' she began abruptly. 'If he ends up crippled or in prison, then I'll go back to him. That's something you should know.'

'Why should he end up in prison?' asked Novikov, frowning.

'Who knows?' said Yevgenia. 'He was a member of the Comintern. Trotsky knew him. He even said about one of his articles: "That's pure marble!"'

'All right then. Go back to him. He'll send you packing.'

'That's my affair.'

He told her that after the war she would be the mistress of a large beautiful house with its own garden.

Was all this final, for ever?

For some reason she wanted Novikov to understand that Krymov was extremely talented and intelligent, that she was attached to him, that she loved him. It wasn't that she consciously wanted to make him jealous, though her words did indeed have that effect. She had even told him, and him alone, what Krymov had once told her, and her alone: those words of Trotsky's. Krymov could hardly have survived the year 1937 if anyone else had known about that. Her feelings for Novikov were such that she had to trust him; she had entrusted him with the fate of the man she had wronged.

Her head was full of thoughts – about the future, about the present, about the past. She felt numb, happy, shy, anxious, sad, appalled . . . Dozens of people – her mother, her sister, Vera, her nephews – would be affected by this change in her life. What would Novikov find to say to Limonov? What would he think of their conversations about poetry and art . . . ? But he wouldn't feel out of place – even if he hadn't heard of Chagall and Matisse . . . He was strong, strong, so strong. And she had given in to him. Soon the war would be over. Would she really never, never see Nikolay again? What had she done? It was best not to think of that now. Who knew what the future might bring?

'I've only just realized: I don't know you at all. You're a stranger – I mean it. What's all this about a house and garden? Are you being serious?'

'All right then. I'll leave the army and work on a construction site in Eastern Siberia. We can live in a hostel for married workers.'

Novikov wasn't joking.

'Perhaps not the hostel for married workers.'

'Yes,' he said emphatically. 'That's an essential part of it.'

'You must be mad. Why are you saying all this to me?' As she said this, she thought to herself: 'Kolenka.'

'What do you mean – why?' Novikov asked anxiously.

But he wasn't thinking about the past or the future. He was happy. He wasn't even frightened by the thought that he'd have to leave her in a few minutes. He was sitting next to her, looking at her . . . Yevgenia Nikolaevna Novikova . . . He was happy. It wasn't important that she was young, intelligent and beautiful. He loved her. At first he'd never even dared hope she might become his wife. Then year after year he had dreamed of nothing else. Even now, he still felt shy and timid as he waited for her smile or for some ironic comment. But he knew that something new had been born.

She watched him get ready to leave and said: 'The time has come for you to rejoin your complaining companions and cast me into the approaching waves.'*

As Novikov said goodbye, he began to realize that she wasn't really so very strong, that a woman was still a woman – for all the sharpness and clarity of her mind.

'There's so much I wanted to say and I haven't said any of it,' she said.

But that wasn't quite so. What really matters, whatever it is that decides people's fates, had become clearer. He loved her.

4

Novikov walked back to the station.

. , . Zhenya, her confused whispering, her bare feet, her tender whispering, her tears as they'd said goodbye, her power over him, her poverty and her purity, the smell of her hair, her modesty, the warmth of her body . . . And his own shyness at being just a worker and a soldier . . . And his pride at being a worker and a soldier.

As Novikov crossed the tracks, a sharp needle of fear suddenly pierced the warm blur of his thoughts. Like every soldier on a journey, he was afraid he had been left behind.

In the distance he caught sight of the open wagons, the rectangular outlines of the tanks under their tarpaulins, the sentries in their black helmets, the white curtains in the windows of the staff carriage.

A sentry corrected his stance as Novikov climbed in.

Vershkov, his orderly, was upset at not having been taken into Kuibyshev. Without a word, he placed on the table a coded message

---

* A quotation from a famous song about the Cossack chieftain, Stenka Razin.

from the *Stavka*: they were to proceed to Saratov and then take the branch-line to Astrakhan . . .

General Nyeudobnov entered the compartment. Looking not at Novikov's face, but at the telegram in his hands, he said: 'They've confirmed our destination.'

'Yes, Mikhail Petrovich. More than that – they've confirmed our fate. Stalingrad . . . ! Oh yes, greetings from Lieutenant-General Ryutin.'

'Mmm,' said Nyeudobnov. It was unclear whether this expression of indifference referred to the general's greetings or Stalingrad itself.

He was a strange man; Novikov sometimes found him quite frightening. Whenever anything had gone wrong on the journey – a delay because of a train coming in the opposite direction, a faulty axle on one of the carriages, a controller being slow to signal them on – Nyeudobnov had said with sudden excitement: 'Take down his name. That's deliberate sabotage. The swine should be arrested immediately.'

Deep down, Novikov felt indifferent towards the kulaks and saboteurs, the men who were called enemies of the people. He didn't hate them. He had never felt the least desire to have anyone flung in prison, taken before a tribunal or unmasked at a public meeting. He himself had always attributed this good-humoured indifference to a lack of political consciousness.

Nyeudobnov, on the other hand, seemed to be constantly vigilant. It was as if, whenever he met someone, he wondered suspiciously: 'And how am I to know, dear comrade, that you're not an enemy of the people yourself?' Yesterday he had told Novikov and Getmanov about the saboteur architects who had tried to convert the main Moscow boulevards into landing strips for enemy planes.

'Sounds like nonsense to me,' Novikov had said. 'It doesn't make sense technically.'

Now Nyeudobnov launched into his other favourite topic – domestic life. After testing the heating pipes in the carriage, he began to describe the central heating system he'd installed, not long before the war, on his dacha. All of a sudden Novikov found this surprisingly interesting; he asked Nyeudobnov to draw a sketch of the system, folded it up and placed it in the inside pocket of his tunic.

'Who knows? One day it might come in useful,' he said.

Soon afterwards Getmanov came in. He greeted Novikov loudly and heartily.

'So our chief's back, is he? We were beginning to think we'd have to choose a new ataman.* We were afraid Stenka Razin had abandoned his companions.'

He looked Novikov up and down good-humouredly. Novikov laughed, but as always, the presence of the commissar made him feel tense.

Getmanov seemed to know a great deal about Novikov, and it was always through his jokes that he allowed this to show. Just now he had even echoed Yevgenia's parting words about rejoining his companions – though that, of course, was pure coincidence.

Getmanov looked at his watch and announced: 'Well, gentlemen, if no one minds, I'll take a look round the town myself.'

'Go ahead,' said Novikov. 'We can manage to entertain ourselves without you.'

'That's for sure. You certainly know how to entertain yourself in Kuibyshev,' said Getmanov, adding from the doorway of the compartment: 'Well, Pyotr Pavlovich? How's Yevgenia Nikolaevna?'

His face was now quite serious; his eyes were no longer laughing.

'Very well, thank you,' said Novikov. 'But she's got a lot of work to do.'

To change the subject, he asked Nyeudobnov: 'Mikhail Petrovich, why don't you go into Kuibyshev yourself for an hour?'

'I've already seen all there is to see.'

They were sitting next to each other. As he listened to Nyeudobnov, Novikov went through his papers, putting them aside one by one and repeating every now and then: 'Very good . . . Carry on . . .'

All his career Novikov had reported to superior officers who had gone on looking through their papers as they repeated absent-mindedly: 'Very good . . . Carry on . . .' He had always found it very offensive and had never expected to end up doing it himself.

'Listen now,' he said. 'We need to make out a request for more maintenance mechanics. We've got plenty for the wheeled vehicles, but hardly any for the tanks.'

'I've already made one out. I think it should be addressed to the

* Cossack chieftain.

335

colonel-general himself. It will go to him anyway to be signed.'

'Very good,' said Novikov, signing the request. 'I want each brigade to check their anti-aircraft weapons. There's a possibility of air-attacks after Saratov.'

'I've already given instructions to that effect to the staff.'

'That's not enough. I want it to be the personal responsibility of each commanding officer. They're to report back in person not later than 1600 hours.'

'The appointment of Sazonov to the post of brigade chief of staff has been confirmed.'

'That's remarkably quick,' said Novikov.

Instead of avoiding his eyes, Nyeudobnov was smiling. He was aware of Novikov's embarrassment and irritation.

Usually Novikov lacked the courage to defend his choice of commanding officers to the end. As soon as anyone cast aspersions on their political reliability, he went sour on them. Their military abilities seemed suddenly unimportant. This time, however, he felt angry. He no longer wanted peace at any price. Looking straight at Nyeudobnov, he said:

'My mistake. I allowed more importance to be attached to a man's biographical data than to his military abilities. But that can be sorted out at the Front. To fight the Germans, you need more than a spotless background. If need be, I'll send Sazonov packing on the first day.'

Nyeudobnov shrugged his shoulders. 'Personally I've got nothing whatsoever against this Basangov. But one should always give preference to a Russian if possible. The friendship of nations is something sacred – but you must realize that there is a considerable percentage, among the national minorities, of people who are unreliable or even positively hostile.'

'We should have thought of that in 1937,' said Novikov. 'One man I knew, Mitka Yevseyev, was always strutting about and repeating: "I'm a Russian, that's all that matters!" A fat lot of good it did him – he was sent to a camp.'

'There's a time for everything,' said Nyeudobnov. 'And if this man was arrested, then he must have been an enemy of the people. People don't get arrested for nothing. Twenty-five years ago we concluded the Treaty of Brest-Litovsk with the Germans – and that was Bolshevism. Today comrade Stalin has ordered us to annihilate the German aggressors who have invaded our Soviet homeland – and that's Bolshevism too.

'Today a Bolshevik is first and foremost a Russian patriot,' he added sententiously.

All this irritated Novikov. His own sense of Russian patriotism had been forged during the most difficult days of the war; Nyeudobnov's appeared simply to have been borrowed from some office – an office to which he himself was denied admittance.

He went on talking to Nyeudobnov, felt irritated, thought about hundreds of different things ... And all the time his heart was thumping, his cheeks burning as though he had been in the wind.

It was as if a whole battalion was marching over his heart, as if thousands of boots were beating out the words: 'Zhenya, Zhenya, Zhenya.'

Vershkov looked into the compartment. By now he had forgiven Novikov and his tone of voice was conciliatory.

'Beg leave to report, comrade Colonel. The cook's giving me a hard time. He's been keeping your dinner hot for over two hours.'

'Very well then, but make it quick!'

The cook rushed in, covered in sweat. With a look of mingled suffering, resentment and happiness on his face he laid out various dishes of pickles that had been brought from the Urals.

'And I'd like a bottle of beer,' said Nyeudobnov languidly.

'Certainly, comrade Major-General,' said the cook.

Novikov suddenly felt so hungry, after his long fast, that tears came to his eyes. 'Yes, the commander has forgotten what it's like to go without meals,' he thought to himself, remembering the cold lilac.

Novikov and Nyeudobnov both looked out of the window. A policeman, a rifle hanging from his shoulder strap, was marching a drunken soldier across the tracks; the soldier was stumbling, lurching about and letting out piercing screams. He tried to hit out and break free, but the policeman just grabbed him firmly by the shoulders. Then – God knows what thoughts were passing through his befuddled mind! – he began kissing the policeman's cheek with sudden tenderness.

'Find out what the hell all that's about,' Novikov ordered Vershkov, 'and report back immediately!'

337

'He's a saboteur. He deserves to be shot,' said Nyeudobnov as he drew the curtain.

You could see a number of different feelings on Vershkov's usually simple face. In the first place, he was sorry that his commanding officer had had his appetite spoiled. At the same time he felt sympathy for the soldier, a sympathy that included nuances of amusement, approval, comradely admiration, fatherly tenderness, sorrow and genuine anxiety. After saluting and saying that of course he'd report back immediately, Vershkov began embroidering:

'His old mother lives here and . . . Well, you know what we Russians are like. He was upset, he wanted to mark his departure and he misjudged the dose.'

Novikov scratched the back of his head and pulled his plate towards him. 'Damn it, that'll be my last chance to get away on my own,' he said to himself, thinking of Zhenya.

Getmanov came back shortly before their departure, red-faced and merry. He said he didn't want supper and just asked for a bottle of fizzy orange, his favourite soft drink. He pulled off his boots with a grunt, lay down and pushed the door shut with his foot.

Then he told Novikov the news he had received from an old comrade, the secretary of an *obkom*, who had recently returned from Moscow; he had been received by someone who had a place on the mausoleum on public occasions in Red Square, though not, of course, at Stalin's side by the microphone. This man didn't know everything and, needless to say, hadn't told all of what he did know to the secretary of the *obkom*, someone he had previously known only as a *raykom* instructor in a small town on the Volga. The secretary of the *obkom*, weighing Getmanov up on some invisible chemical balance, had told him only a small part of what he had heard. And then Getmanov had passed on to Novikov only a small part of what he himself had been told.

Nevertheless, he was speaking in a particularly confidential tone he had never used before with Novikov. He seemed to take it for granted that Novikov was *au fait* with the secrets of the great; he talked as though Novikov must be aware that Malenkov possessed enormous executive power, that Beria and Molotov were the only people who addressed comrade Stalin as '*ty*', that comrade Stalin strongly disliked unauthorized personal initiatives, that comrade Stalin liked *sulguni* cheese, that on account of the poor state of his teeth comrade Stalin always dipped his bread in wine, that his face, incidentally, was very pock-marked from the smallpox he had had as a child, that comrade Molotov had long ago fallen from his position as number two in the Party, that Iosif Vissarionovich had been far from well-disposed towards Nikita Sergeyevich* recently and had even given him a good dressing-down over the telephone . . .

The confidential tone of these remarks about people in positions of supreme power, about the way Stalin had joked and crossed himself during a conversation with Churchill, about Stalin's displeasure at the high-handedness of one of his Marshals – all this somehow seemed more important than Getmanov's veiled hint as to what the man with the place on the mausoleum had said. This news was something Novikov had long and eagerly expected: soon they were to launch a counter-offensive. With a stupid, self-satisfied smile he felt quite ashamed of, he thought to himself: 'Well, I seem to have become part of the *nomenklatura* myself!'

With no warning of any kind, the train moved off.

Novikov walked to the end of the corridor, opened the door and stared out into the darkness that now covered the city. Again he could hear marching boots beating out the words 'Zhenya, Zhenya, Zhenya.' From the front of the train, he could hear snatches of song.

The thunder of steel wheels on steel rails, the clatter of wagons carrying steel tanks to the Front, the young voices, the cold wind from the Volga, the starry sky – suddenly they all took on a different tone, different from that of a moment before, different from that of the whole of the past year. He felt an arrogant happiness, a joyful sense of his own harsh strength. It was as though the face of the war had changed, as though it no longer expressed only hatred and agony. The mournful snatches of song that were wafted out of the darkness suddenly sounded proud and threatening.

This happiness, however, did not make him feel in any way kind or forgiving. On the contrary, it aroused anger, hatred and a desire to show his own strength, to annihilate whatever stood in his way.

He went back to the compartment. Just as he had been surprised

* Khrushchev.

earlier by the charm of the autumn night, so he was now by the stifling closeness, the tobacco smoke, the smell of rancid butter, shoe polish and the sweat of well-fleshed staff officers. Getmanov was still stretched out across the seats; his pyjama top was open and you could see the white skin on his chest.

'Well, how about a game of dominoes? The general's willing.'

'Certainly,' said Novikov. 'Why not?'

Getmanov gave a discreet burp and said anxiously: 'I'm afraid I must have an ulcer somewhere. As soon as I have a bite to eat, I get the most terrible heartburn.'

'We shouldn't have left the medical officer behind to come on the other train,' said Novikov.

Working himself up into a rage, he said to himself: 'I decided to promote Darensky; Fyodorenko frowned and I began to lose confidence. I told Getmanov and Nyeudobnov; they said we could do without former zeks and I quite lost my nerve. I proposed Basangov; they wanted a Russian and I gave way again. Do I have a mind of my own or not?' He looked at Getmanov and thought, with deliberate absurdity: 'Today he offers me my own cognac; tomorrow, if she comes on a visit, he'll be wanting to sleep with my woman.'

Why, if he was so sure that he, and no one else, was destined to break the back of the German war machine, did he always feel so timid and weak when he talked to Getmanov and Nyeudobnov?

He could sense the anger and hatred that had been welling up for years, his resentment at the way people who were militarily illiterate – but accustomed to power, good living and the tinkle of medals – had graciously intervened to help him obtain a room in the officers' mess and perhaps given him small pats of encouragement. All this had seemed quite normal: his superiors had always been men who were ignorant of the calibres of different guns, men who were unable to read without mistakes a speech that had been written for them by someone else, men who were incapable of making sense of a map or even of speaking proper Russian. Why had *he* had to report to *them*? Their illiteracy had nothing to do with their working-class origins; his own father and grandfather had been miners, as was his brother. Sometimes he had wondered whether this ignorance of theirs was in fact their greatest strength, whether his own correct speech and interest in books was really a weakness. Before the war he had thought that these people must be endowed with more faith, more will-power than he was. But the war had shown otherwise.

Although the war had elevated him to a position of importance, he still didn't feel in charge. He still found himself submitting to a force whose presence he was constantly aware of but unable to understand. These two subordinates of his, who themselves had no right to give orders, were representatives of this force. Just now he had been purring with pleasure because Getmanov had told him a few stories about the world where this force was based. But then the war would show who Russia truly had cause to be grateful to – people like Getmanov or people like himself.

His dream had been realized; the woman he had loved for many years was to become his wife . . . And on the same day his tanks had been ordered to Stalingrad.

'Pyotr Pavlovich,' said Getmanov abruptly, 'while you were out and about, Mikhail Petrovich and I had a little discussion.'

He slumped back against the cushions and took a sip of beer.

'I'm a straightforward man myself and I want to talk to you frankly. We were discussing comrade Shaposhnikova. Her brother went under in 1937.' Getmanov jabbed his thumb down at the floor. 'Nyeudobnov knew him personally, and I knew her first husband – Krymov. He only survived – as the phrase goes – by a miracle. He was one of the lecturers attached to the Central Committee. Well, Nyeudobnov was saying that it was wrong of comrade Novikov to become involved with someone whose social and political background was so dubious – especially at a time when the Soviet people and comrade Stalin have expressed such great trust in him.'

'And what concern of his is my private life?' said Novikov.

'Precisely,' said Getmanov. 'That way of thinking is a hangover from 1937. We must learn to take a broader view of such matters. But please don't misunderstand me. Nyeudobnov is a remarkable man, a man of crystal purity, an unshakeable Communist in Stalin's mould. But he does have one slight fault – there are times when he fails to sense the breath of change. What matters to him are quotations from the classics. Sometimes he seems unable to learn from life itself. Sometimes he seems so full of quotations that he's unable to understand the State he's living in. But the war's taught us many things. Lieutenant-General Rokossovsky, General Gorbatov, General Pultus, General Byelov –

they've all done time in a camp. And that hasn't stopped comrade Stalin from appointing them to important posts. Mitrich, the man I went to see today, told me how Rokossovsky was taken straight out of a camp and put in command of an army. He was in his barrack-hut, washing his foot-cloths, when someone came running to fetch him. The day before he'd been maltreated a little during an interrogation. He just said to himself: "Well, they might at least let me finish my washing." And then he found himself being taken straight to the Kremlin in a Douglas . . . Well, there are conclusions to be drawn from stories like that. But our Nyeudobnov's an enthusiast for the methods of 1937 – and nothing will make him budge. I don't know what this brother of Yevgenia Nikolaevna's did, but maybe comrade Beria would have released him too. Maybe he'd be in command of an army himself. As for Krymov – he's at the front right now. He's still a member of the Party and he's doing fine. So what's all the fuss about?'

At these last words Novikov finally exploded.

'To hell with all that!' he said, surprised at the resonance and forcefulness in his own voice. 'What do I care whether Shaposhnikov was or wasn't an enemy of the people? I've never even set eyes on the man. As for this Krymov – Trotsky himself said that one of his articles was pure marble. What do I care? If it's marble, then it's marble. Even if Trotsky, Rykov, Bukharin and Pushkin were all head over heels in love with him, what's that to me? I've never so much as looked at these marble articles of his. And what's it got to do with Yevgenia Nikolaevna? Did *she* work in the Comintern until 1937? Anyone can do your kind of work, dear comrades, but just try doing some real fighting! Some real work! Let me tell you – I've had enough of all this! It makes me sick!'

His cheeks were burning, his heart was pounding, his anger was bright and clear – and yet he felt full of confusion: 'Zhenya, Zhenya, Zhenya.' He had listened to his own words in astonishment. He could hardly believe it: for the first time in his life he had spoken his mind, without fear, to an important Party official. He looked at Getmanov with a sense of joy, choking back any stirrings of fear or remorse.

Getmanov suddenly leapt to his feet and flung open his arms. Addressing Novikov as '*ty*', he cried: 'You're a real man, Pyotr Pavlovich! Let me embrace you!'

Now Novikov no longer knew where he was. They embraced and kissed.

'Vershkov!' Getmanov shouted down the corridor. 'Bring us some cognac! The commanding officer and his commissar are going to drink *Brüderschaft*.'

5

Yevgenia finished cleaning the room and said to herself with a sense of satisfaction: 'Well, now that's over and done with.' It was as though order had been brought back both to the room and to her own soul. The bed was made, the pillow-case was no longer rumpled, there were no more cigarette-ends on the edge of the bookcase, no more ash on the floor . . . Then she realized she was lying to herself and that there was only one thing in the world she really needed – Novikov. And she also wanted to talk to Sofya Osipovna – to her, not to Lyudmila or her mother.

'Oh Sonechka, Sonechka, my little Levinton . . . ,' she said out loud.

Then she remembered that Marusya was dead . . . She realized that she just couldn't live without Novikov and banged her fist on the table in desperation. 'Damn it! Who says I need anyone anyway?' Then she knelt down where Novikov's coat had just been hanging and whispered: 'Stay alive!'

'It's all just a cheap farce,' she thought. 'I'm a bad woman.'

She wanted to hurt herself. Some sexless creature inside her head let loose a flood of cynical accusations:

'So the lady got bored, did she? She wanted a man around, did she? She's used to being spoiled a bit and these are her best years . . . She sent one packing – and quite right! Who needs a man like Krymov? He was on the point of being expelled from the Party. And now she's after the commanding officer of a tank corps. And what a man! Well, why not . . . ? But how are you going to keep hold of him now? You've given him what he was after, haven't you? Well, you'll have plenty of sleepless nights now. You'll be wondering whether he's got himself killed, whether he's found some pretty little nineteen-year-old telephonist . . .'

This mean, cynical creature then came out with a thought that had never even occurred to Yevgenia herself:

'Never mind, you'll be able to fly out and visit him soon.'

What she couldn't understand was why she no longer loved Krymov. But then why should she understand? What mattered was that she now felt happy.

Then she said to herself that Krymov was standing in the way of her happiness. He was always standing between her and Novikov, poisoning her joy. Even now he was still ruining her life. Why all this remorse? Why this self-torture? She no longer loved him – and that was that. What did he want from her? Why did he pursue her so relentlessly? She had the right to be happy. She had the right to love the man who loved her. Why did Nikolay Grigorevich always seem so weak and helpless, so lost, so alone? He wasn't that weak. And he certainly wasn't so very kind.

She felt more and more angry with Krymov. No, no! She wasn't going to sacrifice her own happiness for him . . . He was cruel and narrow-minded. He was a fanatic. She never had been able to accept his indifference to human suffering. How alien it was – to her and to her mother and father. 'There can be no pity for kulaks,' he had said when tens of thousands of women and children were dying of starvation in villages all over Russia and the Ukraine. 'Innocent people don't get arrested,' he had said in the days of Yagoda and Yezhov. Alexandra Vladimirovna had once recounted an incident that had taken place in Kamyshin in 1918. Some property-owners and merchants had been put on a barge and drowned, with all their children. Some of these children had been school-friends of Marusya. Nikolay Grigorevich had just said angrily: 'Well, what would you do with people who hate the Revolution – feed them on pastries?' Why shouldn't she have the right to be happy? Why should she pity someone who had always been so pitiless himself?

For all this, she knew deep down that Nikolay Grigorevich was by no means as cruel as she was making out.

She took off her thick skirt, one she had bought by barter at the market in Kuibyshev, and put on her summer dress. It was the only dress she had left after the fire in Stalingrad. It was the dress she had worn that evening in Stalingrad when she and Novikov had gone for a walk along the banks of the Volga.

Not long before she was deported, she had asked Jenny Genrikhovna if she had ever been in love. Clearly embarrassed, she had replied: 'Yes, I was in love with a boy with golden curls and light blue eyes. He had a white collar and a velvet jacket. I was eleven years old and I knew him only by sight.'

What had happened to the boy with the curls and the velvet jacket? What had happened to Jenny Genrikhovna?

Yevgenia sat down on the bed and looked at the clock. Shargorodsky usually came to see her around this time. No, she wasn't in the mood for intellectual conversation.

She quickly put on her coat and scarf. This was senseless – the train must have left long ago.

There was a huge crowd of people around the station, all sitting on parcels and sacks. Yevgenia walked up and down the little backstreets. One woman asked her if she had any ration coupons, another if she had any coupons for railway tickets. A few people glanced at her sleepily and suspiciously. A goods train thundered past platform number one. The station walls trembled and the glass in the windows rang. She felt as though her heart were trembling too. Then some open wagons went past; they were carrying tanks.

Yevgenia felt suddenly happy. More and more tanks came by. The soldiers sitting on them with their helmets and machine-guns looked as though they had been cast from bronze.

She walked home, swinging her arms like a little boy. She had unbuttoned her coat and she kept glancing at her summer dress. Suddenly the streets were lit up by the evening sun. This harsh, dusty city, this cold city that was now preparing for another winter, seemed suddenly bright, rosy and triumphant. She went into the house. Glafira Dmitrievna, the senior tenant, who had seen the colonel coming to visit Yevgenia, smiled ingratiatingly and said: 'There's a letter for you.'

'This is my lucky day,' thought Yevgenia as she opened the envelope. It was from her mother in Kazan.

She read the first few lines and gave a plaintive cry: 'Tolya! Tolya!'

6

Viktor's sudden inspiration, the idea that had come to him on the street that night, formed the basis of an entirely new theory. The equations he worked out over the following weeks were not an appendix to the classical, generally accepted theory; nor were they even an enlargement of it. Instead, the classical, supposedly all-embracing theory had become a particular instance included in the framework of a wider theory elaborated by Viktor.

He stopped going to the Institute for a while; Sokolov took over the supervision of the laboratory work. Viktor hardly even left the house now; he sat at his desk for hours on end or strode up and down the room. Only in the evening did he sometimes go out for a walk, choosing the deserted streets near the station so as not to meet anyone he knew. At home he behaved the same as ever – making jokes at meals, reading newspapers, listening to Soviet Information Bureau bulletins, teasing Nadya, talking to his wife, asking Alexandra Vladimirovna about her work at the factory.

Lyudmila had the feeling that Viktor was now behaving in the same way as herself: he too did everything he was supposed to, while inwardly not participating in the life of the family at all. What he did came easily to him simply because it was habitual. This similarity, however, was merely superficial and did nothing to bring Lyudmila closer to Viktor. The husband and wife had quite opposite reasons for their alienation from the life of the family – as opposite as life and death.

Uncharacteristically, Viktor had no doubts about his results. As he formulated the most important scientific discovery of his life, he felt absolute certainty as to its truth. When this idea of a system of equations that would allow a new interpretation of a wide group of physical phenomena – when this idea had first come to him, he had sensed its truth immediately, without any of his usual doubts and hesitations. Even now, as he came to the end of the complicated mathematical demonstration, checking and double-checking each step he had taken, his certainty was no greater than at that first moment of inspiration on the empty street.

Sometimes he tried to understand the path he had followed. From the outside it all seemed quite simple.

The laboratory experiments had been intended to confirm the predictions of the theory. They had failed to do this. The contradiction between the experimental results and the theory naturally led him to doubt the accuracy of the experiments. A theory that had been elaborated on the basis of decades of work by many researchers, a theory that had then explained many things in subsequent experimental results, seemed quite unshakeable. Repetition of the experiments had shown again and again that the deflections of charged particles in interaction with the nucleus still failed to correspond with what the theory predicted. Even the most generous allowance for the inaccuracy of the experiments, for the imperfection of the measuring apparatus and the emulsions used to photograph the fission of the nuclei, could in no way account for such large discrepancies.

Realizing that there could be no doubt as to the accuracy of the results, Viktor had then attempted to patch up the theory. He had postulated various arbitrary hypotheses that would reconcile the new experimental data with the theory. Everything he had done had been based on one fundamental belief: that, since the theory was itself deduced from experimental data, it was impossible for an experiment to contradict it.

An enormous amount of labour was expended in an attempt to reconcile the new data with the theory. Nevertheless, the patched-up theory still failed to account for new contradictions in the results from the laboratory. The theory remained as powerless as ever, though it still seemed unthinkable to reject it.

It was at this moment that something had shifted.

The old theory had ceased to be something fundamental and all-embracing. It didn't turn out to be a mistake or an absurd blunder, but simply a particular instance accounted for by the new theory . . . The purple-clad dowager had bowed her head before the new empress . . . All this had taken only a moment.

When Viktor thought about just how the new theory had come to him, he was struck by something quite unexpected. There appeared to be absolutely no logical connection between the theory and the experiments. The tracks he was following suddenly broke off. He couldn't understand what path he had taken.

Previously he had always thought that theories arose from experience and were engendered by it. Contradictions between an existing theory and new experimental results naturally led to a new, broader theory.

But it had all happened quite differently. Viktor was sure of this. He had succeeded at a time when he was in no way attempting to connect theory with experimental data, or vice versa.

The new theory was not derived from experience. Viktor could see this quite clearly. It had arisen in absolute freedom; it had sprung from his own head. The logic of this theory, its chain of reasoning, was quite unconnected to the experiments conducted by Markov in the laboratory. The theory had sprung from the free play of thought. It was this free play of thought – which seemed quite detached from the world of experience – that had made it possible to explain the wealth of experimental data, both old and new.

The experiments had been merely a jolt that had forced him to start thinking. They had not determined the content of his thoughts.

All this was quite extraordinary . . .

His head had been full of mathematical relationships, differential equations, the laws of higher algebra, number and probability theory. These mathematical relationships had an existence of their own in some void quite outside the world of atomic nuclei, stars, and electromagnetic or gravitational fields, outside space and time, outside the history of man and the geological history of the earth. And yet these relationships existed inside his own head.

And at the same time his head had been full of other laws and relationships: quantum interactions, fields of force, the constants that determined the processes undergone by nuclei, the movement of light, and the expansion and contraction of space and time. To a theoretical physicist the processes of the real world were only a reflection of laws that had been born in the desert of mathematics. It was not mathematics that reflected the world; the world itself was a projection of differential equations, a reflection of mathematics.

And his head had also been full of readings from different instruments, of dotted lines on photographic paper that showed the trajectories of particles and the fission of nuclei.

And there had even been room in his head for the rustling of leaves, the light of the moon, millet porridge with milk, the sound of flames in the stove, snatches of tunes, the barking of dogs, the Roman Senate, Soviet Information Bureau bulletins, a hatred of slavery, and a love of melon seeds.

All this was what had given birth to his theory; it had arisen from the depths where there are no mathematics, no physics, no laboratory data, no experience of life, no consciousness, only the inflammable peat of the subconscious . . .

And the logic of mathematics, itself quite unconnected with the world, had become reflected and embodied in a theory of physics; and this theory had fitted with divine accuracy over a complex pattern of dotted lines on photographic paper.

And Viktor, inside whose head all this had taken place, now sobbed and wiped tears of happiness from his eyes as he looked at the differential equations and photographic paper that confirmed the truth he had given birth to.

And yet, if it hadn't been for those unsuccessful experiments, if it hadn't been for the resulting chaos, he and Sokolov would have gone on trying to patch up the old theory. What a joy that that chaos had refused to yield to their demands!

This new explanation had been born from his own head, but it was indeed linked to Markov's experiments. Yes, if there were no atoms and atomic nuclei in the world, there would be none inside a man's brain. If it weren't for those famous glass-blowers the Petushkovs, if there were no power stations, no furnaces and no production of pure reactors, then there would be no mathematics inside the head of a theoretical physicist, no mathematics that could predict reality.

What Viktor found most astonishing was that he had achieved his greatest success at a time of unremitting depression and grief. How was it possible?

And why had it happened after those bold, dangerous conversations that had revived his spirits but which bore no relation to his work – why was it then that everything insoluble had so suddenly been resolved? But that was coincidence . . .

How could he ever make sense of all this . . . ?

Now that it was completed, Viktor wanted to talk about his work. Previously, it hadn't even occurred to him to share his thoughts with anyone else. He wanted to see Sokolov and write to Chepyzhin; he wondered what Mandelstam, Joffe, Landau, Tamm, and Kurchatov would think of his new equations; he tried to guess what response they would evoke in his colleagues both here in the laboratory and in Leningrad. He tried to think of a title for his work. He wondered what Bohr and Fermi would think of it. Maybe Einstein himself would read it and write him a brief nóte. He also wondered who would oppose it and what problems it would help to resolve.

He didn't, however, feel like talking to Lyudmila. In the past he had read even the most ordinary business letter out loud to her before sending it off. If he had unexpectedly bumped into someone he knew on the street, his first thought had always been, 'Well, Lyudmila will be surprised!' If he had come out with some fine sarcasm in an argument with the director, he had thought, 'Yes, I'll tell Lyudmila how I settled him!' And he could never have imagined watching a film or sitting in a theatre without knowing that Lyudmila was there, that he could whisper in her ear, 'God, what rubbish!' He had shared his most secret anxieties with her. As a student, he had sometimes said to her, 'You know, sometimes I think I'm an idiot.'

So why didn't he say anything now? Was it that his compulsion to share his life with her had been founded on a belief that his life mattered more to her than her own, that his life *was* her life? And that now he was no longer sure of this? Did she no longer love him? Or did he no longer love her?

In the end, without really wanting to, he did tell his wife.

'It's a strange feeling, you know. Whatever may happen to me now, I know deep down in my heart that I haven't lived in vain. Now, for the first time, I'm not afraid of dying. Now! Now that this exists!'

He showed her a page covered in scrawls that was lying on his table.

'I'm not exaggerating. It's a new vision of the nature of the forces within the atom. A new principle. It will be the key to many doors that until now have been locked . . . And do you know, when I was little . . . No, it's as though a lily had suddenly blossomed out of still, dark waters . . . Oh, my God . . .'

'I'm very glad, Viktor. I'm very glad,' said Lyudmila with a smile.

Viktor could see that she was still wrapped up in her own thoughts, that she didn't share his joy and excitement.

Indeed, Lyudmila didn't mention any of this to Nadya or her mother. She evidently just forgot about it.

That evening, Viktor set out for the Sokolovs'. It wasn't only about his work that he wanted to talk to Sokolov. He wanted to share his feelings with him. Pyotr Lavrentyevich would understand; he was more than merely intelligent; he had a pure, kind soul.

At the same time, Viktor was afraid that Sokolov would reproach him, that he would remind him of his earlier lack of faith. Sokolov loved explaining other people's behaviour and subjecting them to long lectures.

It was a long time since he had been to the Sokolovs'. His friends had probably been there another three times since his last visit. Suddenly he glimpsed Madyarov's bulging eyes. 'Yes, he's a bold devil,' Viktor said to himself. How peculiar that, during all this time, he'd hardly given a thought to those gatherings. Now he didn't want to. There was some fear, some anxiety, some expectation of imminent doom connected with those late-night discussions. They really had let themselves go. They had croaked away like birds of ill omen – but Stalingrad still stood, the Germans had been halted, evacuees were returning to Moscow.

Last night he had told Lyudmila that he wasn't afraid of dying, not even at that very moment. And yet he was afraid of remembering the criticisms he had voiced. And as for Madyarov ... That didn't bear thinking about. Karimov's suspicions were quite terrifying. What if Madyarov really were a provocateur?

'No, I'm not afraid of dying,' thought Viktor, 'but now I'm a proletarian who has more to lose than his chains.'

Sokolov, in his indoor jacket, was sitting reading a book.

'Where's Marya Ivanovna?' asked Viktor, surprised at his own surprise. He was quite taken aback not to find her at home – as though it was her he had come to talk to about theoretical physics.

Sokolov put his glasses back in their case and smiled. 'Who says Marya Ivanovna has to hang around at home all day long?'

Coughing and stammering with excitement, Viktor began expounding his ideas and showing Sokolov his equations. Sokolov was the first person he had confided in; as he spoke, he relived everything again – though with very different feelings.

'Well,' said Viktor finally, 'that's it.' His voice was shaking. He could feel Sokolov's excitement.

They sat for a while in a silence that to Viktor seemed quite wonderful. He frowned and shook his bowed head from side to side. Finally he stole a timid look at Sokolov. He thought he could see tears in his eyes.

There was a miraculous link that joined these two men – sitting in a miserable little room during a terrible war that enveloped the whole world – to everyone, however distant in space and time, whose pure mind had aspired to these exalted realms.

Viktor hoped that Sokolov would remain silent a while longer. There was something divine in this silence.

They did remain silent for a long time. Then Sokolov went up to Viktor and put his hand on his shoulder. Viktor felt his eyes fill with tears.

'It's wonderful,' said Sokolov, 'quite unbelievable. What elegance! I congratulate you with all my heart. What extraordinary power! What logic, what elegance! Even from an aesthetic point of view your reasoning is perfect.'

Still trembling with excitement, Viktor thought: 'For God's sake! This isn't a matter of elegance. This is bread for the soul.'

'Do you see now, Viktor Pavlovich,' Sokolov continued, 'how wrong you were to lose heart and try to put everything off till our return to Moscow?' Then, just like someone giving a sermon: 'You lack faith, you lack patience. This often hinders you.'

'I know, I know,' Viktor interrupted impatiently. 'But I got very depressed by the way we were so stuck. It made me feel quite ill.'

Then Sokolov began to hold forth. Though he understood the importance of Viktor's work and praised it in superlative terms, Viktor hated every word he said. To him any evaluation seemed trivial and stereotyped.

'Your work *promises* remarkable results.' What a stupid word! He didn't need Pyotr Lavrentyevich to know what his work *promised*. And anyway why '*promises results*'? It was a result in itself. 'You've employed a most original method.' No, it wasn't a matter of originality . . . This was bread, bread, black bread.

Viktor decided to change the subject. He began to talk about the running of the laboratory.

'By the way, Pyotr Lavrentyevich, I received a letter from the Urals. Our order's going to be delayed.'

'Well,' said Sokolov, 'that means we'll already be in Moscow when the apparatus arrives. That's not such a bad thing. We'd never have been able to set it up in Kazan anyway: we'd have been accused of failing to keep up with our schedule.'

He started to talk very pompously about matters connected with their work schedule. Although Viktor had himself initiated this change of topic, he was upset that Sokolov had gone along with it so readily.

It made Viktor feel very isolated. Surely Sokolov understood that his work was more important than the everyday affairs of the Institute? It was probably the most important of all his contributions to science; it would affect the theoretical outlook of physicists everywhere.

Sokolov realized from Victor's expression that he had done the wrong thing. 'It's interesting,' he said. 'You've produced another confirmation of that business with neutrons and a heavy nucleus. We really shall need that new apparatus now.'

'I suppose so,' said Viktor. 'But that's only a detail.'

'No,' said Sokolov. 'It's very important. You know what enormous energy is involved.'

'To hell with all that!' said Viktor. 'What interests me is that it's a new way of seeing the microforces within the atom. That may bring joy to a few hearts and save one or two people from groping around in the dark.'

'Oh yes,' said Sokolov. 'They'll be as glad as sportsmen are when someone else sets a new record.'

Viktor didn't answer. Sokolov was alluding to a recent argument in the laboratory. Savostyanov had compared scientists with athletes; he had claimed that a scientist had to undergo the same daily training as an athlete and that the tension surrounding his attempt to solve a scientific problem was no different from that surrounding an athlete's attempt to break a record. In both cases it was a matter of records.

Viktor had got quite angry with Savostyanov, Sokolov even more so. He had made a long speech and called Savostyanov a young cynic. He had spoken of science as though it were a religion, an expression of man's aspiration towards the divine.

Viktor knew that if he had lost his temper with Savostyanov, it wasn't simply because he was wrong. He too had sometimes felt that same joy, excitement and envy. He also knew, however, that envy, competitiveness and the desire to set records were not in any way fundamental to his attitude towards science.

He had never told anyone, even Lyudmila, of his true feelings about science – feelings that had been born in him when he was still young. And so he had liked the way Sokolov had argued so justly, and so exaltedly, against Savostyanov.

Why then should Pyotr Lavrentyevich himself suddenly compare scientists with sportsmen? What had made him say that? And at a moment of such special importance for Viktor?

Feeling hurt and bewildered, he burst out: 'So, Pyotr Lavrentyevich, someone else has set the record. Has my discovery upset you, then?'

At that moment Sokolov was saying to himself that Viktor's solution was so simple as to be almost self-evident; that it was already there, on the verge of expression, in his own head.

'Yes,' he admitted. 'I'm as pleased as Lawrence must have been when the equations he had established were reworked and transformed by Einstein.'

Sokolov admitted this so frankly that Viktor regretted his animosity. Then, however, Sokolov added:

'I'm joking, of course. Lawrence is neither here nor there. I don't feel anything of the sort. But all the same, I am right – even though I don't feel anything of the sort.'

'Yes,' said Viktor, 'of course, of course.'

His irritation returned. He was sure now that Sokolov did feel envy. 'How devious he is today,' he thought. 'He's as transparent as a child. You can see his insincerity straight away.'

'Pyotr Lavrentyevich,' he said. 'Are you having people round this Saturday?'

Sokolov's thick, fierce-looking nostrils flared. He seemed about to say something, but kept silent. Viktor looked at him questioningly.

'Viktor Pavlovich,' Sokolov said at last. 'Between you and me, I no longer enjoy these evenings of ours.'

Now it was his turn to look questioningly at Viktor. Viktor remained silent. In the end Sokolov went on:

'You know very well why I say that. It's no joke. Some people really let themselves go.'

'You didn't,' said Viktor. 'You kept very quiet.'

'Yes,' said Sokolov. 'And that's why I'm worried.'

'Fine! Let me be the host! I'd be only too delighted,' said Viktor.

It was quite incomprehensible. Now it was he who was being hypocritical. Why was he lying like this? Why should he argue with Sokolov when he knew he agreed with him? He too was afraid of these meetings and would prefer not to continue with them.

'What difference would that make?' asked Sokolov. 'That's not the problem. Let me be quite frank with you. I've quarrelled with Madyarov, our chief orator, my own brother-in-law.'

Viktor wanted very much to ask: 'Pyotr Lavrentyevich, are you quite sure we can trust Madyarov? Can you vouch for him?' Instead he said: 'What is all this nonsense? You've got it into your head that a few bold words somehow endanger the State. I'm sorry you've quarrelled with Madyarov. I like him. Very much.'

'It isn't right,' said Sokolov, 'for us Russians, at such a difficult time, to criticize our own country.'

Again Viktor wanted to ask: 'Pyotr Lavrentyevich, this is something very serious. Are you sure Madyarov's not an informer?' Instead he said: 'Excuse me, but things have just taken a turn for the better. Stalingrad is the beginning of spring. We've already drawn up lists of personnel to return to Moscow. Do you remember what we were thinking two months ago? The Urals, Kazakhstan, the taiga?'

'In that case,' said Sokolov, 'there's even less reason for you to carp and croak.'

'Croak?'

'That's what I said.'

'For heaven's sake, Pyotr Lavrentyevich!'

When he said goodbye to Sokolov, Viktor was feeling depressed and bewildered. Above all, he felt an unbearable loneliness. All day he had been longing to talk to Sokolov. He had thought this meeting would be very special. But almost every word of Sokolov's had seemed trivial and insincere.

And he had been equally insincere himself. That made it even worse.

He went out onto the street. By the outer door a woman's voice quietly called out his name. Viktor knew who it was.

Marya Ivanovna's face was lit up by the street-lamp; her cheeks and forehead were shining with rain. In her old coat, with a woollen scarf round her neck, the professor's wife seemed to embody the poverty of the wartime evacuee.

'She looks like a conductor on one of the trams,' thought Viktor.

'How's Lyudmila Nikolaevna?' she asked, looking questioningly into his eyes.

'The same as usual,' said Viktor, shrugging his shoulders.

'I'll come round earlier tomorrow.'

'You're her guardian angel as it is,' said Viktor. 'It's a good thing Pyotr Lavrentyevich doesn't mind. You spend so much time with Lyudmila. And he's just a child – he can hardly get by without you for even an hour.'

She was still looking at him thoughtfully. She seemed to be listening without really hearing. Then she said: 'Viktor Pavlovich, your face looks quite different today. Has something good happened?'

'What makes you think that?'

'Your eyes have changed,' she said. 'It must be your work. Your work's going well at last. There you are now – and you used to say you were no longer good for anything after all the unhappiness you've been through.'

'Lyudmila must have told her,' thought Viktor. 'Women are such chatterboxes!' At the same time, trying to hide his irritation, he asked with a smile: 'What do you see in my eyes then?'

Marya Ivanovna remained silent for a moment. When she did speak, it was in a serious tone of voice, quite unlike Viktor's.

'Your eyes are always full of suffering – but not today.'

Suddenly Viktor opened up.

'Marya Ivanovna, I don't understand it. I feel that I've done the most important thing of my life. Science is bread, bread for the soul . . . And this has happened at such a sad, difficult time. How strangely tangled our lives are. How I wish I could . . . No, there's no use in saying . . .'

Marya Ivanovna listened, still gazing into Viktor's eyes. Then she said very quietly: 'How I wish I could drive the sorrow out of your home.'

'Thank you, dear Marya Ivanovna,' said Viktor as they parted. He felt suddenly calm – as though it really were her he had come to see and he had now said what he wanted to say.

A minute later, walking down the dark street, Viktor had forgotten the Sokolovs. A cold draught blew from each of the dark entrances; when he came to a crossroads the wind lifted up the tail of his coat. Viktor shrugged his shoulders and frowned. Would his mother never know, would she never know what her son had just achieved?

7

Viktor called a meeting of all the laboratory staff – Markov and Savostyanov the two physicists, Anna Naumovna Weisspapier, Nozdrin the technician, and Perepelitsyn the electrician – and said that the doubts they had all had about the apparatus were quite unfounded. In fact it was the accuracy of their measurements that had led to such uniform results, despite variations in the experimental conditions.

Viktor and Sokolov were both theoreticians; it was Markov who was in charge of the experimental work in the laboratory. He had an astonishing talent for solving difficult problems and could always unerringly determine the principles of any new piece of equipment.

Viktor admired the confidence with which Markov would walk up to some new apparatus and be able, after only a few minutes and without looking at any instructions, to grasp both its essential principles and the tiniest details of its mechanism. He seemed to regard a complex apparatus as a living body; it was as though he were looking at a cat, glancing at its eyes and tail, its ears and claws, feeling its heartbeat, understanding what every part of its body was for.

As for Nozdrin, the haughty technician – he really came into his own when some new apparatus was being assembled in the laboratory. Savostyanov used to joke about Nozdrin, saying, 'When Stepan Stepanovich dies, his hands will be taken to the Brain Institute to be studied.'

Nozdrin didn't like these jokes. He tended to look down on the scientists, knowing that without his strong hands not one of them would be able to do anything at all.

The laboratory favourite was Savostyanov. He was at home in both practical and theoretical matters. Everything he did, he did quickly and effortlessly, almost light-heartedly. Even on the gloomiest of days, his bright corn-coloured hair seemed to be full of sunlight. Viktor would gaze at him admiringly, thinking that his hair reflected the brightness and clarity of his mind. Sokolov thought equally highly of him.

'Yes, he's not like us Talmudists,' Viktor once said to Sokolov. 'He's a match for you and me and Markov put together.'

As for Anna Naumovna – she had an almost superhuman patience and capacity for work; once she had spent eighteen hours on end studying photographs under the microscope.

Many of the other heads of department considered Viktor extremely lucky to have such a brilliant staff. In answer to their comments Viktor replied jokingly: 'Every head of department has the staff he deserves.'

'We have all been through a period of depression and anxiety,' he began. 'Now we can all rejoice. Professor Markov has conducted the experiments faultlessly. The credit for this, of course, also belongs to the laboratory assistants and technicians responsible for so many observations and calculations.'

Markov gave a little cough and said: 'Viktor Pavlovich, we should like you to expound your theory in as much detail as possible.' Lowering his voice, he added: 'I've heard that Kochkurov's research in a similar area holds out great practical possibilities. Apparently Moscow has been asking about his results.'

Markov usually knew all the ins and outs of everything under the sun. When the Institute was being evacuated from Moscow, he had appeared in the railway carriage with all kinds of information – about hold-ups on the line, engine changes, stops where they could get something to eat . . .

Savostyanov, who hadn't yet shaved that morning, said thoughtfully: 'I'll have to drink all the laboratory alcohol to celebrate.' And Anna Naumovna, who was politically very active, sighed: 'Thank God for that! At Party meetings we've already been accused of all kinds of mortal sins.'

Nozdrin remained silent, rubbing his hand over his hollow cheeks. As for Perepelitsyn, the young one-legged electrician, he just turned bright red and let his crutch fall to the floor with a bang.

It had been a good day for Viktor. Pimenov, the young director of the Institute, had telephoned him that morning and showered him with compliments. He was about to fly to Moscow; final preparations were under way for the return of almost the entire Institute.

'Viktor Pavlovich,' Pimenov had announced at the end of their conversations, 'we'll see each other in Moscow soon. I'm both proud and happy to be the director of the Institute at the time when you have brought your remarkable research to a conclusion.'

The meeting of the laboratory staff was equally agreeable.

Markov distrusted theoreticians and liked making jokes about the running of the laboratory. He was always complaining, 'We've got a brigade of doctors and professors, a battalion of research assistants and one private soldier – Nozdrin. We're like some strange pyramid with a wide top and a mere point as its base. Very unstable. What we need is a firm foundation – a whole regiment of Nozdrins.' After Viktor's talk, however, he smiled and said:

'Well, so much for all my talk about regiments and pyramids.'

And as for Savostyanov, who had compared science with sport, his eyes took on a look of extraordinary warmth and joy. This was not how a football player looks at his coach, but the way a believer looks at an evangelist. Remembering Savostyanov's argument with Sokolov and his own recent conversation with him, Viktor said to himself: 'Well, I may understand something about the forces within the atom, but I really don't have a clue about human beings.'

Towards the end of the day, Anna Naumovna came into Viktor's office.

'Viktor Pavlovich, I've just seen the list of people who are to return to Moscow. The new head of the personnel department hasn't included my name.'

'I know,' said Viktor, 'but there's nothing to get upset about. There are two separate lists. You're on the second one. You'll be coming a few weeks later, that's all.'

'But for some reason I'm the only person from our group who isn't on the first list. I've had enough of it here – I think I'm going mad. I dream of Moscow every night. And anyway how are you going to get the laboratory set up without me?'

'I know,' said Viktor. 'But the list has already been authorized. It's very difficult to change it now. Svechin from the magnetic laboratory has already had a word about Boris Israelevich. Boris is in the same position as you, but apparently it's impossible to do anything about it now. I think the best you can do is be patient.'

Then he suddenly lost patience himself.

'Heaven knows what's going on in their heads! They've included people we don't need at all and for some reason they've forgotten you. You're right – we do need you to set the place up.'

'I haven't been forgotten,' said Anna Naumovna, her eyes slowly filling with tears. 'It's worse than that.' She looked round quickly, almost furtively, at the half-open door. 'For some reason it's only Jewish names that have been crossed off the list. And I've heard from Rimma, the secretary of the personnel department, that almost all the Jews have been crossed off the list of the Ukrainian Academy at Ufa. The only ones left are the doctors.'

Viktor gaped at her in momentary astonishment, then burst out laughing.

'My dear woman, have you gone mad? We're not living under the Tsars, thank God! Why this shtetl inferiority complex? It's time you forgot all that.'

8

When he got home, Viktor saw a familiar coat hanging on the peg: Karimov had called round.

Karimov put aside his newspaper. Viktor realized that Lyudmila must have avoided making conversation with him.

'I've just come back from a *kolkhoz*,' he said. 'I was giving a lecture there . . . But please don't worry. I've been very well fed. Our people are extremely hospitable.'

So Lyudmila hadn't even offered him a cup of tea.

It was only if Viktor looked very closely at Karimov's rather crumpled face with its wide nose that he could detect any differences from the usual Slavonic mould. But at odd moments, if he turned his head in a particular way, these slight differences merged into a single pattern, changing his face into that of a Mongol.

In the same way Viktor could sometimes recognize someone with blond hair, blue eyes and a snub nose as a Jew. The signs that revealed a man's Jewish origins were often barely perceptible – a smile, the way he furrowed his brow in surprise, even the way he shrugged his shoulders.

Karimov was telling him about how he had met a wounded lieutenant who had gone back home to his village. He appeared to have come merely to tell this story.

'He was a good lad,' said Karimov. 'He talked about everything very openly.'

'In Tartar?'

'Of course.'

Viktor thought that if he were to meet a wounded Jewish lieutenant, he certainly wouldn't start talking to him in Yiddish. He only knew a dozen words and they were just pleasantries like *bekitser* and *haloimes*.

This lieutenant had been taken prisoner near Kerch in the autumn of 1941. Snow had already fallen and the Germans had sent him to harvest the remaining wheat as fodder for horses. He had waited for the right moment and then disappeared into the winter twilight. The local population, both Russians and Tartars, had helped him escape.

'I now have real hopes of seeing my wife and daughter again,' said Karimov. 'Apparently the Germans have different kinds of ration-cards just as we do. And he said that many of the Crimean Tartars have fled to the mountains – even though the Germans don't harm them.'

'When I was a student, I did some climbing in the Crimea myself,' said Viktor.

As he spoke, he remembered that it was his mother who had sent him the money for the journey.

'Did your lieutenant see any Jews?' he asked.

Just then Lyudmila looked in through the door and said: 'My mother still hasn't come back. I'm quite anxious.'

'Oh dear, I wonder what's happened to her,' said Viktor absent-mindedly. When Lyudmila had closed the door, he repeated his question:

'What did your lieutenant have to say about the Jews?'

'He said he'd seen a Jewish family being taken to be shot – an old woman and two girls.'

'My God!'

'And he said he'd heard of some camps in Poland specially for Jews. First they're killed and then their bodies are cut up – just like in a slaughterhouse. But I'm sure that's only a rumour. I asked him about the Jews because I knew you'd want to know.'

'Why just me?' Viktor said to himself. 'Isn't it going to interest anyone else?'

Karimov thought for a moment and then said:

'I forgot. He also said that the Germans ordered new-born Jewish babies to be taken to the commandant's office. Their lips are then smeared with some kind of colourless preparation and they die at once.'

'New-born babies?'

'But I'm sure that's just someone's imagination – like the camps where corpses are cut up.'

Viktor started to pace up and down the room.

'When you think about new-born babies being killed in our own lifetime,' he said, 'all the efforts of culture seem worthless. What have people learned from all our Goethes and Bachs? To kill babies?'

'Yes,' said Karimov. 'It's terrible.'

Viktor could sense Karimov's sorrow and compassion, but he was also aware of his joy. Karimov now had more hope of seeing his wife again. Whereas he, Viktor, knew only too well that he would never again see his mother.

Karimov got ready to go home. Viktor didn't want to say goodbye and decided to accompany him for part of the way.

'You know one thing,' he said as they were putting on their coats, 'Soviet scientists are very fortunate. Try and imagine the feelings of an honest German chemist or physicist who knows that his discoveries are helping Hitler! Imagine a Jewish physicist whose family are being killed off like mad dogs – imagine what he feels, when, against his will, his discovery is used to reinforce the power of Fascism! He knows that, but he can't help feeling proud of his discovery. It must be terrible!'

'Yes,' agreed Karimov. 'But a thinking person can't just stop thinking.'

They went out onto the street.

'I feel awkward about your coming with me,' said Karimov. 'The weather's terrible and you've only just got back yourself.'

'It's all right,' said Viktor. 'I'll come as far as the corner.' He looked at his friend's face and said: 'I enjoy walking down the street with you – even if the weather is terrible.'

'Soon you'll be going back to Moscow. We'll have to say goodbye. You know, these meetings have meant a lot to me.'

'Believe me,' said Viktor. 'I feel sad too.'

As Viktor was on his way back, someone called out his name. Viktor didn't hear at first. Then he saw Madyarov's dark eyes looking straight at him. The collar of his overcoat was turned up.

'What's happening?' he asked. 'Have our meetings come to an end? You've vanished off the face of the earth. Pyotr Lavrentyevich is angry with me.'

'Yes,' said Viktor, 'it's a pity. But we did both say a lot of things in the heat of the moment.'

'Yes, but no one's going to pay any attention.'

Madyarov drew closer to Viktor. His large, melancholy eyes looked even more melancholy than usual.

'Still,' he said, 'there is one good thing about our not meeting any more.'

'What do you mean?'

'I have to tell you this,' said Madyarov, almost gasping, 'I think old Karimov's an informer. Do you understand? You meet quite often, don't you?'

'That's nonsense. I don't believe a word of it.'

'Can't you see? All his friends and all the friends of his friends are just labour-camp dust. His whole circle has vanished. He's the only one left. What's more, he's flourishing. He's been granted his doctorate.'

'And what of it?' said Viktor. 'I'm a doctor myself. And so are you.'

'The same goes for us. Just think a little about our wonderful fate. You're not a child any more.'

9

'Vitya, Mother's only just got back.'

Alexandra Vladimirovna was sitting at table with a shawl round her shoulders. She moved her cup of tea closer and then pushed it away again.

'Guess what?' she said. 'I spoke to someone who saw Misha just before the war.'

Speaking in a deliberately calm, measured tone because of her excitement, she went on to say that the neighbours of a colleague of hers had had someone to stay from their home-town. The colleague had happened to mention the name Shaposhnikova and he had asked if Alexandra Vladimirovna had a relative called Dmitry.

After work, Alexandra Vladimirovna had gone to her colleague's house. There she had learned that this man had recently been released from a labour camp. He had been a proof-reader on a newspaper and had spent seven years in the camps for missing a misprint in a leading article – the typesetters had got one letter wrong in Stalin's name. Just before the war he had been transferred for an infringement of discipline from a camp in the Komi ASSR to one of the special-regime 'lake camps' in the Far East. There he had slept next to Dmitry Shaposhnikov.

'I knew from the very first word that he really had met Mitya. He said: "Mitya just lay there on the bedboards, whistling 'Little Bird Where Have You Been?'" Mitya came round shortly before he was arrested – and whatever I asked, he just smiled and whistled that same tune . . . This evening the man's going on by lorry to his family in Laishevo. He said Mitya was ill – scurvy and heart trouble. And he said Mitya didn't believe he'd ever get out. Mitya had told him about me and Seryozha. He had a job in the kitchen – apparently that's the best work of all.'

'Yes,' said Viktor. 'It's not for nothing he's got two degrees.'

'You never know,' said Lyudmila. 'This man might be a provocateur.'

'Why should a provocateur bother with an old woman like me?'

'All right, but there is an organization that's interested in Viktor.'

'Lyudmila, you're talking rubbish,' said Viktor impatiently.

'But why was this man released?' asked Nadya. 'Did he say?'

'The things he said are quite incredible. It seems to be a world of its own, or rather a nightmare. He was like someone from a foreign country. They've got their own customs, their own Middle Ages and modern history, their own proverbs . . .

'I asked why he'd been released. He seemed quite surprised. "I was written off," he said. "Don't you understand?" In the end he explained that sometimes, when they're on their last legs, "goners" are released. There are lots of different classes in the camps – "workers",* "trusties", "bitches"** . . . I asked him about the ten years without right of correspondence that thousands of people were sentenced to in 1937. He said he'd been in dozens of camps but he hadn't met one person with that sentence. "Then what's happened to all those people?" I asked. "I don't know," he answered, "but they're not in the camps."'

'Tree-felling. Deportees. People serving additional time . . . It just appals me. And Mitya's lived there. He's used those same words – "goners", "trusties", "bitches" . . . Apparently there's a special way of committing suicide: they don't eat for several days and just drink water from the Kolyma bogs. Then they die of oedema, of dropsy. People just say, "He was drinking water" or "He began drinking". Of course, that's when they have a bad heart already.'

Alexandra Vladimirovna looked round at Nadya's furrowed brow and Viktor's tense, gloomy face. Her head on fire and her mouth quite dry, she went on:

'He said that the journey's even worse than the camp itself. The common criminals have absolute power. They take away people's food and clothes. They even stake the lives of the "politicals" at cards. Whoever loses has to kill someone with a knife. The victim doesn't know till the last moment that his life's just been gambled away. Yes, and apparently the criminals have all the important posts in the camp.

---

* I.e. prisoners still capable of a full day's work.
** Common criminals who have broken the underworld code.

They're the ones in charge of the huts and the work-gangs. The politicals have no rights at all. The criminals call them *"ty"*. They even called Mitya a Fascist.'

In a loud voice, as though she were addressing a crowd, Alexandra Vladimirovna announced:

'This man was transferred from Mitya's camp to Syktyfkar. In the first year of the war a man from Moscow called Kashkotin was appointed director of the lake-camps, including Mitya's. He's been responsible for the execution of tens of thousands of prisoners.'

'Oh my God!' said Lyudmila. 'But does Stalin know of these horrors?'

'Oh my God!' said Nadya angrily, imitating her mother's voice. 'Do you still not understand? It was Stalin who gave the order for the executions.'

'Nadya!' shouted Viktor. 'Cut it out!'

He flew into a sudden rage – the rage of a man who senses that someone else knows his hidden weaknesses.

'Don't you forget,' he shouted at Nadya, 'that Stalin's the commander-in-chief of the army fighting against Fascism. Your grandmother trusted in Stalin to the last day of her life. And if we still live and breathe, it's because of Stalin and the Red Army . . . First learn to wipe your nose properly, then criticize Stalin – the man who's halted the fascists at Stalingrad.'

'Stalin's in Moscow,' said Nadya. 'And you know very well who has really halted the Fascists. You are peculiar. You used to come back from the Sokolovs and say just the same things yourself . . .'

Viktor felt a new surge of anger. He felt as though he would be angry with Nadya for the rest of his life.

'I never said anything of the kind. You're imagining things.'

'Why bring up all these horrors now?' said Lyudmila. 'Soviet children are giving their lives for the Motherland.'

It was at this moment that Nadya showed how well she understood her father's weaknesses.

'No,' she said, 'of course you didn't. Not now – not when your work's going so well and the German advance has been halted.'

'How dare you!' cried Viktor. 'How dare you accuse your own father of being dishonest? Lyudmila, did you hear what the girl said?'

Instead of giving Viktor the support he had asked for, Lyudmila just said: 'I don't know why you should be so surprised. She's picked it up from you. You've said things like that to that Karimov of yours, and that awful Madyarov. Marya Ivanovna's told me all about your conversations. And anyway you've said quite enough here at home. Oh, if only we could go back to Moscow!'

'Enough of that!' said Viktor. 'I know what you're about to say.'

Nadya was silent. Her face looked ugly and shrivelled, like an old woman's. She had turned away from Viktor; when he finally caught her eye he was surprised at the hatred he saw in it.

The air was thick and heavy, almost unbreathable. Everything that lies half-buried in almost every family, stirring up now and then only to be smoothed over by love and trust, had now come to the surface. There it had spread out to fill their lives. It was as though there were nothing between father, mother and daughter save misunderstanding, suspiciousness, resentment and anger.

Had their common fate really engendered nothing but mistrust and alienation?

'Grandmama!' cried Nadya.

Viktor and Lyudmila turned simultaneously towards Alexandra Vladimirovna. She was sitting there, her head in her hands, looking as though she had an unbearable headache.

There was something pitiful about this helplessness of hers. She and her grief were of no use to anyone. All she did was get in the way and stir up quarrels. All her life she had been strong and self-disciplined; now she was lonely and helpless.

Nadya suddenly knelt down and pressed her forehead against Alexandra Vladimirovna's legs.

'Grandmama,' she murmured. 'Dear, kind Grandmama . . . !'

Viktor got up and turned on the radio. The cardboard loudspeaker moaned and wheezed. It could have been the autumn weather, the wind and snow over the front line, over the burnt villages and mass graves, over Kolyma and Vorkuta, over airfields and the wet tarpaulin roofs of first-aid posts.

Viktor looked at his wife's sombre face. He went over to Alexandra Vladimirovna, took her hands and kissed them. Then he bent down to stroke Nadya's head.

To an outsider it would seem as though nothing had changed in those few moments; the same people were in the same room, oppressed by the same grief and led by the same destiny. Only they knew what an extraordinary warmth had suddenly filled their embittered hearts . . .

A booming voice suddenly filled the room:

'During the day our troops have engaged the enemy in the regions of Stalingrad, north-eastern Tuapse and Nalchik. On the other Fronts there has been no change.'

10

Lieutenant Peter Bach was taken to hospital after receiving a bullet-wound in the shoulder. The wound turned out not to be serious; the comrades who had accompanied him to the field-hospital congratulated him on his luck.

Even though he was still groaning with pain, Bach felt blissfully happy. Supported by an orderly, he went to take a bath.

The sensation of the warm water on his skin was a real pleasure.

'Is that better than the trenches then?' asked the orderly. Wanting to cheer up the lieutenant, he gestured towards the continual rumble of explosions. 'By the time you're released, we'll have all that sorted out.'

'Have you only just been posted here?' asked Bach.

'What makes you think that?' replied the orderly, rubbing the lieutenant's back with a flannel.

'Down there no one thinks it will be over soon. People think it will take a very long time indeed.'

The orderly looked at the naked lieutenant. Bach remembered that hospital personnel had instructions to report on the morale of the wounded. And he himself had just expressed a lack of confidence in the might of the armed forces. He said very distinctly: 'Yes, just how it will turn out is anyone's guess.'

What had made him repeat these dangerous words? No one can understand unless he himself lives in a totalitarian empire.

He had repeated these words because he was annoyed with himself for feeling frightened after saying them the first time. And also out of self-defence – to deceive a possible informer by a show of nonchalance.

Then, to dissipate any unfortunate impression he might have produced, he said: 'It's more than likely that this is the most important concentration of forces we've assembled since the beginning of the war. Believe me!'

Disgusted at the sterility of the complex game he was playing, he took refuge in a game played by children – squeezing warm soapy water inside his clenched fist. Sometimes it squirted out against the side of the bath, sometimes straight into his face.

'The principle of the flame-thrower,' he said to the orderly.

How thin he had become! Looking at his bare arms and chest, he thought of the young Russian woman who had kissed him two days before. Could he ever have imagined having an affair, in Stalingrad, with a Russian woman? Though it was hardly an affair. Just a wartime liaison. In an extraordinary, quite fantastic setting. They had met in a cellar. He had had to make his way past ruined buildings that were lit only by the flashes of shell-bursts. It was the kind of meeting that it would be good to describe in a book. He should have seen her yesterday. She probably thought he had been killed. Once he was better, he'd go and see her again. It would be interesting to see who'd taken his place. Nature abhors a vacuum . . .

Soon after his bath he was taken to the X-ray room. The doctor sat him down in front of the screen.

'So, Lieutenant, I hear things have been tough over there,' he said.

'Not as tough as they've been for the Russians,' Bach replied, wishing to please the doctor and be given a good diagnosis, one that would make the operation quick and painless.

The surgeon came in. The two doctors looked at the X-rays. No doubt they could see all the poisonous dissidence that had collected inside his rib-cage over the years.

The surgeon took Bach's hand and began to turn it, moving it towards and away from the screen. His concern was the splinter-wound; it was quite incidental that a young and highly educated man was attached to it.

The doctors talked to each other in a mixture of Latin and jocular curses. Bach realized he was going to be all right – he wasn't going to lose his arm after all.

'Get the lieutenant ready to be operated on,' said the surgeon. 'I'm going to take a look at this skull-wound. It's a difficult case.'

The orderly removed Bach's gown, and the surgeon's assistant, a young woman, told him to sit down on the stool.

'Heavens!' said Bach, smiling pitifully and feeling embarrassed at his nakedness. 'You should warm these stools up, Fräulein, before asking a combatant from the battle of Stalingrad to sit down on them with a bare behind.'

'That's not part of our routine,' she answered in absolute serious-ness. Then she began taking out a terrifying-looking array of instru-ments from a glass-fronted cupboard.

The extraction of the splinter, however, proved quick and simple. Bach even felt a little resentful: the surgeon's contempt for this ridiculously simple operation seemed to extend to the patient.

The assistant asked Bach if he needed to be accompanied back to his ward.

'I'll be all right by myself.'

'Anyway, you won't need to stay here long,' she said reassur-ingly.

'Fine,' he answered. 'I was already beginning to feel bored.'

She smiled.

Her picture of wounded soldiers was obviously derived from newspaper articles. These were full of stories about soldiers who had quietly slipped out of hospital in order to return to their beloved companies and battalions. They apparently felt an overpowering need to be fighting – otherwise life simply wasn't worth living.

Maybe journalists really had found people like that in hospital. Bach, on the other hand, felt shamefully happy to lie on a bed with clean sheets, eat his plate of rice, take a puff at his – strictly forbidden – cigarette, and strike up a conversation with his neighbours.

There were four men in the ward – three officers serving at the Front and a civil servant with a pot belly and a hollow chest. He had been sent from the rear on a mission and had a car accident near Gumrak. When he lay on his back, his hands folded across his stomach, it looked as though someone had jokingly stuffed a football under the blanket. No doubt this was why he had been nicknamed 'the goalkeeper'.

The goalkeeper was the only one to complain about being temporarily disabled. He spoke in an exalted tone about duty, the army, the Fatherland and his pride at being wounded in Stalingrad.

The three officers were amused at his brand of patriotism. One of them, Krap, who was lying on his stomach because of a wound in the buttocks, had been in command of a detachment of scouts. He had a pale face, thick lips and staring brown eyes.

'I guess you're the kind of goalkeeper who's not content just to defend his own goal,' he said, 'but likes to send the ball into his opponent's net as well.'

Wanting to say something stinging in reply, the goalkeeper asked: 'Why are you so pale? I suppose you have to work in an office.'

'No,' said Krap. 'I'm a night bird. That's when I go hunting. Unlike you, I do my screwing during the day.'

Krap was obsessed with sex. It was his chief topic of conversation.

After this, everyone began cursing the bureaucrats who cleared out of Berlin every evening and drove back to their country homes, and those fine warriors, the quartermasters, who were awarded more medals than men serving in the front line. They talked about the sufferings undergone by soldiers' families when their houses were destroyed by bombs. They cursed the Casanovas in the rear who tried to make off with soldiers' wives. They cursed the military stores where you couldn't buy anything except eau-de-Cologne and razor-blades.

In the bed next to Bach was a Lieutenant Gerne. At first Bach had thought he was an aristocrat, but he turned out to be a peasant – one of the men brought to the fore by the National Socialists. He had been the deputy to a regimental chief of staff and had been wounded by a bomb-splinter during a night air-raid.

When the goalkeeper was taken away to be operated on, Lieutenant Fresser, a rather simple man who had the bed in the corner, said: 'People have been shooting at me since 1939, but I've never made a song and dance about my patriotism. I get my food and drink, I get clothed – and I fight. Without philosophising about it.'

'Not entirely,' said Bach. 'When front-line soldiers make fun of a man like the goalkeeper, that's already a kind of philosophy.'

'Really?' said Gerne. 'How very interesting! May I ask just what kind of philosophy?'

Bach could tell from the hostile expression in Gerne's eyes that he was one of those people with a deep hatred of the old German intelligentsia. Bach had had his fill of speeches and articles attacking the intelligentsia for their admiration of American plutocracy, their hidden sympathies for Talmudism and Hebraic abstraction, and for the Jewish styles in literature and painting. Now he felt furious. If he was prepared to bow down before the rude strength of these new men, why then should they look at him with that wolf-like suspicion? Hadn't he been bitten by as many lice as they had? Hadn't he had frost bite? Here he was, a front-line officer – and they still didn't consider him a true German! Bach closed his eyes and turned to the wall.

'Why do you ask with such venom?' he wanted to mutter angrily.

'Do you really not understand?' Gerne would reply with a smile of contemptuous superiority.

'No, I don't understand,' he would say irritably. 'I told you. But perhaps I can guess.'

Gerne, of course, would burst out laughing.

'You suspect me of duplicity,' he would shout.

'That's right! Duplicity!' Gerne would repeat brightly.

'Impotence of the will?'

At this point Fresser would begin to laugh. Krap, supporting himself on his elbows, would stare insolently at Bach.

'You're a band of degenerates!' Bach would thunder. 'And you, Gerne, are half-way between a man and a monkey!'

Numb with hatred, Bach screwed up his eyes still tighter.

'You only have to write some little pamphlet on the most trivial of questions, and you think that gives you the right to despise the men who laid the foundations of German science. You only have to publish some miserable novella, and you think you can spit on the glory of German literature. You seem to imagine the arts and sciences as a kind of Ministry where there's no room for you because the older generation won't make way. Where you and your little book are denied admittance by Koch, Nernst, Planck and Kellerman . . . No, the arts and sciences are a Mount Parnassus beneath an infinite sky! There's room there for every genuine talent that has appeared throughout human history . . . Yes, if there's no place for you and your sterile fruits, it's certainly not for lack of room! You can throw out Einstein, but you'll never take his place yourselves. Yes, Einstein may be a Jew, but – forgive me for saying this – he's a genius. There's no power in the world that could enable you to step into his shoes. Is it really worth expending so much energy destroying people whose places must remain forever unoccupied? If your impotence has made it impossible for you to follow the paths opened up by Hitler, then the fault lies with you and you alone. Police methods and hatred can never achieve anything in the realm of culture. Can't you see how profoundly Hitler and Goebbels understand this? You should learn from them. See with what love, patience and tact, they themselves cherish German science, art and literature! Follow their example! Follow the path of consolidation instead of sowing discord in the midst of our common cause!'

After delivering this imaginary speech, Bach opened his eyes again. His neighbours were all lying quietly under their blankets.

'Watch this, comrades!' said Fresser. With the sweeping gesture of a conjuror, he took out from under his pillow a litre bottle of 'Three Knaves' Italian cognac.

Gerne made a strange sound in his throat. Only a true drunkard – and a peasant drunkard at that – could gaze at a bottle with quite such rapture.

'He's not so bad after all,' thought Bach, feeling ashamed of his hysterical speech.

Fresser, hopping about on one leg, filled the glasses on their bedside tables.

'You're a lion!' said Krap with a smile.

'A true soldier!' said Gerne.

'One of the quacks spotted my bottle,' said Fresser. '"What's that you've got wrapped up in a newspaper?" he asked. "Letters from my mother," I answered. "I carry them with me wherever I go."'

He raised his glass.

'And so, from Lieutenant Fresser, with greetings from the Front!'

They all drank.

Gerne, who immediately wanted more, said: 'Damn it! I suppose we'll have to leave some for the goalkeeper.'

'To hell with the goalkeeper!' said Krap. 'Don't you agree, Lieutenant?'

'We can have a drink – and he can carry out his duty to the Fatherland,' said Fresser. 'After all, we deserve a little fun.'

'My backside's really beginning to come to life,' said Krap. 'All I need now is a nice plump woman.'

They all felt a sense of ease and happiness.

'Well,' said Gerne, raising his glass. 'Let's have another!'

'It's a good thing we landed up in the same ward, isn't it?'

'I thought that straight away. I came in and I thought: "Yes, these are real men. They're hardened soldiers."'

'I must admit that I did have some doubts about Bach,' said Gerne. 'I thought he must be a Party member.'

'No, I've never been a member.'

They began to feel hot and removed their blankets. Their talk turned to the war.

Fresser had been on the left flank, near Okatovka. 'God knows,' he said, 'these Russians just don't know how to advance. But it's already November and we haven't moved forward either. Remember all the vodka we drank in August? All those toasts? "Here's to our continued friendship after the war! We must found an association for veterans of Stalingrad!"'

'They know how to launch an attack all right,' said Krap. He himself had been in the area of the factories. 'What they can't do is hold on. They drive us out of a building and then they just lie down and go to sleep. Or else they stuff themselves while their officers get pissed.'

'They're savages,' said Fresser with a wink. 'And we've wasted more iron on these savages from Stalingrad than on the whole of Europe.'

'And not just iron,' said Bach.

'If nothing's decided by winter,' said Gerne, 'then it will be a real stalemate. It's crazy.'

'We're preparing an offensive in the area of the factories,' said Krap very quietly. 'There's never been such a concentration of forces. Any day now they'll be unleashed. By November 20th we'll be sleeping with girls from Saratov.'

Through the curtained windows came the hum of Russian bombers and the majestic, unhurried thunder of artillery.

'There go the Russian cuckoos,' said Bach. 'They always carry out their raids around this time. Some people call them "nerve-saws".'

'At our HQ we call them "orderly sergeants",' said Gerne.

374

'Quiet!' said Krap, raising one finger. 'Listen! There go the heavy guns.'

'While we have a little drink in the ward for the lightly wounded,' said Fresser.

Their carefree mood returned. They began to talk about Russian women. Everyone had some experience to recount. Bach usually disliked such conversations, but suddenly he found himself telling them about the girl who lived in the cellar of a ruined house. He made a real story out of it and they all had a good laugh.

Then the orderly came in. He glanced at their bright faces and then started to take the sheets off the goalkeeper's bed.

'So has our brave defender of the Fatherland been unmasked as a malingerer?' asked Fresser.

'Say something,' said Gerne. 'We're men here. You can tell us if something's happened.'

'He's dead. Cardiac arrest.'

'That's what comes of too many patriotic speeches,' said Gerne.

'You shouldn't speak like that about a dead man,' said Bach. 'He wasn't just putting on an act. He was being sincere. No, comrades, it's not right.'

'Ah!' said Gerne. 'I wasn't so wrong after all. I thought the lieutenant would give us the Party line. I knew at once he was a true ideologue.'

11

That night Bach felt too comfortable to go to sleep. It was strange to think of his comrades and their bunker, to remember how he and Lenard had drunk coffee and smoked as they watched the sunset through the open door.

Yesterday, as he got into the field-ambulance, he had put his good arm round Lenard's shoulder; they had looked each other in the eye and burst out laughing. No, he'd certainly never have guessed he'd end up drinking with an SS officer in a Stalingrad bunker – or walking through ruins lit up by fires to visit a Russian woman.

What had happened to him was extraordinary. He had hated Hitler for many years. When he had heard grey-haired professors shamelessly claiming that Faraday, Darwin and Edison were nothing but crooks who'd plagiarized the ideas of German scientists, when he had heard them declare Hitler to be the greatest scientist of all times and all nations, he had thought savagely: 'What nonsense! But they'll be unmasked soon enough!' And he had felt the same about those improbable novels about the happiness of ideologically spotless workers and peasants, about the great educational work carried out by the all-wise Party. And as for the miserable poems printed in magazines! These had upset him most of all – as a schoolboy he had written poetry himself.

And now here he was – in Stalingrad – wanting to join the Party! As a child, when he had been afraid his father would get the better of him in an argument, he had put his hands over his ears and shouted: 'No, no, I'm not going to listen!' Well, now he had listened. And his world had been turned upside down.

He still felt as disgusted as ever by the plays and films he saw. Perhaps the people would have to go without poetry for a few years or even a decade? But it was quite possible to write the truth even now! What greater truth could there be today than the truth of the German soul? And the masters of the Renaissance had been able to express the very loftiest of spiritual values in works commissioned by bishops and princes . . .

Although Krap was still asleep, he was evidently still fighting some old battle; in a voice that could probably be heard on the street he screamed: 'Quick! A hand-grenade!' Obviously wanting to crawl forward, he turned over awkwardly, yelled with pain and then began to snore again.

Bach felt differently even about the extermination of the Jews. Previously it had sent shivers down his spine. Even now, if he were in power himself, he would immediately put a stop to this genocide. Nevertheless, though he had several Jewish friends himself, he had to admit that there was such a thing as a German soul and a German character – which meant that there must also be a Jewish soul and a Jewish character.

Marxism had failed! His mother and father had both been Social Democrats and this failure had been hard for him to admit. It was as though Marx were a physicist who had based a theory of the structure of matter on centrifugal forces and had felt only contempt for the universal forces of gravitational attraction. He had defined the centrifugal forces between the different classes and had succeeded more clearly than anyone in showing how they had operated throughout human history. But, like many great theoreticians, he had overestimated the importance of the forces he had discovered; he had believed that these forces alone determined the development of a society and the course of history. He had not so much as glimpsed the powerful forces that hold a nation together in spite of class differences; his social physics, based on a contempt for the universal law of national attraction, was simply absurd.

The State is not an effect; it is a cause!

The law that determines the birth of a nation-state is something miraculous and wonderful. A state is a living unity; it alone has the power to express what is most precious, what is truly immortal in millions of people – a German character, a German hearth, a German will, a German spirit of sacrifice.

Bach lay there for a while with his eyes closed. He began counting sheep – one white, one black, one white, one black, one white, one black . . .

The next morning, after breakfast, he wrote a letter to his mother. Knowing she wouldn't like what he was writing, he frowned and sighed. But it was important to tell her what he had now come to feel. He hadn't said anything during his last spell of leave. But she had noticed his irritability, his unwillingness to go on listening to the same old reminiscences about his father.

She would consider him an apostate from the faith of his father. But that wasn't true. Apostasy was the very thing he was renouncing.

Tired out by the morning routine, the patients were very quiet. During the night a man with serious wounds had been installed in the goalkeeper's bed. He was still unconscious and they didn't yet know what unit he was from.

How could he tell his mother that the people of this new Germany were now closer to him than friends he had known since childhood?

An orderly came in.

'Lieutenant Bach?'

'Yes?' said Bach, covering the letter with the palm of his hand.

'There's a Russian woman asking after you, Lieutenant.'

'Me?' said Bach in surprise. He realized it must be Zina. But how could she have found out where he was? She must have asked the driver of the field-ambulance. He felt touched and delighted. She must have hitched a lift during the night and then walked seven or eight kilometres. He imagined her pale face, her large eyes, her thin neck, the grey shawl she wore round her head.

Meanwhile the ward was in uproar.

'Lieutenant Bach!' said Gerne. 'I take my hat off to you. That's what I call successful work on the native population!'

Fresser waved his hands in the air, as though shaking off drops of water. 'Call her in! The lieutenant's got a good wide bed. We can marry them right now.'

'Women are like dogs,' said Krap. 'They always follow their men.'

All of a sudden Bach felt indignant. What did she think she was doing? How could she come and visit him in hospital? German officers were forbidden to have relationships with Russian women. And what if there'd been relatives of his working in the hospital, or friends of the Forsters? Even a German woman would hardly have come to visit him after such a trivial affair . . .

The man who'd been seriously wounded seemed to be laughing contemptuously in his sleep.

'Tell the woman I'm unable to come out to see her,' he said grimly. Not wanting to take part in the general hilarity, he picked up his pencil and read over what he'd written so far.

'The most extraordinary thing of all is that whereas for years I felt I was being suppressed by the State, I now understand that it alone can give expression to my soul. I don't wish for an easy destiny. If necessary, I'll break with my old friends. I realize those I am turning to will never consider me one of them. But I am ready to suffer for the sake of what is most important in me . . .'

The merriment in the ward continued.

'Sh!' said Gerne. 'Don't disturb him. He's writing to his fiancée.'

Bach began to laugh himself. There were moments when his suppressed laughter sounded like sobs; he realized he could just as easily be crying.

12

Officers who only infrequently saw General Friedrich Paulus – the commander of the Sixth Army – were unaware of any change in his state of mind. His bearing, the style of his orders, the smile with which he listened both to important reports and to trivial points of detail, all seemed to indicate that he was still in control of events.

Only the two men closest to him – his adjutant, Colonel Adam, and his chief of staff, General Schmidt – realized how much he had changed since the beginning of the battle for Stalingrad.

He could still be arrogant, condescending or charmingly witty; he could still enter warmly and intimately into the lives of his officers; he still had the power to throw whole regiments and divisions into battle, to promote and demote his men, to sign orders for decorations. He still smoked his usual cigarettes . . . But deep down something was changing; and this change was on the point of becoming irrevocable.

General Paulus had lost the feeling of being in control of time and events. Until recently he had only cast a quick, unworried glance over the reports furnished by his intelligence section. What did he care about the movements of the Russian reserves? What did their latest plans matter to him?

Now, however, when he looked at the file of documents and reports placed on his desk every morning by Colonel Adam, the reports of Russian troop movements during the night were the first thing he studied. Colonel Adam had noticed this; one day he had changed the order in the file so that the intelligence reports were on top. Paulus had opened the file and looked at the first page; he had then raised his eyebrows and slammed the file shut.

Surprised by the rather pathetic look that had crossed Paulus's face, Colonel Adam realized he had been tactless. A few days later, Paulus had looked through the documents and reports – now once again in their usual order – and smiled.

'You're evidently a very perceptive man, Herr innovator.'

It was a quiet autumn evening. General Schmidt was on his way to report to Paulus. He was feeling triumphant.

He walked down the silent, deserted street. In his head, beneath his heavy-peaked cap, were the plans for the most ruthless offensive yet to be launched in Stalingrad. That was how he described it when Paulus received him and asked him to sit down.

'There have indeed, in German military history, been offensives for which we have mobilized far greater quantities of men and equipment. But I for one have never been asked to organize such a dense concentration of both air and ground forces in such a limited sector of the Front.'

Paulus's attitude, as he listened to Schmidt, was not that of a commander-in-chief. His back was hunched and, as Schmidt's finger pointed to columns of figures and sectors marked on maps, his head turned quickly and obediently from side to side. Paulus himself had conceived this offensive. He had defined its parameters. But now, as he listened to Schmidt – the most brilliant chief of staff he had worked with – he felt unable to recognize his original conception. It was as though Schmidt was imposing his will on him, as though he had planned an offensive that went against his commanding officer's wishes.

'Yes,' said Paulus. 'And this concentration of forces is all the more impressive when you compare it to the void on our left flank.'

'But what can we do about that?' said Schmidt. 'Russia's so vast. We simply don't have enough men.'

'I'm not alone in feeling worried,' said Paulus. 'Von Weichs said to me: "We didn't strike with a fist. We struck with an open hand, our fingers stretching across the infinite spaces of the East." And others are worried too. In fact there's only one man who isn't worried . . .'

He didn't finish the sentence.

Everything was going as it should, and yet somehow failing to go as it should. It was as if the trifling uncertainties and chance misfortunes of the last weeks were beginning to reveal something quite new – the true face of war, the face of war in all its joylessness and hopelessness.

The intelligence section obstinately continued to report a build-up of Soviet forces in the North-West. Air-attacks seemed powerless to prevent this. Von Weichs had no German reserves to cover Paulus's flanks. He was attempting to mislead the Russians by installing

German radio-transmitters in zones occupied by Rumanian troops. But was this enough to turn the Rumanians into Germans?

The campaign in Africa had begun triumphantly. Fierce punishment had been meted out to the English at Dunkirk, in Norway and Greece – and yet the British Isles remained unoccupied. There had been magnificent victories in the East, they had marched thousands of miles to the Volga – and yet the Soviet armed forces had still not been smashed once and for all. It always seemed that what mattered had already been achieved; that only chance, only some trivial delay had prevented a victory from being decisive . . .

What did they matter, these few hundred metres that separated him from the Volga, these half-ruined factories, these burnt-out shells of buildings, compared to the vast spaces conquered during the summer offensive? But then only a few kilometres of desert had separated Rommel from his Egyptian oasis . . . And at Dunkirk they had been only a few kilometres, only a few hours, short of an absolute victory. It was always the same few kilometres . . . And there was always a lack of reserves, a gaping void in the rear of the victorious forces and at their flanks.

Summer 1942! Probably only once in a lifetime is a man allowed to live through days like those. He had felt the breath of India on his face. He had felt what an avalanche would feel – if it had feelings – as it smashes through forests and forces rivers out of their beds.

The idea had occurred to him that perhaps the German ear had grown accustomed to the name Friedrich. He had not really thought this seriously, but still . . . It was just then that a little grain of very hard sand had grated under his foot – or rather, against his teeth.

Headquarters had been full of a general sense of triumph and exultation. He was constantly receiving written reports, oral reports, radio reports, telephone reports, from the commanding officers of his different units. This hadn't seemed like work at all; it had been simply a symbolic expression of German triumph. And then one day the telephone had rung: 'Herr Commander-in-Chief . . .' Somehow this matter-of-fact voice had immediately sounded out of harmony with the peals of triumph filling the ether.

Weller, a divisional commander, had reported that in his sector the Russians had gone over to the offensive. An infantry detachment, equivalent in size to a reinforced battalion, had succeeded in breaking through to the railway station. It was with this seemingly insignificant incident that he had felt his first prickle of anxiety.

Schmidt read the plan of operations out loud. As he did so, he straightened his shoulders and raised his chin. He wanted to indicate that, in spite of the good personal relations between him and Paulus, he was aware of the formality of this meeting.

Quite unexpectedly, Paulus came out with some words that Schmidt found strange and upsetting. In a quiet voice – not that of a commander-in-chief, not that of a soldier at all – he said:

'I believe in victory. But you know what? There's something quite senseless and unnecessary about the whole struggle for this city.'

'That comes a little unexpectedly from the commander-in-chief of the armies around Stalingrad.'

'You think so? But Stalingrad no longer exists as a centre of communications or heavy industry. What do we want it for? We can cover the north-eastern flank of our Caucasian armies along the line Astrakhan-Kalach. We don't need Stalingrad for that . . . I'm confident of victory, Schmidt – we *shall* capture the Tractor Factory. But that won't help us cover our flank. The Russians are going to attack – von Weichs is quite sure. None of our bluffing will stop that.'

'The course of events changes their meaning,' said Schmidt. 'But the Führer has never yet withdrawn without first attaining an objective.'

Paulus himself believed that if the most brilliant victories had failed to bear the expected fruits, this was because they hadn't been carried through with the necessary tenacity and decisiveness. At the same time, he felt that the ability to abandon an objective that had lost its meaning was a sign of strength.

He looked into Schmidt's intelligent, piercing eyes.

'It's not for us to impose our will on a great strategist.'

He picked up the order of operations and signed it.

'Four copies only, in view of its particular secrecy,' said Schmidt.

13

After his visit to Army Headquarters, Darensky went to a unit deployed along the south-eastern flank of the Stalingrad Front, in the waterless sands around the Caspian Sea.

The steppes, with their small rivers and lakes, now seemed like an earthly paradise. Feather-grass grew there, there were horses, an occasional tree . . .

Thousands of men – all of them used to morning dew, the rustle of hay, and humid air – had now taken up quarters in these sandy wastes. The sand cut their skin, got into their ears, found its way into their bread and gruel, grated in the mechanisms of their watches and the bolts of their rifles, penetrated their dreams . . . These were harsh conditions for a human body, for human throats and nostrils, for human calves and thighs. It was as though the human body were a cart that had left the road and was now creaking its way across rough ground.

All day long Darensky visited artillery positions, had discussions, jotted down notes, made sketches, inspected equipment and ammunition dumps. By evening he was exhausted; his ears buzzed and his legs, unaccustomed to these shifting sands, were aching and throbbing.

Darensky had long ago noticed that, during a retreat, generals become particularly sensitive to the needs of their subordinates; commanding officers and Members of the Military Soviet suddenly reveal themselves to be modest, self-critical and full of scepticism. Never does an army prove to be so full of intelligent, all-understanding men as during a forced retreat, when the General Staff are searching for culprits.

But here in the desert people were simply apathetic and lethargic. It was as though the officers were convinced there was nothing for them to do, nothing for them to be concerned about – after all, these sands would be exactly the same tomorrow, the following day, in a year's time . . .

The chief of staff of an artillery regiment, Lieutenant-Colonel Bova, invited Darensky to stay the night with him. Bova was stoop-shouldered, bald and hard of hearing in one ear. His quarters were in a shack made from boards smeared with clay and manure; the floor was covered with ragged sheets of tarred roofing paper. The shack was identical in every detail to those where the other officers were quartered.

'Greetings!' said Bova, shaking Darensky energetically by the hand. 'How's this then?' he asked, gesturing at the walls. 'It looks like I'll be spending the winter in a dog-kennel smeared with shit.'

'I've seen worse lodgings,' said Darensky, surprised at the transformation of the usually quiet Bova.

Bova sat Darensky down on a crate that had once contained cans of food from America, poured out some vodka into a large dirty glass whose rim was smeared with dried toothpaste, and handed him a green pickled tomato on a piece of damp newspaper.

'Make yourself at home, comrade Lieutenant-Colonel!' he insisted. 'We've got vodka and we've got fruit.'

Darensky, who seldom drank, took a small, cautious sip and pushed his glass away. He asked Bova about the state of his troops. Bova, however, didn't want to talk shop.

'Yes, comrade Lieutenant-Colonel,' he said. 'I've had enough of work. In the old days I never took a moment off – not even when there were all those splendid women around in Kuban and the Ukraine. Heavens! And they weren't shy either – believe me! You only had to wink at them. But I just sat on my arse in the Operations Section. I didn't know what I'd missed till I was out here in the desert.'

At first Darensky was annoyed by Bova's reluctance to discuss the average density of troops per square kilometre of front, or to give his opinion on the possible advantages of mortars over artillery in desert conditions. Nevertheless, he was not uninterested by the new turn the conversation had taken.

'You can say that again!' he exclaimed. 'There are some magnificent women in the Ukraine! There's one I used to visit in 1941, when we had our HQ in Kiev . . . She was a real beauty – the wife of someone in the public prosecutor's office . . . And I'm not going to argue about Kuban either. Yes, I rate Kuban very highly indeed – the number of beautiful women there is quite remarkable.'

Darensky's words had an extraordinary effect on Bova; he started to curse and then gave a cry of despair: 'And now we have to make do with Kalmyks!'

'Wrong!' said Darensky emphatically. He then became surprisingly eloquent about the charm of these swarthy and high-cheekboned women who smelt of wormwood and the smoke of the steppes. Remembering Alla Sergeyevna, he concluded: 'You're wrong. There are women everywhere. There may be no water in the desert, but there are always women.'

Bova didn't respond – he was asleep. Only then did Darensky realize that his host was drunk.

Bova's head was hanging off the edge of the camp-bed and his snores were like the groans of a dying man. Darensky, with the special tenderness and patience that a Russian feels towards a drunkard, placed a pillow under his head and some sheets of newspaper under his legs. He then wiped the saliva off Bova's lip and began looking round for somewhere to lie down himself.

He laid his host's greatcoat on the floor, threw his own on top and put his knapsack down to serve as a pillow. When he was out on a mission, this knapsack served as his office, his food store and as a container for his washing kit.

He went outside, drank in the cold night air, and gasped as he gazed at the unearthly flames in the black Asiatic sky. He urinated, still looking at the stars, thought, 'Yes, yes, the cosmos!' and went back in.

He lay down on his host's greatcoat and covered himself with his own. Then, instead of closing his eyes, he gazed pensively and gloomily into the darkness.

What poverty he was surrounded by! Here he was, lying on the floor looking at some left-over marinated tomatoes and a cardboard suitcase that no doubt contained only a skimpy towel with a black stamp on it, some crumpled collars for a soldier's tunic, an empty holster for a revolver and a squashed soap-box.

The hut in Verkhniy-Pogromniy where he had spent the night last autumn now seemed luxurious. And in a year's time, perhaps, this present hut would seem equally luxurious; he would look back on it longingly as he went to sleep at the bottom of some empty pit.

Darensky had changed during his months on the artillery staff. His need for work – something that had once seemed as powerful as his need for food – was now satisfied. His work no longer gave him any particular satisfaction – any more than eating affords any particular satisfaction to someone well-fed.

Darensky was highly regarded by his superior officers. At first this had been a great joy to him – over the years he had become all too used to the opposite. He was probably valued even more highly on the staff of the Stalingrad Front than Novikov had been during his time on the staff of the South-Eastern Front. He had heard that whole pages of his reports were transcribed verbatim in reports addressed by important people in Moscow to still more important people. At a critical period his intelligence and his work had been discovered to be of real use and importance. Five years before the war, however, his wife had left him, considering him to be an enemy of the people who had succeeded in hiding from her the flabbiness and hypocrisy that was his true nature. He had often been turned down for jobs because of his background – he came from an aristocratic family, both on his mother's side and on his father's side. To begin with, he had been upset to learn that someone particularly stupid or ignorant had been appointed instead of him. Then he had begun to feel he really couldn't be trusted with a position of executive responsibility. His spell in camp had made him certain of his inadequacy. And now this terrible war had proved how far this was from the truth.

Darensky pulled his coat up over his shoulders, exposing his feet to the cold draught from the door. He wondered why it was that, at a time when his knowledge and abilities had finally been recognized, he should be lying on the floor in a hen-coop, listening to the piercing screams of camels, dreaming not of dachas and rest-homes but of a clean pair of pants and a decent piece of soap.

He felt proud – and at the same time annoyed – that his promotion hadn't brought him any material advantage. His high opinion of himself went hand in hand with a persistent feeling of timidity. Deep down, he felt he wasn't entitled to the good things of life. This constant lack of both self-assurance and money, this constant sense of being badly dressed, was something he had been used to since childhood, something that still hadn't left him. He was terrified at the thought of going into the Military Soviet canteen and being told by the girl behind the counter: 'Comrade Lieutenant-Colonel, I'm afraid you're only entitled to eat in the general canteen.' Then some witty general would say at a meeting: 'Well, Lieutenant-Colonel, did you enjoy the borshch in the Military Soviet canteen?' He had always been amazed at the brazenness with which not only generals but even mere photographers would eat and drink, or demand petrol, clothes and cigarettes, in places they had no right even to visit.

His father had been unable to find work for years on end; his mother, a stenographer, had been the breadwinner.

Around midnight Bova stopped snoring. Darensky felt worried by the sudden silence. Suddenly Bova asked: 'Are you still awake, comrade Lieutenant-Colonel?'

'Yes, I can't get to sleep.'

'Forgive me for not making you more comfortable,' said Bova. 'I'd had a little too much to drink. But now I feel as clear-headed as ever. And what I keep asking myself is this. What on earth did we do to end up in this godforsaken hole? Whose fault is it?'

'The Germans', of course,' said Darensky.

'You lie on the bed,' said Bova. 'I can go on the floor myself.'

'What do you mean? I'm fine as I am.'

'It's not right. In the Caucasus it's not done for a host to stay in his bed while a guest lies on the floor.'

'Never mind. We're hardly Caucasians.'

'We're not far off it. The foothills are very close. You say the Germans are responsible. But maybe we did our bit too.'

Bova must have sat up – his bed gave a loud squeak. 'Yes,' he said, drawing the word out thoughtfully.

'Yes,' said Darensky non-committally.

Bova had directed the conversation into an unusual channel. They were silent for a moment, each wondering whether he should continue such a conversation with someone he hardly knew. In the end it appeared that they had both decided against it.

Bova lit a cigarette. Darensky glimpsed his face in the light of the match. It looked somehow flabby, sullen, alien . . . He lit a cigarette himself. Bova glimpsed his face as he lay there, resting his head on one elbow. His face looked cold, unkind, alien . . . Then they went on with the conversation.

'Yes,' said Bova. This time he spoke the word sharply and decisively. 'Bureaucrats and bureaucracy – that's what's landed us in this wilderness.'

'Yes,' agreed Darensky. 'Bureaucracy's terrible. My chauffeur said that in his village before the war you couldn't even get a document out of someone without giving them half a litre of vodka.'

'It's no laughing matter,' Bova interrupted. 'In peacetime bureaucracy can be bad enough. But on the front line . . . I heard a story about a pilot whose plane caught fire after a scrap with a Messerschmidt. Well, he parachuted out and was quite unscathed. But his trousers were burnt. And do you know what? They wouldn't give him a new pair! The quartermaster just said: "No, you're not yet due for a new issue." And that was that. For three days he had to do without trousers. Finally the commanding officer found out.'

'Excuse me,' said Darensky, 'but you can hardly make out that we've retreated from Brest to the Caspian desert simply because of some idiot refusing to issue a new pair of trousers.'

'I never said it was because of the trousers,' said Bova sourly. 'Let me give you another example . . . There was an infantry detachment that had been surrounded. The men had nothing to eat. A squadron was ordered to drop them some food by parachute. And then the quartermaster refused to issue the food. He said he needed a signature on the delivery slip and how could the men down below sign for what had been dropped by parachute? And he wouldn't budge. Finally he received an order from above.'

Darensky smiled. 'All right, that's very comic but it's hardly of major importance. Just pedantry. Bureaucracy can be much more terrifying than that. Remember the order: "Not one step back"? There was one place where the Germans were mowing our men down by the hundred. All we needed to do was withdraw over the brow of the hill. Strategically, it would have made no difference – and we'd have saved our men and equipment. But the orders were "Not one step back". And so the men perished and their equipment was destroyed.'

'Yes,' said Bova. 'You're right there. In 1941 we had two colonels sent out to us from Moscow to check on the execution of that very order. They didn't have any transport themselves and during three days we retreated two hundred kilometres from Gomel. If I hadn't taken them in my truck, they'd have been captured by the Germans in no time. And there they were – being shaken about in the back like a sack of potatoes and asking what measures we'd taken to implement the order "Not one step back"! And what else could they do? They couldn't not write their report.'

Darensky took a deep breath, as though preparing to plunge still deeper. 'I'll tell you when bureaucracy really is terrible. It's when a lone machine-gunner has defended a height against seventy Germans. When he's held up the enemy's advance all on his own. When a whole army's bowed down before him after his death. And then his tubercular wife is abused by an official from the district soviet and thrown out of her flat . . . ! It's when a man has to fill in twenty-four questionnaires and then ends up confessing at a meeting: "Comrades, I'm not one of you. I'm an alien element . . ." It's when a man has to say: "Yes, this is a workers' and peasants' State. My mother and father were aristocrats, parasites, degenerates. Go on, throw me out onto the street."'

'I don't see that as bureaucracy,' said Bova. 'The State does belong to the workers and peasants. They're in control. What's wrong with that? That's as it should be. You wouldn't expect a bourgeois State to trust down-and-outs.'

Darensky was taken aback. The man he was speaking to evidently thought very differently to himself.

Bova lit a match. Instead of lighting a cigarette, he just held it up towards Darensky. Darensky screwed up his eyes; he felt like a soldier caught in the beam of an enemy searchlight.

'I'm from the purest of working-class backgrounds myself,' Bova went on. 'My father was a worker, and so was my grandfather. My background's as pure as crystal. But I was no use to anyone before the war either.'

'Why not?'

'I don't look on it as bureaucracy if a workers' and peasants' State treats aristocrats with suspicion. But why did they go for *my* throat? I thought I was going to end up picking potatoes or sweeping the streets. And all I'd done was criticize the bosses – from a class viewpoint. I'd said they were living in the lap of luxury. Well, I really caught it then! That's what I see as the root of bureaucracy – a worker suffering in his own State.'

Darensky had the feeling that Bova had touched on something of great importance. He felt a sudden happiness: he was unaccustomed either to talking about his own deepest preoccupations or to hearing other people talk about theirs. To do this, to speak one's mind freely and without fear, to argue uninhibitedly and without fear, seemed a great joy.

Everything felt different here: as he lay on the floor of this shack, talking to a simple soldier who had only just sobered up, sensing the invisible presence of thousands of men who had retreated from the Western Ukraine to this wilderness, Darensky knew that something had changed. Something very simple and natural, something very necessary – and at the same time quite impossible, quite unthinkable – had come about: he and another man had talked freely and sincerely.

'Yes,' said Darensky. 'But you've got one thing wrong. The bourgeoisie don't allow down-and-outs into the Senate, that's for sure. But if a down-and-out becomes a millionaire, then it's another story. The Fords started out as ordinary workers. We don't trust members of the bourgeoisie and aristocracy with positions of responsibility – and that's fair enough. But it's another matter altogether to stamp the mark of Cain on the forehead of an honest worker simply because his mother and father were kulaks or priests. That's not what I call a class viewpoint. Anyway, do you think I didn't meet workers from the Putilov factory or miners from Donetsk during my time in camp? They were there in their thousands. What's really terrifying is when you realize that bureaucracy isn't simply a growth on the body of the State. If it were only that, it could be cut off. No, bureaucracy is the very essence of the State. And in wartime people don't want to die just for the sake of the head of some personnel department. Any flunkey can stamp "Refused" on some petition. Any flunkey can kick some soldier's widow out of his office. But to kick out the Germans you have to be strong. You have to be a man.'

'That's for sure,' said Bova.

'But don't think I feel any resentment,' said Darensky. 'No, I bow down and take off my hat. I'm happy. A thousand thank-you's. What's wrong is that we had to undergo such terrible tragedies before I could be happy, before I was allowed to devote my energies to my country. If that's the price of my happiness, I'd rather be without it.'

Darensky felt that he still hadn't dug down to what really mattered, that he still hadn't been able to find the simple words that would cast a new, clear light on their lives. But he was happy to have thought and talked about what he had only very seldom thought or talked about.

'Let me say one thing. I can tell you that, whatever happens, I shall never ever regret this conversation of ours.'

14

Mikhail Mostovskoy was kept for over three weeks in the isolation ward. He was fed well, examined twice by an SS doctor, and prescribed injections of glucose.

During his first hours of confinement Mostovskoy expected to be summoned for interrogation at any moment. He felt constantly irritated with himself. Why had he talked with Ikonnikov? That holy fool had betrayed him, planting compromising papers on him just before a search.

The days passed and Mostovskoy still wasn't summoned . . . He went over the conversations he had had with the other prisoners about politics, wondering which of them he could recruit. At night, when he couldn't sleep, he composed a text for some leaflets and began compiling a camp phrase-book to facilitate communication between the different nationalities.

He remembered the old laws of conspiracy, intended to exclude the possibility of a total débâcle if an agent provocateur should denounce them.

Mostovskoy wanted to question Yershov and Osipov about the immediate aims of the organization. He was confident that he would be able to overcome Osipov's prejudice against Yershov.

Chernetsov, who hated Bolshevism and yet longed for the victory of the Red Army, seemed a pathetic figure. Now Mostovskoy felt quite calm about the prospect of his impending interrogation.

One night Mostovskoy had a heart attack. He lay there with his head against the wall, feeling the agony of a man left to die in a prison. For a while the pain made him lose consciousness. Then he came to. The pain had lessened, but his chest, his face and the palms of his hands were all covered in sweat. His thoughts took on a deceptive clarity.

His conversation about evil with the Italian priest became confused with a number of different memories: with the happiness he had felt as a boy when it had suddenly begun to pour with rain and he had rushed into the room where his mother was sewing; with his wife's bright eyes, wet with tears, when she had come to visit him at the time he was in exile by the Yenisey; with pale Dzerzhinsky whom he had once asked at a Party conference about the fate of a young and very kind Social Revolutionary. 'Shot,' Dzerzhinsky had answered . . . Major Kirillov's gloomy eyes . . . Draped in a sheet, the corpse of his friend was being dragged along on a sledge – he had refused to accept his offer of help during the siege of Leningrad.

A boy's dreamy head and its mop of hair . . . And now this large bald skull pressed against the rough boards.

These distant memories drifted away. Everything became flatter and lost its colour. He seemed to be sinking into cold water. He fell asleep – to wake up to the howl of sirens in the early-morning gloom.

In the afternoon he was taken to the sick-bay bath. He sighed as he examined his arms and his hollow chest. 'Yes, old age is here to stay,' he thought to himself.

The guard, who was rolling a cigarette between his fingers, went out for a moment, and the narrow-shouldered, pock-marked prisoner who had been mopping the cement floor sidled over to Mostovskoy.

'Yershov ordered me to tell you the news. The German offensive in Stalingrad has been beaten off. The major told me to tell you that everything is in order. And he wants you to write a leaflet and pass it on when you have your next bath.'

Mostovskoy wanted to say that he didn't have a pencil and paper, but just then the guard came in.

As he was getting dressed, Mostovskoy felt a small parcel in his pocket. It contained ten sugar lumps, some bacon fat wrapped up in a piece of rag, some white paper and a pencil stub. He felt a sudden happiness. What more could he want? How fortunate he was not to have his life drawing to an end in trivial anxieties about indigestion, heart attacks and sclerosis.

He clasped the sugar lumps and the pencil to his breast.

That night he was taken out of the sick-bay by an SS sergeant. Gusts of cold wind blew into his face. He looked round at the sleeping barracks and said to himself: 'Don't worry, lads. You can sleep in peace. Comrade Mostovskoy's got strong nerves – he won't give in.'

They went through the doors of the administration building. Here, instead of the stench of ammonia, was a cool smell of tobacco. Mostovskoy noticed a half-smoked cigarette on the floor and wanted to pick it up.

They climbed up to the second floor. The guard ordered Mostovskoy to wipe his boots on the mat and did so himself at great length. Mostovskoy was out of breath from climbing the stairs. He tried to control his breathing.

They set off down a strip of carpet that ran down the corridor. The lamps – small, semi-transparent tulips – gave a warm, calm light. They walked past a polished door with a small board saying 'Kommandant' and stopped in front of another door with a board saying 'Obersturm-bannführer Liss'.

Mostovskoy had heard the name 'Liss' many times: he was Himmler's representative in the camp administration. Mostovskoy was amused: General Gudz had been annoyed that he had only been interrogated by one of Liss's assistants while Osipov had been interrogated by Liss himself. Gudz had seen this as a slight to the military command.

Osipov had said that Liss had interrogated him without an interpreter; he was a German from Riga with a good knowledge of Russian.

A young officer came out, said a few words to the guard and let Mostovskoy into the office. He left the door open.

The office was almost empty. The floor was carpeted. There was a vase of flowers on the table and a picture on the wall: peasant houses by the edge of a forest, with red tiled rooves.

Mostovskoy thought it was like being in the office of the director of a slaughterhouse. Not far away were dying animals, steaming entrails and people being spattered with blood, but the office itself was peaceful and softly carpeted – only the black telephone on the desk served to remind you of the world outside.

Enemy! That word was so clear and simple. Once again he thought of Chernetsov – what a wretched fate during this time of *Sturm und Drang*! But then he did wear kid gloves . . . Mostovskoy glanced at his own hands, his own fingers.

The door opened at the far end of the office. There was a creak from the door into the corridor – the orderly must have shut it as he saw Liss come in.

Mostovskoy stood there and frowned.

'Good evening!' said the quiet voice of a short man with SS insignia on the sleeves of his grey uniform.

There was nothing repulsive about Liss's face, and for that very reason Mostovskoy found it terrible to look at. He had a snub nose, alert dark-grey eyes, a high forehead and thin pale cheeks that made him look industrious and ascetic.

Liss waited while Mostovskoy cleared his throat and then said:

'I want to talk to you.'

'But I don't want to talk to you,' answered Mostovskoy. He looked sideways into the far corner, waiting for Liss's assistants, the torturers, to emerge and give him a blow on the ear.

'I quite understand,' said Liss. 'Sit down.'

He seated Mostovskoy in the armchair and then sat down next to him.

Liss spoke in the lifeless, ash-cold language of a popular scientific pamphlet.

'Are you feeling unwell?'

Mostovskoy shrugged his shoulders and said nothing.

'Yes, yes, I know. I sent the doctor to you and he told me. I've disturbed you in the middle of the night. But I want to talk to you very badly.'

'Oh yes,' thought Mostovskoy.

'I've been summoned for interrogation,' he said out loud. 'There's nothing for us to talk about.'

'Why do you say that?' asked Liss. 'All you see is my uniform. But I wasn't born in it. The Führer and the Party command; the rank and file obey. I was always a theoretician. I'm a Party member, but my real interest lies in questions of history and philosophy. Surely not all the officers in your NKVD love the Lubyanka?'

Mostovskoy watched Liss's face carefully. He thought for a moment that this pale face with the high forehead should be drawn at the very bottom of the tree of evolution; from there evolution would progress towards hairy Neanderthal man.

'If the Central Committee orders you to step up the work of the

394

Cheka, are you in a position to refuse? You put Hegel aside and get working. Well, we've had to put Hegel aside too.'

Mostovskoy glanced at Liss. Pronounced by unclean lips, the name of Hegel sounded strange and blasphemous . . . A dangerous, experienced thief had come up to him in a crowded tram and started a conversation. He wasn't going to listen, he was just going to watch the thief's hands – any minute now a razor might flash out and slash him across the eyes.

But Liss just lifted up the palms of his hands, looked at them and said: 'Our hands are like yours. They love great work and they're not afraid of dirt.'

Mostovskoy frowned deeply: it was horrible to see this gesture and hear these words that so exactly mimicked his own.

Liss began to speak quickly and with enthusiasm, as though he had talked to Mostovskoy before and was glad to have the opportunity to resume the conversation. The things he said were extraordinary – terrible and absurd.

'When we look one another in the face, we're neither of us just looking at a face we hate – no, we're gazing into a mirror. That's the tragedy of our age. Do you really not recognize yourselves in us – yourselves and the strength of your will? Isn't it true that for you too the world *is* your will? Is there anything that can make *you* waver?'

His face moved closer to Mostovskoy's.

'Do you understand me? I don't know Russian well, but I very much want you to understand me. You may think you hate us, but what you really hate is yourselves – yourselves in us. It's terrible, isn't it? Do you understand me?'

Mostovskoy decided to remain silent. He musn't let Liss draw him into conversation.

But he did think for a moment that, rather than trying to deceive him, the man looking into his eyes was searching for words quite earnestly and sincerely. It was as though he were complaining, asking Mostovskoy to help him make sense of something that tormented him.

It was agonizing. It was as though someone had stuck a needle into Mostovskoy's heart.

'Do you understand me?' Liss repeated, already too excited even to see Mostovskoy. 'When we strike a blow against your army, it's ourselves that we hit. Our tanks didn't only break through your defences – they broke through our own defences at the same time. The tracks of our tanks are crushing German National Socialism. It's terrible – it's like committing suicide in one's sleep. And it might well end tragically for us. Do you understand? Yes, even if we win! As victors we would be left on our own – without you – in a world that is alien to us, a world that hates us.'

It would have been easy enough to refute all this. Liss's eyes had now drawn still closer to Mostovskoy's. But there was something even more dangerous than the words of this experienced SS provocateur. It was what stirred in Mostovskoy's own soul – his own vile, filthy doubts.

He was like a man afraid of an illness – of some malignant tumour – who won't go near a doctor, tries not to notice his indispositions and avoids talking about sickness with anyone close to him. And then suddenly someone comes up to him and says: 'Say, have you ever had such and such a pain, especially in the mornings, usually after . . . ? Yes, yes . . .'

'Do you understand me, teacher?' asked Liss. 'A certain German – I'm sure you know his brilliant work – once said that Napoleon's tragedy was that he embodied the soul of England and yet in England herself found his most deadly foe.'

'If only they'd start beating me up!' thought Mostovskoy. And then: 'Ah, now he's on about Spengler.'

Liss lit a cigarette and held out his cigarette case to Mostovskoy.

'No,' said Mostovskoy abruptly.

He felt somehow calmed by the thought that all the policemen in the world – the ones who'd interrogated him forty years ago and the one talking about Hegel and Spengler right now – should use this same idiotic technique of offering their victim a cigarette. Yes, it was just that his nerves were weak – he'd been expecting to be beaten up and suddenly he'd had to listen to this horrible, absurd talk. But then even some of the Tsarist police had known a little about politics – a few of them were really quite educated, one had even read *Das Kapital*. But had there ever been a moment when a policeman studying Marx had wondered, deep in his heart: 'What if Marx is right?' What had the policeman felt then . . . ? But what of it? Mostovskoy had trampled on his doubts too. Still, that was different – he was a revolutionary.

Not noticing that Mostovskoy had refused the cigarette, Liss muttered: 'Yes, that's right, it's very good tobacco.'

He then closed his cigarette case and began again. He sounded genuinely upset.

'Why do you find this conversation so surprising? What did you expect me to say? Surely you have some educated men at your Lubyanka? People who can talk to Academician Pavlov or to Oldenburg? But I'm different from them. I've got no ulterior motive. I give you my word. I'm tormented by the same anxieties as you are.' He smiled and added: 'My word of honour as a Gestapo officer. And I don't say that lightly.'

'Don't say anything,' Mostovskoy repeated to himself, 'that's the main thing. Don't enter into conversation. Don't argue.'

Liss went on talking. Once again he seemed to have forgotten about Mostovskoy.

'Two poles of one magnet! Of course! If that wasn't the case, then this terrible war wouldn't be happening. We're your deadly enemies. Yes, yes . . . But our victory will be your victory. Do you understand? And if you should conquer, then we shall perish only to live in your victory. It's paradoxical: through losing the war we shall win the war – and continue our development in a different form.'

Why on earth had this all-powerful Liss, instead of watching prize-winning films, drinking vodka, writing reports to Himmler, looking at books on gardening, re-reading his daughter's letters, having fun with young girls from today's transport, or even just taking something for his digestion and going to sleep in his spacious bedroom – why on earth had he decided to summon an old Russian Bolshevik who stank of the camps?

What did he have in mind? Why was he keeping his motives so secret? What was the information he wanted?

Mostovskoy wasn't afraid of torture. What did terrify him was the thought: 'What if the German isn't lying? What if he's sincere? What if he really does just want someone to talk to?'

What a horrible thought! They were both ill, both worn out by the same illness, but one of them hadn't been able to bear it and was speaking out, while the other remained silent, giving nothing away, just listening, listening . . .

Finally, as though answering Mostovskoy's silent question, Liss opened a file on his desk and very fastidiously, with two fingers, took out some sheets of dirty papers. Mostovskoy immediately recognized them as Ikonnikov's scribblings.

Liss evidently expected him to feel consternation at the sight of the papers planted on him by Ikonnikov . . . But he felt quite calm. He even felt glad to see these scribblings: once again everything was clear – as absurdly simple as every police interrogation.

Liss pushed the papers to the edge of the desk and then drew them back again. Suddenly he began to speak in German:

'I've never seen your handwriting, but I knew from the first words that you could never have written rubbish like this.'

Mostovskoy remained silent.

Liss tapped his finger against the papers. He was inviting Mostovskoy to speak, affably, insistently, with good will . . .

Mostovskoy remained silent.

'Have I made a mistake?' asked Liss in surprise. 'No, it's not possible. You and I can feel only disgust at what's written here. We two stand shoulder to shoulder against trash like this!'

'Come on now,' said Mostovskoy hurriedly and angrily. 'Let's get to the point. These papers? Yes, they were taken from me. You want to know who gave them to me? That's none of your business. Maybe I wrote them myself? Maybe you ordered someone to plant them on me . . . ? All right?'

For a moment he thought Liss would accept his challenge, lose his temper and shout: 'We have ways of making you answer!'

He would have liked that so much. That would make everything so straightforward, so easy. What a clear, simple word it was – 'enemy'.

But Liss only said: 'Who cares about these wretched papers? What does it matter who wrote them? I know it was neither of us. Just think for a moment! Who do you imagine fill our camps when there's no war and no prisoners of war? Enemies of the Party, enemies of the People! Yes, and if our Reich Security Administration accepts prisoners of yours in peacetime, then we won't let them out again – your prisoners are our prisoners!'

He grinned.

'The German Communists we've sent to camps are the same ones you sent to camps in 1937. Yezhov imprisoned them: Reichsführer Himmler imprisoned them . . . Be more of a Hegelian, teacher.'

He winked at Mostovskoy.

'I've often thought that a knowledge of foreign languages must be as useful in your camps as it is in ours. Today you're appalled by our hatred of the Jews. Tomorrow you may make use of our experience yourselves. And by the day after tomorrow we may be more tolerant again. I have been led by a great man down a long road. You too have been led by a great man; you too have travelled a long, difficult road. Did you really believe Bukharin was an agent provocateur? Only a very great man could lead people down a road like that . . . I knew Roehm myself; I trusted him. But that's how it had to be . . . What tortures me, though, is the thought that your terror killed millions – and we Germans were the only ones who could understand, the only men in the world who thought: "Yes, that's absolutely right, that's how it has to be!"

'Please try to understand me – as I understand you. This war ought to appal you. Napoleon should never have fought against England.'

Mostovskoy was struck by a new thought. He even screwed up his eyes – either because of a sudden stab of pain or to get rid of this tormenting thought. What if his doubts were not just a sign of weakness, tiredness, impotence, lack of faith, comtemptible shilly-shallying? What if these doubts represented what was most pure and honourable in him . . . ? And he just crushed them, pushed them aside, hated them! What if they contained the seed of revolutionary truth? The dynamite of freedom!

All he need do to defeat Liss, to push aside his sticky, slippery fingers, was stop hating Chernetsov, stop despising that holy fool Ikonnikov! No, no, he had to do more than that! He had to renounce everything he had stood for; he had to condemn what he had always lived by.

No, no, he had to do more than that! With all the strength of his soul, with all his revolutionary passion, he would have to hate the camps, the Lubyanka, bloodstained Yezhov, Yagoda, Beria! More than that . . . ! He would have to hate Stalin and his dictatorship!

More than that! He would have to condemn Lenin . . . ! This was the edge of the abyss.

Yes, this was Liss's victory – not in the war running its course on the battlefields, but in the war of snake venom, the war without gunfire he was waging against him in this office.

For a moment Mostovskoy thought he was about to go mad. Then he let out a sudden joyful sigh of relief. The thought that had horrified and blinded him had turned into dust. It was absurd and pathetic. The hallucination had lasted only a few seconds . . . But still, how was it that for even a second – a fraction of a second – he could have doubted the justice of a great cause?

Liss looked at him and pursed his lips.

'Do you think the world looks on us with horror and on you with hope and love?' he asked. 'No, the world looks on us both with the same horror!'

Mostovskoy was no longer afraid of anything. Now he knew where his doubts led: they didn't lead into a swamp – they led to the abyss.

Liss picked up Ikonnikov's papers.

'How can you have anything to do with people like this? Everything's been turned upside down by this accursed war . . . If only I could unravel this tangle!'

There is no tangle, Herr Liss. Everything's very simple and very clear. We don't need to ally ourselves with Chernetsov and Ikonnikov to overpower you. We can deal with both them and you . . .

Mostovskoy realized that everything dark and sinister was embodied in Liss. All rubbish heaps smelt the same; there was no difference between one lot of splintered wood and crushed brick and another. One shouldn't look to garbage and debris in order to understand similarities and differences; one should look to the thoughts, the design, of the builder.

Mostovskoy found himself gripped by a joyful, triumphant rage – against Liss and Hitler, against the English officer with the colourless eyes who had asked him about criticisms of Marxism, against the sickening speeches of the one-eyed Menshevik, against the mawkish preacher who had turned out to be a police agent. Where would these men ever find people stupid enough to believe that there was the faintest shadow of resemblance between a Socialist State and the Fascist Reich? The Gestapo officer Liss was the only consumer of their rotten goods. Now, as never before, Mostovskoy understood the inner link between Fascism and its agents.

And wasn't this the true genius of Stalin? He had hated and annihilated these people because he alone had seen the hidden brotherhood between Fascism and the Pharisees who advocated a specious freedom. This thought now seemed so obvious that he wanted to explain it – to bring home to Liss the full absurdity of his theories. But he contented himself with a smile: he'd been around a long time; he wasn't like that fool Goldenberg who'd blathered to the Public Prosecutor about the affairs of 'People's Will'.*

He stared straight at Liss. Then, in a voice that could probably be heard by the guard on the other side of the door, he said: 'The best advice I can offer you is to stop wasting your time on me. You can stand me against the wall! You can hang me! You can do me in however you like!'

'No one here wishes to do you in,' Liss answered hurriedly. 'Please calm down.'

'I'm quite calm,' said Mostovskoy brightly. 'I've got nothing to worry about.'

'But you do have something to worry about. You should share my sleeplessness. What is the reason for our enmity? I can't understand . . . Is it that the Führer is a mere lackey of Stinnes and Krupp? That there's no private property in your country? That your banks and factories belong to the people? That you're internationalists and we're preachers of racial hatred? That we set things on fire and you extinguish the flames? That the world hates us – and that its hopes are centred on Stalingrad? Is that what you people say . . . ? Nonsense! There is no divide. It's just been dreamed up. In essence we are the same – both one-party States. Our capitalists are not the masters. The State gives them their plan. The State takes their profit and all they produce. As their salary they keep six per cent of the profit. Your State also outlines a plan and takes what is produced for itself. And the people you call masters – the workers – also receive a salary from your one-party State.'

Mostovskoy watched Liss and thought to himself: 'Did this vile nonsense really confuse me for a moment? Was I really choking in this stream of poisonous, stinking dirt?'

Liss gave a despairing wave of the hand.

* A revolutionary organization of the nineteenth century.

'A red workers' flag flies over our People's State too. We too call people to National Achievement, to Unity and Labour. We say, "The Party expresses the dream of the German worker"; you say, "Nationalism! Labour!" You know as well as we do that nationalism is the most powerful force of our century. Nationalism is the soul of our epoch. And "Socialism in One Country" is the supreme expression of nationalism.

'I don't see any reason for our enmity. But the teacher of genius, the leader of the German people, our father, the best friend of all German mothers, the brilliant and wise strategist, began this war. And I believe in Hitler. And I know that Stalin's mind is in no way clouded by pain or anger. Through all the fire and smoke of war he can see the truth. He knows his true enemy. Yes – even now when he discusses joint military strategy with him and drinks to his health. There are two great revolutionaries in the world – Stalin and our leader. It is their will that gave birth to State National Socialism.

'Brotherhood with you is more important to me than territory in the East. We are two houses that should stand side by side . . . Now, teacher, I want you to live for a while in quiet solitude. I want you to think, think, think before our next conversation.'

'What for? It's all just nonsense. It's absurd and senseless!' said Mostovskoy. 'And why call me "teacher" in that idiotic way?'

'There's nothing idiotic about it,' replied Liss. 'You and I both know that it's not on battlefields that the future is decided. You knew Lenin personally. He created a new type of party. He was the first to understand that only the Party and its Leader can express the spirit of the nation. He did away with the Constituent Assembly. But just as Maxwell destroyed Newton's system of mechanics while thinking he had confirmed it, so Lenin considered himself a builder of inter-nationalism while in actual fact he was creating the great nationalism of the twentieth century . . . And we learnt many things from Stalin. To build Socialism in One Country, one must destroy the peasants' freedom to sow what they like and sell what they like. Stalin didn't shilly-shally – he liquidated millions of peasants. Our Hitler saw that the Jews were the enemy hindering the German National Socialist movement. And he liquidated millions of Jews. But Hitler's no mere student; he's a genius in his own right. And he's not one to be squeamish either. It was the Roehm purge that gave Stalin the idea for the purge of the Party in 1937 . . . You must believe me. You've kept silent while I've been talking, but I know that I'm like a mirror for you – a surgical mirror.'

'A mirror?' said Mostovskoy. 'Every word you've said from beginning to end is a lie. It's beneath me to refute your filthy, stinking, provocative blatherings. A mirror? You must be crazy. But Stalingrad will bring you back to your senses.'

Liss stood up. In painful confusion, feeling both hatred and ecstasy, Mostovskoy thought, 'Now he's going to shoot me. That's it.'

But Liss seemed not to have heard Mostovskoy. He bowed from the waist.

'Teacher,' he said, 'you will continue to teach us and continue to learn from us. We shall think together.'

Liss's face was sad and serious, but his eyes were laughing.

Once again the poisoned needle entered Mostovskoy's heart. Liss looked at his watch and said: 'Well, time will tell.'

He rang a bell and said quietly: 'You can have this back if you want it. We shall meet again soon. *Gute Nacht!*'

Without knowing why, Mostovskoy picked the papers up and thrust them into his pocket.

He was led out of the administration building and back out into the cold night. Cool damp air, the howl of sirens in the gloom before dawn – how pleasant it all was after the Gestapo office and the quiet voice of the National Socialist theoretician.

A car with violet headlamps passed them as they reached the sick-bay. Mostovskoy realized that Liss was on his way home. Once again he was seized by a deep melancholy. The guard took him to his cubicle and locked the door. He sat down on the boards and thought: 'If I believed in God, I would think that terrible interrogator had been sent to me as a punishment for my sins.'

A new day was already beginning and he was unable to sleep. Leaning back against the rough, splintering planks of pine that had been knocked together into a wall, Mostovskoy began to peruse Ikonnikov's scribblings.

15

———◆———

Few people ever attempt to define 'good'. What is 'good'? 'Good' for whom? Is there a common good – the same for all people, all tribes, all conditions of life? Or is my good your evil? Is what is good for my people evil for your people? Is good eternal and constant? Or is yesterday's good today's vice, yesterday's evil today's good?

When the Last Judgment approaches, not only philosophers and preachers, but everyone on earth – literate and illiterate – will ponder the nature of good and evil.

Have people advanced over the millennia in their concept of good? Is this concept something that is common to all people – both Greeks and Jews – as the Apostle supposed? To all classes, nations and States? Even to all animals, trees and mosses – as Buddha and his disciples claimed? The same Buddha who had to deny life in order to clothe it in goodness and love.

The Christian view, five centuries after Buddhism, restricted the living world to which the concept of good is applicable. Not every living thing – only human beings. The good of the first Christians, which had embraced all mankind, in turn gave way to a purely Christian good; the good of the Muslims was now distinct.

Centuries passed and the good of Christianity split up into the distinct goods of Catholicism, Protestantism and Orthodoxy. And the good of Orthodoxy gave birth to the distinct goods of the old and new beliefs.

At the same time there was the good of the poor and the good of the rich. And the goods of the whites, the blacks and the yellow races . . . More and more goods came into being, corresponding to each sect, race and class. Everyone outside a particular magic circle was excluded.

People began to realize how much blood had been spilt in

the name of a petty, doubtful good, in the name of the struggle of this petty good against what it believed to be evil. Sometimes the very concept of good became a scourge, a greater evil than evil itself.

Good of this kind is a mere husk from which the sacred kernel has been lost. Who can reclaim the lost kernel?

But what is good? It used to be said that it is a thought and a related action which lead to the greater strength or triumph of humanity — or of a family, nation, State, class, or faith.

People struggling for their particular good always attempt to dress it up as a universal good. They say: my good coincides with the universal good; my good is essential not only to me but to everyone; in achieving my good, I serve the universal good.

And so the good of a sect, class, nation or State assumes a specious universality in order to justify its struggle against an apparent evil.

Even Herod did not shed blood in the name of evil; he shed blood in the name of his particular good. A new force had come into the world, a force that threatened to destroy him and his family, to destroy his friends and his favourites, his kingdom and his armies.

But it was not evil that had been born; it was Christianity. Humanity had never before heard such words: 'Judge not, that ye be not judged. For with what judgment ye judge, ye shall be judged: and with what measure ye mete, it shall be measured to you again . . . But I say unto you, Love your enemies, bless them that curse you, do good to them that hate you, and pray for them which despitefully use you, and persecute you . . . Therefore all things whatsoever ye would that men should do to you, do ye even so to them: for this is the law and the prophets.'

And what did this doctrine of peace and love bring to humanity? Byzantine iconoclasticism; the tortures of the Inquisition; the struggles against heresy in France, Italy, Flanders and Germany; the conflict between Protestantism and Catholicism; the intrigues of the monastic orders; the conflict between Nikon and Avvakum; the crushing yoke that lay for centuries over science and freedom; the Christians who wiped out the heathen population of Tasmania; the scoundrels who burnt whole Negro villages in Africa. This doctrine caused more suffering than all the crimes of the people who did evil for its own sake . . .

In great hearts the cruelty of life gives birth to good; they then seek to carry this good back into life, hoping to make life itself accord with their inner image of good. But life never changes to accord with an image of good; instead it is the image of good that sinks into the mire of life – to lose its universality, to split into fragments and be exploited by the needs of the day. People are wrong to see life as a struggle between good and evil. Those who most wish for the good of humanity are unable to diminish evil by one jot.

Great ideas are necessary in order to dig new channels, to remove stones, to bring down cliffs and fell forests; dreams of universal good are necessary in order that great waters should flow in harmony . . . Yes, if the sea was able to think, then every storm would make its waters dream of happiness. Each wave breaking against the cliff would believe it was dying for the good of the sea; it would never occur to it that, like thousands of waves before and after, it had only been brought into being by the wind.

Many books have been written about the nature of good and evil and the struggle between them . . . There is a deep and undeniable sadness in all this: whenever we see the dawn of an eternal good that will never be overcome by evil – an evil that is itself eternal but will never succeed in overcoming good – whenever we see this dawn, the blood of old people and children is always shed. Not only men, but even God himself is powerless to lessen this evil.

'In Rama was there a voice heard, lamentation, and weeping, and great mourning, Rachel weeping for her children, and would not be comforted, because they are not.'

What does a woman who has lost her children care about a philosopher's definitions of good and evil?

But what if life itself is evil?

I have seen the unshakeable strength of the idea of social good that was born in my own country. I saw this struggle during the period of general collectivization and again in 1937. I saw people being annihilated in the name of an idea of good as fine and humane as the ideal of Christianity. I saw whole villages dying of hunger; I saw peasant children dying in the snows of Siberia; I saw trains bound for Siberia with hundreds and thousands of men and women from Moscow, Leningrad and every city in Russia – men and women who had been declared enemies of a great and bright idea of social good. This idea was something fine and noble – yet it killed some without mercy, crippled the lives of others, and separated wives from husbands and children from fathers.

Now the horror of German Fascism has arisen. The air is full of the groans and cries of the condemned. The sky has turned black; the sun has been extinguished by the smoke of the gas ovens. And even these crimes, crimes never before seen in the Universe – even by Man on Earth – have been committed in the name of good.

Once, when I lived in the Northern forests, I thought that good was to be found neither in man, nor in the predatory world of animals and insects, but in the silent kingdom of the trees. Far from it! I saw the forest's slow movement, the treacherous way it battled against grass and bushes for each inch of soil . . . First, billions of seeds fly through the air and begin to sprout, destroying the grass and bushes. Then millions of victorious shoots wage war against one another. And it is only the survivors who enter into an alliance of equals to form the seamless canopy of the young deciduous forest. Beneath this canopy the spruces and beeches freeze to death in the twilight of penal servitude.

In time the deciduous trees become decrepit; then the heavyweight spruces burst through to the light beneath their canopy, executing the alders and the beeches. This is the life of the forest – a constant struggle of everything against everything. Only the blind conceive of the kingdom of trees and grass as the world of good . . . Is it that life itself is evil?

Good is to be found neither in the sermons of religious teachers and prophets, nor in the teachings of sociologists and popular leaders, nor in the ethical systems of philosophers . . . And yet ordinary people bear love in their hearts, are naturally full of love and pity for any living thing. At the end of the day's work they prefer the warmth of the hearth to a bonfire in the public square.

Yes, as well as this terrible Good with a capital 'G', there is everyday human kindness. The kindness of an old woman carrying a piece of bread to a prisoner, the kindness of a soldier allowing a wounded enemy to drink from his water-flask, the kindness of youth towards age, the kindness of a peasant hiding an old Jew in his loft. The kindness of a prison guard who risks his own liberty to pass on letters written by a prisoner not to his ideological comrades, but to his wife and mother.

The private kindness of one individual towards another; a petty, thoughtless kindness; an unwitnessed kindness. Something we could call senseless kindness. A kindness outside any system of social or religious good.

But if we think about it, we realize that this private, senseless, incidental kindness is in fact eternal. It is extended to everything living, even to a mouse, even to a bent branch that a man straightens as he walks by.

Even at the most terrible times, through all the mad acts carried out in the name of Universal Good and the glory of States, times when people were tossed about like branches in the wind, filling ditches and gullies like stones in an avalanche – even then this senseless, pathetic kindness remained scattered throughout life like atoms of radium.

Some Germans arrived in a village to exact vengeance for the murder of two soldiers. The women were ordered out of their huts in the evening and set to dig a pit on the edge of the forest. There was one middle-aged woman who had several soldiers quartered in her hut. Her husband had been taken to the police station together with twenty other peasants. She didn't get to sleep until morning: the Germans found a basket of onions and a jar of honey in the cellar; they lit the stove, made themselves omelettes and drank vodka. The eldest then played the harmonica while the rest of them sang and beat time with their feet. They didn't even look at their landlady – she might just as well have been a cat. When it grew light, they began checking their machine-guns; the eldest of them jerked the trigger by mistake and shot himself in the stomach. Everyone began shouting and running about. Somehow the Germans managed to bandage the wounded man and lay him down on a bed. Then they were called outside. They signed to the woman to look after the wounded man. The woman thought to herself how simple it would be to strangle him. There he was, muttering away, his eyes closed, weeping, sucking his lips . . . Suddenly he opened his eyes and said in very clear Russian: 'Water, Mother.' 'Damn you,' said the woman. 'What I should do is strangle you.' Instead she gave him some water. He grabbed her by the hand and signed to her to help him sit up: he couldn't breathe because of the bleeding. She pulled him up and he clasped his arms round her neck. Suddenly there was a volley of shots outside and the woman began to tremble.

Afterwards she told people what she had done. No one could understand; nor could she explain it herself.

This senseless kindness is condemned in the fable about the pilgrim who warmed a snake in his bosom. It is the kindness that has mercy on a tarantula that has bitten a child. A mad, blind, kindness. People enjoy looking in stories and fables for examples of the danger of this senseless kindness. But one shouldn't be afraid of it. One might just as well be afraid of a freshwater fish carried out by chance into the salty ocean.

The harm from time to time occasioned a society, class, race or State by this senseless kindness fades away in the light that emanates from those who are endowed with it.

This kindness, this stupid kindness, is what is most truly human in a human being. It is what sets man apart, the highest achievement of his soul. No, it says, life is not evil!

This kindness is both senseless and wordless. It is instinctive, blind. When Christianity clothed it in the teachings of the Church Fathers, it began to fade; its kernel became a husk. It remains potent only while it is dumb and senseless, hidden in the living darkness of the human heart – before it becomes a tool or commodity in the hands of preachers, before its crude ore is forged into the gilt coins of holiness. It is as simple as life itself. Even the teachings of Jesus deprived it of its strength.

But, as I lost faith in good, I began to lose faith even in kindness. It seemed as beautiful and powerless as dew. What use was it if it was not contagious?

How can one make a power of it without losing it, without turning it into a husk as the Church did? Kindness is powerful only while it is powerless. If Man tries to give it power, it dims, fades away, loses itself, vanishes.

Today I can see the true power of evil. The heavens are empty. Man is alone on Earth. How can the flame of evil be put out? With small drops of living dew, with human kindness? No, not even the waters of all the clouds and seas can extinguish that flame – let alone a handful of dew gathered drop by drop from the time of the Gospels to the iron present . . .

Yes, after despairing of finding good either in God or in Nature, I began to despair even of kindness.

But the more I saw of the darkness of Fascism, the more clearly I realized that human qualities persist even on the edge of the grave, even at the door of the gas chamber.

My faith has been tempered in Hell. My faith has emerged from the flames of the crematoria, from the concrete of the gas chamber. I have seen that it is not man who is impotent in the struggle against evil, but the power of evil that is impotent in the struggle against man. The powerlessness of kindness, of senseless kindness, is the secret of its immortality. It can never be conquered. The more stupid, the more senseless, the more helpless it may seem, the vaster it is. Evil is impotent before it. The prophets, religious teachers, reformers, social and political leaders are impotent before it. This dumb, blind love is man's meaning.

Human history is not the battle of good struggling to overcome evil. It is a battle fought by a great evil struggling to crush a small kernel of human kindness. But if what is human in human beings has not been destroyed even now, then evil will never conquer.

After he had finished reading, Mostovskoy sat there for a few minutes with his eyes half closed.

Yes, the man who had written this was unhinged. The ruin of a feeble spirit!

The preacher declares that the heavens are empty . . . He sees life as a war of everything against everything. And then at the end he starts tinkling the same old bells, praising the kindness of old women and hoping to extinguish a world-wide conflagration with an enema syringe. What trash!

Mostovskoy looked at the grey wall of the cell and remembered the blue armchair and his conversation with Liss. He was overwhelmed by a feeling of heaviness: it wasn't his head that ached but his heart, and he could hardly breathe. He had evidently been wrong to suspect Ikonnikov. The scribblings of this holy fool aroused the same contempt in his night-time interrogator as they did in himself. He thought once again about his own attitude towards Chernetsov, and about the hatred and contempt with which the Gestapo officer had talked about people like him. The confusion and depression that gripped him seemed heavier than any physical suffering.

16

Seryozha Shaposhnikov pointed to a book that was lying on top of a brick, beside a haversack.

'Have you read that?' he asked Katya Vengrova.

'I was looking through it again.'

'Do you like it?'

'I prefer Dickens.'

'Dickens!' said Seryozha in a tone of mockery and condescension.

'What about *La Chartreuse de Parme*? Do you like that?' asked Katya.

'Not much,' replied Seryozha after a moment's thought. Then he added: 'I'm going with the infantry today to clean out the Germans from the shack next door'.

Katya looked at him. Understanding the meaning of this look, Seryozha went on: 'Yes, I've been ordered to by Grekov.'

'What about Chentsov and the rest of the mortar team. Are they going?'

'No. Just me.'

They fell silent for a moment.

'Is he after you, then?' asked Seryozha.

She nodded her head.

'How do you feel about it?'

'You know very well,' she said, thinking of the tribe of Asra who die in silence when they love.

'I'm afraid they'll get me today,' said Seryozha.

'Why are you being sent with the infantry anyway? You're a mortar man.'

'Why's Grekov keeping you here, for that matter? Your wireless set's been smashed to pieces. You should have been sent back to the regiment ages ago. You should have been sent to the left bank. You're just hanging around doing nothing.'

'At least we see each other every day.'

Seryozha gave a wave of the hand and walked away.

Katya looked round and saw Bunchuk looking down from above and laughing. Seryozha must have seen him too. That was why he'd left so abruptly.

The Germans kept the building under artillery fire until evening. Three men were slightly wounded and a partition wall collapsed, blocking the exit from the cellar. They dug out the exit – only for it to be choked with rubble again after another shell smashed into the wall.

They dug their way through a second time. Antsiferov peered into the dust-filled darkness and asked: 'Hey! Comrade radio-operator! Are you still with us?'

'Yes,' answered Katya, sneezing and spitting out red dust.

'Bless you!' said Antsiferov.

When it got dark, the Germans sent up flares and opened up with their machine-guns. A plane flew over several times, dropping incendiary bombs. No one in the building slept. Grekov himself manned a machine-gun; the infantry sallied out twice to repel advancing Germans, swearing for all they were worth and shielding their faces with spades.

It was as though the Germans had foreseen the impending attack on the nearby building they had just occupied.

When the firing died down, Katya could hear the Germans calling out to one another. She could even hear their laughter. Their pronunciation was very different from that of her German teachers.

She noticed that the cat had crawled off its pile of rags. Its back legs were quite motionless; it was dragging itself along on its fore-paws, trying desperately to reach Katya. Then it came to a stop; its jaw opened and closed several times . . . Katya tried to raise one of its eyelids. 'So it's dead,' she thought in disgust. Then she realized that the cat must have thought of her when he realized he was about to die; that he had crawled towards her when he was half-paralysed . . . She put the body in a hole and covered it over with bits of brick.

The cellar was suddenly lit up by a flare. It was as though there were no longer any air, as though she were breathing some blood-coloured liquid that flowed out of the ceiling, oozing out of each little brick.

Maybe the Germans would appear any moment out of the far corners of the cellar. They would come up to her, seize her and drag her away. Or maybe they were cleaning up the first floor right now – the rattle of their tommy-guns sounded closer than ever. Maybe they were about to appear through the hole in the ceiling.

To calm herself down, she tried to picture the list of tenants on the door of her house: 'Tikhimirov – 1 ring; Dzyga – 2 rings; Cheremushkin – 3 rings; Feinberg – 4 rings; Vengrova – 5 rings; Andryushenko – 6 rings; Pegov – 1 long ring.' She tried to imagine the Feinbergs' big saucepan standing on the kerosene stove with its plywood cover, Anastasya's washing tub with its cover made of sacking, the Tikhimirovs' chipped enamel basin hanging from its piece of string . . . Now she would make her bed; where the springs were particularly sharp, she would spread out an old torn coat, a scrap of quilt and her mother's brown shawl.

Then her thoughts turned to house 6/1. Now the Germans were so close, now they were actually tunnelling their way through the ground, she no longer felt upset by the soldiers' foul language. She didn't even feel frightened by the way Grekov looked at her; previously not only her cheeks had blushed, but even her neck and shoulders. Yes, she certainly had heard some obscenities during her months in the army. There had been one particularly unpleasant conversation with a bald lieutenant-colonel who had flashed his metal fillings at her as he had explained what she must do if she wanted to stay on the left bank, at the signals centre . . . She remembered a mournful little song the girls used to sing under their breath:

> Under a fine autumn moon
> The commander took her to bed.
> He kissed her till it was dawn
> And now she belongs to the men.

The first time she had seen Seryozha he had been reading poetry; she had thought to herself, 'What an idiot!' Then he had disappeared for two days. She had kept wondering if he had been killed, but had been too embarrassed to ask. Then he had suddenly reappeared during the

413

night; she'd heard him tell Grekov how he'd left Headquarters without permission.

'Quite right,' said Grekov. 'Otherwise you wouldn't have rejoined us until the next world.'

After that he had walked straight past her without even a glance. She had felt first upset and then angry; once again she had thought, 'What an idiot!'

Soon afterwards she'd heard a discussion about who was likely to be the first man to sleep with her. Someone had said: 'Grekov – that's a certainty!'

'No, that's not for sure,' someone else had said. 'But I can tell you who's at the bottom of the list – young Seryozha. The younger a girl is, the more she needs someone with experience.'

Then she noticed that the other men had stopped joking and flirting with her. Grekov made it very clear that he didn't like anyone else making a play for her. And once Zubarev called out: 'Hey! Mrs house-manager!'

Grekov was in no hurry, but he was very sure of himself. She could feel this all too clearly. After her wireless set had been smashed, he had ordered her to make her home in one of the far corners of the cellar. And yesterday he'd said: 'I've never met a girl like you before. If I'd met you before the war, I'd have made you my wife.'

She'd wanted to reply that he'd have had to ask her view on the matter first. But she'd been too frightened to say anything at all.

He hadn't done anything wrong. He hadn't even said anything coarse or brazen. But she was frightened.

Later on in the day he'd said sadly: 'The Germans are about to launch their offensive. Probably not one of us will be left alive. This building lies right in their path.'

He had then given her a long, thoughtful look – a look that Katya found more frightening than what he'd said about the German offensive – and added: 'I'll come round some time.'

The link between this remark and what he'd said before was by no means obvious, but Katya understood it.

He was very different from any of the officers she'd seen round Kotluban. He never threatened people or shouted at them, but they obeyed him. He just sat there, smoking and chatting away like one of the soldiers. And yet his authority was immense.

She'd never really talked to Seryozha. Sometimes she thought he was in love with her – but as powerless as she herself before the man they admired and were terrified by. She knew he was weak and inexperienced, but she kept wanting to ask for his protection, to say: 'Come and sit by me.' And then there were times when she wanted to comfort him herself. Talking to him was very strange – it often seemed as though there were no war, no house 6/1 at all. Seryozha appeared to understand this and tried to adopt a coarse, soldierly manner. Once he even swore in her presence.

Now she felt that there was some terrible link between her own confused thoughts and feelings and the fact that Seryozha had been ordered to join the storming-party. Listening to the tommy-gun fire, she imagined Seryozha lying across a mound of red brick, his lifeless head and unkempt hair drooping. She felt a heart-rending sense of pity for him. Everything merged together: the many-coloured flares, her memories of her mother, her simultaneous fear and admiration of Grekov – this man who, from a few isolated ruins, was about to launch an assault on the iron-clad German divisions.

She felt ready to sacrifice everything in the world – if only she could see Seryozha again alive.

'But what if I have to choose between him and Mama?' she thought suddenly.

Then she heard footsteps; her fingers tensed against the bricks.

The shooting died down; there was a sudden silence. Her back, her shoulders, her legs all began to itch. She wanted to scratch them but was afraid of making a noise.

People had kept asking Batrakov why he was always scratching himself. He'd always answered: 'It's just nerves.' And then yesterday he'd said: 'I've just found eleven lice!' Kolomeitsev had made fun of him: 'Batrakov's been attacked by nerve-lice!'

She had been killed. Soldiers were dragging her corpse to a pit and saying: 'Poor girl! She's covered in lice!'

But perhaps it really was just her nerves? Then she saw a man coming towards her out of the darkness – and not just someone she had conjured up out of the strange noises and the flickering light.

'Who is it?' she asked.

'Don't be afraid,' said the darkness. 'It's me.'

17

'The attack's been put off till tomorrow. Today it's the Germans' turn. By the way, I wanted to tell you, I've never read *La Chartreuse de Parme*.'

Katya didn't answer.

Seryozha tried to make her out in the darkness; as though in answer to his wish, her face was suddenly lit up by a shell-burst. A second later it was dark again; as though by unspoken agreement they waited for another shell-burst, another flash of light. Seryozha took her by the hand and squeezed her fingers; it was the first time he had held a girl's hand.

The dirty, lice-ridden girl sat there without saying a word. Seryozha could see her white neck in the darkness.

Another flare went up and their heads drew together. He put his arms round her and she closed her eyes. They'd both of them heard the same saying at school: if you kiss with your eyes open, you're not in love.

'This is the real thing, isn't it?' asked Seryozha.

She pressed her hands against his temples and turned his head towards her.

'This is for all our lives,' he said slowly.

'How strange,' she said. 'I'm afraid somebody may come by. Until now I was only too delighted to see any of them: Lyakhov, Kolomeitsev, Zubarev . . .'

'Grekov,' added Seryozha.

'No,' she said firmly.

He kissed her on the neck and undid the metal button on her tunic. He pressed his lips to her thin collar-bone, but didn't touch her breasts. She stroked his wiry unwashed hair as though he were a little boy; she knew that all this was right and inevitable.

He looked at the luminous dial of his watch.

'Who's leading you tomorrow?' she asked. 'Grekov?'

'Why ask now? Who needs a leader anyway?'

He embraced her again. He felt a sudden cold in his fingers and chest, a sudden resolute excitement. She was half lying on her coat; she seemed to be hardly breathing. He felt the coarse, dusty material of her tunic and skirt, then the rough fur of her boots. He sensed the warmth of her body. She tried to sit up, but he began kissing her again. Another flash of light lit up Katya's cap – now lying on some bricks – and her face – suddenly unfamiliar, as though he'd never seen it before. Then it became dark again, very dark . . .

'Katya!'

'What is it?'

'Nothing. I just wanted to hear your voice. Why don't you look at me?'

He lit a match.

'Don't! Don't! Put it out!'

Once again she wondered who she loved most – him or her mother.

'Forgive me,' she said.

Failing to understand her, Seryozha said: 'It's all right. Don't be afraid. This is for life – if we live.'

'No, I was just thinking of my mother.'

'My mother's dead. I've only just realized – she was deported because of my father.'

They went to sleep in each other's arms. During the night the house-manager came and looked at them. Shaposhnikov had his head on the girl's shoulder and his arm round her back; it looked as though he were afraid of losing her. Their sleep was so quiet and so still they might have been dead.

At dawn Lyakhov looked in and shouted:

'Hey, Shaposhnikov! Vengrova! The house-manager wants you. At the double!'

In the cold, misty half-light Grekov's face looked severe and implacable. He was leaning against the wall, his tousled hair hanging over his low forehead. They stood in front of him, shifting from foot to foot, unaware they were still holding hands. Grekov flared his broad nostrils and said: 'Very well, Shaposhnikov, I'm sending you back to Regimental Headquarters.'

Seryozha could feel Katya's fingers trembling; he squeezed them.

She in turn felt his fingers trembling. He swallowed; his tongue and palate were quite dry.

The earth and the clouded sky were enveloped in silence. The soldiers lying in a huddle on their greatcoats seemed wide awake, hardly breathing, waiting. Everything was so familiar, so splendid. Seryozha thought to himself: 'We're being expelled from Paradise. He's separating us like two serfs.' He gave Grekov a look of mingled hatred and entreaty.

Grekov narrowed his eyes as he looked Katya full in the face. Seryozha felt there was something quite horrible about this look, something insolent and merciless.

'That's all,' said Grekov. 'And the radio-operator can go with you. There's no need for her to hang around here with nothing to do. You can show her the way to HQ.'

He smiled.

'And after that you'll have to find your own ways. Here, take this. I can't stand paperwork so I've just written one for the two of you. All right?'

Seryozha suddenly realized that never in all his life had he seen eyes that were so sad and so intelligent, so splendid, yet so human.

18

In the end, Regimental Commissar Pivovarov never visited house 6/1.

Radio contact had been broken off. No one knew if this was because the wireless set was out of action or because the high-handed Grekov was fed up with being ordered about by his superiors.

Chentsov, a Party member, had provided them with some information about the encircled house. He said that 'the house-manager' was corrupting the minds of his soldiers with the most appalling heresies. He didn't, however, deny either Grekov's courage or his fighting abilities.

Just when Pivovarov was about to make his way to house 6/1, Byerozkin, the commanding officer of the regiment, fell seriously ill. He was lying in his bunker; his face was burning and his eyes looked transparent and vacuous. The doctor who examined him was at a loss. He was used to dealing with shattered limbs and fractured skulls. And now here was someone who'd fallen ill all by himself.

'We need cupping-glasses,' he said. 'But where on earth can I find any?'

Pivovarov was about to inform Byerozkin's superiors when the telephone rang and the divisional commissar summoned him to headquarters.

Pivovarov twice dropped flat on his face because of nearby shell-bursts; he arrived somewhat out of breath. The divisional commissar was in conversation with a battalion commissar who had recently been sent across from the left bank. Pivovarov had heard of him before; he had given lectures to the units in the factories.

Pivovarov announced himself loudly: 'Pivovarov reporting!' Then he told him of Byerozkin's illness.

'Yes, that's a bit of a bastard,' said the divisional commissar. 'Well, you'll have to take command yourself, comrade Pivovarov.'

'What about the encircled house?'

'That matter's no longer in your hands. You wouldn't believe what a storm there's been over it. It's even reached Front Headquarters.'

He paused and held up a coded message.

'In fact, that's the very reason I called you. Comrade Krymov here has instructions from the Political Administration of the Front to get through to the encircled house, take over as commissar and establish Bolshevik order. If any problems arise, he is to take over from Grekov . . . Since this is in the sector covered by your regiment, you are to provide comrade Krymov with whatever help he needs to get through and remain in communication. Is that clear?'

'Certainly,' said Pivovarov. 'I'll see to it.'

Then in a conversational tone of voice, he asked Krymov: 'Comrade Battalion Commissar, have you dealt with anything like this before?'

'I have indeed,' smiled Krymov. 'In the summer of '41 I led two hundred men out of encirclement in the Ukraine. Believe me – I know a thing or two about all this partisan nonsense.'

'Very well, comrade Krymov,' said the divisional commissar. 'Get on with it and keep in touch. A State within a State is something we can do without.'

'Yes,' said Pivovarov, 'and there was also an unpleasant story about some girl who was sent as a radio-operator. Byerozkin was very worried when the transmitter went dead. Those lads are capable of anything – believe me!'

'Very well. You can sort that one out when you get there. I wish you luck,' said the divisional commissar.

19

On a cold clear evening, the day after Grekov's dismissal of Shaposhnikov and Vengrova, Krymov, accompanied by a soldier with a tommy-gun, left Regimental HQ on his way to the notorious encircled house.

As soon as he set foot in the asphalt yard of the Tractor Factory, Krymov felt an extraordinarily acute sense of danger. At the same time he was conscious of an unaccustomed excitement and joy. The sudden message from Front Headquarters had confirmed his feeling that in Stalingrad everything was different, that the values and demands placed on people had changed. Krymov was no longer a cripple in a battalion of invalids; he was once again a Bolshevik, a fighting commissar. He wasn't in the least frightened by his difficult and dangerous task. It had been sweet indeed to read in the eyes of Pivovarov and the divisional commissar the same trust in his abilities that had once been displayed by all his comrades in the Party.

A dead soldier was lying on the ground between the remains of a mortar and some slabs of asphalt thrown up by a shell-burst. Now that Krymov was so full of hope and exaltation, he found this sight strangely upsetting. He had seen plenty of corpses in his time and had usually felt quite indifferent. This soldier, so full of his death, was lying there like a bird, quite defenceless, his legs tucked under him as though he were cold.

A political instructor in a grey mackintosh ran past, holding up a well-filled knapsack. Then a group of soldiers came past carrying some anti-tank shells on a tarpaulin, together with a few loaves of bread.

The corpse no longer needed bread or weapons; nor was he hoping for a letter from his faithful wife. His death had not made him strong –

he was the weakest thing in the world, a dead sparrow that not even the moths and midges were afraid of.

Some soldiers were mounting their gun in a breach in the wall, arguing with the crew of a heavy machine-gun and cursing. From their gestures Krymov could more or less guess what they were saying.

'Do you realize how long our machine-gun's stood here? We were hard at it when you lot were still hanging about on the left bank!'

'Well, you are a bunch of cheeky buggers!'

There was a loud whine, and a shell burst in a corner of the workshop. Shrapnel rattled across the walls. Krymov's guide looked round to see if he was still there. He waited a moment and said:

'Don't worry, comrade Commissar, this isn't yet the front line. We're still way back in the rear.'

It wasn't long before Krymov realized the truth of this; the space by the wall was indeed relatively quiet.

They had to run forward, drop flat on the ground, run forward and drop to the ground again. They twice jumped into trenches occupied by the infantry. They ran through burnt-out buildings, where instead of people there was only the whine of metal . . . The soldier said comfortingly: 'At least there are no dive-bombers,' then added: 'Right, comrade Commissar, now we must make for that crater.'

Krymov slid down to the bottom of a bomb-crater and looked up: the blue sky was still over his head and his head was still on his shoulders. It was very strange; the only sign of other human beings was the singing and screaming death that came flying over his head from both sides. It was equally strange to feel so protected in this crater that had been dug out by the spade of death.

Before Krymov had got his breath back, the soldier said, 'Follow me!' and crawled down a dark passage leading from the bottom of the crater. Krymov squeezed in after him. Soon the passage widened, the ceiling became higher and they were in a tunnel.

They could still hear the storm raging on the earth's surface; the ceiling shook and there were repeated peals of thunder. In one place, full of lead piping and cables as thick as a man's arm, someone had written on the wall in red: 'Makhov's a donkey.' The soldier turned on his torch for a moment and whispered: 'Now the Germans are right above us.'

Soon they turned off into another narrow passage and began

making their way towards a barely perceptible grey light. The light slowly grew brighter and clearer; at the same time the roar of explosions and the chatter of machine-guns became still more furious.

For a moment Krymov thought he was about to mount the scaffold. Then they reached the surface and the first thing he saw was human faces. They seemed divinely calm.

Krymov felt a sense of joy and relief. Even the raging war now seemed no more than a brief storm passing over the head of a young traveller who was full of vitality. He felt certain that he had reached an important turning-point, that his life would continue to change for the better. It was as though this still, clear daylight were a sign of his own future – once again he was to live fully, whole-heartedly, with all his will and intelligence, all his Bolshevik fervour.

This new sense of youth and confidence mingled with his regret for Yevgenia. Now, though, he no longer felt he had lost her for ever. She would return to him – just as his strength and his former life had returned to him. He was on her trail.

A fire was burning in the middle of the floor. An old man, his cap pushed forward, was standing over it, frying potato-cakes on some tin-plating. He turned them over with the point of a bayonet and stacked them in a tin hat when they were done. Spotting the soldier who had accompanied Krymov, he asked: 'Is Seryozha with you?'

'There's an officer present,' said the soldier sternly.

'How old are you, Dad?' Krymov asked.

'Sixty,' said the old man. 'I was transferred from the workers' militia.'

He turned to the soldier again. 'Is Seryozha with you?'

'No, he's not in our regiment. He must have ended up with our neighbours.'

'That's bad,' said the old man. 'God knows what will become of him there.'

Krymov greeted various people and looked round the different parts of the cellar with their half-dismantled wooden partitions. In one place there was a field-gun pointing out through a loophole cut in the wall.

'It's like a man-of-war,' said Krymov.

'Yes, except there's not much water,' said the gunner.

Further on, in niches and gaps in the wall, were the mortars. Their long-tailed bombs lay on the floor beside them. There was also an accordion lying on a tarpaulin.

'So house 6/1 is still holding out!' said Krymov, his voice ringing. 'It hasn't yielded to the Fascists. All over the world, millions of people are watching you and rejoicing.'

No one answered.

Old Polyakov walked up to him and held out the tin hat full of potato-cakes.

'Has anyone written about Polyakov's potato-cakes yet?' asked one soldier.

'Very funny,' said Polyakov. 'But our Seryozha's been thrown out.'

'Have they opened the Second Front yet?' asked another soldier. 'Have you heard anything?'

'No,' said Krymov. 'Not yet.'

'Once the heavy artillery on the left bank opened up on us,' said a soldier with his jacket unbuttoned. 'Kolomeitsev was knocked off his feet. When he got up he said: "Well, lads, there's the Second Front for you!"'

'Don't talk such rubbish,' said a young man with dark hair. 'We wouldn't be here at all if it wasn't for the artillery. The Germans would have eaten us up long ago.'

'Where's your commander?' asked Krymov.

'There he is – over there, right in the front line.'

Grekov was lying on top of a huge heap of bricks, looking at something through a pair of binoculars. When Krymov called out his name he turned his head very slowly, put his fingers to his lips and returned to his binoculars. After a few moments his shoulders started shaking; he was laughing. He crawled back down, smiled and said: 'It's worse than chess.'

Then he noticed the green bars and commissar's star on Krymov's tunic.

'Welcome to our hut, comrade Commissar! I'm Grekov, the house-manager. Did you come by the passage we just dug?'

Everything about him – the look in his eyes, his quick movements, his wide, flattened nostrils – was somehow insolent and provocative.

'Never mind,' thought Krymov. 'I'll show you.'

He started to question him. Grekov answered slowly and absent-mindedly, yawning and looking around as though these questions were distracting him from something of genuine importance.

'Would you like to be relieved?' asked Krymov.

'Don't bother,' said Grekov. 'But we could do with some cigarettes. And of course we need mortar-bombs, hand-grenades and – if you can spare it – some vodka and something to eat. You could drop it from a kukuruznik.'* As he spoke, Grekov counted the items off on his fingers.

'So you're not intending to quit?' said Krymov. In spite of his mounting anger at Grekov's insolence, he couldn't help but admire the man's ugly face.

For a brief moment both men were silent. Krymov managed, with difficulty, to overcome a sudden feeling that morally he was inferior to the men in the encircled building.

'Are you logging your operations?'

'I've got no paper,' answered Grekov. 'There's nothing to write on, no time, and there wouldn't be any point anyway.'

'At present you're under the command of the CO of the 176th Infantry Regiment,' said Krymov.

'Correct, comrade Battalion Commissar,' replied Grekov mockingly. 'But when the Germans cut off this entire sector, when I gathered men and weapons together in this building, when I repelled thirty enemy attacks and set eight tanks on fire, then I wasn't under anyone's command.'

'Do you know the precise number of soldiers under your command as of this morning? Do you keep a check?'

'A lot of use that would be. I don't write reports and I don't receive rations from any quartermaster. We've been living on rotten potatoes and foul water.'

'Are there any women in the building?'

'Tell me, comrade Commissar, is this an interrogation?'

'Have any men under your command been taken prisoner?'

'No.'

'Well, where is that radio-operator of yours?'

Grekov bit his lip, and his eyebrows came together in a frown.

'The girl turned out to be a German spy. She tried to recruit me. First I raped her, then I had her shot.'

---

* A light biplane.

He drew himself up to his full height and asked sarcastically: 'Is that the kind of answer you want from me? It's beginning to seem as though I'll end up in a penal battalion. Is that right, Sir?'

Krymov looked at him for a moment in silence.

'Grekov, you're going too far. You've lost all sense of proportion. I've been in command of a surrounded unit myself. I was interrogated afterwards too.'

After another pause, he said very deliberately:

'My orders were that, if necessary, I should demote you and take command myself. Why force me along that path?'

Grekov thought for a moment, cocked his head and said:

'It's gone quiet. The Germans are calming down.'

20

'Good,' said Krymov. 'There are still a few questions to be settled. We can talk in private.'

'Why?' asked Grekov. 'My men and I fight together. We can settle whatever needs settling together.'

Although Grekov's audacity made Krymov furious, he had to admire it. He didn't want Grekov to think of him as just a bureaucrat. He wanted to tell him about his life before the war, about how his unit had been encircled in the Ukraine. But that would be an admission of weakness. And he was here to show his strength. He wasn't an official in the Political Section, but the commissar of a fighting unit.

'And don't worry,' he said to himself, 'the commissar knows what he's doing.'

Now that things were quiet, the men were stretching out on the floor or sitting down on heaps of bricks.

'Well, I don't think the Germans will cause any more trouble today,' said Grekov. He turned to Krymov. 'Why don't we have something to eat, comrade Commissar?'

Krymov sat down next to him.

'As I look at you all,' he said, 'I keep thinking of the old saying: "Russians always beat Prussians".'

425

'Precisely,' agreed a quiet, lazy voice.

This 'precisely', with its condescending irony towards such hack-neyed formulae, caused a ripple of mirth. These men knew at least as much as Krymov about the strength of the Russians; they themselves were the expression of that strength. But they also knew that if the Prussians had now reached the Volga, it certainly wasn't because the Russians always beat them.

Krymov was feeling confused. He felt uncomfortable when political instructors praised Russian generals of past centuries. The way these generals were constantly mentioned in articles in *Red Star* grated on his revolutionary spirit. He couldn't see the point of introducing the Suvorov medal, the Kutuzov medal and the Bogdan Khmelnitsky medal. The Revolution was the Revolution; the only banner its army needed was the Red Flag. So why had he himself given way to this kind of thinking – just when he was once again breathing the air of Lenin's Revolution?

That mocking 'precisely' had been very wounding.

'Well, comrades, you don't need anyone to teach you about fighting. You can give lessons in that to anyone in the world. But why do you think our superior officers have considered it necessary to send me to you? What have I come here for?'

'Was it for a bowl of soup?' asked a voice, quietly and without malice.

This timid suggestion was greeted by a peal of laughter. Krymov looked at Grekov; he was laughing as much as anyone.

'Comrades!' said Krymov, red with anger. 'Let's be serious for a moment. I've been sent to you, comrades, by the Party.'

What was all this? Was it just a passing mood? A mutiny? Perhaps the reluctance of these men to listen to their commissar came from their sense of their own strength, of their own experience? Perhaps there was nothing subversive in all this merriment? Perhaps it sprang from the general sense of equality that was such a feature of Stalingrad.

Previously, Krymov had been delighted by this sense of equality. Why did it now make him so angry? Why did he want to suppress it?

If he had failed to make contact with these men, it was certainly not because they felt crushed, because they were in any way bewildered or frightened. These were men who knew their own strength. How was it that this very consciousness had weakened their bond with

Krymov, giving rise only to mutual alienation and hostility?

'There's one thing I've been wanting to ask someone from the Party for ages,' said the old man who had been frying the potato-cakes. 'I've heard people say that under Communism everyone will receive according to his needs. But won't everyone just end up getting drunk? Especially if they receive according to their needs from the moment they get up.'

Turning to the old man, Krymov saw a look of genuine concern on his face. Grekov, though, was laughing. His eyes were laughing. His flared nostrils were laughing.

A sapper, a dirty, bloodstained bandage round his head, asked:

'And what about the *kolkhozes*, comrade Commissar? Couldn't we have them liquidated after the war?'

'Yes,' said Grekov. 'How about a lecture on that?'

'I'm not here to give lectures,' said Krymov. 'I'm a fighting commissar. I've come here to sort out certain unacceptable partisan attitudes that have taken root in this building.'

'Very good,' said Grekov. 'But who's going to sort out the Germans?'

'Don't you worry about that. We'll find someone. And I haven't come here, as I heard someone suggest, for a bowl of soup. I'm here to give you a taste of Bolshevism.'

'Good,' said Grekov. 'Let's have a taste of it.'

Half-joking, but also half-serious, Krymov continued:

'And if necessary, comrade Grekov, we'll eat you too.'

He now felt calm and sure of himself. Any doubts he had felt about the correct course of action had passed. Grekov had to be relieved of his command.

It was clear that he was an alien and hostile element. None of the heroism displayed in this building could alter that. Krymov knew he could deal with him.

When it was dark, Krymov went up to him again.

'Grekov, I want to talk seriously. What do you want?'

'Freedom. That's what I'm fighting for.'

'We all want freedom.'

'Tell us another! You just want to sort out the Germans.'

'That's enough, comrade Grekov!' barked Krymov. 'You'd do better to explain why you allow your soldiers to give expression to

427

such naïve and erroneous political judgements. With your authority you could put a stop to that as quickly as any commissar. But I get the impression your men say their bit and then look at you for approval. Take the man who asked about *kolkhozes*. What made you support him? Let me be quite frank . . . If you're willing, we can sort this out together. But if you're not willing, it could end badly for you.'

'Why make such a fuss about the *kolkhozes*? It's true. People don't like them. You know that as well as I do.'

'So you think you can change the course of history, do you?'

'And you think you can put everything back just as it was before?'

'What do you mean – everything?'

'Just that. Everything. The general coercion.'

Grekov spoke very slowly, almost reluctantly, and with heavy irony. He suddenly sat up straight and said: 'Enough of all this, comrade Commissar! I was only teasing you. I'm as loyal a Soviet citizen as you are. I resent your mistrust.'

'All right, Grekov. But let's talk seriously then. We must stamp out the evil, anti-Soviet spirit that's taken hold here. You gave birth to it – you must help me destroy it. You'll still get your chance for glory.'

'I feel like going to bed. You need some rest too. Wait till you see what things are like in the morning.'

'Fine. We'll continue tomorrow. I'm in no hurry. I'm not going anywhere.'

'We'll find some way of coming to an agreement,' said Grekov with a laugh.

'No,' thought Krymov, 'this is no time for homeopathy. I must work with a surgeon's knife. You need more than words to straighten out a political cripple.'

'There's something good in your eyes,' said Grekov unexpectedly. 'But you've suffered a lot.'

Krymov raised his hands in surprise but didn't reply. Taking this as a sign of agreement, Grekov went on: 'I've suffered too. But that's nothing. Just something personal. Not something for your report.'

That night, while he was asleep, Krymov was hit in the head by a stray bullet. The bullet tore the skin and grazed his skull. The wound wasn't dangerous, but he felt very dizzy and was unable to stand upright. He kept wanting to be sick.

At Grekov's orders, a stretcher was improvised and Krymov was carried out of the building just before dawn. His head was throbbing and spinning and there was a constant hammering at his temples. Grekov went with him as far as the mouth of the underground passage.

'You've had bad luck, comrade commissar.'

A sudden thought flashed through Krymov's head. Maybe it was Grekov who had shot him?

Towards evening his headache got worse and he began to vomit. He was kept at the divisional first-aid post for two days and then taken to the left bank and transferred to the Army hospital.

21

Commissar Pivovarov made his way into the narrow bunkers that made up the first-aid post. The wounded were lying side by side on the floor. Krymov wasn't there – he had been taken the previous night to the left bank.

'Strange he should have got wounded so quickly!' thought Pivovarov. 'He must be unlucky – or perhaps very lucky indeed!'

Pivovarov had also come to the first-aid post to see if it was worth transferring Byerozkin there. On his return to Regimental HQ – after nearly being killed on the way by a splinter from a German mortar-bomb – he told Glushkov, Byerozkin's orderly, that the conditions in the first-aid post were appalling. Everywhere you looked, there were heaps of bloodstained gauze, bandages and cotton wool – it was frightening.

'Yes, comrade Commissar,' said Glushkov. 'He's certainly better off in his own bunker.'

'No question,' said Pivovarov. 'And they don't even discriminate between a regimental commander and an ordinary soldier. They're all lying on the floor together.'

Glushkov, whose rank only entitled him to a place on the floor, said sympathetically: 'No, that's no good at all.'

'Has he said anything?'

'No,' said Glushkov. 'He hasn't even looked at the letter from his wife. It's just lying there beside him.'

'He won't even look at a letter from his wife?' said Pivovarov. 'He really must be in a bad way.'

He picked up the letter, weighed it in his hand, held it in front of Byerozkin's face and said sternly: 'Ivan Leontyevich, this is a letter from your spouse.'

He paused for a moment, then said in a very different tone: 'Vanya! Look! It's from your wife! Don't you understand? Hey, Vanya?'

Byerozkin didn't understand. His face was flushed, and his staring eyes were bright and empty.

All day long the war knocked obstinately at the door of the bunker. Almost all the telephones had gone dead during the night; Byerozkin's, however, was still working and people were constantly ringing him – Divisional HQ, Army HQ, his battalion commanders Podchufarov and Dyrkin, and his neighbour, the commander of one of Gurov's regiments.

People were constantly coming and going, the door squeaked, and the tarpaulin – hung over the entrance by Glushkov – flapped in the wind. There had been a general sense of anxiety and anticipation since early that morning. In spite of – or perhaps because of – the intermittent artillery fire, the infrequent and carelessly inaccurate air-raids, everyone felt certain that the German offensive was about to be unleashed. This certainty was equally tormenting to Chuykov, to Pivovarov, to the men in house 6/1, and to the commander of the infantry platoon who, to celebrate his birthday, had been drinking vodka all day beside the chimney of the Stalingrad Tractor Factory.

Whenever anyone in the bunker said anything interesting or amusing, everyone immediately glanced at Byerozkin – could he really not hear them?

Company commander Khrenov, in a voice hoarse from the cold, was telling Pivovarov about an incident just before dawn. He'd climbed up from the cellar where his command-post was situated, sat down on a stone and listened to see if the Germans were up to any tricks yet. Suddenly he'd heard a harsh, angry voice in the sky: 'You sod, why didn't you give us any lights?'

Khrenov had felt first amazed, then terrified. How could someone up in the sky know his name?* Then he had looked up and seen a

* The Russian word *khren* is used in an expression meaning 'old sod'.

kukuruznik gliding by with the engine switched off. The pilot was dropping provisions to house 6/1 and was annoyed there hadn't been any markers.

Everyone looked round to see if Byerozkin had smiled; only Glushkov imagined he could see a flicker of life in his glassy eyes. At lunchtime the bunker emptied. Byerozkin still lay there, his long-awaited letter beside him. Glushkov sighed. Pivovarov and the new chief of staff had gone out for lunch. They were tucking in to some first-class borshch and drinking their hundred grams of vodka. Glushkov himself had already been offered some of the borshch. But as the boss, the commander of the regiment, wasn't eating, all he had had was a few drops of water . . .

Glushkov tore open the envelope, went up to Byerozkin's bunk and, very slowly, in a quiet, clear voice, began reading:

'Hello, my Vanya, hello my dearest, hello my beloved . . .'

Glushkov frowned, but he didn't stop reading. This tender, sad, kind letter from Byerozkin's wife had already been read by the censors. Now it was being read out loud to the unconscious Byerozkin, the only man in the world truly able to read it.

Glushkov wasn't so very surprised when Byerozkin turned his head, stretched out his hand and said: 'Give it to me.'

The lines of handwriting trembled between his large fingers.

'Vanya, it's very beautiful here, Vanya, I miss you very much. Lyuba keeps asking where Papa's gone. We're living on the shore of a lake, the house is very warm, the landlady's got a cow, there's lots of milk, and then there's the money you sent us. When I go out in the morning, there are yellow and red maple-leaves all over the cold water, there's already snow on the ground and that makes the water even bluer, and the sky's pure blue and the yellow and red of the leaves are incredibly bright. And Lyuba keeps asking me: "Why are you crying?" Vanya, Vanya, my darling, thank you for everything, for everything, thank you for all your kindness. How can I explain why I'm crying? I'm crying because I'm alive, crying from grief that Slava's dead and I'm still alive, crying from happiness that you're alive. I cry when I think of my mother and sister, I cry because of the morning light, I cry because everything round about is so beautiful and because there's so much sadness everywhere, in everyone's life and in my own. Vanya, Vanya, my dearest, my beloved . . .'

And his head began to spin, everything became blurred, his fingers trembled, the letter itself trembled. Even the white-hot air was trembling.

'Glushkov,' said Byerozkin, 'you must get me back in shape today.' (That was a phrase Tamara didn't like.) 'Tell me, is the boiler still working?'

'The boiler's fine. But how do you think you're going to get better in one day? You've got a fever. Forty degrees — just like vodka. You can't expect that to vanish in a moment.'

An empty petrol-drum was rolled into the bunker with a loud rumble. It was then half-filled — by means of a teapot and a canvas bucket — with steaming-hot river water. Glushkov helped Byerozkin undress and walked him up to the drum.

'The water's very hot, comrade Lieutenant-Colonel,' he said, touching the side of the drum very gingerly with his hand. 'You'll be stewed alive. I called the comrade commissar, but he's at a meeting with the divisional commander. We should wait for him to come back.'

'What for?'

'If anything happens to you, I'll shoot myself. And if I don't have the guts, comrade Pivovarov will do it for me.'

'Give me a hand.'

'Please, let me at least call the chief of staff.'

'Come on now!' Byerozkin's voice was hoarse, he was naked and he could barely stand upright; nevertheless, Glushkov immediately stopped arguing.

As he got into the water, Byerozkin winced and let out a groan. Glushkov paced round the drum, groaning in sympathetic anxiety.

'Just like a maternity home,' he thought suddenly.

Byerozkin lost consciousness for a while. His fever and the general anxiety of war blurred together into a mist. His heart seemed to stop and he could no longer even feel the scalding hot water. Then he came to and said to Glushkov: 'You must mop the floor.'

Glushkov took no notice of the water spilling over the edge. Byerozkin's crimson face had gone suddenly white, his mouth had fallen open, and huge drops of sweat — to Glushkov they looked almost blue — had appeared on his close-shaven head. He began to lose consciousness again. But when Glushkov tried to drag him out of the water, he said very clearly: 'No, I'm not ready yet.'

He was racked by a fit of coughing. As soon as it was over, without even waiting to get his breath back, he said: 'Pour in some more water!'

At last he got out. Looking at him, Glushkov felt even more despondent. He rubbed Byerozkin dry, helped him back into bed, and covered him over with a blanket and some greatcoats. He then began piling on everything he could find – jackets, trousers, tarpaulins . . .

By the time Pivovarov returned everything had been tidied up – though the bunker still felt hot and damp like a bath-house. Byerozkin was sleeping peacefully. Pivovarov stood over his bed for a moment and looked at him.

'He has got a splendid face,' he thought. 'I'm sure he never wrote denunciations.'

For some reason, he had been troubled all day long by the memory of how – five years before – he had helped unmask Shmelyev, a friend and fellow-student of his, as an enemy of the people. All kinds of rubbish came into one's head during this sinister lull in the fighting. He could see Shmelyev's sad, pitiful look as his friend's denunciation was read out at the meeting.

About twelve o'clock, Chuykov himself telephoned, passing over the head of the divisional commander. He was very worried about Byerozkin's regiment – according to the latest intelligence reports the Germans had amassed a particularly heavy concentration of tanks and infantry opposite the Tractor Factory.

'Well, how are things?' he asked impatiently. 'And who's in command? Batyuk said the commanding officer had pneumonia or something. He wanted to have him taken across to the left bank.'

'I'm in command,' answered a hoarse voice. 'Lieutenant-Colonel Byerozkin. I did have something of a cold, but I'm all right now.'

'Yes, you do sound a bit hoarse,' said Chuykov almost gloatingly. 'Well, the Germans will give you some hot milk. They've got it all ready, they won't be long.'

'Yes, comrade,' said Byerozkin. 'I understand you.'

'Very good,' said Chuykov. 'But if you ever think of retreating, remember I can make you an egg-flip at least as good as the Germans' hot milk.'

22

Old Polyakov arranged for Klimov, the scout, to take him at night to Regimental HQ; he wanted to find out how things were with Seryozha.

'That's a splendid idea, old man,' said Grekov. 'You can have a bit of a rest and then come back and tell us how things are in the rear.'

'You mean with Katya?' asked Polyakov, guessing why Grekov had been so quick to agree.

'They left HQ long ago,' said Klimov. 'The commander had them both sent to the left bank. By now they've probably already visited the registry office in Akhtuba.'

'Do you want to cancel our trip then?' asked Polyakov pointedly.

Grekov looked at him sharply, but all he said was: 'Very well, then. Be off with you!'

'Very well,' thought Polyakov.

They set off down the narrow passage about four in the morning. Polyakov kept bumping his head against the supports and cursing Seryozha. He felt a little angry and embarrassed at the strength of his affection for the boy.

After a while the passage widened and they sat down for a rest. Klimov said jokingly:

'What, haven't you got a present for them?'

'To hell with the damned boy!' said Polyakov. 'I should have taken a brick so I could give him a good knock on the head!'

'I see!' said Klimov. 'That's why you wanted to come with me. That's why you're ready to swim the Volga to see him. Or is it Katya you want to see? Are you dying of jealousy?'

'Come on,' said Polyakov. 'Let's get going!'

Soon they came up to the surface and had to walk through no man's land. It was utterly silent.

'Perhaps the war's come to an end?' thought Polyakov. He could picture his own home with an extraordinary vividness: there was a plate of borshch on the table and his wife was gutting a fish he had caught. He even began to feel quite warm . . .

That night General Paulus gave orders for the attack on the Tractor Factory.

Two infantry divisions were to advance through the breach opened by bombers, artillery and tanks . . . Since midnight, cigarettes had been glowing in the soldiers' cupped hands.

The first Junkers flew over the factory an hour and a half before dawn. The ensuing bombardment was quite without respite; any gap in the unbroken wall of noise was immediately filled by the whistle of bombs tearing towards the earth with all their iron strength. The continuous roar was enough to shatter your skull or your backbone.

It began to get light, but not over the factory . . . It was as though the earth itself were belching out black dust, smoke, thunder, lightning . . .

The brunt of the attack was borne by Byerozkin's regiment and house 6/1. All over that sector half-deafened men leapt drunkenly to their feet, dimly realizing that this time the Germans really had gone berserk.

Caught in no man's land, Klimov and Polyakov rushed towards some large craters made by one-ton bombs at the end of September. Some soldiers from Podchufarov's battalion had escaped from their caved-in trenches and were running in the same direction.

The Russian and German trenches were so close together that part of the bombardment fell on the German assault-troops waiting in the front line.

To Polyakov it was as though a fierce wind from downstream was sweeping up the Volga. Several times he was knocked off his feet; he fell to the ground no longer knowing what world he lived in, whether he was old or young, what was up and what was down. But Klimov dragged him along and finally they slid to the bottom of a huge crater. Here the darkness was threefold: the darkness of night, the darkness of dust and smoke, the darkness of a deep pit.

They lay there beside one another; the same soft light, the same prayer for life filled both their heads. It was the same light, the same touching hope that glows in all heads and all hearts – in those of birds and animals as well as in those of human beings.

Klimov couldn't stop swearing at Seryozha, still somehow think-ing this was all his fault. Deep down, though, he felt he was praying.

This explosion of violence seemed too extreme to continue for long. But there was no let-up; as time went by, the black cloud only thickened, linking the earth and the sky still more closely.

Klimov found the roughened hand of the old man and squeezed it; its answering warmth gave him a brief moment of comfort. An explosion nearby threw a shower of earth, stone and brick into the crater; Polyakov was hit in the back by fragments of brick. It was even worse when great chunks of earth began peeling off the walls . . . There they were, cowering in a pit. They would never again see the light of day. Soon the Germans up above would cover them over with earth, then level the edges of the tomb.

Usually Klimov preferred to go on reconnaissance missions alone; he would hurry off into the darkness like an experienced swimmer striking out into the open sea. Now, though, he was glad to have Polyakov beside him.

Time no longer flowed evenly. It had gone insane, tearing forward like a shock-wave, then suddenly congealing, turning back on itself like the horns of a ram.

Finally, though, the men in the pit raised their heads. The dust and smoke had been carried away by the wind and they could see a dim light. The earth quietened; the continual roar separated out into a series of distinct explosions. They felt a numb exhaustion – as though every feeling except anguish had been crushed out of their souls.

As Klimov staggered to his feet, he saw a German soldier lying beside him. Battered, covered in dust, he looked as though he had been chewed up by the war from the peak of his cap to the toes of his boots.

Klimov had no fear of Germans; he had an unshakeable confidence in his own strength, his own miraculous ability to pull a trigger, throw a grenade, strike a blow with a knife or a rifle-butt a second earlier than his opponent. Now, though, he didn't know what to do. He was amazed at the thought that, blinded and deafened as he was, he had been comforted by the presence of this German, had mistaken his hand for Polyakov's. Klimov and the German looked at one another. Each had been crushed by the same terrible force, and each was equally helpless to struggle against it.

They looked at one another in silence, two inhabitants of the war.

The perfect, faultless, automatic reflex they both possessed – the instinct to kill – failed to function.

Polyakov, a little further away, was also gazing at the stubble-covered face of the German. He didn't say anything either – though he usually found it difficult to keep his mouth shut.

Life was terrible. It was as though they could understand, as though they could read in one another's eyes, that the power which had ground them into the mud would continue – even after the war – to oppress both conquered and conquerors.

As though coming to an unspoken agreement, they began to climb to the surface, all three of them easy targets, all three of them quite sure they were safe.

Polyakov slipped; the German, who was right beside him, didn't give him a hand. The old man tumbled down to the bottom, cursing the light of day but obstinately crawling back up towards it. Klimov and the German reached the surface. They both looked round – one to the East, one to the West – to see if any of their superiors had noticed them climbing quite peaceably out of the same pit. Then, without looking back, without a word of goodbye, they set off for their respective trenches, making their way through the newly-ploughed, still smoking, hills and valleys.

'The house has gone. It's been razed to the ground,' said Klimov in a frightened voice as Polyakov hurried after him. 'My brothers, have you all been killed?'

Then the artillery and machine-guns opened fire and the German infantry began to advance. This was to be the hardest day that Stalingrad had known.

'It's all because of that damned Seryozha!' muttered Polyakov. He was unable to understand what had happened, to grasp that there was now no one left in house 6/1. Klimov's cries and sobs merely irritated him.

23

During the initial air-attack, a bomb had fallen on top of the under-ground pipeline that housed one of Byerozkin's battalion command-posts; Byerozkin himself, Battalion Commander Dyrkin and the telephonist had been trapped. Finding himself in complete darkness, deafened and choking with dust, Byerozkin had thought he was no longer in the land of the living. Then, in a brief moment of silence, Dyrkin had sneezed and asked: 'Are you alive, comrade Lieutenant-Colonel?'

'Yes,' Byerozkin had answered.

On hearing his commander's voice, Dyrkin had recovered his customary good humour.

'Well then, everything's fine!' he said, hawking and spitting. In fact, things seemed far from fine. Dyrkin and the telephonist were up to their necks in rubble; it was impossible for them even to check whether they had any broken bones. An iron girder above them prevented them from straightening their backs; it was this girder, however, that had saved their lives. Dyrkin turned on his torch for a moment. What they saw was quite terrifying: there were large slabs of stone hanging right over their heads, together with twisted pieces of iron, slabs of buckled concrete covered in oil, and hacked-up cables. One more bomb and all this would crash down on top of them.

For a while they huddled in silence, listening to the furious force hammering at the workshops above. Even posthumously, these work-shops continued to work for the defence, thought Byerozkin; it was difficult to destroy iron and reinforced concrete.

Then they examined the walls. There was clearly no way they could get out by themselves. The telephone was intact but silent; the line must have been cut.

It was also almost impossible to talk — they were coughing constantly and their voices were drowned by the roar of explosions.

Though it was less than twenty-four hours since he had been in delirium, Byerozkin now felt full of strength. In battle, his strength imposed itself on all his subordinates. Nevertheless, there was nothing essentially military or warlike about it; it was a simple, reasonable and very human strength. Few men were able to display strength of this kind in the inferno of battle; they were the true masters of the war.

The bombardment died down. It was replaced by an iron rumble. Byerozkin wiped his nose, coughed and said: 'Now the wolves are howling. Their tanks are attacking the Tractor Factory . . . And we're right in their path.'

Perhaps because he couldn't imagine anything worse, Dyrkin began singing a song from a film. In a loud voice, he half-sang, half-coughed:

'What a beautiful life we lead, what a beautiful life!
Things can never go wrong, never go wrong with such a
    wonderful chief.'

The telephonist thought Dyrkin had gone mad. All the same, coughing and spitting, he joined in:

'She'll grieve for me, she says she'll grieve for me all her life,
But soon another man, another man, will make her his wife.'

Meanwhile, up in the workshop filled with dust, smoke and the roar of tanks, Glushkov was tearing the skin off his hands and fingers as he rooted up slabs of stone, iron and concrete. He was in a state of frenzy; only this allowed him to clear away heavy girders it would normally have taken ten men even to shift.

The rumble of tanks, the shell-bursts, the chatter of machine-guns grew still louder – and Byerozkin could see light again. It was a dust-laden, smoky light; but it was the light of day. Looking at it, Byerozkin thought: 'See, Tamara? You needn't have worried. I told you it wouldn't be anything terrible.' Then Glushkov embraced him with his powerful, muscular arms.

Gesturing around him, his voice choked with sobs, Dyrkin cried out: 'Comrade Lieutenant-Colonel, I'm in command of a dead battalion. And Vanya's dead. Our Vanya's dead.'

He pointed to the corpse of the battalion commissar. It was lying on its side in a dark crimson puddle of blood and machine-oil.

The regimental command-post was relatively unscathed; there was just a dusting of earth on the bed and the table.

Pivovarov leapt up, swearing happily, as Byerozkin came in. Byerozkin immediately began questioning him.

'Are we still in touch with the battalions? What about the encircled house? How's Podchufarov? Dyrkin and I got caught in a mouse-trap. We couldn't see and we lost touch with everyone. I don't know who's dead and who's alive. Where are the Germans? Where are our men? I'm completely out of touch. We've just been singing songs. Quick, give me a report!'

Pivovarov began by telling him the number of casualties. Everyone in house 6/1, including the notorious Grekov, had perished. Only the scout and one old militiaman had escaped.

But the regiment had withstood the German assault. The men still alive were still alive.

The telephone rang. From the signaller's face, they all realized it was Chuykov himself.

Byerozkin took the receiver. It was a good line; the men in the suddenly quiet bunker recognized Chuykov's low, serious voice.

'Byerozkin? The divisional commander's wounded. His second-in-command and chief of staff are dead. I order you to take command yourself.'

Then, more slowly, and with emphasis:

'You held their attack. You commanded the regiment through hellish, unheard-of conditions. Thank you, my friend. I embrace you. And I wish you luck.'

In the workshops of the Tractor Factory the battle had only just begun. Those who were alive were still alive.

House 6/1 was now silent. Not one shot could be heard from the ruins. It had evidently borne the brunt of the air-attack; the remaining walls had now collapsed and the stone mound had been flattened. The German tanks firing at Podchufarov's battalion were screened by the last remains of the building. What had once been a terrible danger to the Germans was now a place of refuge.

From a distance the heaps of red brick seemed like chunks of raw, steaming flesh. Grey-green German soldiers were buzzing excitedly around the dead building.

'You must take command of the regiment,' said Byerozkin to

Pivovarov. 'Until today, my superiors have never been satisfied with me. Then, after sitting around all day singing songs, I get Chuykov's thanks and the command of a division. Well, I won't let you off the hook now.'

But the Germans were pressing forward. This was no time for pleasantries.

24

It was very cold when Viktor, Lyudmila and Nadya arrived in Moscow. Snow was falling. Alexandra Vladimirovna was still in Kazan; Viktor had promised to get her a job at the Karpov Institute, but she had wanted to stay on at the factory.

These were strange days, days of both joy and anxiety. The Germans still seemed powerful and threatening, as though they were preparing some new offensive.

There was no obvious sign that the war had reached a turning-point. Nevertheless, everyone wanted to return to Moscow. It seemed right and natural – as did the Government's decision to send back various institutions that had been evacuated.

People could sense that spring was in the air, that the worst days of the war were over. Nevertheless, the capital seemed sullen and gloomy during this second winter of the war.

Heaps of dirty snow covered the pavements. The outskirts of the city were just like the country – there were little paths linking each house with tram-stops and food stores. You often saw the iron pipes of makeshift stoves smoking away through a window; the walls of these buildings were covered in a frozen layer of yellow soot. In their short sheepskin coats and scarves, the Muscovites looked very provincial, almost like peasants.

On the way from the station Viktor looked round at Nadya's frowning face; they were both perched on top of their baggage in the back of a truck.

'So, mademoiselle,' he said, 'this isn't the Moscow you dreamed of when we were in Kazan?'

Annoyed that Viktor had guessed her feelings, Nadya didn't answer.

Viktor began to hold forth:

'Man never understands that the cities he has built are not an integral part of Nature. If he wants to defend his culture from wolves and snowstorms, if he wants to save it from being strangled by weeds, he must keep his broom, spade and rifle always at hand. If he goes to sleep, if he thinks about something else for a year or two, then everything's lost. The wolves come out of the forest, the thistles spread and everything is buried under dust and snow. Just think how many great capitals have succumbed to dust, snow and couch-grass.'

Viktor suddenly wanted Lyudmila, who was in the cab with the driver, to have the benefit of his reflections too. He leant over the side of the truck and asked through the half-open window:

'Are you comfortable, Lyuda?'

'What's all this about the death of cultures?' asked Nadya. 'It's just that the janitors haven't been clearing away the snow.'

'Don't be silly!' said Viktor. 'Just look at that ice!'

The truck gave a sudden jolt. The bundles and suitcases flew up into the air, together with Nadya and Viktor. They looked at each other and burst out laughing.

How strange it all was. How could he ever have guessed that he would do his most important work in Kazan, during a war, with all the suffering and homelessness that entailed?

He had expected them to feel only a solemn excitement as they drew near to Moscow. He had expected their sorrow over Tolya, Marusya and Anna Semyonovna, their thoughts of the victims claimed from almost every family, to blend with the joy of homecoming and fill their souls.

But it hadn't been like that at all. On the train Viktor had been upset by all kinds of trivia. He had even been annoyed with Lyudmila for sleeping so much instead of looking out over the earth that her own son had defended. She had snored very loudly; a wounded soldier passing in the corridor had heard her and exclaimed: 'There's a true soldier of the guard!'

He had been equally annoyed with Nadya: she had chosen all the most delicious-looking biscuits out of the bag and left her mother to clear up the remains of her meal. She had put on an absurd, mocking tone of voice whenever she spoke to him; he had overheard her in the next compartment saying: 'My father's a great admirer of music. Sometimes he even tinkles on the piano himself.'

The people they had shared the compartment with talked about such matters as central heating and the Moscow sewers; about people who had gaily neglected to pay their rent and so lost their right to live in Moscow; about what were the best foodstuffs to bring with them. Viktor didn't like these conversations, but in the end he too was talking about janitors and water-pipes; when he couldn't sleep at night, he wondered if the telephone had been cut off and remembered that he must get ration-cards for the Academy store.

The bad-tempered woman in charge of the coach had found a chicken-bone under Viktor's seat when she was sweeping out the compartment.

'What pigs!' she had muttered. 'And they think of themselves as intelligentsia!'

At Mourom, Viktor and Nadya had gone for a walk along the platform and run into some young men wearing long coats with Astrakhan fur collars. One of them had looked round and said: 'Look, Old Father Abraham's coming back from evacuation.'

'Yes,' laughed the other, 'he wants to get his medal for the defence of Moscow.'

At Kanash they had stopped opposite a train full of prisoners. Pressing their pale faces against the tiny barred windows, the prisoners had shouted, 'Tobacco!' or 'Give us a smoke!' The sentries patrolling up and down the train had cursed at the men as they pushed them away from the windows.

In the evening Viktor had gone to the next coach to see the Sokolovs. Marya Ivanovna, a coloured shawl round her head, was getting their bedding ready. She was sleeping in the top bunk, and Pyotr Lavrentyevich down below. Worried about whether Pyotr would be comfortable, she answered Viktor's questions quite randomly and forgot to ask after Lyudmila.

Sokolov himself had just yawned and said how exhausting he found the heat. For some reason Viktor had been offended by this lukewarm welcome.

'It's the first time in my life,' he said in an irritated tone that surprised even himself, 'that I've seen a man sleep below and make his wife climb up on top.'

'It's what we always do,' said Marya Ivanovna, kissing Sokolov on the temple. 'Pyotr Lavrentyevich gets too hot up on top – but it's all the same to me.'

'Well,' said Viktor, 'I'm off.' The Sokolovs didn't ask him to stay; once again he felt offended.

It was very hot in the carriage that night. All kinds of memories had come back to him – Kazan, Karimov, Alexandra Vladimirovna, his conversations with Madyarov, his tiny office at the university . . . What a charming, anxious look had come into Marya Ivanovna's eyes when Viktor had discussed politics at their evening gatherings. Very, very different from their preoccupied look just now.

'Would you believe it?' he said to himself. 'Taking the bottom bunk, where it's cool and comfortable. What a tyrant!'

Then he got angry with kind, meek Marya Ivanovna whom he liked more than any other woman he knew. 'She's a little red-nosed rabbit. But then Pyotr Lavrentyevich is a difficult man. He seems so gentle and measured, but really he's arrogant, secretive and vindictive. Yes, the poor woman has a lot to put up with.'

Viktor hadn't been able to get to sleep. He had tried to imagine the reactions of Chepyzhin and his other friends. Many of them knew about his work already. How would it all go? What would Gurevich and Chepyzhin say? He was, after all, a conquering hero . . .

Then he had remembered that Markov wouldn't be in Moscow for another week. He had made detailed arrangements for setting up the laboratory and it would be impossible to start work without him. It was a pity that he and Sokolov were such theoreticians, that they had such clumsy, insensitive hands.

Yes, a conquering hero . . .

But somehow he hadn't been able to hold on to this train of thought. He kept seeing the prisoners begging for tobacco and the young men who had called him 'Old Father Abraham'. And then there was that strange remark of Postoev's . . . Sokolov had been talking about a young physicist called Landesman and Postoev had said, 'Who cares about Landesman now Viktor Pavlovich has astonished the world with his discovery?' Then he had embraced Sokolov and said, 'Still, what matters is that we're both Russians.'

Would the telephone and the gas be working? And had people thought about trivia like this a hundred years ago – on their way back to Moscow after the defeat of Napoleon?

The truck came to a stop not far from their house. Once again the Shtrums saw the front door, the four windows of their flat with the blue paper crosses that had been pasted on last summer, the linden trees on the edge of the pavement, the sign saying 'Milk' and the board on the janitor's door.

'Well, I don't suppose the lift will be working,' said Lyudmila.

She turned to the driver. 'Can you help take our things up to the second floor?'

'Why not? You can pay me in bread.'

They unloaded the truck; Nadya stayed to watch over their things while Viktor and Lyudmila went up to their apartment. They went up the stairs very slowly, somehow surprised that everything had changed so little: the letter-boxes were still the same, the door on the first floor was still covered with a piece of black oil-cloth. How strange that streets, houses and things you forgot about didn't just disappear; they came back and there you were in the midst of them again.

Once, too impatient to wait for the lift, Tolya had run up to the second floor and shouted down to Viktor: 'Ha ha! I'm home already!'

'Let's stop for a moment on the landing. You're out of breath,' said Viktor.

'My God!' said Lyudmila. 'Just look at the state of the staircase! I'll have to go down tomorrow and get Vasily Ivanovich to have the place cleaned.'

There they were, husband and wife, standing once more before the door of their home.

'Perhaps you'd like to open the door,' said Viktor.

'No, you do it. You're the master of the house.'

They went inside and walked round all the rooms without taking off their coats. Lyudmila took the telephone receiver off the hook, blew into it and said: 'Well, the telephone seems to be working all right.'

Then she went into the kitchen. 'We've even got water. We can use the lavatory.' She went over to the stove and tried to turn on the gas. It had been cut off.

Lord, Lord, it was over at last. The enemy had been halted. They had returned to their home. That Saturday, 21 June, 1941, seemed only yesterday. How much – and how little – everything had changed. The people who had just entered the house were different. Their hearts had changed; their lives had changed; they were living in another epoch. Why was everything so ordinary, and yet such a source of anxiety? Why did their pre-war life, the life they had lost, seem so fine and happy? And why was the thought of tomorrow so oppressive? Ration cards, residence permits, the electricity rental, newspaper subscriptions, the state of the lift . . . And when they were in bed, they would hear that same old clock striking the hour.

Following at his wife's heels, Viktor suddenly remembered how he and pretty young Nina had had a drink here in the summer. The empty wine bottle was still beside the sink.

He remembered the night after he had read the letter from his mother that had been brought by Colonel Novikov; he remembered his own sudden departure to Chelyabinsk. This was where he had kissed Nina; where a pin had fallen out of her hair and they hadn't been able to find it. He felt suddenly anxious. What if the pin suddenly turned up? What if she had forgotten her powder-puff or her lipstick?

Just then the driver came in. Breathing heavily, he looked round the room and asked: 'And all this belongs to you?'

'Yes,' said Viktor guiltily.

'We've got eight square metres for the six of us,' said the driver. 'My old woman sleeps during the day when everyone's out at work. During the night she just sits on a chair.'

Viktor went over to the window. There was Nadya beside their heap of belongings, dancing about and blowing on her fingers.

Dear Nadya, dear helpless daughter, this is the house where you were born.

The driver brought up a sack of food and a hold-all full of toilet things, sat down and began rolling himself a cigarette.

He seemed to be obsessed with the question of living-space. He at once began to regale Viktor with stories about the official hygiene recommendations and the bribe-takers at the local accommodation bureau.

There was a clatter of pans from the kitchen.

'A true housewife,' said the driver, winking at Viktor.

Viktor looked out of the window again.

'A pretty kettle of fish,' said the driver. 'We'll give the Germans a

446

good thrashing at Stalingrad, people will start coming back to Moscow, and it will be even worse. Not long ago, one of our workers came back to the factory after being wounded twice at the front. His home, of course, had been blown up, so he and his wife moved into some awful cellar. And of course his wife was pregnant and his two children had TB. And then the cellar got flooded – the water came right up to their knees. They put wooden boards on top of stools and used them as bridges between the stove, the table and the bed. Then he started making applications. He wrote to the Party committee, he wrote to the district committee, he even wrote to Stalin himself. In reply they just made promises. And then one night, together with his family and all his gear, he moved into a room on the fourth floor that was kept for the district Soviet. Then things really did start to happen. He was summoned by the public prosecutor. He was told he must leave the room within twenty-four hours or he'd get five years in a camp and the kids would be packed off to an orphanage. What do you think he did then? Well, he'd been decorated at the front, so he stuck his medals into his chest, right into the flesh, and tried to hang himself in the lunch-break – there in the workshop. The other lads at work found him, cut the rope and had him rushed to hospital. He got his flat straight away, before he was discharged. Yes, he did well for himself. It's not spacious, but it's got all they need.'

Nadya came in just as he finished.

'What if the baggage gets stolen? Who'll be to blame then?' the driver asked.

Nadya shrugged her shoulders and went off on a tour of the rooms, still blowing on her frozen fingers.

As soon as Nadya came into the house Viktor felt angry again.

'You might at least turn your collar down,' he said.

Nadya paid no attention and shouted towards the kitchen:

'Mama, I'm terribly hungry!'

Lyudmila was extraordinarily active that day. Viktor thought that if she had deployed this energy at the front, the Germans would already have retreated at least a hundred kilometres from Moscow.

The plumber turned on the heating; the pipes were still working, even if they weren't very hot. Getting hold of the gas man was more difficult. Lyudmila finally got the director of the gas board to send someone from the emergency brigade. She lit all the burners and placed irons on top of them. The gas was very weak, but they could at least take off their coats now. After the labours of the driver, the plumber and the gas man, the bag of bread had become extremely light.

Lyudmila carried on working until late at night. She stuck a rag on the end of a broom and started dusting the walls and ceilings. She cleaned the chandelier, took the dead flowers out to the back staircase and assembled a huge heap of rags, old papers and other junk. A grumbling Nadya had to carry three bucket-loads down to the dustbin.

Lyudmila washed all the plates from the kitchen and dining-room. She set Viktor to dry the knives, forks and plates, but refused to trust him with the tea service. She started doing the washing in the bathroom, thawed out the butter on top of the stove and sorted through the potatoes they had brought from Kazan.

Viktor tried to phone Sokolov. Marya Ivanovna answered.

'I've just put Pyotr Lavrentyevich to bed. He's worn out from the journey, but I can wake him up if it's urgent.'

'No, no, I just wanted a chat,' said Viktor.

'I'm so happy,' said Marya Ivanovna. 'I keep wanting to cry.'

'Why not come round? Are you doing anything this evening?'

'You must be mad! Surely you realize how much Lyudmila and I have to do.'

She started to ask how long it had taken to get the electricity and the plumbing sorted out. Viktor cut her short. 'I'll call Lyudmila. If you want to talk about plumbing, she can continue this discussion.'

Then he added teasingly: 'What a pity you can't come round. We could have read Flaubert's poem "Max and Maurice".'

Ignoring his joke, she said: 'I'll phone later. If I've got so much work with just the one room, I can't imagine what it's like for Lyudmila.'

Viktor realized he had offended her. Suddenly he wished he were back in Kazan. How strange people are . . .

Next, Viktor tried to ring Postoev, but his phone seemed to be cut off. He tried Gurevich, but was told by his neighbours that he had gone to his sister in Sokolniki. He rang Chepyzhin, but no one answered.

Suddenly the phone rang. A boyish voice asked for Nadya. She was then on one of her trips to the dustbin.

'Who is it?' asked Viktor severely.

'It doesn't matter. Just someone she knows.'

'Viktor,' called Lyudmila. 'You've been chatting long enough on the phone. Come and help me with this cupboard.'

'I'm not chatting,' said Viktor. 'No one in Moscow wants to speak to me. And you might at least give me something to eat. Sokolov's already stuffed himself and gone to bed.'

Lyudmila seemed only to have increased the chaos in the flat. There were heaps of linen everywhere; the crockery had been taken out of the cupboards and was lying all over the floor; you could hardly move in the rooms and the corridor for all the pans, bowls and sacks.

Viktor hadn't expected Lyudmila to go into Tolya's room at first, but he was wrong. Looking flushed and anxious, she said to him: 'Vitya, put the Chinese vase on Tolya's bookshelf. I've just given the room a good clean.'

The phone rang again. He heard Nadya answer.

'Hello! No, I haven't been out. Mama made me take the rubbish down.'

'Give me a hand, Vitya,' Lyudmila chivvied Viktor. 'Don't just go to sleep. There's still masses to do.'

A woman's instinct is so simple – and so strong.

By evening the chaos was vanquished. The rooms felt warmer and had begun to take on something of their pre-war appearance. They ate supper in the kitchen. Lyudmila had baked some biscuits and fried up some of the millet she had boiled in the afternoon.

'Who was that on the phone?' Viktor asked Nadya.

'Just a boy,' said Nadya and burst out laughing. 'He's been ringing for four days.'

'What, have you been writing to him?' asked Lyudmila. 'Did you tell him we were coming back?'

Nadya looked irritated and shrugged her shoulders.

'I'd be happy if even a dog phoned me,' said Viktor.

During the night Viktor woke up. Lyudmila was in her nightgown, standing outside Tolya's open door.

'Can you see, Tolya?' she was murmuring. 'I've managed to clean everything now. Little one, to look at your room now, no one would think there'd ever been a war.'

25

On their return from evacuation, the University staff met in one of the halls of the Academy of Sciences. All these people – young and old, pale or bald, with large eyes or small piercing eyes, with wide foreheads or narrow foreheads – were conscious, as they came together, of the highest poetry of all, the poetry of prose.

Damp sheets and the damp pages of books left for too long in unheated rooms, formulae noted down by frozen red fingers, lectures delivered in an overcoat with the collar turned up, salads made from slimy potatoes and a few torn cabbage leaves, the crush to get meal tickets, the tedious thought of having to write your name down for salt fish and an extra ration of oil – all this became suddenly unimportant. As people met, they greeted each other noisily.

Viktor saw Chepyzhin standing next to Academician Shishakov.

'Dmitry Petrovich! Dmitry Petrovich!' Viktor repeated, looking at the face that was so dear to him. Chepyzhin embraced him.

'Have you heard from your lads at the front?' asked Viktor.

'Yes, yes, they're fine.'

From the way Chepyzhin frowned as he said this, Viktor realized that he already knew about Tolya's death.

'Viktor Pavlovich,' Chepyzhin went on, 'give my regards to your wife. My sincerest regards. Mine and Nadezhda Fyodorovna's.'

Then he added: 'I've read your work. It's interesting. Very important – even more than it seems. Yes, it's more interesting than we can yet appreciate.'

He kissed Viktor on the forehead.

'No, no, it's nothing,' said Viktor, feeling embarrassed and happy. On his way to the meeting he had been wondering stupidly who would have read his work and what they would say about it. What if no one had read it at all . . . ?

Now he felt certain that no one would speak of anything else.

Shishakov was still standing there. There were lots of things Viktor wanted to say, but not in the presence of a third party – and certainly not in the presence of Shishakov.

When he looked at Shishakov, Viktor was always reminded of Gleb Uspensky's phrase, 'a pyramid-shaped buffalo'. His square fleshy face, his arrogant, equally fleshy lips, his pudgy fingers with their polished nails, his thick silver-grey crewcut, all somehow oppressed Viktor. Every time he met Shishakov, he caught himself thinking, 'Will he recognize me? Will he say hello?' He would then feel angry with himself for feeling glad when Shishakov's fleshy lips slowly pronounced a few words that somehow seemed equally fleshy.

'The arrogant bull,' Viktor once said to Sokolov when Shishakov was mentioned. 'He makes me feel like a Jew from a shtetl in the presence of a cavalry colonel.'

'Just think!' said Sokolov. 'What he's most famous for is failing to recognize a positron on a photograph. All the research students know the story. They call it "Academician Shishakov's mistake".'

Sokolov very rarely spoke ill of people – whether from caution or from some pious principle that forbade him to judge his neighbours. But Shishakov irritated him beyond endurance; Sokolov couldn't help but ridicule and abuse him.

They began to talk about the war.

'The German advance has been halted on the Volga,' said Chepyzhin. 'There's the power of the Volga for you – living water, living power.'

'Stalingrad, Stalingrad,' said Shishakov. 'The triumph of our strategy and the determination of our people.'

'Aleksey Alekseyevich, are you acquainted with Viktor Pavlovich's latest work?' Chepyzhin asked suddenly.

'I know of it, of course, but I haven't yet read it.'

It was by no means clear from Shishakov's face whether he really had heard of it.

Viktor looked for a long time into Chepyzhin's eyes; he wanted his old friend and teacher to see all he had been through, all his doubts and losses. But he saw sadness, depression and the weariness of old age on Chepyzhin's face too.

Sokolov came up. Chepyzhin shook him by the hand, but Shishakov merely glanced carelessly at his rather old jacket. Then

Postoev joined them and Shishakov's large fleshy face broke into a smile.

'Greetings, greetings, my friend. Now you're someone I really am glad to see.'

They asked after each other's health, and after their wives and children. As they talked about their dachas, they sounded like grand lords.

'How are you getting on?' Viktor asked Sokolov quietly. 'Is it warm in your flat?'

'It's not yet any better than Kazan,' answered Sokolov. 'Masha said I must give you her regards. She'll probably come round and see you tomorrow.'

'Splendid! We miss her. In Kazan we got used to seeing her every day.'

'Every day! It seemed more like three times a day. I even suggested she move in with you.'

Viktor laughed, but was conscious of something false in his laughter. Then Academician Leontyev entered the hall, a mathematician with a big nose, an imposing bald skull and enormous glasses with yellow frames. Once, when they had both been staying in Gaspre, they had gone on a trip together to Yalta. They had drunk a lot of wine in a shop and staggered back to the canteen in Gaspre singing a dirty song. This had alarmed the staff and amused the other holiday-makers. Seeing Viktor, Leontyev smiled. Viktor lowered his eyes, expecting Leontyev to say something about his work.

Instead, Leontyev seemed to be remembering their adventures at Gaspre. With a wave of the hand he called out: 'Well, Viktor Pavlovich, how about a song?'

A young man with dark hair came in. He was wearing a black suit. Viktor noticed that Shishakov greeted him immediately.

Suslakov also approached the young man. Suslakov was an important man on the Presidium, though the exact nature of his duties was rather obscure. But if you needed a flat, or if a lecturer needed to get from Alma-Ata to Kazan, then Suslakov could be more useful than the President himself. He had the tired face of a man who works at night and his cheeks seemed to have been kneaded from grey dough. He was the sort of man who is needed by everyone, all the time.

They were all accustomed to the way Suslakov smoked 'Palmyra' at meetings, while the Academicians smoked ordinary tobacco or shag. And he didn't get lifts home from some celebrity; no, he would offer the celebrities a ride in his Zis.

Viktor watched the conversation between Suslakov and the young man with dark hair. He could tell that it wasn't the young man who was asking a favour of Suslakov – however gracefully a man asks for a favour, you can always tell who is asking and who is being asked. On the contrary, the young man seemed quite ready to break off the conversation. And he greeted Chepyzhin coolly, with studied politeness.

'By the way, who is that young grandee?' asked Viktor.

In a low voice Postoev answered: 'He's been working for a while in the scientific section of the Central Committee.'

'Do you know,' said Viktor. 'I've got an extraordinary feeling. As though our determination at Stalingrad is the determination of Newton, the determination of Einstein. As though our victory on the Volga symbolizes the triumph of Einstein's ideas. Well, you know what I mean . . .'

Shishakov gave a perplexed smile and gently shook his head.

'Don't you understand me, Aleksey Alekseyevich?' said Viktor.

'It's as clear as mud,' said the young man from the scientific section, who was now standing beside Viktor. 'But I suppose the so-called theory of relativity can allow one to establish a link between the Russian Volga and Albert Einstein.'

'Why "so-called"?' asked Viktor in astonishment. He turned to the pyramid-shaped Shishakov for support, but Shishakov's quiet contempt seemed to extend to Einstein as well.

Viktor felt a rush of anger. This was the way it sometimes happened – something would needle him and he would find it very difficult to restrain himself. At home in the evening, he would finally allow himself to reply. Sometimes he quite forgot himself, shouting and gesticulating, standing up for what he loved and ridiculing his enemies. 'Papa's making a speech again,' Lyudmila would say to Nadya.

This time, it wasn't only on Einstein's behalf that he was angry. Everyone he knew should be talking about his work – he himself should be the centre of attention. He felt upset and hurt. He knew it was ridiculous to take offence like this, but he did. No one but Chepyzhin had spoken to him about his work.

He began, rather timidly, to explain.

'The Fascists have exiled the brilliant Einstein and their physics has become the physics of monkeys. But we, thank God, have halted the advance of Fascism. It all goes together: the Volga, Stalingrad, Albert Einstein – the greatest genius of our epoch – the most remote little village, an illiterate old peasant woman, and the freedom we all need. This all goes together. I may sound confused, but perhaps there isn't anything clearer than this confusion.'

'I think, Viktor Pavlovich, that your panegyric to Einstein is a trifle exaggerated,' said Shishakov.

'Yes,' said Postoev lightly. 'On the whole I would say the same.'

The young man from the scientific section just looked at Viktor sadly.

'Well, comrade Shtrum,' he began, and Viktor once again felt the malevolence in his voice. 'To you it may seem natural, at a time of such importance for our people, to couple Albert Einstein and the Volga. These days, however, have awoken other sentiments in the hearts of those who disagree with you. Still, no one has power over someone else's heart and there's nothing to argue about there. But there is room for argument as regards your evaluation of Einstein: it does seem inappropriate to regard an idealist theory as the peak of scientific achievement.'

'That's enough,' Viktor interrupted. 'Aleksey Alekseyevich,' he went on in an arrogant and didactic voice, 'contemporary physics without Einstein is the physics of monkeys. It's not for us to trifle with the names of Einstein, Galileo and Newton.'

He raised a finger to silence Shishakov and saw him blink.

A minute later Viktor was standing by the window and recounting this unexpected incident to Sokolov, partly in a whisper and partly quite loudly.

'And you were right next to me and you didn't even hear. Chepyzhin suddenly disappeared too. It was almost as though he did so on purpose.'

He frowned and fell silent. How childishly, how naïvely he had looked forward to today's triumph. As it turned out, it had been some young bureaucrat who had created the most stir.

'Do you know the surname of the young grandee?' Sokolov asked suddenly, as though reading Viktor's thoughts. 'Do you realize whose relative he is?'

'I've no idea.'

Sokolov leant over and whispered in Viktor's ear.

'You don't say!' exclaimed Viktor. He remembered the way both Suslakov and Shishakov had deferred to this youth. 'O-oh' he said. 'So that's what it's all about. Now I understand.'

Sokolov laughed.

'Well, you've already established a cordial relationship with the scientific section and the higher echelons of the Academy. You're like the Mark Twain hero who boasts about his income to the tax-inspector.'

Viktor didn't appreciate this witticism.

'You were standing right beside me,' he replied. 'Did you really not hear our argument? Or did you prefer not to get involved in my conversation with the tax-inspector?'

Sokolov smiled. His small eyes looked suddenly kind and beautiful.

'Don't be upset, Viktor Pavlovich. Surely you didn't really expect Shishakov to appreciate your work? My God, what a lot of nonsense all this is. But your work's different. That's real.'

In his eyes and voice Viktor sensed the warmth and seriousness he had hoped to find that autumn evening in Kazan.

The meeting began. The speakers talked about the task of science during this difficult time, about their own readiness to devote their strength to the popular cause and to help the Army in its struggle against German Fascism. They spoke about the work of the various Institutes of the Academy, about the assistance that would be given to scientists by the Central Committee of the Party, about how comrade Stalin, the leader of the Army and the People, still had time to concern himself with scientific questions, about the duty of every scientist to justify the trust placed in him by the Party and by comrade Stalin himself.

There was also mention of some organizational changes occasioned by the new set-up. The physicists learned with surprise that they themselves were dissatisfied with the projects of their Institute – too much attention, apparently, was being given to purely theoretical matters. Suslakov's words, 'The Institute is cut off from life', were whispered around the hall.

26

The position of scientific research in the country had been discussed by the Central Committee. Apparently the Party was now principally concerned with the development of physics, mathematics and chemistry. The Central Committee considered that science must move closer to industry and become more integrated with real life.

Stalin himself had attended the meeting. Apparently he had walked up and down the hall, pipe in hand, stopping now and then with a pensive look on his face – to listen either to the speaker or to his own thoughts.

There had been fierce attacks on idealism and on any tendency to underestimate Russian science and philosophy. Stalin had spoken twice. When Shcherbakov had proposed a reduction in the Academy's budget, Stalin had shaken his head and said: 'No, we're not talking about making soap. We are not going to economize on the Academy.'

And during a discussion of the danger of idealist theories and the excessive admiration of certain scientists for Western science, Stalin had nodded and said: 'Yes, but we must protect our scientists from Arakcheevs.'*

Having first sworn them to secrecy, the scientists present at this meeting talked about it to their friends. Within a few days, the entire scientific community in Moscow – small groups of friends and close family circles – were discussing every detail of it in hushed voices.

People whispered that Stalin had grey hair, that some of his teeth were black and decayed, that he had beautiful hands with fine fingers, that his face was pock-marked.

Any youngster who happened to be listening was warned: 'And you watch it! Keep your mouth shut or you'll be the ruin of us all.'

Everyone expected a considerable improvement in the position of

* A minister under Alexander I. Here he epitomises a narrow-minded and rigid bureaucracy.

scientists; Stalin's words about Arakcheev held out great hopes.

A few days later an important botanist was arrested, Chetverikov the geneticist. There were various rumours about the reason for his arrest: that he was a spy; that he had associated with Russian émigrés during his journeys abroad; that he had a German wife who had corresponded before the war with her sister in Berlin; that he had tried to instigate a famine by introducing inferior strains of wheat; that it was to do with a remark he had made about 'the finger of God'; that it was on account of a political anecdote he had told to a childhood friend.

Since the beginning of the war there had been relatively little talk of political arrests. Many people, Viktor among them, thought that they were a thing of the past. Now everyone remembered 1937: the daily roll-call of people arrested during the night; people phoning each other up with the news, 'Anna Andreevna's husband has fallen ill tonight'; people answering the phone on behalf of a neighbour who had been arrested and saying, 'He's gone on a journey, we don't know when he'll be back.' And the stories about the circumstances of these arrests: 'they came for him just as he was giving his little boy a bath'; 'they came for him at work . . . at the theatre . . . in the middle of the night'; 'the search lasted forty-eight hours, they turned everything upside down, they even took up the floorboards'; 'they hardly looked at anything at all, they just leafed through a few books for show'.

Victor remembered the names of dozens of people who had left and never returned: Academician Vavilov, Vize, Osip Mandelstam, Babel, Boris Pilnyak, Meyerhold, the bacteriologists Korshunov and Zlatogorov, Professor Pletnyov, Doctor Levin . . .

It wasn't important that these were famous and outstanding people; what mattered was that all those arrested — however famous or however unknown — were innocent.

Was all this going to begin again? Would one's heart sink, even after the war, when one heard footsteps or a car horn during the night?

How difficult it was to reconcile such things with the war for freedom . . . ! Yes, they had been fools to talk so much in Kazan.

A week after Chetverikov's arrest, Chepyzhin announced that he was resigning from the Institute of Physics.

The President of the Academy had called at Chepyzhin's house; apparently Chepyzhin had been summoned by either Beria or

Malenkov, but had refused to alter the Institute's research programme. In view of Chepyzhin's services to science, the authorities had been reluctant to resort to extreme measures. Pimenov, the young administrative director who was something of a liberal, was removed from his post at the same time. Shishakov was then appointed both administrative director and scientific director.

It was rumoured that, as a result of all this, Chepyzhin had had a heart attack. Viktor rang him immediately to arrange to go and see him, but the phone was answered by the housekeeper, who said that Dmitry Petrovich really had been ill during the last few days; on his doctor's advice he and Nadezhda Fyodorovna had gone to the country and would not be back for two or three weeks.

'It's like pushing a boy off a tram,' Viktor said to Lyudmila. 'And they call it defending us from Arakcheevs. What does it matter to physics whether Chepyzhin's a Marxist, a Buddhist or a Lamaist? Chepyzhin's founded his own school. Chepyzhin's a friend of Rutherford. Every street-sweeper knows Chepyzhin's equations.'

'That's putting it a bit strongly,' said Nadya.

'And you watch it,' said Viktor. 'Keep your mouth shut or you'll be the ruin of all of us.'

'I know,' said Nadya. 'Your speeches are only for domestic consumption.'

'Yes, my dear Nadya,' said Viktor meekly, 'but what can I do to change decisions taken by the Central Committee? Anyway Dmitry Petrovich himself said he wanted to resign. Even though, as we say, it was "against the wishes of the people".'

'You shouldn't get so steamed up about it,' said Lyudmila. 'Besides, you were always arguing with Dmitry Petrovich yourself.'

'There's no true friendship without discussion.'

'That's the trouble,' said Lyudmila. 'You and your discussions. You'll end up having your laboratory taken away from you.'

'That's not what worries me,' said Viktor. 'Nadya's right: my speeches are just for domestic consumption . . . Why don't you phone Chetverikov's wife? Or go and see her? You're a friend of hers.'

'That simply isn't done,' said Lyudmila. 'Anyway I don't know her that well. How can I help her? Why should she want to see me? Have you ever phoned anyone in that situation?'

'I think one should,' said Nadya.

Viktor frowned. It was Sokolov, not Lyudmila and Nadya, whom he really wanted to talk to about Chepyzhin's resignation. But he he stopped himself – it really wasn't something to discuss on the phone.

It was odd though. Why Shishakov? It was clear that Viktor's latest work was very important. Chepyzhin had said at the Council of Scientists that it was the most important development in Soviet theoretical physics for the last decade. And then they'd gone and put Shishakov in charge of the Institute. Was it a joke? A man who'd seen hundreds of photographs with the trajectories of electrons going off to the left, and had then been shown photographs with the same trajectories going off to the right ... It was as though he'd been presented, on a silver plate, with the opportunity to discover the positron. Young Savostyanov would not have missed it. But Shishakov had just pouted and said the photographs must be defective.

What was most amazing of all was that no one was in the least surprised by this sort of thing. Somehow it all seemed quite natural. Viktor's wife and friends, even Viktor himself, all considered it the normal state of affairs. Shishakov was a suitable director, and Viktor was not.

What was it Postoev had said? 'Still, what matters is that we're both Russians.' But then it would be difficult to be more Russian than Chepyzhin.

On his way to the Institute the next morning, Viktor imagined that everyone – from doctors to laboratory assistants – would be talking only of Chepyzhin. By the main entrance to the Institute stood a Zis limousine. The chauffeur, a middle-aged man in glasses, was reading a newspaper. On the staircase Viktor met the old caretaker. That summer they'd had tea together in the laboratory.

'The new director's just arrived,' the old man announced. Then he asked sadly: 'What will become of our Dmitry Petrovich?'

The laboratory assistants were discussing how to set up the equipment that had just arrived from Kazan. There were piles of large boxes in the main hall. The new apparatus from the Urals had also arrived. Nozdrin was standing beside a huge crate. Viktor thought he looked very arrogant.

Perepelitsyn was hopping around the crate on his one leg, holding his crutch under his armpit.

'Look, Viktor Pavlovich!' said Anna Stepanovna, pointing at the boxes.

'Even a blind man could see all this,' said Perepelitsyn.

Anna Stepanovna, however, hadn't really been referring to the crates.

'I see,' said Viktor. 'Of course I see.'

'The workers will be arriving in an hour's time,' said Nozdrin. 'Professor Markov and I have made the arrangements.' He spoke in the calm, slow voice of someone who knows he's the boss. This was his hour of glory.

Viktor went into his office. Markov and Savostyanov were sitting on the sofa, Sokolov was standing by the window, and Svechin, the head of the magnetic laboratory next door, was sitting at the desk and rolling a cigarette.

He stood up as Viktor came in.

'This is the boss's chair.'

'No, no, sit down,' said Viktor. 'What are we discussing at the conference?'

'The special stores,' said Markov. 'Apparently Academicians will be allowed to spend fifteen hundred roubles, while us lesser mortals will only be allowed five hundred roubles – the same as People's Artists and great poets like Lebedev-Kumach.'

'We're beginning to set up the equipment,' said Viktor, 'and Dmitry Petrovich is no longer here. The house is burning, but the clock still keeps time, as the saying goes.'

No one responded to this change of subject.

'My cousin passed by yesterday on his way back from hospital to the front,' said Savostyanov. 'We wanted to celebrate, so I bought a half-litre of vodka off a neighbour for 350 roubles!'

'That's amazing!' said Svechin.

'We're not just talking about making soap,' said Savostyanov brightly. He saw from his colleagues' faces that his joke had fallen flat.

'The new boss is here already,' said Viktor.

'A man of great energy,' said Svechin.

'We'll be all right with Aleksey Alekseyevich,' said Markov. 'He's had tea in comrade Zhdanov's own house.'

Markov really was remarkable. He seemed to have very few friends and yet he always knew everything. He knew that Gabrichevskaya from the next-door laboratory was pregnant, that the husband of Lida the cleaning lady was in hospital again, that Smorodintsev's doctoral thesis had been rejected . . .

'That's right,' said Savostyanov. 'We may laugh at Shishakov's notorious "mistake", but, all in all, he's not such a bad type. By the way, do you know the difference between a good type and a bad type? A good type is someone who behaves swinishly in spite of himself!'

'Mistake or no mistake,' said Svechin, 'they don't make someone an Academician for nothing.'

Svechin was a member of the Party bureau of the Institute. He had only joined the Party in autumn 1941 and, like many new members, was unshakeably orthodox. He carried out any task entrusted to him by the Party with an almost religious earnestness.

'There's something I want to talk to you about, Viktor Pavlovich,' Svechin went on. 'The Party bureau wants you to speak at our next meeting on the subject of our new programme.'

'A failure of leadership? The errors of Chepyzhin? Is that what you want me to talk about?' Viktor was very annoyed. The conversation hadn't taken the direction he wanted. 'I don't know if I'm a good type or a bad type myself,' he went on, 'but I'm very reluctant to behave swinishly.'

Turning to his colleagues, he asked: 'What about you, comrades? Are you happy about Chepyzhin's resignation?'

He was counting on his colleagues' support and was quite taken aback when Savostyanov gave a non-committal shrug of the shoulders and said: 'He's getting old now.'

All Svechin said was: 'Chepyzhin refused to undertake any new projects. What else could we do? Anyway, he chose to resign. Everyone wanted him to stay.'

'So an Arakcheev has been uncovered at last,' said Viktor.

'Viktor Pavlovich,' said Markov in a hushed voice, 'I've heard that Rutherford once vowed never to work on neutrons. He was afraid it would lead to the development of a colossal explosive force. Very noble, I'm sure – but that kind of squeamishness is plain senseless. Apparently Dmitry Petrovich was equally holier-than-thou.'

'Heavens!' thought Viktor. 'How on earth does he know all this?'

'Pyotr Lavrentyevich,' he said, 'it seems we're in a minority.'

Sokolov shook his head. 'In my opinion, Viktor Pavlovich, this is no time for individualism and insubordination. We're at war. Chepyzhin was wrong to think only of himself and his personal interests when his superiors asked something of him.

'You too, Brutus!' joked Viktor, trying to mask his confusion.

Curiously, however, as well as feeling confused, Viktor was almost pleased. 'Of course,' he thought, 'just what I expected.' But why 'of course'? He hadn't expected Sokolov to respond like that. And even if he had, why should he be pleased?

'You really must speak,' said Svechin. 'There's no need whatsoever to criticize Chepyzhin. Just a few words about the potential of your research in the light of the decisions taken by the Central Committee.'

Before the war Viktor had met Svechin occasionally at orchestral concerts in the Conservatory. He had heard that in Svechin's youth, when he was a student at the Faculty of Maths and Physics, he had written futurist poetry and worn a chrysanthemum in his button-hole. Now, he spoke about the decisions of the Party bureau as though they were formulations of universal truths.

Sometimes Viktor wanted to dig Svechin in the ribs, wink and say: 'Come on now, let's be frank!' He knew, though, that there was no way of talking frankly with Svechin. Now, however, amazed by Sokolov's speech, Viktor did speak his mind.

'What about Chetverikov's arrest?' he asked. 'Is that linked with our new tasks? And is that why Vavilov was sent to prison? And if I allow myself to say that I consider Dmitry Petrovich a greater authority on physics than comrade Zhdanov, the head of the scientific section of the Central Committee, or even than . . .'

Everyone's eyes were on Viktor, expecting him to pronounce the name of Stalin. He made a dismissive gesture and said: 'All right. Enough of that. Let's go through to the lab.'

The boxes from the Urals had already been opened. The main part of the apparatus, three quarters of a ton in weight, had been carefully teased out from a mass of wood shavings, paper and rough pieces of board. Viktor laid his hand on the polished metal surface.

A stream of particles would gush forth from this metal belly – like the Volga by the small chapel on Lake Seliger.

There was something good about the look in everyone's eyes. Yes, it was good to know the world had room for such a wonderful machine. What more could one ask for?

At the end of the day Viktor and Sokolov were left alone in the laboratory.

'Why strut about like a cock, Viktor Pavlovich?' said Sokolov. 'You lack humility. I told Masha about your success at the meeting of the Academy – how you managed, in only half an hour, to get off on the wrong foot with both the new director and the young grandee from the scientific section. Masha was terribly upset; she couldn't sleep all night. You know the times we live in. And I saw your eyes as you looked at *this*. Why sacrifice everything just for a few words?'

'Wait a moment,' said Viktor. 'I need room to breathe.'

'For heaven's sake!' said Sokolov. 'No one's going to interfere with your work. You can breathe as much as you like.'

'Listen, my friend,' said Viktor with a sour smile. 'You mean well by me and I thank you with all my heart. But please allow me to be equally frank. Why, for the love of God, did you have to talk like that about Dmitry Petrovich? After the freedom of thought we enjoyed in Kazan, I found that very upsetting. As for me, I'm afraid I'm not as fearless as all that. I'm no Danton – as we used to say in my student days.'

'Thank God for that! To be quite honest, I've always thought of political speechmakers as people incapable of expressing themselves in anything creative. We ourselves do have that ability.'

'I don't know,' said Viktor. 'What about that young Frenchman Galois? And what about Kibalchich?'

Sokolov pushed his chair back. 'Kibalchich, as you know very well, ended up on the scaffold. What I'm talking about is empty blather. Like Madyarov's.'

'So you're calling me a blatherer?'

Sokolov shrugged his shoulders and didn't answer.

One might have expected this quarrel to be forgotten as easily as their previous quarrels. But for some reason this particular flare-up was not forgotten. If two men's lives are in harmony, they can quarrel, be wildly unjust to one another and then forget it. But if there is some hidden discord, then any thoughtlessness, any careless word, can be a blade that severs their friendship.

Such discord often lies so deep that it never reaches the surface, never becomes conscious. One violent, empty quarrel, one unkind word, appears then to be the fateful blow that destroys years of friendship.

No, Ivan Ivanovich and Ivan Nikiforovich did not just quarrel over a goose!*

27

When people talked about Kasyan Terentyevich Kovchenko, the new deputy director of the Institute, they always called him 'one of Shishakov's men'. He seemed friendly, he sprinkled his conversation with odd words of Ukrainian, and he managed to obtain both a car and a flat with remarkable speed.

Markov, who knew any number of stories about the different Academicians and senior members of staff, said that Kovchenko had been awarded a Stalin Prize for a work that he had first read through after its publication: his part had been to obtain materials that were in short supply and to smooth over various bureaucratic obstacles.

Shishakov entrusted Kovchenko with the task of filling the various positions that had fallen vacant. Applications were invited for the posts of director of the vacuum laboratory and director of the low temperature laboratory; there were also vacancies for research directors.

The War Department furnished both workers and materials; the mechanical workshop was reorganized and the main building of the Institute restored; the central power station agreed to provide an unlimited supply of electricity; special factories sent in whatever materials were in short supply. All this was arranged by Kovchenko.

Usually when a new director takes over, people say respectfully, 'He's the first to arrive at work and the last to leave.' This was said of Kovchenko. But a new director wins even more respect when people say, 'It's two weeks since he was appointed and he's only appeared once, for half an hour. He just never comes in.' This means that the director is drawing up new canons of law, that he has access to

* The subject of a famous story by Gogol.

the highest circles of government. And this is what was said of Academician Shishakov.

As for Chepyzhin, he went off to his dacha, to work in what he called his laboratory hut. Professor Feinhard, the famous cardiologist, had advised him not to lift anything heavy and to avoid any sudden movements. Chepyzhin, however, chopped wood, dug ditches and felt fine. He wrote to Professor Feinhard that a strict regime suited him.

In cold, hungry Moscow the Institute seemed an oasis of warmth and luxury. When they came in to work, the members of staff took great pleasure warming their hands on the hot radiators; their flats were freezing and damp.

What they liked most of all was the new canteen in the basement. It had a buffet where you could buy yoghurt, sweet coffee and pieces of sausage. And the woman behind the counter didn't tear off the coupons for meat and fat from your ration-cards; this was particularly appreciated.

The canteen had six different menus: one for doctors of science, one for research directors, one for research assistants, one for senior laboratory assistants, one for technicians and one for service personnel. The fiercest passions were generated by the two highest-grade menus, which differed only in their desserts – stewed fruit or a jelly made from powder. Emotions also ran high over the food parcels delivered to the houses of doctors and research directors.

Savostyanov remarked that, in all probability, these parcels had stirred more passions than the theory of Copernicus.

Sometimes it seemed as though higher, more mysterious powers were involved in the arcana of rations allocation; that it did not depend merely on the Party committee and the administrators of the Institute.

'You know, your parcel came today,' Lyudmila announced one evening. 'What I can't understand is why Svechin, a nonentity in the scientific world, should get two dozen eggs, while you, for some reason, only get fifteen. I checked it on the list. You and Sokolov each get fifteen.'

'God knows what it all means,' said Viktor. 'As you are aware, there are various different classes of scientists: very great, great, famous, talented and – finally – very old. Since the very great and the great are no longer with us, they don't need eggs. The others receive varying quantities of eggs, semolina and cabbage according to rank. But then everything gets confused by other questions. Are you active in society? Do you give seminars in Marxism? Are you close to the directors? And it comes out quite crazy. The man in charge of the Academy garage gets the same as Zelinsky – twenty-five eggs. There's a very charming young lady in Svechin's laboratory who was so upset yesterday that she burst into tears and refused to eat anything at all. Like Gandhi.'

Nadya burst out laughing. 'You know, Papa, I'm amazed you're not ashamed to eat your lamb chops with the cleaning ladies right there beside you. Grandmother could never have done that.'

'Each according to his labour,' said Lyudmila. 'That's the principle of Socialism.'

'Come on!' said Viktor. 'There's no trace of Socialism in our canteen. Anyway, I don't give a damn. But do you know what Markov told me today?' he added suddenly. 'At the Institute – and even at the Institute of Mathematics and Mechanics – people are typing out copies of my work and passing them round.'

'Like Mandelstam's poems,' said Nadya.

'Don't make fun of me,' said Viktor. 'And the final-year students are even asking for special lectures on it.'

'That's nothing,' said Nadya. 'Alka Postoeva told me, "Your papa's become a genius."'

'No,' said Viktor, 'I'm not yet a genius.'

He went off to his room. A moment later, however, he came back and said: 'I just can't get this nonsense out of my head. Two dozen eggs for Svechin! It's amazing what ways they find to humiliate people.'

To Viktor's shame, what hurt him most was being put on the same level as Sokolov. 'Yes, they should have recognized my merits by allowing me at least one extra egg. They could have given Sokolov fourteen – just as a symbolic distinction.'

He tried to laugh at himself, but he couldn't get rid of his pathetic sense of irritation. He was more upset at being given the same as Sokolov than at being given less than Svechin. With Svechin everything was clear enough: he was a member of the Party bureau. This was something Viktor could accept. But with Sokolov it was a matter of relative scientific standing. That was something he couldn't ignore. He felt quite tormented; his indignation sprang from the very depths of his

466

soul. What an absurd way for the authorities to show their appreciation of people! But what could he do? There are times when everyone behaves pathetically.

As he was getting into bed, Viktor remembered his conversation with Sokolov about Chepyzhin and said in a loud, angry voice: 'Homo lackeyus!'

'Who do you mean?' asked Lyudmila, who was already in bed, reading a book.

'Sokolov. He's a born lackey.'

Lyudmila put a finger in her book to mark the page and said, without even turning her head:

'Soon you'll be thrown out of the Institute – and all for a few fine words. You're so irritable, you're always telling everyone what to do . . . You've already quarrelled with everyone else and now you want to quarrel with Sokolov. Soon no one will even set foot in our house.'

'No, Lyuda darling, that's not it at all. How can I explain? Don't you understand? The same fear as before the war, the same fear over every word, the same helplessness . . . Chepyzhin! Lyuda, we're talking about a great man. I thought the whole Institute would be seething, but the only person who said anything was the old caretaker. And then that strange remark Postoev made to Sokolov: "What matters is that we're both Russians." Why, why on earth did he say that?'

He wanted to have a long talk with Lyudmila; he wanted to share all his thoughts with her. He was ashamed at being so preoccupied with things like rations. He had grown dull. Why? Why had he somehow become older now that they were back in Moscow? Why had these trivialities, these petty-bourgeois concerns suddenly become so important? Why had his spiritual life in Kazan been so much deeper and purer, so much more significant? Why was it that even his scientific work – and his joy in it – was now contaminated with vanity and pettiness?

'It's all very difficult, Lyuda. I'm not well. Lyuda? Why don't you say anything?'

Lyudmila was asleep. Viktor laughed quietly. It seemed amusing that one woman should lose sleep over his troubles and another fall asleep while he talked about them. He could see Marya Ivanovna's thin face before him. He repeated what he had just said to his wife.

'Don't you understand? Masha?'

'Goodness, what nonsense gets into my head!' he said to himself as he fell asleep.

What nonsense indeed.

Viktor was very clumsy with his hands. If the electric iron burnt out or the lights fused, it was nearly always Lyudmila who sorted things out. During their first years together, Lyudmila had found this helplessness of Viktor's quite endearing; now, however, she found it irritating. Once, seeing him putting an empty kettle on the burner, she snapped: 'What's the matter with you? Are your hands made of clay or something?'

While they were assembling the new apparatus in the laboratory, these words of Lyudmila's came back to him; they had upset him and made him angry.

Markov and Nozdrin now ruled the laboratory. Savostyanov was the first to sense this. At one of their meetings he announced: 'There is no God but Professor Markov, and Nozdrin is his prophet!'

Markov's reticence and arrogance had quite disappeared. Viktor was amazed at his bold thinking, delighted by the ease with which he could solve any problem as it came up. He was like a surgeon applying his scalpel to a network of blood-vessels and nerve-fibres. It was as though he were bringing some rational being to life, some creature with a quick and penetrating mind of its own. This new metallic organism, the first in the world, seemed endowed with a heart and feelings, seemed able to rejoice and suffer along with the people who had made it.

In the past Viktor had been a little amused by Markov's unshakeable conviction that his work, the apparatus he had set up, was of more importance than the works of Tolstoy or Dostoyevsky or the futile occupations of a Buddha or a Mohammed.

Tolstoy had doubted the value of his own enormous labours. Tolstoy, a genius, had been unsure whether what he did was of any use to anyone. Not so the physicists. They had no doubts. And Markov least of all.

Now, however, this assurance of Markov's no longer made Viktor laugh.

Viktor also loved to watch Nozdrin working away with a file, a screwdriver or a pair of pliers, or sorting through skeins of flex as he helped the electricians wire up the apparatus.

The floor was covered in bundles of wire and thin leaves of matt blueish lead. On a cast-iron platform in the middle of the hall stood the main part of the new apparatus, patterned with small circles and rectangles that had been punched out of the metal. There was something heart-breakingly beautiful about the apparatus, this huge slab of metal that would allow them to study the nature of matter with fantastic refinement.

In the same way, one thousand or two thousand years ago, a small group of men had gathered together on the shore of the sea to build a raft, lashing thick logs together with ropes. Their workbenches and winches had been set up on a sandy beach and pots of tar were boiling over fires. Soon they would set sail.

In the evening the builders of the raft had left; they had once again breathed in the scent of their homes, felt the warmth of their hearths and listened to the laughter and curses of their women. Sometimes they had got drawn into domestic quarrels, shouting, threatening their children and arguing with their neighbours. But in the warm darkness of night the sound of the sea had come back to them; their hearts beat faster as they dreamed of travelling into the unknown.

Sokolov usually watched the progress of the work in silence. Often Viktor caught his eye and saw the seriousness and intentness of his gaze; it seemed then that nothing had changed and that there was still something good and important between them.

He longed to talk to Sokolov. It really was very strange. All these humiliating emotions unleashed by the allocation of rations, all these petty thoughts about the exact measure of the authorities' esteem for you. But there was still room in his soul for what did not depend on the authorities, on some prize or other, on his professional recognition or lack of it.

Once again those evenings in Kazan seemed young and beautiful, almost like pre-revolutionary student gatherings. As long as Madyarov could be trusted ... How peculiar, though! Karimov suspected Madyarov, and Madyarov Karimov. They were both trustworthy! Viktor was sure of it. Unless, in the words of Heine, 'They both stank'.

Sometimes he remembered a strange conversation he had once had with Chepyzhin. Why, now he was back in Moscow, were the things he recalled so trivial and insignificant? Why did he think so often of people he had no respect for? And why were the most talented people, the most trustworthy people, unable to help him?

'It is odd,' Viktor said to Sokolov. 'People come from all the different laboratories to watch the new apparatus being assembled. But Shishakov hasn't once honoured us with his presence.'

'He's very busy.'

'Of course, of course,' Viktor agreed hurriedly.

Now that they were in Moscow, it was impossible to have a sincere, friendly conversation with Sokolov. It was as though they no longer knew each other.

Viktor no longer tried to seize every pretext for an argument with Sokolov. On the contrary, he tried to avoid arguments. But this was difficult; sometimes arguments seemed to flare up of their own accord.

Once Viktor ventured:

'I've been thinking of our talks in Kazan . . . By the way, do you know how Madyarov is? Does he write?'

Sokolov shook his head.

'I don't know. I don't know anything about Madyarov. I told you that we stopped seeing one another. I find it increasingly unpleasant to even think of those conversations. We were so depressed that we tried to lay the blame for temporary military setbacks on entirely imaginary failings in the Soviet State itself. And what we thought of as failings have now shown themselves to be strengths.'

'Like 1937, for example?'

'Viktor Pavlovich, for some time now you've been trying to turn every conversation of ours into an argument.'

Viktor wanted to say that it was the other way round, that it was Sokolov who was always irritable and that this irritation of his made him seek every opportunity for a quarrel. Instead, he just said:

'It may well be that the fault lies in my bad character, Pyotr Lavrentyevich. It gets worse every day. Lyudmila has noticed it too.'

At the same time he thought to himself: 'How alone I am. I'm alone at home and alone with my friend.'

28

Reichsführer Himmler had arranged a meeting to discuss the special measures being undertaken by the RSHA, the headquarters of the Reich Security Administration. The meeting was an important one: after it Himmler had to visit the headquarters of the Führer himself.

Obersturmbannführer Liss had been instructed by Berlin to report on the progress of the special building being constructed next to the camp administration centre. Before inspecting the building itself, Liss was to visit the chemical and engineering firms responsible for filling the Administration's orders. He then had to go to Berlin to report to SS Obersturmbannführer Eichmann, the man responsible for organizing the meeting.

Liss was delighted to be entrusted with this mission. He was tired of the atmosphere in the camp, of constant dealings with men of a coarse, primitive mentality.

As he got into his car, he thought of Mostovskoy. Day and night, the old man must be racking his brains, trying vainly to understand why on earth Liss had summoned him. He was probably waiting anxiously and impatiently for their next meeting. And all Liss had wanted was to check out a few ideas in connection with an article he hoped to write: 'The Ideology of the Enemy and Their Leaders'.

What an interesting old man! Yes, once you get inside the nucleus of the atom, the forces of attraction begin to act on you as powerfully as the centrifugal forces.

They drove out through the camp gates and Liss forgot Mostovskoy.

Early next morning he arrived at the Voss engineering works. After breakfast, Liss talked in Voss's office with the designer, Praschke, and then with the engineers in charge of production. The commercial director gave him a cost estimate for the equipment that had been ordered. He spent several hours in the din of the workshops themselves; by the end of the day he was exhausted.

The Voss works had been entrusted with an important part of the order and Liss was satisfied with their work. The directors had devoted considerable thought to the project and were keeping precisely to the specifications. The mechanical engineers had improved the construction of the conveyors, and the thermal technicians had developed a more economical system for heating the ovens.

After his long day at the factory, the evening he spent with the Voss family was particularly agreeable.

His visit to the chemical factory, on the other hand, was a disappointment: production had reached barely 40 per cent of the scheduled quantity. Liss was irritated by the countless complaints of the personnel involved: the production of these chemicals was a complex and uncertain process; the ventilation system had been damaged during an air-raid and a large number of workers had been poisoned; the supplies of infusorial earth – with which the stabilized product had to be treated – were erratic; the hermetic containers had been held up on the railways . . .

The directors, however, seemed to be fully aware of the importance of the order. The chief chemist, Doctor Kirchgarten, assured Liss that the order would be completed on time. It had even been decided to delay orders placed by the Ministry of Munitions, something unprecedented since September 1939.

Liss refused an invitation to observe the experiments being conducted in the laboratory. He did, however, look through pages of records signed by various physiologists, chemists and biochemists. He also met the young researchers responsible for the experiments: a physiologist and a biochemist (both women), a specialist in pathological anatomy, a chemist who specialized in organic compounds with a low boiling-point, and Professor Fischer himself, the toxicologist who was in charge of the group.

Liss found these people very impressive. Although they were obviously concerned that he should approve of their methods, they nevertheless admitted their doubts and made no attempt to conceal the weak points in their work.

On the third day Liss flew to the site itself, accompanied by an engineer from the Oberstein construction firm. He felt good; the trip was proving entertaining. The best part of it – the visit to Berlin with the technical directors of the construction work – was still to come.

The weather was foul – cold November rain. It was only with some difficulty that they managed to land at the central camp airfield – there was mist on the ground, and the wings had begun to freeze as they reached a low altitude. Snow had fallen at dawn; here and there, in spite of the rain, grey frozen patches still clung to the clay. Impregnated with the leaden rain, the brims of the engineers' felt hats had begun to droop.

A railway track had been laid down, leading directly off the main line to the construction site. The tour of inspection began with the depots alongside the railway line. First, under an awning, was the sorting depot. This was filled with component parts of a variety of machines, tubes and pipes of every diameter, unassembled conveyor belts, fans and ventilators, ball-mills for human bones, gas and electricity meters soon to be mounted on control panels, drums of cable, cement, tip-wagons, heaps of rails, and office furniture.

Non-commissioned SS officers guarded a special building studded with softly humming ventilators and air-extractors. Here were housed the supplies that were beginning to arrive from the chemical factory: cylinders with red taps and fifteen-kilogram canisters with red and blue labels that looked from a distance like pots of Bulgarian jam.

The last building was partly below ground level. As they emerged, Liss and his companions met Professor Stahlgang, the chief architect of the project, who had just arrived by train from Berlin. He was accompanied by von Reineke, the chief site engineer, a vast man in a yellow leather jacket.

Stahlgang was having difficulty breathing; the damp air had brought on an attack of asthma. The engineers began reproaching him for not taking enough care of himself; they all knew that there was an album of his work in Hitler's personal library.

The site itself was no different from that of any other gigantic construction of the mid-twentieth century. Round the excavations you could hear the whistles of sentries, the grinding of excavators, the creaking of cranes as they manoeuvred, and the bird-like hoots of the locomotives.

Liss and his companions then went up to a grey rectangular building without windows. The whole group of buildings – the

473

red-brick furnaces, the wide-mouthed chimneys, the control-towers, the watch-towers with their glass hoods – was centred on this faceless rectangle.

The roadmen were just finishing laying asphalt over the paths. Clouds of hot grey steam rose from beneath the rollers to mingle with the cold grey mist.

Von Reineke told Liss that recent tests had revealed that the hermetic qualities of number one complex were still inadequate. Then, forgetting his asthma, Stahlgang began outlining the architectural principles of the building; his voice was hoarse and excited.

For all its apparent simplicity and small dimensions, the ordinary industrial hydro-turbine is the point of concentration of enormous masses, forces and speeds. Within its spirals the geological power of water is transformed into work.

Number one complex was constructed according to the principle of the turbine. It was capable of transforming life itself, and all forms of energy pertaining to it, into inorganic matter. This new turbine had to overcome and harness the power of psychic, nervous, respiratory, cardiac, muscular and circulatory energy. And in this building the principle of the turbine was combined with those of the slaughter-house and the garbage incineration unit. His task had been to find a way of integrating these various factors in one architectural solution.

'Even when he's inspecting the most mundane of industrial installations,' said Stahlgang, 'our beloved Hitler, as you know, never forgets questions of architectural form.'

He lowered his voice so that only Liss could hear him.

'An excessive mysticism in the architectural realization of the camps near Warsaw – as I'm sure you know – caused our Führer grave annoyance. All these things have to be taken into account.'

The interior of the building corresponded perfectly to the epoch in which it was built, the epoch of the industry of mass and speed.

Once life had entered the supply canals, it was impossible for it to stop or turn back; its speed of flow down the concrete corridor was determined by formulae analogous to that of Stokes regarding the movement of liquid down a tube (a function of its density, specific gravity, viscosity and temperature, and of the friction involved).

Electric lights, protected by thick, almost opaque glass, were set into the ceiling. The light grew brighter as you walked down the corridor; by the polished steel door that closed off the chamber, it was cold and blinding.

Here you could sense the peculiar excitement which always grips builders and fitters when a new installation is about to be tested. Some labourers were washing down the floor with hoses. A middle-aged chemist in a white coat was measuring the pressure. Reineke gave orders for the door to be opened. As they entered the vast chamber with its low concrete ceiling, several of the engineers took off their hats. The floor consisted of heavy, movable slabs in metal frames; the joints between these frames were close and perfect. A mechanism operated from the control-room allowed the slabs to be raised on end in such a way that the contents of the chamber were evacuated into a hall beneath. Here the organic matter was examined by teams of dentists who extracted any precious metals used in dental work. Next, a conveyor-belt leading to the crematoria themselves was set in motion; there the organic matter, already without thought or feeling, underwent a further process of decomposition under the action of thermal energy and was transformed into phosphate fertilizer, lime, cinders, ammoniac, and sulphurous and carbonic acid gas.

A liaison officer came up to Liss and handed him a telegram. They all watched Liss's face darken as he read that Obersturmbannführer Eichmann was to meet him not in Berlin, but at the site that very evening: he had already set out by car down the Munich autobahn.

So much for Liss's trip to Berlin. He had counted on spending the night at his country house, together with his sick wife who missed him very badly. He'd have sat for an hour or two in his armchair, in warmth and comfort, wearing his fur slippers, and forgotten about the harsh times he lived in. It would have been very pleasant to go to bed in peace, listening to the distant rumble of the anti-aircraft guns in Berlin.

And during the quiet period before the air-raids, before he left for the country after the meeting on Prinz-Alberstrasse, he had meant to visit a young student at the Institute of Philosophy. She was the only person who understood how difficult his life was, what confusion reigned in his soul. At the bottom of his briefcase, ready for this meeting, lay a bottle of cognac and a box of chocolates. Well, so much for that.

The engineers, chemists and architects all looked at him, wondering what anxieties could be troubling a man of Liss's importance.

There were moments when they felt the chamber might already have broken free of its creators, might already be about to live its own concrete life, feeling its own concrete hunger, secreting toxins, masticating with its steel jaws, beginning the long process of digestion.

Stahlgang winked at von Reineke and whispered: 'Liss has probably only just been told that the Gruppenführer wishes to hear his report here and not in Berlin. I heard this morning. And he'd hoped to visit his family – and probably some pretty young lady as well!'

29

Liss met Eichmann that night.

Eichmann was thirty-five years old. His gloves, cap and boots – embodiments of the poetry, arrogance and superiority of the German armed forces – were similar to those worn by Reichsführer Himmler himself.

Liss had known the Eichmanns since before the war; they came from the same town. During his years at Berlin University, working at the same time first on a newspaper and then on a philosophical journal, Liss had made occasional visits to his home town and had heard what had become of his contemporaries at school. Some had been carried up on the wave of success, only to be cast down when Fame and Fortune smiled unexpectedly on others. The life of the young Eichmann, however, had been monotonously drab and uniform. The guns of Verdun, the seemingly imminent victory, the final defeat and ensuing inflation, the political struggles in the Reichstag, the whirl of leftist and extreme-leftist movements in painting, theatre and music, the dizzying changes of fashion – all these had left him untouched.

He worked as an agent for a provincial firm. He behaved with moderate rudeness and moderate attentiveness towards his family and towards people in general. He was cut off from all avenues of advancement by a noisy, gesticulating, hostile crowd. Wherever he went, he saw himself pushed aside by brisk, lively men with dark, shining eyes, men of experience and ability who looked at him with condescending smiles.

After leaving school, he had found it impossible to get work in Berlin. The owners and directors of the different firms and offices informed him that the post had already, unfortunately, been filled – and then Eichmann would hear on the grapevine that the job had been given to some putrid little man of obscure nationality, a Pole perhaps, or an Italian. He had wanted to enter Berlin University, but the same discrimination had prevented his application from being accepted. He had felt the examiners lose interest the moment they set eyes on his full face, his blond crew-cut, his short straight nose, his light-coloured eyes. They seemed interested only in people with long faces, dark eyes, narrow shoulders and hunched backs – in degenerates. Nor had he been alone in being rejected by the capital; it had been the fate of many.

The particular breed that held sway in Berlin could be met with at every level of society, but they were to be found most plentifully among the cosmopolitan intelligentsia, now bereft of any national characteristics and incapable of distinguishing between a German and an Italian, a German and a Pole. They were a strange breed, a strange race. Whoever tried to compete with them in the realms of culture and the intellect was crushed with mocking indifference. The worst thing of all was the feeling one got of their intellectual power – a lively, unaggressive power that showed in their strange tastes, in the way they respected fashion while seeming indifferent or careless towards it, in the way they loved animals yet followed a totally urban life-style, in their gift for abstract speculation that was somehow combined with a passion for everything crude and primitive in both life and art . . .

It was these men who were responsible for Germany's advances in dye chemistry and the synthesis of nitrogen, who researched the properties of gamma rays and refined the production process of high-quality steel. It was to see them that foreign scientists, artists, philosophers and engineers visited Germany. And yet these were the men who were the least German of all. Their home was anywhere in the world. Their friendships were not with Germans. And their German origins were exceedingly doubtful.

So how could a mere office-worker in a provincial firm hope to make a better life for himself? He could count himself lucky not to be going hungry . . .

And now here he was, leaving his office after locking away papers whose existence was known only to three other men in the world – Hitler, Himmler and Kaltenbrunner. A limousine was waiting for him outside. The sentries saluted, the orderly flung open the door and Obersturmbannführer Eichmann was on his way. Accelerating quickly, the powerful Gestapo limousine made its way through the streets of Berlin, passing policemen who saluted respectfully as they hurriedly changed the lights to green, and sped onto the autobahn. And then rain, mist, road-signs and the long smooth curves of the highway . . .

Smolevichi is full of quiet little houses with gardens; grass grows on the pavements. In the slums of Berdichev there are dirty hens running around in the dust, their yellowish legs marked with red and violet ink. In Kiev – on Vassilievskaya Avenue and in the Podol – there are tall buildings with dirty windows, staircases whose steps have been worn down by millions of children's shoes and old men's slippers.

In yards all over Odessa stand tall plane trees with peeling bark. Brightly-coloured clothes and linen are drying on the line. Pans of cherry jam are steaming on cookers. New-born babies with swarthy skin – skin that has yet to see the sun – are screaming in cradles.

On the six floors of a gaunt, narrow-shouldered building in Warsaw live seamstresses, book-binders, private tutors, cabaret-singers, students and watchmakers . . .

In Stalindorf people light fires in their huts in the evening. The wind blows from Perekop, smelling of salt and warm dust. Cows shake their heavy heads and moo . . .

In Budapest and Fastov, in Vienna, Melitopol and Amsterdam, in detached houses with sparkling windows, in hovels swathed in factory smoke, lived people belonging to the Jewish nation.

The barbed wire of the camps, the clay of the anti-tank ditches and the walls of the gas ovens brought together millions of people of different ages, professions and languages, people with different material concerns and different spiritual beliefs. All of them – fanatical believers and fanatical atheists, workers and scroungers, doctors and tradesmen, sages and idiots, thieves, contemplatives, saints and idealists – were to be exterminated.

The Gestapo limousine sped down the autumn autobahn.

30

Eichmann marched into the office, firing off questions before he'd even sat down.

'I've got very little time. I have to be in Warsaw by tomorrow at the latest.'

He had already spoken to the camp-commandant and the chief engineer.

'How are the factories getting on? What are your impressions of Voss? Do you think the chemists are up to it?' he asked rapidly.

His large white fingers – with correspondingly large pink nails – turned over the papers on the desk. From time to time he made brief notes with a fountain-pen. Liss had the feeling that to him this project was no different from any other – though it aroused a secret shiver of horror in even the most hardened hearts.

Liss had drunk a lot over these last few days. He was constantly short of breath and he could feel his heart pounding during the night. In spite of this, he felt that alcohol was less damaging to his health than the constant nervous tension that was the alternative.

He dreamed of returning to his research on important figures who had shown hostility towards National Socialism; of studying questions that, for all their complexity and cruelty, could at least be solved without the shedding of blood. Then he would smoke only two or three cigarettes a day and he would stop drinking. Not long ago, he had played a game of political chess with an old Russian Bolshevik; he had gone back home afterwards, fallen asleep without having to take any tablets and not woken up until nine in the morning.

A small surprise had been laid on for Eichmann and Liss during their tour of inspection. In the middle of the gas chamber, the engineers had laid a small table with hors-d'oeuvres and wine. Reineke invited Eichmann and Liss to sit down.

Eichmann laughed at this charming idea and said: 'With the greatest of pleasure.'

He gave his cap to his bodyguard and sat down. His large face suddenly took on a look of kindly concentration, the same look that appears on the faces of millions of men as they sit down to a good meal.

Reineke poured out the wine and they all reached for their glasses, waiting for Eichmann to propose a toast.

The tension in this concrete silence, in these full glasses, was so extreme that Liss felt his heart was about to burst. What he wanted was some ringing toast to clear the atmosphere, a toast to the glory of the German ideal. Instead, the tension grew stronger – Eichmann was chewing a sandwich.

'Well, gentlemen?' said Eichmann. 'I call that excellent ham!'

'We're waiting for the master of ceremonies to propose a toast,' said Liss.

Eichmann raised his glass.

'To the continued success of our work! Yes, that certainly deserves a toast!'

Eichmann was the only man to eat well and drink very little.

The following morning, wearing only a pair of underpants, Eichmann did his exercises in front of an open window. Through the mist he could make out the orderly rows of barrack-huts and hear the whistles of steam-engines.

Liss wasn't usually envious of Eichmann. He himself enjoyed an important position without excessive responsibilities. He was considered one of the most intelligent men in the Gestapo. Himmler himself liked to chat with him.

Important dignitaries usually avoided pulling their rank with him. He was used to being treated with respect – and not only within the Gestapo. The presence of the Gestapo could be felt everywhere – in universities, in the signature of the director of a children's nursing-home, in auditions for young opera-singers, in the jury's choice of pictures for the spring exhibition, in the list of candidates for elections to the Reichstag. It was the axis around which life turned. It was thanks to the Gestapo that the Party was always right, that its philosophy triumphed over any other philosophy, its logic – or lack of logic – over any other logic. Yes, this was the magic wand. If it were dropped, a great orator would be transformed into a mere windbag, a renowned scientist would be exposed as a common plagiarist. The magic wand must never be dropped.

As he looked at Eichmann, Liss, for the first time in his life, felt a twinge of envy.

A few minutes before his departure, Eichmann said thoughtfully: 'We're from the same town, Liss.'

They started to reel off the names of familiar streets, restaurants and cinemas.

'There are, of course, places I never visited,' said Eichmann, naming a club that wouldn't have admitted the son of an artisan.

Liss changed the subject. 'Can you give me some idea – just a rough estimate – of the number of Jews we're talking about?'

He knew this was the million-dollar question, a question that perhaps only three men in the world, other than Himmler and the Führer, could answer. But it was the right moment – after Eichmann's reminiscences about his difficult youth during the period of democracy and cosmopolitanism – for Liss to admit his ignorance, to ask about what he didn't know.

Eichmann answered his question.

'*What?*' Liss gasped in astonishment. 'Millions?'

Eichmann shrugged his shoulders.

They remained silent for some time.

'I very much regret that we didn't meet during our years as students,' said Liss, 'during our years of apprenticeship – as Goethe put it.'

'You needn't. I studied out in the provinces,' said Eichmann, 'not in Berlin.'

After a pause he went on: 'It's the first time, my friend, that I've pronounced that figure out loud. If we include Berchtesgaden, the Reichskanzler and the office of our Führer, it may have been pronounced seven or eight times.'

'I understand,' said Liss. 'It won't be printed in tomorrow's newspapers.'

'That's precisely what I mean,' said Eichmann.

He looked at Liss mockingly. Liss suddenly had a disturbing feeling he was talking to someone more intelligent than himself.

'Apart from the fact that the quiet little town where we were born is so full of greenery,' Eichmann continued, 'I had another reason for naming that figure. I would like it to unite us in our future collaboration.'

'Thank you,' said Liss. 'It's a very serious matter. I need to think about it.'

'Of course. This proposal doesn't come only from me,' said Eichmann, pointing towards the ceiling. 'If you join me in this task and Hitler loses, then we'll hang for it together.'

'A charming prospect!' said Liss. 'I need to give it some thought.'

'Just imagine! In two years' time, we'll be sitting at a comfortable table in this same office and saying: "In twenty months we've solved a problem that humanity failed to solve in the course of twenty centuries."'

They said their farewells. Liss watched the limousine disappear.

He had some ideas of his own about personal relations within the State. Life in a National Socialist State couldn't just be allowed to develop freely; every step had to be directed. And to control and organize factories and armies, reading circles, people's summer holidays, their maternal feelings, how they breathe and sing – to control all this you need leaders. Life no longer has the right to grow freely like grass, to rise and fall like the sea. In Liss's view, there were four main categories of leaders.

The first were the simple, undivided natures, usually people without particular intelligence or finesse. These people were full of slogans and formulae from newspapers and magazines, of quotations from Hitler's speeches, Goebbels's articles and the books of Franck and Rosenberg. Without solid ground under their feet, they were lost. They seldom reflected on the connections between different phenomena and they were easily moved to intolerance and cruelty. They took everything seriously: philosophy, National Socialist science and its obscure revelations, the new music, the achievements of the new theatre, the campaign for the elections to the Reichstag. Like schoolchildren, they got together in little groups to mug up *Mein Kampf* and to make précis of pamphlets and articles. They usually lived in relatively modest circumstances, sometimes experiencing actual need; they were more ready than the other categories to volunteer for posts that would take them away from their families. To begin with, Liss had thought that Eichmann belonged to this category.

The second category were the intelligent cynics, the people who knew of the existence of the magic wand. In the company of friends they trusted, they were ready to laugh at most things – the ignorance of newly appointed lecturers and professors, the stupidity and the lax morals of Leiters and Gauleiters. The only things they never laughed at were grand ideals and the Führer himself. These men usually drank a lot and lived more expansively. They were to be met with most frequently on the higher rungs of the Party hierarchy; the lower rungs were usually occupied by men of the first category.

The men of the third category held sway at the very top of the hierarchy. There was only room for nine or ten of them, and they admitted perhaps another fifteen or twenty to their gatherings. Here were no dogmas. Here everything could be discussed freely. Here were no ideals, nothing but serenity, mathematics and the pitilessness of these great masters.

It sometimes seemed that all the activities of the country were centred around them, around their well-being.

Liss had also noticed that the appearance of more limited minds in the higher echelons always heralded some sinister turn of events. The controllers of the social mechanism elevated the dogmatists only in order to entrust them with especially bloody tasks. These simpletons became temporarily intoxicated with power, but on the completion of their tasks they usually disappeared; sometimes they shared the fate of their victims. The serene masters then remained in control undisturbed.

The simpletons, the men of the first category, were endowed with one exceptionally valuable quality: they came from the people. Not only were they able to cite the classics of National Socialism, but they did so in the language of the people. At workers' meetings, they were able to make people laugh; their coarseness made them seem like workers or peasants themselves.

The fourth category were the executives, people who were indifferent to dogma, ideas and philosophy and equally lacking in analytic ability. National Socialism paid them and they served it. Their only real passion was for dinner-services, suits, country houses, jewels, furniture, cars and refrigerators. They were less fond of money as they never fully believed in its solidity.

Liss was drawn to the true leaders, the men of the third category. He dreamed of their company and their intimacy. It was in that kingdom of elegant logic, of irony and intelligence, that he felt most fully himself.

But at some terrifying height, above even these leaders, above the stratosphere, was yet another world, the obscure, incomprehensible and terrifyingly alogical world of Adolf Hitler himself.

What Liss found most terrifying about Adolf Hitler was that he seemed to be made up of an inconceivable fusion of opposites. He was the master of masters, he was the great mechanic, his mathematical cruelty was more refined than that of all his closest lieutenants taken together. And at the same time, he was possessed by a dogmatic frenzy, a blindly fanatical faith, a bullish illogicality that Liss had only met with at the very lowest, almost subterranean levels of the Party. The high priest, the creator of the magic wand, was also one of the faithful, a mindless, frenzied follower.

Watching Eichmann's car disappear, Liss felt at once afraid of him and attracted to him. Until now, such a confusion of feelings had only been evoked in him by the Führer himself.

31

Anti-Semitism can take many forms – from a mocking, contemptuous ill-will to murderous pogroms.

Anti-Semitism can be met with in the market and in the Presidium of the Academy of Sciences, in the soul of an old man and in the games children play in the yard. Anti-Semitism has been as strong in the age of atomic reactors and computers as in the age of oil-lamps, sailing-boats and spinning-wheels.

Anti-Semitism is always a means rather than an end; it is a measure of the contradictions yet to be resolved. It is a mirror for the failings of individuals, social structures and State systems. Tell me what you accuse the Jews of – I'll tell you what you're guilty of.

Even Oleinichuk, the peasant fighter for freedom who was imprisoned in Schlüsselburg, somehow expressed his hatred for serfdom as a hatred for Poles and Yids. Even a genius like Dostoyevsky saw a Jewish usurer where he should have seen the pitiless eyes of a Russian serf-owner, industrialist or contractor. And in accusing the Jews of racism, a desire for world domination and a cosmopolitan indifference towards the German fatherland, National Socialism was merely describing its own features.

Anti-Semitism is also an expression of a lack of talent, an inability to win a contest on equal terms – in science or in commerce, in craftsmanship or in painting. States look to the imaginary intrigues of World Jewry for explanations of their own failure.

At the same time anti-Semitism is an expression of the lack of consciousness of the masses, of their inability to understand the true reasons for their sufferings. Ignorant people blame the Jews for their troubles when they should blame the social structure or the State itself. Anti-Semitism is also, of course, a measure of the religious prejudices smouldering in the lower levels of a society.

An aversion for the physical appearance of a Jew, for his way of speaking and eating, is certainly not a genuine cause of anti-Semitism. The same man who speaks with disgust of a Jew's curly hair or of the way he waves his arms about, will gaze admiringly at the black curly hair of children in paintings by Murillo, will be quite undisturbed by the gesticulating and the guttural speech of Armenians, and will look without aversion at the thick lips of a Negro.

Anti-Semitism has a place to itself in the history of the persecution of national minorities. Anti-Semitism is a unique phenomenon – just as the history of the Jews is unique.

Just as a man's shadow can give an idea of his stature, so anti-Semitism can give an idea of the history and destiny of the Jews. One trait that distinguishes the Jews from other national minorities is that their history has been bound up with a large number of religious and political issues of world importance. Another distinguishing trait is the extraordinary degree to which they are dispersed throughout both Eastern and Western hemispheres; there are Jews in nearly every country of the world.

It was during the dawn of capitalism that Jewish tradesmen and usurers made their first appearance. During the industrial revolution many Jews made names for themselves in the realms of industry and mechanics. During the atomic age many talented Jews have been nuclear physicists. And during the epoch of revolutionary struggle, many of the most important revolutionary leaders were Jews. Rather than relegating themselves to the periphery, Jews have always chosen to play a role at the centre of a society's industrial and ideological development. This constitutes a third distinguishing trait of Jewish minorities.

Part of the Jewish minority becomes assimilated into the indigenous population, but the general mass retain their peculiar religion, language and way of life. Anti-Semitism always accuses the assimilated Jews of secret nationalist and religious aspirations; at the same time, it holds the general mass of non-assimilated Jews – the manual labourers and artisans – responsible for the actions of their fellows who become revolutionary leaders, captains of industry, atomic physicists and important administrators. This is a fourth distinguishing trait.

Each of these traits taken singly may be characteristic of some other minority, but it is only the Jews who are characterized by all of them.

Anti-Semitism, as one might expect, reflects these traits. It too has always been bound up with the most important questions of world politics, economics, ideology and religion. This is its most sinister characteristic: the flame of its bonfires has lit the most terrible periods of history.

When the Renaissance broke in upon the Catholic Middle Ages, the forces of darkness lit the bonfires of the Inquisition. These flames, however, not only expressed the power of evil, they also lit up the spectacle of its destruction.

In the twentieth century, an ill-fated nationalist regime lit the bonfires of Auschwitz, the gas ovens of Lyublinsk and Treblinka. These flames not only lit up Fascism's brief triumph, but also foretold its doom. Historical epochs, unsuccessful and reactionary governments, and individuals hoping to better their lot all turn to anti-Semitism as a last resort, in an attempt to escape an inevitable doom.

In the course of two millennia, have there ever been occasions when the forces of freedom and humanitarianism made use of anti-Semitism as a tool in their struggles? Possibly, but I do not know of them.

There are also different levels of anti-Semitism. Firstly, there is a relatively harmless everyday anti-Semitism. This merely bears witness to the existence of failures and envious fools.

Secondly, there is social anti-Semitism. This can only arise in democratic countries. Its manifestations are in those sections of the press that represent different reactionary groups, in the activities of these groups – for example, boycotts of Jewish labour and Jewish goods – and in their ideology and religion.

Thirdly, in totalitarian countries, where society as such no longer exists, there can arise State anti-Semitism. This is a sign that the State is looking for the support of fools, reactionaries and failures, that it is seeking to capitalize on the ignorance of the superstitious and the anger of the hungry.

The first stage of State anti-Semitism is discrimination: the State limits the areas in which Jews can live, the choice of professions open to them, their right to occupy important positions, their access to higher education, and so on.

The second stage is wholesale destruction. At a time when the forces of reaction enter into a fatal struggle against the forces of freedom, then anti-Semitism becomes an ideology of Party and State – as happened with Fascism.

32

The newly-formed units moved up to the front line under cover of darkness.

One concentration of forces was along the River Don, to the north-west of Stalingrad. The trains unloaded in the steppe itself, along a newly constructed railway-line.

Just before dawn, these iron rivers suddenly congealed; all you could see then was a light cloud of dust over the steppe. Gun-barrels were camouflaged with dry grass and handfuls of straw so that they blended into the autumn steppe; nothing in the world could have seemed quieter or more peaceful. Aircraft lay on the ground like dried insects, their wings spread, draped in camouflage-netting.

Every day the network of figures grew more complex; every day the diamonds, circles and triangles spread more thickly over the secret map. The armies of the newly-formed South-Western Front – to the north-west of Stalingrad itself – were taking up their positions in readiness to advance.

Meanwhile, on the left bank of the Volga, avoiding the smoke and thunder of Stalingrad, tank corps and artillery divisions were making their way through the empty steppe towards quiet creeks and backwaters. They then crossed the Volga and took up position in the Kalmyk steppe, in the salt-flats between the lakes. These forces were being concentrated on the Germans' right flank. The Soviet High Command was planning the encirclement of Paulus's army.

During dark nights, under the autumn clouds and stars, Novikov's tank corps was transferred to the right bank, south of Stalingrad, by barge, steamer and ferry . . .

Thousands of people saw the names of famous Russian generals – Kutuzov, Suvorov, Alexander Nevsky – painted in white on the armour-plating of the tanks. And millions of people had seen the heavy guns, the mortars and the columns of lend-lease Fords and Dodges. Nevertheless, this vast build-up of forces in readiness for the offensive remained secret.

How was this possible? The Germans knew about these troop movements. It would have been no more possible to hide them than to hide the wind from a man walking through the steppe.

Any German lieutenant, looking at a map with approximate positions for the main concentrations of Russian forces, could have guessed the most important of all Soviet military secrets, a secret known only to Stalin, Zhukov and Vasilevsky. How was it then that the Germans were taken by surprise, lieutenants and field marshals alike?

Stalingrad itself had continued to hold out. For all the vast forces involved, the German attacks had still not led to a decisive victory. Some of the Russian regiments now only numbered a few dozen soldiers; it was these few men, bearing all the weight of the terrible fighting, who confused the calculations of the Germans.

The Germans were simply unable to believe that all their attacks were being borne by a handful of men. They thought the Soviet reserves were being brought up in order to reinforce the defence. The true strategists of the Soviet offensive were the soldiers with their backs to the Volga who fought off Paulus's divisions.

The remorseless cunning of History, however, lay still more deeply hidden. Freedom engendered the Russian victory. Freedom was the apparent aim of the war. But the sly fingers of History changed this: freedom became simply a way of waging the war, a means to an end.

33

A marvellous but somehow exhausting silence lay over the Kalmyk steppe. Did the men hurrying, that very morning, along Unter den Linden know what was about to happen? Did they know that Russia had now turned her face towards the West? That she was about to strike, about to advance?

'Don't forget the coats,' Novikov called out from the porch to Kharitonov, his driver. 'Mine and the commissar's. We won't be back till late.'

Getmanov and Nyeudobnov followed him out.

'Mikhail Petrovich,' said Novikov, 'if anything happens, phone Karpov. Or if it's after three o'clock, get hold of Byelov and Makarov.'

'What do you think could happen here?' asked Nyeudobnov.

'Who knows? Maybe a visit from one of the brass hats.'

Two small points appeared out of the sun and swooped down over the village. The whine of engines grew louder; the still silence of the steppe was shattered.

Kharitonov leapt out of the jeep and ran for shelter behind the wall of a barn.

'Fool!' shouted Getmanov. 'They're our own planes.'

At that very moment, one plane released a bomb and the other let out a burst of machine-gun fire. The air howled, there was the sound of shattering glass, a woman let out a piercing scream, a child began to cry, and clods of earth rained down on the ground.

Novikov ducked as he heard the bomb fall. For a moment everything was drowned in dust and smoke; all he could see was Getmanov standing beside him. Then Nyeudobnov emerged, standing very upright, shoulders straight and head erect. It was as though he were carved out of wood.

A little pale, but animated and full of excitement, Getmanov brushed the dust off his trousers. With an endearing boastfulness he said: 'That's a mercy. My trousers are still dry. And as for our general, he didn't even bat an eyelid.'

Getmanov and Nyeudobnov went off to look at the bomb crater and to see how far the earth had been thrown. They examined a piece of smashed fencing and were surprised to see that the windows of the more distant houses had been broken, but not those of the nearer ones.

Novikov watched the two men with curiosity. It was as though they were surprised that the bomb should have been made in the factory, carried into the sky and dropped to earth with only one aim – that of killing the fathers of the little Getmanovs and Nyeudobnovs. It was as though they were thinking: 'So that's what people get up to during a war.'

Getmanov was still talking about the raid when they set off. Then he cut himself short and said: 'You must find it amusing to listen to me, Pyotr Pavlovich. You've already seen thousands of them, but that was my first time.'

Then another thought struck him.

'Listen, Pyotr Pavlovich. This Krymov fellow, tell me, was he ever taken prisoner?'

'Krymov? Why do you ask?'

'It's just that I heard an interesting conversation about him at Front Headquarters.'

'His unit was once encircled, but no, I don't think he was ever taken prisoner. What was this conversation anyway?'

As though he hadn't heard, Getmanov tapped Kharitonov on the shoulder and said: 'That road there. It goes straight to the HQ of 1st Brigade – and we avoid the ravine. See if I haven't learnt to orient myself!'

Novikov was already used to the way Getmanov could never follow one train of thought. He would begin telling a story, suddenly ask a question, carry on with the story, then interrupt himself with another question. His thoughts appeared to move in zigzags, with no rhyme or reason; Novikov knew, however, that this was by no means the case.

Getmanov often talked about his wife and children. He carried a thick packet of family photographs around with him and he had twice sent men off to Ufa with parcels of food. But as soon as he'd arrived he'd begun an affair – and quite a serious one at that – with Tamara

Pavlovna, a swarthy, bad-tempered doctor from the first-aid post. One morning Vershkov had announced in a tragic voice: 'Comrade Colonel, the doctor's spent the night with the commissar. He didn't let her go until dawn.'

'That's none of your business, Vershkov,' Novikov had answered. 'And I'd rather you stopped bringing me sweets on the sly.'

Getmanov made no secret of this affair. There in the jeep, he nudged Novikov and whispered: 'Pyotr Pavlovich, I know a lad who's fallen in love with our doctor.'

'A commissar, I believe,' said Novikov, glancing at the driver.

'Well, Bolsheviks aren't monks,' Getmanov explained in a whisper. 'What could the poor fool do? He's fallen in love.'

They were silent for a few minutes. Then, in a quite different tone of voice, Getmanov said: 'And as for you, Pyotr Pavlovich, you're certainly not getting any thinner. You must be in your element here. The same as I'm in my element working for the Party. That's what I was made for. I arrived at my *obkom* at the most difficult moment. Anyone else would have had a heart attack. The plan for grain deliveries was in tatters. Stalin himself spoke to me twice on the telephone . . . And I just put on weight – for all the world as though I were on holiday.'

'God only knows what I was made for,' said Novikov. 'Maybe I really was made for war.'

He laughed.

'One thing I've noticed – whenever anything interesting happens, I immediately think: "I must remember to tell Yevgenia Nikolaevna." After that raid I thought: "I mustn't forget to tell her – Getmanov and Nyeudobnov have seen their first bomb."'

'So you're drawing up political reports, are you?' asked Getmanov.

'That's right.'

'I can understand,' said Getmanov. 'There's no one closer than one's wife.'

They reached Brigade HQ and got out of the jeep.

Novikov's head was always full of names of people and places, of problems, difficulties, questions to be resolved and questions that had just been resolved, orders to be given and orders to be countermanded.

Sometimes he would wake up at night and begin wondering anxiously whether or not it was right to open fire at distances exceeding the range of the sighting gear. Was it really worth firing while on the move? And would his officers be able to take stock of a changing situation quickly and accurately? Would they be able to take decisions independently, on the spot?

Then he imagined his tanks breaking through the German and Rumanian defences. Column after column, they entered the breach and set off in pursuit of the enemy. In liaison with ground-support aircraft, self-propelled guns and motorized infantry they drove further and further towards the West, seizing fords and bridges, avoiding minefields, crushing pockets of resistance . . . Out of breath with joy and excitement, Novikov would sit up in bed, his bare feet touching the floor.

He never felt any desire to tell Getmanov about such moments. Here in the steppe, he felt even more irritated with him and Nyeudob-nov than he had in the Urals. 'They've arrived just in time for dessert,' he would sometimes say to himself.

He himself was no longer the man he had been in 1941. He drank more, swore a lot and had become quick-tempered. Once he had almost hit the officer responsible for fuel supplies. People were afraid of him – and he knew it.

'I don't know if I really am made for war,' he said to Getmanov. 'The best thing in the world would be to live in a hut in the forest together with the woman you love. You'd go hunting during the day and come back home in the evening. She'd cook you a meal and then you'd go to bed. War's no nourishment for a man.'

Getmanov, his head cocked, watched him attentively.

Colonel Karpov, the commander of the 1st Brigade, was a man with puffy cheeks, red hair and piercingly blue eyes. He met Novikov and Getmanov by the field wireless-set.

He had seen service on the North-Western Front. There he had more than once had to dig in his tanks and use them simply as guns.

He accompanied Novikov and Getmanov on their inspection of the 1st Brigade. His movements were as calm and unhurried as if he were himself the senior officer.

From his build, you would have expected him to be a good-natured man who drank too much beer and enjoyed a good meal. In fact he was cold, taciturn, suspicious and petty-minded. He was a far from generous host and had a reputation for miserliness.

Getmanov praised the conscientiousness with which bunkers, artillery emplacements and tank shelters had been constructed. He had indeed taken everything into consideration: types of terrain over which an enemy attack would be practicable, the possibility of a flanking movement . . . All he had forgotten was that he would now be required to lead his brigade into the attack, to break through the enemy front, to take up the pursuit.

Novikov was annoyed by Getmanov's repeated nods and words of approval. Meanwhile Karpov, as though intentionally adding fuel to the flames, was saying:

'Comrade Colonel, let me tell you how things were in Odessa. Well, we were quite splendidly entrenched. We counter-attacked in the evening and dealt the Rumanians a good blow. And then that night the army commander had us all embark on board ship, right down to the last man. Around nine o'clock in the morning the Rumanians finally came to and stormed the empty trenches. By then we were already on the Black Sea.'

'Well, I just hope you don't hang around in front of empty Rumanian trenches,' said Novikov.

Would Karpov be capable of pressing on ahead, day and night, leaving pockets of enemy resistance behind him? Would he be able to forge on, exposing his head, his neck, his flanks? Would he be seized by the fury of pursuit? No, no, that was not his nature.

Everything was still parched by the heat of summer; it was strange to find the air so cool. The soldiers were all busy with everyday concerns: one, sitting on top of his tank, was shaving in front of a mirror he had propped against the turret; another was cleaning his rifle; another was writing a letter; there was a group playing dominoes on a tarpaulin they had spread out; another, larger, group had gathered, yawning, around the nurse. The sky was vast and the earth was vast; this everyday picture was full of the sadness of early evening.

Suddenly a battalion commander rushed up. Putting his tunic straight as he ran, he shouted: 'Battalion! Attention!'

'At ease, at ease,' said Novikov.

Getmanov walked about among the men, saying a few words here and there. They all laughed, their faces brightening as they exchanged glances. He asked whether they were missing the girls from the Urals, whether they'd wasted a lot of paper in writing letters, whether their copies of *Red Star* came regularly. Then he turned on the quarter-master.

'What did the soldiers have to eat today? And yesterday? And the day before yesterday? Is that what you've had to eat for the last three days? Soup made from green tomatoes and barley?

'Let me have a word with the cook!' he demanded to the accompaniment of general laughter. 'I'd like to know what the quartermaster had to eat today.'

Through these questions about the everyday life of the soldiers and their material welfare, Getmanov seemed almost to be reproaching their commanding officers. It was as though he were saying: 'Why do you go on and on all the time about the ordnance? What about the men themselves?'

The quartermaster himself, a thin man with the red hands of a washerwoman, just stood there in his old, dusty boots. Every now and then he cleared his throat nervously.

Novikov felt sorry for him. 'Comrade Commissar,' he said, 'shall we visit Byelov's together?'

Getmanov had always, with reason, been considered a man of the masses, a born leader. He only had to open his mouth for people to laugh; his vivid, direct way of talking, his sometimes vulgar language quickly bridged the distance between the secretary of an *obkom* and a worker in overalls.

He always began by asking about material matters. Did they get their wages on time? Was the shop in the factory or village well supplied, or were some items always unobtainable? Was the workers' hostel well-heated? How was the food from the field-kitchen?

He had a particular gift for talking to middle-aged women in factories and collective farms. They liked the way he showed himself to be a true servant of the people, the way he was ready to attack managers, food suppliers, wardens of hostels, managers of tractor-stations and factories, if they failed to take into account the interests of the working man. He was the son of a peasant, he had worked in a factory himself – and the workers could sense this.

In his office at the *obkom*, however, he was a different man. There his sole concern was his responsibility towards the State. There his only preoccupations were the preoccupations of Moscow. The factory managers and secretaries of rural *raykoms* knew this very well.

'You realize that you're disrupting the State plan, do you? Do you want to surrender your Party membership card right now? Are you aware that the Party has placed its trust in you? Need I say more?'

There were no jokes or pleasantries in his office, no talk of providing boiling water in hostels or more greenery in the factories. Instead, people gave their approval to tight production schedules, agreed that the construction of new housing should be postponed, that the workers would have to increase their daily output and that they would all have to tighten their belts, slash costs and increase retail prices.

It was during the meetings held in his office that Getmanov's power could be felt most tangibly. Other people seemed to come to these meetings not to express ideas and demands of their own, but simply to help Getmanov. It was as though the whole course of these meetings had been determined in advance by Getmanov's will and intelligence.

He spoke quietly and unhurriedly, confident of his listeners' agreement.

'Let's hear about your region then. First, comrades, we'll have a word from the agronomist. And we'd like to hear your point of view, Pyotr Mikhailovich. I think Lazko has something to tell us – he's had certain problems in that area. Yes, Rodionov, I know you've got something on the tip of your tongue, but in my opinion the matter's quite clear. It's time we began to sum up, I don't think there can be any objections. Perhaps I can call on you, Rodionov, to read out this draft resolution.' And Rodionov – who had intended to express certain doubts or even disagreements – would conscientiously read out the resolution, glancing now and again at the chairman to see if he was reading it clearly enough. 'Well, comrades, it seems we're all in favour.'

What was most extraordinary of all was that Getmanov always seemed to be absolutely sincere. He was fully himself when he was commiserating with old women in a village Soviet or expressing regret at the cramped conditions in a workers' hostel; he was equally himself when he insisted to the secretary of a *raykom* on 100 per cent fulfilment of the plan, when he deprived workers on a collective farm of their entitlement to a few last grains of corn, when he decreased wages, increased retail prices and demanded lower overheads.

All this was far from easy to understand. But is life ever easy to understand?

As they made their way back to the jeep, Getmanov said jokingly to Karpov: 'We'll have to have lunch at Byelov's. It's hardly worth waiting for a meal from you and your quartermaster.'

'Comrade Commissar,' replied Karpov, 'the quartermaster still hasn't received anything from the HQ stores. And he hardly eats anything at all himself – he's got a bad stomach.'

'A bad stomach. Ay! Poor man!' yawned Getmanov as he signed to the driver to start.

Byelov's brigade was positioned some distance to the west of Karpov's. He was a thin man with a large nose and the crooked legs of a cavalryman. He spoke rapidly and he had a sharp, intelligent mind. Novikov liked him, and he seemed the ideal man to effect a sudden breakthrough and a swift pursuit. He was thought highly of, despite his relative lack of experience. Last December, near Moscow, he had led a raid on the enemy rear.

Now, though, Novikov was anxiously conscious only of Byelov's failings: he was forgetful and frivolous, he drank like a fish, he was too much of a womanizer, and he was disliked by his subordinates. He had prepared no defensive positions whatsoever. He seemed quite uninterested in logistics – with the exception of fuel and ammunition supplies. He hadn't given enough thought to the matter of the evacuation of damaged tanks from the battlefield and their subsequent repair.

'We're not in the Urals any longer, comrade Byelov,' said Novikov.

'Yes,' said Getmanov. 'We're encamped on the steppes, like gypsies.'

'I've taken measures against attack from the air,' Byelov pointed out. 'But at this distance from the front line, a ground attack seems hardly probable. 'Anyway, comrade Colonel,' he announced with a loud sigh, 'what my soul thirsts for is an offensive.'

'Very good, Byelov, very good!' said Getmanov. 'You're a true commander, a real Soviet Suvorov!' Then, addressing him as '*ty*', he added in a quiet, good-humoured tone of voice: 'The head of the Political Section says you're having an affair with a nurse. Is that so?'

At first, misled by Getmanov's friendly tone, Byelov didn't understand the question.

'I'm sorry. What did he say?'

Then Getmanov's meaning became clear. With obvious embarrassment, he said: 'I'm a man, comrade Commissar. And we are in the field.'

'You've got a wife and child.'

'Three children,' said Byelov sullenly.

'Three children then. Well, you know what happened to Bulanovich in the 1st Brigade. He's a fine officer, but he was relieved of his command because of an affair like this. What kind of an example are you setting your subordinates? A Russian officer and the father of three children!'

Suddenly furious, Byelov protested: 'Seeing as I didn't use force, it's of no concern to anyone else. And as for setting an example – it's been done before you and me and before your father.'

Without raising his voice, but now addressing him as '*vy*', Getmanov said: 'Remember your Party membership card, comrade Byelov. And you should stand to attention when a superior officer addresses you.'

Standing rigidly to attention, Byelov said: 'Excuse me, comrade Commissar. I understand. I realize my error.'

'The corps commander and I are confident of your fighting abilities. But take care not to disgrace yourself in your personal life.'

Getmanov looked at his watch and turned to Novikov.

'Pyotr Pavlovich, I haven't got time to go with you to Makarov's. I have to be at Headquarters. I'll borrow a jeep from Byelov.'

They left the bunker. Unable to restrain himself, Novikov asked: 'Can't you wait to see your Tamara then?'

Two frosty eyes looked at him in astonishment. An irritated voice said: 'I've been called to Front Headquarters by the Member of the Military Soviet.'

Novikov went on by himself to visit Makarov, the commander of the 3rd Brigade and a favourite of his.

They walked together towards a lake; one of the battalions was disposed on its shores. Makarov, a man with a pale face and improbably sad eyes for the commander of a brigade of heavy tanks, said: 'Comrade Colonel, do you remember how the Germans chased us through that bog in Byelorussia?'

Novikov did indeed remember. He thought for a moment of Karpov and Byelov. It obviously wasn't just a matter of experience, but of a man's nature. You can give a man all the experience in the world, but you can't change his nature. It was no good trying to make a sapper out of a fighter pilot. Not everyone can be like Makarov – equally competent both in attack and in defence.

Getmanov had said he had been made for Party work. Well, Makarov was a soldier – and he would always remain a soldier. That was his nature.

Novikov didn't need to hear any reports from Makarov. What he wanted was to talk things over with him, to ask for his advice. During the offensive, how could they liaise most effectively with the infantry, the motorized infantry, the sappers and the self-propelled guns? Did they agree as to the possible actions of the enemy after the beginning of the offensive? Did they have the same opinion of the strength of his anti-tank defences? Were the lines of deployment correctly drawn?

They came to the shallow ravine that housed the battalion command-post. Fatov, the battalion commander, was taken aback to see such important visitors. His bunker seemed somehow inadequate. A soldier had just used gunpowder to light the stove and it smelt vile.

'Comrades,' said Novikov. 'I want you to remember one thing. This corps will be assigned a crucial role in the coming engagements. I shall assign the most difficult part of this role to you, Makarov. And I have a feeling you will assign the most difficult part of your role to Fatov. You'll have to solve your problems yourselves – I won't go foisting my own ideas on you in battle.'

He then asked Fatov about his liaison with Regimental HQ and with his squadron commanders, about the functioning of the radio, his supplies of ammunition, the quality of the fuel and the condition of the engines.

Before saying goodbye, Novikov asked: 'Are you ready, Makarov?'

• 'Not quite, comrade Colonel.'

'Will three days be enough for you?'

'Yes, comrade Colonel.'

On the way back, Novikov said to his driver: 'Well, Kharitonov, Makarov seems to be on top of things, doesn't he?'

Kharitonov glanced at Novikov. 'Yes, comrade Colonel, absolutely on top of things. The brigade quartermaster got dead drunk and went off to bed leaving everything locked up. Someone came to pick up the rations for his battalion and found no one at home. And a sergeant-major told me that his squadron commander got hold of his squadron's vodka ration and had himself a birthday party. He got through the whole lot. And I wanted to repair an inner tube and get a spare wheel off them. They didn't even have any glue.'

34

Nyeudobnov was delighted when, looking out of the window, he saw Novikov's jeep arrive in a cloud of dust.

He had felt like this once when he was a child. His parents were going out and he had been full of excitement at the thought of being left alone in the house. And then as soon as the door closed, he had felt terrified: he had seen thieves in every corner, he had been afraid the house would catch fire . . . He had paced back and forth between the door and the window, listening, wondering if he could smell smoke.

Alone in the hut that served as Corps HQ, he had felt helpless. His usual ways of controlling the world had become suddenly ineffectual. What if the enemy appeared? After all, they were only sixty kilometres from the front line. What would he do then? It would be no good threatening to dismiss them from their posts or accusing them of conspiring with enemies of the people. How could he stop their tanks? Nyeudobnov was struck by something blindingly obvious: here at the front, the terrible rage of the State, before which millions of people bowed down and trembled, was of no effect. The Germans didn't have to fill in questionnaires. They didn't have to stand up at meetings and relate their biographies. They weren't afraid to admit the nature of their parents' occupations before 1917.

His own fate and the fate of his children, everything he loved and would be unable to live without, was no longer under the protection of the great, terrible and beloved State. For the first time he thought of Novikov with a mixture of warmth and timidity.

'Makarov, comrade General! Makarov's the man!' said Novikov as he came in. 'He'll be able to make quick decisions in any circumstances. Byelov will just tear on ahead without looking back – that's all he understands. And as for Karpov – he's a real slowcoach. He'll need a good kick up the arse.'

'Yes, cadres decide everything. Comrade Stalin has taught us to study them tirelessly,' said Nyeudobnov. 'I keep thinking there must be a German agent in the village,' he went on in a more lively tone of voice. 'The swine must have given our position away to the German bombers.'

Nyeudobnov told Novikov what had happened in his absence.

'Our neighbours and the commanders of the reinforcements are coming round to say hello. Just to introduce themselves.'

'A pity Getmanov won't be here,' said Novikov. 'I wonder why they wanted him at Front HQ.'

They agreed to have lunch together. Novikov went off to his billet to wash and change his dust-covered tunic.

The wide village street was almost completely deserted; there was just one old man, the owner of the hut where Getmanov was billeted, standing by the bomb-crater. Holding his hands wide apart, he seemed to be measuring something – as though this crater had been dug for some purpose of his own. As he came up to him, Novikov asked: 'What are you doing, father? Casting spells?'

The old man saluted. 'Comrade commander, I was taken prisoner by the Germans in 1915. There was one woman I worked for there . . .' He pointed first to the pit, then to the sky, and winked. 'And I wondered if it wasn't my son, the little rascal, flying by to pay me a visit.'

Novikov burst out laughing. 'You old devil!'

He glanced at Getmanov's shuttered windows, nodded at the sentry by the porch and suddenly thought anxiously: 'What the hell's Getmanov doing at HQ? What fish is he frying now? The hypocrite! He gives Byelov a dressing down for immoral behaviour – then freezes up as soon as I even mention his Tamara.'

But all this was soon forgotten. Novikov's wasn't a suspicious nature.

He turned a corner and saw several dozen young lads sitting on a patch of grass. They were obviously new recruits, having a rest by the well on their way to the district military commissariat.

The soldier in charge had covered his face with his forage cap and gone to sleep. Beside him lay a heap of packs and bundles. They must have walked quite a distance over the steppe; some of them had blisters and had taken off their shoes. They hadn't had their hair cut yet and from a distance they looked like village schoolboys having a rest during the break between lessons. Their thin faces and necks, their long light-brown hair, their patched clothes – evidently fashioned from trousers and jackets that had belonged to their fathers before them – all this belonged to the world of childhood. Some of them were playing an old game he himself had once played – throwing five-kopeck bits into a little hole in the ground, narrowing their eyes as they took aim. The rest were just watching. Everything about them was childish except for their sad, anxious eyes.

They caught sight of Novikov and glanced at the still sleeping soldier. They seemed to want to ask if it was all right to go on playing games while an important officer went by.

'It's all right, my warriors, carry on!' said Novikov softly. He walked past with a wave of the hand.

He was taken aback by the heart-rending pity they aroused in him. Their thin little faces, their staring eyes, the shabbiness of their clothes had suddenly reminded him that the men under his command were also mere children. Normally, in the army, all this was covered over by the shell of discipline, by the squeak of boots, by words and movements that were polished and automatic. Here it was transparent.

Novikov arrived at his billet. Strangely, this meeting with the new recruits troubled him more than all the other thoughts, impressions and anxieties of the day.

'Men,' he kept repeating to himself. 'Men, men . . .'

All his life as a soldier he had been afraid of having to account for lost ammunition and ordnance, lost fuel, lost time; afraid of having to explain why he had abandoned a summit or crossroads without permission. Not once had he known a superior officer show real anger because an operation had been wasteful in terms of human lives. He had even known officers send their men under fire simply to avoid the anger of their superiors, to be able to throw up their hands and say: 'What could I do? I lost half my men, but I was unable to reach the objective.'

Men, men . . .

He had also seen officers send their men under fire out of pure obstinacy and bravado – not even for the sake of covering themselves by formal compliance with an order. That was the mystery and tragedy of war: that one man should have the right to send another to his death. This right rested on the assumption that men were only exposed to fire for the sake of a common cause.

Yet one officer Novikov had known, a sober and level-headed man, had been used to having fresh milk for breakfast. He had been posted to an observation-post in the front line and a soldier from a support unit had had to bring him a thermos every morning, exposing himself to enemy fire on the way. There had been days when the soldier had been picked off by the Germans and the officer had had to do without milk. On the following day the milk would be brought by another orderly. And the man who drank this milk was both good-natured and fair-minded. He showed great concern for the well-being of his subordinates. His soldiers referred to him as 'father'. How could one ever make sense of all this?

Soon Nyeudobnov arrived. Hurriedly and painstakingly combing his hair, Novikov said: 'War's a terrible business, comrade General. Did you see those new recruits?'

'Yes, they're a green lot. Second-rate material. I woke that soldier up and promised to send him to a penal battalion. I've never seen such slovenliness. It looked more like a tavern than a military unit.'

In his novels, Turgenev often describes calls paid by neighbours on a landlord who has just settled down on his estate . . . That evening, two jeeps stopped outside Corps HQ and the hosts came out into the porch to receive their guests: the commanders of an artillery division, a howitzer regiment and a rocket-launcher brigade.

. . . Take my hand, dear reader. Today is the name-day of Tatyana Borisovna and we must go to pay her a visit . . .

Colonel Morozov was the commander of an artillery division; Novikov had heard of him several times. He had had a clear picture of him in his mind: someone red-faced and round-headed. In fact he was a middle-aged man with a pronounced stoop.

His bright eyes seemed to have nothing to do with his sullen face; it was as though they had been placed there by mere chance. Sometimes, however, their quick laughing intelligence made it seem as though they were the true expression of the Colonel's being; then it was the wrinkles, the despondent stoop that seemed the chance appendage.

Lopatin, the commander of the howitzer regiment, could have been Morozov's son – or even his grandson.

Magid, the commander of the 'Katyusha' rocket-launchers, was very swarthy. He had a high, prematurely balding forehead and a black moustache on his protruding upper lip. He seemed witty and talkative.

Novikov invited his guests to come through. The table had already been laid.

'Greetings from the Urals!' he said, pointing to some plates of pickled and marinated mushrooms.

The cook had been standing beside the table in a theatrical pose. He suddenly went bright red, gasped and left the room. The tension had proved too much for him.

Vershkov took Novikov aside, pointed at the table and whispered something in his ear.

'Yes, of course!' said Novikov. 'Why keep vodka locked up in a cupboard?'

Morozov held his fingernail against his glass, a quarter of the way up, and explained: 'I can't have any more because of my liver.'

'How about you, Lieutenant-Colonel?'

'Fill it right up! My liver's doing fine, thank you!'

'Our Magid's a true Cossack.'

'How about you, Major? How's your liver?'

Lopatin covered his glass with one hand.

'Thank you, but I don't drink.'

Then he took his hand away and added: 'Well, a symbolic drop. For the toast.'

'Lopatin's a baby. He just likes sweets.'

They drank to the success of their common task. Then, as always happens, they discovered they had friends in common from their days at military school or the Academy. They went on to talk about their superior officers, about how cold and unpleasant the steppes were in autumn.

'Well,' said Lopatin. 'Is the wedding going to be soon?'

'It won't be long,' said Novikov.

'There's sure to be a wedding if there are Katyushas around,' said Magid.

Magid was convinced that the rocket-launchers would play a

decisive role. After a glass of vodka he became condescending, sarcastic, sceptical and distant. Novikov took a strong dislike to him.

Now, whenever he met people, Novikov tried to imagine what Yevgenia Nikolaevna would think of them. He also tried to imagine how they would behave with her, what they would find to talk about.

Magid, he decided, would at once start to flirt, putting on airs, boasting and telling tall stories. He suddenly felt anxious and jealous – as though Zhenya really was listening to Magid's witticisms.

Wanting to make an impression on her himself, he began to explain how important it is to understand the men you're fighting alongside, to know in advance how they're likely to behave in battle. He talked about Karpov, who would need egging on, about Byelov, who would need holding back, and about Makarov, who was equally at home in attack and in defence.

A series of rather empty remarks – as often happens with a group of officers representing different arms of the service – gave rise to a heated but equally empty argument.

'Yes,' said Morozov. 'Sometimes you need to correct people a little, to give them some kind of orientation. But you should never impose your will on them.'

'People should be led firmly,' said Nyeudobnov. 'One should never be afraid of taking responsibility on oneself.'

Lopatin changed the subject.

'If you haven't fought in Stalingrad, then you haven't seen war.'

'Excuse me!' exclaimed Magid. 'But why Stalingrad? No one could deny the stubbornness and heroism of its defenders. That would be absurd. But I've never been in Stalingrad and I still have the cheek to say that I've seen war. My element is the offensive. I've taken part in three offensives. And let me tell you something – I've been the one who's broken through the enemy line. I've been the one who's entered the breach. Yes, the artillery really showed what it can do. We were ahead of the infantry, ahead of the tanks, we were even ahead of the air force.'

'Come on now!' said Novikov fiercely. 'Everyone knows that the tank is the master of mobile warfare. That's something there can be no two opinions about.'

'There's one other possibility,' said Lopatin, taking up an earlier thread of the conversation. 'In the event of success, you can take the credit yourself. But if you fail, you can blame it on your neighbours.'

'Don't talk to me of neighbours!' said Morozov. 'There was this general, the commander of an infantry unit, who asked for a supporting barrage. "Go on, old man, just give those heights a little dusting for me!" I asked him what calibres I should use. He called me every name in the book and repeated: "Open fire! And don't waste time about it." I discovered afterwards he couldn't tell one calibre from another, had no idea of the different ranges and could hardly even read a map. "Open fire, you motherfucker!" And he'd shout out to his subordinates: "Forward! Or I'll smash your teeth in. Forward! Or I'll put you against the wall and have you shot!" And of course he was convinced he was a great strategist. There's a fine neighbour for you! And often you end up being put under someone like that. After all, he was a general.'

'I'm surprised to hear you talking like that,' said Nyeudobnov. 'There are no officers like that in the Soviet armed forces – and certainly no generals.'

'What do you mean?' asked Morozov. 'I've met hundreds over the last year. They curse, wave their pistols about and expose their men to enemy fire just for the fun of it. Why, not long ago I saw a battalion commander burst out crying. "How can I lead my men straight into those machine-guns?" he said. "Don't worry," I told him. "First let's neutralize those gun emplacements. The artillery can do that." And what do you think the general in command of the division did? He went for the battalion commander with his fists. "Either you attack right now," he shouted, "or I'll have you shot like a dog!" So he led his men forward to be slaughtered.'

'Yes,' said Magid. ' "I'll do as I please and don't you dare contradict me!" That's their motto. And these generals don't, incidentally, propagate themselves just by budding. They get their dirty hands on pretty little telephonists.'

'And they can't write two words without making five mistakes,' said Lopatin.

'That's just it!' said Morozov, who hadn't heard this last remark. 'Try sparing your men with people like that around. They don't care about their men – and that's the only strength they have.'

Novikov sympathized with everything Morozov had said. He'd

seen all too many incidents like that himself. And yet he suddenly blurted out:

'Spare your men! How do you think you can spare your men? If that's what you want, then you've got no business to be fighting.'

Those young recruits had upset him; he'd wanted to talk about them. But instead of letting the officers see his true kindness, he burst out with a violence that surprised even himself: 'Spare your men indeed! You don't spare your men in war any more than you spare yourself. I'll tell you what upsets me. It's when we have to entrust precious equipment to a bunch of greenhorns. And then I wonder: is it really men we need to be so careful of?'

Nyeudobnov himself had been responsible for the death of more than one man similar to those who were now sitting at table. Novikov suddenly thought that this man was no less of a danger than the enemy front line.

Nyeudobnov had been watching Novikov and Morozov as they spoke. Now he said sententiously: 'That's not what comrade Stalin says. Comrade Stalin tells us that nothing is more precious than men. Our men, our cadres, are the most precious capital of all. One must watch over them like the apple of one's eye.'

Sensing that everyone agreed with Nyeudobnov, Novikov thought: 'How strange. Now they all think of me as a brute and Nyeudobnov as someone who looks after his men. A pity Getmanov isn't here – he's even more of a saint.'

He broke in on Nyeudobnov's homily and barked out even more fiercely:

'We've got more than enough men. What we don't have is equipment. Any idiot can make a man. It's another matter to make a tank or a plane. If you're so sorry for your men, then you've got no business to call yourself an officer!'

35

Lieutenant-General Yeremenko, the Commander-in-Chief of the Stalingrad Front, had summoned Novikov, Getmanov and Nyeudobnov for an interview. He had inspected the individual brigades on the previous day, but hadn't called at Corps HQ. The three of them sat in his bunker, glancing now and again at Yeremenko as they wondered what was in store for them.

Yeremenko noticed Getmanov looking at the crumpled pillow on the bunk.

'Yes, my leg's very sore.'

They watched Yeremenko in silence while he cursed his bad leg.

'Your corps seems well prepared. You seem to have made good use of the time.'

He looked at Novikov as he said this, a little surprised at the corps commander's apparent indifference to the compliment. He knew he was considered grudging in his praise of subordinates.

'Comrade Lieutenant-General,' said Novikov. 'I've already reported to you that our ground-support aircraft have twice bombed the 137th Tank Brigade in the area of the ravines. That brigade forms part of my corps.'

Narrowing his eyes, Yeremenko wondered what Novikov was after. Did he have it in for the officer responsible, or was he just trying to cover himself?

Novikov frowned and added: 'It's a good thing there weren't any direct hits. They haven't yet learnt their trade.'

'Very well,' said Yeremenko. 'But you'll be glad of their support later. You can be sure they'll make up for their error.'

'Of course, comrade Commander-in-Chief,' Getmanov joined in. 'We've no intention of picking a quarrel with Stalin's air force.'

'That's right, comrade Getmanov,' said Yeremenko. 'Well, have you seen Khrushchev?'

'Nikita Sergeyevich has ordered me to visit him tomorrow.'

'You know each other from Kiev, don't you?'

'Yes, I worked with Nikita Sergeyevich for nearly two years.'

'Tell me, comrade General,' said Yeremenko, turning to Nyeudobnov, 'did I once see you at Titsian Petrovich's?'

'That's right,' said Nyeudobnov. 'That was when he'd called you up, together with Marshal Voronov . . .'

'Oh yes, I remember.'

'And I, at Titsian Petrovich's request, was temporarily serving in the capacity of People's Commissar. That's why I was there.'

'So we've met before,' said Yeremenko. 'Well, I hope you're not bored in the steppes, comrade General. Have you managed to make yourself comfortable?'

Without waiting for an answer, he gave a satisfied nod of the head.

As the three men were going out of the door, Yeremenko called out: 'One moment, Colonel.'

Novikov went back into the room. Yeremenko half got up, leaning his stout peasant body over the desk, and said: 'So there we are. One of them's worked with Khrushchev, and the other with Titsian Petrovich. But don't you forget, you damn son of a bitch – you're the soldier, you're the one who's going to lead your tank corps into the breach.'

36

Krymov was released from hospital on a cold dark morning. Without even going home, he went straight to General Toshcheyev, the head of the Political Administration of the Front, to report on his visit to Stalingrad.

Krymov was in luck. Toshcheyev had been in his office – a small hut faced with grey planks – since early morning; he received his visitor without delay.

Toshcheyev, squinting constantly at his brand-new general's uniform, turned up his nose at the smell of carbolic acid that emanated from his visitor.

'After being wounded,' said Krymov, 'I was unable to complete my mission to house 6/1. I can go back there straight away.'

Toshcheyev gave him an irritated look.

'No, just write me a detailed report.'

Toshcheyev didn't ask a single question. Nor did he utter one word of approval or disapproval.

As always, a general's uniform and medals seemed out of place in a simple village hut. But that wasn't the only thing that was odd. Krymov was unable to understand why the general should seem so sullen and dissatisfied.

He went into the administrative section to obtain lunch coupons, to register his rations certificate, and to sort out various formalities to do with his mission and the days he had spent in hospital. While this was being attended to, he sat on a stool and studied the faces of the people in the office.

No one showed the least interest in him. His visit to Stalingrad, his wound, all he had seen and done, seemed quite without meaning. The people here had work to get on with. Typewriters clattered, papers rustled, people's eyes slid rapidly over Krymov before returning to the sheaves of paper spread out over their desks.

What a lot of furrowed brows, what tension in everyone's eyes! How absorbed they all seemed in their work, how quickly and deftly their fingers leafed through the papers! Only the odd convulsive yawn or furtive glance at the clock, only a bleary, haggard look that appeared fleetingly on one face or another spoke of the deadly boredom of this stuffy office.

Someone Krymov knew, an instructor from the seventh department, looked in through the door. Krymov went out into the corridor with him for a smoke.

'So you're back, are you?'

'As you see,' said Krymov.

As the instructor didn't ask anything about Stalingrad, Krymov asked: 'So what's new in the Political Administration?'

The main piece of news was that Brigade Commissar Toshcheyev had finally – under the new system to which they were changing over – been given the rank of general. The instructor laughed as he told Krymov how Toshcheyev had fallen ill with anxiety. He had had a general's uniform made up for him by the best tailor at the front – and then Moscow had kept delaying the announcement. It hadn't been at all funny. There were dark rumours that, under this new system, some of the regimental commissars and senior battalion commissars would only be given the ranks of captain or senior lieutenant.

'Just imagine!' said the instructor. 'After eight years in the army political organs – to be made a lieutenant!'

There were other items of news. The deputy head of the Information Section had been summoned to Moscow; there he had been promoted to deputy head of the Political Administration of the Kalinin Front.

The Member of the Military Soviet had decreed that senior

instructors were now to eat in the general canteen rather than in the canteen for heads of sections. Instructors sent on missions were to have their meal-tickets withdrawn without any compensatory issue of field-rations. The poets Kats and Talalayevsky had been put forward for the 'Red Star' medal – but according to comrade Shcherbakov's new decree, awards to members of the press had to be approved by the Central Political Administration. The poets' dossiers had been sent to Moscow; meanwhile, Yeremenko had signed the list of soldiers to be decorated – everyone except the poets was already celebrating.

'Have you had lunch yet?' asked the instructor. 'Come on, then.'

Krymov said he was waiting for his documents.

'Well, I'm off,' said the instructor. 'There's no time to lose,' he added with a trace of irony. 'Soon we'll be eating in the canteen for civilian workers and typists.'

Krymov got his documents back and went outside. He took in a deep breath of the damp autumn air.

Why had the head of the Political Administration received him so coldly? Why did he seem so annoyed? Because Krymov hadn't completed his mission? Did he suspect him of cowardice? Did he doubt that he really had been wounded? Or was Toshcheyev annoyed that Krymov had come straight to him, without first seeing his own immediate superior – and at a time when he didn't usually receive visitors? Or was it that Krymov had twice called him 'Comrade Brigade Commissar' instead of 'Comrade Major-General'? Or maybe it wasn't anything to do with Krymov? Maybe he'd had a letter saying his wife had fallen ill? Perhaps he'd hoped to be put forward for the Order of Kutuzov? There were, after all, any number of reasons why he might be in a bad mood.

During his weeks in Stalingrad Krymov had forgotten what it was like in Akhtuba. He'd forgotten the way your superiors, your colleagues, even the waitresses in the canteen, looked at you as if you barely existed.

In the evening he went back to his room. The landlady's dog was very glad to see him. It seemed to be made up of two halves – a shaggy, reddish-brown behind, and a long black-and-white face – and both halves were equally welcoming. The shaggy brown tail wagged, and the black-and-white face thrust itself into Krymov's hands, looking at him tenderly with its brown eyes. In the twilight it seemed there were two dogs, both of them making up to Krymov. The dog came with him as far as the door. Then the landlady appeared and shouted: 'Get out of it, you filthy creature!' Only then did she greet Krymov – and her welcome was as sullen as Toshcheyev's.

His quiet little room seemed very lonely after the friendly warmth of the trenches, the grey, smoky, tarpaulin-covered bunkers that were like the lairs of animals. The bed itself, the pillow in its white pillow-case, and the lace curtains all seemed equally unwelcoming.

Krymov sat down and started to compile his report. He wrote quickly, glancing only briefly at the notes he had made in Stalingrad. The most difficult part was house 6/1. He got up, walked about the room and sat down. Then he got up again, went out into the corridor and coughed. Surely that damned woman would offer him some tea? Instead he ladled out some water from the barrel. It was very pleasant, better than the water in Stalingrad. He went back into his room and sat down for a while to think, pen in hand. Then he lay down on the bed and closed his eyes.

How had it happened? Grekov had fired at him . . .

In Stalingrad he had felt a rapport with the men around him. He had been at ease there; people had no longer looked at him with blank indifference. In house 6/1 he had expected to feel the spirit of Lenin still more strongly. Instead he had immediately encountered mockery and hostility; he had lost his poise and begun lecturing people and making threats. What could have made him talk about Suvorov? And then Grekov had shot at him!

Today his isolation, the condescending arrogance of people whom he thought of as semi-literates, as mere greenhorns in the Party, had been more distressing than ever. Why should he have to bow and scrape before a man like Toshcheyev? What right did Toshcheyev have to look at him with such disdain and ill humour? In terms of the work he'd done for the Party he couldn't hold a candle to Krymov – for all his medals and high rank. What did people like him have to do with the Party and the Leninist tradition? Many of them had come to the fore only in 1937 – by writing denunciations and unmasking enemies of the people.

Then Krymov remembered the wonderful sense of faith, strength and light-heartedness he had felt as he walked down the underground passage towards that tiny point of daylight. He felt choked with anger

– Grekov had exiled him from the life he yearned for. On his way to the building he had been joyfully conscious of a new turn in his destiny. He had believed that the spirit of Lenin was alive there. And then Grekov had fired at a Leninist, at an Old Bolshevik! He had sent Krymov back to the stifling offices of Akhtuba. The swine!

Krymov sat down. Every word he then wrote was the absolute truth.

He read the report over. Toshcheyev, of course, would pass it on to the Special Department. Grekov had subverted and demoralized the military sub-unit under his command. He had committed an act of terrorism: he had fired at a representative of the Party, a military commissar. Krymov would have to give evidence. Probably he would be summoned for a personal confrontation with Grekov – who by then would have been arrested.

He imagined Grekov in front of the investigator's desk, unshaven, without his belt, his face pale and yellow.

What was it Grekov had said? 'But you've suffered a lot.'

The Secretary General of the party of Marx and Lenin had been declared infallible, almost divine. And he certainly hadn't spared the Old Bolsheviks in 1937. He had infringed the very spirit of Leninism – that fusion of Party democracy and iron discipline.

How could Stalin have settled accounts so ruthlessly with members of Lenin's own party . . . ? Grekov would be shot in front of the ranks. It was terrible to kill one's own men. But then Grekov was an enemy.

Krymov had never doubted the sacred right of the Revolution to destroy its enemies. The Party had a right to wield the sword of dictatorship. He had never been one to sympathize with the Opposition. He had never believed that Bukharin, Rykov, Zinoviev and Kamenev were true followers of Lenin. And Trotsky, for all his brilliance and revolutionary fervour, had never outlived his Menshevik past; he had never attained the stature of Lenin. Stalin, though, was a man of true strength. It wasn't for nothing he was known as 'the boss'. His hand had never trembled – he had none of Bukharin's flabby intellectuality. Crushing its enemies underfoot, the party of Lenin now followed Stalin. Grekov's military competence was of no significance. There was no point in listening to one's enemies, no point in arguing with them . . .

It was no good. Krymov could no longer bring himself to feel angry with Grekov.

Once again he remembered those words of Grekov's: 'But you've suffered a lot.'

'Have I gone and written a denunciation?' Krymov asked himself. 'All right, it may be true, but that doesn't make it any the less a denunciation . . . But what can you do about it, comrade? You're a member of the Party. You must do your duty.'

The following morning Krymov handed in his report.

Two days later, he was summoned by Regimental Commissar Ogibalov, the head of the agit-prop section, who was acting for the head of the Political Administration. Toshcheyev himself was busy with the commissar of a tank corps and was unable to see Krymov.

Ogibalov was a slow, methodical man with a pale face and a large nose.

'In a few days we're sending you off to the right bank, comrade Krymov,' he said. 'This time you'll be going to Shumilov's – the 64th Army. One of our cars will be going to the command post of the *obkom*. From there you can get across to Shumilov's yourself. The *obkom* secretaries are going to Beketovka to celebrate the anniversary of the Revolution.'

Very slowly, he dictated Krymov's instructions. The tasks he had been assigned were humiliatingly boring and trivial – of no importance except for official records.

'What about my lecture?' asked Krymov. 'At your request, I prepared a lecture, to be read to the different units during the October celebrations.'

'We'll have to leave that for the moment,' said Ogibalov, and went on to explain the reasons for this decision.

As Krymov was getting up to leave, the commissar said:

'As for that report of yours . . . Well, my boss has just put me in the picture.'

Krymov's heart sank. So the wheels were already turning . . .

'Our brave warrior's been lucky,' the commissar went on. 'We were informed yesterday by the head of the Political Section of the 62nd Army that Grekov, together with all his men, was killed during the German assault on the Tractor Factory.'

As though to console Krymov, he added:

'The Army commander nominated him posthumously for the title of Hero of the Soviet Union. We'll certainly squash that.'

Krymov shrugged his shoulders, as if to say: 'So he's had a stroke of luck. Well, that's that.'

Ogibalov lowered his voice.

'The head of the Special Section thinks he may still be alive. He may have gone over to the enemy.'

Krymov found a note waiting for him at home: he was to report to the Special Section. So the Grekov affair wasn't yet over and done with.

Krymov decided to postpone what was bound to be a very disagreeable conversation until his return. After all, a posthumous affair could hardly be so very urgent.

37

The Stalingrad *obkom* had decided to celebrate the twenty-fifth anniversary of the Revolution with a special meeting at the 'Sudoverf' factory. This was situated in the hamlet of Beketovka to the south of the city.

Early on the morning of 6 November, the *obkom* officials met in their underground command-post in 2 small oak wood on the left bank of the Volga. After an excellent hot breakfast, the first secretary, the secretaries of the different sections and the members of the bureau set out by car along the main road leading to the Volga.

It was the same road that had been used during the night by tank and artillery units on their way to the Tumansk crossing. Ploughed up by the war, dotted with frozen mounds of brown dirt and puddles that seemed like sheets of tin, the steppe looked painfully sad. As you approached the Volga, you could hear the grating of drift-ice. A strong wind was blowing from downstream – crossing the Volga on an open iron barge would be no joy-ride.

The soldiers waiting to cross had already taken their places in the barge. Their coats whipped by the wind, they huddled together and tried to avoid touching the icy metal. They drew in their legs under the bench and beat out a mournful tap-dance with their heels. When the wind got up, they just sat there and froze; they no longer had the strength to wipe their noses, to blow on their fingers, to clap their sides. Wisps of smoke from the tug's funnel spread out across the river. Against the ice, the smoke seemed very black indeed; the ice itself, under the low curtain of smoke, seemed very white. As it drifted across from Stalingrad, the ice seemed to be bringing the war with it.

A crow with a large head was sitting thoughtfully on a block of ice. On the neighbouring block lay the tail of a burnt greatcoat; on a third block stood a stone-hard felt boot and a carbine whose twisted barrel had frozen into the ice.

The cars from the *obkom* drove onto the barge. The secretaries and members of the bureau got out and stood by the railings, listening to the ice as it moved slowly by. The old soldier in charge of the barge came over to the *obkom* transport-secretary, Laktionov. His lips were quite blue and he was wearing a black sheepskin coat and an army cap. In a hoarse voice – brought about by the damp of the river on top of many years of vodka and tobacco – he announced:

'The first trip we made this morning, comrade Secretary, there was this soldier lying there on the ice. The boys needed pick-axes to get him out – some of them almost got drowned themselves. Look, there he is – on the bank, under that tarpaulin.'

The old man indicated the bank with a dirty mitten. Unable to see the corpse and feeling somewhat ill at ease, Laktionov pointed at the sky and asked abruptly: 'So what's he up to these days? Does he have any favourite time?'

The old man gave a dismissive wave of the hand.

'Hm! He's not up to real bombing any more.' He began to curse the now feeble Germans, his voice suddenly becoming clear and ringing.

Meanwhile the tug drew slowly closer to the Stalingrad bank. Covered with small booths, huts and supply-dumps, it seemed quite ordinary and peaceful.

The *obkom* officials soon tired of standing in the wind. They got back into their cars, lit cigarettes, scratched themselves and started chatting. The soldiers gazed at them through the glass as though they were fish in a warm aquarium.

The special meeting took place that evening.

The invitations were no different from those sent in peacetime – except for the poor quality of the soft grey paper and the fact that there was no mention of the venue.

The Stalingrad Party leaders, the guests from the 64th Army, the workers and engineers from nearby factories were all accompanied by guides who had a good knowledge of the way: 'Left here, and again here. Careful now – there's a bomb crater. And now some rails. And very careful here – there's a lime-pit . . .'

The darkness was full of voices and the tramping of boots.

Krymov arrived with the representatives of the 64th Army; he had visited their Political Section immediately after crossing the river.

Something about the way all these people were walking through the labyrinth of the factory, in small groups and under cover of night, made Krymov think of clandestine celebrations before 1917. He was almost breathless with excitement. He was an experienced orator and he knew he could give an impromptu speech there and then; he could share with everyone his excitement and joy at the similarity between the defence of Stalingrad and the revolutionary struggle of the Russian workers.

Yes, yes! This war, and the patriotic spirit it aroused, was indeed a war for the Revolution. It had been no betrayal of the Revolution to speak of Suvorov in house 6/1. Stalingrad, Sebastopol, the fate of Radishchev, the power of Marx's manifesto, Lenin's appeals from the armoured car near the Finland station – all these were part of one and the same thing.

He caught sight of Pryakhin, the first secretary of the *obkom* and an old friend of his. He seemed as calm and unhurried as ever, but somehow Krymov was unable to find an opportunity to talk to him.

There were a lot of things he wanted to talk about; he'd gone to see him as soon as he'd arrived at the command-post of the *obkom*. But the telephone had kept ringing and people had kept dropping in. Pryakhin had spoken to him only once, asking suddenly: 'Did you ever know someone by the name of Getmanov?'

'Yes. In the Ukraine. He was a member of the bureau of the Central Committee. Why do you ask?'

Pryakhin hadn't answered. Then there had been all the bustle of departure. Krymov had been offended that Pryakhin hadn't offered him a lift in his own car. Twice they had almost bumped into each other, but Pryakhin had looked straight through him.

The soldiers were now going down a lighted corridor: Shumilov, the Army commander, a flabby man with a large chest and a large stomach; General Abramov, a Siberian with brown, bulging eyes, the Member of the Military Soviet . . . In this group of men, in the good-hearted comradeliness between them, in the steam rising from their tunics, padded jackets and coats, Krymov again sensed the spirit of the first years of the Revolution, the spirit of Lenin. He had felt it as soon as he returned to the right bank.

The members of the Presidium took their places. Piksin, the chairman of the Stalingrad Soviet, leant forward and directed a slow, chairmanlike cough towards the noisiest part of the hall. He then announced the opening of this special meeting of the Stalingrad Soviet and Party organizations, attended also by representatives of the military units and workers from the local factories, in celebration of the twenty-fifth anniversary of the Great October Revolution.

You could tell from the sound of the applause that the hands clapping belonged to men, to soldiers and workers.

Then Pryakhin spoke, as slow and ponderous as ever . . . Any connection between the present moment and what had happened in the past vanished at once. It was as though Pryakhin had entered into a polemic with Krymov, as though he had deliberately adopted these measured tones in order to dash Krymov's excitement.

The factories in the *oblast* were fulfilling the State plan. The agricultural districts on the left bank had satisfactorily, though with slight delays, provided their quota of grain for the State. The factories within the city and to the north of it were situated within the zone of military operations; their failure to carry out their obligations to the State could therefore be understood . . .

And this was the same man who had once stood beside Krymov during a revolutionary meeting at the front, who had torn off his cap and shouted: 'Comrades, soldiers, brothers, to hell with this war and its blood! Long live freedom!'

Now he gazed calmly around the hall and explained that the sudden drop in the quantity of grain supplied to the State was caused by the fact that the Zimovnichesky and Kotelnichesky districts had been unable to furnish supplies because they were part of the arena of military operations – while the Kalach and Kurmoyarsk regions were partially or completely occupied by the enemy.

He went on to say that the population of the *oblast*, while continuing to work hard to fulfil their obligations to the State, had at the same time played an important part in military operations against the Fascist invaders. He quoted figures: first, the number of workers from the city enrolled in militia units, and second – with the proviso that his data was incomplete – the number who had been decorated for their exemplary courage and valour while carrying out the tasks entrusted to them.

As Krymov listened to the calm voice of the first secretary, he thought that the glaring disparity between his words and his real thoughts and feelings was far from senseless. It was the very coldness of his speech that confirmed just how absolute was the State's triumph.

The faces of the workers and soldiers were grave and sullen.

How strange and painful it was to remember people like Tarasov and Batyuk, to recall his conversations with the soldiers in house 6/1. It was particularly unpleasant to think of Grekov and how he had met his death.

But why should Grekov matter to him? Why was that remark of his so troubling? Grekov had fired a shot at him . . . And why should the words spoken by Pryakhin, his old comrade, the first secretary of the Stalingrad *obkom*, sound cold and alien? How complicated it all was.

Pryakhin was summing up.

'And so we are delighted to be able to report to the great Stalin that the workers of the *oblast* have carried out their obligations to the Soviet State . . .'

Krymov looked out for Pryakhin as he made his way through the crowd towards the exit. No, that was not the sort of speech to deliver in the middle of this terrible battle.

Suddenly Krymov caught sight of him. He had stepped down from the dais and was standing beside Shumilov. He was staring straight at Krymov. When he saw Krymov looking at him, he turned away.

'What on earth does that mean?' wondered Krymov.

38

After the meeting, Krymov got a lift to the Central Power Station. That night, after a recent raid by German bombers, it looked particularly sinister. The explosions had blasted out huge craters and thrown up great ramparts of earth. Some of the windowless workshops had subsided; the three-storey administrative building was in ruins.

The transformers were still smoking. Little fangs of flame were playing lazily about them.

A young Georgian sentry took Krymov through the yard, still lit up by the fire. Krymov saw his guide's fingers shake as he lit a cigarette – stone buildings weren't the only things to have been devastated by the massive bombs.

Krymov had been hoping to see Spiridonov ever since he had received instructions to go to Beketovka. Perhaps Zhenya would be here. Perhaps Spiridonov would know something about her. Perhaps he had had a letter from her and at the end she had written: 'Have you heard anything about Nikolay Grigorevich?'

He felt excited and happy. Perhaps Spiridonov would say: 'But Yevgenia Nikolaevna seemed very sad.' Or perhaps: 'She was crying, you know.'

He had been getting more and more impatient all day. He had wanted to drop in on Spiridonov during the afternoon. Instead he had gone to the command-post of the 64th Army – despite the fact that a political instructor had whispered to him, 'There's no point in hurrying, you know. The Member of the Military Soviet's been drunk since morning.'

It had indeed been a mistake to visit the general. As he sat in the waiting-room of the underground command-post, he had overheard the general, on the other side of the thin plywood partition, dictating a letter of congratulation to his neighbour, Chuykov.

'Vasily Ivanovich, soldier and friend!' he began solemnly.

Then he burst into tears and, sobbing, repeated the words several times: 'Soldier and friend, soldier and friend.'

'What's that you've written down?' he asked the typist, his voice suddenly severe.

'Vasily Ivanovich, soldier and friend.'

Her bored tone must have seemed inappropriate. By way of correcting her, he repeated, with still greater exaltation:

'Vasily Ivanovich, soldier and friend!'

Once again he was overwhelmed by emotion. Then, with the same severity as before: 'What have you written?'

'Vasily Ivanovich, soldier and friend,' replied the typist.

There had indeed been no point in hurrying.

The dim flames served more to obscure the way than to illuminate it. They seemed to be coming from the depths of the earth; or perhaps the earth itself had caught fire – the low flames were certainly heavy and damp enough.

They reached the director's command-post. Bombs had fallen nearby and thrown up great mountains of earth; the path had not yet been properly trodden down and was barely distinguishable.

'You've got here just in time for the party,' said the guard.

Krymov knew he wouldn't be able to speak freely to Spiridonov in the presence of other people. He told the guard to tell the director that a commissar from Front Headquarters was here to see him. Left on his own, a wave of uncontrollable anguish swept over him.

'What is all this?' he said to himself. 'I thought I was cured. Can't even the war exorcize her? What can I do?'

'Drive her away, drive her away! Get out of it or it will be the end of you!' he muttered.

But he didn't have the strength to leave – any more than he had the strength to drive her away.

Then Spiridonov appeared.

'Yes, comrade, what can I do for you?' he asked impatiently.

'Don't you recognize me, Stepan Fyodorovich?'

'Who is it?' Spiridonov sounded nervous. He looked Krymov in the face and suddenly cried out: 'Nikolay! Nikolay Grigorevich!'

His arms were trembling as he flung them round Krymov's neck.

'My dearest Nikolay!' he said with a loud sniff.

Krymov felt himself beginning to cry. He was shaken by this

strange meeting in the middle of the ruins. And he felt alone, utterly alone . . . Spiridonov's trust and joy brought home to him how close he was to Yevgenia Nikolaevna's family. And this brought home his pain. Why, why had she left him? Why had she caused him so much suffering? How could she?

. 'You know what the war's done?' said Spiridonov. 'It's destroyed my life. My Marusya's dead.'

He told Krymov about Vera. About how, only a few days before, she had finally crossed to the left bank. 'The girl's a fool.'

'What about her husband?' asked Krymov.

'He probably died long ago. He's a fighter pilot.'

Unable to restrain himself any longer, Krymov asked:

'What about Yevgenia Nikolaevna? Is she still alive? Where is she?'

'She's alive all right. She's either in Kuibyshev or Kazan.'

He looked at Krymov and said:

'She's still alive. That's what matters.'

'Yes, yes, of course,' said Krymov.

He himself no longer knew what really mattered. All he knew was that he was in pain. Everything to do with Yevgenia Nikolaevna brought him pain. It would hurt him to know that some tragedy had happened to her; it would hurt him to be told that she was well and happy.

Spiridonov began to talk about Alexandra Vladimirovna, Lyudmila and Seryozha. Krymov just nodded and muttered: 'Yes, yes . . . Yes, yes . . .'

'Come on, Nikolay!' said Spiridonov. 'You must come and visit my home. It's all I have left.'

The cellar was crammed with pallets, cupboards, equipment, sacks of flour and huge bottles. The flickering oil lamps lit up only a small part of it. There were people sitting everywhere – on the pallets, on boxes and benches, along the walls. The air was stifling and full of the buzz of conversation.

Spiridonov started to pour alcohol into glasses, mugs and the lids of pots. Everyone fell silent, watching him attentively. The look in their eyes was calm and serious, full of faith.

As he looked round, Krymov said to himself: 'It's a pity Grekov's not here. He deserves a drink.' But Grekov had already drunk all he was ever to drink.

Glass in hand, Spiridonov got up.

'Now he'll go and spoil everything,' thought Krymov, 'like Pryakhin.'

But Spiridonov just sketched a figure of eight in the air with his glass and said: 'Well, lads, it's time for a drink. Cheers!'

There was a clinking of glasses and tin mugs. The drinkers cleared their throats and nodded their heads.

There were all sorts of people here. Before the war, the State had somehow kept them apart; they had never sat down at one table, clapped each other on the shoulder and said: 'No, you just listen to what I'm saying!' Here, though, beneath the remains of the burning power station, they had become brothers. And this simple brotherhood was so important that they would happily have given their lives for it.

A grey-haired night-watchman began to sing an old song. Before the Revolution, when Stalingrad was still called Tsaritsyn, it had been a favourite of the young lads from the French factory. He sang in the thin, high voice of his youth. This voice was unfamiliar to him now and he listened to himself with the amused astonishment of a man listening to a stranger who's had too much to drink.

Another old man, with black hair, frowned as he listened to this song about love and the pain of love.

There was something wonderful about this singing, about this terrible moment that had brought together the director, the orderly from the bakery, the night-watchman and the sentry, that had brought together the Kalmyk, the Georgian and the Russians.

When the song was over, the old man with black hair frowned still more fiercely and himself began to sing, very slowly and quite out of tune.

> 'Away with the old world,
> Let's shake its dust from our feet . . .'

Spiridonov and Nikolayev, the delegate from the Central Committee, both laughed and shook their heads. Krymov grinned at Spiridonov.

'So the old man was once a Menshevik?'

Spiridonov knew all there was to know about Andreyev. He would gladly have told Krymov, but he was afraid Nikolayev would overhear. For a moment the feeling of simplicity and brotherhood disappeared.

'Pavel Andreyevich, that's the wrong song,' he interrupted gently.

Andreyev fell silent, looked at him and said:

'I'd never have thought it. I must have been dreaming.'

The Georgian sentry was showing Krymov where he had rubbed the skin off his hand.

'That's from digging out my friend, Seryozha Vorobyov.'

His black eyes glittered. Then, rather breathlessly, he said:

'I loved that Seryozha more than my own brother.'

The words were almost a scream.

Meanwhile the grey-haired night-watchman, covered in sweat and a little the worse for drink, had fastened onto Nikolayev.

'No, you listen to me now! Makuladze says he loved Seryozha Vorobyov more than his own brother. I once worked in an anthracite mine. You should have seen the boss we had there. He really did love me. We drank together and I used to sing. He said straight out: "You're just like a brother to me, even if you are only a miner." We used to talk, we used to eat our lunch together.'

'A Georgian, was he?' asked Nikolayev.

'What do you mean? He was Mr Voskresensky, the owner of all the mines. But you'll never understand how much he respected me. A man who had a capital of millions. Is that clear?'

Nikolayev and Krymov exchanged glances. They both winked and shook their heads.

'Well, well,' said Nikolayev. 'Now that really is something. You live and learn.'

'That's right,' said the old man, apparently unaware that he was being made fun of.

It was a strange evening. Late at night, as people were beginning to leave, Spiridonov said to Krymov: 'Don't start looking for your coat, Nikolay. You're staying here for the night.'

He started preparing a place for Krymov to sleep. He did this very slowly, thinking carefully what to put where: the blanket, the padded jacket, the ground sheet. Krymov went outside; he stood for a while in the darkness, looking at the dancing flames, then went back down again. Spiridonov was still at it.

Krymov finally took off his boots and lay down.

'Well, are you comfortable?' Spiridonov asked. He patted Krymov on the head and smiled a kindly, drunken smile.

To Krymov, the fire in the power station was somehow reminiscent of the bonfires in Okhotniy Ryad on that night in January 1924 when they had buried Lenin.

Everyone else who had stayed behind seemed to be already asleep. It was pitch-dark. Krymov lay there with his eyes open, thinking and remembering . . .

There had been a harsh frost for some days. The dark winter sky over the cupolas of Strastny monastery . . . Hundreds of men in greatcoats, leather jackets, caps with ear-flaps, pointed helmets . . . At one moment Strastnaya Square had suddenly turned white. There were leaflets, government proclamations, lying all over it.

Lenin's body had been taken from Gorki to the railway station on a peasant sledge. The runners had squeaked, the horses snorted. The coffin had been followed by his widow, Krupskaya, wearing a round fur cap held on by a grey headscarf, by his two sisters, Anna and Maria, by his friends, and by some of the village peasants. It might have been the funeral of some agronomist, of a respected village doctor or teacher.

Silence had fallen over Gorki. The polished tiles of the Dutch stoves had gleamed; beside the bed with its white summer bedspread stood a small cupboard full of little bottles with white labels; there was a smell of medicine. A middle-aged woman in a white coat had come into the room; out of habit she walked on tiptoe. She had gone past the bed and picked up a ball of twine with a piece of newspaper tied to the end. The kitten asleep in the empty armchair had looked up as it heard the familiar rustle of its toy; it had looked at the empty bed, yawned and then settled down again.

As they followed the coffin, Lenin's relatives and close comrades had begun reminiscing. His sisters remembered a little boy with fair hair and a difficult character. He had teased them a lot and been impossibly demanding. Still, he had been a good boy and he had loved his mother and his brothers and sisters.

His widow remembered him in Zurich, squatting on the floor and talking to the little granddaughter of Tilly the landlady. Tilly had said, in the Swiss accent that Volodya found so amusing:

'You should have children yourselves.'

He had stolen a quick, sly look at Nadyezhda Konstantinovna.

Workers from the 'Dynamo' factory had come to Gorki. Volodya had forgotten his condition and got up to meet them. He had wanted to say something, but had only managed to give a pitiful moan and a despairing wave of the hand. The workers had stood around in a circle; watching him cry, they had started to cry themselves. And then that frightened, pitiful look of his at the end – like a little boy turning to his mother.

Then the station buildings had come into view. The locomotive, with its tall funnel, had seemed even blacker against the snow.

Lenin's comrades – Rykov, Kamenev and Bukharin – had walked just behind the sledge, their beards white with hoar-frost. From time to time they had glanced absent-mindedly at a swarthy, pock-marked man wearing a long greatcoat and boots with soft tops. They had always felt a contemptuous scorn for his Caucasian style of dress. And had he been a little more tactful, he wouldn't have come to Gorki at all; this was a gathering for Lenin's very closest friends and relatives. None of them understood that this man was the true heir of Lenin, that he would supplant every one of them, even Krupskaya herself.

No, it wasn't Bukharin, Rykov and Zinoviev who were the heirs of Lenin. Nor Trotsky. They were all mistaken. None of them had been chosen to continue Lenin's work. But even Lenin himself had failed to understand this.

Nearly two decades had passed since that day, since the body of Lenin – the man who had determined the fate of Russia, of Europe, of Asia, of humanity itself – had been drawn through the snow on a creaking sledge.

Krymov couldn't stop thinking about those days. He remembered the bonfires blazing in the night, the frost-covered walls of the Kremlin, the hundreds of thousands of weeping people, the heart-rending howl of factory hooters, Yevdokimov's stentorian voice as he stood on a platform and read an appeal to the workers of the world, the small group who had carried the coffin into the hastily-built wooden mausoleum.

Krymov had climbed the carpeted steps of the House of Unions and walked past the mirrors draped in black and red ribbons; the warm air had been scented with pine-needles and full of mournful music. He had gone into the hall and seen the bowed heads of the men he was used to seeing on the tribune at the Smolny or at Staraya Ploshchad. In 1937 he had seen the same bowed heads in the same building. As they listened to the sonorous, inhuman tones of Prosecutor Vyshinsky, the accused had probably remembered how they had walked behind the sledge and stood beside Lenin's coffin, listening to that mournful music.

Why, on this anniversary of the Revolution, had he suddenly remembered that distant January? Dozens of men who had helped Lenin to create the Bolshevik Party had proved to be foreign spies and provocateurs; and someone who had never occupied a central position in the Party, who had never been highly thought of as a theoretician, had proved to be the saviour of the Party's cause, the bearer of its truth. Why had they all confessed?

Questions like these were best forgotten. But tonight Krymov was unable to forget them . . . Why did they all confess? And why do I keep silent? Why have I never found the strength to say: 'I really don't believe that Bukharin was a saboteur, provocateur and assassin.' I even raised my hand to vote. I signed. I gave a speech and wrote an article. And I still believe that my zeal was genuine. But where were my doubts then? Where was all my confusion? What is it that I'm trying to say? That I am a man with two consciences? Or that I am two men, each with his own conscience? But then that's how it's always been – for all kinds of people, not just for me.

Grekov had merely given voice to what many people felt without admitting it. He had put into words the thoughts that most worried Krymov, that sometimes most attracted him. But Krymov had at once been overwhelmed with hatred and anger. He had wanted to make Grekov lick his boots; he had wanted to break him. If it had come to it, he would have shot him without hesitation.

Pryakhin's words were spoken in the cold language of officialdom. He had talked, in the name of the State, about grain procurements, workers' obligations and percentages of the plan. Krymov had always disliked the soulless speeches delivered by soulless bureaucrats – but these soulless bureaucrats were his oldest comrades, the men he had marched in step with. The work of Lenin was the work of Stalin; it had become embodied in these men, in this State. And Krymov wouldn't hesitate to give his life for the glory of this work.

What about Mostovskoy? He too was an Old Bolshevik. But not

once had he spoken out, even in defence of people whose revolutionary honour he had never questioned. He too had kept silent. Why?

And Koloskov, that kind, upright young fellow who'd attended Krymov's courses in journalism. Coming from a village in the country, he'd had a lot to say about collectivization. He'd told Krymov about the scoundrels who included someone's name on a list of kulaks simply because they had their eye on his house or garden, or because they were personal enemies. He'd told Krymov about the terrible hunger, about the ruthlessness with which the peasants' last grain of corn had been confiscated. He'd begun to cry as he talked about one wonderful old man who'd given his life to save his wife and granddaughter . . . Not long afterwards, Krymov had read an article by Koloskov on the wall-newspaper: apparently the kulaks felt a violent hatred for everything new and were burying their grain in the ground.

Why, after crying his heart out, had Koloskov written such things? Why had Mostovskoy never said anything? Out of cowardice? Krymov had said things that went against his deepest feelings. But he had always believed what he said in his speeches and articles; he was still convinced that his words were a true reflection of his beliefs. Though there had been times when he'd said: 'What else can I do? It's for the sake of the Revolution.'

Yes, yes . . . Krymov had indeed failed to defend friends whose innocence he had felt sure of. Sometimes he had said nothing, sometimes he had mumbled incoherently, sometimes he had done still worse. There were occasions when he had been summoned by the Party Committee, the District Committee, the City Committee or the *Oblast* Committee – by the security organs themselves. They had asked his opinion about people he knew, people who were members of the Party. He had never said anything bad about his friends, he had never slandered them, he had never written denunciations . . .

What about Grekov? But Grekov was an enemy. Where enemies were concerned, Krymov had never felt a trace of pity. He had never worn kid gloves in dealing with them.

But why had he had nothing more to do with the families of comrades who had been arrested? He had stopped phoning or visiting them. Of course, if he had met them by chance, he had always said hello; he had never crossed over to the other side of the street.

But then there were some people – usually old women, lower-middle-class housewives – who would help you send parcels to someone in camp. You could arrange for someone in camp to write to you at their address. And for some reason they were quite unafraid. These same old women, these superstitious domestics and illiterate nannies, would even take in children whose mothers and fathers had been arrested, saving them from orphanages and reception-centres. Members of the Party, on the other hand, avoided these children like the plague. Were these old women braver and more honourable than Old Bolsheviks like Mostovskoy and Krymov?

People are able to overcome fear: children pluck up their courage and enter a dark room, soldiers go into battle, a young man can leap into an abyss with only a parachute to save him. But what about this other fear, this fear that millions of people find insuperable, this fear written up in crimson letters over the leaden sky of Moscow – this terrible fear of the State . . . ?

No, no! Fear alone cannot achieve all this. It was the revolutionary cause itself that freed people from morality in the name of morality, that justified today's pharisees, hypocrites and writers of denunciations in the name of the future, that explained why it was right to elbow the innocent into the ditch in the name of the happiness of the people. This was what enabled you to turn away from children whose parents had been sent to camps. This was why it was right for a woman – because she had failed to denounce an innocent husband – to be torn away from her children and sent for ten years to a concentration camp.

The magic of the Revolution had joined with people's fear of death, their horror of torture, their anguish when the first breath of the camps blew on their faces.

Once, if you took up the cause of the Revolution, you could expect prison, forced labour, years of homelessness, the scaffold . . . But now – and this was the most terrible thing of all – the Revolution paid those who were still faithful to its great ideal with supplementary rations, with dinners in the Kremlin canteen, with special food parcels, with private cars, trips to holiday resorts and tickets for first-class coaches.

'Are you still awake, Nikolay Grigorevich?' asked Spiridonov out of the darkness.

'Just,' said Krymov. 'I'm just falling asleep.'

'Oh! I'm sorry. I won't disturb you again.'

39

It was over a week since the night when Mostovskoy had been summoned by Obersturmbannführer Liss. His feeling of tension, of feverish expectancy, had been replaced by a heavy depression. There were moments when he began to think he had been completely forgotten by both his friends and his enemies; that they looked on him as a weak, half-senile old man, a goner.

One clear still morning he was taken to the bath-house. This time the SS guard sat down on the steps outside, putting his tommy-gun down beside him, and lit a cigarette. The sky was clear and the sun was warm; the soldier obviously preferred not to enter the damp building.

The prisoner on duty inside came up to Mostovskoy.

'Good morning, dear comrade Mostovskoy.'

Mostovskoy let out a cry of astonishment: in front of him stood Brigade Commissar Osipov; he was wearing a uniform jacket with a band on the sleeve and waving an old rag in his hand.

They embraced.

'I managed to get myself a job in the bath-house,' Osipov explained hurriedly. 'I'm standing in for the usual cleaner. I wanted to see you. Kotikov, the general and Zlatokrylets all send their greetings. But first, how are they treating you, how are you feeling, what do they want from you? You can talk while you're undressing.'

Mostovskoy told him about his interrogation.

Osipov stared at him with his dark, prominent eyes.

'The blockheads think they'll be able to win you over.'

'But why? Why? What's the point of it all?'

'They may be interested in information of a historical nature, in the personalities of the founders and leaders of the Party. Or they may be intending to ask you to write letters, statements and appeals.'

'They're wasting their time.'

'They may torture you, comrade Mostovskoy.'

'The fools are wasting their time,' repeated Mostovskoy. 'But tell me – how are things with you?'

'Better than could have been expected,' said Osipov in a whisper. 'The main thing is that we've made contact with the factory workers. We're stockpiling weapons – machine-guns and hand-grenades. People bring in the components one by one and we assemble them in the huts at night. For the time being, of course, the quantities are insignificant.'

'That's Yershov's doing,' said Mostovskoy. 'Good for him!'

Then he shook his head sadly as he took off his shirt and looked at his bare chest. Once again he felt angry with himself for being so old and weak.

'I have to inform you as a senior comrade that Yershov is no longer with us.'

'What do you mean? How come?'

'He has been transferred to Buchenwald.'

'Why on earth? He was a splendid fellow.'

'In that case he'll still be a splendid fellow in Buchenwald.'

'But how did this happen? And why?'

'A split appeared in the leadership. Yershov enjoyed a widespread popularity that quite turned his head. Nothing would make him submit to the centre. He's a doubtful individual, an alien element. The position became more confused with every step we took. The first rule in any underground work is iron discipline – and there we were with two different centres, one of them outside the Party. We discussed the position and came to a decision. A Czech comrade who worked in the office slipped Yershov's card into the pile for Buchenwald. He was put on the list automatically.'

'What could be simpler?' said Mostovskoy.

'It was the unanimous decision of all the Communists,' said Osipov.

He stood in front of Mostovskoy in his miserable clothes, holding a rag in one hand – stern, unshakeable, certain of his rectitude, of his terrible, more than divine, right to make the cause he served into the supreme arbiter of a man's fate.

And the naked skinny old man, one of the founders of a great Party, sat there in silence, his shoulders hunched and his head bowed.

It was night and he was back in Liss's office. He was overwhelmed by terror. What if Liss hadn't been lying . . . ? What if he had had no ulterior motive, if he had simply wanted to talk to another human being?

He drew himself up to his full height. Then – just as ten years before during the period of collectivization, just as during the political trials when the comrades of his youth had been condemned to the scaffold – he said:

'I submit to this decision; I accept it as a member of the Party.'

He took his jacket from the bench and removed several scraps of paper from the lining. They were texts he had drawn up for leaflets.

Suddenly, in his mind's eye, he saw Ikonnikov's face and large cow-like eyes. If only he could listen once again to the preacher of senseless kindness.

'I wanted to ask about Ikonnikov,' he said. 'Did the Czech slip his card in too?'

'The holy fool? The man you used to call the blancmange? He was executed. He refused to work on the construction of an extermination camp. Keyze was ordered to shoot him.'

That night Mostovskoy's leaflets about Stalingrad were stuck up on the walls of the barrack-huts.

40

Soon after the end of the war a dossier was found in the archives of the Munich Gestapo relating to the investigation into an underground organization in one of the concentration camps of Western Germany. The final document stated that the sentence passed on the members of the organization had been carried out and their bodies burnt in the crematorium. The first name on the list was Mostovskoy's.

It was impossible to ascertain the name of the provocateur who had betrayed his comrades. Probably he was executed by the Gestapo together with the men he betrayed.

41

The hostel belonging to the special unit assigned to the gas chambers, crematorium and stores of poisonous substances was both warm and quiet.

The prisoners who worked permanently in number one complex enjoyed good living conditions. Beside each bed stood a small table with a carafe of boiled water. There was even a strip of carpet down the central passageway. The prisoners here were all trusties; they ate in a special building.

The Germans in the special unit were able to choose their own menus as though in a restaurant. They were paid almost three times as much as officers and soldiers of corresponding rank on active service. Their families were granted rent reductions, maximum discounts on groceries and the right to be the first evacuees from areas threatened by air-raids.

Private Roze's job was to watch through the inspection-window; when the process was completed, he gave the order for the gas chamber to be emptied. He was also expected to check that the dentists worked efficiently and honestly. He had written several reports to the director of the complex, Sturmbannführer Kaltluft, about the difficulty of carrying out these two tasks at once. While Roze was up above watching the gassing, the workers down below were left unsupervised; the dentists and the men loading bodies onto the conveyor-belt could steal and loot to their hearts' content.

Roze had grown accustomed to his work; looking through the inspection-window no longer disturbed or excited him as it had during the first few days. His predecessor had once been found engaged in a pastime more suitable for a twelve-year-old boy than an SS soldier entrusted with a special assignment. At first Roze hadn't understood why his comrades kept hinting at certain improprieties; only later had he understood what they were talking about.

Roze did not, however, enjoy his work. He was unnerved by the esteem that now surrounded him. The waitresses in the canteen kept asking why he was so pale.

As far back as he could remember, Roze's mother had always been in tears. And time and again his father had been fired from work; he seemed to have been sacked from more jobs than he had actually had. It was from his parents that Roze had learned his quiet, sidling walk – intended not to disturb anyone – and the anxious smile with which he greeted his neighbours, his landlord, his landlord's cat, the headmaster and the policeman on the corner of the street. Gentleness and friendliness had seemed the fundamental traits of his character; even he was surprised how much hatred lay inside him and how long he had kept it hidden.

He had been seconded to the special unit; the commander, a man with a fine understanding of people, had at once sensed his gentle, effeminate nature.

There was nothing pleasant about watching the convulsions of the Jews in the gas chambers. The soldiers who enjoyed working in the complex filled Roze with disgust. He especially disliked Zhuchenko, the prisoner-of-war on duty by the door of the gas-chambers during the morning shift. He always had a childish and particularly unpleasant smile on his face. Roze didn't like his work, but he was well aware of the many official and unofficial perks it brought him.

At the end of each day one of the dentists would hand Roze a small packet containing several gold crowns. Although this represented only an insignificant fraction of the precious metal taken every day to the camp authorities, Roze had twice handed over almost a kilo of gold to his wife. This was their bright future, their dream of a peaceful old age. As a young man, Roze had been weak and timid, unable to play an active part in life's struggle. He had never doubted that the Party had set itself one aim only: the well-being of the small and weak. He had already experienced the benefits of Hitler's policies; life had improved immeasurably for him and his family.

42

Sometimes, deep in his heart, Anton Khmelkov was appalled by his work. As he lay down in the evening and listened to Trofima Zhuchenko's laughter, he would be overcome by a cold, heavy fear.

It was Zhuchenko's job to close the hermetically sealed doors of the gas chamber. His large, strong hands and fingers always looked as though they hadn't been washed; Khmelkov didn't even like to take a piece of bread from the same basket as Zhuchenko.

Zhuchenko looked happy and excited as he went out to work in the morning and waited for the column of prisoners from the railway-line. But the slow progress of the column seemed to incense him; he would twitch his jaws and make a thin, complaining sound in his throat – like a cat watching sparrows from behind a pane of glass.

Khmelkov found Zhuchenko very disturbing. Not that he himself was above having a few drinks and then going off for a bit of fun with one of the women in the queue. There was a little door through which members of the special unit could go into the changing-room and pick out a woman. A man's a man, after all. Khmelkov would choose a woman or a girl, take her off to an empty corner, and half an hour later hand her back to the guard. Neither he nor the woman would say anything. Still, he wasn't in this job for the wine or the women, for gabardine riding-breeches or box-calf boots.

Khmelkov had been taken prisoner in July 1941. He had been beaten over the head and neck with a rifle-butt, he had suffered from dysentery, he had been forced to march through the snow in tattered boots, he had drunk yellow water tainted with fuel-oil, he had torn off hunks of black, stinking meat from the carcass of a horse, he had eaten potato peelings and rotten swedes. All he had asked for, all he had wanted, was life itself. He had fought off dozens of deaths – from cold, from hunger, from bloody flux . . . He didn't want to fall to the ground with nine grams of metal in his skull. He didn't want to swell up till his heart choked in the water rising from his legs. He wasn't a criminal – just a hairdresser from the town of Kerchi. No one – neither his relatives, his neighbours, his fellow workers or the friends with whom he drank wine, ate smoked mullet and played dominoes – had ever thought badly of him. There was a time when he thought he had nothing whatever in common with Zhuchenko; now, though, he sometimes thought that the differences between them were insignificant and trifling. What did it matter what the two of them felt? If the job they did was the same, what did it matter if one felt happy and the other felt sad?

What Khmelkov didn't understand was that it wasn't Zhuchenko's greater guilt that made him so disturbing. What was disturbing was that Zhuchenko's behaviour could be explained by some terrible, innate depravity – whereas he himself was still a human being. And he was dimly aware that if you wish to remain a human being under Fascism, there is an easier option than survival – death.

43

The director of the complex, Sturmbannführer Kaltluft, had arranged for the controller's office to provide him each evening with a schedule of the next day's arrivals. He was able to inform his workers in advance of the number of wagons and the quantity of people expected. Depending what country the train was from, the appropriate auxiliary units would be called up – barbers, escort-guards, porters . . .

Kaltluft disliked slovenliness of any kind. He never drank and was furious if he found any of his subordinates the worse for drink. Only once had anyone seen him bright and animated: sitting in his car, about to go and stay with his family over Easter, he had beckoned to Sturmführer Hahn and showed him photographs of his daughter – a little girl with large eyes and a large face like her father's.

Kaltluft enjoyed work and disliked wasting his time; he never went to the club after supper, he never played cards and he never watched films. At Christmas the special unit had had their own tree and arranged for a performance by an amateur choir; a free bottle of

French cognac had been given out to every two men. Kaltluft had dropped in for half an hour and everyone had seen the fresh ink-stains on his fingers – he had been working on Christmas Eve.

He had grown up in his parents' old home in the country. He wasn't afraid of hard work and he enjoyed the peace of the village; it had seemed he would live there for ever. He had dreamed of increasing the size of the holding, but – no matter what he earned from his wheat, swedes and pigs – he had expected to stay on in the quiet, comfortable house. His life, however, had followed a different course: at the end of the First World War he had been sent to the front. It seemed as though nothing less than fate itself had decreed his progression from the village to the army, from the trenches to HQ company, from clerk to adjutant, from the central apparatus of the RSHA to the administration of the camps – and finally to his appointment as commander of a Sonderkommando in an extermination camp.

If, on the day of judgment, Kaltluft had been called upon to justify himself, he could have explained quite truthfully how fate had led him to become the executioner of 590,000 people. What else could he have done in the face of such powerful forces – the war, fervent nationalism, the adamancy of the Party, the will of the State? How could he have swum against the current? He was a man like any other; all he had wanted was to live peacefully in his father's house. He hadn't walked – he had been pushed. Fate had led him by the hand . . . And if they had been called upon, Kaltluft's superiors and subordinates would have justified themselves in almost the same words.

But Kaltluft was not asked to justify himself before a heavenly court. Nor was God asked to reassure him that no one in the world is guilty.

There is divine judgment, there is the judgment of a State and the judgment of society, but there is one supreme judgment: the judgment of one sinner over another. A sinner can measure the power of the totalitarian State and find it limitless: through propaganda, hunger, loneliness, infamy, obscurity, labour camps and the threat of death, this terrible power can fetter a man's will. But every step that a man takes under the threat of poverty, hunger, labour camps and death is at the same time an expression of his own will. Every step Kaltluft had taken – from the village to the trenches, from being a man-in-the-street to being a member of the National Socialist Party – bore the imprint of his will. A man may be led by fate, but he can refuse to follow. He may be a mere tool in the hands of destructive powers, but he knows it is in his interest to assent to this. Fate and the individual may have different ends, but they share the same path.

The man who pronounces judgment will be neither a pure and merciful heavenly being, nor a wise justice who watches over the interests of society and the State, neither a saint nor a righteous man – but a miserable, dirty sinner who has been crushed by Fascism, who has himself experienced the terrible power of the State, who has himself bowed down, fallen, shrunk into timidity and submissiveness. And this judge will say:

'Guilty! Yes, there are men in this terrible world who are guilty.'

44

It was the last day of the journey. There was a grinding of brakes and the wagons squealed to a halt. A moment of quiet was followed by the rattle of bolts and the order 'Alle heraus!'

They began to make their way out onto the platform. It was still wet from the recent rain.

How strange people's faces seemed in the light!

Their clothes had changed less than the people themselves. Coats, jackets and shawls called to mind the houses where they had been put on, the mirrors in front of which they had been measured.

The people emerging from the wagons clustered in groups. There was something familiar and reassuring in the closeness of the herd, in the smell and the warmth, in the exhausted eyes and faces, in the solidity of the vast crowd emerging from the forty-two goods wagons.

Two SS guards walked slowly up and down the platform, the nails of their boots ringing on the asphalt. They seemed haughty and thoughtful, looking neither at the young Jews carrying out the corpse of an old woman with streaks of white hair over her white face, nor at the curly-headed man on all fours drinking from a puddle, nor at the hunch-backed woman lifting up her skirt to adjust the torn elastic of her knickers.

Now and again the SS guards glanced at each other and exchanged a few words. Their passage along the platform was like the sun's through the sky. The sun doesn't need to watch over the wind and clouds, to listen to the sound of leaves or of a storm at sea; it knows as it follows its smooth path that everything in the world depends on it.

Men in caps with large peaks and blue overalls with white bands on the sleeves chivvied on the new arrivals, shouting at them in a strange mixture of Russian, Yiddish, Polish and Ukrainian. They organized the crowd quickly and efficiently. They weeded out people who could no longer stand up and got the stronger men to load the dying into vans. Then they moulded the milling throng into a column, inspired it with the idea of movement and gave this movement direction and purpose.

As they were formed up into ranks of six, the news ran down the column: 'The bath-house! First we're going to the bath-house!'

No merciful God could have thought of anything kinder.

'Very well, Jews, let's be off!' shouted the man in a cape who commanded the unit responsible for unloading the train.

The men and women were picking up their bags; the children were clinging to their mothers' skirts and the lapels of their fathers' jackets. 'The bath-house . . . ! The bath-house . . .' The words were like a hypnotic charm that filled their consciousness.

There was something attractive about the tall man in the cape. It was as if he were one of them, closer to their unhappy world than to the men in helmets and grey greatcoats. Carefully, entreatingly, an old woman stroked the sleeves of his overalls with the tips of her fingers and asked in Yiddish: 'You're a Jew, aren't you, my child? A Litvak?'

'That's right, mother, that's right.'

Suddenly, in a hoarse, resonant voice, bringing together words used by the two opposing armies, he shouted:

'*Die Kolonne marsch! Shagom marsh!*'

The platform emptied. The men in overalls began sweeping up pieces of rag, scraps of bandages, a broken clog and a child's brick that had been dropped on the ground. They slammed the doors of the wagons. A grinding wave ran down the train as it moved off to the disinfection point.

After they had finished work, the unit returned to the camp through the service gates. The trains from the East were the worst –

538

you got covered in lice and there was a foul stench from the corpses and invalids. No, they weren't like the wagons from Hungary, Holland or Belgium where you sometimes found a bottle of scent, a packet of cocoa or a tin of condensed milk.

45

A great city opened out before the travellers. Its western outskirts were lost in the mist. The dark smoke from the distant factory chimneys blended with the damp to form a low haze over the chequered pattern of the barrack-huts; there was something surprising in the contrast between the mist and the angular geometry of the streets of barracks.

To the north-east there was a dark red glow in the sky; it was as though the damp autumn sky had somehow become red-hot. Sometimes a slow, creeping flame escaped from this damp glow.

The travellers emerged into a spacious square. In the middle of this square were several dozen people on a wooden bandstand like in a public park. They were the members of a band, each of them as different from one another as their instruments. Some of them looked round at the approaching column. Then a grey-haired man in a colourful cloak called out and they reached for their instruments. There was a burst of something like cheeky, timid bird-song and the air – air that had been torn apart by the barbed wire and the howl of sirens, that stank of oily fumes and garbage – was filled with music. It was like a warm summer cloud-burst ignited by the sun, flashing as it crashed down to earth.

People in camps, people in prisons, people who have escaped from prison, people going to their death, know the extraordinary power of music. No one else can experience music in quite the same way.

What music resurrects in the soul of a man about to die is neither hope nor thought, but simply the blind, heart-breaking miracle of life itself. A sob passed down the column. Everything seemed transformed, everything had come together; everything scattered and fragmented – home, peace, the journey, the rumble of wheels, thirst, terror, the city rising out of the mist, the wan red dawn – fused together, not into a memory or a picture but into the blind, fierce ache of life itself. Here, in the glow of the gas ovens, people knew that life was more than happiness – it was also grief. And freedom was both painful and difficult; it was life itself.

Music had the power to express the last turmoil of a soul in whose blind depths every experience, every moment of joy and grief, had fused with this misty morning, this glow hanging over their heads. Or perhaps it wasn't like that at all. Perhaps music was just the key to a man's feelings, not what filled him at this terrible moment, but the key that unlocked his innermost core.

In the same way, a child's song can appear to make an old man cry. But it isn't the song itself he cries over; the song is simply a key to something in his soul.

As the column slowly formed into a half-circle round the square, a cream-coloured car drove through the camp gates. An SS officer in spectacles and a fur-collared greatcoat got out and made an impatient gesture; the conductor, who had been watching him, let his hands fall with what seemed like a gesture of despair and the music broke off.

A number of voices shouted 'Halt.' The officer walked down the ranks; sometimes he pointed at people and the guard called them out. He looked them over casually while the guard asked in a quiet voice – so as not to disturb his thoughts: 'Age? Occupation?'

Thirty people altogether were picked out.

Then there was another command:

'Doctors, surgeons!'

No one responded.

'Doctors, surgeons, come forward!'

Again – silence.

The officer walked back to his car. He had lost interest in the thousands of people in the square.

The chosen were formed up into ranks of five and wheeled round towards the banner on the camp gates: '*Arbeit mach frei*'. A child in the main column screamed, then some women; their cries were wild and shrill. The chosen stood there in silence, hanging their heads.

How can one convey the feelings of a man pressing his wife's hand for the last time? How can one describe that last, quick look at a beloved face? Yes, and how can a man live with the merciless memory of how, during the silence of parting, he blinked for a moment to hide the crude joy he felt at having managed to save his life? How can he ever bury the memory of his wife handing him a packet containing her wedding ring, a rusk and some sugar-lumps? How can he continue to exist, seeing the glow in the sky flaring up with renewed strength? Now the hands he had kissed must be burning, now the eyes that had admired him, now the hair whose smell he could recognize in the darkness, now his children, his wife, his mother. How can he ask for a place in the barracks nearer the stove? How can he hold out his bowl for a litre of grey swill? How can he repair the torn sole of his boot? How can he wield a crowbar? How can he drink? How can he breathe? With the screams of his mother and children in his ears?

Those who were to remain alive were taken towards the camp gates. They could hear the other people shouting and they were shouting themselves, tearing at the shirts on their breasts as they walked towards their new life: electric fences, reinforced concrete towers with machine-guns, barrack-huts, pale-faced women and girls looking at them from behind the wire, columns of people marching to work with scraps of red, yellow and blue sewn to their chests.

Once again the orchestra struck up. The people chosen to work entered the town built on the marshes.

Dark water forced its way sullenly and mutely between heavy blocks of stone and slabs of concrete. It was a rusty black and it smelt of decay; it was covered in green chemical foam, filthy shreds of rag, bloodstained clothes discarded by the camp operating-theatres. It disappeared underground, came back to the surface, disappeared once more. Nevertheless, it forced its way through – the waves of the sea and the morning dew were still present, still alive in the dark water of the camp.

Meanwhile, the condemned went to their death.

46

Sofya Levinton was walking with heavy, even steps; the little boy beside her was holding her hand. His other hand was in his pocket, clutching a matchbox containing a dark brown chrysalis, wrapped in cotton wool, that had just emerged from the cocoon. The machinist, Lazar Yankevich, walked beside them; his wife, Deborah Samuelovna, was carrying a child in her arms. Behind him, Rebekka Bukhman was muttering: 'Oh God, oh God, oh God!' The fifth person in the row was the librarian Musya Borisovna. She had put up her hair and the nape of her neck seemed quite white. Several times during the journey she had exchanged her ration of bread for half a mess-tin of warm water. She never grudged anyone anything. In the wagon she had been looked on as a saint; the old women, good judges of character, used to kiss her dress. The rank in front consisted of only four people; during the selection the officer had called out two men from this rank straight away, a father and son, the Slepoys. In reply to the question about profession, they had shouted out, 'Zahnarzt'.* The officer had nodded; the Slepoys had guessed right, they had won life. Three of the men left in the rank walked with their arms dangling by their sides; it was as though they no longer needed them. The fourth walked with a carefree gait, the collar of his jacket turned up, his hands in his pockets and his head thrown back. Four or five ranks in front was a huge man in a soldier's winter cap.

Just behind Sofya Levinton was Musya Vinokur, who had celebrated her fourteenth birthday in the goods-wagon.

Death! It had become sociable, quite at home; it called on people without ceremony, coming into their yards and workshops, meeting a housewife at the market and taking her off together with her sack of potatoes, joining in children's games, peeping into a shop where some tailors were hurrying to finish a coat for the wife of a commissar, waiting in a bread queue, sitting down beside an old woman darning stockings.

Death carried on in its own everyday manner, and people in theirs. Sometimes it allowed them to finish a cigarette or eat up a meal; sometimes it came up on a man with comradely bluffness, slapping him on the back and guffawing stupidly.

It was as though people had now understood death, as though it had at last revealed how humdrum it was, how childishly simple. Really it was an easy crossing, just a shallow stream with planks thrown across from one bank – where there was smoke coming out of

* Dentist.

the wooden huts – to the other bank and its empty meadows. It was a mere five or six steps. That was all. What was there to be afraid of? A calf was just going over the bridge – you could hear its hooves – and there were some little boys running across in bare feet.

Sofya Levinton listened to the music. She had first heard this piece when she was a child; she had listened to it again as a student, and then as a young doctor. It always filled her with a keen sense of the future.

But this time the music was deceptive. Sofya Levinton had no future, only a past.

For a moment this sense of her past blotted out everything present, blotted out the abyss. It was the very strangest of feelings, something you could never share with any other person – not even your wife, your mother, your brother, your son, your friend or your father. It was the secret of your soul. However passionately it might long to, your soul could never betray this secret. You carry away this sense of your life without having ever shared it with anyone: the miracle of a particular individual whose conscious and unconscious contain everything good and bad, everything funny, sweet, shameful, pitiful, timid, tender, uncertain, that has happened from childhood to old age – fused into the mysterious sense of an individual life.

When the music began, David had wanted to take the matchbox out of his pocket, open it just for a moment – so the chrysalis wouldn't catch cold – and let it see the musicians. But after a few steps he forgot the people on the bandstand. There was nothing left but the music and the glow in the sky. The sad, powerful melody filled his soul with longing for his mother – a mother who was neither strong nor calm, a mother who was ashamed at having been deserted by her husband. She had made David a calico shirt and the people in the other rooms along the corridor had laughed at him because it had flowers on it and the sleeves weren't straight. She had been everything to him. He had always relied on her without thinking. But now, perhaps because of the music, he no longer relied on her. He loved her, but she was weak and helpless – just like the people walking beside him now. And the music was quiet and sleepy; it was like the little waves he had seen when he had had a fever, when he had crawled off his burning pillow onto warm, damp sand.

The band howled; it was as though some huge, dried-up throat had started to wail. The dark wall, the wall that had risen out of the water when he was ill, was hanging over him now, filling the whole sky.

Everything that had ever terrified his little heart now became one. The fear aroused by the picture of a little goat who hadn't noticed the shadow of a wolf between the trunks of the fir-trees, the blue eyes of the dead calves at market, his dead grandmother, Rebekka Bukhman's suffocated daughter, his first unreasoning terror at night that had made him scream out desperately for his mother. Death was standing there, as huge as the sky, watching while little David walked towards him on his little legs. All around him there was nothing but music, and he couldn't cling to it or even batter his head against it.

As for the cocoon, it had no wings, no paws, no antennae, no eyes; it just lay there in its little box, stupidly trustful, waiting.

David was a Jew . . .

He was choking and hiccuping. He would have strangled himself if he had been able to. The music stopped. His little feet and dozens of other little feet were hurrying along. He had no thoughts and he was unable to weep or scream. His fingers were wet with sweat; they were squeezing a little box in his pocket, he no longer even remembered what it was. There was nothing except his little feet, walking, hurrying, running.

If the horror that gripped him had lasted only a few more minutes, he would have fallen to the ground, his heart broken.

When the music stopped, Sofya Levinton wiped away her tears and said angrily: 'Yes, it's just what that poor man said!'

Then she glanced at the boy's face; even here, its peculiar expression made it stand out.

'What is it? What's the matter with you?' she shouted, gripping his hand. 'What is it? What's the matter? We're just going to the bath-house to wash.'

When they had called for the doctors and surgeons, she had remained silent, fighting against some powerful force that she found repugnant.

The machinist's wife was walking along beside her; in her arms the pathetic little baby, its head too large for its body, was looking around with a calm, thoughtful expression. It was this woman, Deborah, who one night in the goods-wagon had stolen a handful of sugar for her baby. The injured party had been too feeble to do anything, but old

Lapidus had stood up for her . . . No one had wanted to sit near him – he was always urinating on the floor.

And now Deborah was walking along beside her, holding her baby in her arms. And the baby, who had cried day and night, was quite silent. The woman's sad dark eyes stopped one from noticing the hideousness of her dirty face and pale crumpled lips.

'A madonna!' thought Sofya Levinton.

Once, about two years before the war, she had watched the sun as it rose behind the pine-trees on Tyan-Shan, catching the white squirrels in its light; the lake lay there in the dawn as though it had been chiselled out of some pure blue condensed to the solidity of stone. She had thought then that there was probably no one in the world who wouldn't envy her; and at the same moment, with an intensity that burnt her fifty-year-old heart, she had felt ready to give up everything if only in some shabby, dark, low-ceilinged room she could be hugged by the arms of a child.

She had always loved children, but little David evoked some special tenderness in her that she had never felt before. In the goods-wagon she had given him some bread and he had turned his little face towards her in the half-light; she had wanted to weep, to hug him, to smother him with kisses like a mother kissing her child. In a whisper that no one else could hear, she had said:

'Eat, my son, eat.'

She seldom spoke to the boy; some strange shame made her want to hide the maternal feelings welling up inside her. But she had noticed that he always watched anxiously if she moved to the other side of the wagon and that he calmed down when she was near him.

She didn't want to admit why she hadn't answered when they had called for doctors and surgeons, why she had been seized at that moment by a feeling of exaltation.

The column moved on beside the barbed wire and the ditches, past the reinforced concrete towers with their machine-guns; to these people, who no longer remembered freedom, it seemed that the barbed wire and the machine-gunes were there not to stop the in-mates from escaping, but to stop the condemned from hiding away in the camp.

The path turned away from the barbed wire and led towards some low squat buildings with flat roofs; from a distance, these rectangles with grey windowless walls looked like the children's bricks David had once glued together to make pictures.

As the column turned, a gap appeared in the ranks and David saw that some of the buildings had their doors flung wide open. Not knowing why, he took the little box out of his pocket and, without saying goodbye to the chrysalis, flung it away. Let it live!

'Splendid people, these Germans!' said the man in front – as though the guards might hear and appreciate his flattery.

The man with the raised collar shrugged his shoulders in a manner that was somehow peculiar, gave a quick glance to either side of him and seemed to grow taller and more imposing; with a sudden nimble jump, as though he had spread his wings, he punched an SS guard in the face and knocked him to the ground. Sofya Levinton leapt after him with an angry shout. She stumbled and fell. Several hands grabbed her and helped her up. The people behind were pressing on; David glanced round, afraid of being knocked over, and caught a glimpse of the man being dragged away by the guards.

In the brief instant when Sofya had attempted to attack the guard, she had forgotten about David. Now once more she took him by the hand. David saw how clear, fierce and splendid human eyes can be when – even for a fraction of a second – they sense freedom.

By now the front ranks had already reached the asphalt square in front of the bath-house; their steps sounded different as they marched through the wide-open doors.

47

The warm, damp changing-room was quiet and gloomy; the only light came through some small rectangular windows.

Benches made from thick bare planks disappeared into the half-darkness. A low partition ran down the middle of the room to the wall opposite the entrance; the men were undressing on one side, the women and children on the other.

This division didn't cause any anxiety: people were still able to see each other and call out: 'Manya, Manya, are you there?' 'Yes, yes, I can see you.' One man shouted out: 'Matilda, bring a flannel so you can rub my back for me!' Most people felt a sense of relief.

Serious-looking men in gowns walked up and down the rows, keeping order and giving out sensible advice: socks, foot-cloths and stockings should be placed inside your shoes, and you mustn't forget the number of your row and place.

People's voices sounded quiet and muffled.

When a man has no clothes on, he draws closer to himself. 'God, the hairs on my chest are thicker and wirier than ever – and what a lot of grey!' 'How ugly my fingernails look!' There's only one thing a naked man can say as he looks at himself: 'Yes, here I am. This is me!' He recognizes himself and identifies his 'I', an 'I' that remains always the same. A little boy crosses his skinny arms over his bony chest, looks at his frog-like body and says, 'This is me'; fifty years later he looks at a plump, flabby chest, at the blue, knotted veins on his legs and says, 'This is me'.

But Sofya Levinton noticed something else. It was as though the body of a whole people, previously covered over by layers of rags, was laid bare in these naked bodies of all ages: the skinny little boy with the big nose over whom an old woman had shaken her head and said, 'Poor little Hassid!'; the fourteen-year-old girl who was admired even here by hundreds of eyes; the feeble and deformed old men and women who aroused everyone's pitying respect; men with strong backs covered in hair; women with large breasts and prominently veined legs. It was as though she felt, not just about herself, but about her whole people: 'Yes, here I am.' This was the naked body of a people: young and old, robust and feeble, with bright curly hair and with pale grey hair.

Sofya looked at her own broad, white shoulders; no one had ever kissed them – only her mother, long ago when she was a child. Then, with a feeling of meekness, she looked at David. Had she really, only a few minutes ago, forgotten about him and leapt furiously at an SS guard? 'A foolish young Jew and an old Russian pupil of his once preached the doctrine of non-violence,' she thought. 'But that was before Fascism.' No longer ashamed of the maternal feelings that had been aroused in her – virgin though she was – she bent down and took David's narrow little face in her large hands. It was as though she had taken his warm eyes into her hands and kissed them.

'Yes, my child,' she said, 'we've reached the bath-house.'

For a moment, in the gloom of the concrete changing-room, she glimpsed the eyes of Alexandra Vladimirovna Shaposhnikova. Was she still alive? They had said goodbye. Sofya had gone on her way, and now reached the end of it; so had Anya Shtrum.

The machinist's wife wanted to show her little son to her husband, but he was on the other side of the partition. Instead she held him out, half-covered in diapers, to Sofya Levinton and said proudly: 'He's only just been undressed and he's already stopped crying.'

Behind the partition, a man with a thick black beard, wearing torn pyjama bottoms instead of underpants, called out, his eyes and his false teeth glittering, 'Manechka, there's a bathing-costume for sale here. Shell we buy it?'

Musya Borisovna smiled at the joke; her low-cut shift revealed her breasts and she was covering them with one hand.

Sofya Levinton knew that these witticisms were anything but an expression of strength. It was just that terror became less terrible if you laughed at it.

Rebekka Bukhman's beautiful face looked thin and exhausted; she turned her huge, feverish eyes aside and ran her fingers through her thick curls, hiding away her rings and ear-rings.

She was in the grip of a cruel, blind life-force. Helpless and unhappy though she was, Fascism had reduced her to its own level: nothing could break her determination to survive. Even now she no longer remembered how, with these same hands, she had squeezed her child's throat, afraid that its crying would reveal their hiding-place.

But as Rebekka Bukhman gave a long sigh, like an animal that had finally reached the safety of a thicket, she caught sight of a woman in a gown cutting Musya Borisovna's curls with a pair of scissors. Beside her someone else was cutting a little girl's hair. A silky black stream fell silently onto the concrete floor. There was hair everywhere; it was as though the women were washing their legs in streams of bright and dark water.

The woman in the gown unhurriedly took Rebekka's hand away and seized the hair at the back of her head; the tips of her scissors clinked against the rings. Without stopping work, she deftly ran her fingers through Rebekka's hair, removed the rings and whispered:

'Everything will be returned to you.' Then, still more quietly, she whispered: '*Ganz ruhig*. The Germans are listening.'

Rebekka at once forgot the woman's face; she had no eyes, no lips, just a blue-veined, yellowish hand.

A grey-haired man appeared on the other side of the partition; his spectacles sat askew on his crooked nose and he looked like a sick, unhappy demon. He glanced up and down the benches. Articulating each syllable like someone used to speaking to the deaf, he asked:

'Mother, mother, how are you?'

A little wrinkled old woman, recognizing her son's voice amid the general hubbub, guessed what he meant and answered:

'My pulse is fine, no irregularity at all, don't worry!'

Someone next to Sofya Levinton said:

'That's Helman. He's a famous doctor.'

A naked young woman was holding a thick-lipped little girl in white knickers by the hand and screaming:

'They're going to kill us, they're going to kill us!'

'Quiet, quiet! Calm her down, she's mad,' said the other women. They looked round – there were no guards in sight. Their eyes and ears were able to rest in the quiet semi-darkness. What pleasure there was, a pleasure they hadn't experienced for months on end, in taking off their half-rotten socks, stockings and foot-cloths, in being free of clothes that had become almost wooden with dirt and sweat. The haircutters finished their job and went away; the women breathed still more freely. Some began to doze, others checked the seams on their clothes for lice, still others started to chat quietly among themselves.

'A pity we haven't got a pack of cards!' said one voice. 'We could play Fool.'

At this moment Kaltluft, a cigar between his teeth, was picking up the telephone receiver; the storeman was loading a motor-cart with jars of 'Zyklon B' that had red labels on them like pots of jam; and the special unit orderly was sitting in the office, waiting for the red indicator lamp on the wall to light up.

Suddenly the order 'Stand up!' came from each end of the changing-room.

Germans in black uniforms were standing at the end of the benches. Everyone made their way into a wide corridor, lit by dim ceiling-lamps covered by ovals of thick glass. The muscular strength of the smoothly curving concrete sucked in the stream of people. It was quiet; the only sound was the rustle of bare feet.

Before the war Sofya Levinton had once said to Yevgenia Nikolaevna Shaposhnikova, 'If one man is fated to be killed by another, it would be interesting to trace the gradual convergence of their paths. At the start they might be miles away from one another – I might be in Pamir picking alpine roses and clicking my camera, while this other man, my death, might be eight thousand miles away, fishing for ruff in a little stream after school. I might be getting ready to go to a concert and he might be at the railway station buying a ticket to go and visit his mother-in-law – and yet eventually we are bound to meet, we can't avoid it . . .'

Sofya looked up at the ceiling: the thick concrete would never again allow her to listen to a storm or glimpse the overturned dipper of the Great Bear . . . She was walking in bare feet towards a bend in the corridor, and the corridor was noiselessly, stealthily floating towards her. The movement went on by itself, without violence; it was as if she were gliding along in a dream, as if everything inside her and round her had been smeared with glycerine . . .

The door to the gas chamber opened gradually and yet suddenly. The stream of people flowed through. An old couple, who had lived together for fifty years and had been separated in the changing-room, were again walking side by side; the machinist's wife was carrying her baby, now awake; a mother and son looked over everyone's heads, scrutinizing not space but time. Sofya Levinton caught a glimpse of the doctor's face; right beside her she saw Musya Borisovna's kind eyes, then the horror-filled gaze of Rebekka Bukhman. There was Lusya Shterental – nothing could lessen the beauty of her young eyes, her nose, her neck, her half-open mouth; and there was old Lapidus walking beside her with his wrinkled blue lips. Again, Sofya Levinton hugged David's shoulders. Never before had she felt such tenderness for people.

Rebekka Bukhman, now walking at Sofya's side, gave a sudden scream – the scream of someone who is being turned into ashes.

A man with a length of hosepipe was standing beside the entrance to the gas chamber. He wore a brown shirt with a zip-fastener and short sleeves. It was seeing his childish, mindless, drunken smile that had caused Rebekka Bukhman to let out that terrible scream.

His eyes slid over Sofya Levinton's face. There he was; they had met at last!

Sofya felt her fingers itching to seize hold of the neck that seemed to creep up from his open collar. The man with the smile raised his club. Through the ringing of bells and the crunch of broken glass in her head, she heard the words: 'Easy now, you filthy Yid!'

She just managed to stay on her feet. With slow, heavy steps, still holding David, she crossed the steel threshold.

48

David passed his hand over the steel frame of the door; it felt cool and slippery. He caught sight of a light-grey blur that was the reflection of his own face. The soles of his bare feet told him that the floor here was colder than in the corridor – it must have just been washed.

Taking short, slow steps, he walked into a concrete box with a low ceiling. He couldn't see any lamps but there was a grey light in the chamber, a stone-like light that seemed unfit for living beings – it was as though the sun were shining through a concrete sky.

People who had always stayed together now drifted apart, began to lose one another. David glimpsed the face of Lusya Shterental. When he had first seen it in the goods-wagon he had felt the sweet sadness of being in love. A moment later a short woman with no neck was standing where Lusya had been. She was replaced by an old man with blue eyes and white fluff on his neck, then by a young man with a fixed wide-eyed stare.

This wasn't how people moved. It wasn't even how the lowest form of animal life moved. It was a movement without sense or purpose, with no trace of a living will behind it. The stream of people flowed into the chamber; the people going in pushed the people already inside, the latter pushed their neighbours, and all these countless shoves and pushes with elbows, shoulders and stomachs gave rise to a form of movement identical in every respect to the streaming of molecules.

David had the impression that someone was leading him, that he had to move. He reached the wall; first one knee, then his chest, came up against its bare cold. He couldn't go any further. Sofya Levinton was already there, leaning against the wall.

For a few moments they watched the people moving away from the door. The door seemed very far away; you could guess its position by the particular density of the white human bodies; they squeezed through the entrance and were then allowed to spread out into the chamber.

David saw people's faces. Since the train had been unloaded that morning he had only seen people's backs; now it was as though the faces of the whole trainload were moving towards him. Sofya Levinton had suddenly become strange; her voice sounded different in this flat concrete world; she had changed since entering the gas chamber. When she said, 'Hold on to my hand, son,' he could feel that she was afraid of letting him go, afraid of being left alone. They didn't manage to stay by the wall; they were pushed away from it and forced to shuffle forward. David felt he was moving faster than Sofya Levinton. Her hand was gripping his, pulling him towards her. But some gentle, imperceptibly growing force was pulling David away; Sofya Levinton's grip began to loosen.

The crowd grew steadily denser; people began to move more and more slowly, their steps shorter and shorter. No one was controlling the movement of people in the concrete box. The Germans didn't care whether the people in the chamber stood still or moved in senseless zigzags and half-circles. The naked boy went on taking tiny, senseless steps. The curve traced by his slight body no longer coincided with the curve traced by Sofya Levinton's large heavy body; they were being pulled apart. She shouldn't have held him by the hand; they should have been like those two women – mother and daughter – clasping each other convulsively, with all the melancholy obstinacy of love, cheek to cheek and breast to breast, fusing into one indivisible body.

Now there were even more people, packed in so tightly they no longer obeyed the laws of molecular movement. The boy screamed as he lost hold of Sofya Levinton's hand. But immediately Sofya Levinton receded into the past. Nothing existed except the present moment. Beside him, mouths were breathing, bodies were touching each other, people's thoughts and feelings fusing together.

David had been caught by a sub-current which, thrown back by the wall, was now flowing towards the door. He glimpsed three people joined together: two men and an old woman – she was defending her children, they were supporting their mother. Suddenly a new, quite different movement arose beside David. The noise was new too, quite distinct from the general shuffling and muttering.

'Let me through!' A man with strong muscular arms, head bent forward over a thick neck, was forcing his way through the solid mass of bodies. He wanted to escape the hypnotic concrete rhythm; his body was rebelling, blindly, thoughtlessly, like the body of a fish on a kitchen table. Soon he became quiet again, choking, taking tiny steps like everyone else.

This disruption changed people's trajectories; David found himself beside Sofya Levinton again. She clasped the boy to her with the peculiar strength familiar to the Germans who worked there – when they emptied the chamber, they never attempted to separate bodies locked in a close embrace.

There were screams from near the entrance; seeing the dense human mass inside, people were refusing to go through the door.

David watched the door close: gently, smoothly, as though drawn by a magnet, the steel door drew closer to its steel frame. Finally they became one.

High up, behind a rectangular metal grating in the wall, David saw something stir. It looked like a grey rat, but he realized it was a fan beginning to turn. He sensed a faint, rather sweet smell.

The shuffling quietened down; all you could hear were occasional screams, groans and barely audible words. Speech was no longer of any use to people, nor was action; action is directed towards the future and there no longer was any future. When David moved his head and neck, it didn't make Sofya Levinton want to turn and see what he was looking at.

Her eyes – which had read Homer, *Izvestia*, *Huckleberry Finn* and Mayne Reid, that had looked at good people and bad people, that had seen the geese in the green meadows of Kursk, the stars above the observatory at Pulkovo, the glitter of surgical steel, the *Mona Lisa* in the Louvre, tomatoes and turnips in the bins at market, the blue water of Issyk-Kul – her eyes were no longer of any use to her. If someone had blinded her, she would have felt no sense of loss.

She was still breathing, but breathing was hard work and she was running out of strength. The bells ringing in her head became deafening; she wanted to concentrate on one last thought, but was unable to articulate this thought. She stood there – mute, blind, her eyes still open.

The boy's movements filled her with pity. Her feelings towards him were so simple that she no longer needed words and eyes. The half-dead boy was still breathing, but the air he took in only drove life away. His head was turning from side to side; he still wanted to see. He could see people settling onto the ground; he could see mouths that were toothless and mouths with white teeth and gold teeth; he could see a thin stream of blood flowing from a nostril. He could see eyes peering through the glass; Roze's inquisitive eyes had momentarily met David's. He still needed his voice – he would have asked Aunt Sonya about those wolf-like eyes. He still even needed thought. He had taken only a few steps in the world. He had seen the prints of children's bare heels on hot, dusty earth, his mother lived in Moscow, the moon looked down and people's eyes looked up at it from below, a teapot was boiling on the gas-ring . . . This world, where a chicken could run without its head, where there was milk in the morning and frogs he could get to dance by holding their front feet – this world still preoccupied him.

All this time David was being clasped by strong warm hands. He didn't feel his eyes go dark, his heart become empty, his mind grow dull and blind. He had been killed; he no longer existed.

Sofya Levinton felt the boy's body subside in her hands. Once again she had fallen behind him. In mine-shafts where the air becomes poisoned, it is always the little creatures, the birds and mice, that die first. This boy, with his slight, bird-like body, had left before her.

'I've become a mother,' she thought.

That was her last thought.

Her heart, though, still had life in it; it still beat, still ached, still felt pity for the dead and the living. Sofya Levinton felt a wave of nausea. She was hugging David to her like a doll. Now she too was dead, she too was a doll.

49

When a person dies, they cross over from the realm of freedom to the realm of slavery. Life is freedom, and dying is a gradual denial of freedom. Consciousness first weakens and then disappears. The life-processes – respiration, the metabolism, the circulation – continue for some time, but an irrevocable move has been made towards slavery; consciousness, the flame of freedom, has died out.

The stars have disappeared from the night sky; the Milky Way has vanished; the sun has gone out; Venus, Mars and Jupiter have been extinguished; millions of leaves have died; the wind and the oceans have faded away; flowers have lost their colour and fragrance; bread has vanished; water has vanished; even the air itself, the sometimes cool, sometimes sultry air, has vanished. The universe inside a person has ceased to exist. This universe is astonishingly similar to the universe that exists outside people. It is astonishingly similar to the universes still reflected within the skulls of millions of living people. But still more astonishing is the fact that this universe had something in it that distinguished the sound of its ocean, the smell of its flowers, the rustle of its leaves, the hues of its granite and the sadness of its autumn fields both from those of every other universe that exists and ever has existed within people, and from those of the universe that exists eternally outside people. What constitutes the freedom, the soul of an individual life, is its uniqueness. The reflection of the universe in someone's consciousness is the foundation of his or her power, but life only becomes happiness, is only endowed with freedom and meaning when someone exists as a whole world that has never been repeated in all eternity. Only then can they experience the joy of freedom and kindness, finding in others what they have already found in themselves.

50

Semyonov, an army driver, was taken prisoner at the same time as Mostovskoy and Sofya Levinton. After ten weeks in a camp near the front, he was sent with a large party of captured Red Army soldiers in the direction of the western border. During these ten weeks he wasn't beaten or kicked with fists, rifle-butts or boots; all he suffered from was hunger.

Like water, hunger is part of life. Like water, it has the power to destroy the body, to cripple the soul, to annihilate millions of lives.

Hunger, ice, snowfalls, droughts, floods and epidemics can decimate flocks of sheep and herds of horses. They can kill wolves, foxes, song-birds, camels, perch and vipers. During natural disasters, people become like animals in their suffering.

The State has the power to dam life up. Like water squeezed between narrow banks, hunger will then cripple, smash to pieces or exterminate a man, tribe or people.

Molecule by molecule, hunger squeezes out the fats and proteins from each cell. Hunger softens the bones, twists the legs of children with rickets, thins the blood, stiffens the muscles, makes the head spin, gnaws at the nerves. Hunger weighs down the soul, drives away joy and faith, destroys thought and engenders submissiveness, base cruelty, indifference and despair.

All that is human in a man can perish. He can turn into a savage animal that murders, commits acts of cannibalism and eats corpses.

The State can construct a barrier that separates wheat and rye from the people who sowed it. The State has the power to bring about a famine as terrible as those which killed millions of people during the siege of Leningrad and in the cattle-pens of Hitler's camps.

Food! Victuals! Grub! Nourishment! Rations! Hard tack! Bread! A fry-up! Something to eat! A rich diet! A meat diet! An invalid diet! A thin diet! A rich, generous spread! A refined dish! Something simple! A peasant dish! A blow-out! Food! Food . . . !

Potato peelings, dogs, young frogs, snails, rotten cabbage leaves, stale beet, decayed horse-meat, cat-meat, the flesh of crows and jackdaws, damp rotting grain, leather from belts and shoes, glue, earth impregnated with slops from the officers' kitchen – all this is food. This is what trickles through the dam. People struggle to obtain all this; they then divide it up, exchange it and steal it from one another.

On the eleventh day of the journey, at Khutor Mikhailovsky, the guards dragged the now unconscious Semyonov out of the wagon and handed him over to the station authorities. The commandant, a middle-aged German, glanced at the half-dead soldier lying by the wall and turned to his interpreter.

'Let him crawl to the village. He'll be dead by tomorrow. There's no need to shoot him.'

Semyonov dragged himself to the village. At the first hut he was refused entrance.

'There's nothing here for you. Go away!' said an old woman's voice from behind the door.

No one answered when he knocked at the second hut. Either it was empty or the door was bolted on the inside.

The door of the third hut was half-open. He walked into the porch; no one challenged him. He went inside.

He could smell the warmth. He felt dizzy and lay down on the bench by the door. Breathing heavily, he looked round at the white walls, the icons, the table and the stove. After the cattle-pen of the camp, all this seemed very strange.

A shadow passed by the window. A woman walked in, caught sight of Semyonov and screamed.

'Who are you?'

Semyonov didn't say anything. The answer was obvious enough.

That day his life and fate was decided not by the merciless forces of warring States, but by a human being – old Khristya Chunyak.

She gave him a mug of milk. He drank, swallowing it greedily but with difficulty. After he finished the mug, he felt sick. He vomited over and over again; he felt he was being torn apart. He wept, sucking in each breath as though it were his last.

He tried to control himself. There was only one thought in his mind. He was unclean, foul – the woman would throw him out.

Through his swollen eyes he saw her fetch a rag and start to wipe the floor. He wanted to say that he'd clear it up himself, that he'd do anything she wanted – if only she didn't throw him out! But he could only mutter incoherently and point with his trembling fingers. Time passed; the old woman went in and out of the hut several times. She still hadn't tried to throw him out. Perhaps she was asking a neighbour to call a German patrol or the Ukrainian police?

She put an iron pot on the stove. The room grew hotter. Clouds of steam began to appear. The old woman's face looked hard, hostile.

'She's going to throw me out and then disinfect the place,' he thought to himself.

She took some trousers and some underwear out of a trunk. She helped Semyonov undress and made his clothes into a bundle. He could smell his filthy body and the stench of his pants; they were soaked with urine and bloody excrement.

She helped him into a bathtub. He felt the strong, rough touch of her palms on his louse-eaten body. Warm, soapy water ran over his chest and shoulders. He suddenly began to choke and tremble. He felt dizzy. Whining, swallowing down snot, he howled: 'Máma . . . ! Mámanka . . . ! Mámanka . . . !'

She wiped the tears from his eyes with a thick grey towel and dried his hair and shoulders. She put her hands under his armpits and lifted him onto a bench. She bent down to dry his thin, stick-like legs, slipped a shirt and some drawers over him and did up the white cloth-covered buttons.

She poured the filthy black water into a bucket and carried it away. She spread a sheepskin jacket over the stove, covered it with a piece of striped cloth, and put a large pillow at one end. Then she lifted Semyonov into the air, as easily as if he were a chicken, and laid him out on the stove.

He lay there in semi-delirium. His body knew that an unimaginable change had taken place: the merciless world was no longer trying to destroy a tormented beast. But he had never experienced such pain, neither in the camp nor on the journey . . . His legs ached, his fingers ached, his bones ached. His head kept filling with some damp, black sludge, then suddenly emptying and starting to spin. There were moments when he felt a twinge of pain in his heart, when it seemed to stop beating, when his insides filled with smoke and he thought Death had come for him.

Four days passed. Semyonov climbed down from the stove and began to walk about the room. He was amazed how much food there was in the world. In the camp there had been nothing but rotten beet. He had forgotten that there were other foods than that thin, cloudy, putrid-smelling soup. And now he could see millet, potatoes, cabbage, lard . . . He could hear a cock crow.

He was like a child who thought that the world was ruled by two magicians – one good and the other evil. He couldn't rid himself of the fear that the evil magician might once again overpower the good magician, that the kind, warm world would vanish with all its food, that he would again be left to chew at his leather belt.

He busied himself with trying to repair the small hand-mill; it was appallingly inefficient. His forehead would be dripping with sweat after he had ground a mere handful of damp grey flour.

He cleaned the drive with a file and some sandpaper and then tightened the bolt between the mechanism and the grindstones. He did everything that could be expected of an intelligent mechanic from Moscow; at the end of his labours the mill worked worse than ever.

He lay down on the stove, trying to work out how best to grind wheat. In the morning he took the mill to pieces again and rebuilt it using some cogs from an old grandfather clock.

'Look, Aunt Khristya!' he boasted, showing her the double train of gears he had contrived.

They spoke to each other very little. She never mentioned her husband who had died in 1930, her sons who had disappeared without trace, or her daughter who had moved to Priluki and quite forgotten her. Nor did she ask him how he had been taken prisoner or where he was from – the city or the country.

He didn't dare go out onto the street. He would always look long and carefully through the window before going out into the yard – and then hurry back inside. If the door slammed or a mug fell to the floor, he took fright; it seemed as though everything good would come to an end, as though the magic of old Khristya Chunyak would lose its power.

Whenever a neighbour came in, he climbed up onto the stove and tried not to breathe too loudly or sneeze. But the neighbours very seldom called round. As for the Germans – they never stayed long in the village; their billets were in the settlement by the station.

Semyonov didn't feel any guilt at the thought that he was enjoying warmth and peace while the war raged on around him. What he did feel was fear – fear that he might be dragged back into the world of the camps, the world of hunger.

He always hesitated before opening his eyes in the morning. The magic might have run out during the night. He might see camp guards and barbed wire; he might hear the clang of empty tins. He would listen for a while with his eyes closed, checking that Khristya was still there.

He seldom thought about the recent past – about Commissar Krymov, Stalingrad, the camp or the train journey. But every night he cried out and shouted in his sleep. Once he even climbed down from the stove, crawled along the floor, squeezed under the bench and slept there till morning. He was unable to remember what it was he had dreamed.

Sometimes he saw trucks drive down the village street with potatoes and sacks of grain; once he saw a car, an Opel Kapitan. It had a powerful engine and the wheels didn't skid in the mud. His heart missed a beat as he imagined guttural voices in the porch and a German patrol bursting into the hut.

When he asked Aunt Khristya about the Germans, she answered:

'Some of them aren't bad at all. When the front came this way, I had two of them in here. One was a student and the other an artist. They used to play with the children. Then there was a driver. He had a cat with him. When he came back, she would run out to meet him. She must have come all the way from the frontier with him. He would sit at the table nursing her and giving her lumps of butter and bacon-fat . . . He was very good to me. He brought me firewood. Once he got me a sack of flour. But there are other Germans who kill children. They killed the old man next door. They don't treat us like human beings – they make a filthy mess in the house and they walk around naked in front of women. And some of our own police from the village are just as bad.'

'There are no beasts like German beasts,' said Semyonov. 'But aren't you afraid to keep me here, Aunt Khristya?'

She shook her head and said there were lots of freed prisoners in the countryside – though of course they were mostly Ukrainians who'd come back to their own homes. But she could say Semyonov was her nephew, the son of her sister who'd gone to Moscow with her husband.

Semyonov knew the neighbours' faces by now; he even knew the old woman who'd refused to let him in on the first day. He knew that in the evening the girls went to the cinema at the station, that every Saturday there was a dance. He wanted to know what films the Germans showed, but only the old people called round and none of them ever went there.

One neighbour showed him a letter from her daughter who'd been deported to Germany. There were several passages he had to have explained to him. In one paragraph the girl had written: 'Vanka and Grishka flew in; they mended the windows.' Vanya and Grisha were in the air force: there must have been Soviet air-raids. Later in the same letter she wrote: 'It rained just like in Bakhmach.' That was another way of saying the same thing – at the beginning of the war the railway station at Bakhmach had been bombed.

That evening a tall, thin old man came to see Khristya. He looked Semyonov up and down and said, with no trace of a Ukrainian accent:

'Where are you from, young man?'

'I was a prisoner.'

'We're all of us prisoners now.'

The old man had served in the artillery under Tsar Nikolay and he could recall the commands with astonishing accuracy. He began to rehearse them in front of Semyonov, giving the commands in Russian, in a hoarse voice, and then reporting their execution in a young, ringing voice with a Ukrainian accent. He had obviously remembered his own voice and that of his commanding officer as they had sounded years ago.

Then he began abusing the Germans. He told Semyonov that people had hoped they would do away with the *kolkhozes* – but they must have realized that the system had its advantages for them too. They had set up five-hut and ten-hut co-operatives, the same old 'sections' and 'brigades' under another name.

'*Kolkhozes, kolkhozes*,' Aunt Khristya repeated mournfully.

'Why do you say that?' asked Semyonov. 'Of course there are *kolkhozes*. What do you expect?'

'You be quiet!' said the old woman. 'Remember what you were like when you first arrived? Well, in 1930 the whole of the Ukraine was like that. When there were no more nettles, we ate earth . . . Every last grain of corn was taken away. My man died. As for me – I couldn't walk, my whole body swelled up, I lost my voice . . .'

Semyonov was astonished that old Khristya could once have starved just like he had. He had imagined hunger and death to be powerless before the mistress of the good hut.

'Were you kulaks?' he asked.

'What do you mean? Everyone was dying. It was worse than the war.'

'Are you from the country?' asked the old man.

'No, I was born in Moscow and so was my father.'

'Well,' said the old man, 'if you'd been here during collectivization, you'd have kicked the bucket in no time. You know why I stayed alive? Because I know plants. And I'm not talking about things like acorns, linden leaves, goosefoot and nettles. They all went in no time. I know fifty-six plants a man can eat. That's how I stayed alive. It was barely spring, there wasn't a leaf on the trees – and there was I digging up roots. I know everything, brother – every root, every grass, every flower, every kind of bark. Cows, sheep and horses can die of hunger – but not me. I'm more herbivorous than any of them.'

'You're from Moscow?' said Khristya very slowly. 'I hadn't realized you were from Moscow.'

The old man left and Semyonov went to bed. Khristya sat there, her head in her hands, gazing into the black night sky.

There had been a fine harvest in 1930. The wheat stood like a tall, thick wall. It was taller than she was. It came right up to the shoulders of her Vasily . . .

A low wailing hung over the village; the little children kept up a constant, barely audible whine as they crawled about like living skeletons. The men wandered aimlessly around the yards, exhausted by hunger, barely able to breathe, their feet swollen. The women went on searching for something to eat, but everything had already gone – nettles, acorns and linden leaves, uncured sheepskins, old bones, hooves and horns that had been lying around on the ground . . .

Meanwhile the young men from the city went from house to house, hardly glancing at the dead and the dying, searching cellars, digging holes in barns, prodding the ground with iron bars ... They were searching for the grain hidden away by the kulaks.

One sultry day Vasily Chunyak had breathed his last breath. Just then the young men from the city had come back to the hut. One of them, a man with blue eyes and an accent just like Semyonov's, had walked up to the corpse and said:

'They're an obstinate lot, these kulaks. They'd rather die than give in.'

Khristya gave a sigh, crossed herself and laid out her bedding.

51

Viktor had expected his work to be appreciated by only a narrow circle of theoretical physicists. In fact, people were constantly telephoning him – and not only physicists, but also mathematicians and chemists whom he hadn't even met. Often they asked him to clarify certain points; his equations were of some complexity.

Delegates from one of the student societies came to the Institute to ask him to give a lecture to final-year students of physics and mathematics; he gave two lectures at the Academy itself. Markov and Savostyanov said that his work was being discussed in most of the Institute's laboratories. In the special store, Lyudmila overheard an exchange between the wives of two scientists: 'Where are you in the queue?' 'Behind Shtrum's wife.' '*The* Shtrum?'

Viktor was by no means indifferent to this sudden fame – though he tried not to show it. The Scientific Council of the Institute decided to nominate his work for a Stalin Prize. Viktor didn't attend the meeting himself, but that evening he couldn't take his eyes off the phone; he was waiting for Sokolov to say what had happened. The first person to speak to him, however, was Savostyanov.

With not even a trace of his usual mockery or cynicism, Savostyanov repeated: 'It's a triumph, a real triumph!'

Academician Prasolov had said that the walls of the Institute had seen no work of such importance since the research of his late friend Lebedev on the pressure of light. Professor Svechin had talked about Viktor's mathematics, showing that there was an innovative element even in his methods. He had said that it was only the Soviet people who were capable of devoting their energy so selflessly to the service of the people at a time of war. Several other men, Markov among them, had spoken, but the most striking and forceful words of all had been Gurevich's.

'He's a good man,' said Savostyanov. 'He didn't hold back – he said what needed to be said. He called your work a classic, of the same importance as that of the founders of atomic physics, Planck, Bohr and Fermi.'

'That is saying something,' thought Viktor.

Sokolov phoned immediately afterwards.

'It's impossible to get through to you today. The line's been engaged for the last twenty minutes.'

He too was excited and enthusiastic.

'I forgot to ask Savostyanov how the voting went,' said Viktor.

Sokolov explained that Professor Gavronov, a specialist in the history of physics, had voted against Viktor; in his view Viktor's work lacked a true scientific foundation, was influenced by the idealist views of Western physicists and held out no possibilities of practical application.

'It might even help to have Gavronov against it,' said Viktor.

'Maybe,' agreed Sokolov.

Gavronov was a strange man. He was referred to in jest as 'The Slav Brotherhood', on account of the fanatical obstinacy with which he tried to link all the great achievements of physics to the work of Russian scientists. He ranked such little-known figures as Petrov, Umov and Yakovlev higher than Faraday, Maxwell and Planck.

Finally, Sokolov said jokingly:

'You see, Viktor Pavlovich, Moscow's recognized the importance of your work. Soon we'll be banqueting in your house.'

Marya Ivanovna then took the receiver from Sokolov and said:

'Congratulations to both you and Lyudmila Nikolaevna. I'm so happy for you.'

'It's nothing,' said Viktor, 'vanity of vanities.'

Nevertheless, that vanity both excited and moved him.

Later, when Lyudmila Nikolaevna was about to go to bed, Markov rang. He was always very *au fait* with the ins and outs of the official world and he talked about the Council in a different way from Sokolov and Savostyanov. Apparently, after Gurevich's speech, Kovchenko had made everyone laugh by saying:

'They're ringing the bells in the Institute of Mathematics to celebrate Viktor Pavlovich's work. The procession round the church hasn't yet begun, but the banner's been raised.'

The ever-suspicious Markov had sensed a certain hostility behind this joke. As for Shishakov, he hadn't said what he thought of Viktor's work. He had merely nodded his head as he listened to the speakers – perhaps in approval, perhaps as if to say, 'Hm, so it's your turn now, is it?' Indeed, he even appeared to favour the work of young Professor Molokanov on the radiographic analysis of steel. If nothing else, his research had immediate practical applications in the few factories producing high-quality metals. After the meeting, Shishakov had gone up to Gavronov and had a word with him.

When Markov finished, Viktor said to him:

'Vyacheslav Ivanovich, you should be in the diplomatic service.'

'No,' replied Markov, who had no sense of humour, 'I'm an experimental physicist.'

Viktor went in to Lyudmila's room. 'I've been nominated for a Stalin Prize. I've just heard the news.'

He told her about the various speeches. 'Of course, all this official recognition means nothing. Still, I've had enough of my eternal inferiority complex. You know, if I go into the conference hall and see free seats in the front row, I never dare go and sit there. Instead I hide away in some distant corner. While Shishakov and Postoev go and sit on the platform without the least hesitation. I don't give a damn about the actual chair, but I do wish I could feel the right to sit in it.'

'How glad Tolya would have been,' said Lyudmila.

'Yes, and I'll never be able to tell my mother,' said Viktor.

Lyudmila then said:

'Vitya, it's already after eleven and Nadya still isn't home. Yesterday she didn't get back till eleven either.'

'What of it?'

'She says she's at a girl-friend's, but it makes me anxious. She says

565

that Mayka's father has a permit to use his car at night and that he drives her right to the corner.'

'Why worry then?' said Viktor. At the same time he thought to himself: 'Good God! We're talking about a real success, about a Stalin Prize, and she has to bring up trivia like this.'

Two days after the meeting of the Scientific Council, Viktor phoned Shishakov at home. He wanted to ask him to accept the young physicist Landesman on the staff: the personnel department were dragging their feet. At the same time he wanted to ask Shishakov to speed up the formalities for Anna Naumovna Weisspapier's return from Kazan. Now that the Institute was recruiting again, it was ridiculous to leave qualified staff behind in Kazan.

All this had been on Viktor's mind for a long time, but he had been afraid that Shishakov was not well disposed towards him and would just say, 'Have a word with my deputy.' As a result he had kept postponing the conversation.

But today he was riding the wave of his success. Ten days ago he had felt awkward about visiting Shishakov at work; now it seemed quite simple and natural to phone him at home.

'Who's speaking?' a woman's voice answered.

Viktor was pleased by the way he announced his name: he sounded so calm, so unhurried.

The woman paused for a moment and then said in a friendly voice: 'Just a minute.'

A minute later, in the same kindly voice, she said:

'Please phone him tomorrow morning at the Institute, at ten o'clock.'

'Thank you, I'm sorry for troubling you.'

Viktor felt a burning embarrassment spread over his skin and through every cell of his body. He thought wearily that this feeling would stay with him even while he slept; when he woke up in the morning, he would think, 'Why do I feel so awful?' and then he would remember, 'Oh yes, that stupid telephone call.'

He went in to Lyudmila's room and told her about his attempt to speak to Shishakov.

'Yes,' said Lyudmila. 'You certainly have got off on the wrong foot – as your mother used to say about me.'

Viktor began to curse the woman who had answered the phone.

'To hell with the bitch! I hate that way of asking who's speaking and then saying that the boss is busy.'

Lyudmila usually shared Viktor's indignation at incidents like this; that was why he had come to talk to her.

'Do you remember?' said Viktor. 'I had thought that Shishakov was so distant because he couldn't get any credit for himself out of my work. Now he's realized that there is a way – by discrediting me. He knows that Sadko doesn't love me.'*

'God, you are suspicious!' said Lyudmila. 'What time is it?'

'A quarter past nine.'

'You see. Nadya's still out.'

'God, you are suspicious!' said Viktor.

'By the way,' said Lyudmila, 'I heard something at the store today: apparently Svechin's been nominated for a prize too.'

'Well, I like that! He never said a word about it. What for, anyway?'

'For his theory of diffusion.'

'That's impossible! It was published before the war.'

'You wait – he'll be the one who wins it! And you're doing all you can to help him.'

'Don't be a fool, Lyuda.'

'You need your mother. She'd have said what you wanted to hear.'

'What are you so angry about? I just wish that you'd shown my mother a fraction of the warmth I've always felt for Alexandra Vladimirovna.'

'Anna Semyonovna never loved Tolya,' said Lyudmila.

'That's not true,' said Viktor.

His wife had become a stranger. He found her obstinacy and her unfairness quite frightening.

---

* An allusion to a passage in Rimsky-Korsakov's opera. Viktor is referring to the political authorities, perhaps to Stalin himself.

52

In the morning Viktor had news from Sokolov. Shishakov had invited some of the Institute staff round to his home the previous evening; Kovchenko had come to fetch Sokolov in his car. One of the guests had been young Badin, the head of the Scientific Section of the Central Committee.

Viktor felt even more mortified; he must have rung Shishakov when his guests were already there. He gave a little smile and said: 'So Count St Germain was one of the guests. And what did the gentlemen discuss?'

He suddenly remembered the velvet tone of voice he had used to give his name; he had been certain that Shishakov would come running delightedly to the phone as soon as he heard the name 'Shtrum'. He groaned. He then thought that only a dog could have groaned so pitifully, a dog scratching at a particularly annoying flea.

'I must say,' said Sokolov, 'you'd never have thought it was wartime. Coffee, dry Georgian wine. And not many people at all – less than a dozen.'

'How strange,' said Viktor. Sokolov understood the meaning of his thoughtful tone of voice.

'Yes, I don't really understand,' he said equally thoughtfully, 'or rather I don't understand at all.'

'Was Gurevich there?'

'No, they phoned him but he had a session with some of the postgraduates.'

'Yes, yes, yes,' said Viktor, drumming one finger on the table. Then, to his surprise, he heard himself asking:

'Pyotr Lavrentyevich, was anything said about my work?'

Sokolov hesitated for a moment.

'I get the feeling, Viktor Pavlovich, that the people who sing your praises so unreservedly are doing you a disservice. It upsets the authorities.'

'Yes?' said Viktor. 'Go on. Finish what you're saying.'

Sokolov said that Gavronov had asserted that Viktor's work contradicted the Leninist view of the nature of matter.

'Well?' said Viktor. 'What of it?'

'Gavronov doesn't matter. You know that. But what does matter is that Badin supported him. His line seemed to be that for all its brilliance, your work contradicts the guidelines laid down at that famous meeting.'

He glanced at the door, then at the telephone, and said very quietly:

'You know, I'm afraid our bosses are going to pick you as a scapegoat in a campaign to strengthen Party spirit in science. You know what that sort of campaign's like. They choose a victim and then crush him. It would be terrible. And your work's so remarkable, so unique.'

'And so no one stood up for me?'

'I don't think so.'

'And you, Pyotr Lavrentyevich?'

'There seemed no point in arguing. One can't refute that kind of demagogy.'

Viktor sensed his friend's embarrassment and began to feel embarrassed himself.

'No, no, of course not. You're quite right.'

They fell into an uncomfortable silence. Viktor felt a shiver of fear, the fear that was always lurking in his heart – fear of the State's anger, fear of being a victim of this anger that could crush a man and grind him to dust.

'Yes,' he said pensively. 'It's no good being famous when you're dead.'

'How I wish you understood that,' said Sokolov quietly.

'Pyotr Lavrentyevich,' asked Viktor in the same hushed voice, 'how's Madyarov? Is he all right? Have you heard from him? Sometimes I get very anxious. I don't know why.'

His question, unprompted and spoken in a whisper, was a way of saying that some relationships are special, and have nothing to do with the State.

'No, I've had no news from Kazan at all.'

Sokolov's reply, delivered in a loud, unruffled voice, was a way of saying that such a relationship was no longer appropriate for them.

Then Markov and Savostyanov came into the office and the topic of conversation changed. Markov was citing examples of women who had poisoned their husbands' lives.

'Everyone gets the wife he deserves,' said Sokolov.

He looked at his watch and left the room. Savostyanov laughed and called after him:

'If there's one seat in a trolleybus, then Marya Ivanovna stands and Pyotr Lavrentyevich sits. If the doorbell rings during the night, he stays in bed and Mashenka rushes out in her dressing-gown to find out who's there. No wonder he thinks a wife is a man's best friend.'

'I wish I was as lucky,' said Markov. 'My wife just says, "What's the matter with you? Have you gone deaf or something? Open the door!"'

Feeling suddenly angry, Viktor said: 'What are you talking about? Pyotr Lavrentyevich is a model husband.'

'You've no reason to complain, Vyacheslav Ivanovich,' said Savostyanov. 'You're in your laboratory day and night. You're well out of range.'

'And do you think I don't have to pay for that?' asked Markov.

'I see,' said Savostyanov, savouring a new witticism. 'Stay at home! As they say – "My home is my Peter and Paul fortress".'*

Viktor and Markov burst out laughing. Obviously afraid that there might be more of these jokes, Markov got up and said to himself: 'Vyacheslav Ivanovich, it's time you were back at work!'

When he'd gone, Viktor said: 'And he used to be so prim, so controlled in all his movements. Now he's like a drunkard. He really is in his laboratory day and night.'

'Yes,' said Savostyanov. 'He's like a bird building a nest. He's totally engrossed.'

'And he's even stopped gossiping,' laughed Viktor. 'A bird building a nest. Yes, I like that.'

* A Tsarist political prison.

Very abruptly, Savostyanov turned to face Viktor. There was a serious look on his young face.

'By the way,' he said, 'there's something I must tell you. Viktor Pavlovich, Shishakov's evening – to which you weren't invited – was absolutely appalling. It quite shocked me.'

Viktor frowned. He felt humiliated by this expression of sympathy.

'All right. Leave it at that,' he said drily.

'Viktor Pavlovich,' Savostyanov went on, 'I know you don't care whether you were invited or not. But has Pyotr Lavrentyevich told you the filth Gavronov came out with? He said your work stinks of Judaism and that Gurevich only called it a classic because you are a Jew. And the authorities just gave a quiet smile of approval. That's "the Slav Brotherhood" for you.'

Instead of going to the canteen at lunchtime, Viktor paced up and down his office. Who would have thought people could stoop so low? Good for Savostyanov, anyway! And he seemed so empty and frivolous with his endless jokes and his photos of girls in swimming costumes. Anyway it was all nonsense. Gavronov's blatherings didn't matter. He was just a petty, envious psychopath. And if no one had replied, it was because what he'd said was patently absurd.

All the same, he was upset and worried by this nonsense. How could Shishakov not invite him? It was really very rude and stupid of him. What made it worse was that Viktor didn't give a damn for that fool Shishakov and his evenings. And yet he was as upset as if he'd been struck by some irreparable tragedy. He knew he was being foolish, but he couldn't help it . . . And he'd wanted to be given one more egg than Sokolov! Well, well!

But there was one thing that hurt him deeply. He wanted to say to Sokolov, 'Aren't you ashamed of yourself, my friend? Why didn't you tell me how Gavronov slandered me? That's twice you've kept silent: once then and once with me.'

He was very distressed indeed; but this didn't stop him from saying to himself:

'Yes, but who's talking? You didn't tell your friend Sokolov about Karimov's suspicions of Madyarov – a relative of his. You kept your mouth shut too. Out of embarrassment? Tact? Nonsense! Out of cowardice, Jewish cowardice!'

It was obviously one of those days. Next, Anna Stepanovna Loshakova came into his office, looking very upset. 'Surely she hasn't heard of my troubles already,' thought Viktor.

'What's the matter, my dear Anna Stepanovna?'

'What is all this, Viktor Pavlovich?' she began. 'Acting like that behind my back! What have I done to deserve it?'

During the lunch-break Anna Stepanovna had been told to go to the personnel department. There she had been asked to write a letter of resignation. The director had ordered them to dismiss any laboratory assistant without further education.

'I've never heard such nonsense,' said Viktor. 'Don't worry, I'll sort it out for you.'

Anna Stepanovna had been particularly hurt when Dubyonkov had said that the administration had nothing against her personally.

'What *could* they have against me, Viktor Pavlovich? Oh God, forgive me, I'm interrupting your work.'

Viktor threw a coat over his shoulders and walked across the courtyard to the two-storey building that housed the personnel department.

'Very well,' he said to himself, 'very well.' He didn't articulate his thoughts any further – this 'very well' had many meanings.

Dubyonkov greeted Viktor and said: 'I was just about to phone you.'

'About Anna Stepanovna?'

'What makes you think that? No, what I wanted to say is that in view of various circumstances senior members of staff are being asked to fill in this questionnaire here.'

Viktor looked at the sheaf of papers.

'Hm! That looks as though it'll keep me busy for a week.'

'Nonsense, Viktor Pavlovich. Just one thing though: in the event of a negative answer, rather than putting a dash, you must write out in full, "No, I have not," "No, I was not," "No, I do not," and so on.'

'Listen, my friend,' said Viktor. 'It's quite absurd to be dismissing our senior laboratory assistant, Anna Stepanovna Loshakova. I want that order cancelled.'

'Loshakova?' repeated Dubyonkov. 'But, Viktor Pavlovich, how can I cancel an order that comes from the director himself?'

'But it's mad,' said Viktor. 'She saved the Institute. She looked after everything during the bombing. And now she's being dismissed on purely administrative grounds.'

'Members of staff are never dismissed from the Institute *without* administrative grounds,' said Dubyonkov pompously.

'Anna Stepanovna is not only a wonderful person, she's one of the finest workers in our laboratory.'

'If she really is irreplaceable,' said Dubyonkov, 'then you must speak to Kasyan Terentyevich. By the way, there are two other points concerning your laboratory that have to be settled.'

Dubyonkov held out two sheets of paper that had been stapled together.

'This is about the nomination for the position of research assistant of . . .' He looked down at the paper and read out very slowly, 'Landesman, Emiliy Pinkhusovich.'

'Yes,' said Viktor, recognizing the paper in Dubyonkov's hands, 'I wrote that.'

'And this is Kasyan Terentyevich's decision: "Lacking the necessary qualifications."'

'What on earth do you mean? He's got perfect qualifications. How's Kovchenko to know who I need?'

'Then you'll have to discuss that with Kasyan Terentyevich too,' said Dubyonkov. 'And this is a statement made by our members of staff still in Kazan – together with your petition.'

'Yes?'

'Kasyan Terentyevich considers it inappropriate for them to return now since they are working productively at Kazan University. The matter will be reviewed at the end of the academic year.'

Dubyonkov spoke very quietly and softly, as though he wanted to tone down this bad news; his face, however, expressed only inquisitiveness and ill-will.

'Thank you, comrade Dubyonkov,' said Viktor.

For a second time Viktor walked across the yard, repeating to himself, 'Very well, very well.' No, he didn't need the authorities' support, his friends' affection or his wife's understanding; he could fight on alone.

He went up to the first floor of the main building. The secretary announced him, and Kovchenko, in a black jacket and an embroidered Ukrainian shirt, came out of his office.

'Welcome, Viktor Pavlovich, come through into my hut.'

Viktor went in. It was furnished with red sofas and armchairs. Kovchenko motioned Viktor towards one of the sofas and sat down beside him.

Kovchenko smiled as he listened to Viktor. His apparent friendliness was very like Dubyonkov's. And no doubt he had given a similar smile when Gavronov had spoken about Viktor's work.

'But what can we do?' Kovchenko gestured helplessly. 'We didn't think this up ourselves. She stayed here during the bombing, you say? That can't be considered of especial merit now, Viktor Pavlovich. Every Soviet citizen will put up with bombing if that's what his country orders.'

He thought for a moment, then said:

'There is one possibility, however, though it will attract criticism. We can give Loshakova the position of junior assistant. And she can keep her card for the special store. Yes – that I can promise you.'

'No,' said Viktor. 'That would be insulting.'

'Viktor Pavlovich, are you saying that the Soviet State should be governed by one set of laws and Shtrum's laboratory by another?'

'No, I'm simply asking for Soviet law to be applied. According to Soviet law, Loshakova cannot be dismissed. And while we're on the subject of law, Kasyan Terentyevich,' Viktor went on, 'why did you refuse to confirm the appointment of young Landesman? He's extremely talented.'

Kovchenko bit his lip.

'Viktor Pavlovich, he may have the abilities you require, but you must understand that there are other circumstances to be considered by the Institute.'

'Very good,' said Viktor. 'I see.'

Then he asked in a whisper:

'The questionnaire, I suppose? Has he got relatives abroad?'

Kovchenko shrugged his shoulders.

'Kasyan Terentyevich,' said Viktor, 'let me continue this very pleasant conversation. Why are you delaying the return from Kazan of my colleague Anna Naumovna Weisspapier? She has, incidentally, completed a thesis. What contradiction are you going to find now between my laboratory and the State?'

A martyred expression appeared on Kovchenko's face.

'Viktor Pavlovich, why this interrogation? Please understand that choice of personnel is my responsibility.'

'Very good,' said Viktor. 'I see.'

He knew he was about to get extremely rude.

'With all due respect, Kasyan Terentyevich,' he went on, 'I just can't go on like this. Science isn't at Dubyonkov's beck and call – or yours. And I'm here for my work, not just to serve the obscure interests of the personnel department. I shall write to Aleksey Alekseyevich Shishakov – he can put Dubyonkov in charge of the nuclear laboratory.'

'Calm down, Viktor Pavlovich. Please calm down.'

'No, I can't go on like this.'

'Viktor Pavlovich, you've no idea how much the Institute values your work. And no one values it more than I do.'

'What do I care how much you value my work?' Viktor looked at Kovchenko's face. Rather than humiliation, however, he saw on it an expression of eager pleasure.

'Viktor Pavlovich, there is no question of your being allowed to leave the Institute,' Kovchenko said sternly. 'And that's not because you're indispensable. Do you really think that no one can replace Viktor Pavlovich Shtrum?'

His final words were spoken almost tenderly.

'You can't do without Landesman and Weisspapier – and you think there's no one in all Russia who can replace you?'

He looked at Viktor. Viktor felt that at any moment Kovchenko might come out with the words that had been hovering between them all along, brushing against his eyes, hands and brain like an invisible mist.

He bowed his head. He was no longer a professor, a doctor of science, a famous scientist who had made a remarkable discovery, a man who could be forthright and independent, arrogant and condescending. He was just a man with curly hair and a hooked nose, with a stooped back and narrow shoulders, screwing up his eyes as though he was expecting a blow on the cheek. He looked at the man in the embroidered Ukrainian shirt, and waited.

Very quietly, Kovchenko said:

'Calm down, Viktor Pavlovich, calm down. You really must calm down. Heavens, what a fuss over such a trifle!'

53

That night, after Lyudmila and Nadya had gone to bed, Viktor began filling in the questionnaire. Nearly all the questions were the same as before the war. Their very familiarity, however, somehow renewed Viktor's anxiety.

The State was not concerned about the adequacy of Viktor's mathematical equipment or the appropriateness of the laboratory apparatus for the complex experiments he was conducting; the State didn't want to know whether the staff were properly protected from neutron radiation, whether Sokolov and Shtrum had a good working relationship, whether the junior researchers had received adequate training for their exhausting calculations, whether they realized how much depended on their constant patience, alertness and concentration.

This was the questionnaire royal, the questionnaire of question-naires. It wanted to know everything about Lyudmila's father and mother and about Viktor's grandfather and grandmother – where they had been born, where they had died, where they had been buried. In what connection had Viktor Pavlovich's father, Pavel Iosifovich, travelled to Berlin in 1910? There was something sinister about the State's anxious concern. Reading the questionnaire, Viktor began to doubt himself: was he really someone reliable?

1. Surname, name and patronymic . . . Who was he, who was this man filling in a questionnaire at the dead of night? Shtrum, Viktor Pavlovich? His mother and father had never been properly married, they had separated when Viktor was only two; and on his father's papers he had seen the name Pinkhus – not Pavel. So why was he Viktor *Pavlovich*? Did he know himself? Perhaps he was someone quite different – Goldman . . . or Sagaydachny? Or was he the Frenchman Desforges, alias Dubrovsky?

Filled with doubt, he turned to the second question.

2. Date of birth ... year ... month ... day ... (to be given according to both old and new styles). What did he know about that dark December day? Could he really claim with any confidence to have been born at that precise moment? To disclaim responsibility, should he not add the words, 'according to'?

3. Sex ... Viktor boldly wrote, 'Male'. Then he thought, 'But what kind of man am I? A real man would never have kept silent after the dismissal of Chepyzhin.'

4. Place of birth ... (according to both old and new systems of administration – province, county, district, village and *oblast*, region, rural or urban district). Viktor wrote, 'Kharkov'. His mother had told him he had been born in Bakhmut, but she had filled in his birth certificate two months later, after moving to Kharkov. Should he be more precise?

5. Nationality ... Point five. This had been so simple and insignificant before the war; now, however, it was acquiring a particular resonance.

Pressing heavily on his pen, Viktor wrote boldly and distinctly, 'Jew'. He wasn't to know what price hundreds of thousands of people would soon have to pay for answering Kalmyk, Balkar, Chechen, Crimean Tartar or Jew. He wasn't to know what dark passions would gather year by year around this point. He couldn't foresee what fear, anger, despair and blood would spill over from the neighbouring sixth point: 'Social origin'. He couldn't foresee how in a few years' time many people would answer this fifth point with a sense of fatedness – the same sense of fatedness with which the children of Cossack officers, priests, landlords and industrial magnates had once answered the sixth point.

Nevertheless, Viktor could already sense how the lines of force were shifting, how they were now gathering around this point. The previous evening, Landesman had phoned; Viktor had told him of his failure to secure his nomination. 'Just as I expected!' Landesman had said angrily and reproachfully. 'Is there something awkward in your background?' Viktor had asked. Landesman had snorted and said, 'There's something awkward in my surname.'

And while they were drinking tea that evening, Nadya had said:

'Do you know, Papa, Mayka's father said that next year they're not going to accept a single Jew in the Institute of International Relations.'

'Well,' thought Viktor, 'if one's a Jew, then one's a Jew – and one must say so.'

6. Social origin . . . This was the trunk of a mighty tree; its roots went deep into the earth while its branches spread freely over the spacious pages of the questionnaire: social origin of mother and father, of mother's and father's parents . . . social origin of wife and wife's parents . . . if divorced, social origin of former wife together with her parents' occupation before the Revolution.

The Great Revolution had been a social revolution, a revolution of the poor. Viktor had always felt that this sixth point was a legitimate expression of the mistrust of the poor for the rich, a mistrust that had arisen over thousands of years of oppression.

Viktor wrote, 'Petit bourgeois'. Petit bourgeois! What kind of petit bourgeois was he? Suddenly, probably because of the war, he began to doubt whether there really was such a gulf between the legitimate Soviet question about social origin and the bloody, fateful question of nationality as posed by the Germans. He remembered their evening discussions in Kazan and Madyarov's speech about Chekhov's attitude towards humanity.

He thought to himself: 'To me, a distinction based on social origin seems legitimate and moral. But the Germans obviously consider a distinction based on nationality to be equally moral. One thing I am certain of: it's terrible to kill someone simply because he's a Jew. They're people like any others – good, bad, gifted, stupid, stolid, cheerful, kind, sensitive, greedy . . . Hitler says none of that matters – all that matters is that they're Jewish. And I protest with my whole being. But then we have the same principle: what matters is whether or not you're the son of an aristocrat, the son of a merchant, the son of a kulak; and whether you're good-natured, wicked, gifted, kind, stupid, happy, is neither here nor there. And we're not talking about the merchants, priests and aristocrats themselves – but about their children and grandchildren. Does noble blood run in one's veins like Jewishness? Is one a priest or a merchant by heredity? Nonsense! Sofya Perovskaya was the daughter of a general, the daughter of a provincial governor. Have her banished! And Komissarov, the Tsarist police stooge who grabbed Karakozov, would have answered the sixth point:

"petit bourgeois". He would have been accepted by the University. Stalin said: "The son isn't responsible for the father." But he also said: "An apple never falls far from the tree . . ." Well, petit bourgeois it is.'

7. Social position . . . White-collar worker? But clerks and civil servants are white-collar workers. A white-collar worker called Shtrum had elaborated the mathematics of the disintegration of atomic nuclei. Another white-collar worker called Markov hoped, with the aid of their new apparatus, to confirm the theories of the white-collar worker called Shtrum.

'That's it,' he thought. 'White-collar worker.'

Viktor shrugged his shoulders and got up. Making a gesture as if to brush someone off, he paced around the room. Then he sat down and went on with the questionnaire.

29. Have you or your closest relative ever been the subject of a judicial inquiry or trial? Have you been arrested? Have you been given a judicial or administrative sentence? When? Where? Precisely what for? If you were reprieved, when?

Then the same question regarding Viktor's wife. Viktor felt his heart miss a beat. They showed no mercy. Different names flashed through his mind. I'm certain he's innocent . . . he's simply not of this world . . . she was arrested for not denouncing her husband, I think she got eight years, I'm not sure, I don't write to her, I think she was sent to Temniki, I found out by chance, I met her daughter on the street . . . I don't remember exactly, I think he was arrested in early 1938, yes, ten years without right of correspondence . . .'

My wife's brother was a Party member, I met him only occasionally . . . my wife and I don't write to him . . . I think my wife's mother visited him, yes, long before the war . . . his second wife was exiled for failing to denounce her husband, she died during the war, her son volunteered for the front, for the defence of Stalingrad . . . my wife separated from her first husband . . . her son by that marriage – my own stepson – died during the defence of Stalingrad . . . her first husband was arrested, my wife has heard nothing of him from the moment of his arrest, I don't know the reason for his arrest, I've heard vague talk of his belonging to the Trotskyist opposition, but I'm not sure, I wasn't in the least interested . . .

He was seized by a feeling of irreparable guilt and impurity. He remembered a meeting at which a Party member, confessing his faults, had said: 'Comrades, I'm not one of us.'

Suddenly Viktor rebelled. No, I'm not one of the obedient and submissive. I'm all on my own, my wife is no longer interested in me, but so what . . . ? I won't renounce those unfortunates who died for no reason.

You should be ashamed of yourselves, comrades! How can you bring up such things? These people are innocent – what can their wives and children be guilty of? It's you who should repent, you who should be begging for forgiveness. And you want to prove my inferiority, to destroy my self-confidence – simply because I'm related to these innocent victims? All I'm guilty of is failing to help them.

At the same time, another, quite opposite train of thought was running through Viktor's mind . . . I didn't keep in touch with them, I never corresponded with enemies of the Party, I never received letters from camps, I never gave them material help, I met them only infrequently and by chance . . .

30. Do any of your relatives live abroad? (Where? Since when? Their reasons for emigrating?) Do you remain in touch with them?

This question increased Viktor's depression.

Comrades, surely you understand that emigration was the only possible choice under the Tsarist regime? It was the poor, the lovers of freedom, who emigrated. Lenin himself lived in London, Zurich and Paris. Why are you exchanging winks as you read the list of my uncles and aunts living, together with their sons and daughters, in New York, Paris and Buenos Aires? A friend of mine once joked: 'I've got an aunt in New York. I always knew that hunger's no friendly aunt; now I know that aunts mean hunger.'

The list of his relatives abroad turned out to be almost as long as the list of his scientific works. And if one added the list of those who had been arrested . . .

This was how to flatten a man. He's an alien! Throw him out! But it was all a lie. Science needed *him* – not Gavronov or Dubyonkov. And he was ready to give his life for his country. And were people with spotless questionnaires incapable of deception or betrayal? And were there no people who had written, 'Father – swindler' or 'Father – landowner' – and then given their own lives in battle, joined the partisans, been executed?

What was all this? He knew only too well. The statistical method! Probability theory! There was a greater probability of finding enemies among people of a non-proletarian background. And it was on these same grounds – probability theory – that the German Fascists had destroyed whole peoples and nations. The principle was inhuman, blind and inhuman. There was only one acceptable way of relating to people – a human way.

If he were choosing staff for his laboratory, he would draw up a very different questionnaire – a human questionnaire.

It was all the same to him whether his future colleague was a Russian, a Jew, a Ukrainian or an Armenian, whether his grandfather had been a worker, a factory-owner or a kulak; his relationship with him would not depend on whether or not his brother had been arrested by the organs of the NKVD; it didn't matter to him whether his future colleague's sister lived in Geneva or Kostroma.

He would ask at what age someone had first become interested in theoretical physics, what he thought of the criticisms Einstein had made of Planck when the latter was an old man, whether he was interested only in mathematical theory or whether he also enjoyed experimental work, what he thought of Heinsenberg, did he believe in the possibility of a unified field theory? What mattered was talent, fire, the divine spark . . .

He would like to know – but only if his future colleague were happy to say – whether he enjoyed long walks, whether he drank wine, whether he went to orchestral concerts, whether he liked Seton Thompson's children's books, whether he felt more drawn to Tolstoy or to Dostoyevsky, whether he enjoyed gardening, whether he went fishing, what he thought of Picasso, which was his favourite story of Chekhov's.

He would also like to know whether this future colleague was taciturn or talkative, whether he was good-natured, witty, resentful, irritable, ambitious, whether he was likely to start an affair with the pretty young Verochka Ponamariova . . .

Madyarov had spoken extraordinarily well about all this – perhaps he really was a provocateur . . . Oh my God . . . !

Viktor took his pen and wrote: 'Esther Semyonovna Dashevskaya, my aunt on my mother's side, has lived since 1909 in Buenos Aires, working as a teacher of music.'

54

Viktor entered Shishakov's office determined to remain calm and composed, not to utter a single aggressive word. He knew very well how stupid it was to take offence simply because he and his work were held in such low esteem by a mere bureaucrat.

As soon as he saw Shishakov's face, however, he felt a sense of uncontrollable irritation.

'Aleksey Alekseyevich,' he began, 'one can't of course go against one's own nature, but you haven't once shown the least interest in the assembly of our new apparatus.'

In a conciliatory tone Shishakov answered: 'I shall certainly visit you in the immediate future.'

The boss had graciously promised to honour Viktor with a visit.

'I think that in general the administration has been sufficiently attentive to your needs,' Shishakov added.

'Especially the personnel department.'

'What difficulty has been occasioned you by the personnel department?' asked Shishakov in the same conciliatory tone. 'You're the first head of a laboratory to make any complaint.'

'Aleksey Alekseyevich, I've been trying in vain to have Weisspapier recalled from Kazan – in the field of nuclear photography she's quite irreplaceable. I protest categorically against the dismissal of Loshakova: she's an exceptional worker and an exceptional human being. I can't imagine how you can dismiss Loshakova – it's inhuman. And finally, I wish to have my nomination of Landesman confirmed; he's a very talented young man. You underestimate the importance of our laboratory. Otherwise I wouldn't be wasting my time on conversations of this nature.'

'I am wasting my own time too,' said Shishakov.

Viktor felt glad that Shishakov had abandoned his conciliatory tone; now he could give free rein to his anger.

'What strikes me as particularly unpleasant is that these conflicts have arisen principally around people with Jewish surnames.'

'Very well, Viktor Pavlovich,' said Shishakov, taking the offensive. 'The Institute is faced with a number of very important tasks. As you know, we have been entrusted with these tasks at a very difficult time. I consider your laboratory unable at present to assist us with these tasks. And your own work – as disputable as it is interesting – has received far too much attention.

'This is not merely a personal point of view,' he went on, a note of authority appearing in his voice. 'There are comrades who consider that the excessive attention paid to your work has disrupted scientific research. All this was discussed in considerable detail only yesterday. The view was put forward that your theories contradict the materialist view of the nature of matter and need to be reconsidered. You are to be asked to give a speech to that effect yourself. Certain people – for reasons that are obscure to me – would like to establish various doubtful theories as central tenets of our science – and at a time when we need to focus all our energies on the tasks imposed on us by the war. All this is extremely serious. And now here you are making terrible insinuations concerning a certain Loshakova. Excuse me, but I was unaware that Loshakova was a Jewish name.'

At this, Viktor lost his head. No one had ever spoken to him about his work with such undisguised hostility – least of all an Academician who was the director of his own Institute! No longer afraid of the consequences, Viktor blurted out everything that was on his mind.

He said that it was of no concern to physics whether or not it confirmed philosophy; that the logic of mathematical proof was more powerful than that of Engels and Lenin; that it was for Badin of the Scientific Section of the Central Committee to accommodate Lenin's views to mathematics and physics, not for mathematicians and physicists to accommodate their views to Lenin's. He said that an excessive pragmatism would always be the death of science – though it were commanded 'by the Lord himself': only a great theory could give birth to great practical achievements. He was confident that the principal technical problems – and not only technical problems – of the twentieth century would be resolved through the theory of nuclear reactions. He was only too willing to give a speech to that effect if this should be considered necessary by the comrades whose names Shishakov preferred not to reveal.

'As for the matter of people with Jewish surnames, that's not something you can laugh off quite so easily – not if you consider yourself a member of the intelligentsia. If my requests are denied, I shall be compelled to resign from the Institute immediately. I am unable to work under these conditions.'

Viktor took a breath, looked at Shishakov, thought for a moment and said: 'It's very difficult for me to work under these conditions. I am a human being as well as a physicist. I feel ashamed before people who expect my help, who count on my protection against injustice.'

This time, Viktor had only said: 'It's *very difficult*.' He no longer had the nerve to repeat his threat of immediate resignation.

Shishakov obviously noticed this. Perhaps for this very reason he insisted: 'There's no point in continuing this conversation in the language of ultimata. It is my duty, of course, to take your requests into consideration.'

Throughout the rest of the day Viktor had a strange feeling of both joy and depression. The laboratory equipment, the new apparatus – already nearly assembled – seemed a part of his life, a part of his brain, a part of his body. How could he exist without them?

It was terrifying even to think what heresies he had uttered to the director. At the same time, however, Viktor felt strong. His very helplessness was a source of strength. How could he ever have guessed that on his return to Moscow, at the moment of his scientific triumph, he would be having a conversation like this?

Although no one could have heard about his confrontation with Shishakov, his colleagues seemed to be treating him with a particular warmth.

Anna Stepanovna took his hand, squeezed it and said:

'Viktor Pavlovich, I don't want to appear to be thanking you – but I do know that you've been true to yourself.'

Viktor stood beside her in silence. He felt very moved, almost joyful.

'Mother, mother,' he thought suddenly, 'can you see?'

On the way home Viktor decided not to say anything to Lyudmila. However, his habit of sharing everything with her proved too strong; as he came through the door and began taking off his coat, he said:

'Well, Lyudmila, it's happened. I'm leaving the Institute.'

Lyudmila was very upset, but she still managed to say something wounding.

'You're behaving as though you were Lomonosov or Mendeleev. If you leave, then Sokolov or Markov will just take your place.'

She looked up from her sewing.

'Besides, why can't your Landesman go to the Front? Otherwise it really does look to a prejudiced observer as though one Jew's looking after another.'

'All right, all right,' said Viktor. 'That's enough. Do you remember that line of Nekrasov's? "He hoped to be admitted to the temple of fame – and then was glad to be admitted to hospital." I thought I had earned my daily bread – and now they're asking me to repent my sins and heresies. More than that – they want me to make a public confession! It's madness. And at a time when I've been nominated for a Stalin Prize, when students are seeking me out . . . It's all Badin's doing. No, it's nothing to do with Badin. Sadko doesn't love me!'

Lyudmila came up to him, straightened his tie and turned down the collar of his jacket.

'You look pale. Did you have any lunch?'

'I don't feel like eating.'

'Have some bread and butter while I warm up your supper.'

She poured out a few drops of his heart-medicine and said:

'I don't like the look of you. Drink this. And let me check your pulse.'

They went through to the kitchen. As he chewed his bread, Viktor kept glancing at the mirror Nadya had hung by the gas-meter.

'How strange it all is,' he said. 'How could I ever have guessed that I'd have to answer drawerfuls of questionnaires and hear what I've heard today? What power! The State and the individual . . . The State raises a man up, then throws him effortlessly into the abyss.'

'Vitya,' said Lyudmila, 'I want to talk to you about Nadya. Almost every night she comes home after curfew.'

'You told me about that the other day.'

'I know I did. Well, yesterday evening I happened to go up to the window and lift up the black-out curtain. What do you think I saw? Nadya and some soldier! They walked down the street, stopped outside the dairy and began kissing.'

'Well I never!' Viktor was so astonished he stopped chewing the food in his mouth.

Nadya kissing a soldier! After a few moments' silence, Viktor began to laugh. He was quite stunned; probably nothing else could have distracted him from his own sombre preoccupations. For a moment their eyes met; to her surprise, Lyudmila burst out laughing as well. Their empathy was complete, that rare understanding that needs neither thoughts nor words.

It was no surprise to Lyudmila when Viktor, apparently apropos of nothing at all, said: 'Mila, I was right to have it out with Shishakov, wasn't I?'

His train of thought was quite simple, though not so easy for an outsider to follow. Several things had come together: memories of his past; the fate of Tolya and Anna Semyonovna; the war; the fact that, however rich and famous a man may be, he will still grow old, die and yield his place to the young; that perhaps nothing matters except to live one's life honestly.

And so he asked: 'I was right, wasn't I?'

Lyudmila shook her head. Decades of intimacy can also divide people.

'Lyuda,' said Viktor humbly, 'people who are in the right often don't know how to behave. They lose their tempers and swear. They act tactlessly and intolerantly. Usually they get blamed for everything that goes wrong at home and at work. While those who are in the wrong, those who hurt others, always know how to behave. They act calmly, logically and tactfully – and appear to be in the right.'

Nadya came in after ten o'clock. As she heard the key in the lock, Lyudmila said: 'Go on, have a word with her.'

'It's easier for you,' said Viktor.

But as Nadya came into the room, with dishevelled hair and a red nose, it was Viktor who said: 'Who were you kissing opposite the front door?'

Nadya looked round as though about to run away. For a moment she just gaped at Viktor. Then she shrugged her shoulders and said calmly: 'A-Andryusha Lomov. He's at military school. He's a lieutenant.'

'Are you going to marry him then?' asked Viktor, astonished at Nadya's self-possession. He looked round to see Lyudmila's reaction.

'Marry him?' Nadya sounded very grown-up: irritated, but basically unconcerned. 'Maybe. I'm thinking of it . . . And then maybe not. I haven't made up my mind yet.'

At last Lyudmila said something.

'Nadya, why did you tell all those lies about Mayka's father and his lessons? I never told lies to my mother.'

Viktor remembered how, when he was courting Lyudmila, she would come to meet him and say: 'I've left Tolya with Mother. I told her I was going to the library.'

All of a sudden, Nadya was a child again. In an angry, whining voice, she shouted: 'And do you think it's right to spy on me? Did your mother spy on you?'

'Don't you dare be so insolent to your mother, you little fool!' roared Viktor.

Nadya gave him a look of patient boredom.

'So, Nadezhda Victorovna, it seems you haven't yet decided whether to marry the young colonel or to become his concubine?'

'No, I haven't – and he's not a colonel.'

Could some young lad in a military greatcoat really be kissing his daughter? Could he be falling in love with this brat of a girl, this ridiculous, sharp-witted little idiot? Could he be kissing her puppy-like eyes?

But then, this was an old story . . .

Lyudmila said nothing more. She knew that Nadya would only get angry and clam up. She also knew that, when they were alone, she would run her fingers through her daughter's hair and Nadya would sob without knowing why. She herself would feel a sharp pang of pity for Nadya, also without knowing why – after all, there were worse things for a young girl than to be kissing a young man. Then Nadya would tell her all about this Lomov; she would continue to run her fingers through Nadya's hair, all the time remembering her own first kisses and thinking of Tolya – yes, now she linked everything to Tolya.

There was something terribly sad about this girlish love, this love poised over the abyss of war. Tolya, Tolya . . .

Viktor was still ranting away, consumed by fatherly anxiety.

'Where's this man serving? I'm going to have a word with his commanding officer. Chasing after babes-in-arms! He'll teach him a lesson!'

587

Nadya didn't say anything. As though bewitched by her haughtiness, Viktor fell silent too. Then he asked: 'Why are you staring at me like that? You look like some member of a higher race studying an amoeba.'

Somehow, the way Nadya was looking at him reminded him of Shishakov. He had watched Viktor with the same calm self-confidence, looking down from his position of academic and political grandeur; his clear gaze had at once brought home to Viktor the futility of his indignation, the futility of his protests and ultimatums. The power of the State reared up like a cliff of basalt. Yes, Shishakov could well afford to watch Viktor's struggles with such indifference.

In some strange way this girl in front of him seemed also to understand the senselessness of his anger and indignation. She too seemed to understand that he was trying to achieve the impossible, to halt the flow of life itself.

That night Viktor felt as though he had ruined his whole life. His resignation from the Institute would be seen as a political gesture. He would be considered a source of dangerous oppositional tendencies – at a time when Russia was at war, when the Institute had been granted Stalin's special favour . . .

And then that terrible questionnaire. And that senseless conversation with Shishakov. And those discussions in Kazan. And Madyarov . . .

Suddenly he felt so terrified that he wanted to write to Shishakov and beg for forgiveness. He wanted the events of the day to be forgotten, blotted out.

55

Returning from the store in the afternoon, Lyudmila saw a white envelope in the letter-box. Her heart, already fluttering after climbing the stairs, began to beat still faster. Holding the letter in her hand, she went down the corridor, opened Tolya's door and looked in – the room was still empty, he hadn't returned.

Lyudmila glanced through pages covered in a handwriting she had known since childhood — her own mother's. She saw the names Zhenya, Vera and Stepan Fyodorovich, but the name of her son was not there. Once again hope ebbed away — for the time being.

Alexandra Vladimirovna said almost nothing about her own life — only a few words about her difficulties with the landlady; apparently Nina Matveevna had behaved very unpleasantly since Lyudmila's departure. She wrote that she had heard nothing from Seryozha, Stepan Fyodorovich or Vera. And she was worried about Zhenya — something quite serious seemed to have happened to her. She had written a letter hinting at various problems and saying she might have to go to Moscow.

Lyudmila didn't know how to feel sad. She only knew how to grieve. Tolya, Tolya.

Stepan Fyodorovich was now a widower . . . Vera was a homeless orphan. Seryozha might or might not be alive. Perhaps he was crippled? Perhaps he was lying in some military hospital? His father had either died in a camp or been shot; his mother had died in exile . . . Alexandra Vladimirovna's house had burnt down; she was alone, with no news of either her son or her grandson.

Alexandra Vladimirovna didn't say a word about her own health. She didn't say whether her room was heated. She didn't say whether her rations had been increased. Lyudmila understood the reason for this all too well.

Lyudmila's home was now cold and empty. The warmth had drained out of it; it was a ruin. It was as though it had been destroyed by terrible, invisible bombs.

She thought a lot about Viktor that day. Their relationship had gone sour. Viktor was angry and treated her coldly. The saddest thing of all was that she didn't mind. She knew him too well. From the outside everything about him seemed exalted and poetic — but she didn't see people that way. Masha saw Viktor as a noble sage, as a martyr. Masha loved music and would go pale when she listened to the piano. Sometimes Viktor played for her. She obviously needed someone to adore. She had created for herself an exalted image, a Viktor who had never existed. But if she were to watch Viktor day in and day out, she'd be disenchanted soon enough.

Lyudmila knew that Viktor was moved only by egotism, that he cared for no one. Even now – though his confrontation with Shishakov filled her with fear and anxiety on his behalf – she felt the usual irritation: he was ready to sacrifice both his work and the peace of his family for the selfish pleasure of strutting about and posing as the defender of the weak.

Yesterday, in his anxiety about Nadya, he had forgotten his egotism. But was he capable of forgetting his troubles and showing the same anxiety on Tolya's behalf? She herself had been mistaken yesterday. Nadya hadn't been fully open with her. Was it just a childish infatuation? Or was this her destiny?

Nadya had spoken quite freely about the circle of friends where she had first met Lomov. She had told Lyudmila how they read futurist and symbolist poetry, how they argued about art, even about their contemptuous mockery for things which, in Lyudmila's eyes, deserved neither contempt nor mockery.

Nadya had answered Lyudmila's questions with good grace and seemed to be speaking the truth: 'No, we don't drink – apart from one evening when someone was leaving for the front'; 'We talk about politics now and then. No, not in the same language as *Pravda* . . . but only occasionally, just once or twice.'

But as soon as Lyudmila began asking about Lomov himself, Nadya had become edgy: 'No, he doesn't write poetry'; 'How do you expect me to know about his parents? I've never even met them. What's strange about that? Lomov doesn't know anything about Father. He probably thinks he works in a food store.'

What was all this? Was it Nadya's destiny? Or would it be quite forgotten in a month's time?

As she got the supper ready and did the washing, she thought in turn about her mother, Vera, Zhenya and Seryozha. She rang Marya Ivanovna, but no one answered. She rang the Postoevs – the domestic answered that her employer was out shopping. She rang the janitor about the broken tap, but apparently the plumber hadn't come in to work.

She sat down to write a long letter to her mother. She meant to say how sad she was that she had failed to make Alexandra Vladimirovna feel at home, how much she regretted her decision to stay on alone in Kazan. Lyudmila's relatives had given up coming to stay with her before the war. Now not even the very closest of them came to visit her in her large Moscow flat. Lyudmila didn't write the letter – all she did was spoil four sheets of paper.

Towards the end of the afternoon Viktor phoned to say that he'd be staying late at the Institute; the technicians he'd wanted from the military factory were coming that evening.

'Is there any news?' asked Lyudmila.

'You mean about all that? No, nothing.'

In the evening Lyudmila read through her mother's letter again and then got up and went over to the window.

The moon was shining and the street was quite empty. Once again she saw Nadya arm in arm with her lieutenant; they were walking down the road towards the flat. Suddenly Nadya started to run and the young man in the military greatcoat stood there in the middle of the road, gazing after her. Everything most incompatible suddenly fused together in Lyudmila's heart: her love for Viktor, her resentment of Viktor, her anxiety on Viktor's behalf; Tolya who had died without ever kissing a girl's lips; the lieutenant standing there in the road; Vera climbing happily up the staircase of her house in Stalingrad; poor homeless Alexandra Vladimirovna . . .

Her soul filled with the sense of life that is man's only joy and his most terrible pain.

56

Outside the main door of the Institute, Viktor met Shishakov getting out of his car. Shishakov raised his hat and said hello; he clearly didn't want to talk.

'That's bad,' thought Viktor.

At lunch Professor Svechin was sitting at the next table, but he looked straight past Viktor without saying a word. Stout Doctor Gurevich talked to Viktor with particular warmth on his way out of the canteen; he pressed his hand for a long time, but as the door of the director's reception room opened, he quickly said goodbye and walked off down the corridor.

In the laboratory, Markov, who was talking to Viktor about

setting up the equipment for photographing atomic particles, suddenly looked up from his notes and said:

'Viktor Pavlovich, I've heard that you were the subject of a very harsh discussion during a meeting of the Party bureau. Kovchenko really had it in for you. He said: "Shtrum doesn't want to be a part of our collective."'

'Well,' said Viktor, 'that's that.' He felt one of his eyelids beginning to twitch.

While they were discussing the photographs, Viktor got the feeling that it was now Markov who was in charge of the laboratory. He had the calm voice of someone who is in control; Nozdrin twice came up to him to ask questions about the equipment.

Then Markov's face took on a look of pathetic entreaty.

'Viktor Pavlovich, if you say anything about this Party meeting, please don't mention my name. I'll be accused of revealing Party secrets.'

'Of course not.'

'It's just a storm in a teacup.'

'I don't know,' said Viktor. 'You'll get by without me. And the ambiguities surrounding the operation of psi are quite impossible.'

'I think you're wrong,' said Markov. 'I was talking to Kochkurov yesterday. You know what he's like – he's certainly got his feet on the ground. Well he said, "I know Shtrum's mathematics have overtaken his physics, but somehow I find his work very illuminating, I don't know why."'

Viktor understood what Markov was saying. Young Kochkurov was particularly interested in the action of slow neutrons on the nuclei of heavy atoms. In his view, work in this area had great practical possibilities.

'It's not the Kochkurovs of this world who decide things,' said Viktor. 'The people who matter are the Badins – and he wants me to repent of leading physicists into Talmudic abstraction.'

Everyone in the laboratory seemed to know about yesterday's meeting and Viktor's conflict with the authorities. Anna Stepanovna kept giving Viktor sympathetic looks.

Viktor wanted to talk to Sokolov, but he had gone to the Academy in the morning and then rung up to say that he'd been delayed and probably wouldn't return that day.

Savostyanov, for some reason, was in an excellent mood.

'Viktor Pavlovich,' he said, 'you have before you the esteemed Gurevich – a brilliant and outstanding scientist.' He put his hands on his head and stomach to denote Gurevich's bald head and pot belly.

On his way home in the evening, Viktor suddenly met Marya Ivanovna on Kaluga Street. She saw him first and called out his name. She was wearing a coat he hadn't seen before and he took a moment to recognize her.

'How extraordinary!' he said. 'What's brought you to Kaluga Street?'

For a moment she just looked at him in silence. Then she shook her head and said: 'It's not a coincidence. I wanted to see you – that's all.'

Viktor didn't know what to say. For a moment his heart seemed to stop beating. He thought she was going to say something terrible, to warn him of some danger.

'Viktor Pavlovich, I just wanted a word with you. Pyotr Lavrentyevich has told me what happened.'

'You mean my latest success,' said Viktor.

They were walking side by side – but in silence, almost as though they didn't know one another. Viktor again felt embarrassed. He looked at Marya Ivanovna out of the corner of one eye and said: 'Lyudmila's very angry with me. I suppose you feel the same.'

'Not at all,' she said. 'I know what compelled you to act in that way.'

Viktor gave her a quick look.

'You were thinking of your mother.'

He nodded.

'Pyotr Lavrentyevich didn't want to tell you . . . He's heard that the Party organization and the Institute authorities have really got it in for you . . . Apparently Badin said: "It's not just a case of hysteria. It's political hysteria, anti-Soviet hysteria." '

'So that's what's the matter with me,' said Viktor. 'Yes, I thought that Pyotr Lavrentyevich was keeping something back.'

'Yes. That upset me very much.'

'Is he afraid?'

'Yes. And he considers you to be in the wrong.

'Pyotr Lavrentyevich is a good man,' she added quietly. 'He's suffered a lot.'

'Yes,' said Viktor. 'And that's what's upsetting. Such an audacious, brilliant scientist – and such a cowardly soul.'

'He's suffered a lot,' repeated Marya Ivanovna.

'All the same, he should have told me.'

He took her arm. 'Listen, Marya Ivanovna, what is all this about Madyarov? I just don't understand.'

He was haunted by the thought of their conversations in Kazan. He kept remembering odd words, odd phrases, Karimov's alarming warning and Madyarov's own suspicions. He was afraid that his blatherings in Kazan would soon be added to what was already brewing in Moscow.

'I don't understand myself,' she replied. 'The registered letter we sent Leonid Sergeyevich was returned to us. Has he changed his address? Has he left Kazan? Has the worst happened?'

'Yes, yes,' muttered Viktor. For a moment he felt quite lost.

Marya Ivanovna obviously thought that her husband had told Viktor about the letter that had been returned. But Sokolov hadn't said a word. When Viktor had asked that question, he had been thinking of the quarrel between Madyarov and Pyotr Lavrentyevich.

'Let's go into the park,' he said.

'We're going in the wrong direction.'

'There's a way in off Kaluga Street.'

He wanted to know more about Madyarov, and to tell her of his and Karimov's suspicions of one another. The park would be empty; no one would disturb them there. Marya Ivanovna would understand the import of such a conversation. He would be able to talk freely and openly about everything that troubled him, and she would be equally frank.

A thaw had set in. On the slopes you could see damp rotting leaves peeping out from under the melting snow; in the gullies, however, the snow was still quite thick. The sky above was cloudy and sombre.

'What a beautiful evening,' said Viktor, breathing in the cool, damp air.

'Yes, and there isn't a soul around. It's like being in the country.'

They walked down the muddy paths. When they came to a puddle, he held out his hand and helped her across.

For a long time they didn't say a word. Viktor didn't want to talk about the war, the Institute, Madyarov, or any of his fears and

594

premonitions. All he wanted was to keep on walking, without saying a word, beside this small woman with the light yet awkward step – and to prolong this feeling of lightness and peace that had suddenly come over him.

Marya Ivanovna didn't say a word. She just walked on beside him, her head slightly bowed.

They came out onto the quay. The river was covered with a layer of dark ice.

'I like this,' said Viktor.

'Yes,' she agreed, 'it's good.'

The asphalt path along the quay was quite dry and they walked more quickly, like travellers on a long journey. A wounded lieutenant and a stocky young girl in a ski-suit were coming towards them. They had their arms round one another and were stopping every now and then to kiss. As they passed Viktor and Marya Ivanovna, they kissed again, looked round and burst out laughing.

'Who knows?' thought Viktor. 'Perhaps Nadya came for a walk here with her lieutenant.'

Marya Ivanovna looked round at the young couple and said:

'How sad it all is.'

She smiled. 'Lyudmila Nikolaevna told me about Nadya.'

'Yes, yes,' said Viktor. 'It is all very strange.'

Then he added:

'I've decided to phone the director of the Electro-Mechanical Institute and offer my services. If they don't accept me, I'll have to go somewhere like Novosibirsk or Krasnoyarsk.'

'Yes, that's the best thing you can do,' she said. 'What can I say? You couldn't have acted any other way.'

'How sad it all is.'

He wanted to say what a deep love he felt now for his work and his laboratory. He wanted to say that when he looked at the new apparatus – now almost complete – he felt a strange blend of joy and sorrow; that he sometimes felt he would come back to the Institute at night and peer through the windows. But he didn't say anything; he was afraid Marya Ivanovna would think he was putting on an act.

As they came to the exhibition of war-trophies, they slowed down to look at an aeroplane with black swastikas and at the grey German tanks, field-guns and mortars.

'They look terrifying enough even like this,' said Marya Ivanovna.

'They're not so bad,' said Viktor. 'By the time the next war comes, they'll seem as innocent as muskets and halberds.'

They reached the gate.

'So our walk's come to an end,' said Viktor. 'What a pity this park's so small. You're not tired?'

'Not at all. I do a lot of walking.'

Either she was pretending not to understand or she really didn't.

'It's strange,' he said. 'Our meetings always seem to depend on your meetings with Lyudmila or mine with Pyotr Lavrentyevich.'

'Yes,' she agreed, 'but how else could it be?'

They left the park; the noise of the city surrounded them again, destroying the charm of their quiet walk. They came out onto a square not far from where they had first met.

Looking up at him – as though she were a little girl and he were an adult – she said:

'Just now you probably feel a special love for your work, for your laboratory and equipment. But you couldn't have acted in any other way. Another man could – but not you. I've brought you bad news, but I always think it's best to know the truth.'

'Thank you, Marya Ivanovna,' said Viktor, squeezing her hand. 'And not only for that.'

He thought he could feel her fingers trembling in his hand.

'How strange,' she said. 'We're saying goodbye almost exactly where we met.'

Viktor smiled. 'It's not for nothing that the ancients said, "In my beginning is my end."'

Marya Ivanovna frowned as she puzzled over this. Then she laughed and said: 'I don't understand.'

Viktor watched as she walked down the street: a short, skinny woman, not someone a passer-by would turn round to look at.

57

Darensky had seldom been so bored or depressed as during these weeks in the Kalmyk steppe. He had sent a telegram to Front Head-quarters, saying that he had completed his mission and that his continued presence on the extreme left flank – where there was in any case no activity – served no purpose. With an obstinacy he found incomprehensible, his superiors had still not recalled him.

It wasn't so bad when he was working; what was most difficult was when he was off duty.

There was sand everywhere; dry, rustling, slippery sand. Of course, even this supported life. You could hear the rustle of lizards and tortoises and see the tracks left by the lizards' tails. Here and there you came across small thorn bushes, themselves the colour of sand. Kites hovered in the air, searching for refuse or carrion. Spiders ran past on long legs.

The stern poverty, the cold monotony of the snowless November desert, seemed to have devastated the men who had been posted here. Their way of life, even their thoughts, seemed to have become equally dreary.

Little by little, Darensky had submitted to this monotony. He had always been indifferent to food, but now he thought of little else. The endless meals of sour-tasting soup made from pearl barley and mari-nated tomatoes – followed by pearl-barley porridge – had become a nightmare. Sometimes he found it unbearable to sit in the gloom of the small barn, in front of puddles of soup splashed over a table knocked together from a few planks, watching everyone sipping this soup from flat tin bowls; all he wanted was to get out – to escape the rattle of spoons and the nauseating smell. But as soon as he left, he began to count the hours till the next day's meal.

The huts were cold at night. Darensky slept badly; his back froze, his ears and legs froze, his fingers froze, his cheeks froze. He went to bed without undressing, with two pairs of foot-cloths round his feet and a towel round his head.

At first he had been amazed at the way people he met seemed almost to have forgotten the war; they seemed to have no room in their minds for anything except food, tobacco and clean laundry. But soon he noticed himself thinking of all kinds of trivia, all kinds of petty hopes and disappointments as he talked to the commanders of divisions and batteries about axle-grease, ammunition supplies and how best to prepare the guns for the winter.

Front Headquarters now seemed impossibly distant; his dream was to spend a day at Army Headquarters, near Elista. But it wasn't Alla Sergeyevna and her blue eyes that he dreamed of: he dreamed of a bath, clean underwear and soup with white noodles.

Even the night he had spent at Bova's now seemed pleasant and agreeable. It hadn't been such a bad hut after all. And they hadn't talked only about soup and clean laundry.

The worst torment of all was the lice.

It had taken him some time to realize why he was always itching; he had failed to understand people's knowing smiles when he had furiously begun scratching his thigh or armpit in the middle of a serious discussion. Every day he had scratched with increasing zeal. He had felt a constant burning under his armpits.

He had thought he had eczema, that the dust and sand must be irritating his dry skin. Sometimes, on his way somewhere, he would stop and suddenly begin scratching his legs, his stomach, the small of his back. It was worst of all at night. He would wake up and scratch furiously at his chest. Once, when he was lying on his back, he had stuck his legs up in the air and moaned as he scratched at his thighs. His eczema seemed to be aggravated by heat. Under the blankets, it became unbearable; if he went out into the frost, it calmed down. He decided to go to the first-aid post and ask for some ointment.

One morning he had turned down his shirt collar and seen a row of sleepy, full-grown lice along the seam. There were dozens of them. He had looked round in embarrassment at the captain who slept in the next bed. He was sitting there with a ferocious expression on his face; he had spread out his pants and was squashing the lice that infested them. He was moving his lips silently, evidently keeping a tally.

Darensky took off his shirt and began doing the same. It was a quiet, misty morning. There was no shooting, and no planes going by overhead. You could hear distinct cracks as the lice perished, one after another, beneath the fingernails of the two officers. The captain glanced at Darensky and muttered:

'There's a fine one for you – a real bear of a louse! A breeding sow!'

His eyes still on his shirt collar, Darensky said:

'Don't they issue any powder?'

'They do,' said the captain. 'But it's a waste of time. What we need is a good wash, but there isn't even enough water to drink. They can't even wash the plates properly in the canteen. There's certainly no chance of a bath.'

'What about the ovens?'

'That's no use either. The uniforms come back scorched, and the lice just get a sun-tan ... And when I think of the time we were quartered in Penza! I never even went to the canteen. The landlady fed me herself. She was a nice plump woman – and not too old. We had baths twice a week, beer every day ...'

'I know,' said Darensky. 'But what's to be done? It's a long way to Penza.'

The captain looked at him seriously and said, as if revealing a secret:

'There is one good method, comrade Lieutenant-Colonel. Snuff! You grind up a brick, mix it with snuff and sprinkle it on your underwear. The lice begin sneezing. That makes them jump – and then they bash their heads in against the brick.'

The captain kept such a straight face that it took Darensky some time to realize this was a joke.

During the next few days, he heard at least a dozen stories in a similar vein. The folklore of lice was evidently a rich field of study.

Day and night, his mind was occupied with a host of questions: food, a change of underwear, clean uniform, louse-powder, extermination of lice by ironing them with a heated bottle, by freezing them to death, by burning them to death ... He no longer thought of women at all. He remembered a saying the criminals had used in the camps:

'You may live, but you won't love.'

58

Darensky had spent all day inspecting the guns of the artillery division. He hadn't seen a single plane or heard a single shot.

The division's commander, a young Kazakh, said very clearly and without a trace of an accent:

'You know what? Next year I'm going to grow some melons. You must come back and try one.'

The divisional commander was at home in the desert. He cracked jokes, bared his white teeth in a smile, and moved with quick and effortless steps through the deep sand. He even glanced amiably at the camels standing in harness by the huts with their corrugated-iron roofs.

Darensky found his cheerfulness irritating. In search of solitude, he decided to return to the emplacements of the 1st battery – though he had already been there during the day.

An enormous moon had risen; it seemed more black than red. Growing crimson with effort, it climbed up into the transparent black of the sky; the mortars, anti-tank weapons and the barrels of the guns looked strangely threatening in this angry light. Along the road stretched a caravan of camels; they were harnessed to squeaking village carts loaded with hay and boxes of shells. It was an unlikely scene: tractors, the lorry with the printing press for the Army journal, a thin radio mast, the long necks of the camels – and their undulating walk that made it seem as though their whole body was made out of rubber, without a single hard bone.

The camels passed by, leaving a smell of hay in the frosty air. The same huge moon – more black than red – had shone over the deserted fields where Prince Igor was to give battle. The same moon had shone when the Persian hosts marched into Greece, when the Roman legions invaded the German forests, when the battalions of the first consul had watched night fall over the pyramids . . .

Darensky, his head sunk into his shoulders, was sitting on a box of shells and listening to two soldiers who lay stretched out under their greatcoats beside the guns. The battery commander and his political instructor had gone to Divisional HQ; the lieutenant-colonel from Front HQ – the soldiers had found out who he was from a signaller – seemed to be fast asleep. The soldiers puffed blissfully at the cigarettes they had rolled, letting out clouds of smoke.

They were obviously close friends; you could tell from their certainty that whatever happened to one was of equal interest to the other.

'So what happened?' said one of them, feigning mockery and indifference.

'You know the bastard as well as I do,' said the second soldier with pretended reluctance. 'How *can* he expect a man to walk in boots like these?'

'So what happened?'

'So here I am in the same old boots. I'm not going to walk barefoot, am I?'

'So he wouldn't give you new boots,' said the second gunner. His voice was now full of interest; every trace of mockery and indifference had disappeared.

Their talk turned to their homes.

'What do you expect a woman to write about? This is out of stock and that's out of stock. If the boy isn't ill, then it's the girl. You know what women are like.'

'Mine's quite straightforward about it. She says: "You lot at the front are all right – you've got your rations. As for us, we really are having a hard time."'

'That's woman's logic for you,' said the first gunner. 'There she is, sitting in the rear, and she hasn't got a clue what it's like at the front. All she knows about are your rations.'

'That's right. She can't get hold of any kerosene, and she thinks it's the end of the world.'

'Sure. It's a thousand times more difficult to wait in a queue than to sit here in the desert and fight off enemy tanks with empty bottles.'

They were both well aware that there had been no tank attacks anywhere near them.

Interrupting the eternal discussion – who has the hardest role in life, man or woman? – one of them said hesitantly:

'Mine's fallen ill, though. She's got something wrong with her back. She only has to lift something heavy and she's in bed for a week.'

Once again the conversation seemed to take a different direction. They began to talk about the accursed, waterless desert around them.

The second gunner, the one lying closest to Darensky, said:

'She didn't write that to upset me. She just doesn't understand.'

Wanting to take back – but not completely take back – his harsh words about soldiers' wives, the first gunner said:

'I know. I was just being stupid.'

They smoked for a while in silence, then started discussing the respective merits of safety-razors and cut-throats, the battery commander's new jacket, and how you still want to go on living no matter how hard things may be.

'Just look at the night! You know, I once saw a picture like this when I was at school: a full moon over a field and dead warriors lying on the ground.'

'That doesn't sound much like us,' said the other with a laugh. 'We're not warriors. We're more like sparrows.'

59

The silence was suddenly broken by an explosion to Darensky's right. 'A hundred and three millimetres,' he said to himself at once. All the usual thoughts immediately went through his mind: 'Was that a stray shot? Are they registering? I hope they haven't already bracketed us. Is it going to be a full-scale barrage? Are they preparing the ground for a tank-attack?'

Every experienced soldier was asking the same questions.

An experienced soldier can distinguish one genuinely alarming sound from among a hundred others. Whatever he's doing – eating, cleaning his rifle, writing a letter, scratching his nose, reading a newspaper; even if his mind is as empty as only that of an off-duty soldier can be – he cocks his head and listens intently and avidly.

The answer came straight away. There were explosions to the right of them, then to the left of them – and suddenly everything began shaking, smoking and thundering.

A full-scale barrage.

The flames of the explosions pierced the clouds of smoke, dust and sand; at the same time, smoke poured out of the flames. Everywhere people were running for cover, dropping to the ground.

The desert was filled by a terrible howl. Mortar-bombs had begun falling near the camels; they were running wild, upsetting their carts and dragging their broken harnesses along the ground. Darensky just stood there, forgetting the whistling shells, gazing in horror at the appalling spectacle.

He couldn't rid himself of the thought that these were the last days of his motherland. He felt a sense of doom. The terrible howl of maddened camels, the anxious Russian voices, the men running for shelter! Russia was dying! Here she was, driven into the cold sands of Asia, dying under a sullen, indifferent moon. The Russian language he so cherished had become mingled with the terrified screams of wounded camels.

What he felt at this bitter moment was not anger or hatred, but a feeling of brotherhood towards everything poor and weak. For some reason he glimpsed the dark face of the old Kalmyk he had met in the steppe; he seemed very close – as though they had known one another for a long time.

'We're in the hands of Fate,' he thought, realizing that he'd rather not stay alive if Russia was defeated.

He looked round at the soldiers; they were lying prone in whatever hollows they had been able to find. He drew himself up to his full height, ready to take command of the battery, and called out:

'Where's the telephonist? Quick! I want you right here.'

At that very moment the thunder of explosions ceased.

That night, on Stalin's orders, the commanders of three Fronts, Vatutin, Rokossovsky and Yeremenko, launched the offensive that, within a hundred hours, was to decide the battle of Stalingrad and the fate of Paulus's 330,000-strong army, the offensive that was to mark a turning-point in the war.

A telegram was waiting for Darensky at headquarters. He was to attach himself to Colonel Novikov's tank corps and keep the General Staff informed of its operations.

60

Soon after the anniversary of the Revolution, there had been another massive air-raid on the Central Power Station; eighteen bombers took part.

Clouds of smoke covered the ruins; the power station had finally been brought to a standstill.

After the raid, Spiridonov's hands had begun to tremble convulsively. He splashed tea everywhere if he tried to lift a mug to his lips; sometimes he had to put it straight back on the table, knowing he couldn't hold it any longer. His hands only stopped trembling when he drank vodka.

He and Kamyshov began allowing the workers to leave; they crossed the Volga and made their way through the steppe to Akhtuba and Leninsk. At the same time, they themselves asked Moscow for permission to leave; there was little sense in their remaining in the front line among these ruins. Moscow was slow to reply and Spiridonov became increasingly nervous. Nikolayev, the Party organizer, had already been summoned by the Central Committee; he had left for Moscow in a Douglas.

Spiridonov and Kamyshov spent their time wandering through the ruins, telling one another that there was nothing left for them to do and that they had better get the hell out of it. But Moscow still didn't reply.

Spiridonov was particularly worried about Vera. She had begun to feel ill after crossing to the left bank and had been unable to make the journey to Leninsk. She was in the last stages of pregnancy and there was no question of her travelling nearly a hundred kilometres in the back of a truck along frozen, pot-holed roads.

Some workers she knew took her to a barge that had been converted into a hostel; it was moored close to the bank, fast in the ice.

Soon after the bombing of the power station, Vera had sent her father a note by a mechanic on one of the launches. She told him that he wasn't to worry and that she'd been given a comfortable little corner in the hold, behind a partition. Among the other evacuees on the barge were a nurse from the Beketovka clinic and an old midwife; if there were any complications, they could call a doctor from the field-hospital four kilometres away. They had hot water on the barge, and a stove. The *obkom* supplied them with food and they all ate together.

Although she told him not to worry, every word of her note filled Spiridonov with anxiety. The only crumb of comfort was that as yet the barge hadn't been bombed.

If he could only get across to the left bank himself, he could get hold of a car or ambulance and take her at least as far as Akhtuba. But there was no word from Moscow. They still hadn't authorized the departure of the director and chief engineer – though there was no longer any need for anyone at the power station except a small armed guard. The workers and engineers had had no wish to hang around there with nothing to do; they had all crossed to the left bank as soon as Spiridonov gave his permission.

Only old Andreyev refused to accept the official permit bearing the director's round stamp. When Spiridonov suggested he join his daughter-in-law and grandson in Leninsk, he just said: 'No, I'm staying here.'

He felt that as long as he stayed on the Stalingrad bank he still had some link with his former life. Maybe in a little while he'd be able to get to the Tractor Factory. He'd make his way through the houses that had been burnt down or blown apart and come to the garden laid out by his wife. He'd straighten the young, injured trees, check whether the things they had buried were still in their hiding-place and sit down on a stone by the broken fence.

'Well, Varvara, the sewing-machine's still in its place and it hasn't even got rusty. But I'm afraid the apple-tree by the fence has had its day. It must have been caught by a splinter. As for the sauerkraut in the cellar – that's fine, it's just got a tiny bit of mould on top.'

Spiridonov very much wanted to talk things over with Krymov, but Krymov hadn't once looked in since the anniversary of the Revolution.

Spiridonov and Kamyshov agreed to wait until 17 November and then leave; there really was nothing whatever for them to do. The

Germans were still shelling the power station now and again. Kamyshov, who had lost his nerve after the last air-raid, said:

'Stepan Fyodorovich, if they're still shelling us, then their intelligence service is a dead loss. They may bomb us again any moment. You know the Germans. They're like bulls — they'll just carry on pounding away.'

On 18 November, without waiting for permission from Moscow, Spiridonov said goodbye to the guard, embraced Andreyev, looked for a last time at the ruins and left.

He had worked hard and honourably. His achievement was all the more worthy of respect in that he was afraid of war, was unaccustomed to conditions at the front, had lived in constant fear of air-raids and gone completely to pieces during the bombardments themselves.

He had a suitcase in one hand and a bundle over his shoulder. He waved to Andreyev, who was standing by the ruined gates, then looked round at the engineers' building with its broken windows, at the gloomy walls of the turbine-workshop and at the smoke from the still-burning insulators.

He left the power station when there was nothing more that he could do there, only twenty-four hours before the beginning of the Soviet offensive. But in the eyes of many people those twenty-four hours outweighed all he had done before; ready to greet him as a hero, they branded him a coward and a deserter.

Long afterwards he was to be tormented by the memory of how he had turned round and waved; of how he had seen a solitary old man standing by the gate, watching him.

61

Vera gave birth to a son.

She lay in the hold on a plank bed; the other women had thrown a heap of rags on top so she wouldn't be quite so cold; beside her, wrapped in a sheet, lay her baby. When someone came in and parted the curtains, she saw the other men and women and the rags hanging down from the upper bunks; she heard the cries of children, the continual commotion and the buzz of voices. She felt as though her head was as full of fog and confusion as the fetid air.

The hold was both stuffy and extremely cold; here and there you could see patches of frost on the plank walls. People slept in their felt boots and padded jackets. All day long the women sat huddled up in shawls and strips of blanket, blowing on their freezing fingers.

The tiny window, almost on a level with the ice, hardly let in any light; it was dark even in the daytime. At night they lit oil-lamps, but the glass covers were missing and their faces were covered in soot. Clouds of steam came in when they opened the trap-door from the bridge; it was like a shell-burst.

Old women combed their long grey hair; old men sat on the floor, holding mugs of hot water to warm their hands. Children, wrapped up in shawls, crawled about among the jumble of pillows, bundles and plywood suitcases.

Vera felt that her body, her thoughts, and her attitude towards other people had all been changed by the baby at her breast. She thought about her friend Zina Melnikova, about Sergeyevna – the old woman who looked after her here – about spring, about her mother, about the hole in her shirt, about the quilted blanket, about Seryozha and Tolya, about washing-powder, about German planes, about the bunker at the power station and her own unwashed hair. All these thoughts were somehow infused with her feelings for her baby; it was only in relation to him that they had meaning.

She looked at her hands, her legs, her breasts, her fingers. They were no longer the same hands that had played volleyball, written essays and turned the pages of books. They were no longer the same legs that had run up the school steps, that had been stung by nettles, that had kicked against the warm water of the river, that passers-by had turned to stare at.

When she thought about her son, she thought simultaneously of Viktorov. There were airfields not far away. He was probably very close. The Volga no longer separated them. Any moment some pilots might come into the hold.

'Do you know Lieutenant Viktorov?'

'Yes, we certainly do.'

'Tell him that his son's here – and his wife.'

The other women came to visit her in her little corner. They shook their heads, smiled and sighed; some of them cried as they bent over the baby. It was themselves they were crying over and the baby they were smiling at; this went without saying.

The questions people asked Vera all centred around one thing: how she could best serve her child. Did she have enough milk? Was she getting mastitis? Was she suffering from the damp?

Her father appeared two days after the baby's birth. Unshaven, his nose and cheeks burnt by the icy wind, his collar turned up, his coat fastened at the waist by a tie, carrying a small suitcase and a bundle, no one would have taken him for the director of the Central Power Station.

She noticed that when he came up to her bunk, his trembling face turned first of all to the creature beside her. Then he turned away; she could tell from his back and shoulders that he was crying. She realized that he was crying because his wife would never know about their grandson, would never bend over him as he himself had just done. Only then, angry and ashamed that dozens of people had seen him crying, did he say in a hoarse voice:

'So . . . You've made me a grandfather.'

He bent down, kissed her on the forehead and patted her shoulder with a cold, dirty hand. Then he said:

'Krymov came round on the anniversary of the Revolution. He didn't know your mother had died. And he kept asking about Zhenya.'

An old man, wearing a torn jacket that was losing its padding, came up and wheezed:

'Comrade Spiridonov, people are awarded the Order of Kutuzov, the Order of Lenin, the Red Star – and all for killing as many men as they can. Just think how many men have died on both sides. Well, I think your daughter deserves a medal that weighs a good two kilos – for giving birth to new life in a hell-hole like this.'

It was the first time since the baby's birth that anyone had said anything about Vera herself.

Spiridonov decided to stay on the barge till Vera was stronger. Then they could go to Leninsk together. It was on the way to Kuibyshev; he'd have to go there for a new appointment. The food on the barge was obviously quite appalling. Once he'd warmed up a bit, he set off into the forest to find the command post of the *obkom*; he knew it was somewhere nearby. He hoped he'd be able to get hold of some fat and some sugar through his friends there.

62

It had been a difficult day on the barge. The clouds lay heavily on the Volga. There were no children playing outside, no women washing clothes in the holes in the ice; the icy Astrakhan wind tore at the frozen rags and bits of rubbish, forcing its way through crevices in the walls of the barge, whistling and howling through the hold.

Everyone sat there without moving, numb, wrapped up in shawls and blankets. Even the most talkative of the women had fallen silent, listening to the howl of the wind and the creaking boards. When night came, it was as though the darkness had sprung from the unbearable sadness, from the terrible cold and hunger, from the filth, from the endless torments of the war.

Vera lay with a blanket up to her chin. On her cheeks she could feel the draught that whistled into the hold with each gust of wind. Everything seemed hopeless: her father would never be able to get her out of here; the war would never come to an end; next spring the Germans would spread right over the Urals and into Siberia; there would always be the whine of planes in the sky and the thunder of bombs on the earth.

She began to doubt, for the first time, whether Viktorov really was nearby. After all, there were airfields in every sector of the front. And he might no longer even be at the front – or even in the rear.

She moved the sheet aside and looked at her baby's face. Why was he crying? She must be passing her sadness to him, just as she passed on her milk and her warmth.

That day everyone felt crushed by the mercilessness of the cold and wind, by the vastness of the war that had stretched out over the Russian steppes.

How long can one bear a life of continual cold and hunger?

Old Sergeyevna, the midwife, came over to Vera.

'I don't like the look of you today. You looked better on the first day.'

'It doesn't matter,' said Vera. 'Papa will be back tomorrow. He'll bring some food with him.'

Even though Sergeyevna wanted the nursing mother to have some fats and sugar, she replied sourly:

'Yes, it's all right for you lot, you leaders and directors. You always get enough to eat. All we ever get is half-frozen potatoes.'

'Quiet there!' someone shouted. 'Quiet!'

All they could hear was an indistinct voice at the other end of the hold. Then the voice rang out loud and clear, drowning every other sound. Someone was reading a news bulletin by the light of the oil-lamp.

'. . . A successful offensive in the Stalingrad area . . . Several days ago our forces on the outskirts of Stalingrad launched an offensive against the German Fascists . . . Our forces are advancing along two axes – to the north-west and to the south of Stalingrad . . .'

Everyone stood there and cried. A miraculous link joined them both to the men marching through the snow, shielding their faces from the wind, and to the men who now lay on the snow, spattered with blood, their eyes growing dim as their lives ran out.

Everyone was crying: workers, old men, women, even the children – whose faces had become suddenly adult and attentive.

'Our forces have taken the town of Kalach on the east bank of the Don, Krivomuzginskaya railway station, the town and station of Abgasarovo . . .'

Vera was crying with everyone else. She too could feel the link between the exhausted listeners in the barge and the men marching through the darkness of the winter night, falling and standing up again, falling and never standing up again.

It was for her and her son, for these women with chapped hands, for these old men, for these children wrapped in their mothers' torn shawls, that the men were going to their death.

She thought with ecstasy how her husband might suddenly come in. Everyone would gather round him and call him 'My son!'

The man came to the end of the bulletin. 'The offensive launched by our troops is still continuing.'

63

The duty-officer had just given a report to the general in command of the 8th Air Army on the sorties made by their fighter squadrons during the day.

The general looked through the papers spread out in front of him.

'Zakabluka's having a hard time. Yesterday he lost his commissar and today he's lost two pilots.'

'I've just phoned his HQ, comrade General,' said the duty-officer. 'Comrade Berman's going to be buried tomorrow. The Member of the Military Soviet has promised to fly in and give a speech.'

'He does like giving speeches,' said the general with a smile.

'As for the pilots, comrade General, Lieutenant Korol was shot down over the area held by the 38th division. And Senior Lieutenant Viktorov was set on fire over a German airfield. He couldn't get back to our lines – he came down on a hill in no man's land. The infantry tried to get him out, but the Germans stopped them.'

'Yes, yes . . .,' said the general, scratching his nose with a pencil. 'I know what: you phone Front Headquarters and remind them that Zakharov promised us a new jeep. Soon we won't be able to get about at all.'

The dead pilot lay there all night on a hill covered with snow; it was a cold night and the stars were quite brilliant. At dawn the hill turned pink – the pilot now lay on a pink hill. Then the wind got up and the snow covered his body.

PART THREE

1

A few days before the beginning of the Stalingrad offensive Krymov arrived at the underground command-post of the 64th Army. Abramov's aide was eating a pie and some chicken soup.

He put down his spoon; you could tell from his sigh that it was good soup. Krymov's eyes went moist; he desperately wanted a bite of cabbage-pie.

Behind the partition, the aide announced his arrival. After a moment's silence Krymov heard a familiar voice; it was too quiet for him to make out the words.

The aide came out and announced:

'The member of the Military Soviet is unable to receive you.'

Krymov was taken aback.

'But I never asked to see him. Comrade Abramov summoned me himself.'

The aide just looked at his soup.

'So it's been cancelled, has it? I can't make head or tail of all this,' said Krymov.

He went back up to the surface and plodded along the gully towards the bank of the Volga. He had to call at the editorial office of the Army newspaper.

He felt annoyed by the senseless summons and by his sudden greed for someone else's pie. At the same time he listened attentively to the intermittent gunfire coming from the Kuporosnaya ravine.

A girl walked past on her way to the Operations Section. She was wearing a forage cap and a greatcoat. Krymov looked her up and down and said to himself: 'She's not bad at all.'

The memory of Yevgenia came back to him, and as always his heart sank. As always he immediately reproved himself: 'Forget her! Forget her!' He tried to call to mind a young Cossack girl he had spent the night with in a village they had passed through. Then he thought of Spiridonov: 'He's a fine fellow – even if he isn't a Spinoza!'

For a long time afterwards Krymov was to remember these thoughts with piercing clarity – together with the gunfire, the autumn sky and his irritation with Abramov.

A staff officer with a captain's green stripes on his greatcoat called out his name. He had followed him from the command-post.

Krymov gave him a puzzled look.

'This way please,' the captain said quietly, pointing towards the door of a hut.

Krymov walked past the sentry and through the doorway. They entered a room with a large desk and a portrait of Stalin on the plank wall.

Krymov expected the captain to say something like this: 'Excuse me, comrade Battalion Commissar, but would you mind taking this report to comrade Toshcheev on the left-bank?' Instead, he said:

'Hand over your weapon and your personal documents.'

Krymov's reply was confused and meaningless.

'But what right . . . ? Show me your own documents first . . . !'

There could be no doubt about what had happened – absurd and senseless though it might be. Krymov came out with the words that had been muttered before by many thousands of people in similar circumstances:

'It's crazy. I don't understand. It must be a misunderstanding.'

These words were no longer those of a free man.

2

'You're playing the fool. I want to know who recruited you when your unit was surrounded.'

He was now on the left bank, being interrogated in the Special Section at Front HQ.

The painted floor, the pots of flowers by the window, the pendulum-clock on the wall, all seemed calm and provincial. The rattling of the window-panes and the rumble of bombs from Stalingrad seemed pleasantly humdrum.

How little this lieutenant-colonel behind the wooden kitchen-table corresponded to the pale-lipped interrogator of his imagination.

But the lieutenant-colonel, one of his shoulders smudged with whitewash from the stove, walked up to the man sitting on the wooden stool – an expert on the workers' movement in the colonies of the Far East, a man with a commissar's star on the sleeves of his uniform, a man who had been brought up by a sweet, good-natured mother – and punched him in the face.

Krymov ran his hand over his lips and nose, looked at his palm and saw a mixture of blood and spittle. He tried to move his jaw. His lips had gone numb and his tongue was like stone. He looked at the painted floor – yes, it had just been washed – and swallowed his blood.

Only during the night did he begin to feel hatred for his interrogator. At first he had felt neither hatred nor physical pain. The blow on the face was the outward sign of a moral catastrophe. He could respond only with dumbfounded amazement.

The lieutenant-colonel looked at the clock. It was time for lunch in the canteen for heads-of-departments.

Krymov was taken across the dirty, frozen snow that covered the yard towards a rough log building that served as a lock-up. The sound of the bombs falling on Stalingrad was very clear.

His first thought as he came to his senses was that the lock-up might be destroyed by a German bomb . . . He felt disgusted with himself.

In the stifling, log-walled cell he was overwhelmed by despair and fury: he was losing himself. He was the man who had shouted hoarsely as he ran to the aeroplane to meet his friend Georgiy Dimitrov, he was the man who had borne Clara Zetkin's coffin – and just now he had given a furtive glance to see whether or not a security officer would hit him a second time. He had led his men out of encirclement; they had called him 'Comrade Commissar'. And now a peasant with a tommy-gun had looked at him – a Communist being beaten up and interrogated by another Communist – with squeamish contempt.

He had not yet taken in the full meaning of the words 'loss of freedom' . . . He had become another being. Everything in him had to change. He had lost his freedom . . .

He felt giddy . . . He would appeal to Shcherbakov, to the Central Committee! He would appeal to Molotov! He wouldn't rest until that scoundrel of a lieutenant-colonel had been shot. 'Yes – pick up that phone! Ring up Krasin! Stalin has heard my name. He knows who I am. Comrade Stalin once asked comrade Zhdanov: "Is that the same Krymov who used to work in the Comintern?"'

Then Krymov felt the quagmire beneath his feet: a dark, gluey, bottomless swamp was sucking him in. He had come up against something insuperable, something more powerful than the German Panzer divisions. He had lost his freedom.

Zhenya! Zhenya! Can you see me? Zhenya! Look at me – I'm in trouble, terrible trouble! I'm alone and abandoned. You too have abandoned me.

A degenerate had been beating him. His head span; his fingers were almost in spasm: he wanted to throw himself at the security officer.

Never had he felt such hatred towards the Tsarist police, the Mensheviks or even towards the SS officer he had once interrogated.

No, the man now trampling over him was not someone alien. Krymov could see himself in this officer, could recognize in him the same Krymov who as a boy had wept with happiness over those astonishing words of the *Communist Manifesto*: 'Workers of the World Unite!' And this feeling of recognition was appalling.

3

Darkness fell. Intermittently, the rumble of Stalingrad boomed through the close, evil air of the prison. Perhaps the Germans were going for Batyuk and Rodimtsev.

From time to time there were movements out in the corridor. The doors of the general cell – for deserters, traitors to the Motherland, looters and rapists – opened and closed. When the prisoners asked to go to the lavatory, the sentry would argue for a long time before opening the door.

Krymov himself had been put in the general cell after being brought over from Stalingrad. No one had paid any attention to the commissar with the red star still sewn on his sleeve: all the men cared about was whether he had any paper for rolling their dusty tobacco.

All they wanted was to be able to eat, smoke and carry out their natural functions.

Who had denounced him? What a torment it was: to know that he was innocent and yet to suffer from this chilling sense of irreparable guilt. Rodimtsev's conduit, the ruins of house 6/1, the White-Russian bogs, the Voronezh winter, the rivers they'd had to ford – everything light and joyful was lost for ever.

How he wanted simply to go out onto the street, stroll around, crane his neck and look up at the sky . . . And then buy a newspaper, have a shave, write a letter to his brother. He wanted a cup of tea. He had to return a book he'd borrowed for the evening. He wanted to look at his watch, go to the bath-house, take a handkerchief out of his suitcase. But he couldn't do anything. He had lost his freedom.

Then he had been taken out into the corridor. The commandant had shouted at the guard:

'I told you in plain Russian! Why the hell did you go and put him in the general cell? And don't just stand there gaping! Do you want to be sent to the front line?'

When the commandant had gone, the guard had complained:

'It's always the same. The solitary cell's occupied. He told us to keep it for people sentenced to death. If I put you there, what can I do with the fellow who's already there?'

Soon Krymov saw the firing-squad taking the man out to be executed. His fair hair clung to the narrow, scrawny nape of his neck. He could have been anything from twenty years old to thirty-five.

Krymov was then transferred to the solitary cell. In the semi-darkness he made out a pot on the table. Next to it he could feel a hare moulded from the soft inside of a loaf of bread. The condemned man must have just put it down – it was still soft. Only the hare's ears had had time to grow stale.

Krymov, his mouth hanging open, sat down on the plank-bed. He had too much on his mind to be able to sleep. Nor could he think. His temples were throbbing. He felt deafened. Everything was whirling around in his head. There was nothing he could catch hold of, no firm point from which to begin a line of thought.

During the night there was a commotion in the corridor. The guards called the corporal. There was a tramping of boots. The commandant – Krymov recognized his voice – said: 'To hell with that battalion commissar. Put him in the guard-room.' Then he added: 'What a story! I bet it'll get to the CO.'

The door of his cell opened and a soldier shouted: 'Out!'

Krymov went out. In the corridor stood a bare-footed man in his underwear.

Krymov had seen many terrible things in his life, but nothing so terrible as this small, dirty yellow face. Its lips, wrinkles, and trembling cheeks were all crying; everything was crying except for the eyes; and so terrible was the expression in those eyes, it would have been better never even to have glimpsed them.

'Come on, come on!' said the guard.

When Krymov was in the guard-room, he learned what had happened.

'They keep threatening to send me to the front, but this place is a thousand times worse. Your nerves get worn to a frazzle . . . A soldier's to be executed for self-mutilation – he'd shot himself in the left hand through a loaf of bread. They shoot him, cover him over with earth – and during the night he comes to life again and finds his way back!'

The guard avoided addressing Krymov directly – so as not to have to choose between the polite and impolite forms of the second person.

'They make a hash of everything they set their hands to. It wears your nerves to a frazzle. Even a pig gets slaughtered better than that! What a mess! The ground's frozen – so they rake up some weeds, sprinkle them over him and off they go. And then he gets up. What do you expect? He couldn't have done that if he'd been buried according to the rule-book.'

Krymov – who had always answered questions, given explanations, set people back on the true path – was bewildered.

'But why did he come back here?'

The guard laughed.

'And now the sergeant-major wants him to be given some bread and tea while they sort out his papers. The head of the catering section's raising hell. How can they give him tea when they've already written him off? And why should the sergeant-major be allowed to bungle everything and then expect the catering department to bail him out?'

'What did you do before the war?' Krymov asked suddenly.

'I was a beekeeper on a State farm.'

'I see,' said Krymov. At that moment everything – both inside him and outside him – was equally incomprehensible.

At dawn Krymov was taken back to the solitary cell. The hare was still standing beside the pot; its skin was now hard and rough. Krymov could hear a wheedling voice in the general cell:

'Come on, comrade guard! Take me along for a piss.'

A reddish-brown sun was rising over the steppe. It was like a frozen beetroot with lumps of earth still clinging to it.

Soon afterwards Krymov was taken out and put in the back of a truck. A young lieutenant sat down beside him, the sergeant-major handed over his suitcase and the truck set off for the airfield, grinding and jolting over the frozen mud.

Krymov took a deep breath of cool, damp air. His heart filled with faith and light. The nightmare seemed to be over.

4

Krymov got out of the car and looked round at the narrow grey passage leading into the Lubyanka. His head was buzzing, full of the roar of aeroplane engines, of glimpses of streams, forests and fields, of moments of despair, doubt and self-assurance.

The door opened. He entered an X-ray world of stifling official air and glaring official light. It was a world that existed quite independently of the war, outside it and above it.

He was taken to an empty, stifling room and ordered to strip. The light was as dazzling as a searchlight. A man in a doctor's smock ran his fingers thoughtfully over Krymov's body. Krymov twitched; it was clear that the war and all its thunder could never disturb the methodical work of these shameless fingers . . .

A dead soldier, a note in his gas-mask that he'd written before the attack: 'I died for the Soviet way of life, leaving behind a wife and six children . . .' A member of a tank-crew who had burned to death – he had been quite black, with tufts of hair still clinging to his young head . . . A people's army, many millions strong, marching through bogs and forests, firing artillery and machine-guns . . .

Calmly and confidently, the fingers went on with their work . . . They were under enemy fire. Commissar Krymov was shouting: 'Comrade Generalov, do you not want to defend the Soviet Motherland?'

'Turn round! Bend down! Legs apart!'

He was photographed in a soldier's tunic with its collar unbuttoned, full-face and in profile. With almost indecent diligence he pressed his fingerprints onto a sheet of paper. Someone bustled up, removed his belt and cut off his trouser buttons.

He went up in a brightly lit lift and walked down a long carpeted corridor, past a row of doors with round spy holes. They were like the wards of a cancer clinic. The air was warm. It was government air, lit by a mad electric light. This was a Radiological Institute for the Diagnosis of Society . . .

'Who had me arrested?'

He could hardly even think in this blind, stifling air. Reality and delirium, past and future, were wrestling with each other. He had lost his sense of identity . . . Did I ever have a mother? Maybe not, maybe I never had one. Zhenya no longer mattered. Stars caught in the tops of pine-trees, the ford over the Don, a green German flare, Workers of the World Unite, there must be people behind each door, I'll remain a Communist to my death, my head's buzzing, did Grekov really fire at me? Grigory Yevseevich Zinoviev, the President of the Comintern, walked down this same corridor, what close, suffocating air, damn this blinding light . . . Grekov fired at me, the man from the Special Section punched me in the jaw, the Germans fired at me, what will happen tomorrow, I swear I'm not guilty, I need a piss, the old men singing songs at Spiridonov's were quite splendid, the Cheka, the Cheka, the Cheka, Dzerzhinsky had been the first master of this house, then Heinrich Yagoda, then Menzhinsky, then that little proletarian from Petersburg, Nikolay Ivanovich Yezhov with the green eyes – and now kind, intelligent Lavrentiy Pavlovich Beria . . . Yes, we've already met – greetings to you! What was it we sang? 'Stand up, proletarian, and fight for your cause!' But I'm not guilty, I need a piss, they're not really going to shoot me, are they . . . ?

How strange it was to walk down this long, straight corridor. Life itself was so confusing – with all its winding paths, its bogs, streams and ravines, its dust-covered steppes, its unharvested corn . . . You squeezed your way through or made long detours – but fate ran straight as an arrow. Just corridors and corridors and doors in corridors.

Krymov walked at an even pace, neither quick nor slow – as though the guard was walking in front of him, not behind him.

Something had happened. Something had changed the moment he set foot in this building.

'A geometrical arrangement of points,' he had said to himself as he had his fingerprints taken. He hadn't understood these words, but they expressed what had happened.

He was losing himself. If he had asked for water, he would have been given something to drink. If he had collapsed with a heart attack, a doctor would have given him the appropriate injection. But he was no longer Krymov; he didn't understand this yet, but he could feel it. He was no longer the comrade Krymov who could dress, eat lunch, buy a cinema ticket, think, go to bed – and remain the same person. What distinguished him from everyone else was his soul, his mind, his articles in *The Communist International*, the fact that he had joined the Party before the Revolution, his various personal habits, the different tones of voice he adopted when he talked to Komsomol members, secretaries of Moscow *raykoms*, workers, old Party members, friends of his and petitioners. His body was still like any other body; his thoughts and movements were still like anyone else's thoughts and movements; but his essence, his freedom and dignity had disappeared.

He was taken into a cell – a rectangle with a clean parquet floor and four bunks. The blankets on the bunks had been pulled tight and there were no creases. He at once felt that three human beings were looking with human interest at a fourth human being.

They were people. He didn't know whether they were good or bad, whether they would be hostile, indifferent or welcoming. All he knew was that their feelings were human feelings.

He sat down on the empty bunk. The three men watched him in silence. They were sitting on their bunks with open books on their knees. Everything he had lost came back to him.

One of the men was quite massive. He had a craggy face and a mass of Beethoven-like curls – some of them quite grey – that swept down over his low, bulging forehead. The second was an old man. His hands were as white as paper, his skull was bald and gaunt, and his face was like a metal bas-relief. What flowed in his veins and arteries might have been snow rather than blood. The third, Krymov's neighbour, had just taken off his spectacles and had a red mark on the bridge of his nose. He looked kind, friendly and unhappy. He pointed at the door, gave a faint smile and shook his head. Krymov understood: the guard was still looking through the spy-hole and they should keep quiet.

The man with the dishevelled hair spoke first.

'Well,' he said in a good-natured drawl, 'on behalf of our community let me welcome the armed forces. Where have you just come from, comrade?'

'Stalingrad,' said Krymov with an embarrassed smile.

'Oh! I'm glad to meet someone who's taken part in our heroic resistance. Welcome to our hut!'

'Do you smoke?' the white-faced old man asked hurriedly.

'Yes.'

The old man nodded and stared at his book.

'It's because I let the two of them down,' Krymov's kindly neighbour explained. 'I said I didn't smoke. Otherwise they could have had my ration themselves. But tell me – how long is it since you left Stalingrad?'

'I was there this morning.'

'I see,' said the giant. 'You were brought here by Douglas?'

'That's right.'

'Tell us about Stalingrad. We haven't managed to get any papers yet.'

'You must be hungry,' said Krymov's neighbour. 'We've already had supper here.'

'I don't want anything to eat,' replied Krymov. 'And the Germans aren't going to take Stalingrad. That's quite clear.'

'That always was clear,' said the giant. 'The synagogue stands and will continue to stand.'

The old man closed his book with a bang.

'You must be a member of the Communist Party?'

'Yes, I am a Communist.'

'Sh! Sh! You must always whisper,' said Krymov's neighbour.

'Even about being a Party member,' added the giant.

The giant's face seemed familiar. Finally Krymov remembered

him. He was a famous Moscow compere. He and Zhenya had once seen him on stage during a concert in the Hall of Columns.

The door opened. A guard looked in.

'Anyone whose name begins with K?'

'Yes,' answered the giant. 'Katsenelenbogen.'

He got up, brushed back his dishevelled hair with one hand and walked unhurriedly to the door.

'He's being interrogated,' whispered Krymov's neighbour.

'Why "Anyone whose name begins with K"?'

'It's a rule of theirs. Yesterday the guard called out, "Any Katsenelenbogen whose name begins with K?" It was quite funny. He's a bit cracked.'

'Yes, we had a good laugh,' said the old man.

'I wonder what they put you inside for,' thought Krymov. And then: 'My name begins with K too.'

The prisoners got ready to go to sleep. The light continued to glare down; Krymov could feel someone watching through the spy-hole as he unwound his foot-cloths, pulled up his pants and scratched his chest. It was a very special light; it was there not so that they could see, but so that they could be seen. If it had been found more convenient to observe them in darkness, they would have been kept in darkness.

The old man – Krymov imagined him to be an accountant – was lying with his face to the wall. Krymov and his neighbour were talking in whispers; they didn't look at one another and they kept their hands over their mouths. Now and again they glanced at the empty bunk. Was the compere still cracking jokes?

'We've all become as timid as hares,' whispered Krymov's neighbour. 'It's like in a fairy-tale. A sorcerer touches someone – and suddenly he grows the ears of a hare.'

He told Krymov about the other two men in the cell. The old man, Dreling, turned out to be either a Social Revolutionary, a Social Democrat or a Menshevik. Krymov had come across his name before. He had spent over twenty years in prisons and camps; soon he'd have done longer than the prisoners in the Schlüsselburg in the last century. He was back in Moscow because of a new charge that had been brought against him: he'd taken it into his head to give lectures on the agrarian question to the kulaks in his camp.

The compere's experience of the Lubyanka was equally impressive. Over twenty years before, he'd begun working in Dzerzhinsky's Cheka. He had then worked under Yagoda in the OGPU, under Yezhov in the NKVD and under Beria in the MGB. Part of the time he had worked in the central apparatus; part of the time he had been at the camps, in charge of huge construction projects.

Krymov's neighbour was called Bogoleev. Krymov had imagined him to be a minor official; in fact he was an art historian who worked in the reserve collection of a museum. He also wrote poetry that was considered out of key with the times and had never been published.

'But that's all finished with,' whispered Bogoleev. 'Now I'm just a timid little hare.'

How strange it all was. Once there had been nothing except the crossing of the Bug and the Dnieper, the encirclement of Piryatinsk, the Ovruch marshes, Mamayev Kurgan, house number 6/1, political reports, shortages of ammunition, wounded political instructors, night attacks, political work on the march and in battle, the registration of guns, tank raids, mortars, General Staffs, heavy machineguns . . .

And at the same time there had been nothing but night interrogations, inspections, reveilles, visits to the lavatory under escort, carefully rationed cigarettes, searches, personal confrontations with witnesses, investigators, sentences decreed by a Special Commission . . .

These two realities had co-existed.

But why did it seem natural, even inevitable, that his neighbours should be confined within a cell in the Lubyanka? And why did it seem senseless, quite inconceivable that he should be confined in the same cell, that he should now be sitting on this bunk?

Krymov wanted desperately to talk about himself. In the end he gave in and said:

'My wife's left me. No one's going to send me any parcels.'

The bunk belonging to the enormous Chekist remained empty till morning.

5

One night before the war, Krymov had walked past the Lubyanka and tried to guess what was going on inside that sleepless building. After being arrested, people would be kept there for eight months, a year, a year and a half – until the investigation had been completed. Their relatives would then receive letters from camps and see the words Komi, Salekhard, Norilsk, Kotlas, Magadan, Vorkuta, Kolyma, Kuznetsk, Krasnoyarsk, Karaganda, Bukhta-Nagaevo . . .

But many thousands would disappear for ever after their spell in the Lubyanka. The Public Prosecutor's office would inform their relatives that they had been sentenced to 'ten years without right of correspondence'. But no one in the camps ever met anyone who had received this sentence. What it meant was: 'shot'.

When a man wrote to his relatives from a camp, he would say that he was feeling well, that it was nice and warm, and could they, if possible, send him some garlic and onions. His relatives would understand that this was in order to prevent scurvy. Never did anyone write so much as a word about his time in the Lubyanka.

It had been especially terrible to walk down Komsomolskiy Alley and Lubyanka Street during the summer nights of 1937 . . .

The dark, stifling streets were deserted. For all the thousands of people inside, the buildings seemed quite dead; they were dark and the windows were wide open. The silence was anything but peaceful. A few windows were lit up; you could glimpse faint shadows through the white curtains. From the main entrance came the glare of headlights and the sound of car-doors being slammed. The whole city seemed to be pinned down, fascinated by the glassy stare of the Lubyanka. Krymov had thought about various people he knew. Their distance from him was something that couldn't even be measured in space – they existed in another dimension. No power on earth or in heaven could bridge this abyss, an abyss as profound as death itself. But these people weren't yet lying under a nailed-down coffin-lid – they were here beside him, alive and breathing, thinking, weeping.

The cars continued to bring in more prisoners. Hundreds, thousands, tens of thousands of prisoners disappeared into the Inner Prisons, behind the doors of the Lubyanka, the Butyrka and the Lefortovo.

New people came forward to replace those who had been arrested – in *raykoms*, Peoples' Commissariats, War Departments, the office of the Public Prosecutor, industrial enterprises, surgeries, trade-union committees, land departments, bacteriological laboratories, theatre managements, aircraft-design offices, institutes designing vast chemical and metallurgical factories.

Sometimes the people who had replaced the arrested terrorists, saboteurs and enemies of the people were arrested as enemies of the people themselves. Sometimes the third wave of appointments was arrested in its turn.

A Party member from Leningrad had told Krymov in a whisper how he had once shared a cell with three ex-secretaries of the same Leningrad *raykom*; each had unmasked his predecessor as a terrorist and enemy of the people. They had lain side by side, apparently without the least ill-feeling.

Dmitry Shaposhnikov, Yevgenia Nikolaevna's brother, had once entered this building. He had carried under his arm a small white bundle put together for him by his wife: a towel, some soap, two changes of underwear, a toothbrush, socks and three handkerchiefs. He had walked through these doors, remembering the five-figure number of his Party card, his writing-desk at the trade delegation in Paris and the first-class coach bound for the Crimea where he had had things out with his wife, drunk a bottle of mineral water and yawned as he flipped through the pages of *The Golden Ass*.

Mitya certainly hadn't been guilty of anything. Still, it wasn't as though Krymov had been put in prison himself.

Abarchuk, Lyudmila Nikolaevna's first husband, had once walked down the brightly-lit corridor leading from freedom to confinement. He had gone to be interrogated, anxious to clear up an absurd misunderstanding . . . Five months had passed, seven months, eight months – and then he had written: 'The idea of assassinating comrade Stalin was first suggested to me by a member of the German Military

Intelligence Service, a man I was first put in touch with by one of the underground leaders . . . The conversation took place after the May Day demonstration, on Yauzsky Boulevard. I promised to give a final answer within five days and we agreed on a further meeting . . .'

The work carried out behind these windows was truly fantastic. During the Civil War, Abarchuk hadn't so much as flinched when one of Kolchak's officers had fired at him.

Of course Abarchuk had been coerced into making a false confession. Of course he was a true Communist, a Communist whose strength had been tested under Lenin. Of course he hadn't been guilty of anything. But still, he had been arrested and he had confessed . . . And Krymov had not been arrested and had not confessed . . .

Krymov had heard one or two things about how these cases were fabricated. He had learned a few things from people who had told him in a whisper: 'But remember! If you pass this on to anyone – even your wife or your mother – then I'm done for.'

He had learned a little from people who had had too much to drink. Infuriated by someone's glib stupidity, they had let slip a few careless words and suddenly fallen silent. The following day they had yawned and said in the most casual of tones: 'By the way, I seem to remember coming out with all kinds of nonsense yesterday. You don't remember? Well, so much the better.'

He had learned a little from wives of friends who had travelled to camps in order to visit their husbands . . . But all this had been gossip, mere tittle-tattle. Nothing like this had ever happened to Krymov . . .

And now it had. He was in prison. It was absurd, crazy, unbelievable – but it was true.

When Mensheviks, Social Revolutionaries, officers in the White Guard, priests and kulak agitators had been arrested, he had never, for one moment, wondered what it must be like to be awaiting sentence. Nor had he thought about the families of these men.

Of course he had felt less indifferent when the shells had begun to fall closer, when people like himself – true Soviet citizens and members of the Party – had been arrested. And he had been very shaken when several close friends, people of his own generation whom he looked on as true Leninists, had been arrested. He had been unable to sleep; he had questioned Stalin's right to deprive people of freedom, to torment them and shoot them. He had thought deeply about the sufferings of these men and their families. After all, they weren't just kulaks or White officers; they were Old Bolsheviks.

But he had managed to reassure himself. It wasn't as though *he* had been imprisoned or exiled. *He* hadn't signed anything; *he* hadn't pleaded guilty to false charges.

But now it had happened. He, an Old Bolshevik, was in prison. And he had no explanation for it, no interpretation, no way of reassuring himself.

He was learning already. The principal focus of a search was a naked man's teeth, ears, nostrils and groin. A pitiful, ridiculous figure, he would have to hold up his now buttonless trousers and underpants as he walked down the corridor. If he wore spectacles, they would be taken away from him; he would be anxiously screwing up his eyes and rubbing them. He then entered a cell where he was transformed into a laboratory rat. New reflexes were conditioned into him. He spoke only in a whisper. He got up from his bunk, lay down on his bunk, relieved himself, slept and dreamed under incessant observation. It was all monstrously cruel. It was absurd and inhuman. Now he realized what terrible things were done in the Lubyanka. They were tormenting an Old Bolshevik, a Leninist. They were tormenting Comrade Krymov.

6

The days passed. Krymov still hadn't been called for interrogation.

He already knew what they were fed and when, what time they had their walk, what days they were taken to the bath-house. He knew the times of inspections, the smell of prison tobacco and the titles of the books in the library. He would wait anxiously for his cell-mates to return from interrogations. It was Katsenelenbogen who was called most often. And Bogoleev was always summoned in the afternoon.

Life without freedom! It was an illness. Losing one's freedom was like losing one's health. There was still light, water still flowed from the tap, you still got a bowl of soup – but all these things were different, they were merely something allocated to you. Sometimes, in the interests of the investigation, it was necessary to deprive a prisoner of light, food and sleep. And if you were allowed them, that was also in the interests of the investigation.

Once, as he returned from an interrogation, the bony old man announced haughtily:

'After three hours of silence, the investigator finally accepted that my surname was Dreling.'

Bogoleev was very friendly and gentle. He always spoke respectfully to his cell-mates, asking how they were feeling and whether they had slept well. Once he began reading some poems to Krymov, but then broke off and said: 'I'm sorry. You're probably not in the least interested.'

Krymov grinned. 'To be quite honest, I couldn't understand a word of it. But I read all of Hegel once – and I could understand that.'

Bogoleev was very frightened of interrogations. He got quite flustered when the guard came in and asked: 'Anyone whose name begins with B?' When he came back, he looked smaller, thinner and older.

His accounts of his interrogations were always very confused. It was impossible to make out whether he was being charged with an attempt on Stalin's life or a dislike of socialist-realist literature.

Once the giant Chekist advised him:

'You should help the man formulate the charge. How about this? "Feeling a wild hatred for everything new, I groundlessly criticized works of art that had been awarded a Stalin Prize." You'll get ten years for that. And don't denounce too many people you know – that doesn't help at all. On the contrary – you'll be charged with conspiracy and sent to a strict-regime camp.'

'What do you mean?' asked Bogoleev. 'They know everything. How can I help?'

He often extemporized in whispers on his favourite theme: that they were all of them characters in a fairy-tale . . . 'Whoever we are – fierce divisional commanders, parachutists, admirers of Matisse and Pissarro, Party members, pilots, designers of vast factories, creators of five-year plans – and however self-assured, however arrogant we may seem, we only have to cross the threshold of an enchanted house, to be touched by a magic wand – and we're transformed into piglets and squirrels, into little dicky-birds . . . We should be fed on midges and ants' eggs.'

Bogoleev's mind was unusual, clearly capable of profound thoughts, but he was obsessed with petty, everyday matters. He was always worrying that he'd been given less to eat than other people, that what he had been given wasn't as good, that his walk had been cut short, that someone had eaten his rusks while he was out . . .

Their life in the cell seemed to be full of events and at the same time an empty sham. They were living in a dried-up river-bed. The investigator studied the pebbles, the clefts, the unevenness of the bank. But the water that had once shaped the bed was no longer there.

Dreling rarely spoke. If he did, it was usually to Bogoleev – obviously because he wasn't a member of the Party. But he often got irritated even with him.

'You're an odd one,' he said once. 'First of all, you're friendly and respectful towards people you despise. Secondly, you ask after my health every day – though it's a matter of complete indifference to you whether I live or die.'

Bogoleev looked up at the ceiling and gave a helpless shrug of the shoulders. He then recited in a sing-song voice:

> ' "What's your shell made out of, mister tortoise?"
> I said and looked him in the eye.
> "Just from the lessons fear has taught us."
> Were the words of his reply.'

'Did you make up that doggerel yourself?' asked Dreling.

Bogoleev just gave another shrug of the shoulders.

'The man's afraid. He's learnt his lessons well,' said Katsenelenbogen.

After breakfast Dreling showed Bogoleev the cover of a book.

'Do you like it?'

'To be quite honest – no.'

'I'm no admirer of the work myself,' said Dreling with a nod of the head. 'Georgiy Valentinovich Plekhanov once said: "The image of mother created by Gorky is an ikon. The working class doesn't need ikons." '

'What's all this about ikons?' said Krymov. 'Generation after generation reads *Mother*.'

Sounding like a schoolmistress, Dreling replied:

'You only need ikons if you wish to enslave the working class. In your Communist ikon-case you have ikons of Lenin and ikons of the revered Stalin. Nekrasov didn't need ikons.'

Not only his forehead, but his whole skull, his nose, his hands looked as if they had been carved from white bone. Even his words had a bony ring to them.

Bogoleev suddenly flared up – Krymov had never seen this meek, gentle, depressed man in such a state – and said:

'You've still only got as far as Nekrasov in your understanding of poetry. Since then we've had Blok. We've had Mandelstam. We've had Khlebnikov.'

'I've never read Mandelstam,' said Dreling. 'But as for Khlebnikov – that's just decadence!'

'To hell with you!' said Bogoleev, raising his voice for the first time. 'I've had enough of you and your maxims from Plekhanov. Everyone in this cell's a Marxist of one persuasion or another. What you all have in common is that you're deaf to poetry. You don't know a thing about it.'

It was a strange business. It especially upset Krymov to think that – as far as the sentries and duty officers were concerned – there was no difference between a sick old man like Dreling and a Bolshevik, a commissar, like himself.

At this moment – though he had always loved Nekrasov and hated the Symbolists and the Decadents – he was ready to side with Bogoleev. And if the bony old man had said a word against Yezhov, he would without hesitation have defended everything – the execution of Bukharin, the banishment of wives who had failed to denounce their husbands, the terrible sentences, the terrible interrogations . . .

Dreling didn't say anything. Just then a guard appeared, to take him to the lavatory. Katsenelenbogen turned to Krymov and said:

'For ten whole days there were just the two of us in here. He was as silent as the grave. Once I said: "It's enough to make a cat laugh – two middle-aged Jews in the Lubyanka whiling away their evenings without exchanging a single word!" And he didn't say a word. No, not one word! Why? Why's he so scornful? Why won't he speak to me? Is it some way of getting his revenge?'

'He's an enemy,' said Krymov.

Dreling really seemed to have got under the Chekist's skin. 'It's quite unbelievable,' he went on. 'It's certainly not for nothing that he's inside. He's got the camp behind him, the grave ahead – and he's as firm as a rock. I envy him. The guard calls out: "Anyone whose name begins with D?" And what do you think he does? He just sits there, he doesn't say a word. Now he's got them to call him by name. And even if they had him shot then and there, he still wouldn't stand up when the authorities come into the cell.'

After Dreling had come back, Krymov said to Katsenelenbogen:

'You know, all this will seem insignificant before the judgment of history. Here in prison both you and I continue to hate the enemies of Communism.'

Dreling glanced at Krymov with amused curiosity.

'The judgment of history!' he said to no one in particular. 'You mean its summary proceedings.'

Katsenelenbogen was wrong to envy Dreling his strength. It was no longer a human strength. What warmed his empty, desolate heart was the chemical warmth of a blind, inhuman fanaticism.

He seemed uninterested in the war or anything to do with it. He never asked about the situation in Stalingrad or on any of the other fronts. He knew nothing of the new cities and the power of the new heavy industry. He no longer lived a human life; he was merely playing an abstract, never-ending game of prison draughts, a game that concerned no one but himself.

Krymov was intrigued by Katsenelenbogen. He joked and chattered away, but his eyes – for all their intelligence – were tired and lazy. They were the eyes of someone who knows too much, who is tired of life and unafraid of death.

Once, when he was talking about the construction of the railway line along the shores of the Arctic, he said:

'A strikingly beautiful project! True, it did cost ten thousand lives.'

'Isn't that rather terrible?' said Krymov.

Katsenelenbogen shrugged his shoulders.

'You should have seen the columns of zeks marching to work. In dead silence. The blue and green of the Northern Lights above them, ice and snow all around them, and the roar of the dark ocean. There's power for you.'

Sometimes he gave Krymov advice.

'You should help your interrogator. He's a recent appointment. It's hard work for him too. And if you just prompt him a little, you'll be helping yourself. At least you'll avoid the "conveyor-belts" – the five-day interrogations. And it will all be the same in the end – the Special Commission will just give you the usual.'

Krymov tried to argue, but Katsenelenbogen answered:

'The concept of personal innocence is a hangover from the Middle Ages. Pure superstition! Tolstoy declared that no one in the world is guilty. We Chekists have put forward a more advanced thesis: "No one in the world is innocent." Everyone is subject to our jurisdiction. If a warrant has been issued for your arrest, you are guilty – and a warrant can be issued for everyone. Yes, everyone has the right to a warrant. Even if he has spent his whole life issuing warrants for others. The Moor has ta'en his pay and may depart.'

He had met a number of Krymov's friends – several of them when they were being interrogated in 1937. He had a strange way of talking about the people whose cases he had supervised. Without the least hint of emotion he would say: 'He was a nice guy . . .'; 'An interesting fellow . . .'; 'A real eccentric . . .'

He often alluded to Anatole France and Shevchenko's 'Ballad of Opanas', he loved quoting Babel's Benya Krik and he referred to the singers and ballerinas of the Bolshoy Theatre by first name and patronymic. He was a collector of rare books; he told Krymov about a precious volume of Radishchev he had acquired not long before he was arrested.

'I'd like my collection to be donated to the Lenin Library,' he once said. 'Otherwise it will just be split up by fools who've got no idea what it's worth.'

He was married to a ballerina, but he seemed less concerned about her than about the fate of his volume of Radishchev. When Krymov said as much, he replied:

'My Angelina's no fool. She knows how to look after herself.'

He seemed to understand everything but feel nothing. Simple things like parting, suffering, freedom, love, grief, the fidelity of a woman, were mysteries to him. It was only when he spoke about his early years in the Cheka that you could sense any emotion in his voice. 'What a time that was! What people!' He dismissed Krymov's own beliefs as mere propaganda. He once said about Stalin:

'I admire him even more than I admire Lenin. He's the one man I truly love.'

But how could this man – someone who had taken part in the preparations for the trial of the leaders of the Opposition, someone whom Beria had put in charge of a colossal camp construction project inside the Arctic Circle – feel so unperturbed about having to hold up his buttonless trousers as he was taken along at night to be interrogated in his own home? And why, on the other hand, was he so upset by the punishment of silence inflicted on him by the old Menshevik?

Sometimes Krymov himself began to doubt. Why did he turn hot and cold, why did he break out in sweat as he composed a letter to Stalin? The Moor has ta'en his pay and may depart. All this had happened to tens of thousands of Party members in 1937 – men as good as him or better than him. The Moor has ta'en his pay and may depart. Why was he so appalled now by the word 'denunciation'? Just because he himself was in prison as a result of a denunciation? He himself had received political reports from his informers in the ranks. The usual thing. The usual denunciations. 'Soldier Ryaboshtan wears a cross next to the skin and refers to Communists as atheists.' Did he survive long after being transferred to a penal battalion? 'Soldier Gordeev doesn't believe in the strength of the Soviet armed forces and considers Hitler's final victory to be inevitable.' Did he survive long in a penal company? 'Soldier Markeevich said: "The Communists are just thieves. One day we'll prong the whole lot of them on our bayonets and the people will be free."' He had been sent to a firing squad by a military tribunal. And he had denounced people himself. He had denounced Grekov to the Political Administration of the Front. If it hadn't been for the German bombs, Grekov would have been shot in front of the other officers. What had all these people felt, what had they thought when they had been transferred to penal companies, sentenced by military tribunals, interrogated in Special Departments?

And how many times before the war had he done exactly the same? How many times had he listened calmly while a friend said: 'I informed the Party Committee about my conversation with Peter'; 'Like an honest man he summarized the content of Ivan's letter to the Party meeting'; 'He was sent for. As a Communist he had to tell all. He said how the lads felt and he mentioned Volodyas's letters'?

Yes, yes, yes.

And had any of his written or oral explanations ever got anyone out of prison? Their only purpose had been to help him keep his distance, to save him from the quagmire.

Yes, Krymov had been a poor defender of his friends – even if he had hated these affairs, even if he had been afraid of them, even if he had done all he could not to get entangled in them. What was he getting so worked up about now? What did he want? Did he want the duty-officers in the Lubyanka to know about his loneliness? Did he want his investigators to commiserate with him about being abandoned by the woman he loved? Did he expect them to take into consideration that he called out for her at night, that he had bitten his hand, that his mother had called him Nikolenka?

Krymov woke up during the night, opened his eyes and saw Dreling standing beside Katsenelenbogen's bunk. The glaring electric light shone down on the old jailbird's back. Bogoleev had woken up too; he was sitting on his bunk with a blanket round his legs.

Dreling rushed to the door and banged on it with his bony fists. He shouted in his bony voice:

'Quick! Send us a doctor! One of the prisoners has had a heart attack.'

'Quiet there! Cut it out at once!' shouted the duty-officer who had come running to the spy-hole.

'What do you mean?' yelled Krymov. 'There's a man dying.'

He jumped up from his bunk, ran to the door and banged at it with his fists. He noticed that Bogoleev was now lying down again under the blankets, evidently afraid of playing an active role in this sudden emergency.

Soon the door was flung open and several men came in.

Katsenelenbogen was unconscious. It took the men a long time to lift his vast body onto the stretcher.

In the morning Dreling suddenly asked Krymov:

'Tell me, did you, as a Communist commissar, often hear expressions of discontent at the front?'

'What do you mean?' demanded Krymov. 'Discontent with what?'

'With the collectivization policy of the Bolsheviks, with the military leadership – any expression of political discontent.'

'Not once. I never came across the least hint of any such attitude.'

'Yes, yes, I see. Just as I thought,' said Dreling with a satisfied nod of the head.

7

Two hammers, one to the north and one to the south, each composed of millions of tons of metal and flesh, awaited the signal to advance.

It was the forces to the north-west of Stalingrad that launched the attack. On 19 November, 1942, at 7.30 a.m., a massive artillery bombardment began along the entire length of the South-Western and Don Fronts; it lasted for eighty minutes. A wall of fire came down over the positions held by the 3rd Rumanian Army.

The tanks and infantry went into the attack at 8.50 a.m. The morale of the Soviet troops was exceptionally high. The 76th Division went into the attack to the strains of a march played by its brass band.

By the afternoon they had broken through the enemy front line. Fighting was taking place over an enormous area.

The 4th Rumanian Army Corps had been smashed. The 1st Rumanian Cavalry Division near Krainyaya had been isolated from the remaining units of the Army.

The 5th Tank Army advanced from the heights thirty kilometres to the south-west of Serafimovich and broke through the positions held by the 2nd Rumanian Army Corps. Moving quickly towards the south, it had taken the heights north of Perelasovskaya by midday. The Soviet Tank and Cavalry Corps then turned to the south-west; by evening they had reached Gusynka and Kalmykov, sixty kilometres to the rear of the 3rd Rumanian Army.

The forces concentrated to the south of Stalingrad, in the Kalmyk steppes, went into the attack twenty-four hours later, at dawn on 20 November.

8

Novikov woke up long before dawn. His excitement was so great he was no longer aware of it.

'Do you want some tea, comrade Colonel?' asked Vershkov solemnly.

'Yes,' said Novikov. 'And you can tell the cook to do me some eggs.'

'How would you like them, comrade Colonel?'

Novikov didn't answer for a moment. Vershkov imagined he was lost in thought and hadn't even heard the question.

'Fried,' said Novikov. He looked at his watch and added: 'Go and see if Getmanov's up yet. We'll be starting in half an hour.'

He wasn't thinking – or so at least it seemed to him – about the artillery barrage that would be starting in an hour and a half, about the bombers and ground-support aircraft that would be filling the sky with the roar of their engines, about the sappers who would creep forward to clear the barbed wire and the minefields, about the infantry who would soon be dragging their machine-guns up the misty hills he had looked at so often through his binoculars. He was no longer conscious of any link with Byelov, Makarov and Karpov. He seemed to have forgotten the tanks to the north-west of Stalingrad that had already penetrated the breach in the enemy front opened up by the infantry and artillery, that were already advancing rapidly towards Kalach; he seemed to have forgotten that soon his own tanks would advance from the south to meet them and surround Paulus's army.

He wasn't thinking about Yeremenko, about the fact that Stalin might cite his name in tomorrow's order of the day. He seemed to have forgotten Yevgenia Nikolaevna, to have forgotten that dawn in Brest-Litovsk when he had run towards the airfield and seen the first flames of war in the sky.

He wasn't thinking about any of these things, but they were all of them inside him.

He was thinking simply about whether he should wear his old boots or his new ones; that he mustn't forget his cigarette-case; that his swine of an orderly had yet again given him cold tea. He sat there, eating his fried eggs and mopping up the butter still left in the pan with a piece of bread.

'Your orders have been carried out,' reported Vershkov. He went on in confiding disapproval: 'I asked the soldier if the commissar was there and he said: "Where d'you think he is? He's with that woman of his."'

The soldier had used a more expressive word than 'woman', but Vershkov preferred not to repeat this to the corps commander's face.

Novikov didn't say anything; he went on gathering up the crumbs of bread on the table, squeezing them together with one finger.

Soon Getmanov arrived.

'Tea?' asked Novikov.

'It's time we were off, Pyotr Pavlovich,' said Getmanov abruptly. 'We've had enough tea and enough sugar. Now it's time to deal with the Germans.'

'Oh,' Vershkov said to himself, 'we are tough today!'

Novikov went into the part of the house that served as their headquarters, glanced at the map and had a word with Nyeudobnov about various matters of liaison.

The deceptive silence and darkness reminded Novikov of his childhood in the Donbass. Everything had seemed just as calm, just as sleepy, only a few minutes before the whistles and hooters started up and the men went out to the mines and factories. But Petya Novikov had known that hundreds of hands were already groping for foot-cloths and boots, that women were already walking about in bare feet, rattling pokers and crockery.

'Vershkov,' he said, 'you can take my tank to the observation post. I'll be needing it today.'

'Yes, comrade Colonel, said Vershkov. 'And I'll put your gear in – and the commissar's.'

'Don't forget the cocoa,' said Getmanov.

Nyeudobnov came out onto the porch, his greatcoat thrown over his shoulders.

'Lieutenant-General Tolbukhin just phoned. He wanted to know whether the corps commander had set off for the observation post yet.'

Novikov nodded, tapped his driver on the shoulder and said: 'Let's be off, Kharitonov.'

The road left the last house behind, turned sharply to the right, to the left and then ran due west, between patches of snow and dry grass.

They passed the dip in the ground where the 1st Brigade was waiting. Novikov suddenly told Kharitonov to stop, jumped out and walked towards the tanks. They showed up as black shapes surrounded by semi-darkness. Novikov looked at the men's faces as he passed by, but he didn't say a word to anyone.

He remembered the young recruits he had seen the other day on the village square. They really were just children, and the whole world had conspired to expose these children to enemy fire: the plans of the General Staff, the orders given by Yeremenko, the order he himself would give to his brigade commanders in an hour's time, what they heard from their political instructors, what they read in poems and articles in the newspapers. Into battle! Into battle! And to the west men were waiting to blow them up, to cut them apart, to crush them under the treads of their tanks.

'Yes, there is going to be a wedding!' he thought. But with no harmonicas, no sweet port wine. Novikov would shout 'Bitter! Bitter!'* — and the nineteen-year-old bridegrooms would dutifully kiss their brides.

Novikov felt as though he were walking among his own brothers and nephews, among the sons of his own neighbours, and that thousands of invisible girls and women were watching him.

Mothers contest a man's right to send another man to his death. But, even in war, you find men who join the mothers' clandestine resistance. Men who say, 'Stay here a moment. Can't you hear the firing outside? They can wait for my report. You just put the kettle on.' Men who say on the telephone to their superior officer, 'Yes, Colonel, we're to advance the machine-gun,' but then hang up and say, 'There's no point in moving it forward, and it will just mean the death of a good soldier.'

* A traditional custom: if guests at a wedding party shout, 'Bitter', then the bride and groom have to kiss.

Novikov strode back to his jeep. His face looked harsh and grim, as though it had absorbed some of the raw darkness of this November dawn. The jeep started up again. Getmanov looked sympathetically at Novikov.

'You know what I want to say to you right now, Pyotr Pavlovich? I love you, yes, and I believe in you.'

9

The silence was dense and unbroken; it was as though there were no steppe, no mist, no Volga, nothing in the world but silence. And then the clouds grew lighter, the grey mist began to turn crimson – and the earth and sky suddenly filled with thunder.

The nearby guns joined those in the distance; the echoes reinforced this link, and the whole battlefield was covered by a dense pattern of sound.

In the steppe villages the mud walls of the houses began to shake; pieces of clay fell silently to the floor and doors started to open and close of their own accord. The thin ice on the lakes began to crack.

A fox took flight, waving its thick silky tail in the air; a hare for once ran after it rather than away from it. Birds of prey of both day and night flew heavily up into the sky, brought together for the first time. A few field mice leapt sleepily out of their holes – like startled, dishevelled old men running out of a hut that had just caught fire.

The damp morning air over the artillery batteries probably grew a degree or two warmer from the hundreds of burning-hot gun barrels.

You could see the shell-bursts very clearly from the observation post, together with the oily black and yellow smoke twisting into the air, the fountains of earth and muddy snow and the milky whiteness of steely fire.

The artillery fell silent. The clouds of hot smoke slowly mingled with the cold, clammy mist.

Then the sky filled with another sound, a broad, rumbling sound. Soviet planes were flying towards the West. The hum and roar of the planes made tangible the true height of the sky: the fighters and ground-support aircraft flew beneath the low clouds, almost at ground level, while in and above the clouds you could hear the bass note of the invisible bombers.

The Germans in the sky over Brest-Litovsk, the Russians over the steppe . . . Novikov didn't make this comparison. What he felt then went deeper than any thoughts, memories or comparisons.

The silence returned. The silence was quite suffocating, both for the men who had been waiting to launch the attack on the Rumanian lines and for the men who were to make that attack.

This silence was like the mute, turbid, primeval sea . . . How joyful, how splendid, to fight in a battle that would decide the fate of your motherland. How appalling, how terrifying, to stand up and face death, to run towards death rather than away from it. How terrible to die young . . . You want to stay alive. There is nothing stronger in the world than the desire to preserve a young life, a life that has lived so little. This desire is stronger than any thought; it lies in the breath, in the nostrils, in the eyes, in the muscles, in the haemoglobin and its greed for oxygen. This desire is so vast that nothing can be compared to it; it cannot be measured . . . It's terrible. The moment before an attack is terrible.

Getmanov gave a loud, deep sigh. He looked in turn at Novikov, at the telephone and at the radio.

He was surprised at the expression on Novikov's face. During the last months he had seen it take on many different expressions – anger, worry, anxiety, gaiety, sullenness – but it had never looked anything like this.

One by one, the Rumanian batteries that hadn't yet been neutralized returned to life. From their emplacements in the rear, they were firing on the Russian front line. The powerful anti-aircraft guns were now being used against targets on the ground.

'Pyotr Pavlovich!' said Getmanov anxiously. 'It's time! You can't make an omelette without breaking eggs.'

To him, the necessity of sacrificing men to the cause had always seemed natural and incontestible – in peace as well as in war.

But Novikov held back. He ordered his telephonist to get Lopatin, the commander of the heavy artillery regiment that had been clearing the path for his tanks.

'Take care, Pyotr Pavlovich!' said Getmanov, looking at his watch. 'Tolbukhin will eat you alive.'

Novikov was reluctant to admit his deepest feelings even to himself, let alone to Getmanov; they were ridiculous, almost shameful.

'I'm worried about the tanks,' he said. 'We could lose a large number of them. It's only a matter of a few minutes and the T-34s are such splendid machines. We've got those anti-tank and anti-aircraft batteries in the palm of our hand.'

The steppe was still smoking. The men beside him in the observation post were staring at him, wide-eyed. The brigade commanders were waiting for their orders over the radio.

He was a colonel and a true craftsman; he was in the grip of his passion for war. But Getmanov was pushing him on, he was afraid of his superiors, and his pride and ambition were at stake. He knew very well that the words he had said to Lopatin would never be studied by the General Staff or enter the history books. No, they wouldn't win him any words of praise from Zhukov or Stalin; they wouldn't bring any nearer the Order of Suvorov he coveted.

There is one right even more important than the right to send men to their death without thinking: the right to think twice before you send men to their death. Novikov carried out this responsibility to the full.

10

In the Kremlin Stalin was waiting for a report from Yeremenko. He looked at his watch; the artillery barrage had just finished, the infantry had gone forward and the mobile units were about to enter the breach cleared by the artillery. The aeroplanes would now be bombing the German rear, the roads and airfields.

Ten minutes before, he had spoken to Vatutin. The tank and cavalry units to the north of Stalingrad were advancing even more rapidly than planned.

He picked up his pencil and glanced at the silent telephone. He wanted very much to mark the movement of the southern claw of the pincer on his map. But a superstitious anxiety made him put down the pencil. At that moment he could feel very clearly that Hitler — conscious of Stalin's thoughts — was thinking about him.

Churchill and Roosevelt trusted him; but he knew that their trust was by no means unconditional. What annoyed him most was the way, although they were only too willing to confer with him, they always first discussed everything between themselves. They knew very well that wars came and went, but politics remained politics. They admired his logic, his knowledge, the clarity of his reasoning; but he knew they saw him as an Asiatic potentate, not as a European leader.

He suddenly remembered Trotsky's piercing eyes, their merciless intelligence, the contempt in the narrowed lids. For the first time he regretted that Trotsky was no longer alive; he would have liked him to know of this day.

Stalin felt happy, full of strength; he no longer had that taste of lead in his mouth, that ache in his heart. To him, the sense of life itself was inseparable from a sense of strength. Since the first days of the war he had felt a constant weariness. It hadn't left him even when he'd seen his marshals freeze with fear at his anger, even when thousands of people stood up to greet him as he entered the Bolshoy Theatre. He always had the impression that people were laughing at him behind his back, that they remembered his confusion during the summer of 1941.

Once, in Molotov's presence, he had seized his head in his hands and muttered: 'What can we do . . . what can we do?' And during a meeting of the State Defence Committee his voice had suddenly broken; everyone had looked the other way. He had several times given absurd orders and realized that everyone was aware of their absurdity. On 3 July, he had nervously sipped mineral water as he gave his speech on the radio; his nervousness had gone out over the waves. Once, at the end of June, Zhukov had contradicted him to his face. He had felt quite taken aback; all he had been able to say was: 'All right, do as you think best.' Sometimes he wished he could yield his responsibilities to the men he had shot in 1937, that Rykov, Kamenev and Bukharin could take over the running of the army and the country.

Sometimes a strange and terrifying feeling came over him: that it wasn't only his current enemy who had defeated him on the battlefield. Behind Hitler's tanks, in a cloud of dust and smoke, he could see all those he thought he had brought low, chastised and destroyed. They were climbing out of the tundra, breaking through the layer of permafrost that had closed over them, forcing their way through the entanglements of barbed wire. Trainloads of the condemned, newly returned to life, were on their way from Kolyma and the Komi republic. Old peasant women and children were crawling out of the earth with terrifying, emaciated, sorrowful faces. They were coming towards him, looking for him; there was no anger in their eyes, only sadness. Yes, Stalin knew better than anyone that not only history condemns the defeated.

Beria's presence was sometimes quite unbearable: he seemed to understand what Stalin was going through.

This weakness didn't last long – just a few days, to return only at odd moments. But his feeling of depression was constant. He was troubled by indigestion. He had an aching feeling at the back of his neck and there were moments when he felt dizzy.

He looked at the telephone again. By now Yeremenko should have reported that the tanks had gone into the attack.

This was his hour of strength. What was being decided now, what was at stake, was the fate of the State Lenin had founded: now the rational, centralized force of the Party would be able to realize itself in the construction of huge factories, atomic power stations, jetplanes, intercontinental missiles, space rockets, immense buildings and palaces of culture, new canals and seas, new roads and cities north of the Arctic Circle.

What was at stake was the fate of France, Belgium, Italy and the countries Hitler had occupied in Scandinavia and the Balkans. It was now that the death sentence was passed on Auschwitz, Buchenwald and the nine hundred other German labour camps and concentration camps.

What was at stake was the fate of the German prisoners-of-war who were to be sent to Siberia; what was at stake was the fate of the Soviet prisoners-of-war in Hitler's camps who were also to be sent to Siberia.

What was at stake was the fate of the Kalmyks and Crimean Tartars, the Balkars and Chechens who were to be deported to Siberia and Kazakhstan, who were to lose the right to remember their history or teach their own children to speak their mother-tongue.

What was at stake was the fate of the actors Mikhoels and Zuskin, the writers Bergelson, Markish, Fefer, Kvitko and Nusinov, whose execution was to precede the sinister trial of Professor Vovsi and the Jewish doctors. What was at stake was the fate of the Jews saved by the Red Army: on the tenth anniversary of this victory Stalin was to raise over their heads the very sword of annihilation he had wrested from the hands of Hitler.

What was at stake was the fate of Poland, Hungary, Czechoslovakia and Rumania.

What was at stake was the fate of the Russian peasants and workers, the freedom of Russian thought, literature and science.

Stalin was moved. At this moment the future power of the State had merged with his will.

His greatness and genius did not exist independently of the greatness of the State and the armed forces. Only if the State was victorious would his scientific and philosophical works remain an object of study and admiration for millions of people.

He was connected to Yeremenko.

'What's up then?' said Stalin abruptly. 'Have the tanks gone in yet?'

Sensing the irritation in Stalin's voice, Yeremenko quickly put out his cigarette.

'No, comrade Stalin. Tolbukhin's just finishing the softening-up barrage. The infantry have cleaned up the front line, but the tanks haven't yet entered the breach.'

Stalin cursed loudly and put down the receiver. Yeremenko relit his cigarette and telephoned the commander of the 51st Army.

'Why haven't the tanks gone in yet?'

Holding the receiver in one hand, Tolbukhin was mopping the sweat from his chest with the other. His jacket was unbuttoned; under the open collar of his immaculately white shirt you could see the heavy folds of fat at the base of his neck. A little short of breath, he answered with the unhurried calm of an overweight man who understands in every cell of his body that too much exertion is bad for him.

'The commander of the tank corps has just reported to me: there are enemy batteries on his path that are still operational. He asked for a few minutes' delay to neutralize them with artillery fire.'

'Send the tanks in at once,' said Yeremenko curtly. 'And report back in three minutes.'

'Yes, comrade Colonel-General.'

Yeremenko wanted to curse Tolbukhin. Instead, he asked suddenly:

'How come you're breathing so heavily? Is something the matter with you?'

'No, no. I'm fine, Andrey Ivanovich. I've only just had breakfast.'

'Get on with it then,' said Yeremenko and put down the receiver. 'He's just had breakfast – he's out of breath. I ask you!' He launched into a volley of expressive and imaginative curses.

The phone rang at the observation post. You could barely hear it over the artillery fire. Novikov knew it was the army commander and that he would order him to send in his tanks at once.

He heard Tolbukhin through, thought, 'Just as I guessed,' and said: 'Yes, comrade Lieutenant-General. Immediately.'

Then he smiled in the direction of Getmanov. 'All the same, we do just need another four minutes.'

Three minutes later, Tolbukhin phoned again. Now he was no longer gasping for breath.

'Is this a joke, comrade Colonel? Why is it I can still hear artillery fire? Carry out my orders at once!'

Novikov ordered his telephonist to connect him to Lopatin, the commander of the artillery regiment. He heard Lopatin's voice, but remained silent himself; watching the second-hand of his watch, he waited for the four minutes to elapse.

'What a man!' exclaimed Getmanov with unfeigned admiration.

A minute later, when the artillery fire had died down, Novikov put on his headphones and called the commander of the leading brigade.

'Byelov?'

'Yes, comrade Corps Commander.'

Twisting his mouth into a furious, drunken cry, Novikov screamed:

'Byelov! Attack!'

The mist thickened with blue smoke. The air was alive with the rumble of motors as the tank corps entered the breach in the enemy front.

11

The aims of the Russian offensive became evident to the German commanders when, at dawn on 20 November, the artillery opened fire in the Kalmyk steppe and the shock units disposed to the south of Stalingrad attacked the 4th Rumanian Army on Paulus's right flank.

The tank corps on the extreme left of the Soviet grouping entered the breach in the front between Lakes Tsatsa and Barmantsak, turned to the north-west, and advanced towards Kalach where it was to link up with the tank and cavalry corps from the Don and South-Western Fronts.

On the afternoon of 20 November, the Soviet units advancing from Serafimovich reached a point slightly to the north of Surovikino, threatening Paulus's lines of communication.

Paulus's 6th Army was, however, still unaware that it was threatened with encirclement. At six o'clock that evening Paulus's headquarters informed Baron von Weichs, the commanding officer of Army Group B, that they were intending to continue reconnaissance activities in Stalingrad on the following day.

Later that evening Paulus received an order from von Weichs to break off offensive operations in Stalingrad. He was to concentrate tank units, infantry units and anti-tank weapons along his left flank, disposing them in depth in order to withstand an attack from the north-west.

This order, received by Paulus at 9.00 p.m., marked the end of the German offensive in Stalingrad. It was, however, rendered meaningless by the speed of events.

On 21 November the Soviet units advancing from Serafimovich and Kletskaya effected a ninety-degree turn, joined together, and moved towards the Don to the north of Kalach, directly in Paulus's rear.

That same day, forty Soviet tanks appeared on the high west bank of the Don, only a few kilometres from Paulus's command-post at Golubinskaya. Another group of tanks seized a bridge over the Don without firing a shot: the German defenders mistook them for a training detachment equipped with captured Soviet tanks that often used this bridge. Soviet tanks then entered Kalach itself. And so the first lines of the encirclement of the two German armies in Stalingrad, Paulus's 6th Army and Hoth's 4th Tank Army, were sketched in. One of Paulus's finest units, the 384th Infantry Division, was disposed to the north-west to defend Paulus's rear.

Meanwhile, Yeremenko's forces were advancing from the south. They had crushed the 29th German Motorized Division, smashed the 6th Rumanian Army Corps, and were now advancing, between the Chervlennaya and Donskaya Tsaritsa rivers, on the Stalingrad-Kalach railway line.

At dusk, Novikov's tanks reached a strongly fortified Rumanian outpost. This time Novikov did not delay. He chose not to make use of the darkness in order to concentrate his forces before attacking.

At Novikov's orders, the tanks, self-propelled guns, armoured transports and troop-carriers all simultaneously switched on their headlights. Hundreds of dazzling lights tore through the darkness. A vast mass of vehicles appeared out of the steppes, deafening the Rumanian defences with the rumble of engines, the chatter of machine-gun fire and the roar of guns, blinding them with stabbing light, paralysing them with panic.

After a few brief skirmishes, the tanks continued their advance.

On the morning of 22 November, they reached Buzinovka. That same evening, east of Kalach, in the rear of the two German armies, the vanguard linked up with the tanks that had broken through from the north. By 23 November Soviet infantry units had taken up position on the rivers Shir and Aksay, securing the flanks of the shock units.

The objective defined by the Supreme Command had been attained: the German armies had been encircled within 100 hours.

What then determined the final outcome of these manoeuvres? What human will became the instrument of destiny?

At 6.00 p.m. on 22 November Paulus radioed the following message to the Headquarters of Army Group B:

'The army has been encircled. Despite heroic resistance, the whole Tsaritsa valley, the railway line from Sovietskaya to Kalach, the bridge across the Don and the high ground on the west bank are now in Russian hands . . . The ammunition situation is acute. We have six days' rations. I request a free hand in case we should fail to establish a perimeter defence. The situation may compel me to abandon Stalingrad itself together with the northern sector of the front . . .'

On the night of 22–23 November Paulus received orders from Hitler to name the zone occupied by his troops 'Fortress Stalingrad'. The preceeding order had read: 'The Army Commander will transfer his headquarters to Stalingrad itself. The 6th Army will establish a perimeter defence and await further orders.'

After a conference between Paulus and his corps commanders, Baron von Weichs telegraphed the Supreme Command: 'In spite of the terrible weight of responsibility I feel in taking this decision, I have to inform you that I fully support General Paulus's request to withdraw the 6th Army.'

General Zeitzler, the Chief of the General Staff of the German land forces, who had been in constant liaison with von Weichs, fully shared the views of Paulus and von Weichs. He considered it quite impossible to supply such vast numbers of troops by air.

At 2.00 a.m. on 24 November, Zeitzler informed von Weichs that he had finally succeeded in persuading Hitler to abandon Stalingrad. The order for the 6th Army to break out would be given by Hitler later that morning.

The only telephone link between Army Group B and the 6th Army was cut soon after 10.00 a.m.

They were expecting to receive Hitler's order to withdraw at any minute. As it was essential to act quickly, von Weichs decided to take the responsibility upon himself.

As the radio message was being prepared, the director of the signals centre heard the following message addressed to Paulus by the Führer himself:

'The 6th Army has been temporarily encircled by Russian troops. I have decided to concentrate the Army in the following zone: North Stalingrad, Kotluban, heights 137 and 135, Marinovka, Tsybenko, South Stalingrad. The Army can be assured that I shall do everything in my power both to keep it supplied and to break the encirclement. I know the bravery of the 6th Army and its commanding officer and I am confident that it will do its duty.'

The will of Hitler was the instrument of destiny for both Paulus's Army and the Third Reich itself. At his command, a new page of German military history was written by Paulus, von Weichs and Zeitzler, by the commanding officers of corps and battalions, by the German soldiers themselves, by all those who, albeit reluctantly, executed his orders.

12

After a hundred hours of combat, units from the South-Western Front, the Don Front and the Stalingrad Front had linked up.

The Soviet tanks met under a dark winter sky on the outskirts of Kalach. The snow-covered steppes were scorched by shell-bursts and ploughed up by the treads of hundreds of vehicles. The heavy machines tore on through clouds of snow, sending up a white veil into the air. Where they turned particularly sharply, the veil was dotted with fragments of frozen dirt.

The fighters and ground-support aircraft from the other side of the Volga flew low over the steppe. You could hear the thunder of heavy artillery from the north-east; the dark, cloudy sky was lit by flashes of dim lightning.

Two T-34s stopped next to one another beside a small wooden house. Excited by their success and the nearness of death, the dirty soldiers greedily gulped in the frosty air; after the stench of oil and fumes in their tanks this was a great joy. Pushing back their black leather helmets, they entered the house. The commander of the tank that had come from Lake Tsatsa took a half-litre bottle of vodka out of his pocket. A woman in huge felt boots and a padded jacket put some glasses on the table. Her hands were trembling.

'Oy, oy! We never thought we'd come out alive,' she sobbed. 'How the guns fired and fired! I spent two days and one night in the cellar.'

Two more soldiers came into the room. They were squat and broad-shouldered – like pegtops.

'Valera! See what they've brought? Well, I think we've got something to go with it,' said the commander of the tank that had come from the north.

Valera plunged his hand into a deep pocket in his overalls and pulled out a piece of smoked sausage wrapped up in a dirty page from an army newspaper. He began to divide it up, carefully picking up the pieces of white fat that fell out and pressing them back into place with his dirty fingers.

The soldiers happily began drinking. One of them, his mouth full of sausage, smiled and said: 'Your vodka and our sausage – we've linked up!'

This joke went down well. Full of warmth and comradeliness, the soldiers repeated it to one another and laughed.

13

The commander of the tank from the south reported by radio to his squadron commander that the link-up had been effected near Kalach. He added that the crew of the other tank were splendid fellows and that they'd drunk a bottle of vodka together.

This report was rapidly passed back. Three minutes later Karpov repeated it to Novikov.

Novikov could sense the love and admiration that now surrounded him at headquarters. They had carried out their task according to schedule, and they had sustained almost no casualties.

After reporting to Yeremenko, Nyeudobnov gave Novikov a long squeeze of the hand. His usually bilious and irritable eyes looked bright and gentle.

'You see what miracles our lads can accomplish when we've eliminated the hidden enemies and saboteurs,' he said.

Getmanov embraced Novikov. He looked round at all the officers, orderlies, drivers, radio operators and cypher clerks, gave a sob and said in a loud voice:

'Thank you, Pyotr Pavlovich! A Russian thank-you, a Soviet thank-you! I thank you as a Communist. I take off my hat to you.'

Once again he embraced and kissed a deeply-moved Novikov.

'You prepared everything. Your foresaw everything. You studied your men. And this is the fruit of your labour.'

Novikov felt both overjoyed and embarrassed. He waved a file of reports at Getmanov.

'I'll tell you what I foresaw! The man I counted on was Makarov. But Makarov dawdled, deviated from his assigned route and wasted an hour and a half in an unnecessary skirmish on his flank. As for Byelov, I was quite certain that he would just forge straight ahead without paying the least attention to his flanks and rear. And what did he do? On the second day, instead of outflanking a centre of enemy resistance, he got bogged down in an operation he undertook against some artillery and infantry units and even went over to the defensive. He wasted eleven hours. It was Karpov who was the first to arrive in Kalach. He went flat out! He didn't once look back. He didn't give a damn what was happening on his flanks. He was the one who broke through the Germans' lines of communication. So much for my study of men! So much for what I foresaw! I thought he'd be so busy securing his flanks that I'd have to drive him on with a cudgel.'

Getmanov smiled.

'All right, all right. We all know the value of modesty. That's something Stalin's taught us.'

Novikov was happy. He thought he really must love Yevgenia Nikolaevna if he thought of her so much on a day like this. He kept looking round as if she might appear any moment.

'And what I'll never forget, Pyotr Pavlovich,' Getmanov went on, his voice lowered to a whisper, 'is the way you hung fire for eight minutes at the beginning. The army commander was waiting. Yeremenko was waiting. I've heard that Stalin himself phoned to ask why the tanks hadn't gone in yet. You made Stalin wait. And then you breached the enemy front without losing one tank, without losing one man. That's something I'll never forget.'

That night, when Novikov was in his tank on the way to Kalach, Getmanov called to see Nyeudobnov.

'Comrade General, I've written a letter about the way the corps commander delayed for eight minutes at the start of a crucial operation, the operation to decide the outcome of the Great Patriotic War. I'd like you to take a look at this document.'

14

Stalin's secretary, Poskrebyshev, was present when Vasilevsky reported by radio that the encirclement of the German armies had been completed. For a few moments Stalin just sat there, his eyes half-closed as though he were going to sleep. Poskrebyshev held his breath and tried not to move.

This was his hour of triumph. He had not only defeated his current enemy; he had defeated the past. In the village the grass would grow thicker over the tombs of 1930. The snow and ice of the Arctic Circle would remain dumb and silent.

He knew better than anyone that no one condemns a victor.

He wished he had his children beside him. He wished he could see his little granddaughter, the daughter of the wretched Yakov. He would have just stroked her quietly on the head, not so much as glancing at the world that stretched out beyond the threshold of the hut. His beloved daughter; his quiet, sickly granddaughter; memories of childhood; the cool of a garden; the distant sound of a river. What did anything else matter? His strength existed independently of the Soviet State, independently of his great divisions.

Very slowly and gently, his eyes still closed, he repeated the words of a song:

> 'You're caught in the net, my pretty little bird,
> I won't let you go for anything in the world.'

Poskrebyshev looked at Stalin, at his grey, thinning hair, his pock-marked face, his closed eyes; suddenly he felt the ends of his fingers grow cold.

15

The success of the Stalingrad offensive filled in a number of gaps in the Soviet line of defence: between the Stalingrad Front and the Don Front; between Chuykov's army and the divisions disposed to the north of it; between the companies and platoons ensconced in the buildings of Stalingrad and the forces in the rear from which they had been cut off. At the same time this success altered people's consciousness: a feeling of being cut off, of being wholly or partially surrounded, was replaced by a feeling of wholeness, of unity. It is precisely this sense of fusion between the individual and the mass which engenders the morale that leads to victory.

The exact opposite, of course, took place in the hearts and minds of the encircled German soldiers. A huge piece of flesh, composed of hundreds of thousands of sensitive, intelligent cells, had been torn from the main body of the German armed forces.

Tolstoy claimed that it was impossible fully to encircle an army. This claim was borne out by the experience of his time.

The years 1941–1945 proved that it is indeed possible to encircle an entire army, to nail it to the ground, to fetter it in a hoop of iron. A large number of armies, Soviet and German alike, were encircled during these years.

Tolstoy's claim was indisputably true for his time. But, like most of the thoughts of great men about war and politics, it was by no means an eternal truth.

What made encirclements possible was the combination of the extraordinary mobility of shock troops and the vast, unwieldy rears on which they depended. The encircling forces have all the advantages of mobility on their side. The encircled forces entirely lose this mobility: it is impossible for an encircled army to organize its vast, complex and factory-like rear. The encircled forces are paralysed; the encircling forces have motors and wings.

An encircled army loses more than just mobility and technical resources. Its soldiers and officers are somehow excluded from the contemporary world, thrust back into the past. They begin to reappraise not only the strength of the enemy and the likely development of the war; they also begin to reappraise the politics of their own country, the appeal of their political leaders, their laws and constitution, their characteristics as a nation, their past and their future. The encircling forces go through a similar reappraisal – but inversely.

The victory of Stalingrad determined the outcome of the war, but the silent quarrel between the victorious people and the victorious State was not yet over. On the outcome of this quarrel depended the destiny, the freedom, of Man.

16

A gentle drizzle was falling in the forest of Görlitz, on the frontier between Eastern Prussia and Lithuania. A man of average height, wearing a grey raincoat, was walking down a path between the tall trees. As the sentries caught sight of him, they held their breath, freezing into perfect immobility, allowing the raindrops to run down their cheeks.

Hitler had wanted to be alone for a moment, to have a breath of fresh air. The fine, gentle drizzle was very pleasant. He loved the silent trees. And he enjoyed walking over the soft carpet of fallen leaves.

All day he had found the staff of his field headquarters quite unbearable . . . He had never felt any respect for Stalin. His actions before the war had always seemed crude and stupid. There was a peasant simplicity even in his cunning and treachery. His Soviet State was absurd. One day Churchill would understand the tragic role played by the Reich – with its own body it had defended Europe from Stalin's Asiatic Bolshevism . . . He thought of the men on his staff who had insisted on the withdrawal of the 6th Army from Stalingrad; they would now be particularly reserved and respectful. He was equally irritated by those whose faith in him was unconditional; they would use eloquent words to assure him of their fidelity. He kept trying to think scornfully of Stalin. He wanted somehow to despise him, and he knew this was because he no longer had a sense of his own superiority over him . . . that cruel, vengeful little shopkeeper from the Caucasus. Anyway, this one success of his changed very little . . . Had he sensed a veiled mockery today in the eyes of that old gelding Zeitzler? He was annoyed at the thought that Goebbels would probably report the witticisms of the English prime minister about his gifts as a military leader. 'You've got to admit it – he *is* quite witty!' Goebbels would laugh. At the bottom of his intelligent, handsome eyes he would glimpse the envious light of a triumphant rival – something he had thought extinguished for ever.

This trouble over the 6th Army somehow prevented him from feeling fully himself. What mattered was not the loss of Stalingrad or the encirclement of the Army; what mattered was that Stalin had gained the upper hand.

Well, he would soon see to that.

Hitler had always had ordinary thoughts and ordinary, endearing weaknesses. But while he had seemed great and omnipotent, they had evoked only love and admiration. He had embodied the national élan of the German people. But if the power of the armed forces and the Reich wavered for even a moment, then his wisdom began to seem tarnished, his genius vanished.

He had never envied Napoleon. He couldn't bear people whose greatness endured even in solitude, poverty and impotence, people who were able to remain strong even in a dark cellar or attic.

He had found it impossible during this solitary walk in the forest to rise above everyday trivia and find the true, just solution that was beyond the plodders of the General Staff and the Party leadership. He found it unbearably depressing to be reduced again to the level of ordinary men.

It had been beyond the capacities of a mere man to found the New Germany, to kindle the war and the ovens of Auschwitz, to create the Gestapo. To be the founder of the New Germany and its Führer, one had to be a superman. His thoughts and feelings, his everyday life, had to exist outside and above those of ordinary men.

The Russian tanks had brought him back to his starting-point. His thoughts, decisions and passions were no longer directed towards God and the destiny of the world. The Russian tanks had brought him back among men.

At first he had found it soothing to be alone in the forest, but now he began to feel frightened. Without his bodyguards and aides, he felt like a little boy in a fairy-tale lost in a dark, enchanted forest.

Yes, he was like Tom Thumb; he was like the goat who had wandered into the forest, unaware that the wolf had stolen up on him through a thicket. His childhood fears had re-emerged through the thick darkness of decades. He could see the picture in his old book of fairy-tales: a goat in the middle of a glade and, between the damp, dark trees, the red eyes and white teeth of the wolf.

He wanted to scream, to call for his mother, to close his eyes, to run.

This forest, however, hid only the regiment of his personal guard: thousands of strong, highly-trained men whose reflexes were instantaneous. Their sole aim in life was to stop the least breath disturbing a single hair on his head. The telephones buzzed discreetly, passing on from zone to zone, from sector to sector, each movement of the Führer who had decided to go for a walk on his own in the woods.

He turned round. Restraining his desire to run, he began to walk back towards the dark-green buildings of his field headquarters.

The guards noticed he was hurrying and thought he must have urgent matters to attend to. How could they have imagined that the gathering twilight had reminded the Führer of a wolf in a fairy-tale?

Through the trees he could see the lights of the buildings. For the first time, he felt a sense of horror, human horror, at the thought of the crematoria in the camps.

17

The men in the bunkers and command-posts of the 62nd Army felt very strange indeed; they wanted to touch their faces, feel their clothes, wiggle their toes in their boots. The Germans weren't shooting. It was quiet.

The silence made their heads whirl. They felt as though they had grown empty, as though their hearts had gone numb, as though their arms and legs moved in a different way from usual. It felt very odd, even inconceivable, to eat *kasha* in silence, to write a letter in silence, to wake up at night and hear silence. This silence then gave birth to many different sounds that seemed new and strange: the clink of a knife, the rustle of a page being turned in a book, the creak of a floorboard, the sound of bare feet, the scratching of a pen, the click of a safety-catch on a pistol, the ticking of the clock on the wall of the bunker.

Krylov, the chief of staff, entered Chuykov's bunker; Chuykov himself was sitting on a bed and Gurov was sitting opposite him at the table. He had hurried in to tell them the latest news: the Stalingrad Front had gone over to the offensive and it would be only a matter of hours before Paulus was surrounded. Instead, he looked at Chuykov and Gurov and then sat down without saying a word. What he had seen on his comrades' faces must have been very special – his news was far from unimportant.

The three men sat there in silence. The silence had already given birth to sounds that had seemed erased for ever. Soon it would give birth to new thoughts, new anxieties and passions that had been uncalled-for during the fighting itself.

But they were not yet aware of these new thoughts. Their anxieties, ambitions, resentments and jealousies had yet to emerge from under the crushing weight of the fighting. They were still unaware that their names would be forever linked with a glorious page of Russian military history.

These minutes of silence were the finest of their lives. During these minutes they felt only human feelings; none of them could understand afterwards why it was they had known such happiness and such sorrow, such love and such humility.

Is there any need to continue this story? Is there any need to describe the pitiful spectacle many of these generals then made of themselves? The constant drunkenness, the bitter disputes over the sharing-out of the glory? How a drunken Chuykov leapt on Rodimtsev and tried to strangle him at a victory celebration – merely because Nikita Khrushchev had thrown his arms round Rodimtsev and kissed him without so much as a glance at Chuykov?

Is there any need to say that Chuykov and his staff first left the right bank in order to attend the celebrations of the twenty-fifth anniversary of the Cheka? And that the following morning, blind drunk, he and his comrades nearly drowned in the Volga and had to be fished out by soldiers from a hole in the ice? Is there any need to describe the subsequent curses, reproaches and suspicions?

There is only one truth. There cannot be two truths. It's hard to live with no truth, with scraps of truth, with a half-truth. A partial truth is no truth at all. Let the wonderful silence of this night be the truth, the whole truth ... Let us remember the good in these men; let us remember their great achievements.

Chuykov left the bunker and climbed slowly up to the top of the slope; the wooden steps creaked under his boots. It was dark. Both the east and the west were quiet. The silhouettes of factories, the ruined buildings, the trenches and dug-outs all merged into the calm, silent darkness of the earth, the sky and the Volga.

This was the true expression of the people's victory. Not the ceremonial marches and orchestras, not the fireworks and artillery salutes, but this quietness – the quietness of a damp night in the country ...

Chuykov was very moved; he could hear his heart thumping in his breast. Then he realized the silence was not total. From Banniy Ovrag and the 'Red October' factory came the sound of men singing. Below, on the banks of the Volga, he could hear quiet voices and the sound of a guitar.

He went back to the bunker. Gurov was waiting for him so they could have supper.

'What silence, Nikolay Ivanovich!' said Gurov. 'I can't believe it.'

Chuykov sniffed and didn't answer.

They sat down at table. Gurov said:

'Well, comrade, you must have had a hard time if a happy song makes you cry.'

Chuykov looked at him in astonishment.

18

In a dug-out on the slope leading down to the Volga, a few soldiers were sitting around a table fashioned from a few planks. The sergeant-major was pouring out mugs of vodka by the light of an oil-lamp; the soldiers watched as the precious liquid slowly mounted to the level indicated by his horny fingernail.

They drank and then reached out for some bread.

One of the soldiers finished chewing his piece of bread and said:

'Yes, he gave us a hard time. But we were too much for him in the end.'

'He's certainly quietened down now. You can't hear a sound.'

'He's had enough.'

'The epic of Stalingrad is over.'

'He's done a lot of damage, though. He's set half of Russia on fire.'

They chewed their bread very slowly. It was as though they were breaking off for a meal, after a long and difficult job of work.

Their heads grew hazy, but somehow this haziness left them clear-headed. The taste of bread, the crunch of onion, the weapons piled beside the mud wall, the Volga, this victory over a powerful enemy, a victory won by the same hands that had stroked the hair of their children, fondled their women, broken bread and rolled tobacco in scraps of newspaper – they experienced all this with extraordinary clarity.

19

The Muscovites who were now preparing to return home were probably rejoicing more at the thought of escaping their life as evacuees than at the thought of seeing Moscow again. Everything in Sverdlovsk, Omsk, Tashkent and Krasnoyarsk had become unbearable: the streets and houses, the stars in the autumn sky, even the taste of bread.

If there was a hopeful Soviet Information Bureau bulletin, they said: 'Well, it won't be much longer now.'

If the news was bad, they said: 'Oh, that means they'll interrupt the re-evacuation of families.'

Countless stories sprang up about people who'd managed to get back to Moscow without a pass – you had to change trains several times, using local and suburban trains where there were no inspectors.

People had forgotten that only a year before, in October 1941, every extra day spent in Moscow had seemed a torment. How enviously they had looked at their fellow citizens who were about to exchange the dangerous skies of their birthplace for the peace and safety of Tartary and Uzbekhistan . . .

They had forgotten how some of the men and women not included on the lists of evacuees had abandoned their bundles and suitcases and walked to Zagorsk on foot – anything to get out of Moscow. Now people were ready to abandon their work and belongings, abandon their ordered lives, and walk back to Moscow.

In the second half of November the Soviet Information Bureau announced first that a blow had been struck against the German Fascist forces in the region of Vladikavkaz, and then that a successful offensive had been launched in the Stalingrad area. There were nine announcements in the course of two weeks: 'The offensive continues . . . A new blow struck against the enemy . . . Our forces near Stalingrad, overcoming enemy resistance, have broken through his new line of defence on the east bank of the Don . . . Our forces, continuing their offensive, have advanced another twenty kilometres . . . Our troops in the Central Don region have now taken the offensive against the German Fascist forces . . . The offensive launched by our forces in the Central Don region continues . . . The offensive launched by our forces in the Northern Caucasus . . . A new blow struck by our forces to the south-west of Stalingrad . . . The offensive launched by our forces to the south of Stalingrad . . .'

On New Year's eve, the Soviet Information Bureau published a report entitled 'A Summary of the Past Six Weeks of the Stalingrad

Offensive'. This finally announced the encirclement of the German armies in Stalingrad.

A change in popular consciousness was about to become manifest; the first stirrings of this had taken place subconsciously; as secretly as the preparations for the offensive itself. For all the apparent similarities, this change in consciousness was to prove very different indeed from that which had followed the earlier victories near Moscow.

The Moscow victory had served chiefly to change people's attitudes towards the Germans. After December 1941, the mystical fear aroused by the German Army disappeared.

The Stalingrad victory, on the other hand, served mainly to change people's attitudes towards themselves, to develop a new form of self-consciousness in the army and in the population as a whole. Soviet Russians began to think of themselves differently, to adopt a different manner towards other nationalities. The history of Russia was no longer the history of the sufferings and humiliations undergone by the workers and peasantry; it was the history of Russian national glory.

People's way of thinking at the time of the Moscow victory was still fundamentally the same as it had been before the war. The reinterpretation of the events of the war, the new consciousness of the power of the Russian armed forces, of the power of the Russian State, was part of a long and complex process. This process had begun long before the war, but only on an unconscious level.

Three major events formed the basis for this new vision of human relationships and of life itself: collectivization, industrialization and the year 1937. These events, like the October Revolution itself, involved the displacement of vast sections of the population, displacements accompanied by the physical extermination of numbers of people far greater than had accompanied the liquidation of the Russian aristocracy and the industrial and commercial bourgeoisie.

These events, presided over by Stalin himself, marked the economic triumph of the builders of the new Soviet State, the builders of 'Socialism in One Country'. At the same time, these events were the logical result of the October Revolution itself.

This new social order – this order which had triumphed during the period of collectivization, industrialization and the year 1937 with its almost complete change of leading cadres – had preferred not to renounce the old ideological concepts and formulae. The fundamental characteristic of the new order was State nationalism, but it still made use of a phraseology that went back to the beginning of the twentieth century and the formation of the Bolshevik wing of the Social Democratic Party.

The war accelerated a previously unconscious process, allowing the birth of an overtly national consciousness. The word 'Russian' once again had meaning.

To begin with, during the retreat, the connotations of this word were mainly negative: the hopelessness of Russian roads, Russian backwardness, Russian confusion, Russian fatalism . . . But a national self-consciousness had been born; it was waiting only for a military victory.

National consciousness is a powerful and splendid force at a time of disaster. It is splendid not because it is nationalist, but because it is human. It is a manifestation of human dignity, human love of freedom, human faith in what is good. But this consciousness can develop in a variety of ways.

No one can deny that the head of a personnel department protecting his Institute from 'cosmopolitans' and 'bourgeois nationalists' is expressing his national consciousness in a different manner to a Red Army soldier defending Stalingrad.

This awakening of national consciousness can be related to the tasks facing the State during the war and the years after the war: the struggle for national sovereignty and the affirmation of what is truly Russian, truly Soviet, in every area of life. These tasks, however, were not suddenly imposed on the State; they appeared when the events in the countryside, the creation of a national heavy industry and the complete change in the ruling cadres marked the triumph of a social order defined by Stalin as 'Socialism in One Country'.

The birthmarks of Russian social democracy were finally erased.

And this process finally became manifest at a time when Stalingrad was the only beacon of freedom in the kingdom of darkness.

A people's war reached its greatest pathos at the time of the defence of Stalingrad; the logic of events was such that Stalin chose this moment to proclaim openly his ideology of State nationalism.

20

A new article, 'Always with the People', appeared on the wall-newspaper in the hall of the Physics Institute.

This article said that the Soviet Union – under the leadership of the great Stalin, who was guiding the country through the tempest of war – attached immense significance to science; that the Party and Government honoured and respected scientists as nowhere else in the world; and that even during the current difficult times the Soviet state was providing scientists with all the conditions necessary for normal, productive work.

It went on to list the great tasks now facing the Institute: the new building work, the expansion of the old laboratories, the bringing together of theory and practice, and the importance of scientific research for the armaments industry.

Mention was made of the patriotic élan that had seized the collective of scientists; the collective was determined to justify the concern and trust of the Party and of comrade Stalin himself, determined not to disappoint the hope with which the people looked on this glorious vanguard of the Soviet intelligentsia.

The final part of the article was about the unfortunate fact that there were certain individuals in this healthy and fraternal collective who lacked a sense of responsibility to the People and the Party – individuals who were isolated from the great Soviet family. These individuals were opposed to the collective and considered their personal interests of greater importance than the tasks entrusted to them by the Party; they tended to exaggerate their own scientific achievements, real or imaginary. Deliberately or not, some of these individuals became mouthpieces for alien, anti-Soviet views and attitudes; the ideas they spread were politically dangerous. These individuals often called for an 'objective attitude' towards the idealist, reactionary and obscurantist theories of foreign idealists. They even boasted of their links with these idealists, thus belittling the achievements of Soviet science and offending the patriotic pride of Russian scientists.

Sometimes these individuals posed as defenders of a supposedly flouted justice, trying to win a cheap popularity among the short-sighted, the gullible and the naïve; in fact they were sowing seeds of discord, seeds of a lack of faith in Russian science, of a lack of respect for its splendid past and great names. The article called on scientists to liquidate every sign of decadence, everything alien and hostile, everything that might hinder the fulfilment of the tasks with which, during the Great Patriotic War, they had been entrusted by the Party and the People. The article ended: 'Forward, towards new peaks of science, following the splendid path lit by the searchlight of Marxist philosophy, the path we have been shown by the great Party of Lenin and Stalin.'

No names were mentioned, but the article was obviously about Viktor. It was Savostyanov who first told him about it. At that moment Viktor was with a group of colleagues putting the last touches to the new apparatus. Instead of going to read it immediately, he threw his arms round Nozdrin's shoulders and said: 'Come what may, this giant will do its work.'

Nozdrin responded with a volley of curses. For a moment Viktor wasn't sure who they were aimed at.

Towards the end of the afternoon Sokolov came up to Viktor.

'Viktor Pavlovich, I admire you. You've been working all day as though nothing had happened. You're a real Socrates.'

'If a man's born blond, his hair won't turn brown just because he's been abused on a wall-newspaper,' said Viktor.

He was by now so accustomed to his feeling of resentment towards Sokolov as to be almost unconscious of it. He no longer reproached him for his excessive caution. Sometimes he said to himself, 'He does have many good qualities – and, besides, we all have our failings.'

'Yes,' said Sokolov, 'but there are articles and articles. Anna Stepanovna felt quite ill after reading it. First she went to the first-aid post and then she was sent home.'

'What on earth have they written?' thought Viktor. He preferred not to ask Sokolov, and no one else mentioned it to him. He might just as well have had terminal cancer.

That evening Viktor was the last to leave the laboratory. Alexey

Mikhailovich, the old caretaker now working as a cloakroom attendant, said:

'That's how it is, Viktor Pavlovich. There's no peace in this world for an honest man.'

Viktor put on his coat, went back up the stairs and stopped in front of the board.

When he had read the article, he looked round in confusion. For a moment he thought he was going to be arrested then and there – but the hall was quiet and empty.

He could feel quite tangibly the difference in weight between the fragile human body and the colossus of the State. He could feel the State's bright eyes gazing into his face; any moment now the State would crash down on him; there would be a crack, a squeal – and he would be gone.

The street was full of people, but there seemed to be a strip of no man's land between them and Viktor.

In the trolleybus a man in a soldier's winter cap turned excitedly to his companion. 'Have you heard the latest news?'

'Stalingrad!' someone else shouted from one of the front seats. 'The enemy's been crushed.'

A middle-aged woman stared at Viktor. She seemed to be reproaching him for his silence.

Viktor thought about Sokolov almost tenderly now. 'Yes, we all of us have our failings.'

But no one ever sincerely believes his own failings to be equal to those of other people. Soon Viktor was thinking: 'Yes, but his views depend on his success, on the love shown him by the State. Now the tide's turning, now it looks like victory, he won't utter a word of criticism. But I'm not like that: whether the State's strong or weak, whether it beats me or caresses me, my convictions remain the same.'

When he got home, he would tell Lyudmila all about the article. Yes, they really did have it in for him now. 'So much for the Stalin Prize, Lyudochka', he would say. 'An article like that means you're going to be arrested.'

'We share one destiny,' he thought. 'She'd accompany me if I was invited to lecture at the Sorbonne – and she'll accompany me to a camp in Kolyma.'

'Well, you can't say you haven't brought it on yourself,' Lyudmila would say.

He would reply coolly: 'I don't need criticism. I've had enough of that at the Institute. I need understanding and affection.'

Nadya opened the door. She flung her arms round him and buried her face in his breast.

'What's the matter? Let me take my coat off. I'm cold and wet.'

'Haven't you heard yet? Stalingrad! There's been a tremendous victory! The Germans have been surrounded! Come on, come on!'

She helped him off with his coat, took him by the hand and dragged him down the corridor.

'This way. Mama's in Tolya's room.'

She opened the door. Lyudmila was sitting at Tolya's desk. Slowly she turned her head and gave Viktor a sad, solemn smile.

He couldn't bring himself to talk about what had happened at the Institute. Instead, they all sat down at Tolya's desk; Lyudmila drew a diagram showing how the Germans had been encircled and explained her plan of operations to Nadya.

That night, when Viktor was alone in his room, he thought:

'Oh God! Why don't I write a letter of repentance? That's what everyone else does in a situation like this.'

21

It was several days since the article had first appeared. Work in the laboratory was going on as usual. Sometimes Viktor sank into depression; sometimes his spirits revived and he paced animatedly up and down the laboratory, tapping out his favourite tunes on the windowsill and the metal pipes.

He said jokingly that an epidemic of shortsightedness had broken out in the Institute; people he knew looked straight through him and passed by without so much as a word. Once, on the street, Gurevich caught sight of Viktor in the distance; he looked thoughtful, crossed to the other side and started reading a notice. Viktor had seen all this; he and Gurevich then looked round at the same moment and their eyes met. Gurevich waved at him, pretending to look pleased and surprised. All this was far from amusing.

Svechin said hello when they met. He even made an effort to walk more slowly. But from the look on his face he might have been greeting the ambassador of a hostile power. Viktor kept count of who turned away, who just nodded and who shook hands with him.

As soon as he got home, he would ask his wife: 'Has anyone rung?'

And Lyudmila would nearly always answer: 'Only Marya Ivanovna.'

Knowing what he usually asked next, she would add: 'And there's still no letter from Madyarov.'

'Do you see?' said Viktor. 'The people who used to ring up every day now only ring occasionally – and the people who used to ring occasionally have stopped altogether.'

He even thought he was being treated differently at home. On one occasion he was drinking tea and Nadya walked past without saying anything.

'You might say hello,' he called out. 'Do you think I'm an inanimate object?'

He looked quite pathetic. Instead of coming out with some harsh retort, Nadya said hurriedly: 'Dear Papa, I'm very sorry!'

That same day he asked: 'Listen, Nadya, are you still seeing your great strategist?'

She simply shrugged her shoulders.

'I just wanted to warn you. Please don't talk politics with him. All I need is to be criticized on that count too.'

Again, instead of replying sarcastically, Nadya said: 'You don't need to worry, Papa.'

On his way to the Institute in the morning, Viktor tried to avoid meeting people; he would look round to assess the situation, then walk either more quickly or more slowly. When he arrived he would make sure the corridor was empty and then rush down it as quickly as he could, his head bowed. If one of the doors opened, his heart almost stopped beating. As he reached the laboratory, he would heave a sigh of relief – like a soldier regaining his trench under enemy fire.

One day Savostyanov came into Viktor's office and pleaded with him.

'Viktor Pavlovich, I entreat you, we all of us entreat you: write a letter, say you repent! I can assure you that will help. Just think: you're throwing away everything – and at a time when an important – no, a truly great – work lies before you, a time when all that is genuine in our science looks to you with hope. Write a letter, admit your errors.'

'What errors? What do you want me to repent of?'

'Who cares? It's what everyone does – writers, scientists, political leaders, even your beloved Shostakovich. He admits his errors, writes letters of repentance – and then returns to work. It's like water off a duck's back.'

'But what do you want me to repent of? And who to?'

'The director, the Central Committee . . . It doesn't matter – as long as you repent! Something like this: "I have committed errors and I admit my guilt. I am now conscious of this and I promise to mend my ways." That sort of thing – you know what's expected. That's bound to help; it always helps.'

Savostyanov's bright, laughing eyes were for once quite serious. They even seemed to be a different colour.

'Thank you, thank you, my friend,' said Viktor. 'I'm grateful to you for your concern.'

An hour later Sokolov said:

'Viktor Pavlovich, there's going to be an open meeting of the Scientific Council next week. I think you should say something.'

'What about?'

'I think you need to make some explanations. To be more precise, you must make a confession of error.'

Viktor paced up and down the room. Suddenly he stopped by the window, his eyes on the door.

'What if I write a letter, Pyotr Lavrentyevich? That would be easier than spitting at myself in public.'

'No, I think you need to make a speech. I spoke to Svechin yesterday. He led me to understand that they . . .' Sokolov made a vague gesture in the direction of the cornice above the door, 'require a speech rather than a letter.'

Viktor turned round to face Sokolov.

'No, I'm not going to make a speech and I'm not going to write a letter.'

In the patient voice of a psychiatrist talking to someone mentally ill, Sokolov said:

'Viktor Pavlovich, for you to remain silent is the equivalent of suicide. There are political accusations hanging over your head.'

'You know what torments me most of all?' said Viktor. 'Why does all this have to happen at a moment of victory, a moment of general rejoicing? Now any son of a bitch can say that I openly attacked the foundations of Leninism at a time when I imagined the Soviet regime was about to collapse. As though I attacked people when they were down.'

'I have heard that opinion expressed.'

'No,' said Viktor. 'To hell with it. I'm not going to repent.'

That night he locked himself in his room and began to write the letter. Suddenly overwhelmed with shame, he tore it up – and began writing the text of his speech to the Scientific Council. He then read it over, thumped his elbow on the table, and tore that up too.

'Well that's it!' he said out loud. 'If they want to arrest me, they can.'

He sat there for a while without moving, mulling over the import of this decision. Then he had the idea of writing a rough draft of the letter he would have sent if he had repented. There was nothing humiliating about that. No one would ever see it. No one.

He was alone, the door was locked, everyone in the house was asleep, and it was quiet outside. There was no traffic, no car horns.

But an invisible force was crushing him. He could feel its weight, its hypnotic power; it was forcing him to think as it wanted, to write as it dictated. This force was inside him; it could dissolve his will and cause his heart to stop beating; it came between him and his family; it insinuated itself into his past, into his childhood memories. He began to feel that he really was untalented and boring, someone who wore out the people around him with dull chatter. Even his work seemed to have grown dull, to be covered with a layer of dust; the thought of it no longer filled him with light and joy.

Only people who have never felt such a force themselves can be surprised that others submit to it. Those who have felt it, on the other hand, feel astonished that a man can rebel against it even for a moment – with one sudden word of anger, one timid gesture of protest.

It was for himself that Viktor wrote this letter. He intended to hide it away and never show it to anyone. Deep down, though, he knew that it might come in useful. He would hang on to it.

Next morning, as he drank his tea, he kept looking at the clock; it was time to go to the laboratory. He felt a chilling sense of isolation. It was as though no one would ever come round to see him again. And it wasn't simply fear that stopped people from ringing him up; it was the fact that he was so dull, so boring and talentless.

'I don't suppose anyone asked for me yesterday,' he said to Lyudmila. Then he quoted the lines: 'I'm alone at the window, I don't expect guests or friends.'

'Oh yes, I forgot to say. Chepyzhin's back. He phoned and said he wants to see you.'

'How could you forget to tell me?' He began to tap out a solemn tune on the table-top.

Lyudmila went over to the window. Viktor was walking unhurriedly down the road – tall, bent forward, giving his briefcase an occasional swing. She could tell that he was thinking about his coming meeting with Chepyzhin. In his imagination, they had already exchanged greetings and were now deep in conversation.

She felt very sorry for Viktor, very anxious about him, but she couldn't forget his faults, least of all his egotism. How could he declaim, 'I'm alone at the window' – and then go off to a laboratory where he had real work to do, where he was surrounded by people? In the evening he'd go and see Chepyzhin; he probably wouldn't be back before midnight. And would he give her a moment's thought? Would it occur to him that she would be alone all day, that she would be standing by the window in an empty flat, that she was the one who wasn't expecting friends or guests?

She went into the kitchen to do the washing-up. She felt more depressed than ever. Marya Ivanovna wouldn't be phoning; she had gone to see her elder sister in Shabolovka.

How anxious she felt about Nadya! She still went out every evening, even though it had been forbidden. And of course she didn't say a word about it. As for Viktor, he was wrapped up in his own troubles. He didn't have time to think of Nadya.

Suddenly the bell rang. It must be the carpenter she had spoken to yesterday. He was coming to repair the door of Tolya's room. Human company – how wonderful!

Lyudmila opened the door. A woman in a grey fur hat was standing in the half-lit corridor, suitcase in hand.

'Zhenya!' she cried.

Her voice was so loud and so tragic that it took even her aback. She kissed her sister, flinging her arms round her shoulders and sobbing: 'He's dead, he's dead. My Tolya's dead.'

22

A thin stream of hot water dribbled into the bath; if you turned the tap any further, the water became cold. The bath was filling very slowly, but the two sisters felt as though they'd hardly had time to exchange a word.

While Yevgenia was in the bath, Lyudmila kept coming to the door and asking: 'Are you all right in there? Do you want me to rub your back for you? Keep an eye on the gas – it might go out.'

A few minutes later she'd be back, banging on the door and asking impatiently: 'What's going on in there? Have you gone to sleep or something?'

Yevgenia came out of the bathroom in her sister's towelling dressing-gown.

'You look like a witch,' said Lyudmila.

Yevgenia remembered how Sofya Osipovna had once called her a witch – on the night of Novikov's visit to Stalingrad.

'It's strange,' she said. 'After two days in a crowded train I've at last had a bath. I feel as though I should be in ecstasy, and yet . . .'

'What's brought you here so suddenly? Is something wrong?'

'I'll tell you in a moment,' said Yevgenia with a wave of the hand.

Lyudmila told her sister about Viktor's troubles and about Nadya's unexpected and amusing romance; she told her about their friends who no longer rang up and pretended not to recognize Viktor on the street. Yevgenia in turn told Lyudmila about Spiridonov; he was now in Kuibyshev and he wouldn't be offered a new job until the commission had completed its report. Somehow he seemed both noble and pathetic. Vera and her son were in Leninsk; Spiridonov couldn't so much as mention his little grandson without crying. Yevgenia went on to tell how Jenny Gerikhovna had been exiled, how Limonov had helped her to get a residence permit and what a sweet old man Shargorodsky was.

Her head was still full of tobacco smoke, conversations from the journey and the rumble of wheels; it was strange to be looking into her sister's face, to feel the soft dressing-gown against her newly-washed body, to be in a room with a carpet and a piano.

In every word the two sisters said, in all the sad, joyful, absurd or touching events they related, they could sense the presence of friends and family who had died but who would always be bound to them. Whatever they said about Viktor evoked the shade of his mother Anna Semyonovna; Dmitry and his wife, who had both died in camps, loomed behind any mention of their son Seryozha; and Lyudmila herself was always accompanied by the steps of a shy young man with broad shoulders and full lips. But neither of them mentioned any of this out loud.

'I haven't heard any news of Sofya Osipovna. She seems to have vanished into thin air,' said Yevgenia.

'The Levinton woman?'

'Yes, of course.'

'I never did like her . . . Are you doing any drawing?'

'I did in Stalingrad. But not since I moved to Kuibyshev.'

'Viktor took two of your pictures when we were evacuated. You should be flattered.'

'I am,' said Yevgenia with a smile.

'Well, madam general, you haven't said a word about what matters most of all. Are you happy? Do you love him?'

Fingering her dressing-gown, Yevgenia replied:

'Yes, I am happy. I'm fine. We love each other . . .'

She glanced quickly at Lyudmila.

'Shall I tell you why I came to Moscow? Nikolay Grigorevich has been arrested. He's in the Lubyanka.'

'Good Lord! What on earth for? He's such a hundred-per-cent Communist.'

'What about our Dmitry? Or your Abarchuk? He was a two-hundred-per-cent Communist.'

'But your Nikolay was so harsh. He was quite ruthless at the time of general collectivization. I remember asking what on earth was happening. And he just said: "The kulaks can go to the devil for all I care." He had a lot of influence on Viktor.'

'Lyuda,' said Yevgenia, a reproachful note in her voice, 'you remember only the worst about people and you always bring it up at the wrong moment.'

'What do you expect of me? I've always been one to call a spade a spade.'

'Fine,' said Yevgenia, 'but don't imagine that's always a virtue.' She lowered her voice to a whisper.

'Lyuda, I was summoned for interrogation.'

She took her sister's scarf and draped it over the telephone. 'Apparently the mouthpieces can be bugged. Yes, I've had to make a statement.'

'You and Nikolay were never officially married, were you?'

'No, but what of it? They interrogated me as though I were his wife. Let me start from the beginning. I was sent a summons to appear at the office and to bring my passport. I went through hundreds of names – Dmitry, Ida, Abarchuk, everyone I knew who'd ever been arrested – but I can tell you I didn't once think of Nikolay. I was told to come at five o'clock. It was just an ordinary office with huge portraits of Stalin and Beria on the wall. The investigator was a very ordinary-looking young man, but he looked straight through me as if he knew everything and said: "Are you aware of the counter-revolutionary activities of Nikolay Grigorevich Krymov?" Several times I thought I'd never be allowed out of the building. Once – can you imagine it? – he even hinted that Novikov . . . that I had become involved with Novikov in order to elicit information from him, and report it to Krymov. I felt quite paralysed. I said: "But Krymov's such a fanatical Communist. Just to be in his company was like attending a Party meeting." The investigator replied: "If I understand you correctly, you're implying that Novikov himself isn't a true Soviet citizen." I said: "You are strange. At the front people are fighting the Fascists, while you, young man, sit in the rear and sling mud at them.' I thought I'd get a slap in the face, but he actually blushed and looked embarrassed. So, Nikolay's been arrested. The accusations are quite crazy: Trotskyism and links with the Gestapo.'

'How appalling!' said Lyudmila, thinking to herself: 'What if Tolya's unit had got surrounded? Then he'd have had the same accusations levelled against him.'

'Vitya will take this very badly,' she said. 'He's incredibly nervous at present. He thinks he's about to be arrested. He keeps going back over everything he's ever said, who he said it to and when. Especially during that unfortunate time in Kazan.'

Yevgenia stared at her sister for a while. Finally she said:

'Shall I tell you the most terrible thing of all? This investigator said to me: "How can you claim to be ignorant of your husband's Trotskyism when he himself told you Trotsky's verdict on one of his articles: 'Splendid, that's pure marble'?" On my way home I remembered Nikolay saying to me, "You're the only person who knows those words." That night it suddenly hit me – I told that story to Novikov when he came to Kuibyshev in the autumn. I was horrified. I thought I was going out of my mind . . .'

'You poor woman. But then that's the sort of thing that would happen to you.'

'What do you mean?' asked Yevgenia. 'It could just as well have happened to you.'

'No. You left one man for another. Then you told the second man about the first. What do you expect?'

'You've probably done the same. You left Tolya's father. I'm sure you've talked about him to Viktor Pavlovich.'

'You're wrong,' said Lyudmila emphatically. 'Anyway that's different.'

'Why's it different?' asked Yevgenia, feeling suddenly irritated. 'What you're saying now is just plain stupid.'

'Maybe it is,' answered Lyudmila calmly.

'Have you got the time?' asked Yevgenia. 'I've got to go to 24 Kuznetsky Most.'

Giving vent to her anger, she went on:

'You've got a difficult character, Lyuda. I can understand why Mama lives like a gypsy in Kazan instead of staying with you in your four-room flat.'

Yevgenia immediately regretted these harsh words. Wanting Lyudmila to understand that the trust between them was stronger than any chance misunderstanding, she said:

'I do want to trust Novikov. But still . . . Who else could have told the security organs? It's terrible. It's like being lost in a fog.'

Yevgenia would have given so much to have her mother beside her. She would have leant her head on her shoulder and said: 'Dearest, I'm so tired.'

'You know what might have happened?' said Lyudmila. 'Your general might have mentioned this conversation to someone else who then reported it.'

'Yes,' said Yevgenia, 'of course! How strange I never thought of something as simple as that.'

In the quiet calm of Lyudmila's home, Yevgenia felt even more conscious of the confusion inside her . . . The thoughts and feelings she had repressed, the secret pain and anxiety from the time she and Krymov had separated, the tenderness she still felt for him, the way she still felt somehow accustomed to him – everything had flared up with renewed intensity during these last weeks.

She thought of Krymov when she was at work, when she was in a tram, when she was queuing for food. She dreamed of him almost every night, moaning, crying out in her sleep, waking up repeatedly.

She had terrible nightmares, full of fires and scenes of war. There was always some danger threatening Nikolay Grigorevich – and she was always powerless to protect him.

And when she got washed and dressed in the morning, afraid of being late for work, she would still be thinking of him.

She didn't think she loved him. But is it possible to think so incessantly of someone you don't love? And if she didn't love him, how could she feel such distress over the tragedy that had overtaken him? And why – when Limonov and Shargorodsky made fun of the supposed non-entities who were his favourite artists and poets – did she always want to see Nikolay, to run her fingers through his hair, to comfort and fondle him?

She no longer remembered his fanaticism, his lack of concern over people who had been arrested, the anger and hatred in his voice when he had talked about the kulaks. Now she only remembered his good side; she only remembered what was sad, touching and romantic about him. It was his weakness that gave him power over her. There had always been something helpless in the way he smiled, his movements were awkward and his eyes were those of a child.

She saw him sitting there with his shoulder-tabs torn off and his face covered in grey stubble; she saw him lying on a plank bed at night; she saw his back as he walked up and down the prison yard . . . He must be thinking she had had a premonition of his fate and that was why she had left him. All night he was thinking about her. Madam general . . .

She had no idea whether these thoughts sprang from love, pity, a guilty conscience or a sense of duty.

Novikov had sent her a pass and arranged by radio for a pilot he knew to take her by Douglas to Front HQ. Her superiors had given her three weeks' leave to visit him.

She tried to reassure herself, telling herself over and over again, 'He'll understand. He's sure to understand. There just wasn't anything else I could do.'

She knew very well how badly she had behaved towards Novikov. There he was, still waiting for her.

She had written him a mercilessly truthful letter. After sending it off, she had realized that the letter would be read by the military censors. All this could make terrible problems for him.

'No, no, he'll understand,' she repeated to herself.

Yes, of course he would understand – and leave her for ever.

Did she really love him, or was it just his love for her that she loved?

When she thought about the inevitable break with him, she was overwhelmed by fear, melancholy and a sense of horror at the thought of being left on her own. It was unbearable to think that she had destroyed her happiness with her own hands. It was equally unbearable, on the other hand, to think that there was nothing she could do about it, that it was now up to Novikov whether or not they finally separated.

When the thought of Novikov became unbearable, she tried to imagine Nikolay Grigorevich. Perhaps she would be summoned for a confrontation . . . Hello, my poor darling . . .

Novikov was tall, strong, broad-shouldered and in a position of power. He didn't need her support; he could take care of himself. She thought of him sometimes as her knight in armour. She would never forget his handsome, charming face. She would always grieve for him, always grieve for the happiness she had destroyed. But what of it? She wasn't sorry for herself. She wasn't afraid of suffering.

But then she knew that Novikov wasn't really so very strong. Sometimes she had glimpsed a timid, almost helpless look on his face . . . Nor was she really so pitiless towards herself, so indifferent to her own sufferings.

As though she had just read her sister's thoughts, Lyudmila asked:

'So what's going to happen about this general of yours?'

'I can't bear to think.'

'What you need is a good hiding.'

'But there just wasn't anything else I could do,' pleaded Yevgenia.

'I don't like your continual wavering. If you leave someone, you should make a clean break of it.'

'Oh yes,' said Yevgenia. 'Take good care of yourself and keep out of trouble. I'm afraid I can't live like that.'

'That's not what I mean. I don't like Krymov, but I respect him. And I haven't even set eyes on your general. But now you've decided to be his wife, you do have a certain responsibility towards him. And you're not behaving responsibly at all. An important officer with a wife sending parcels to someone in camp? You know how that could end.'

'I do.'

'Do you love him or not?'

'Leave me alone!' said Yevgenia, sounding as though she were about to cry. At the same time she asked herself, 'But which of them do I love?'

'No, I want you to answer.'

'There was nothing else I could do. People don't cross the threshold of the Lubyanka just for the fun of it.'

'You shouldn't think only of yourself.'

'I'm not thinking only of myself.'

'Viktor agrees with me. Really, it's just pure egotism.'

'You do have the most extraordinary sense of logic. It's amazed me ever since I was a child. Is this what you call egotism?'

'But what can you do to help? You can't change his sentence.'

'If you ever get arrested, then you'll learn what someone who loves you can do to help.'

To change the subject, Lyudmila asked:

'Have you got any photographs of Marusya?'

'Just one. Do you remember? It was taken when we were in Sokolniki.'

Yevgenia put her head on Lyudmila's shoulder. 'I'm so tired,' she said plaintively.

'Go and lie down for a while. You need a rest. You shouldn't go anywhere today. I've made up the bed.'

Yevgenia shook her head. Her eyes were still half-closed.

'No, no. There's no point. I'm just tired of living.'

Lyudmila went to fetch a large envelope and emptied a heap of photographs onto her sister's lap. Yevgenia went through them, exclaiming:

'My God, my God . . . yes, I remember that, it was when we were at the dacha . . . How funny little Nadya looks . . . That was after Papa had come back from exile . . . There's Dmitry as a schoolboy, Seryozha looks so like him, especially the upper part of his face . . . And there's Mama with Marusya in her arms, that was before I was even born . . .'

She noticed that there weren't any photographs of Tolya, but didn't say anything.

'Well, Madam,' said Lyudmila, 'I must give you something to eat.'

'Yes, I've got a good appetite. Nothing affects that. It was the same when I was a child.'

'I'm glad to hear it,' said Lyudmila, giving her sister a kiss.

23

Yevgenia got off the trolleybus by the Bolshoy Theatre, now covered in camouflage, and walked up Kuznetsky Most. Without even noticing them, she went past the exhibition rooms of the Artists' Foundation; friends of hers had exhibited there before the war and her own paintings had once been shown there.

It was very strange. Her life was like a pack of cards shuffled by a gypsy. Now she had drawn 'Moscow'.

She was still a long way away when she recognized the towering granite wall of the Lubyanka. 'Hello, Kolya,' she thought. Perhaps

Nikolay Grigorevich would sense her presence. Without knowing why, he would feel disturbed and excited.

Her old fate was now her new fate. What had seemed lost for ever had become her future.

The spacious new reception-room, whose polished windows looked out onto the street, had been closed; visitors now had to go to the old room. She walked into a dirty courtyard, past a dilapidated wall, and came to a half-open door. Everything inside looked surprisingly normal – tables covered in ink-stains, wooden benches along the walls, little information-windows with wooden sills.

There seemed to be no connection between this ordinary waiting-room and the vast, many-storeyed stone building that looked out over Lubyanka Square, Stretenka, Furkasovsky Lane and Malaya Lubyanka Street.

There were lots of people there; the visitors, mostly women, were standing in line in front of the windows. A few were sitting on the benches, and there was one old man, wearing glasses with thick lenses, who was filling in a form at a table. Looking at these faces – young and old, male and female – Yevgenia noticed that the expression in their eyes and the set of their mouths all spoke of one thing. If she had met any of these people on the street or in a tram, she could have guessed that they frequented 24 Kuznetsky Most.

She turned to the young man by the door. He was dressed in an army greatcoat, but for some reason he looked very unlike a soldier. 'Your first time?' he asked, and pointed to one of the windows. Yevgenia took her place in the queue, passport in hand, her fingers and palms damp with sweat. A woman in a beret who was standing in front of her said quietly:

'If he's not here in the Inner Prison, you must go to Matrosskaya Tishina and then to the Butyrka – but that's only open on certain days and they see people in alphabetical order. If he's not there, you must go to the Lefortovo military prison, and then back here again. I've been looking for my son for six weeks now. Have you been to the military prosecutor yet?'

The queue was moving very quickly. That seemed a bad sign – the answers people were getting must be vague and laconic. Then it was the turn of a smart, middle-aged woman and there was a delay; the word went round that the man on duty had gone to check something in person – a mere telephone call hadn't been enough. The woman had turned round and was half-facing the queue; her slightly narrowed eyes seemed to be saying that she had no intention of letting herself be treated in the same manner as this miserable crowd of relatives of the repressed.

Soon the queue began to move again; a young woman who had just left the window said quietly: 'Everyone's getting the same answer: 'Parcel not accepted.'

'That means the investigation's still not completed,' explained the woman in front of Yevgenia.

'What about visits?'

'Visits?' The woman smiled at Yevgenia's naïvety.

Yevgenia had never realized that the human back could be so expressive, could so vividly reflect a person's state of mind. People had a particular way of craning their necks as they came up to the window; their backs, with their raised, tensed shoulders, seemed to be crying, to be sobbing and screaming.

When Yevgenia was seventh in the queue, the window slammed shut and a twenty-minute break was announced. Everyone sat down on the chairs and benches.

There were wives and mothers; there was a middle-aged engineer whose wife – an interpreter in the All Union Society for Cultural Relations – had been arrested; there was a girl in her last year at school whose mother had been arrested and whose father had been sentenced in 1937 to 'ten years without right of correspondence'; there was an old blind woman who had been brought here by a neighbour to enquire after her son; there was a foreigner, the wife of a German Communist, who spoke very poor Russian. She wore a foreign-looking checked coat and carried a brightly-coloured cloth handbag, but her eyes were the eyes of an old Russian woman.

There were Russian women, Armenian women, Ukrainian women and Jewish women. There was a woman who worked on a *kolkhoz* near Moscow. The old man who had been filling in the form turned out to be a lecturer at the Timiryazev Academy; his grandson, a schoolboy, had been arrested – apparently for talking too much at a party.

Yevgenia learnt a great deal during those twenty minutes.

The man on duty today was one of the good ones . . . They don't accept tinned food in the Butyrka . . . You really must bring onion and garlic, they're good for scurvy . . . There was a man here last Wednesday who'd come to pick up his documents, he'd been three years in the Butyrka without once being interrogated and had then been released . . . Usually people are sent to a camp about a year after they've been arrested . . . You mustn't bring anything too good — at the transit prison in Krasnaya Presnaya the 'politicals' are put together with the common criminals and everything gets stolen . . . There was a woman here the other day whose elderly husband, an important engineer and designer, had been arrested. Apparently he'd had a brief affair in his youth and gone on sending the woman alimony for a son he'd never even set eyes on. The son, now adult, had deserted to the Germans. And the old man had got ten years for fathering a traitor to the Motherland . . . Most people were sentenced under article 58-10: Counter-Revolutionary Agitation, or not keeping their mouths shut . . . There had been arrests just before the first of May, there were always a lot just before public holidays . . . There was one woman who'd been phoned at home by the investigator and had suddenly heard her husband's voice . . .

How strange it all was. Here, in the waiting-room of the NKVD, Yevgenia somehow felt calmer, less depressed, than after her bath in Lyudmila's house.

What wonderful good fortune to have a parcel accepted!

One of the people near her said in a stifled whisper: 'When it comes to people who were arrested in 1937, they just say whatever comes into their head. One woman was told: "He's alive and working." She came back a second time and the same person gave her a certificate saying that her husband had died in 1939.'

Now it was Yevgenia's turn. The man behind the window looked up at her. His face was like that of any other clerk; yesterday he might have been working on the desk at a fire station, and tomorrow, if he was ordered to, he might be filling in forms for military decorations.

'I want to enquire about someone who's been arrested — Krymov, Nikolay Grigorevich,' said Yevgenia. She had the feeling that even people who didn't know her would be able to tell that she wasn't speaking in her normal voice.

'When was he arrested?'

'November.'

The man took out a form. 'Fill this in. You don't need to queue again – just hand it straight in. And come back tomorrow for the answer.'

As he handed her the form, the man looked at her again. This time his rapid glance was not that of an ordinary clerk at all – it was the glance of a Chekist, an intelligent glance that remembers everything.

She filled in the form with trembling fingers – just like the old man from the Timiryazev Academy who not long before had been sitting on the same chair. When she came to the question about her relationship to the person arrested, she wrote 'Wife', underlining the word heavily.

She handed the form in, sat down on the bench and put her passport back in her bag. She kept moving it from one part of the bag to another; finally she realized this was because she didn't want to leave the people in the queue.

At that moment she wanted only one thing: to let Krymov know that she was here, that she had given up everything for him, that she had come to him.

If only he could find out that she was here, so near him!

She walked down the street. It was already evening. Most of her life had been spent in this city. But that life – with its theatres, art exhibitions, orchestral concerts, dinners in restaurants and visits to dachas – was now so distant as to be no longer her own. Stalingrad and Kuibyshev had disappeared – as had the handsome, sometimes divinely handsome, face of Novikov himself. All that was left was 24 Kuznetsky Most. It was as though she was walking down the unfamiliar streets of a city she had never seen before.

24

Viktor took off his galoshes in the hall and said hello to the old housekeeper. At the same time, he glanced at the half-open door of Chepyzhin's study.

'Go on then,' said old Natalya Ivanovna helping him off with his coat, 'he's waiting for you.'

'Is Nadezhda Fyodorovna at home?'

'No, she went to the dacha yesterday with her nieces. Viktor Pavlovich, do you know if the war will soon be over?'

'There's a story going round,' Viktor answered, 'that some people told Zhukov's driver to ask him when the war would be over. And then Zhukov got into his car and said, "Can you tell me when the war will be over?"'

'What are you doing – taking my guests away from me like that?' Chepyzhin came out to meet Viktor. 'Invite your own friends, my dear.'

Viktor nearly always felt happier when he saw Chepyzhin. Now he felt a lightness of heart he had quite forgotten. And when he saw the rows of books in Chepyzhin's study, he did as he had always done and quoted a line from *War and Peace*: 'Yes, they didn't just waste their time, they wrote.'

The apparent chaos of the bookshelves was similar to that of the workshops in the factory at Chelyabinsk.

'Have you heard from your sons?' he asked Chepyzhin.

'I had a letter from the older one, but the young one's in the Far East.'

He took Viktor's hand and pressed it silently, saying what could never be said in words. Old Natalya Ivanovna came over to Viktor and kissed him on the shoulder.

'What news have you got, Viktor Pavlovich?' asked Chepyzhin.

'The same as everyone – Stalingrad. There's no doubt about it now. Hitler's kaput. But as for my own life, well, that's a mess.'

He began to tell Chepyzhin about his troubles. 'My friends and my wife are all telling me to repent. To repent my rightness.'

Viktor talked about himself greedily and at length. He was like an invalid who thinks of his illness day and night.

Then he grimaced and shrugged his shoulders.

'I keep remembering that conversation of ours about a mixing-tub and all the scum that comes up to the surface . . . Never in my life have I been surrounded by so much filth. And what's particularly painful, almost unbearable, is that for some reason all this has to coincide with the Russian victories.'

He looked Chepyzhin in the eye.

'What do you think? Is that just coincidence?'

Chepyzhin had an extraordinary face. It was simple, coarse, with high cheekbones and a snub nose, the face of a peasant – yet at the same time so fine and intelligent as to be the envy of any Englishman, even Lord Kelvin.

'Wait till the war's over,' he answered gloomily. 'Then we'll know what's coincidence and what isn't.'

'The swine may have finished me off by then. Tomorrow my fate's being decided by the Scientific Council. That is, it's already been decided by the Institute authorities and the Party Committee. The Scientific Council's just a formality. You know – the voice of the people, the demands of the community.'

It was strange talking to Chepyzhin – the things they were discussing were very painful, but somehow it wasn't in the least depressing.

'And I thought they'd be offering you everything you wanted on a silver platter – on a *golden* platter,' said Chepyzhin.

'Why? I've been "dragging science into the swamp of Talmudic abstraction", cutting it off from reality.'

'Yes, I know,' said Chepyzhin. 'It's amazing. You know, sometimes a man loves a woman. She's what gives his life meaning, she's his happiness, his joy, his passion. But for some reason all this is considered almost indecent; he has to pretend he sleeps with her simply because she prepares his meals, darns his socks and washes his clothes.'

He held up his hands, the fingers spread, in front of his face. They too were extraordinary – powerful, worker's hands, like claws and yet somehow aristocratic.

'But I don't feel ashamed,' he cried angrily. 'And it isn't just so I can have my meals prepared that I need her. The value of science lies in the happiness it brings to people. Our fine Academicians think that science is the domestic servant of practice, that it can be put to work according to Shchedrin's principle: "Your wish is my command." That's the only reason why science is tolerated at all. No! Scientific discoveries have an intrinsic value! They do more for the perfection of man than steam-engines, turbines, aeroplanes or the whole of metallurgy from Noah to the present day. They perfect the soul! The human soul!'

'I quite agree with you, Dmitry Petrovich, but I'm afraid comrade Stalin thinks differently.'

'Yes, but he's wrong. Besides, there's another side to all this. Maxwell's abstract idea can be tomorrow's military radio signal.

Einstein's theory of gravitational fields, Schrödinger's quantum mechanics and the conceptions of Bohr can all yield very concrete applications. That is what these people don't realize. And yet it's so simple you'd think even a goose could understand.'

'Yes,' said Viktor, 'of course today's theory is tomorrow's practice. But I don't need to tell *you* how reluctant our authorities are to accept that.'

'No,' said Chepyzhin, 'it was the other way round for me. It was because I know that today's theories are tomorrow's practice that I didn't want to be director of the Institute. But there's one thing I don't understand. I was quite sure that Shishakov had been appointed to carry out research into nuclear reactions. And in that field they can't get by without you . . . In fact I still do feel sure of that.'

'I don't understand your reasons for leaving the Institute,' said Viktor. 'I can't make out what you're saying. I understand that the authorities set the Institute various tasks which you find disturbing. That's clear enough. But the authorities have made mistakes in less esoteric realms than ours. Look at the way the boss was always strengthening our ties of friendship with the Germans; only a few days before the outbreak of war he was sending Hitler whole trainloads of rubber and other raw materials of strategic importance. And in our field – well, even a great politician can be pardoned for failing to understand what's going on there . . . As for my life – everything's been back to front. My work before the war was closely linked to practice. In Chelyabinsk I used to go to the factory and help set up the electronic apparatus. But since the war began . . .'

He waved his hand in mock despair.

'I'm lost in a labyrinth. Sometimes I feel awkward, sometimes I feel quite terrified. Heavens . . . ! All I wanted was to establish the physics of nuclear reactions. What's happened is that time, mass and gravity have collapsed and space has become two different things; it no longer really exists and has no meaning except in terms of magnetism. There's a clever young man in my laboratory called Savostyanov. Well, once I got talking to him about my work. He asked lots of questions; I replied that all this wasn't yet a theory – just a few ideas and a general direction of research. Parallel space is merely an exponent in an equation, not a physical reality. The only symmetry so far is in a mathematical equation; I don't yet know if there's a corresponding symmetry of particles. Mathematics has left physics behind; I don't know whether or not the physics of particles will ever fit into my equations. Savostyanov listened for a long time and then said: "All this reminds me of a fellow-student of mine. He got hopelessly muddled with some equation and said: 'You know, this isn't science − it's a blind couple trying to screw in a patch of nettles.'"'

Chepyzhin burst out laughing.

'It's odd that even you can't see the significance to physics of your own mathematics,' he said. 'It's like the cat in *Alice in Wonderland* − first you see the smile, then the cat itself.'

'Dear God . . . !' said Viktor. 'But deep down I know that this is the central axis of human life. No, I'm not going to give in. I'm not going to betray the faith.'

'I can appreciate what a sacrifice it must be to part with the laboratory at the very moment when the link between physics and your mathematics is about to emerge,' said Chepyzhin. 'It must be hard for you, but I'm very glad: honesty is never just wiped off the slate and forgotten.'

'I just hope I'm not wiped off the slate myself,' said Viktor.

Natalya Ivanovna brought in the tea and shifted the books to make room on the table.

'Ah! Lemon!' said Viktor.

'You're an honoured guest,' said Natalya Ivanovna.

'A nonentity,' said Viktor.

'Come on!' protested Chepyzhin. 'What do you mean by that?'

'Dmitry Petrovich, tomorrow my fate's being decided. I'm sure of it. Where will I be the day after tomorrow?'

He moved his glass of tea closer. Beating out the rhythm of his despair with a teaspoon, he said absent-mindedly, 'Ah! Lemon!', then felt embarrassed at having repeated the same words in exactly the same intonation.

For a while neither of them spoke. Then Chepyzhin said: 'I've got some thoughts I'd like to share with you.'

'Of course,' said Viktor as absent-mindedly as before.

'Nothing special,' said Chepyzhin, 'just a few whimsical notions . . . As you know, the idea of an infinite universe is already a truism. A metagalaxy will one day seem like a sugar-lump that some thrifty Lilliputian takes with his tea. While an electron or a neutron will seem like a whole world populated by Gullivers. Even schoolboys understand this.'

Viktor nodded and thought to himself: 'Yes, this isn't anything special. The old man's not on form today.' His thoughts turned to Shishakov and tomorrow's meeting: 'No, I'm not going. If I do go, then I have to either repent or argue about politics – and that's the equivalent of suicide.' He gave a slight yawn and thought: 'A weak heart. That's what makes people yawn.'

'One might think that only God was able to limit Infinity,' Chepyzhin went on. 'Beyond a cosmic boundary, we have to admit the presence of a divine power. Right?'

'Of course,' said Viktor, thinking to himself: 'I may be arrested any day, Dmitry Petrovich. I'm not in the mood for philosophy. Yes, I'm probably done for. I talked too much when I was in Kazan. I said things I shouldn't have said to a fellow called Madyarov. Either he's an informer, or else he's been arrested and they've made him talk. It's a mess, a terrible mess.'

He looked at Chepyzhin. Aware that Viktor was only pretending to pay attention, Chepyzhin continued:

'I think there is a boundary limiting the infinity of the universe – life itself. This boundary's nothing to do with Einstein's curvature of space; it lies in the opposition between life and inanimate matter. In my opinion, life can be defined as freedom. Life is freedom. Freedom is the fundamental principle of life. That is the boundary – between freedom and slavery, between inanimate matter and life.

'Now, as soon as freedom first appeared, it began to evolve. It evolved along two lines. First: man has more freedom than protozoa. The whole evolution of the living world has been a movement from a lesser to a greater degree of freedom. This is the very essence of evolution – the highest being is the one which has the most freedom.'

Viktor was now watching Chepyzhin thoughtfully. Chepyzhin nodded as though approving of his attentiveness.

'And then there's a second, quantitative, line of evolution. If we assume the weight of an average man to be fifty kilos, then humanity now weighs 100 million tons. That's a great deal more than, say, a thousand years ago. The mass of animate matter will constantly increase at the expense of that of inanimate matter. The terrestrial globe will gradually come to life. After settling the Arctic and the deserts, man will burrow under the earth, continually pushing back the horizons of his underworld cities and fields. Eventually there will be a predominance of animate matter on earth. Then the other planets will come to life. If we try to imagine the evolution of life over infinity, then the animation of inanimate matter will take place on a galactic scale. Inanimate matter will be transformed into free, living matter. The universe will come to life. Everything in the world will become alive and thus free. Freedom – life itself – will overcome slavery.'

'Yes,' said Viktor with a smile. 'You can even take the integral.'

'Listen now,' said Chepyzhin. 'I used to study the evolution of stars, but now I've come to understand the importance of the slightest movement of a spot of living mucus. Take the first line of evolution – from the lowest to the highest form of life. One day man will be endowed with all the attributes of the deity – omnipresence, omnipotence and omniscience. The coming century will bring a solution to the problem of the transformation of matter into energy and the creation of life itself. There will be a parallel development towards the attainment of extreme speeds and the conquest of space. More distant millennia will see progress towards the harnessing of the very highest form of energy – psychic energy.'

Suddenly Viktor realized that this wasn't just idle chatter and that he strongly disagreed with it.

'Man will learn to materialize in his laboratory the content and rhythm of the psychic activity of rational beings throughout the metagalaxy. Psychic energy will cross millions of light-years of space instantaneously. Omnipresence – formerly an attribute of God – will have become one more conquest of reason. But man won't just stop there. After attaining equality with God, he will begin to solve the problems that were beyond God. He will establish communication with rational beings from the highest level of evolution, beings from another space and another time to whom the whole history of humanity seems merely a dim flicker. He will establish communication with the life of the microcosm whose whole evolution occurs within the twinkling of a man's eye. The abyss of time and space will be overcome. Man will finally be able to look down on God.'

Viktor shook his head.

'Dmitry Petrovich,' he said, 'when you began, I was thinking that I might be arrested any day and that I wasn't in the mood for philosophy. Suddenly I quite forgot about Kovchenko, Shishakov and comrade Beria; I forgot that I might be thrown out of my laboratory tomorrow and into prison on the following day. But what I felt as I listened to you was not joy, but utter despair. We think we're so wise – to us Hercules seems like a child with rickets. And yet on this very day the Germans are slaughtering Jewish children and old women as though they were mad dogs. And we ourselves have endured 1937 and the horrors of collectivization – famine, cannibalism and the deportation of millions of unfortunate peasants . . . Once, everything seemed simple and clear. But these terrible losses and tragedies have confused everything. You say man will be able to look down on God – but what if he also becomes able to look down on the Devil? What if he eventually surpasses *him*? You say life is freedom. Is that what people in the camps think? What if the life expanding through the universe should use its power to create a slavery still more terrible than your slavery of inanimate matter? Do you think this man of the future will surpass Christ in his goodness? That's the real question. How will the power of this omnipresent and omniscient being benefit the world if he is still endowed with our own fatuous self-assurance and animal egotism? Our class egotism, our race egotism, our State egotism and our personal egotism? What if he transforms the whole world into a galactic concentration camp? What I want to know is – do you believe in the evolution of kindness, morality, mercy? Is man capable of evolving in that way?'

He gave Chepyzhin a rueful look.

'Forgive me for throwing a question like that at you. It seems even more abstract than the equations we were just talking about.'

'No,' said Chepyzhin. 'It's not so very abstract. It's a question that's had a very real effect on my life. I took a decision not to take part in any research relating to nuclear fission. You said yourself that man isn't yet kind enough or wise enough to lead a rational life. Just think what would happen now if he was presented with the power within the atom! Man's spiritual energy is still at a lamentable level. But I do believe in the future. I believe that it is not only man's power that will evolve, but also his soul, his capacity for love.'

Chepyzhin fell silent, troubled by the expression on Viktor's face.

'I have thought about all this,' said Viktor. 'And I ended up feeling quite appalled. You and I are concerned about the imperfection of man. But take my laboratory – who else there has ever thought about these questions? Sokolov? He's very clever – but very timid. He prostrates himself before the State and believes that there is no power except that of God. Markov? Markov hasn't the slightest inkling of questions of good and evil, of love and morality. His is a strictly practical talent. His attitude to scientific problems is that of a chess-player. Savostyanov – the man I was just talking about? He's charming and witty and a splendid physicist. But at the same time he's just a gay young fellow without a thought in his head. When we were evacuated, he took with him a whole pile of photos of young women in bathing costumes. He likes playing the dandy, he likes dancing and getting drunk. He sees science as another kind of sport – understanding some particular phenomenon, solving a particular problem is the same as setting a new athletic record. All he cares about is getting there first. And I'm no better. I've never thought seriously about these matters myself. Science today should be entrusted to men of spiritual under-standing, to prophets and saints. But instead it's been left to chess-players and scientists. They don't know what they're doing. You do. But there's only one of you. If there's a Chepyzhin in Berlin, *he* won't refuse to do research on neutrons. What then? And what about me? What's going to happen to me? Once everything seemed quite simple, but now, now . . . You know that Tolstoy considered his works of genius to be just a trivial game. Well, we physicists are no geniuses but we aren't half pleased with ourselves.'

Viktor's eyelids had started to twitch.

'Where can I find faith, strength, determination?'

He was speaking very quickly and with a strong Jewish accent.

'What can I say? You know what's happened – and now I'm being persecuted just because . . .'

He jumped up without finishing the sentence; his teaspoon fell to the floor. His hands were trembling; his whole body was trembling.

'Calm down, Viktor Pavlovich! Please calm down!' said Chepyzhin. 'Let's talk about something else.'

'No, no, I must go now. I'm sorry. Something's the matter with my head. Forgive me.'

He thanked Chepyzhin and took his leave. Afraid he could no longer control himself, he avoided looking him in the face. There were tears on his cheeks as he went down the stairs.

25

The others were already asleep when Viktor got back. He had the feeling he'd be sitting at his desk until morning, rewriting his letter of repentance and reading it over yet again, trying for the hundredth time to decide whether or not to go into the Institute.

He hadn't been able to think during the long walk home – not even about his tears on the staircase or his abruptly terminated conversation with Chepyzhin; not even about what might happen on the following day or about the letter from his mother in the side-pocket of his jacket. He was under the spell of the silent darkness of the streets; his mind was as vacant and windswept as the deserted alleys of Moscow at night. He felt no emotion: neither shame at his tears nor dread of what was to come, nor even hope that everything would come right in the end.

In the morning, when he wanted to go to the bathroom, he found the door locked from the inside.

'Is that you, Lyudmila?' he called.

He was astonished to hear Yevgenia's voice.

'Heavens! Zhenechka! What's brought you here?' He was so taken aback that he asked stupidly: 'Does Lyuda know that you're here?'

Yevgenia came out. They kissed each other.

'You don't look well,' said Viktor. 'That's what's called a Jewish compliment.'

There and then she told him about Krymov's arrest and the reason for her visit. Viktor was shocked. But after news like that, her visit seemed all the more precious. A bright happy Yevgenia, full of thoughts of her new life, would have seemed less close to him, less dear.

Viktor talked away, asking lots of questions, but continually looking at his watch.

'How senseless and absurd it all is,' he said. 'Just think of all the

694

times I've argued with Nikolay, all the times he's tried to put me right. Now he's in prison – and I'm still at large.'

'Viktor,' interrupted Lyudmila, 'don't forget – the clock in the dining-room's ten minutes slow.'

Viktor muttered something and went off to his room. He looked at his watch twice as he walked down the corridor.

The meeting of the Scientific Council was due to begin at eleven o'clock. Surrounded by his books and other belongings, Viktor had an intensified, almost hallucinatory awareness of the bustle and tension there must be in the Institute. It was half-past ten. Sokolov was taking off his jacket. Savostyanov was whispering to Markov: 'Well, it seems our madman's decided not to show up.' Gurevich was scratching his stout behind and looking out of the window. A limousine was drawing up outside; Shishakov, wearing a hat and a long fur coat, was just getting out. Another car drew up and Badin got out. Kovchenko was going down the corridor. There were already about fifteen people in the hall, all of them looking through newspapers. They'd known it would be crowded and had come early to get a good place. Svechin and Ramskov, the secretary of the Institute Party Committee 'with the stamp of secrecy on his brow', were standing by the door of the Committee office. Old Academician Prasolov was gazing into the air as he floated down the corridor; he always made unbelievably vile speeches at meetings like this. The junior research assistants had formed a large noisy group of their own.

Viktor looked at his watch, took his statement out of the drawer, stuffed it into his pocket, and looked at his watch again.

He could go to the meeting and not say anything . . . No . . . If he did go, it would be wrong not to speak – and if he did speak, he would have to repent. But if he didn't go at all, if he just burnt his boats . . .

Yes, he knew what people would say – 'He didn't have the courage . . . openly defying the collective . . . a political challenge . . . after this we must adopt a different language in dealing with him . . .' Once again Viktor took his statement out of his pocket and put it back without reading it. He had read these lines dozens of times: 'I have realized that in expressing a lack of confidence in the Party leadership I have behaved in a manner incompatible with what is expected of a Soviet citizen, and therefore . . . Also, without realizing it, I have deviated in my researches from the central tenets of Soviet science and involuntarily opposed myself . . .'

Viktor kept wanting to reread his statement, but as soon as he picked it up, every letter of it seemed hatefully familiar . . . Krymov was in the Lubyanka and he was a Communist. As for Viktor – with his doubts, with his horror of Stalin's cruelty, with all he had said about freedom and bureaucracy, with his lurid political history – he should have been packed off to Kolyma long ago . . .

These last few days, Viktor had felt more and more frightened: he was sure they were coming to arrest him. There was usually more to an affair like this than just being fired from one's job. First you're taught a lesson, then you're fired – and then you're arrested.

Viktor looked at his watch again. The hall was already full. People were sitting there, looking at the door and whispering: 'Still no Shtrum . . .' One person said: 'It's already midday and Viktor's still not here.' Shishakov sat down in the chairman's place and put his briefcase on the table. A secretary was standing beside Kovchenko; she had brought him some urgent papers to sign.

Viktor felt crushed by the impatience and irritation of the dozens of people waiting in the hall. There was probably someone waiting in the Lubyanka too; the man in charge of his case was saying to himself: 'Is he really not going to come?' Viktor could see the grim figure from the Central Committee saying: 'So he's chosen not to show up, has he?' He could see people he knew talking to their wives and calling him a lunatic. He knew that Lyudmila resented what he had done: the State that Viktor had challenged was the one that Tolya had given his life for.

Previously, when he had counted the number of his and Lyudmila's relatives who had been arrested and deported, he had reassured himself with the thought: 'At least I can tell them not all my friends are like that. Look at Krymov – he's a close friend and he's an Old Bolshevik who worked in the underground.'

So much for Krymov. Maybe they'd interrogate him in the Lubyanka and he'd tell them all Viktor's heresies. But then Krymov wasn't that close to him – Zhenya and he had divorced. And his conversations with Krymov hadn't been that dangerous – it was only since the beginning of the war that Viktor's doubts had been so pressing. If they spoke to Madyarov, though . . .

The cumulative force of dozens of pushes and blows, dozens of fierce struggles, seemed to have bent his ribs, to be unstitching the bones of his skull.

As for those senseless words of Doctor Stockmann's: 'He who is alone is strong . . . !' Was he strong? Looking furtively over his shoulder with the pathetic grimaces of someone from a shtetl, Viktor hurriedly put on his tie, transferred his papers to the pockets of his new jacket and put on his new yellow shoes.

Just then, as he was standing fully-dressed by the table, Lyudmila looked into the room. She walked up to him silently, kissed him and went out again.

No, he wasn't going to recite these stereotyped formulae! He would tell the truth, he would say what came from his heart: 'My friends, my comrades, I have listened to you with pain; I have asked myself with pain how it is that at this joyful time, the time of this great and hard-won breakthrough at Stalingrad, I find myself alone, listening to the angry reproaches of my comrades, my brothers, my friends . . . I swear to you – with my blood, with my brain, with all my strength . . .' Yes, yes, now he knew what he would say . . . Quick, quick, there was still time . . . 'Comrades . . . Comrade Stalin, I have lived falsely, I have had to reach the edge of the abyss to see my mistakes in their full horror . . .' Yes, what he said would come from the depths of his soul. 'Comrades, my own son died at Stalingrad . . .'

He went to the door.

Everything had been resolved. All that remained was to get to the Institute as quickly as possible, leave his coat in the cloakroom, enter the hall, hear the excited whispering of dozens of people, look round the familiar faces and say: 'A word if you please. Comrades, I wish to share with you my thoughts and feelings of the last few days . . .'

But at the same moment, Viktor slowly took off his jacket and hung it on the back of a chair. He took off his tie, folded it and placed it on the edge of the table. He then sat down and began unlacing his shoes.

He felt a sense of lightness and purity. He felt calm and thoughtful. He didn't believe in God, but somehow it was as though God were looking at him. Never in his life had he felt such happiness, such humility. Nothing on earth could take away his sense of rightness now.

He thought of his mother. Perhaps she had been standing beside him when he had so unaccountably changed his mind. Only a minute before he had sincerely wanted to make a hysterical confession. Neither God nor his mother had been in his mind when he had come to that last unshakeable decision. Nevertheless, they had been there beside him.

'How good, how happy I feel,' he thought.

Once again he imagined the meeting, the faces, the speakers' voices.

'How good, how light everything is,' he said to himself once again.

He seemed never to have thought so deeply about life, about his family, about himself and his fate.

Lyudmila and Yevgenia came into the room. Seeing him there without his shoes and his jacket, with an open collar, Lyudmila said: 'Good God! You're still here. What will become of us now?' She sounded like an old woman.

'I've no idea.'

'Maybe it's still not too late.' She looked at him again and added: 'I don't know – you're a grown man. But when it comes to matters like this, there are other things to think about than your principles.'

Viktor just sighed.

'Lyudmila!' said Yevgenia.

'All right, all right,' said Lyudmila. 'Whatever will be, will be.'

'Yes, Lyudochka,' said Viktor. 'One way or another, we'll get by.'

He put his hand to his neck and smiled. 'Forgive me, Zhenya. I haven't got a tie on.'

Viktor looked at Lyudmila and Yevgenia. It was as though he had only now, for the first time, fully understood the difficulty and seriousness of life on earth, the true importance of close relationships. At the same time he knew that life would go on in its usual way, that he would still get upset over trifles, that he would still be infuriated by his wife and daughter.

'That's enough about me,' he said. 'Let's have a game of chess, Zhenya. Remember how you checkmated me twice running?'

They set out the pieces. Viktor was white. He opened with the king's pawn. Yevgenia said:

'Nikolay always opened with the king's pawn when he was white. What do you think they'll say to me today at Kuznetsky Most?'

Lyudmila bent down and put Viktor's slippers beside his feet. He tried to slip his feet into them without looking; Lyudmila gave a querulous sigh, knelt down on the floor and put them on for him. Viktor kissed her on the head and said absent-mindedly:

'Thank you, Lyudochka. Thank you!'

Yevgenia still hadn't made her first move. She shook her head and said: 'No, I just don't understand. Trotskyism's old hat. Something must have happened – but what?'

Lyudmila straightened the white pawns. 'I hardly slept last night. Such a right-thinking, devoted Communist!'

'You slept very well last night,' said Yevgenia. 'I woke up several times and you were always snoring.'

'That's not true,' said Lyudmila angrily. 'I literally didn't close my eyes.'

Then, answering the question that was troubling her, she said to her husband: 'As long as they don't arrest you! I'm not afraid of anything else. We can sell our possessions, we can move to the dacha. I can teach chemistry in a school.'

'You won't be able to keep your dacha,' said Yevgenia.

'But don't you understand that Nikolay's quite innocent?' said Viktor. 'It's a different way of thinking, another generation.'

They sat there talking over the chess-board, glancing now and again at the pieces and the solitary pawn that had made one move.

'Zhenya, my dear,' said Viktor, 'you've acted according to your conscience. Believe me – that's the highest thing a man can do. I don't know what life has in store for you, but I'm sure of one thing: you listened to your conscience – and the greatest tragedy of our age is that we don't listen to our consciences. We don't say what we think. We feel one thing and do another. Remember Tolstoy's words about capital punishment? "I can't remain silent." But we remained silent in 1937 when thousands of innocent people were executed. Or rather some of us – the best of us – remained silent. Others applauded noisily. And we remained silent during the horrors of general collectivization . . . Yes, we spoke too soon about Socialism – it's not just a matter of heavy industry. Socialism, first of all, is the right to a conscience. To deprive a man of his conscience is a terrible crime. And if a man has the strength to listen to his conscience and then act on it, he feels a surge of happiness. I'm glad for you – you've acted according to your conscience.'

'That's enough sermonizing, Vitya,' said Lyudmila. 'Stop confusing the poor girl. You're not the Buddha . . . What's conscience got to do with it anyway? She's ruining her life, tormenting a good man – and what good will it do Krymov? He won't be happy even if they do set him free. And he was doing fine when they separated – she's got nothing to feel guilty about.'

Yevgenia picked up one of the kings, twirled it around, examined the felt on its base, then put it back again.

'Who's talking of happiness, Lyuda?' she asked. 'I'm not thinking of happiness.'

Viktor looked at the clock. The dial now looked peaceful, the hands calm and sleepy.

'The discussion must be in full swing now. They're abusing me for all they're worth – but I'm not in the least upset or angry.'

'I'd punch the whole lot of them in the snout,' said Lyudmila. 'They're quite shameless. First you're the bright hope of Soviet science, then they're spitting in your face . . . Zhenya, when are you going to Kuznetsky Most?'

'About four o'clock.'

'Well, you must have something to eat first.'

'What's for lunch today?' asked Viktor. He smiled. 'Ladies, you know what I'd like to ask you?'

'I know, I know. You want to go and work,' said Lyudmila as she got up.

'Anyone else would be banging his head against the wall on a day like this,' said Yevgenia.

'It's not a strength, but a weakness,' said Viktor. 'Yesterday I had a long talk about science with Chepyzhin. But I don't agree with him. Tolstoy was the same. He was tormented by doubts. He didn't know whether people needed literature. He didn't know whether people needed the books he wrote.'

'You know something?' said Lyudmila. 'Before talking like that, you should write the *War and Peace* of physics.'

Viktor felt horribly embarrassed.

'Yes, Lyuda, yes, you're quite right. I let my tongue run away with me,' he muttered. At the same time he gave his wife a look of reproach: 'Even at a time like this she has to pounce on every slip I make.'

Once again Viktor was left alone. He reread the notes he had made yesterday; at the same time he pondered what had just happened.

Why did he feel more comfortable now that Yevgenia and Lyud-mila had left the room? Somehow he had been behaving unnaturally. There had been something false in the way he'd asked Yevgenia for a game of chess, in the way he'd said he wanted to do some work. And Lyudmila must have sensed it; that was the reason for her remark about the Buddha. He himself had been conscious of something wooden in his voice as he made his speech about conscience. He had tried to talk about everyday matters so as not to be thought smug, but that had seemed equally forced and unnatural.

He felt a vague sense of anxiety; something was missing, but he didn't know what. He kept getting up and walking over to the door to eavesdrop on Lyudmila and Yevgenia.

He hadn't the slightest wish to know what had been said at the meeting, who had made the most vicious or intolerant speech, what resolution had finally been passed. He would just write a short note to Shishakov, saying that he was ill and wouldn't be able to come to the Institute for the next few days. After that, things would sort themselves out. He was always ready to be of service in any way that was required . . .

Why, recently, had he felt so afraid of being arrested? He hadn't done anything that awful. He had talked too much. But not so very much.

Viktor still felt anxious. He kept looking impatiently at the door. Was it that he wanted something to eat? Yes, he'd have to say goodbye to the special store. And to the famous canteen.

There was a quiet ring at the door. Viktor rushed out into the corridor, shouting in the direction of the kitchen, 'I'll go, Lyudmila.'

He flung open the door. Marya Ivanovna peered anxiously at him through the gloom.

'So you're still here,' she said quietly. 'I knew you wouldn't go.'

Viktor began helping her off with her coat. As his fingers touched the collar, as he felt the warmth from the back of her head and neck, he suddenly realized that he had been waiting for her. That was why he had been watching the door and listening so anxiously.

He knew this from the sense of joy and ease he had felt as soon as he saw her. It must have been her he wanted to meet all the times he had walked back gloomily from the Institute, staring anxiously at the passers-by, studying women's faces behind the windows of trams and trolley-buses. And when he had got back and asked Lyudmila, 'Has anyone been round?', what he had really wanted to know was whether she had been round. Yes, it had been like this for a long time. She had come round, they had talked and joked, she had gone away and he seemed to have forgotten her. She had only come to mind when he was talking to Sokolov or when Lyudmila had passed on her greetings. She seemed to have existed only when he was with her or when he was talking about how charming she was. Sometimes, when he was teasing Lyudmila, he had said that she hadn't even read Pushkin and Turgenev.

He had been for a walk with her in the park; he had enjoyed looking at her and had liked the way she understood him so quickly and so perfectly. He had been very touched by her childlike attentiveness. Then they had said goodbye and he had stopped thinking about her. He had thought of her again on his way back – only to forget her once more.

Now Viktor felt that she had been with him all the time; that she had only appeared to be absent. She had been with him even when he wasn't thinking of her. Even when he hadn't seen her or thought of her, she had still been with him. He had been aware of her absence without realizing it; he hadn't known that he had constantly and unwittingly been upset by it. Today he understood himself and the people close to him very deeply; now he understood his feelings towards her. He had been glad to see her because this had brought to an end the constant ache of her absence. Now that she was with him, he felt at ease. He had felt lonely talking to his daughter, talking to his friends, to Chepyzhin, to his wife . . . Seeing Marya Ivanovna had been enough to bring this sense of loneliness to an end.

There was nothing surprising about this discovery; it seemed natural and self-evident. How was it he had failed to understand this a month ago, two months ago, while they were still in Kazan? And of course today, when he had felt her absence particularly strongly, this feeling had broken through to the surface and become conscious.

As it was impossible to hide anything from her, he frowned and said to her there and then: 'I thought I must be as hungry as a wolf. I kept looking at the door to see if they'd call me for lunch. But what I was really waiting for was Marya Ivanovna.'

Marya Ivanovna didn't say anything; she just walked straight through as though she hadn't heard what he said.

They introduced her to Yevgenia and she sat down next to her on the sofa. Viktor looked from Yevgenia to Marya Ivanovna, and then at Lyudmila.

How beautiful the two sisters were! There was something particularly attractive about Lyudmila today. Her face had none of the harshness that often disfigured it. Her large bright eyes looked sad and gentle.

Sensing that Marya Ivanovna was looking at her, Yevgenia straightened her hair.

'Forgive me saying this, Yevgenia Nikolaevna, but I never imagined that a woman could be so beautiful. I've never seen a face like yours.' Marya Ivanovna blushed as she said this.

'But look at her hands, Mashcnka!' said Lyudmila. 'And her neck and her hair!'

'And her nostrils!' said Viktor. 'Her nostrils!'

'Do you think I'm a horse or something?' said Yevgenia. 'As if all that mattered to me.'

'The horse is off its food,' said Viktor. It was far from clear what this meant, but they all laughed.

'Do you want to eat, Vitya?' asked Lyudmila.

'No, no,' he answered. He saw Marya Ivanovna blush. So she *had* heard what he'd said to her in the hall.

Marya Ivanovna sat there, as thin and grey as a little sparrow. Her forehead was slightly protuberant, she had a hairdo like a village schoolteacher's, and she wore a woollen dress patched at the elbows. To Viktor every word she spoke seemed full of intelligence, kindness and sensitivity; every movement she made was an embodiment of sweetness and grace.

Instead of talking about the meeting of the Scientific Council, she asked after Nadya. She asked Lyudmila if she could borrow *The Magic Mountain*. She asked Yevgenia about Vera and her little boy and what news she'd heard from Alexandra Vladimirovna in Kazan.

It took a while for Viktor to realize how unerringly Marya Ivanovna had chosen the right subjects to talk about. It was as though she were affirming that no power in the world could stop people from being people; that even the most powerful State was unable to intrude on a circle of parents, sisters and children; and that her admiration for the people she was sitting with gave her the right to talk not about what had been imposed on them from outside, but about their own inner concerns.

Marya Ivanovna had indeed chosen correctly. The women talked about Nadya and Vera's little boy and Viktor sat there in silence. He could sense the light inside him burning warmly and evenly, never flickering or growing dim.

Viktor thought Yevgenia had been conquered by Marya Ivanovna's charm. When Lyudmila and Marya Ivanovna went off to the kitchen, he said thoughtfully: 'What a charming woman!'

'Vitka! Vitka!' said Yevgenia teasingly.

He was quite taken aback. It was over twelve years since anyone had called him that.

'The young lady's head over heels in love with you.'

'Don't be stupid,' he said. 'And what do you mean – *the young lady*? That's the last thing one can say of her. And she's Lyudmila's only friend. She and Marya Ivanovna are very close.'

'What about *you* and Marya Ivanovna?' enquired Yevgenia, her eyes twinkling.

'I'm being serious,' said Viktor.

Realizing that he was angry, she looked straight at him, her eyes still full of laughter.

'You know what, Zhenechka?' said Viktor. 'You can go to hell!'

Just then Nadya came in. Still in the hall, she asked quickly: 'Has Papa gone off to repent?'

She came into the room. Viktor hugged her and gave her a kiss.

Yevgenia looked her up and down; her eyes were quite moist.

'Well,' she said, 'there isn't a single drop of Slav blood in you. You're a true Hebrew maiden.'

'Papa's genes,' said Nadya.

'You know, Nadya, I've a weakness for you,' said Yevgenia. 'Like Grandmama has for Seryozha.'

'Don't worry, Papa, we won't let you die of hunger,' said Nadya.

'What do you mean – *we*? You and your lieutenant?' said Viktor. 'And don't forget to wash your hands when you come back from school.'

'Who's Mama talking to?'

'Marya Ivanovna.'

'Do you like Marya Ivanovna?' asked Yevgenia.

'I think she's the best person in the whole world,' said Nadya. 'I'd like to marry her.'

'Very kind, quite angelic?' asked Yevgenia in the same mocking tone.

'Don't you like her, Aunt Zhenya?'

'I don't like saints. There's usually some kind of hysteria underneath,' said Yevgenia. 'I'd rather have an outright bitch.'

'Hysteria?' repeated Viktor.

'I was just talking in general, Viktor. I don't mean her in particular.'

Nadya went out to the kitchen. Yevgenia said to Viktor: 'Vera had a lieutenant when I was in Stalingrad. And now Nadya's got one too. Here today and gone tomorrow. They die so easily, Viktor. It's so sad.'

'Zhenechka, Zhenevyeva, do you really not like Marya Ivanovna?'

'I don't know,' she said hurriedly. 'Some women seem so accommodating, so ready to sacrifice themselves. They never say, "I'm going to bed with this man because I want to." Instead they say, "It's my duty, I pity him, I'm sacrificing myself for him." It's of her own free will that a woman like that goes to bed with a man, lives with him, or decides to leave him. But the way she explains it is very different: "I had to, it was my duty, I acted according to my conscience, I made a sacrifice, I renounced him . . ." And she hasn't made any sacrifice at all – she's done just as she pleased. The worst of it is that she sincerely believes in this willingness of hers to make sacrifices. I can't stand women like that. And do you know why . . . ? Because I sometimes think I'm like that myself.'

While they were eating, Marya Ivanovna said to Yevgenia:

'Let me go with you, Yevgenia Nikolaevna. I have, sadly, got some experience of these matters. And it's always easier with someone else.'

Yevgenia looked very embarrassed.

'No, no,' she said, 'but thank you very much. There are things one has to do on one's own, burdens one can never share.'

Lyudmila looked at her sister out of the corner of her eye. As though to prove that she and Marya Ivanovna had no secrets from one another, she said: 'Mashenka's got it into her head that you don't like her.'

Yevgenia didn't answer.

'Yes,' said Marya Ivanovna, 'I can feel it. But you must forgive me for saying that. It's stupid of me. What does it matter to you, anyway? Lyudmila should have kept quiet. Now it looks as though I'm forcing myself on you, trying to make you change your mind. Really I just said it without thinking. And anyway . . .'

To her surprise, Yevgenia found herself saying quite sincerely:

'No, my dear. No. It's just that I'm very upset. Please forgive me. You're very kind.'

Then she got up and said: 'Now, my children – as Mama used to say – it's time.'

26

There were a lot of people on the street.

'Are you in a hurry?' Viktor asked Marya Ivanovna. 'We could go to the park again.'

'But people are already coming home from work. I must be back before Pyotr Lavrentyevich.'

Viktor was expecting her to ask him round. Then Sokolov could tell him about the meeting. But she didn't say anything. He began to wonder if Sokolov was afraid to meet him.

He felt hurt that Marya Ivanovna was in such a hurry. But of course it was only natural. They passed a little square not far from the road leading to the Donskoy Monastery. Suddenly Marya Ivanovna stopped and said: 'Let's sit down for a minute. Then I can get the trolleybus.'

They sat there in silence. Viktor could sense that she was very troubled. Her head slightly bent, she looked straight into his eyes.

They remained silent. Her lips were tightly closed, but he seemed able to hear her voice. Everything was quite clear – as though it had already been said. What difference could words make?

Viktor knew that something very serious was happening, that a new imprint lay on his life, that he was entering a time of deep and painful confusion. He didn't want to make anyone suffer. It would be better if no one knew of their love; perhaps they shouldn't talk of it even to one another. Or perhaps . . . But they couldn't conceal what was happening now, they couldn't hide their present joy and sorrow – and this alone would have deep and inevitable consequences. What was happening depended only on them, but it seemed like a fate they were powerless to oppose. What lay between them was true and natural, they were no more responsible for it than a man is responsible for the light of day – and yet this truth inevitably engendered insincerity, deceit and cruelty towards those dearest to them. It was in their power to avoid deceit and cruelty; all they had to do was renounce this clear and natural light.

One thing was plain: he had lost his peace of mind for ever. Whatever happened, he would never know peace. Whether he hid his love for the woman beside him or whether it became his destiny, he would not know peace. Whether he was with her, feeling guilty, or whether he was apart from her, aching for her, he would have no peace.

She was still staring at him. Viktor found her look of mingled happiness and despair almost unbearable.

He hadn't given in, he had stood firm against a vast and merciless force – but how weak, how helpless he felt now . . .

'Viktor Pavlovich,' she said. 'It's time for me to go. Pyotr Lavrentyevich will be waiting.'

She took him by the hand. 'We won't be able to see each other any more. I gave Pyotr Lavrentyevich my word not to see you.'

Viktor felt like someone dying of a heart attack. His heart, whose beating had never depended on his will, was stopping; the universe was swaying, turning upside down; the air and the earth were disappearing.

'But why, Marya Ivanovna?'

'Pyotr Lavrentyevich made me promise to stop seeing you. I gave him my word. I know that's terrible, but he's in such a state, he's quite ill, I'm afraid he might die.'

'Masha,' said Viktor.

There was an invincible power in her voice and her face – the same power that he had been struggling against everywhere.

'Masha,' he repeated.

'Dear God, you can see everything, you understand all too

I'm not hiding anything – but why talk about it all? I can't, I just can't. Pyotr Lavrentyevich has been through so much. You know that yourself. And think of Lyudmila's sufferings. It's impossible.'

'Yes, yes, we have no right,' said Viktor.

'My dearest, my unhappy friend, my light,' said Marya Ivanovna.

Viktor's hat fell to the ground. People were probably looking at them.

'Yes, yes, we have no right,' he repeated.

He kissed her hands. As he held her small cold fingers, he felt that the unshakeable strength of her resolve went hand in hand with weakness, submissiveness, helplessness . . .

She got up from the bench and walked away without looking back. He sat there, thinking that for the first time in his life he had seen happiness, light – and now it had left him. This woman whose fingers he had just kissed could have replaced everything he had ever wanted, everything he had dreamed of – science, fame, the joy of recognition . . .

27

The following day Savostyanov phoned Viktor and asked after his and Lyudmila's health.

When Viktor asked about the meeting, Savostyanov answered: 'I don't want to upset you, Viktor Pavlovich, but there are more nonentities around than even I ever imagined.'

'Surely Sokolov can't have spoken?' thought Viktor. 'Was a resolution passed?' he asked.

'Yes, a harsh one. That certain things were considered incompatible . . . That the directors should be asked to reassess . . .'

'I see,' said Viktor. He had known very well that such a resolution would be adopted, but now it seemed somehow unexpected. He felt quite taken aback.

'I'm innocent,' he thought, 'but still, I'm sure to be arrested. They knew very well that Krymov was innocent, and he was arrested.'

'Did anyone vote against?' he asked. In reply he heard an embarrassed silence.

'No. Viktor Pavlovich, I think it was unanimous. You did yourself a lot of harm by not attending.' Savostyanov's voice was barely audible; he must have rung from a call-box.

The same day, Anna Stepanovna telephoned. She had already been dismissed and no longer went in to the Institute; she didn't know about the meeting. She said she was going to stay with her sister in Murom for two months and invited him to join them. Viktor felt touched.

'Thank you, thank you,' he said. 'But if I go to Murom, it won't be for a rest; it will be to teach physics in a technical college.'

'Heavens, Viktor Pavlovich!' said Anna Stepanovna. 'What made you do all that just for me? You make me despair. I'm not worth it.'

She had obviously taken what he had said about the technical college as a reproach. Her voice was also very faint; she too must be ringing from a call-box.

'Did Sokolov really speak?' Viktor asked himself.

Late that night, Chepyzhin rang. All day Viktor had been like an invalid who came to life only when people spoke about his disease. Chepyzhin obviously sensed this.

'Did Sokolov speak? Can he really have done so?' Viktor asked Lyudmila. But she, of course, knew no more than he did.

A veil seemed to have fallen between him and everyone close to him.

Savostyanov had been afraid to talk about what most concerned Viktor. He hadn't wanted to be the one who told him. He was probably worried that Viktor would meet people from the Institute and say: 'I know everything already. Savostyanov's given me a detailed report.'

Anna Stepanovna had been very affectionate, but she should have done more than just phone him; at a time like this she should have called at his home. And as for Chepyzhin, he should have offered Viktor a job at the Astro-Physics Institute, or at least mentioned it as a possibility.

'They all upset me, and I upset them,' thought Viktor. 'It would be better if they didn't phone at all.'

He felt still more offended, however, with the people who hadn't phoned. He waited all day long for calls from Gurevich, Markov and

Pimenov. He even felt a sudden burst of anger at the electricians and technicians who were setting up the new apparatus. 'The swine!' he said to himself. 'They've got nothing to fear. The workers are all right.'

As for Sokolov – Viktor couldn't bear even to think about him. He had told Marya Ivanovna never to phone! Viktor could pardon everyone else – colleagues, old acquaintances, relatives. But his friend! He felt so angry when he thought about Sokolov, so deeply and painfully upset, that he could hardly breathe. Without realizing it, however, he was pleased to find in Sokolov's betrayal a justification for his own betrayal of Sokolov.

Viktor was so nervous that he wrote a quite unnecessary letter to Shishakov asking to be informed of the decision taken by the directors of the Institute; he himself was ill and would be unable to come to work for several days.

The phone didn't ring once during the whole of the following day.

'What does it matter? I'm going to be arrested anyway.' By now, this thought was more of a consolation than a torment. Invalids console themselves in the same way, saying: 'Illness or no illness, we all die in the end.'

'The only person we hear any news from is Zhenya,' Viktor said to Lyudmila. 'But then that's from the NKVD – straight from the horse's mouth.'

'I'm sure of it now,' said Lyudmila. 'Sokolov must have spoken at the Scientific Council. That's the only way I can explain Marya Ivanovna's silence. She feels ashamed. In that case, I'll phone her myself – while he's out at work.'

'No!' shouted Viktor. 'You mustn't do that. You absolutely mustn't.'

'Your relations with Sokolov have nothing to do with me,' said Lyudmila. 'I'm friends with Masha.'

Viktor couldn't explain why she must not phone Marya Ivanovna, but he felt ashamed at the idea of Lyudmila unwittingly becoming a link between them.

'Lyuda, from now on our contact with people has to be one-sided. If a man's been arrested, his wife can only visit people who've invited her. She doesn't have the right to say: "I want to come round." That would be humiliating for both her and her husband. You and I have entered a new epoch. We can no longer write to anyone ourselves; we can only reply to letters. We can no longer phone anyone; we can only pick up the receiver when it rings. We don't even have the right to greet acquaintances – they may prefer not to notice us. And if someone does greet me, I don't have the right to speak first. He might consider it possible to give me a nod of the head, but not to talk to me. I can only answer if he speaks first. You and I are pariahs.'

He paused for a moment. 'Fortunately for the pariahs, however, there are exceptions. There are one or two people – I'm not talking about family, about Zhenya or your mother – whom a pariah can trust. He can contact these people without first waiting for a sign. People like Chepyzhin.'

'Yes, Vitya,' answered Lyudmila, 'you're absolutely right.'

Viktor was amazed. It was a long time since Lyudmila had agreed with anything he said.

'And I have a friend like that myself – Marya Ivanovna,' she went on.

'Lyuda!' said Viktor. 'Do you realize that Marya Ivanovna's given her word to Sokolov not to go on seeing us? Now phone her! Go on! Phone her after that!'

He snatched up the receiver and held it out to Lyudmila. As he did so, a small part of him was hoping: 'Perhaps she will phone. Then at least one of us will hear Marya Ivanovna's voice.'

'So it's like that, is it?' said Lyudmila, putting down the receiver.

'What can have happened to Zhenevyeva?' said Viktor. 'Our troubles have brought us together. I've never felt such tenderness towards her as I do now.'

When his daughter came in, Viktor said: 'Nadya, I've had a talk with Mama. She'll tell you about it in detail herself. Now I'm a pariah, you must stop going to the Postoevs'.'

[....]

28

Darensky felt a strange mixture of feelings as he looked at the German tanks and lorries that had been abandoned in the snow, at the frozen corpses, at the column of men being marched under escort to the East.

This was retribution indeed.

He remembered stories about how the Germans had made fun of the poverty of the peasant huts, how they had gazed in surprise and disgust at the simple cradles, the crude stoves, the earthenware pots, the pictures on the walls, the wooden tubs, the painted clay cocks, at the beloved and wonderful world in which the boys then fleeing from their tanks had been born and brought up.

'Look, comrade Lieutenant-Colonel!' said his driver.

Four Germans were carrying one of their comrades on a greatcoat. You could tell from their faces, from their straining necks, that soon they too would fall to the ground. They swayed from side to side. They tripped over the tangled rags wound round their feet. The dry snow lashed their mindless eyes. Their frozen fingers gripped the corners of the greatcoat like hooks.

'So much for the Fritzes,' said the driver.

'We never asked them to come here,' said Darensky.

Suddenly he felt a wave of happiness. Straight through the steppe, in a cloud of mist and snow, Soviet tanks were making their way to the West. They looked quick and fierce, strong and muscular . . .

Soldiers were standing up in the hatches. He could see their faces and shoulders, their black helmets and their black sheepskins. There they were, tearing through the ocean-like steppe, leaving behind them a foaming wake of dirty snow. Darensky caught his breath in pride and happiness.

Terrible and sombre, a steel-clad Russia had turned her face to the West.

There was a hold-up as they came to a village. Darensky got out of his jeep and walked past two rows of trucks and some tarpaulin-covered Katyushas. A group of prisoners was being herded across the road. A full colonel who had just got out of his car was watching; he was wearing a cap made from silver Astrakhan fur, the kind you can only obtain if you are in command of an army or if you have a quartermaster as a close friend. The guards waved their machine-guns at the prisoners and shouted: 'Come on, come on! Look lively there!'

An invisible wall separated these prisoners from the soldiers and lorry-drivers. A cold still more extreme than the cold of the steppes prevented their eyes from meeting.

'Look at that!' said a laughing voice. 'One of them's got a tail.'

A German soldier was crawling across the road on all fours. A scrap of torn quilt trailed along behind him. The soldier was crawling as quickly as he could, moving his arms and legs like a dog, his head to the ground as though he were following a scent. He was making straight for the colonel. The driver standing beside the colonel said: 'Watch out, comrade Colonel. He's going to bite you.'

The colonel stepped to one side. As the German came up to him, he gave him a push with his boot. The feeble blow was enough to break him. He collapsed on the ground, his arms and legs splayed out on either side.

The German looked up at the man who had just kicked him. His eyes were like those of a dying sheep; there was no reproach or suffering in them, nothing at all except humility.

'A fine warrior that shit makes!' said the colonel, wiping the sole of his boot on the snow. There was a ripple of laughter among the onlookers.

Everything went dark. Darensky was no longer his own master; another man, someone who was at once very familiar to him and yet utterly alien, someone who never hesitated, was directing his actions.

'Comrade Colonel,' he said, 'Russians don't kick a man when he's down.'

'What do you think I am then?' asked the colonel. 'Do you think I'm not a Russian?'

'You're a scoundrel,' said Darensky. He saw the colonel take a step towards him. Forestalling the man's angry threats, he shouted: 'My surname's Darensky. Lieutenant-Colonel Darensky – inspector of the Operations Section of Stalingrad Front Headquarters. I'm ready to repeat what I said to you before the commander of the Front and before a military tribunal.'

In a voice full of hatred, the colonel said: 'Very well, Lieutenant-Colonel Darensky. You will be hearing from me.'

He stalked away. Some prisoners came up and dragged their comrade to one side. After that, wherever Darensky turned, he kept meeting the eyes of the prisoners. It was as though something attracted them to him.

As he walked slowly back to his jeep, he heard a mocking voice say: 'So the Fritzes have found a defender!'

713

Soon Darensky was on his way again. But they were held up by another column of prisoners being marched towards them, the Germans in grey uniforms, the Rumanians in green.

Darensky's fingers were trembling as he lit a cigarette. The driver noticed this out of the corner of his eye and said: 'I don't feel any pity for them. I could shoot any one of them just like that.'

'Fine,' said Darensky. 'But you should have shot them in 1941 instead of taking to your heels like I did.'

He said nothing more for the rest of the journey.

This incident, however, didn't open his heart. On the contrary, it was as though he'd quite exhausted his store of kindness.

What an abyss lay between the road he was following today and the road he had taken to Yashkul through the Kalmyk steppe. Was he really the same man who, beneath an enormous moon, had stood on what seemed to be the last corner of Russian earth? Who had watched the fleeing soldiers and the snake-like necks of the camels, tenderly making room in his heart for the poor, for the weak, for everyone whom he loved?

29

The command-post of the tank corps lay on the outskirts of the village. Darensky drove up to the hut. It was already dark. They'd obviously only recently moved in: soldiers were unloading suitcases and mattresses from a truck and signallers were installing telephones.

The soldier on sentry-duty reluctantly went inside and called for the duty-officer. He came reluctantly out onto the porch. Like all duty-officers, he looked at the new arrival's epaulettes rather than his face.

'Comrade Lieutenant-Colonel, the corps commander's only just got back from visiting one of the brigades. He's having a rest. He can see you later.'

'Report to the corps commander that Lieutenant-Colonel Darensky has arrived. Is that clear?'

The officer sighed and went back into the hut.

A minute later he came out again and called: 'This way please, comrade Lieutenant-Colonel.'

Darensky climbed the steps up onto the porch and saw Novikov coming to meet him. For a few moments they just looked at one another, laughing.

'So we meet again,' said Novikov.

It was a good meeting.

Two intelligent heads bent over the map, just as they had in the old days.

'I'm advancing as fast as I once retreated,' said Novikov. 'Even faster on this bit of the course.'

'And this is winter,' said Darensky. 'Just wait till the summer!'

'I know.'

It was wonderful to study the map with Darensky. He grasped things immediately and he was interested in details that no one except Novikov ever seemed to notice.

Lowering his voice, as though he were about to come out with some personal confidence, Novikov said: 'Of course we have scouts in the zone of operations. Of course we have a co-ordinated system of reference points for the terrain. Of course we liaise with other arms of the service. But the operations of every other arm are subordinated to one god – the T-34. She's the queen!'

Darensky was familiar with the maps of the other military operations then in progress. He told Novikov about the campaign in the Caucasus, the contents of the intercepted conversations between Hitler and Paulus, and about the movement of General Fretter-Piko's artillery units.

'You can already see the Ukraine through the window,' said Novikov. He pointed to the map. 'I think I'm nearer than anyone else. But Rodin's corps is right on my heels.'

Then he pushed the map aside and said: 'Well, that's enough tactics and strategy for one day.'

'How's everything else?' asked Darensky. 'Still the same?'

'No,' said Novikov, 'very different indeed.'

'You haven't got married, have you?'

'I'm expecting to any day. She should be here soon.'

'Well, well,' said Darensky. 'Another good man gone. But I congratulate you with all my heart! As for me, I'm still single.'

'How's Bykov?' asked Novikov abruptly.

'Bykov? He's surfaced with Vatutin. Doing the same job.'

'He's a tough bastard, isn't he?'

'A rock.'

'To hell with him,' said Novikov. He shouted in the direction of the other room: 'What's up, Vershkov? Have you decided to starve us to death? And you can call the commissar. We'll all eat together.'

There was no need to call Getmanov. He opened the door, looked sadly at Novikov and said: 'What's all this, Pyotr Pavlovich? Rodin seems to have overtaken us. You watch it – he'll beat us to the Ukraine yet!'

He turned to Darensky.

'See what a pass things have come to, Lieutenant-Colonel? Now we're more afraid of our neighbours than of the enemy. You're not a neighbour, are you? No, I can see – you're an old comrade.'

'You seem to be obsessed with the Ukrainian question,' said Novikov.

Getmanov reached out for a tin of food and said in a tone of mock threat:

'Very well, Pyotr Pavlovich. But remember this! I won't marry you and your Yevgenia Nikolaevna till we're on Ukrainian soil. The Lieutenant-Colonel's my witness.'

He held out his glass towards Novikov. 'Anyway, let's drink to his Russian heart!'

'That's a good toast,' said Darensky in all sincerity.

Remembering Darensky's dislike of commissars, Novikov said: 'Yes, comrade Lieutenant-Colonel, it's a long time since we last met.'

Getmanov glanced at the table. 'We've got nothing to offer our guest – only a few tins. The cook barely has time to light the stove before we move our command-post. We're on the go day and night. You should have come round before the offensive began. Now we only stop for one hour in every twenty-four. We'll soon be overtaking ourselves.'

'You might at least give us a fork,' said Novikov to his orderly.

'You told us not to unload all that,' he replied.

Getmanov began giving his impressions of the newly-liberated territory.

'The Russians and the Kalmyks are like day and night,' he began.

'The Kalmyks danced to the Germans' tune. They even got issued with green uniforms. They roamed over the steppes, rounding up our men. And just think of what they've been given by Soviet power! They were just a crowd of ragged, illiterate, syphilitic nomads. But it's no good – you can't change a leopard's spots. Even during the Civil War the vast majority were on the side of the Whites. And just think how much money we spent on all those weeks dedicated to the friendship of nations. We'd have done better to spend it on building another tank factory in Siberia. I met one young woman, a Don Cossack, who told me what she went through during these months. No, there's no doubt about it – the Kalmyks have betrayed the confidence of the Russians. That's what I'm going to say in my report to the Military Soviet.'

He turned to Novikov.

'Do you remember what I said about Basangov? My intuition as a Communist didn't let me down. But don't you be offended, Pyotr Pavlovich. That's not meant as a reproach. Do you think I've never made mistakes in my life? But you can't overestimate the importance of nationality. That's what we've been taught by the experience of the war. And you know the name of a Bolshevik's best teacher? Experience.'

'As for what you say about the Kalmyks,' said Darensky, 'I couldn't agree more. I've just been in the Kalmyk steppe myself. I can tell you – I've had enough of driving through all these Shebeners and Kicheners.'

What made him say that? He had spent a long time in the steppes and never once felt the least antipathy toward the Kalmyks. On the contrary, he had felt a genuine interest in their customs and way of life.

It was as if the commissar was endowed with some magnetic power. Darensky felt a need to agree with everything he said. Novikov looked at him with a mocking smile; he knew Getmanov's power only too well.

'I know you've suffered injustice in your time,' said Getmanov to Darensky unexpectedly. 'But don't you go nursing a grudge against us Bolsheviks. What we want is the good of the people.'

Darensky, who had always thought that military commissars did nothing but spread confusion, said: 'But of course. How could I fail to understand that?'

'Certainly there have been times when we've gone too far,' Getmanov continued. 'But the people will pardon us. They will! We're good fellows. And we mean well. Isn't that so?'

Novikov gave the two men a friendly look and said: 'Don't you think we've got a fine commissar?'

'You have indeed,' said Darensky.

'That's right,' said Getmanov. They all three began to laugh.

As though reading the thoughts of the two officers, Getmanov looked at his watch and said: 'Well, I'm going to go and lie down. I should be able to get a decent night's sleep for once. We're like gypsies – always on the road. It's ten days since I've taken off my boots. Where's the chief of staff? Is he asleep?'

'Asleep!' said Novikov. 'He's already taking a look at our new quarters. We'll be off again in the morning.'

Novikov and Darensky were left on their own.

'You know,' said Darensky, 'there's one thing I've never quite managed to understand . . . Not long ago I was in the sands near the Caspian. I felt very depressed. I felt it was the end of everything. And then what? I find we've achieved this. What power! What does anything else matter beside this?'

'As for me,' said Novikov, 'I'm really beginning to understand what we Russians can do. We're a fierce breed. We're real wolves.'

'What power!' repeated Darensky. 'And the important thing is this: under the leadership of the Bolsheviks we Russians are the vanguard of humanity. Everything else is just an insignificant detail.'

'I'll tell you what,' said Novikov. 'Would you like me to ask again to have you transferred here? You could be the deputy chief of staff. We'd be fighting shoulder to shoulder again. How about it?'

'Thank you,' said Darensky. 'Who would I be deputy to?'

'General Nyeudobnov. That's as it should be – a lieutenant-colonel as deputy to a general.'

'Nyeudobnov? The one who was abroad just before the war? In Italy?'

'That's right. He's no Suvorov, but it's possible to work with him.'

Darensky didn't say anything. Novikov looked at him. 'Well?'

Darensky put his hand up to his mouth and pulled up his upper lip.

'See these crowns?' he said. 'That's Nyeudobnov's work. He

knocked out two teeth of mine when he was interrogating me in 1937.'

They looked at each other, didn't say anything, and looked at each other again.

'A very competent man,' said Darensky. 'Certainly.'

'Of course,' said Novikov with an ironic smile. 'After all, he's not one of those Kalmyks. He's a Russian!'

'And now let's have a real drink,' he bellowed. 'Let's drink like Russians!'

Darensky had never drunk so much in his life. Nevertheless, but for the two empty bottles on the table, no one would have guessed quite how much the two men had accounted for. They were now addressing each other as '*ty*'.

As he refilled the glasses for the hundredth time, Novikov said: 'Come on! Don't hold back now!'

For once, Darensky didn't hold back.

They talked about the first days of the war and the retreat, about Blücher and Tukhachevsky, about Zhukov. Darensky spoke about his interrogation.

Novikov told Darensky how he'd delayed for a few minutes at the very beginning of the offensive. He didn't tell him how very mistaken he'd been concerning his brigade commanders. Their talk turned to the Germans. Novikov said how he'd thought the summer of 1941 would have hardened him for ever. But, as soon as he'd seen the first columns of prisoners, he'd given orders to improve their rations and to have anyone wounded or frostbitten taken to the rear by truck.

'Just now your commissar and I were abusing the Kalmyks,' said Darensky. 'And we were quite right. But it's a pity your Nyeudobnov isn't here. I'd like to have a few words with him. Yes, I certainly would.'

'And were there no collaborators among the Russians in Kursk and Orel?' asked Novikov. 'What about General Vlasov? He's hardly a Kalmyk. As for my Basangov – he's a fine soldier. And Nyeudobnov's a Chekist. He's not a soldier at all. My commissar told me that. But we Russians are going to conquer. Yes, I'll get to Berlin myself. The Germans will never be able to stop us now.'

'I know about Nyeudobnov and Yezhov and all that,' said Darensky. 'But there's only one Russia now – Soviet Russia. And even if they knock out every one of my teeth, that won't change my love for

Russia. I'll love Russia till my dying day. But I won't be deputy to a prostitute like that. No, comrade, you must be joking!'

Novikov poured out some more vodka. 'Come on! Don't hold back!'

Then he said: 'But who knows what else will happen? One day I'll be in disgrace myself.'

Changing the subject again, he said:

'A horrible thing happened the other day. A driver had his head blown off but he still had his foot on the accelerator. The tank drove on. Forward! Forward!'

'Your commissar and I were abusing the Kalmyks,' said Darensky. 'But there's one old Kalmyk I just can't get out of my head. How old's that Nyeudobnov? How about driving to your new quarters and paying him a visit?'

'I've been granted a great happiness.' said Novikov in a thick, drawling voice. 'The greatest of all happinesses.'

He took a photograph out of his pocket and passed it to Darensky. Darensky looked at it for a long time. 'Yes, she's a real beauty.'

'Beauty?' said Novikov. 'Who cares about beauty? No one could love a woman like I do just for her beauty.'

Vershkov appeared in the doorway. He looked at Novikov questioningly.

'Get the hell out of here!' said Novikov very slowly.

'Why treat him like that?' said Darensky. 'He just wanted to know if you needed him for anything.'

'All right, all right . . . But I can be a swine too. And I don't need you to tell me how to behave. And why are you calling me "*ty*" anyway? You're just a lieutenant-colonel.'

'So it's like that, is it?'

'Don't you know how to take a joke?' said Novikov, thinking to himself that it was a good thing Zhenya hadn't yet seen him drunk.

'I don't know how to take stupid jokes,' said Darensky.

They went on wrangling for a long time. They only made peace when Novikov suggested driving to their new quarters and giving Nyeudobnov a good whipping. Needless to say, they didn't drive anywhere at all but just went on drinking.

30

Alexandra Vladimirovna received three letters all on the same day: one from each of her two daughters and one from her granddaughter Vera. She guessed by the handwriting who these letters were from, and sensed immediately that they contained bad news. Many years of experience had taught her that children don't write to their mothers just to share their joys.

Each letter contained an invitation to come and stay: with Lyudmila in Moscow, with Zhenya in Kuibyshev, with Vera in Leninsk. This made Alexandra Vladimirovna still more certain that the three women were in trouble.

Vera wrote mostly about her father. His difficulties with the Party had brought him to the end of his tether. He had been summoned to Kuibyshev by the People's Commissariat and had only returned a few days ago. This journey had exhausted him more than all the months in Stalingrad. His case still awaited a decision. He had been ordered to return to Stalingrad and make a start on rebuilding the power station; it was uncertain, however, whether he would be allowed to remain in the employ of the Commissariat.

Vera herself had decided to go back to Stalingrad with her father. The centre of the city hadn't yet been liberated, but the Germans were no longer shooting. Apparently the house where Alexandra Vladimirovna had lived was just an empty shell with a caved-in roof. Stepan Fyodorovich's flat was still there – undamaged save that the windows were broken and the plaster had come off the walls. He and Vera were intending to move back in, together with her son.

Alexandra Vladimirovna found it very strange that her little granddaughter Vera should now sound so adult, so like a woman. The letter was full of information about the baby's rashes, about his stomach-upsets and disturbed nights. These were all things she should have been writing about to her husband or her mother, but she no longer had either.

She also wrote about old Andreyev and his daughter-in-law Natalya, and about Aunt Zhenya, whom Stepan Fyodorovich had seen in Kuibyshev. She said almost nothing about herself – as though her own life were of no interest to Alexandra Vladimirovna. In the margin of the last page, however, was a note saying: 'Grandmama, we've got a large flat in Stalingrad and there's plenty of room. Please, I beg you to come.' This sudden appeal expressed everything Vera hadn't written in the rest of the letter.

Lyudmila's letter was very brief indeed. At one point she said: 'My life seems quite meaningless. Tolya's dead. And as for Viktor and Nadya – they don't need me at all, they can get on fine without me.'

Lyudmila had never written her mother a letter like this before. Alexandra Vladimirovna realized she must be getting on very badly indeed with her husband. After inviting her to stay, Lyudmila went on: 'Vitya's in trouble – and he always talks more readily to you about his troubles than he does to me.' A little further on she wrote: 'Nadya's become very secretive. She doesn't tell me anything at all. That seems to be the norm in this family.'

The last letter, from Zhenya, was quite incomprehensible. It was full of vague hints at various difficulties and tragedies. She invited her mother to Kuibyshev – and then said she would have to go to Moscow almost immediately. She wrote about Limonov and how highly he always spoke of Alexandra Vladimirovna. He was an interesting and intelligent man and Alexandra Vladimirovna would enjoy meeting him. She then wrote that he had gone to Samarkand. Alexandra Vladimirovna found it hard to understand how she was to meet him in Kuibyshev.

There was one thing she could understand. As she came to the end of the letter, she said to herself: 'My poor little girl!'

Alexandra Vladimirovna was very upset by these letters.

All three women had asked after her own health and whether her room wasn't too cold. She was touched by their concern, but realized that none of them had wondered whether she herself might not be in need of them.

They needed her. But it could very well have been the other way round. Why wasn't she asking for her daughters' help? Why was it her daughters who were asking her for help? After all, she was alone. She had no real home. She was an old woman. She had lost her son and daughter. She didn't know anything about Seryozha.

And she was finding her work increasingly difficult. She had a constant pain around her heart and she always felt dizzy. She had even asked the technical director to have her transferred from the shop-floor to the laboratory. She found it very difficult to spend the whole day taking control samples from one machine after another.

In the evening she stood in the food queues, went home, lit the stove and prepared something to eat.

Life was so bare, so harsh! It wasn't standing in a queue that was difficult. It was worse when the shop was empty and there was no queue. It was worse when she went home and lay down in her cold, damp bed without lighting the stove, without preparing anything to eat.

Everyone around her was suffering. A woman doctor from Leningrad told her how she'd spent the winter with two children in a village a hundred kilometres from Ufa. They'd lived in a hut that had once belonged to a kulak; there were no windows and the roof had been partly dismantled. To get to work she had had to walk six kilometres through the forest; at dawn she had sometimes glimpsed the green eyes of wolves through the trees. It had been a very poor village. The *kolkhoz* had failed to fulfil the plan; the peasants said that however hard they worked, they'd still have their grain taken away from them. Her neighbour's husband had gone to the war, leaving her alone with her hungry children; she had one pair of torn felt boots for all six of them.

The doctor told Alexandra Vladimirovna how she'd bought a goat. Late at night she used to walk through the deep snow to a distant field; there she would steal buckwheat and dig up the rotten hay that had never been gathered in. Listening to the villagers, her children had learnt to swear. The teacher in Kazan had said to her: 'It's the first time I've heard seven-year-olds swearing like drunks. And you say you're from Leningrad!'

Alexandra Vladimirovna lived in the small room that had once been Viktor Pavlovich's. The official tenants, who had moved to an annexe while the Shtrums had been there, now lived in the main room. They were tense, irritable people, always quarrelling over trivia.

What Alexandra Vladimirovna resented was not the noise or the quarrels, but the fact that they should demand two hundred roubles a month – more than a third of her salary – from a woman whose own home had been burnt down by the Germans. And the room was minute. Sometimes she thought their hearts must be made out of tin and plywood. All day long they talked about potatoes, salt beef, what you could buy and sell at the flea-market. During the night they talked in whispers. The landlady would tell her husband that honey had been very cheap that day in the market, or that their neighbour, a foreman in a factory, had been to a village and brought back a whole sack of sunflower seeds and half a sack of hulled maize.

The landlady, Nina Matveyevna, was very good-looking – tall and slim, with grey eyes. Before getting married, she had worked in a factory, sung in a choir and taken part in amateur theatricals. Her husband, Semyon Ivanovich, worked as a blacksmith's striker in a military factory. In his youth he had served on a destroyer and been the middleweight boxing champion of the Pacific fleet. The distant past of this couple now seemed very improbable.

Before going to work in the morning, Semyon Ivanovich fed the ducks and prepared some swill for the piglet. When he came back in the evening, he pottered about the kitchen, cleaning millet, repairing shoes, sharpening knives, washing out bottles, and talking about drivers at work who had managed to get hold of flour, eggs and goat-meat from distant *kolkhozes*. Nina Matveyevna would interrupt him with stories of her countless illnesses and visits to famous doctors; then she would talk about lard and margarine, about how she had exchanged a towel for some beans, how a neighbour had bought a pony-skin jacket and five china saucers from an evacuee.

They weren't bad people, but they never said one word to Alexandra Vladimirovna about the war, about Stalingrad, or about the bulletins of the Soviet Information Bureau.

They both pitied and despised Alexandra Vladimirovna for living in such penury. Since the Shtrums had left, she had no sugar or butter, she drank hot water instead of tea, and ate the soup in the public canteen that even the piglet had refused. She had no money for firewood and no personal belongings to sell. Her poverty was a nuisance to them. Once she heard Nina Matveyevna say to her husband: 'Yesterday I had to give the old woman a biscuit. I don't like eating when she's sitting there watching me with her hungry eyes.'

Alexandra Vladimirovna no longer slept well. Why was there still no news from Seryozha? She slept on the iron bed that had once been Lyudmila's; it was as though her daughter's anxieties had now been transferred to her.

How easily death annihilated people. How hard it was to go on living. She thought of Vera. Her child's father had either forgotten her or been killed. Stepan Fyodorovich was constantly depressed and anxious. As for Lyudmila and Viktor, all their griefs and losses had done nothing to bring them together.

Alexandra Vladimirovna wrote to Zhenya that evening. 'My dearest daughter . . .' She kept thinking of her during the night. What sort of mess was she in? What lay in store for her?

Anya Shtrum, Sonya Levinton, Seryozha . . . What had become of them all?

Next door she could hear two hushed voices.

'We should kill the duck for the October anniversary,' said Semyon Ivanovich.

'Do you think I've been feeding it on potatoes just to have it killed?' snapped Nina Matveyevna. 'Oh yes, once the old woman's out of the way I'd like to paint the floors. Otherwise the boards will start rotting.'

All they ever spoke of was food and material things; the world they lived in had room only for objects. There were no human feelings in this world – nothing but boards, paint, millet, buckwheat, thirty-rouble notes. They were hard-working, honest people; the neighbours all said that neither of them would ever take a penny that didn't belong to them. But somehow they were quite untouched by the wounded in hospital, by blind veterans, by homeless children on the streets, by the Volga famine of 1921.

In this they were quite the opposite of Alexandra Vladimirovna. She herself could get upset, overjoyed or angry over matters that had nothing to do with her or anyone close to her. The period of general collectivization, the events of 1937, the fate of women who had been sent to camps because of their husbands, the children who had been put in orphanages after their parents had been sent to camps, the summary execution of Russian prisoners-of-war, the many tragedies of the war – all these troubled her as deeply as the sufferings of her own family.

This wasn't something she had learnt from books, from the

populist and revolutionary traditions of her family, from her friends, from her husband, or even from life itself. It was something she couldn't help; it was just the way she was. She always ran out of money six days before pay-day. She was always hungry. Everything she owned could be wrapped up in a handkerchief. But not once in Kazan had she thought of her belongings that had been burnt in Stalingrad – her furniture, her piano, her tea-service, her spoons and forks. She didn't even think about her books.

It was very strange that she should now be so far from the people who needed her, living under one roof with people who were so alien to her.

Two days after she had received the letters, Karimov came round. Alexandra Vladimirovna was glad to see him and offered him some rose-hip tea.

'How long since you last heard from Moscow?' he asked.

'Two days.'

'Really?' said Karimov with a smile. 'Tell me, how long does a letter take?'

'Have a look at the postmark,' said Alexandra Vladimirovna.

Karimov examined the envelope for some time. 'Nine days,' he said in a preoccupied tone of voice. He sat there thoughtfully – as though the slowness of the postal service was a matter of great importance to him.

'They say it's the censors,' said Alexandra Vladimirovna. 'They're quite snowed under.'

Karimov looked at her with his beautiful dark eyes.

'So they're all right, are they? They're not having any problems?'

'You don't look at all well,' said Alexandra Vladimirovna. 'Are you ill?'

'What do you mean? I'm fine!' he replied hurriedly, as though denying some accusation.

They began to talk about the war.

'We've come to a real turning-point now,' said Karimov. 'Even a child can see that.'

'Yes, and last summer it was just as obvious that the Germans were going to win,' said Alexandra Vladimirovna sarcastically.

'Is it very difficult for you on your own?' Karimov asked abruptly. 'I see you have to light the stove yourself.'

Alexandra Vladimirovna frowned – as though this were a question she could only answer after deep thought. Finally she said: 'Akhmet Usmanovich, have you really called on me just to ask if I find it difficult to light the stove?'

Karimov looked down at his hands. He waited for a long time before replying.

'The other day I was summoned to you-know-where. I was questioned about the meetings and conversations we had.'

'Why didn't you tell me that at the beginning?' asked Alexandra Vladimirovna. 'Why did you have to start asking about the stove?'

Trying to catch her eye, Karimov went on:

'Naturally, I was unable to deny that we had talked about politics and the war. It would have been absurd to try and make out that four adults had spoken exclusively about the cinema. Naturally I said that we had always talked like true Soviet patriots. I said we were all of us certain that, under the leadership of comrade Stalin and the Party, the Soviet people would be victorious. In general, the questions weren't particularly hostile. But after a few days I began to worry. I couldn't sleep at all. I began thinking that something must have happened to Viktor Pavlovich. And then there's this strange business with Madyarov. He went off for ten days to the Pedagogical Institute in Kazan. And he still hasn't come back. His students are waiting for him. The dean's sent him a telegram. And not a word. Well, you can imagine what goes through my head at night.'

Alexandra Vladimirovna said nothing.

'Just think,' he went on in a quiet voice, 'you only have to get talking over a glass of tea and everyone's full of suspicion, you get summoned you know where . . .'

Alexandra Vladimirovna said nothing. Karimov looked at her questioningly, as though inviting her to speak. He realized that she was waiting for him to tell her the rest.

'So there we are,' he said.

Alexandra Vladimirovna still didn't say anything.

'Oh yes,' he said. 'There's one thing I forgot. This comrade asked if we'd ever talked about the freedom of the press. We had indeed. Yes, and then they asked if I knew Lyudmila Nikolaevna's younger sister and her ex-husband . . . Krymov or something? I've never set eyes on them in my life and Viktor Pavlovich has never so much as mentioned them to me. And that's what I told them. Yes, and then they asked if Viktor Pavlovich had ever talked to me personally about the situation of the Jews. I asked why he should have talked about that to me. They answered: "You understand. You're a Tartar and he's a Jew . . ."'

Later, after Karimov had put on his hat and coat and was standing in the doorway, tapping the letter-box where Lyudmila had once found the letter telling her that Tolya had been wounded, Alexandra Vladimirovna said: 'It's strange. Why should they ask about Zhenya?'

But neither she nor Karimov had any idea why a Chekist in Kazan should suddenly take an interest in Zhenya, who lived in Kuibyshev, or in her ex-husband, who was now at the front.

People trusted Alexandra Vladimirovna and she had heard many similar stories and confessions. She had grown all too used to feeling that something important had been left unsaid. She didn't see any point in warning Viktor; it would merely cause him fruitless anxiety. Nor was there any point in trying to guess which of the group had talked carelessly or had informed. In situations like this it nearly always turned out to be the person you least suspected. And very often the matter had come to the attention of the NKVD in some quite unexpected manner: through a veiled hint in a letter, a joke, a few careless words in the communal kitchen . . . But why should the investigator have asked Karimov about Zhenya and Nikolay Grigorevich?

That night she was unable to sleep. She wanted something to eat. She could smell food in the kitchen. They must be frying potato-cakes – she could hear the clatter of tin plates and the calm voice of Semyon Ivanovich. God, how hungry she felt! What awful soup they'd served for lunch in the canteen! Now, though, she very much regretted not having finished it. She couldn't even think clearly; her desire for food kept interrupting her train of thought.

On her way in to work next morning she met the director's secretary, a middle-aged woman with an unpleasantly masculine face.

'Comrade Shaposhnikova,' she said, 'come round to my office during the lunch-break.'

Alexandra Vladimirovna felt surprised. Surely the director couldn't already have answered her request for a transfer? She walked through the yard. Suddenly she said out loud:

'I've had enough of Kazan. It's time to go home, to Stalingrad.'

Chalb, the head of the military police, had called company commander Lenard to the Headquarters of the 6th Army.

Lenard arrived late. A new order of Paulus's had forbidden the use of petrol for personal transport. All their supplies of fuel were now at the disposition of General Schmidt, the chief of staff. And he'd rather see you die ten deaths than sign you an order for five litres of petrol. There wasn't enough fuel for the officers' cars, let alone for the soldiers' cigarette-lighters.

Lenard had to wait till evening, when he could get a lift with the courier. The small car drove slowly over the frost-covered asphalt. The air was still and frosty; thin wisps of almost transparent smoke rose from the dug-outs and trenches of the front line. There were wounded soldiers walking along the road with towels and bandages round their heads. And then there were other soldiers, also with bandages round their heads and rags round their feet, who were being transferred to the area round the factories.

The driver stopped the car near the corpse of a dead horse and began digging about inside the engine. Lenard watched the anxious, unshaven men hewing off slabs of frozen horsemeat with hatchets. One soldier, standing between the horse's exposed ribs, looked like a carpenter up in the rafters of an unfinished roof. A few yards away, in the middle of a ruined building, was a fire with a black cauldron hanging down from a tripod. Round it stood a group of soldiers wrapped up in shawls and blankets, helmets and forage caps on their heads, tommy-guns and hand-grenades hanging from their shoulders and belts. The cook prodded with his bayonet at the pieces of meat that came to the surface. A soldier sitting on the roof of a dug-out was gnawing at a large bone; it looked for all the world like an improbably vast harmonica.

Suddenly the road and the ruined house were caught in the rays of the setting sun. The empty eye-sockets of the burnt-out building seemed to fill with frozen blood. The ploughed-up, soot-covered snow turned golden. The dark red cave of the horse's innards was lit up. The snow eddying across the road turned into a whirl of bronze.

The light of evening can reveal the essence of a moment. It can bring out its emotional and historical significance, transforming a mere impression into a powerful image. The evening sun can endow patches of soot and mud with thousands of voices; with aching hearts we sense past joys, the irrevocability of loss, the bitterness of mistakes and the eternal appeal of hope.

It was like a scene from the Stone Age. The grenadiers, the glory of the nation, the builders of the New Germany, were no longer travelling the road to victory. Lenard looked at these men bandaged up in rags. With a poetic intuition he understood that this twilight was the end of a dream.

Life must indeed conceal some strangely obtuse inertial force. How was it that the dazzling energy of Hitler and the terrible power of a people moved by the most progressive of philosophies had led to the quiet banks of a frozen Volga, to these ruins, to this dirty snow, to these windows filled with the blood of the setting sun, to the quiet humility of these creatures watching over a steaming cauldron of horsemeat?

32

Paulus's headquarters were now in the cellar of a burnt-out department store. The established routine continued as usual: superior officers came and went; orderlies prepared reports of any change in the situation or any action undertaken by the enemy.

Telephones rang and typewriters clattered. Behind the partition you could hear the deep laughter of General Schenk, the head of the second section. The boots of the staff officers still squeaked on the stone floors. As he walked down the corridor to his office, the monocled commanding officer of the tank units still left behind him a smell of French perfume – a smell that blended with the more usual smells of tobacco, shoe-polish and damp, and yet somehow remained distinct from them. Voices and typewriters still suddenly fell silent as Paulus walked down the narrow corridor in his long, fur-collared greatcoat; dozens of eyes still stared at his thoughtful face and aquiline nose. Paulus himself still kept to the same habits, still allowed the same amount of time after meals for a cigar and a talk with his chief of staff. The junior radio-officer still burst into Paulus's office with the same plebeian insolence, walking straight past Colonel Adam with a radio message from Hitler marked: 'To be delivered personally.'

This continuity, of course, was illusory; a vast number of changes had imposed themselves since the beginning of the encirclement. You could see these changes in the colour of the coffee, in the lines of communication stretching out to new sectors of the front, in the new instructions regarding the expenditure of ammunition, in the cruel, now daily spectacle of burning cargo-planes that had been shot down as they tried to break the blockade. And a new name was now on everyone's lips – the name of Manstein.

There is no need to list all these changes; they are obvious enough. Those who had previously had plenty to eat now went hungry. As for those who had previously gone hungry – their faces were now ashen. And there were changes in attitude: pride and arrogance softened, there was less boasting, even the most determined optimists had now started to curse the Führer and question his policies.

But there were also the beginnings of other, deeper changes, in the hearts and minds of the soldiers who until now had been spellbound by the inhuman power of the nation-state. These changes took place in the subsoil of human life and mostly went unnoticed.

This process was as difficult to pin down as the work of time itself. The torments of fear and hunger, the awareness of impending disaster slowly and gradually humanized men, liberating their core of freedom.

The December days grew still shorter, the icy seventeen-hour nights still longer. The encircling forces pressed still closer; the fire of their guns and machine-guns grew still fiercer. And then there was the pitiless cold – a cold that was unbearable even for those who were used to it, even for the Russians in their felt boots and sheepskins.

Over their heads hung a terrible frozen abyss. Frosted tin stars stood out against a frostbound sky.

Who among these doomed men could have understood that for

millions of Germans these were the first hours, after ten years of complete inhumanity, of a slow return to human life?

33

Lenard approached Army Headquarters. He felt his heart beat faster as he saw the ashen face of the sentry standing beside the grey wall. And as he made his way down the underground corridor, everything he saw filled him with tenderness and sorrow.

He read the Gothic script on the door-plates: '2nd Section', 'ADCs' Office', 'General Koch', 'Major Traurig'. He heard voices and the clatter of typewriters. All this brought home to him the strength of his filial, fraternal bond with his brothers-in-arms, his Party comrades, his colleagues in the SS. But it was twilight and their life was fading away.

He had no idea what Chalb wanted to talk about, whether or not he would wish to confide his personal anxieties. As was often the case with people who had been brought together by their work in the Party before the war, they paid little attention to their difference in rank and talked with comradely straightforwardness. Their meetings were usually a mixture of serious discussion and friendly chat.

Lenard had a gift for laying bare the essence of a complicated matter with the utmost concision. His words were sometimes relayed from one report to another right up to the most important offices in Berlin.

He entered Chalb's office. It took him a moment to recognize him. And he had to look hard at his still plump face before he realized that all that had changed was the look in his dark, intelligent eyes.

A map of Stalingrad hung on the wall. The 6th Army was encircled by a merciless band of flaming crimson.

'We're on an island, Lenard,' said Chalb, 'surrounded not by water, but by the hatred of brutes.'

They talked about the Russian frost, about Russian felt boots, about Russian bacon fat and the treacherous nature of Russian vodka – how it first warmed you up only to freeze you later.

Chalb asked if there had been any changes in the relations between officers and soldiers in the front line.

'When it comes down to it,' said Lenard, 'I can't really see much difference between the thoughts of a colonel and the thoughts of the privates. There's precious little optimism in either.'

'It's the same story at HQ,' said Chalb. He paused to give his words greater effect and then added: 'And the Commander-in-Chief's the worst of all.'

'Nevertheless,' said Lenard, 'there have been no deserters.'

'I've got a question for you,' said Chalb. 'It has a bearing on something very important. Hitler wants the 6th Army to stand firm, while Paulus, Weichs and Zeitzler are in favour of capitulating in order to save the lives of the soldiers and officers. My task is to make discreet soundings as to the possibility of disobedience on the part of the encircled troops.'

Aware of the gravity of this question, Lenard thought for a moment in silence. He then said he'd like to begin with a particular example and said a few words about a certain Lieutenant Bach.

'There's one rather doubtful character in Bach's company. He used to be a general laughing-stock, but now everyone's trying to get in with him ... That made me start thinking about the company and its commanding officer. When things were going well, this Lieutenant Bach was wholeheartedly in agreement with the policies of the Party. But I've got a feeling he's begun to think differently. And I've been wondering what it is that draws the soldiers in his company to someone they used to look on as a cross between a clown and a madman. How would that character behave at a critical moment? What would he say to the other soldiers? How would their commanding officer react ... ? There are no easy answers to these questions. But there's one thing I can say: the soldiers won't mutiny.'

'Now we can see the wisdom of the Party more clearly than ever,' said Chalb. 'We never hesitated not only to cut out infected tissue from the body of the people, but also to cut out apparently healthy tissue that might become infected at a critical moment. Rebellious spirits and hostile ideologues were purged from the Army, from the Church, from the cities, from the villages. There may be any amount of grumbling and anonymous letters, but there will never be a rebellion – not even if the enemy encircles us in Berlin itself. For that we can thank Hitler. We should give thanks to heaven for sending us such a man at this time.'

He stopped for a moment and listened to the slow rumbling over their heads. In the deep cellar it was impossible to tell whether this was the German artillery or the explosion of Soviet bombs. After the rumbling had gradually subsided, Chalb said: 'It's quite unthinkable that you should merely be receiving the rations of an ordinary officer. I've entered you on a list of security officers and especially valued friends of the Party. You will receive regular parcels by courier at your divisional headquarters.'

'Thank you,' said Lenard. 'But I'd prefer to eat what everyone else does.'

Chalb spread his hands in helpless surprise.

'What about Manstein?' asked Lenard. 'I've heard he's received some new weapons.'

'I don't believe in Manstein,' said Chalb. 'On that subject I share the views of our commander-in-chief.'

In the hushed voice of a man who for years on end has dealt mainly with classified information, he went on:

'There's another list, also in my keeping, of security officers and valued friends who will be allowed a place on a plane in the event of a catastrophe. I've included your name. In the event of my absence, Colonel Osten will be in possession of the instructions.'

Noticing the questioning look in Lenard's eyes, he explained: 'I may have to fly to Germany – in connection with a matter too confidential to be entrusted either to paper or to a radio code.

'I can tell you one thing,' he said with a wink, 'I'll have a few stiff drinks before we take off. Not to celebrate, but because I'll be frightened. A very large number of our planes are being shot down.'

'Comrade Chalb,' said Lenard, 'I don't want a seat in the plane. I'd be ashamed to abandon men whom I myself have urged to fight to the bitter end.'

Chalb sat a little straighter in his chair. 'I have no right to attempt to dissuade you.'

Wanting to lighten the over-solemn atmosphere, Lenard asked: 'If it's possible, I'd be very grateful if you could help me return to my regiment. I've no car.'

'There's nothing I can do,' said Chalb. 'For the first time in my life I'm quite powerless. The petrol's in the hands of that dog Schmidt. I can't get a single litre out of him. Do you understand? I'm powerless.'

His face had resumed the helpless expression that had made him unrecognizable when Lenard first came in. It was quite unlike him. Or did it perhaps reveal his true self?

34

It got warmer towards evening and a fresh snowfall covered the soot and dirt of the war. Bach was doing the rounds of the front-line fortifications. The white snow of Christmas glittered in the flashes of gunfire, turning pink or green in the light of the signal-flares.

The stone ridges, the caves, the mounds of brick, the fresh hare-tracks that covered the ground where people ate, relieved themselves, went in search of shells and cartridges, carried away their wounded, buried their dead – all this looked very strange in the brief flashes of light. And at the same time it looked all too familiar.

Bach reached a spot that was covered by the Russian guns installed in the ruins of a three-storey building. He could hear the sound of a harmonica and their slow, wailing singing. Through a gap in the wall he could see the Soviet front line, the silhouettes of factories and the frozen Volga.

Bach called out to the sentry, but his answer was drowned by a sudden explosion followed by the drumming of clods of frozen earth against the wall. A low-flying Russian plane, its engine cut out, had just dropped a bomb.

'Another lame Russian crow,' said the sentry, pointing up at the dark winter sky.

Bach squatted down, leaning his elbows on the familiar stone ledge, and looked round. A faint pink shadow trembled against the high wall – the Russians had lit their stove and the chimney was now white-hot. It seemed they had nothing to do all day except eat, eat, eat and slurp down huge mouthfuls of hot coffee.

Further to the right, where the Russian and German trenches were closest together, he could hear the quiet, unhurried sound of metal striking frozen earth.

Very slowly, without ever coming up to the surface, the Russians were bringing their trench forward. This slow movement through the frozen, stony earth bore witness to a fierce, obtuse passion; it was as though the earth itself were advancing.

That afternoon Sergeant Eisenaug had reported that a grenade from a Russian trench had smashed the chimney pipe of the company stove and filled the dug-out with dirt. Later on a Russian soldier wearing a white sheepskin and a new fur hat had leapt out from his trench, cursing and shaking his fist.

Realizing instinctively that this was a spontaneous act, none of the Germans had opened fire.

'Hey! Chicken, eggs, Russian glug-glug?' the soldier had shouted.

A German had then jumped up and, in a quiet voice that wouldn't be heard in the officers' trench, called out:

'Hey! Russian! Don't shoot! Must see Mother again. You have my tommy-gun, I have your hat.'

The reply from the Russian trench had been curt and monosyllabic. Its sense had been unmistakeable and had enraged the Germans.

Still later a hand-grenade had exploded in the communication trench. But no one had been bothered by this.

All this had been reported by Sergeant Eisenaug. Bach had said: 'Let them shout if that's what they want. As long as no one deserts . . .'

Eisenaug, his breath stinking of raw beetroot, had gone on to report that Private Petenkoffer had somehow managed to do a deal with the enemy: some Russian bread and lump sugar had been found in his knapsack. He had promised to exchange a friend's razor for a chunk of fat bacon and two packets of buckwheat. For this he had demanded a commission of 150 grams of fat bacon.

'That's simple enough,' Bach had replied. 'Order him to report to me at once!'

It had then emerged that Petenkoffer had been killed that morning while carrying out a dangerous mission.

'What do you expect me to do about it?' Bach had said in exasperation. 'In any case, Russians and Germans have always been trading partners.'

Eisenaug, however, had been in no mood for pleasantries. He had been wounded in France in May 1940 and his wound still hadn't healed. He had then served in a police battalion in South Germany. He had been flown to Stalingrad only two months before. Hungry, frozen, eaten up by lice and by fear, he had lost whatever sense of humour he might once have had.

It was over there, where he could just make out the lacework of ruined buildings, that Bach had begun his life in Stalingrad. The black September sky and its huge stars, the turbid waves of the Volga, the huge walls that were still hot from the fire – and then the steppes of the South-East, the frontier of Asia . . .

The buildings to the west were buried in darkness. He could only make out the outlines of a few snow-covered ruins.

Why had he written that letter to his mother from hospital? She'd almost certainly have shown it to Hubert. Why had he had those conversations with Lenard?

Why do people have memories? It would be easier to die – anything to stop remembering. How could he have taken that moment of drunken folly for the deepest truth of his life? Why had he finally given in after holding back for all those long, difficult years?

He had never killed a child; he had never arrested anyone. But he had broken the fragile dyke that had protected the purity of his soul from the seething darkness around him. The blood of the camps and ghettos had gushed over him and carried him away . . . There was no longer any divide between him and the darkness; he himself was a part of the darkness.

What had happened to him? Was it folly, chance? Or was it the deepest law of his soul?

35

It was warm inside the bunker. A few of the soldiers were asleep, their bare yellow feet sticking out from under the overcoats they had pulled up over their heads; the rest were sprawled on the floor.

'Do you remember?' asked one particularly thin soldier, pulling his shirt across his chest and examining the seam with the fierce look characteristic of soldiers the world over as they inspect their shirts and underclothes. 'Do you remember that wonderful cellar where we were quartered in September?'

A second soldier, lying on his back, said: 'You were already here when I joined you.'

'That was a splendid cellar,' several other voices confirmed. 'You can take our word for it. It was a real home, with proper beds . . .'

'Some of the fellows were beginning to despair when we were outside Moscow. And look what happened: we reached the Volga!'

Another soldier split a board with his bayonet and opened the door of the stove to throw in a few bits of wood. The flames lit up his large, grey, unshaven face, turning it a reddish copper.

'And a lot of good that's done us!' he said. 'We've swapped a hole near Moscow for an even worse hole near the Volga.'

A gay voice rang out from the dark corner where the soldiers' packs were piled. 'Horsemeat! You couldn't think of a better Christmas dinner if you tried!'

The talk turned to food and everyone grew more animated. First they discussed the best way of getting rid of the smell of sweat in boiled horsemeat. Some said you just needed to scoop the black scum off the top of the boiling water. Others said it was important to simmer the broth very gently; still others said you should only use the meat from the hind-quarters and put it straight into the boiling water while it was still frozen.

'It's the scouts who really have a good time of it,' said one young soldier. 'They steal provisions from the Russians and then share them with their women in the cellars. And people wonder why the scouts always get off with the youngest and prettiest ones!'

'That's one thing I no longer think about,' said the soldier stoking the stove. 'I don't know whether it's just my mood, or not having anything to eat. But what I would like is to see my children before I die. Just for one hour!'

'The officers think about it, though. I met the lieutenant himself in one of their cellars. He was quite at home, almost one of the family.'

'What were you doing there?'

'I'd gone to get my washing done.'

'You know, I was once a guard in a camp. I saw prisoners-of-war picking up bits of potato-peel, fighting over a few rotten cabbage

leaves. I said to myself: "They're not human beings – they're beasts."
And now we've become beasts ourselves.'

Suddenly the door was flung open. The mist swirled in and a loud,
ringing voice shouted: 'On your feet! Attention!'

These words of command sounded the same as ever, calm and
unhurried.

The men in the bunker made out the face of Lieutenant Bach
through the mist. Then there was an unfamiliar squeak of boots and
they caught sight of the light blue greatcoat of the general in command
of the division. He was screwing up his myopic eyes and wiping his
monocle with a dirty piece of chamois. There was a gold wedding-ring
on his white hand.

A voice accustomed to ringing out over vast parade-grounds said:
'Good evening! Stand at ease!'

The soldiers answered in a ragged chorus. The general sat down on
a crate; the yellow light from the stove flickered over the black Iron
Cross on his chest.

'I wish you a happy Christmas Eve,' he said.

The soldiers who were accompanying him dragged another crate
up to the stove, prised open the lid with their bayonets and began
taking out tiny Christmas trees wrappped in cellophane. Each tree,
only a few inches long, was decorated with gold tinsel, beads and tiny
fruit-drops.

The general watched as the soldiers unwrapped the cellophane,
then beckoned the lieutenant towards him and mumbled a few words
in his ear. The lieutenant announced in a loud voice:

'The lieutenant-general would like you to know that this Christmas present from Germany was flown in by a pilot who was mortally
wounded over Stalingrad itself. The plane landed in Pitomnik and he
was found dead in the cabin.'

36

The soldiers were holding the trees in the palms of their hands. As they
warmed up, a fine dew appeared on the needles and the bunker was

filled with the smell of resin. The usual smell of the front line – a cross between that of a morgue and that of a blacksmith's – was quite blotted out. To the soldiers it was as if this smell of Christmas emanated from the grey-haired general sitting beside the stove.

Bach felt the beauty and sadness of the moment. These men who defied the power of the Russian heavy artillery, these coarse, hardened soldiers who were dispirited by their lack of ammunition and tormented by vermin and hunger had all understood at once that what they needed more than anything in the world was not bread, not bandages, not ammunition, but these tiny branches twined with useless tinsel, these orphanage toys.

The soldiers sat in a circle round the old man on the crate. Only that summer he had led the vanguard of the motorized infantry to the Volga. Everywhere, all his life, this man had been an actor. He had played a role not only in front of the soldiers or during conversations with a superior officer, but also when he was at home, when he was with his wife, his daughter-in-law or his grandson, when he went for a walk in the garden. He had played a role when he lay alone in bed at night, his general's uniform spread out on the chair beside him. And of course he had been playing a role when he had asked the soldiers about their mothers, when he had made coarse jokes about their affairs with women, when he had looked inside their cooking-pots and tasted their soup with exaggerated seriousness, when he had bowed his head austerely before still uncovered graves, when he had given heartfelt, fatherly speeches to the new recruits. And all this hadn't been a pose; it had been a part of his inner nature, infused into all his thoughts. He was quite unconscious of it; it could no more be separated from him than salt can be filtered out of sea-water. It had been there as he entered the bunker, as he flung open his greatcoat, as he sat down on the crate in front of the stove, as he looked calmly and sorrowfully at the soldiers and wished them a happy Christmas Eve. But now, for the first time in his life, he became conscious of this theatricality; and – just as salt crystallizes when water freezes – it deserted him, leaving him to his melancholy, to his sense of pity for these hungry, exhausted men. Now he was just a weak, helpless old man sitting with a group of other men who were equally helpless, equally unhappy.

One soldier quietly began to sing.

'O, Tannenbaum, O, Tannenbaum,
wie grün sind deine Blätter.'

Two or three more voices joined in. The scent of pine-needles was enough to make you feel dizzy; the words of the children's song were like fanfares of heavenly trumpets.

'O, Tannenbaum, O, Tannenbaum . . .'

Out of the cold darkness of oblivion, as though from the depths of the sea, long-dead thoughts and feelings rose slowly up to the surface. They brought no joy, no relief, but their strength was a human strength, the greatest strength in the world . . .

One after another came the explosions of large-calibre Soviet shells. Ivan must have been annoyed about something – perhaps he had guessed that the besieged soldiers were celebrating Christmas. None of these soldiers, however, paid the least attention to the plaster falling from the ceiling or to the clouds of red sparks belched out by the stove.

Then there was a burst of furious, metallic hammering; the earth seemed to be screaming. That was Ivan playing with his beloved Katyushas. Then came a crackle of machine-gun fire.

The old man sat there with his head bowed; he looked like thousands of other men who have been exhausted by a long life. The footlights had faded; the actors had taken off their make-up and gone out into the grey light of day. Now they all looked the same: the legendary general, an insignificant corporal, even Private Schmidt who had been suspected of harbouring dissident thoughts . . . Bach suddenly thought of Lenard. A man like him would never have surrendered to the charm of this moment. There was too much in him that was German, that was dedicated only to the State; now it was too late for that to be made human.

Bach looked up towards the door and caught sight of Lenard.

37

Stumpfe, once the finest soldier in the company, a man the new recruits had regarded with frightened admiration, was now unrecognizable. His large, blue-eyed face was thin and sunken. His uniform and greatcoat were just crumpled rags that barely kept out the wind and frost. He had lost his sharp intelligence and his jokes no longer made anyone laugh.

An enormous man with a vast appetite, he suffered more acutely from hunger than anyone else in the company. His constant hunger drove him out foraging early in the morning. He dug about in the ruins, begged, gathered up crumbs, hung around outside the kitchen. Bach had grown used to his tense, watchful face. Stumpfe thought about food incessantly; he searched for it even when they were fighting.

As he made his way back to the bunker, Bach caught sight of the huge back and shoulders of this eternally hungry soldier. He was digging in a patch of wasteland where the kitchens and supply-depot had once stood. Here and there he found old cabbage leaves and tiny acorn-sized potatoes that had escaped the pot. Then an old woman appeared from behind a stone wall. She was very tall and was wearing a ragged man's coat, tied with a piece of string, and a pair of down-at-heel hobnailed boots.

She walked towards the soldier, staring down at the ground as she stirred around in the snow with a hook made from a thick piece of twisted wire.

Their two shadows met on the snow; otherwise they would have been unaware of each other's presence.

Finally the vast German looked up at the old woman. Trustingly holding out a cabbage leaf that was stone-hard and full of holes, he said slowly and solemnly: 'Good day, madam.'

The old woman pushed back the piece of rag that had fallen

forward onto her forehead, looked at him with dark eyes that were full of kindness and intelligence, and said equally slowly and majestically: 'Good day, sir.'

It was a summit meeting between the representatives of two great peoples. Bach was the only witness; the soldier and the old woman forgot the meeting immediately.

As it grew warmer, big flakes of snow settled on the ground, on the red brick-dust, on the crosses of graves, on the turrets of abandoned tanks, in the ears of dead men waiting to be buried.

The snow filled the air with a soft grey-blue mist, softening the wind and gunfire, bringing the earth and sky together into one swaying blur.

The snow fell on Bach's shoulders; it was as though flakes of silence were falling on the still Volga, on the dead city, on the skeletons of horses. It was snowing everywhere, on earth and on the stars; the whole universe was full of snow. Everything was disappearing beneath it: guns, the bodies of the dead, filthy dressings, rubble, scraps of twisted iron.

This soft, white snow settling over the carnage of the city was time itself; the present was turning into the past, and there was no future.

38

Bach was lying on a bunk behind a cotton curtain that screened off a small corner of the cellar. A woman was sleeping beside him, her head on his shoulder. Her face was very thin and looked somehow both childish and withered. Bach looked at her thin neck and at the outline of her breasts under her dirty grey blouse. Very gently, so as not to disturb her, he lifted an untidy tress of hair to his lips. It was springy and smelt of life and warmth.

The woman opened her eyes.

On the whole she was a sensible, practical woman. At different moments she could be tender, sly, patient, calculating, submissive, quick-tempered. Sometimes she seemed morose and stupid – as though something had broken her; sometimes she sang arias from *Faust* and *Carmen* in Russian.

Bach had never tried to find out what she had done before the war. He had come to see her when he felt like sleeping with her; otherwise he had never given her a thought. He had never worried about whether she had enough to eat, whether she might have been killed by a Russian sniper. Once he had given her a biscuit he happened to find in his pocket; she had seemed grateful and had then offered the biscuit to her elderly neighbour. At the time he had been touched, but he had seldom remembered to bring her anything to eat.

She had a strange, very un-European name – Zina.

Until the war, Zina seemed not to have known the woman who lived with her. She was an unpleasant old woman, amazingly hypocritical, full of insincere flattery, and obsessed with food. At this moment, with a wooden pestle and mortar, she was methodically grinding some mouldy grains of wheat that smelt of petrol.

Until the encirclement, the Germans had quite ignored the Russian civilians; now they visited their cellars frequently and got the old women to help with all kinds of tasks: washing clothes – with cinders instead of soap – cooking up bits of garbage, darning uniforms . . . The most important people in the cellars were the old women, but the soldiers did call on the younger women as well.

Bach had always thought that no one knew of his visits to this cellar. One day, however, he had been sitting on the bunk, holding Zina's hand between his own, when he had suddenly heard German being spoken behind the curtain. A voice that seemed familiar was saying: 'No, no, don't go behind that curtain. That's the lieutenant's Fraülein.'

They lay there, side by side, without saying a word. His friends, his books, his romance with Maria, his childhood, his ties with his birthplace, his school, his university, the Russian campaign itself – his whole life had become insignificant . . . All that was simply the path he had followed on his way to this bunk fashioned from the remains of a charred door . . . The thought that he might lose this woman was appalling. He had found her, he had come to her; everything that had happened in Germany, in the whole of Europe, had been merely a prelude to this meeting. Until now he had failed to understand this. He had often forgotten her. He had enjoyed seeing her simply because he had thought there was nothing serious between them. But now she was all that remained of the world. Everything else lay buried under the snow . . . There was only this wonderful face, these slightly dilated nostrils, these strange eyes, the tired, helpless, childish look on her face that drove him so crazy. In October she had visited him in hospital; she had found out where he was and had come all the way on foot. And he hadn't even got out of bed to see her.

She knew he wasn't drunk. But he was on his knees, kissing her hands, kissing her feet, pressing his forehead and cheeks against her knees; he was talking quickly, passionately, but she couldn't understand, he knew she couldn't understand, she didn't know that terrible language of his.

Soon the wave which had carried him to this woman would tear him away from her, would separate them for ever. Still on his knees, he threw his arms round her legs and looked into her eyes. She listened, trying to guess what he was saying, trying to understand what had happened to him.

She had never seen such an expression on the face of a German. She had thought that only the eyes of a Russian could look so tender, so imploring, so mad, so full of suffering.

He was telling her that here, in this cellar, as he kissed her feet, he had understood love for the first time – not just from other people's words, but in his heart, in his blood. She was dearer to him than all his past, dearer to him than his mother, than Germany, than his future with Maria . . . He had fallen in love with her. Great walls raised up by States, racist fury, the heavy artillery and its curtain of fire were all equally insignificant, equally powerless in the face of love . . . He gave thanks to Fate for having allowed him to understand this before he died.

She couldn't understand what he was saying. All she knew, all she had ever heard was '*Halt, komm, bring, schneller, kaputt, brot, zucker*'. But she could see how moved he was; she could guess what he was feeling. The German officer's hungry, frivolous mistress sensed his helplessness and felt both tender and indulgent. She knew Fate would separate them and she was reconciled to this. But now, seeing his despair, she sensed that their liaison was developing into something unexpectedly deep and powerful. She could hear it in his voice, she could see it in his eyes, in the way he kissed her.

As she played dreamily with his hair, she felt a sudden fear that this obscure force might seize hold of her too, might cause her to stumble, might be her ruin . . . Her heart was throbbing; it didn't want to listen to the cynical voice of warning.

<p style="text-align: center;">

39

Yevgenia got to know a new circle of people – people from the prison queues. On seeing her, they would ask: 'Well? Any news yet?' By now she had become quite experienced; instead of listening to advice, she gave it to others: 'Don't worry. Maybe he's in hospital. The conditions in hospital are very good. Everyone in the cells dreams of being sent there.'

She had managed to find out that Krymov was in the Lubyanka. None of her parcels had been accepted, but she hadn't lost hope: at Kuznetsky Most they would often refuse a parcel the first time, even the second time, and then suddenly say: 'Come on then, give us your parcel.'

Yevgenia went to Krymov's flat. A neighbour said that the house-manager had come round two months before with two soldiers; they had gone into Krymov's room, taken a lot of books and papers, put a seal on the door and left. Yevgenia looked at the wax seals and the bits of string; the neighbour, who was standing beside her, said: 'But for the love of God – I never told you anything.'

Then, as she showed Yevgenia to the door, she plucked up courage and whispered: 'What a fine man he was! He even volunteered to go to the front.'

Yevgenia didn't once write to Novikov.

How confused she was! She felt pity, love, repentance, joy at the Russian victories, guilt about Novikov, anxiety on his behalf, fear that she would lose him forever, an aching feeling of having surrendered all her rights . . .

Only a little while ago she had been living in Kuibyshev. She had been about to go to the front to visit Novikov; the bond between them seemed as necessary, as inevitable, as Fate itself. Yevgenia had been horrified at the idea that she was bound to him for ever, separated for ever from Krymov ... There had been moments when everything about Novikov had seemed alien to her. His hopes, his worries, his circle of friends had nothing whatsoever in common with hers. There was something absurd about the idea of her pouring out tea at his table, receiving his friends, talking to the wives of colonels and generals.

She remembered Novikov's indifference towards Chekhov's 'The Bishop' and 'A Boring Story'. He preferred the tendentious novels of a Dreiser or a Feuchtwanger. But now that she knew her separation from Novikov was final, she felt a surge of tenderness; she thought many times of his obedient readiness to agree with everything she said. Then she felt overwhelmed by grief – would his hands never again touch her shoulders, would she really never see his face again?

Never before had she met such an unusual combination of shy kindness and rough strength. She was so drawn to him -- he was so free of harshness and fanaticism, there was such a special, wise, peasant kindness in him. But as soon as she thought this, Yevgenia felt the presence of something dark and unclean. How had the NKVD found out what Krymov had said about Trotsky? Everything that tied her to Krymov was so desperately serious; it had been impossible to draw a line through their life together.

She would follow Krymov. What did it matter if he didn't forgive her – she deserved his never-ending reproaches. She knew that he needed her, that in prison he thought of her all the time.

Novikov would find the inner strength to get over their separation. But she had no idea what she needed for her own peace of mind. The knowledge that he no longer loved her, that he had calmly forgiven her? The knowledge that he was quite inconsolable, that he still loved her and would never forgive her? And was it easier to believe they had separated for ever, or to trust that one day they would be reunited?

What suffering she had caused everyone close to her. Could she really have done all this not for other people, but for herself, to gratify her own whims? Was she just a neurotic intellectual?

That evening, when they were all sitting at table, Yevgenia suddenly looked at her sister and asked: 'Do you know what I am?'

'You?' asked Lyudmila in surprise.

'Yes, me,' said Yevgenia. Then she explained: 'I'm a small dog of female gender.'

'A bitch?' said Nadya gaily.

'Precisely,' said Yevgenia.

They all burst out laughing – though they knew very well that Yevgenia was not joking.

'You know,' said Yevgenia, 'an admirer of mine in Kuibyshev, Limonov, once gave me a definition of middle-aged love. He said it was a spiritual vitamin deficiency. A man lives for a long time with his wife and develops a kind of spiritual hunger – he's like a cow deprived of salt, or an Arctic explorer who's gone without vegetables for years on end. A man with a forceful, strong-willed wife begins to long for a meek, gentle soul, someone timid and submissive.'

'This Limonov of yours sounds a fool,' said Lyudmila.

'What if a man needs several different vitamins – A, B, C and D?' asked Nadya.

Later, as they were about to go to bed, Viktor said:

'Zhenevyeva, we often make fun of intellectuals for their doubts, their split personalities, their Hamlet-like indecisiveness. When I was young I despised that side of myself. Now, though, I've changed my mind: humanity owes many great books and great discoveries to people who were indecisive and full of doubts; they have achieved at least as much as the simpletons who never hesitate. And when it comes to the crunch, they too are prepared to go to the stake; they stand just as firm under fire as the people who are always strong-willed and resolute.'

'Thank you, Vitenka,' said Yevgenia. 'Are you thinking of the small female dog?'

'Precisely,' said Viktor.

He wanted to say something that would please Yevgenia.

'I was looking again at your painting, Zhenechka. I like it because of the feeling in it. Avant-garde art is nothing but novelty and audacity; there's no God in any of it.'

'You can say that again!' said Lyudmila. 'Green men, blue huts . . . It's totally cut off from reality.'

'Listen, Milka,' said Yevgenia. 'Matisse once said, "If I use green, that doesn't mean I'm about to paint some grass; if I use blue, that doesn't mean I'm painting a sky." Colour is simply an expression of the inner world of the artist.'

Viktor had wanted to please Yevgenia, but he couldn't help adding mockingly:

'Eckerman, on the other hand, said: "If Goethe were God, if he had created the world, he too would have made the grass green and the sky blue." Those words mean a lot to me. After all, I'm not entirely a stranger to the material God formed the world from ... Though of course I also know that there are no paints or colours, only atoms and the void between them.'

Such conversations were rare, however. Usually they talked either about the war or about the Public Prosecutor.

It was a difficult time. Yevgenia's leave was coming to an end; soon she would have to return to Kuibyshev.

She dreaded having to explain herself to her boss. She had gone off to Moscow without saying a word; day after day she had hung around prisons and written petitions to the Public Prosecutor and the People's Commissar for Internal Affairs.

Yevgenia had always been terrified of official institutions and of having to write official requests; even the need to renew her passport had been enough to give her insomnia. Recently, though, her whole life seemed to have been made up of meetings with policemen, difficulties with passports and residence permits, statements and petitions addressed to the Public Prosecutor ...

There was a deathly calm in Lyudmila's house. Viktor no longer went out to work; he just sat in his room for hours on end. Lyudmila came back from the special store looking angry and upset – the other wives no longer even said hello to her.

Yevgenia was very conscious of Viktor's nervousness. If the phone rang, he shuddered and rushed to pick up the receiver. While they were talking during meals, he often interrupted with a sudden: 'Sh! Sh! I think there's someone at the door.' He would go out into the hall and come back again with an embarrassed smile. The two sisters were well aware of the reason for this constant anxiety.

'That's how you develop persecution mania,' said Lyudmila. 'The psychiatric hospitals were full of people like that in 1937.'

In view of Viktor's constant apprehension, Yevgenia was particularly touched by the way he treated her. Once he even said: 'Remem-

749

ber, Zhenevyeva, I don't care in the least what anyone thinks of the fact that someone living in my house is trying to help a person who's been arrested. Do you understand? You must look on this as your own home.'

Yevgenia enjoyed talking to Nadya in the evenings.

'You're too clever for your own good,' she said once. 'You don't sound a bit like a young girl; you sound more like a member of a society for former political prisoners.'

'Future political prisoners,' said Viktor. 'I suppose you talk politics with your lieutenant too.'

'And what of it?' asked Nadya.

'You should stick to kissing,' said Yevgenia.

'That's what I was going to say myself,' said Viktor. 'It's less dangerous.'

Nadya was drawn to dangerous subjects; one moment she'd suddenly ask about Bukharin, the next she'd ask whether it was true that Lenin had thought highly of Trotsky and hadn't wanted to see Stalin during the last months of his life. Had he really written a testament that Stalin had kept secret?

When they were alone together, Yevgenia avoided asking Nadya about Lieutenant Lomov. Nevertheless, she soon knew more about him and Nadya's relationship with him than Lyudmila did – from listening to Nadya talk about politics, about the war, about conversations she'd had with her friends, about the poetry of Mandelstam and Akhmatova.

Lomov was obviously sharp-witted and difficult; his attitude towards everything generally accepted was one of cynicism. He wrote poetry himself; it was from him that Nadya had learnt her indifference towards Sholokhov and Nikolay Ostrovsky and her contempt for Demyan Byedniy and Tvardovsky. And Nadya was obviously parroting him when she said with a shrug of the shoulders: 'Revolutionaries are either stupid or dishonest – how can one sacrifice the life of a whole generation for some imaginary future happiness?'

Once Nadya said to Yevgenia:

'Why is it that the older generation always has to believe in something? Krymov believes in Lenin and Communism, Papa believes in freedom, Grandmother believes in the people and the workers ... But to us, to the younger generation, all that just seems stupid. It's stupid to believe in things. One should live without beliefs.'

'The lieutenant's philosophy?' Yevgenia interrupted.

She was taken aback by Nadya's answer:

'In three weeks he'll be at the front. There's philosophy for you: alive today, dead tomorrow.'

Talking to Nadya, Yevgenia often remembered Stalingrad. Vera had also talked to her; Vera had also fallen in love. But what a difference between the clear simplicity of Vera's feelings and the confusion of Nadya's! And how her own life had changed! What a difference between her view of the war then and her view of it now, in these days of victory. Nevertheless, the war went on, and what Nadya had said was still true: 'Alive today, dead tomorrow.' What did the war care whether a lieutenant played the guitar and sang, whether he believed in the bright future of Communism and volunteered for work on the great construction sites, or whether he read the poetry of Annensky and had no faith whatsoever in the imaginary happiness of future generations?

Once Nadya showed Yevgenia a handwritten copy of a song written in one of the camps. It was about the freezing holds of the transport ships, the roar of the ocean, the way 'the zeks, suffering from seasickness, embraced like blood-brothers,' and how Magadan, the capital of Kolyma, rose up out of the mist.

When they first got back to Moscow, Viktor had lost his temper if Nadya so much as mentioned these subjects. Now, however, he had changed completely. Unable to restrain himself, he would complain in Nadya's presence how impossible it was to read these unctuous letters addressed to 'the great teacher, the best friend of all gymnasts, the wise father, the powerful coryphaeus, the brilliant genius,' a man who in addition to all this was kind, compassionate and modest. It began to seem as though Stalin himself ploughed fields, forged metal, fed babies in their cradles and handled a machine-gun – while the workers, students and scientists did nothing but pray to him. But for Stalin, a whole great nation would have perished long ago like helpless cattle.

One day Viktor counted eighty-six mentions of Stalin's name in one issue of *Pravda*; the following day he counted eighteen mentions in one editorial. He railed against the illegal arrests, the absence of freedom, and the way semi-literate Party members had the right to give orders to scientists and writers, to correct them and tick them off.

Something had indeed changed in Viktor. His growing horror at the destructive fury of the State, his increasing isolation and helplessness, his sense of doom – all this sometimes engendered fits of recklessness, a contempt for the dictates of prudence.

One morning Viktor ran into Lyudmila's room. She felt quite taken aback by his unaccustomed look of excitement and joy.

'Lyuda, Zhenya! I've just heard on the radio. We've set foot once more in the Ukraine!'

That afternoon, when Yevgenia came back from Kuznetsky Most, Viktor saw the expression on her face and asked – just as Lyudmila had asked him in the morning: 'What's happened?'

'They've taken my parcel! They've taken my parcel!' said Yevgenia.

Even Lyudmila could understand how much a parcel from Yevgenia would mean to Krymov.

'A resurrection from the dead,' she said, and added: 'I think you really must still love him. I've never seen you with eyes like that before.'

'Probably I really am mad,' Yevgenia whispered to her sister. 'I'm happy first because Nikolay will get my parcel, and secondly because I've realized today that there's absolutely no question of Novikov having informed. Do you understand?'

'You're not just mad,' said Lyudmila angrily. 'You're worse than mad.'

'Vitya, darling, do play us something on the piano,' said Yevgenia.

Viktor hadn't sat down at the piano for a long time. But now, instead of making excuses, he fetched some music, showed it to Yevgenia and asked: 'Is that all right?' Lyudmila and Nadya both disliked music; they went out into the kitchen. Viktor began, and Yevgenia listened. He played for a long time. When he'd finished, he just sat there without saying a word or even looking at Yevgenia; then he began another piece. There were moments when Yevgenia had the impression that Viktor was sobbing, but she couldn't see his face. Suddenly Nadya flung open the door and shouted:

'Turn on the radio! That's an order!'

The music stopped and was replaced by the metallic roar of Levitan's voice; at that moment he was announcing: 'The town was taken by storm, together with an important railway junction . . .'

752

Then he listed the generals and units which had distinguished themselves in combat, beginning with General Tolbukhin. Suddenly he said in an exultant voice: 'And also the tank corps commanded by Colonel Novikov.'

Yevgenia gave a quiet sigh. Then, as the announcer went on in his powerful, measured voice, 'Eternal glory to the heroes who have died for the freedom and independence of the Motherland,' she began to cry.

40

Yevgenia left. Now there was nothing to lighten the gloom in the house.

Viktor just sat at his writing desk for hours on end; often whole days went by without him even leaving the house. He was frightened: he felt sure he would meet people who had it in for him; he would be unable to avoid their merciless eyes.

The telephone was now absolutely silent. If it did ring – once every two or three days – Lyudmila would say: 'That's for Nadya.' And she would be right.

Viktor hadn't immediately understood the gravity of what had happened. At first he had even felt relieved to be sitting among his beloved books, in silence, far away from those morose, hostile faces. Soon, however, the silence at home began to oppress him; it made him feel anxious and gloomy. What was happening in the laboratory? How was the work going? What was Markov doing? He grew quite feverish at the thought that he was just sitting at home doing nothing at a time when he might be needed. But it was equally unbearable to imagine them getting on fine without him.

Lyudmila bumped into a friend of hers on the street – Stoinikova, who had a secretarial job in the Academy. She told Lyudmila every detail of the meeting of the Scientific Council; she had taken it down in shorthand from beginning to end.

The most important thing was that Sokolov hadn't spoken. Shishakov had said: 'We'd like to hear what you think, Pyotr Lavrentyevich.

You've been a colleague of Shtrum's for a long time.' Sokolov had answered that he had had heart trouble during the night and found it difficult to speak.

Strangely, this news brought Viktor no joy whatsoever.

Markov had spoken on behalf of the laboratory. He had been more measured than anyone else, avoiding political accusations and dwelling instead on Shtrum's unpleasant personality. He even mentioned his talent.

'He's a Party member. He had to speak,' said Viktor. 'He's not to blame.'

Most of the speeches, however, were terrible. Kovchenko had called him a cheat and a rogue. 'And now this Shtrum hasn't even deigned to appear,' he had said. 'He really has gone too far now. We'll have to speak to him in a different language. He's asking for it, after all.'

Grey-haired Prasolov, who used to compare Viktor's researches with those of Lebedev, had said: 'Certain people have managed to draw a quite indecent amount of attention to Shtrum's dubious theorizings.'

Doctor Gurevich had delivered a particularly unpleasant speech. After admitting his own grave mistake in overestimating Shtrum's work, he had remarked on his racial intolerance and said that a man who goes astray in politics must also go astray in the realm of science.

Svechin had spoken of 'the worthy Shtrum' and had quoted words of his to the effect that physics was a unity, that there was no German physics, American physics or Soviet physics.

'I did say something of the sort,' said Viktor. 'But to quote from a private conversation at that kind of meeting is a form of denunciation.'

Viktor was surprised that Pimenov had spoken: he wasn't directly connected with the Institute and no one had compelled him to speak. He confessed to having attached excessive importance to Shtrum's research and to overlooking its faults. It was quite extraordinary. Pimenov had once said that he bowed down before Viktor's work and that it was a joy to be able to assist in its realization.

Shishakov had spoken only briefly. A resolution had been proposed by Ramskov, the Secretary of the Institute Party Committee. It was a harsh one, asking the Administration to amputate the decaying limbs from a healthy collective. What was most hurtful was that the resolution didn't so much as mention Viktor's scientific achievements.

'So Sokolov behaved quite impeccably,' said Lyudmila. 'Where's Marya Ivanovna then? Surely he can't be that frightened?'

Viktor didn't answer.

How peculiar it was. Although the Christian notion of forgiveness was quite alien to him, Viktor didn't feel in the least angry with Shishakov or Pimenov. Nor did he feel resentful towards Svechin, Gurevich or Kovchenko. But one person made him speechless with fury; as soon as he thought of him, he felt such an oppressive rage that he could hardly breathe. It was as though Sokolov were to blame for all the injustice, all the cruelty, that Viktor had suffered. How could Pyotr Lavrentyevich forbid his wife to visit the Shtrums! What base cowardice! What vile cruelty!

What Viktor was unable to admit was that this fury stemmed as much from his own secret guilt concerning Sokolov, as from Sokolov's behaviour towards him.

Lyudmila talked more and more about material matters. Their excess living space, ration cards, salary attestations for the house management committee, the need to transfer to a different store, a ration book for the coming quarter, Viktor's out-of-date passport, the fact that he needed a certificate of employment in order to renew it – all these questions weighed on her day and night. How could they get enough money to live on?

At first Viktor had pooh-poohed all this, saying, 'I'll stay at home and concentrate on theory. I'll build my own laboratory hut.' Now, though, it was no longer a laughing matter. The money Viktor received as a corresponding member of the Academy of Sciences was barely enough to pay for the flat, the dacha and the communal expenses. And he was weighed down by his sense of isolation.

But they had to live!

The idea that he could teach in an Institute of Higher Education now seemed impossible. There was no question of a politically dubious individual having contact with the young.

What could he do?

His position as a well-known scientist made it difficult for him to obtain a more modest post. No personnel officer would be willing to appoint a Doctor of Science as a technical editor or a secondary-school physics teacher. They would just gasp in astonishment.

When the thought of the work he had lost, the humiliations he had undergone and his state of dependency and need became quite unbearable, he thought: 'If only they'd arrest me right now!' But then what about Lyudmila and Nadya? They would still need something to live on.

As for selling strawberries from the dacha . . . They only had the dacha until May – then the lease had to be renewed. The dacha went with his job, not with being a member of the Academy. And out of pure negligence he'd forgotten to pay the rent; he'd meant to settle his arrears at the same time as he paid for the first six months of the next year. But sums of money that had then seemed trivial now seemed horrifyingly vast.

How could he get some money? Nadya needed a new coat.

By borrowing? But one can't borrow unless one has some hope of repaying. By selling off their belongings? But who'd want to buy china or a piano in the middle of a war? And anyway, he didn't want to do that. Lyudmila loved her collection of porcelain; even now, after Tolya's death, she sometimes took it out and admired it.

He often thought of going to the Military Commissariat, renouncing the exemption he was entitled to as an Academician, and volunteering to serve in the ranks. This thought somehow made him feel calmer.

But then he would feel anxious and tormented again. How would Lyudmila and Nadya make a living without him? By teaching? By renting out a room? But that would immediately bring in the house management committee and the police. There'd be interrogations, fines, searches at night . . .

How wise, how powerful, how threatening all these officials suddenly appeared – these house managers, district police-inspectors, housing inspectors, secretaries of personnel departments! To a man with no place in the world, even a slip of a girl at a desk in a rations office seems endowed with a vast, unshakeable power.

A sense of fear, indecisiveness and helplessness hung over Viktor all day long. But this feeling was by no means unchanging and uniform; on the contrary, each part of the day had its own particular melancholy, its own particular terror. Early in the morning, after the warmth of his bed, when the windows were still veiled by a cold, opaque semi-darkness, he felt like a helpless child faced with some awesome power that was about to crush him; he wanted to burrow under the blankets, curl up, screw up his eyes and keep absolutely still.

Later on in the morning he would think sadly about his work, longing to go into the Institute again. He felt then that he was someone useless, stupid and talentless.

It was as though the State, in its fury, was able to take away not only his freedom and peace of mind, but even his intelligence, his talent and his belief in himself. It had transformed him into a grey, stupid, miserable bourgeois.

Before lunch he would come to life for a while and even feel quite cheerful. But immediately afterwards his melancholy would return – as empty, thoughtless and tedious as ever.

The worst moments of terror came as twilight set in. Viktor had become terrified of the dark, as terrified as Stone Age man caught at dusk in the middle of a forest. His terror grew as he sat there and mulled over his memories. Out there in the darkness beyond the window a cruel and inevitable fate was watching. Any moment now he would hear a car in the street, a ring at the door, and then the scraping and squeaking of boots here in the room. There was nowhere he could escape to . . . And then suddenly, with a flash of joy and anger, Viktor no longer cared . . .

'It was all very well for those nobles who criticized the Tsarist regime,' he told Lyudmila. 'If one of them fell into disfavour, he just got into his carriage and left the capital for his estate in Penza. Everything was waiting for him – his neighbours, the park, all the joys of the country. He could go out hunting or sit down and write his memoirs. I wonder how those Voltairians would have got on with two weeks' redundancy pay and a reference in a sealed envelope that wouldn't even get them a job as a janitor.'

'Don't worry, Vitya,' said Lyudmila. 'We'll survive. I'll work at home. I'll do embroidery and make painted scarves. Or I might work as a laboratory assistant. I'll find a way of feeding you.'

Viktor kissed her hands. She couldn't understand why his face had taken on such a guilty, martyred expression, why a look of such pitiful entreaty should suddenly have come into his eyes.

Viktor paced up and down the room, singing the words of an old romance under his breath:

'. . . he lies forgotten, quite alone . . .'

When Nadya heard about Viktor's idea of volunteering for the front, she said: 'There's one girl I know, Tonya Kogan, whose father volunteered. He was a specialist in Ancient Greek. He ended up in a reserve regiment near Penza, cleaning latrines. He was very short-sighted; once the captain came in and he swept some rubbish straight at him. The captain gave him a punch that burst his ear-drum.'

'Very well,' said Viktor. 'I won't sweep rubbish at captains.'

These days, Viktor talked to Nadya as though she were an adult. Never before, it seemed, had he got on so well with her. She had taken to coming home straight after school; Viktor thought it was because she didn't want to cause him anxiety and felt very moved. When she talked to him now, she no longer had that mocking look in her eyes; instead, they took on an expression of warmth and seriousness.

One evening Viktor got dressed and set off for the Institute; he wanted to look in through the windows. Perhaps the lights would be on for the second shift? Perhaps Markov had already finished installing the new apparatus?

Suddenly he felt afraid of meeting someone he knew and turned into a side-street. It was dark and deserted. He felt strangely happy. The snow, the night sky, the cool fresh air, the trees and their dark branches, the narrow strip of light escaping through the black-out curtain of a one-storey wooden house – everything was so beautiful. He was breathing in the night air, he was walking down a quiet side-street and no one was looking at him. He was alive, he was free. What more did he need? What more could he want? Then Viktor returned home and his happiness evaporated.

At first he had waited anxiously for Marya Ivanovna to get in touch. The days passed and she still didn't ring. Everything had been taken away from him – his work, his honour, his peace of mind, his belief in himself. Could they really have taken away the last refuge of all – love?

There were moments when he would sit there in despair, his head in his hands, thinking that it was impossible for him to go on living without her. Sometimes he would mutter: 'Well then, well then.' Or he would ask himself: 'Does anyone need me?'

There was, however, one glimmer of brightness at the bottom of his despair – he and Marya Ivanovna had behaved honourably. They had suffered themselves, but they hadn't tormented anyone else. But Viktor knew very well that these thoughts – whether resentful, resigned or philosophical – had very little to do with his deepest feelings. His anger with Marya Ivanovna, his self-mockery, his sorrowful acceptance of the inevitable, his thoughts about his conscience and his duty to Lyudmila – all these were simply a way of combating despair. When he remembered her eyes and her voice, he was overwhelmed by longing for her. Would he never see her again?

When he could no longer bear his sense of loss, his sense of the finality of their separation, he turned to Lyudmila, feeling quite ashamed of himself as he did so, and said: 'You know, I keep worrying about Madyarov. Do you think he's all right? Does anyone know what's happened to him? Maybe you ought to phone Marya Ivanovna after all. What do you think?'

What was most surprising of all was that Viktor went on working. This didn't, however, diminish his anxiety, his grief, or his longing for Marya Ivanovna. His work didn't help him combat grief and terror; he didn't turn to it for relief from his gloom and despair. His work was more to him than just a psychological prop: he worked simply because he was unable not to.

41

Lyudmila told Viktor that she had met the house-manager; he wanted Viktor to call on him in his office.

They tried to guess what he might want. Was it about their excess living space? Viktor's out-of-date passport? Or was it a check-up by the Military Commissariat? Or perhaps some informer had told them that Yevgenia had been living there without being registered?

'You should have asked,' said Viktor. 'Then we wouldn't be sitting here racking our brains like this.'

'Of course I should,' agreed Lyudmila. 'But I was quite taken aback. All he said was: "Ask your husband to come round. He can come in the morning now he no longer goes to work."'

759

'Heavens! They already know everything.'

'Of course they do. They're all spying on us – the janitors, the lift attendants, the neighbours' daily helps . . . What's there to be surprised about?'

'Yes, you're right. Do you remember the young man with a Party membership card who came round before the war? The one who asked you to keep an eye open and tell him who visited the neighbours?'

'I certainly do! I gave him such a dressing-down that he was already out in the passage before he had time to say, "But I thought you were socially conscious."'

Lyudmila had told this story hundreds of times. In the past Viktor had always tried to hurry her on; now, though, he kept asking her to tell him more details.

'You know what?' said Lyudmila. 'It might be something to do with the two tablecloths I sold in the market.'

'I don't think so,' said Viktor. 'Then it would be you they wanted to see.'

'Maybe there's something they want you to sign,' said Lyudmila uncertainly.

Viktor sank into the depths of depression. He kept remembering everything he had come out with during his conversations with Shishakov and Kovchenko. Then he thought back to his student days. How he had talked! He had argued with Dmitry. He had argued – though he had also sometimes agreed – with Krymov. But he had never, for even one minute, been an enemy of the Party, an enemy of Soviet power. Suddenly he remembered some particularly outspoken remark he had once made; he went quite cold at the mere thought of it. And then what about Krymov? He was as pure and dedicated a Communist as anyone. He certainly hadn't had any doubts – he was a fanatic. Yet even he had been arrested. And then there had been those terrible evenings with Karimov and Madyarov.

How strange everything was! Usually, as twilight set in, Viktor was haunted by the thought that he was about to be arrested. His feeling of terror grew more and more oppressive. But when at last the end seemed quite inevitable, he would feel a sense of joy and relief. No, he couldn't make head or tail of it.

And sometimes, thinking about the unjust reception his work had met with, he felt as though he were about to go out of his mind. But when the thought that he himself was stupid and talentless and that his work was nothing more than an obtuse, colourless mockery of reality – when this thought ceased to be a mere thought and became instead a fact of life, then he would all of a sudden feel happy.

He no longer even played with the idea of confessing his faults in public. He was a pitiful ignoramus and, even if he did repent, it wouldn't change anything. He was of no use to anyone. Whether he repented or not, he was of equally little significance to the furious State.

How Lyudmila had changed over these last weeks. She no longer phoned up the house-manager to say: 'I need a locksmith at once.' She no longer initiated a public inquiry on the staircase, demanding: 'Who's emptied their rubbish on the floor again?' Even the way she dressed was somehow nervous. One day she put on an expensive fur coat just to go and buy some oil; another day she wrapped herself up in an old grey dress and put on a coat she had meant to give to the lift attendant long before the war had even begun.

Viktor looked at his wife, wondering what the two of them would be like in ten or fifteen years.

'Do you remember Chekhov's story "The Bishop"? The mother used to take her cow out to graze and tell the other women how her son had once been a bishop. No one believed her.'

'No, I don't remember', said Lyudmila. 'I read it when I was a little girl.'

'Well, read it again,' said Viktor irritably. He had always resented Lyudmila's indifference towards Chekhov; he suspected she hadn't even read most of his stories.

How very strange! The weaker and more helpless he became, the nearer he seemed to a state of complete entropy, the more of a nonentity he felt he had become in the eyes of the caretaker and the girls in the rations office, in the eyes of passport inspectors, personnel managers, laboratory assistants, scientists and friends, even in the eyes of his family, perhaps even in the eyes of Chepyzhin and Lyudmila – then the more certain he felt that Masha loved and treasured him. They didn't see one another, but he knew this for sure. After each new humiliation, after each new blow of fate, he would say, 'Can you see me, Masha?'

And so there he was, sitting next to his wife, talking to her, and all the time thinking his own secret thoughts.

The telephone rang. Its ringing now made Viktor as anxious as if it were the middle of the night and a telegram had arrived with news of some tragedy.

'I know what it is,' said Lyudmila. 'Someone promised to phone me about a job in a co-operative.'

She picked up the receiver. Raising her eyebrows, she said: 'He's just coming.'

'It's for you,' she said to Viktor.

Viktor looked at her questioningly.

She covered the receiver with the palm of her hand and said: 'It's a voice I don't know. I can't think . . .'

He took the receiver from her.

'Certainly,' he said. 'I'll hold on.'

Now it was Lyudmila's turn to look questioningly at him. He groped on the table for a pencil and scrawled a few letters on a scrap of paper. Very slowly, not knowing what she was doing, Lyudmila made the sign of the cross first over herself and then over Viktor. Neither of them said a word.

'This is a bulletin from all the radio services of the Soviet Union.'

A voice unbelievably similar to the voice that had addressed the nation, the army, the entire world on 3 July, 1941, now addressed a solitary individual holding a telephone receiver.

'Good day, comrade Shtrum.'

At that moment everything came together in a jumble of half-formed thoughts and feelings – triumph, a sense of weakness, fear that all this might just be some maniac playing a trick on him, pages of closely written manuscript, that endless questionnaire, the Lubyanka . . .

Viktor knew that his fate was now being settled. He also had a vague sense of loss, as though he had lost something peculiarly dear to him, something good and touching.

'Good day, Iosif Vissarionovich,' he said, astonished to hear himself pronouncing such unimaginable words on the telephone.

The conversation lasted two or three minutes.

'I think you're working in a very interesting field,' said Stalin.

His voice was slow and guttural and he placed a particularly heavy stress on certain syllables; it was so similar to the voice Viktor had heard on the radio that it sounded almost like an impersonation. It was like Viktor's imitation of Stalin when he was playing the fool at home. It was just as everyone who had ever heard Stalin speak – at a conference or during a private interview – had always described it.

Perhaps it really was a hoax after all?

'I believe in my work,' said Viktor.

Stalin was silent for a moment. He seemed to be thinking over what Viktor had said.

'Has the war made it difficult for you to obtain foreign research reports?' asked Stalin. 'And do you have all the necessary laboratory equipment?'

With a sincerity that he himself found astonishing, Viktor said: 'Thank you very much, Iosif Vissarionovich. My working conditions are perfectly satisfactory.'

Lyudmila was still standing up, as though Stalin could see her. Viktor motioned to her to sit down. Stalin was silent again, thinking over what Viktor had said.

'Goodbye, comrade Shtrum, I wish you success in your work.'

'Goodbye, comrade Stalin.'

He put down the phone.

There they both were, still sitting opposite each other – just as when they had been talking, a few minutes before, about the table-cloths Lyudmila had sold at the Tishinsky market.

'I wish you success in your work,' said Viktor with a strong Georgian accent.

There was something extraordinary about the way nothing in the room had changed. The sideboard, the piano, the chairs, the two unwashed plates on the table, were exactly the same as when Viktor and Lyudmila had been talking about the house-manager. It was enough to drive one insane. Hadn't their whole lives been turned upside down? Wasn't a new destiny now awaiting them?

'What did he say to you?'

'Nothing special. He just asked if I was having difficulty in obtaining foreign research literature,' said Viktor, trying to sound calm and unconcerned.

For a moment he felt almost embarrassed at his sudden feeling of happiness.

'Lyuda, Lyuda,' he said. 'Just think! I didn't repent. I didn't bow down. I didn't write to him. He phoned me himself.'

The impossible had happened. Its significance was incalculable. Was this really the same Viktor Pavlovich who had tossed about in bed and been unable to sleep, who had lost his head over some questionnaire, who had scratched himself as he wondered anxiously what had been said about him at the Scientific Council, who had gone over his sins one by one, who had repented – at least in thought – and begged for forgiveness, who had expected to be arrested or to live the rest of his life in poverty, who had trembled at the thought of talking to a girl at the passport office or the rations desk?

'My God, my God!' said Lyudmila. 'And to think that Tolya will never know!' She went to Tolya's room and opened the door.

Viktor picked up the telephone receiver and put it down again.

'But what if the whole thing was a hoax?' he said, going over to the window.

The street was deserted. A woman went by, dressed in a quilted coat.

He returned to the telephone and drummed on the receiver with his finger. 'How did my voice sound?'

'You spoke very slowly. You know, I've no idea what made me suddenly stand up like that.'

'Stalin himself!'

'Perhaps it really was just a hoax?'

'No one would dare. You'd get ten years for a joke like that.'

It was only an hour since Viktor had been pacing up and down the room, humming the old romance by Golenishchev-Kutuzov:

'. . . he lies forgotten, quite alone . . .'

Stalin and his telephone calls! Rumours would go round Moscow once or twice every year: 'Stalin's phoned Dovzhenko, the film director! Stalin's phoned Ilya Ehrenburg!'

There was no need for Stalin to give direct orders – to ask that a prize be awarded to X, a flat be allocated to Y, or an Institute be set up for Z. Stalin was above such matters; they were dealt with by subordinates who divined Stalin's will through his tone of voice and the look in his eyes. If Stalin gave a man a quick smile, his life would be transformed overnight; he would suddenly rise up out of the outer darkness to be greeted with power, fame and showers of honours. Dozens of notables would bow down before him – Stalin had smiled at him, Stalin had joked with him on the phone.

People repeated these conversations to one another in detail; every word of Stalin's seemed astonishing. And the more banal his words, the more astonishing they seemed. It was as if Stalin was incapable of saying anything ordinary.

Apparently he had phoned a famous sculptor and said, laughing: 'Hello, you old drunkard!'

He had rung a famous writer, a very decent man, and asked about a comrade of his who had been arrested. Taken aback, the writer had mumbled something quite inaudible in reply. Stalin had then said: 'You don't know how to defend your friends.'*

He had phoned up a newspaper for the young. The deputy editor had said: 'Bubyekin speaking.'

'And who is Bubyekin?' Stalin had asked.

'You should know,' Bubyekin had answered. He had then slammed down the receiver.

Stalin had called back and said: 'Comrade Bubyekin, this is Stalin speaking. Please explain who you are.'

After this, Bubyekin had apparently spent two weeks in hospital recovering from shock.

One word of his could annihilate thousands, tens of thousands, of people. A Marshal, a People's Commissar, a member of the Central Committee, a secretary of an *obkom* – people who had been in command of armies and fronts, who had held sway over vast factories, entire regions, whole Republics – could be reduced to nothing by one angry word. They would become labour-camp dust, rattling their tin bowls as they waited outside the kitchen for their ration of gruel.

One night Stalin and Beria had visited an Old Bolshevik from Georgia who had recently been released from the Lubyanka; they had stayed till morning. The other tenants hadn't dared use the toilet and hadn't even gone out to work in the morning. The door had been opened by a midwife, the senior tenant. She was wearing a nightdress and holding a pug-dog in her arms; she was very angry that the visitors

---

* The famous writer was Boris Pasternak, his comrade Osip Mandelstam.

hadn't rung the bell the correct number of times. As she put it herself: 'I opened the door and saw a portrait. Then the portrait started walking towards me.' Apparently Stalin had gone out into the corridor and looked for a long time at the sheet of paper by the phone where the tenants noted how many calls they had made.

It was the very banality of all these incidents that people found so amusing – and so unbelievable. Just imagine! Stalin himself had walked down the corridor of a communal flat.

It *was* unbelievable. It needed only one word from Stalin for vast buildings to rise up, for columns of people to march out into the taiga and fell trees, for hundreds of thousands of men and women to dig canals, build towns and lay down roads in a land of permafrost and polar darkness. He was the embodiment of a great State. The Sun of the Stalinist Constitution . . . The Party of Stalin . . . Stalin's five-year plans . . . Stalin's construction works . . . Stalin's strategy . . . Stalin's aviation . . . A great State was embodied in him, in his character, in his mannerisms.

'I wish you success in your work . . . ,' Viktor kept repeating. 'You're working in a very interesting field . . .'

One thing was quite clear: Stalin knew about the importance attributed to nuclear physics in other countries.

Viktor was aware of the strange tension that was beginning to surround this area of research. He could sense this tension between the lines of articles by English and American physicists; he could sense it in the odd hiatuses that sometimes interrupted their chains of reasoning. He had noticed that the names of certain frequently-published researchers had disappeared from the pages of physics journals. Everyone studying the fission of heavy nuclei seemed to have vanished into thin air; no one even cited their work any longer. This silence, this tension, grew still more palpable when it came to anything relating to the fission of uranium nuclei.

Chepyzhin, Sokolov and Markov had discussed this more than once. Only the other day Chepyzhin had talked about the short-sightedness of people who couldn't see the practical application of the reactions of heavy nuclei to bombardment by neutrons. He himself had chosen not to work in this field . . .

The air was still full of the fire and smoke of battle, the rumble of tanks and the tramping of boots, but a new, still silent tension had appeared in the world. The most powerful of all hands had picked up a telephone receiver; a theoretical physicist had heard a slow voice say: 'I wish you success in your work.'

A new shadow, still faint and mute, barely perceptible, now hung over the ravaged earth, over the heads of children and old men. No one knew of it yet, no one was aware of the birth of a power that belonged to the future.

It was a long way from the desks of a few dozen physicists, from sheets of paper covered with alphas, betas, gammas, ksis and sigmas, from laboratories and library shelves to the cosmic and satanic force that was to become the sceptre of State power. Nevertheless, the journey had been begun; the mute shadow was thickening, slowly turning into a darkness that could envelop both Moscow and New York.

Viktor didn't think at this moment about the success of his work – work that had seemed abandoned for ever in the drawer of his writing-desk, but which would now once again see the light and be incorporated into lectures and scientific papers. Nor did he think about the triumph of scientific truth; nor about how he could once again help the progress of science, have his own students, be mentioned in the pages of textbooks and journals, wait anxiously to see whether his theory corresponded to the truth revealed by calculating machines and photographic emulsions.

No, what Viktor felt was a sense of pride – pride that he had been victorious over his persecutors. Not long ago he had felt quite free of resentment. Even now, he had no desire to occasion these people harm, to get his revenge. But he did take great joy in remembering their acts of dishonesty, cowardice and cruelty. The worse someone had behaved, the sweeter it was to think of him now.

When Nadya arrived back from school, Lyudmila shouted out: 'Nadya, Stalin's just telephoned Papa!'

Nadya rushed into the room, her scarf trailing on the floor, her coat half on and half off. Seeing her reaction made it easier for Viktor to imagine everyone's consternation when, later today or tomorrow, they heard what had happened.

They sat down to lunch. Viktor suddenly pushed his spoon away and said: 'I really don't want anything to eat.'

'It's a complete rout for all your detractors and persecutors,' said

Lyudmila. 'Just think what must be going on now in the Institute and the Academy!'

'Yes, yes.'

'And the other women in the special store will say hello to you again, Mama, and smile at you,' said Nadya.

'That's right,' replied Lyudmila with a little laugh.

Viktor had always detested bootlickers. Still, it pleased him to think how obsequiously Shishakov would smile at him now.

There was just one thing he didn't understand. Mixed with his joy and his feeling of triumph was a sadness that seemed to well up from somewhere deep underground, a sense of regret for something sacred and cherished that seemed to be slipping away from him. For some reason he felt guilty, but he had no idea what of or before whom.

He sat there, eating his favourite buckwheat-and-potato soup and remembering a spring night in Kiev when he was a child; he had watched the stars looking down at him between the chestnut blossoms and wept. The world had seemed splendid then, the future quite vast, full of goodness and radiant light. Today his fate had been decided. It was as though he were saying goodbye to that pure, childish, almost religious love of science and its magic, saying goodbye to what he had felt a few weeks before as he overcame his terror and refused to lie to himself.

There was only one person he could have talked to about all this; but she wasn't there.

There was one other strange thing. He felt impatient and greedy; he wanted the whole world to know what had happened. He wanted it to be known in the Institute, in the auditoriums of the University, in the Central Committee, in the Academy, in the house management office, in the dacha office, in the different scientific societies. But Viktor felt quite indifferent as to whether or not Sokolov knew. And deep down, quite unconsciously, he would have preferred Marya Ivanovna not to know. He had the feeling it was better for their love that he should be persecuted and unhappy.

He told Nadya and Lyudmila a story they had all known even before the war. One night Stalin appeared in the metro, slightly drunk, sat down beside a young woman, and asked: 'What can I do for you?'

'I'd love to look round the Kremlin,' the woman replied.

Stalin thought for a moment and said: 'Yes, I can certainly arrange that for you.'

'See!' exclaimed Nadya. 'You're such a great man now that Mama let you finish the story without interrupting. She's already heard it a hundred and ten times.'

Once again, for the hundred and eleventh time, they all laughed at the simple-minded woman in the metro.

'Vitya,' said Lyudmila. 'Maybe we should have something to drink to celebrate the occasion?' She went to fetch a box of sweets that had been set aside for Nadya's birthday. 'There,' she said. 'But calm down, Nadya. There's no need to throw yourself on them like a starving wolf!'

'Papa,' said Nadya, 'what right have we got to laugh at the woman in the metro? After all, you could have asked Stalin about Krymov and Uncle Dmitry.'

'What do you mean? How could I?'

'I think you could. Grandmother would have said something straight away. That's for sure.'

'Maybe,' said Viktor. 'Maybe.'

'Don't be silly,' said Lyudmila.

'We're not being silly,' said Nadya. 'We're talking about the life of your own brother.'

'Vitya,' said Lyudmila. 'You must phone Shishakov.'

'I don't think you've quite taken in what's happened,' said Viktor. 'There's no need for me to phone anyone.'

'You should phone Shishakov,' said Lyudmila obstinately.

'Me phone Shishakov? When Stalin's wished me success in my work?'

Something had changed in Viktor. Until now he had always felt indignant at the way Stalin was idolized, the way his name appeared again and again in every column of every newspaper. And then there were all the portraits, busts, statues, oratorios, poems, hymns . . . And the way he was called a genius, the father of the people . . .

What had made Viktor particularly indignant was the way even Lenin's name had been eclipsed; Stalin's military genius was often contrasted with Lenin's more civic genius. There was a play of Aleksey Tolstoy's where Lenin obligingly lit a match so Stalin could have a puff at his pipe. One artist had portrayed Stalin striding up the steps of the

Smolny with Lenin darting along behind him like a bantam cock. And if Lenin and Stalin were portrayed together in public, then the children and old people would be gazing tenderly at Lenin while a procession of armed giants – workers and sailors festooned with machine-gun belts – marched towards Stalin. Historians describing critical moments in the life of the Soviet State made it seem as though Lenin were constantly asking Stalin for advice – during the Kronstadt rebellion, during the defence of Tsaritsyn, even during the invasion of Poland. The strike at Baku, which Stalin had participated in, and the newspaper *Bdzola*, which he had edited, seemed more important in the history of the Party than the whole of the revolutionary movement that had gone before.

'*Bdzola, Bdzola*,' Viktor had repeated angrily. 'What about Zhelayabov, Plekhanov and Kropotkin? What about the Decembrists? All we ever hear about now is *Bdzola*.'

For a thousand years Russia had been governed by an absolute autocracy, by Tsars and their favourites. But never had anyone held such power as Stalin.

Now, though, Viktor no longer felt angry or horrified. The greater Stalin's power, the more deafening the hymns and trumpets, the thicker the clouds of incense at the feet of the living idol, the happier Viktor felt.

It was getting dark and Viktor didn't feel afraid.

Stalin had spoken to him. Stalin had said: 'I wish you success in your work.'

When it was fully dark, Viktor went out for a walk. He no longer felt helpless and doomed. No, he felt calm. The people who counted already knew everything. He found it strange even to think about Krymov, Abarchuk and Dmitry, about Madyarov and Chetverikov. Their fate was not his fate. He felt sad for them, but he felt no empathy.

Viktor was happy in his triumph: his intelligence, his moral strength had brought him victory. It didn't matter that this happiness was so different from what he had felt when he had been on trial, when he had felt his mother standing there beside him. He no longer cared whether Madyarov had been arrested or whether Krymov had informed on him. For the first time in his life he was free of anxiety about his careless talk and seditious jokes.

Late at night, when Lyudmila and Nadya were already in bed, the telephone rang.

'Hello,' said a quiet voice. Viktor felt an even greater excitement than he had earlier in the day.

'Hello,' he answered.

'I need to hear your voice. Say something to me.'

'Masha, Mashenka,' Viktor began. Then he fell silent.

'Viktor, darling,' she said. 'I can't lie to Pyotr Lavrentyevich. I told him I love you. I promised never to see you.'

The following morning Lyudmila came into the room, ruffled his hair, kissed him on the forehead and said: 'Did you phone someone last night? I thought I heard you in my sleep.'

'No, you must have been dreaming,' said Viktor, looking her straight in the eye.

'Don't forget. You have to go and see the house-manager.'

42

The investigator's jacket looked strange to Krymov, accustomed as he was to a world of soldiers' tunics and military uniforms. His face, however, was quite ordinary; Krymov had seen any number of political officers whose faces had the same sallow colour.

The first questions were easy enough; it began to seem as though the whole thing would be as straightforward as his first name, patronymic and surname.

The prisoner answered the investigator's questions quickly, as though anxious to assist him. After all, the investigator didn't know anything about him. The official-looking table that stood between them in no way divided them. They had both paid their Party membership dues, both watched the film *Chapayev* and both listened to briefings by the Central Committee; they had both been sent to make speeches in the factories during the week before May Day.

There were a number of preliminary questions and Krymov began to feel more at ease. Soon they would get to the heart of the matter and he would explain how he had led his men out of encirclement.

Finally it was established beyond doubt that the unshaven creature sitting at the desk in a soldier's open-collared tunic and a pair of trousers with the buttons torn off had a first name, patronymic and surname, had been born in the autumn, was of Russian nationality, had fought in two World Wars and one Civil War, had not been a member of any White Army bands, had not been involved in any court cases, had been a member of the All-Union Communist Party (Bolshevik) for twenty-five years, had been chosen as a delegate to a Comintern Congress and to the Pacific Ocean Trade Union Congress, and had not been awarded any orders or medals.

Krymov's main anxiety was centred on his time in encirclement, on the men he had led across the bogs of Byelorussia and the fields of the Ukraine.

Which of them had been arrested? Which of them had broken down under interrogation, had lost all sense of conscience? Krymov was taken aback by a sudden question concerning other, more distant, years.

'Tell me, when did you first become acquainted with Fritz Hacken?'

After a long silence, he replied:

'If I'm not mistaken, it was at the Central Trade Union Headquarters, in Tomsky's office. In spring 1927, if I'm not mistaken.'

The investigator nodded as though he had already known about this far-distant event. He sighed, opened a file inscribed 'To be kept in perpetuity', slowly loosened the white tapes and began leafing through pages covered in writing. Krymov caught a glimpse of different colours of ink, single- and double-spaced typescript and occasional appended notes in red and blue crayon and ordinary pencil.

The investigator turned the pages over slowly; he was like a prize-winning student glancing through a textbook, already certain he knows it from cover to cover. Sometimes he glanced at Krymov. At these moments he was like an artist checking his sketch against the model: the physical characteristics, the moral characteristics, even the window of the soul – the eyes . . .

But how evil he looked now. His very ordinary face – since 1937 Krymov had seen many such faces in *raykoms*, *obkoms*, district police stations, libraries and publishing houses – suddenly lost its ordinariness. He seemed to be made up of distinct cubes that had yet to be gathered into the unity of a human being. His eyes were on one cube, his slow hands on another; his mouth that kept opening to ask questions was on a third. Sometimes the cubes got mixed up and out of proportion. His mouth became vast, his eyes were set in his wrinkled forehead and his forehead was in the place that should have been occupied by his chin.

'So that's what happened,' said the investigator. His face became human again. He closed the file, but without tying up the curling tapes.

'Like a shoe with the laces undone,' thought the creature with no buttons on his trousers.

Very slowly and solemnly the investigator pronounced the words, 'The Communist International.' Then, in his usual voice: 'Nikolay Krymov, Comintern official.' And then, slowly, solemnly: 'The Third Communist International.' After that he remained silent for some time, apparently lost in thought.

Then, with sudden animation, in a frank, man-to-man voice, he said:

'That Muska Grinberg's a dangerous woman, isn't she?'

Krymov blushed, surprised and deeply embarrassed.

Yes! But what a long time ago that had been – even if he was still embarrassed. He must have already been in love with Zhenya. He had dropped in on an old friend after work. It must have been to return some money he had borrowed to go on a journey. After that he could remember everything clearly, without any 'must have's'. His friend Konstantin had been out . . . But he had never really liked her – a woman with the hoarse voice of a chain-smoker, whose judgments were always sweeping and assured. She was the Deputy Party Secretary in the Institute of Philosophy. She was, admittedly, beautiful – 'a fine figure of a woman'. Yes, he had indeed pawed Kostya's wife on the couch. They'd even met a couple of times afterwards . . .

An hour before, he had thought that his investigator knew nothing about him, that he had recently been promoted from some village. But time passed and the investigator kept on asking questions about the foreign Communists who had been Krymov's comrades; he knew the familiar forms of their forenames, their nicknames, the names of their wives and lovers. There was something sinister in the extent of his knowledge. Even if Krymov had been a very great man, whose every word was important to history, it would still not have been worth gathering so many trifles, so much junk, into this great file.

But nothing was considered trifling.

Wherever he had been, he had left footprints behind him: a whole retinue had followed on his heels, committing his life to memory.

A mocking remark he had made about one of his comrades, a word or two about a book he had read, a comic toast he had made on someone's birthday, a three-minute telephone conversation, an angry note he had addressed to the platform at a conference – everything had been gathered together into the file.

A great State had busied itself over his affair with Muska Grinberg. Meaningless trifles and empty, careless words had become intertwined with his deepest convictions; his love for Yevgenia Nikolaevna didn't mean anything – what mattered were his most casual, shallow affairs. He himself could no longer distinguish between what was important and what was trivial. One disrespectful remark he had made about Stalin's knowledge of philosophy appeared to mean more than ten years of ceaseless work on behalf of the Party. Had he really, in 1932, in Lozovsky's office, told a visiting comrade from Germany that the Soviet Trade Union Movement represented the State more than the proletariat? A visiting comrade who had informed on him?

Heavens, what a tissue of lies it all was! A cobweb that was gumming up his mouth and nostrils.

'Please understand, comrade investigator . . .'

'Citizen investigator.'

'Yes, of course – citizen. Please – this is just a lie, a fabrication. I've been a Party member for more than twenty-five years. I incited soldiers to mutiny in 1917. I was four years in China. I worked day and night. Hundreds of people know me . . . In the present war I volunteered for the front. Even at the worst moments, people trusted me and followed me . . . I . . .'

'Do you think you're here to receive a testimonial?' asked the investigator. 'Are you applying for a citation?' He shook his head. 'And he even has the nerve to complain that his wife doesn't bring him any parcels. What a husband!'

That was something he had mentioned to Bogoleev in their cell. Oh God! He remembered that Katsenelenbogen had once joked: 'A

774

certain Greek once said, "All things flow"; we say, "All people inform".'

Inside the file, his life had somehow lost its proportions, lost its true scale. The whole of his life had coagulated into grey, sticky vermicelli and he no longer knew what mattered: his four exhausting years of underground work in the sultry heat of Shanghai, the river-crossing at Stalingrad, his faith in the Revolution – or a few exasperated words he had said at 'The Pines' sanatorium, to a journalist he didn't know very well, about the wretchedness of Soviet newspapers.

And then, in a quiet, good-natured tone of voice, the investigator said:

'And now tell me how the Fascist Hacken inveigled you into sabotage and espionage.'

'You don't mean that seriously, do you?'

'Don't play the fool, Krymov. You've already seen that we know every step of your life.'

'But, that's just why . . .'

'Cut it out, Krymov. You can't fool the security organs.'

'But the whole thing's a lie.'

'Listen, Krymov. We've got Hacken's own confession. He repented of his crime and told us of his criminal association with you.'

'You can show me ten of Hacken's confessions. They're all forgeries. It's madness! And if you have got this confession of Hacken's, then why was I, a spy and a saboteur, trusted to act as a military commissar, to lead people into battle? What were you doing then, where were you looking?'

'So you think you've been called here to teach us how to do our work, do you? You want to supervise the work of the organs?'

'What's all that got to do with it? It's just a matter of logic. I know Hacken. He couldn't have said he recruited me. It's not possible.'

'Why not?'

'He's a Communist, a fighter for the Revolution.'

'Have you always been certain of that?'

'Yes,' answered Krymov. 'Always.'

Nodding his head, the investigator leafed through the file, repeating to himself in apparent confusion: 'Well, that does change things, that does change things . . .'

Then he held out a sheet of paper to Krymov, covering part of it with the palm of his hand. 'Read through that.'

Krymov read what was written and shrugged his shoulders.

'It's pretty poor stuff,' he said, raising his eyes from the page.

'Why?'

'The man's neither brave enough to declare firmly that Hacken's an honest Communist, nor is he cowardly enough to level accusations against him. So he worms his way out of saying anything.'

The investigator took his hand away and showed Krymov his own signature next to the date, February 1938.

They both fell silent. Then the investigator asked sternly:

'Perhaps you were being beaten then and that's why you gave such testimony.'

'No, no one beat me.'

The investigator's face broke up into separate cubes: his eyes watched Krymov with exasperated contempt, while his mouth said:

'And so, during the time you were encircled, you left your unit for two days. You were taken by air to the German Army HQ where you handed over important information and received your new instructions.'

'Raving nonsense,' muttered the creature in the soldier's tunic with the unbuttoned collar.

The investigator carried on. Now Krymov no longer saw himself as a man of high principles, strong, clear-minded, ready to go to the scaffold for the sake of the Revolution. Instead he felt weak and indecisive; he had said things he shouldn't; he had allowed himself to mock the reverence of the Soviet people for comrade Stalin. He had been undiscriminating in his associates: many of his friends had been victims of repression. His theoretical views were totally confused. He had slept with his friend's wife. He had given cowardly, dishonest testimony about Hacken.

Was it really him sitting here? Was all this really happening to him? It was a dream, a midsummer nightmare . . .

'Before the war you supplied an émigré Trotskyist centre with information about the thinking of leading figures in the international revolutionary movement.'

You didn't have to be a scoundrel or an idiot to suspect such a filthy, pathetic creature of treachery. If Krymov had been in the

investigator's shoes, he certainly wouldn't have trusted such a creature
... He knew the new type of Party official very well – those who had
replaced the Old Bolsheviks liquidated or dismissed from their posts in
1937. They were people of a very different stamp. They read new
books and they read them in a different way: they didn't read them,
they 'mugged them up'. They loved and valued material comforts:
revolutionary asceticism was alien to them, or, at the very least, not
central to their character. They knew no foreign languages, were
infatuated with their own Russian-ness – and spoke Russian ungram-
matically. Some of them were by no means stupid, but their power
seemed to lie not so much in their ideas or intelligence, as in their
practical competence and the bourgeois sobriety of all their opinions.

Krymov could understand that both the new and the old cadres
were bound together by a great common goal, that this gave rise to
many similarities, and that it was unity that mattered, not differences.
Nevertheless, he had always been conscious of his own superiority
over these new people, the superiority that was his as an Old Bolshevik.

What he hadn't noticed was that it was no longer a matter of his
own willingness to accept the investigator, to recognize him as a fellow
Party member. Now his longing to be one with his investigator was
really a pathetic hope that the latter would accept him, would accept
Nikolay Grigorevich Krymov, or would at least admit that not
everything about him was wretched, dishonest and insignificant.

Krymov hadn't noticed how it had happened, but now it was
his investigator's self-assurance that was the assurance of a true
Communist.

'If you are genuinely capable of sincere repentance, if you still feel
any love at all for the Party, then help the Party with your confession.'

Suddenly, shaking off the terrible impotence that was eating into
his cerebral cortex, Krymov shouted: 'No, you won't get anything out
of me! I'm not going to give false testimony! Do you hear? I won't sign
even if you torture me!'

'Think about it for a while,' said the investigator.

He began leafing through some papers. He didn't once look at
Krymov. The minutes went by. He moved Krymov's file to one side
and took a sheet of paper out of a drawer. He seemed to have forgotten
about Krymov. He was writing calmly, unhurriedly, screwing up his

eyes as he collected his thoughts. Then he read through what he had written, thought about it, took an envelope out of a drawer and started writing an address on it. It was possible that this wasn't an official letter at all. He read through the address and underlined the surname twice. He filled his fountain-pen, spending a long time wiping off the drops of ink. He began sharpening pencils over an ashtray. The lead in one of the pencils kept breaking. Without showing the least sign of irritation, the investigator began sharpening it again. Then he tried the point on his finger.

Meanwhile the creature thought. It had a lot to think about.

How can there have been so many informers? I must remember everything. I must work out who can have denounced me. But why bother? Muska Grinberg . . . The investigator will come to Zhenya in time . . . But it is strange that he hasn't asked about her at all, that he hasn't said a word . . . Surely Vasya didn't inform on me? But what, just what am I supposed to confess . . . ? What's hidden will remain hidden, but here I am. Tell me what all this is for, Party. Iosif, Koba, Soso. What can have made him kill so many fine, strong people? Katsenelenbogen's right – it's not the investigator's questions I should be afraid of, but his silences, the things he keeps silent about. Yes, soon he'll come to Zhenya. She must have been arrested too. Where had all this started, how had it begun? Can it really be me sitting here? How awful. What a lot of shit there is in my life. Forgive me, comrade Stalin! Just say one word to me, Iosif Vissarionovich! I'm guilty, I've been confused, I've said things I shouldn't, I've doubted, the Party knows everything, the Party sees everything. Why, why did I ever talk to that literary critic? What does it matter anyway? But how does my time in encirclement fit into all this? The whole thing's quite mad. It's a lie, a slander, a provocation. Why on earth didn't I say about Hacken, 'My brother, my friend, I have no doubt at all of your purity . . .'? Hacken had averted his unhappy eyes.

Suddenly the investigator asked: 'Well, have you remembered yet?'

Krymov threw up his hands helplessly. 'There isn't anything for me to remember.'

The telephone rang.

'Hello.' The investigator glanced cursorily at Krymov. 'Yes, you can get everything ready. It will soon be time.' For a moment Krymov thought the conversation was about him.

The investigator put down the receiver and picked it up again. The ensuing conversation was extraordinary: it was as though the creature sitting next to the investigator were not a man, but some quadruped.

He was obviously talking to his wife. First of all they discussed household matters: 'At the special store? Goose – that's fine. But they should have given it to you on your first coupon. Sergey's wife rang the department. She got a leg of lamb on her first coupon. They've asked us . . . By the way I got some cottage cheese in the canteen. Eight hundred grams. No, it's not sour . . . How's the gas been today? And don't forget about the suit.'

After this he said: 'Well then, take care, don't miss me too much. Did you dream about me? What did I look like? In my underpants again? Pity! Well, I'll teach you a thing or two when I get home. Now you be careful – housework's all very well, but you mustn't lift anything heavy.'

There was something improbable about how very bourgeois and ordinary it all was: the more normal, the more human the conversation, the less the speaker seemed like a human being. There's something ghastly about a monkey imitating the ways of a man . . . At the same time Krymov had a clear sense that he himself was no longer a human being – when had people ever had conversations like this in front of a third person . . . ? 'Want a big fat kiss? No? Oh well . . .'

Of course, if Bogoleev's theory was correct, if Krymov was a Persian cat, a frog, a goldfinch or a beetle on a stick, then there wasn't anything in the least surprising about this conversation.

Towards the end, the investigator said: 'Something burning? Run then, run. So long.'

Then he took out a book and a writing pad and began to read. From time to time he noted something down in pencil. He might be preparing for a meeting of some study-group, or perhaps he was going to give a lecture . . .

Suddenly, in extreme exasperation, he said: 'Why do you keep tapping your feet like that? This isn't a gymnastics exhibition.'

'I've got pins and needles, citizen investigator.'

But the investigator had already buried himself again in his book.

After another ten minutes he asked absent-mindedly: 'Well? Have you remembered?'

'Citizen investigator, I need to go to the lavatory.'

The investigator sighed, walked to the door and gave a quiet call. His face was just like that of a dog-owner whose dog asks to go out for a walk at the wrong time. A young soldier in battledress walked in. Krymov looked him up and down with a practised eye: everything was in order – his belt was properly tucked in, his collar was clean and his forage cap was tilted at the right angle. It was only his work that was not that of a soldier.

Krymov got up. His feet were numb from sitting so long on the chair; at his first steps they almost gave way under him. He thought hurriedly, both while he was in the lavatory with the soldier watching him, and on his way back. He had a lot to think about.

When he got back the investigator was no longer there. A young man was sitting in his place. He had a captain's blue epaulettes on his uniform, bordered with red braid. He looked sullenly at Krymov as though he had known and hated him all his life.

'What are you standing up for?' he barked. 'Go on, sit down. And sit up straight, you sod. You'll catch it in the guts if you keep on slouching like that. That'll straighten you out.'

'So now we've introduced ourselves,' thought Krymov. He felt terrified, more terrified than he had ever felt during the war.

'Now it's going to begin in earnest,' he thought.

The captain let out a cloud of tobacco smoke. Through the haze, his voice continued: 'Here's a pen and some paper. Do you think I'm going to do your writing for you?'

The captain obviously enjoyed insulting him. Or was he just doing his duty? Perhaps he was like an artillery officer ordered to keep on firing day and night simply to fray the enemy's nerves.

'Don't slouch like that! Do you think you're here to have a good sleep?'

A few minutes later the captain shouted: 'Didn't you hear what I said? Have you gone deaf?'

He went up to the window, raised the black-out blind and switched off the light. A grey morning looked gloomily into Krymov's eyes. It was the first time he had seen daylight since he had arrived in the Lubyanka.

'So we've whiled the whole night away,' he thought.

Had he ever known a worse morning? Had he really, only a few weeks ago, been lying in a bomb-crater, happy and free, while friendly pieces of iron whistled over his head?

Time had become confused: it was only very recently that he had left Stalingrad, yet he had been sitting here in this office for an interminable length of time.

What a grey, stony light it was. The windows looked out onto the central pit of the Inner Prison. It wasn't light at all – it was just dirty water. Objects looked still more hostile, still more sullen and official than they had under the electric light.

No, it wasn't that his boots were too small; it was simply that his feet had swollen.

How had his past life and work become linked to the time he had been surrounded in 1941? Whose fingers had joined together things that could never be joined? And what was this for? Who needed all this? Why?

His thoughts burned so fiercely that there were moments when he quite forgot the aching pain in his spine and the small of his back. He no longer even felt how his swollen legs were bursting open the tops of his boots.

Fritz Hacken . . . How could he forget that in 1938 he had been sitting in a room just like this? Yes, but there was something very different in the way he had been sitting then – inside his pocket he had had a pass. What was worst of all was the way he had been so anxious to please everyone – the official in charge of issuing passes, the janitors, the lift attendant in military uniform. The investigator had said: 'Comrade Krymov, please assist us.'

No, there was something still more vile – his desire to be sincere! Yes, now he did remember. All that had been required of him was sincerity. And he had indeed been sincere: he had remembered Hacken's mistaken appraisal of the Spartakist movement, the ill-will he had felt towards Thälman, the way he had wanted royalties for his book, the way he had divorced Else when Else was pregnant . . . He had, of course, remembered good things as well . . . The investigator had noted down the sentence: 'On the basis of many years' acquaintance I consider it improbable that he should have been involved in any direct sabotage against the Party; nevertheless, I am not able totally to exclude the possibility that he is a double agent . . .'

Yes. He had informed . . . Yes, and all the information about him in this file – this file that was to be kept in perpetuity – had been gathered from comrades of his who had also no doubt wished to be sincere. Why had he wanted to be sincere? His duty towards the Party? Nonsense! The really sincere thing to do would have been to bang his fist furiously on the table and shout: 'Hacken's my brother, my friend. He's innocent!' But instead he had fumbled about in odd corners of his memory, catching fleas, remembering all kinds of trifles, playing up to the man without whose signature his permit to leave the large grey building would remain invalid. He could remember very well his happy, greedy feeling when the investigator had said to him: 'Just a minute, comrade Krymov, let me sign your pass for you.' He himself had helped to pull the noose round Hacken's neck. And where had the seeker after truth gone when his exit-pass had been signed and validated? Hadn't it been to see Muska Grinberg, the wife of his friend? But then everything he had said about Hacken was true. Maybe, but then so was everything that had been said about him. He really had told Fedya Yevseev that Stalin had an inferiority complex about his ignorance of philosophy. Even the mere list of people he had associated with was quite terrifying: Nikolay Ivanovich Bukharin, Grigory Yevseevich Zinoviev, Lomov, Shatskin, Pyatnitsky, Lominadze, Ryutin, Shlyapnikov with the red hair; he'd been to the Institute to see Lev Borisovich Deborin in the 'Academy'; Lashevich, Yan Gamarnik, Luppol; he'd been to the Institute to see Ryazanov when he was an old man; he'd twice stayed with his old friend Ekhe when he was in Siberia; and then in their day he'd seen Skrypnik in Kiev, Stanislav Kossior in Kharkhov, and Ruth Fischer; and yes . . . Well, thank God the investigator hadn't mentioned the most important thing of all: Trotsky himself had thought well of him . . .

He was rotten all the way through. Why though? And were they any more guilty than he was? But he hadn't signed any confessions. Just wait, Nikolay, you will! Just like they did! Probably the real horrors are kept till later. They keep you for three days without sleep and then start beating you up. None of this seems much like Socialism, does it? Why does my Party need to destroy me? We were the ones who made the Revolution – not Malenkov, Zhdanov and Shcherbakov. We were merciless towards the enemies of the Revolution. Why has the Revolution been so merciless towards us? Perhaps for that very reason. Or maybe it hasn't got anything to do with the Revolution. What's this captain got to do with the Revolution? He's just a thug, a member of the Black Hundreds.

There he had been, just milling the wind, while time had been passing.

He was exhausted. The pain in his back and legs was crushing him . . . All he wanted was to lie down on his bunk, stick his legs in the air, flex his bare toes, scratch his calves.

'Stay awake!' shouted the captain, for all the world as though he were shouting out orders in battle.

It was as though the Front would break and the whole Soviet State collapse if Krymov were to close his eyes for one moment.

Krymov had never in all his life heard so many swear-words.

His friends, his closest associates, his secretaries, the people he had had the most intimate conversations with, had gathered together his every word and action. He was appalled when he remembered, 'Ivan was the only person I told about that'; 'That was when I was talking to Grishka – I've known him since 1920'; 'That was when I was talking to Mashka Kheltser, oh Mashka, Mashka!'

Suddenly he remembered the investigator saying that he shouldn't expect any parcels from Yevgenia Nikolaevna . . . That was a reference to a conversation in his cell with Bogoleev. People had been adding to the Krymov collection as recently as that.

In the afternoon someone brought him some soup. His hand was trembling so badly that he had to bend forward and sip from the rim of the bowl, leaving the spoon tapping away by itself.

'You eat like a pig,' said the captain sadly.

After that, one other thing happened: Krymov asked to go to the lavatory. This time he walked down the corridor without thinking anything at all, but he did have one thought as he stood over the lavatory-pan: it was a good thing his buttons had been ripped off – his fingers were far too shaky to be able to cope with fly-buttons.

Time passed, slowly doing its work. The State – the captain and his epaulettes – was victorious. A dense grey fog filled Krymov's head. It was probably the same fog that filled the brain of a monkey. Past and future had disappeared; even the file with its curling tapes had disappeared. There was only one thing left in the world – his need to take off his boots, have a good scratch and go to sleep.

The investigator came back.

'Did you sleep?' asked the captain.

'Your superior officer doesn't sleep,' replied the investigator in a schoolmasterly tone of voice. 'He takes a rest.' This was a very old chestnut.

'Of course,' agreed the captain.

The investigator was just like a worker coming on shift who looks over his bench and exchanges a few businesslike words with the man he is relieving; he glanced first at Krymov, then at his writing-desk, and said: 'Very well, comrade Captain.'

He looked at his watch, took the file out of his drawer, and said, in a voice full of animation: 'Now then, Krymov, let's continue.'

They got down to work.

Today, it was the war that most concerned the investigator. Once again he turned out to have a vast fund of knowledge: he knew about Krymov's different postings; he knew the numbers of the regiments and armies concerned; he mentioned the names of people who had fought beside him; he quoted remarks Krymov had made at the Political Section, together with his comments on an illiterate memorandum of the general's.

All Krymov's work at the front, the speeches he had made under fire, the faith he had been able to impart to his soldiers through the constant hardships of the retreat – all this had suddenly ceased to exist.

He was a miserable chatterbox who had demoralized his comrades, destroying their faith and infecting them with a feeling of hopelessness. How could it be doubted that German Intelligence had helped him to cross the lines in order to continue his work as a saboteur and spy?

During the first few minutes of the new session the investigator's lively enthusiasm communicated itself to Krymov too.

'Say what you like,' he said, 'but I'll never admit to being a spy.'

The investigator glanced out through the window. It was getting dark; he could no longer clearly make out the papers on his desk.

He turned on his desk-lamp and let down the blue black-out blind.

From outside the door came a sullen, animal-like howl. It broke off as suddenly as it had begun.

'Now then, Krymov,' he said as he sat down again at his desk.

He asked Krymov if he knew why he had never been promoted. Krymov's answer was somewhat confused.

'You just stayed on as a battalion commissar, when you should have been the Member of the Military Soviet for an Army or even a Front.'

For a moment he just stared at Krymov in silence. It was perhaps the first time he had really gazed at him as an investigator should. Then, very solemnly, he announced: 'Trotsky himself said, "That's pure marble!" about one of your works. If that reptile had seized power, you'd be doing well for yourself. "Pure marble" indeed!'

'Now he's playing trumps,' thought Krymov. 'The ace itself!'

All right then, he'd describe the whole incident – when and where it had taken place – but one could just as well put the same questions to comrade Stalin himself: Krymov had never had the least connection with Trotskyism; he had always, without exception, voted against any Trotskyist resolutions.

All he really wanted was to take off his boots, lie down, put up his bare feet, and scratch himself in his sleep.

Quietly, almost affectionately, the investigator said:

'Why won't you help us? Do you really think it's just a matter of whether or not you committed crimes before the war, whether or not you renewed contacts and agreed on rendezvous during the time you were surrounded? It's something more serious and deep-rooted than that. It's a matter of the new direction of the Party. You must help the Party in this new stage of its struggle. To do that, you must first renounce your past opinions. Only a Bolshevik is capable of such a task. That's why I'm talking to you now.'

'Very well,' Krymov said slowly and sleepily. 'I can allow that, in spite of myself, I may have given expression to views hostile to the Party. My own internationalism may have contradicted the policies of a sovereign Socialist State. I may have been out of touch with the way things were going after 1937, out of touch with the new people. Yes, I can admit all this. But espionage, sabotage . . .'

'Why that "but"? Can't you see that you're already on the way towards realizing your hostility to the cause of the Party? What does the mere form matter? Why that "but", when you've already admitted what's most important?'

'No, I deny that I'm a spy.'

'So you don't want to help the Party? Just when we get to the point, you try and hide. It's like that, is it? You're shit, real dogshit!'

Krymov jumped up, grabbed the investigator's tie, and banged his fist on the table. Something inside the telephone clicked and tinkled.

'You son of a bitch, you swine,' he cried out in a piercing howl, 'where were you when I led people into battle in the Ukraine and the Bryansk forests? Where were you during the winter I was fighting outside Voronezh? Were you ever in Stalingrad, you bastard? Who are you to say I never did anything for the Party? I suppose you were defending our Motherland here in the Lubyanka, you . . . you Tsarist gendarme! And you don't believe I fought for Socialism in Stalingrad! Were you ever nearly executed in Shanghai? Were you shot in the left shoulder by one of Kolchak's soldiers in 1917?'

After that he was beaten up. He wasn't just beaten up any old how; he wasn't just punched in the face like in the Special Section at the front; he was beaten up carefully, intelligently, by two young men in new uniforms who had an understanding of anatomy and physiology. As they beat him up, he shouted:

'You swine, you should be sent to a penal detachment . . . You should be sent to face a tank-attack with nothing but rifles . . . Deserters . . .'

They carried on with their work, quite without anger and leaving nothing to chance. They didn't seem to be hitting him at all hard, to be putting any force behind their punches; nevertheless, there was something terrible about each blow, just as there is in a wounding remark delivered with icy calm.

They hadn't once hit Krymov in the teeth, but blood was pouring out of his mouth. The blood hadn't come from his nose or his jaw; it wasn't that he had bitten his tongue like in Akhtuba . . . This was blood from deep inside him, blood from his lungs. He could no longer remember where he was or what was happening to him . . . Then he caught sight of the investigator's face looming over him; he was pointing at the portrait of Gorky above the desk and asking: 'What was it the great proletarian writer Maxim Gorky once said?'

He answered his question himself, sounding like a schoolmaster again: 'If an enemy won't yield, he must be destroyed.'

After that Krymov saw a light on the ceiling and a man with narrow epaulettes.

'Very well,' said the investigator. 'You don't need any more rest, thanks to medical science.'

Soon Krymov was back at the desk, listening to the investigator's wise exhortations.

'We can sit like this for a week, a month, a whole year . . . Let me put things very simply for you. You may not be guilty but you can still sign what I tell you to. Then you won't be beaten up any more. Is that clear? You may be sentenced by the Special Commission but you won't be beaten up again – and that's quite something! Do you think I enjoy seeing you being beaten up? And we'll let you sleep. Do you understand?'

Time passed; the interrogation dragged on. It seemed as though nothing would be able to shock Krymov out of his stupor now. Nevertheless, the investigator did once make him jerk back his head and gape at him in astonishment.

'These are all things that happened a long time ago,' said the investigator, pointing at Krymov's file. 'We can forget about them. But what we cannot forget is your base treachery towards the Motherland during the battle for Stalingrad. Our witnesses and documents all say the same thing. You tried to weaken the political consciousness of the soldiers in the surrounded house 6/1. You incited Grekov, a true patriot, to treachery: you tried to make him go over to the enemy. You betrayed the trust shown in you both by the Party and by your commanding officers when they chose to send you to this house as a military commissar. How did you behave when you got there? Like an enemy agent!'

Krymov was beaten up again in the small hours. He seemed to be drowning in warm black milk. Once again the man with the narrow epaulettes nodded as he wiped the needle of his syringe. Once again the investigator said: 'Well then, thanks to medical science . . .'

They were sitting opposite one another again. Krymov looked at the investigator's tired face and felt surprised at his own lack of anger. Could he really have seized this same man by the tie and tried to strangle him? Now he was beginning to feel quite close to his investigator again. The desk no longer separated them from one another: they were two comrades, two disappointed men.

Suddenly Krymov remembered how the man in bloodstained underwear who hadn't been shot properly had come back from the steppe at night, back to the Front Special Section.

'That's my fate too,' he thought. 'I've got nowhere to go. It's too late.'

Later he asked to go to the lavatory. The captain from the previous day appeared again. He raised the blind, turned out the light and lit a cigarette.

Once again Krymov saw the light of day, a sullen light that seemed to come not from the sun, or even the sky, but from the grey brick of the Inner Prison.

43

The other bunks were all empty: his neighbours must have been transferred to another cell, or else they were being interrogated.

He lay there, frayed. He was quite lost; his whole life had been smeared with filth. He had a terrible pain in the small of his back; they must have injured his kidneys.

At this bitter moment, his whole life shattered, he understood the power of a woman's love. A wife! No one else could love a man who had been trampled on by iron feet. She would wash his feet after he had been spat on; she would comb his tangled hair; she would look into his embittered eyes. The more they lacerated his soul, the more revolting and contemptible he became to the world, the more she would love him. She would run after a truck; she would wait in the queues on Kuznetsky Most, or even by the camp boundary-fence, desperate to hand over a few sweets or an onion; she would bake shortbread for him on an oil-stove; she would give whole years of her life just to be able to see him for half an hour . . .

Not every woman you sleep with can be called a wife.

The despair that cut into him like a knife made him want to reduce someone else to despair.

He composed several lines of a letter to her: 'Doubtless you were glad to hear what has happened, not because I have been crushed, but because you managed to run away from me in time; you must be blessing your rat's instinct that made you desert a sinking ship . . . I am alone . . .'

He glimpsed the telephone on the investigator's desk . . . a great lout was punching him in the side, under his ribs . . . the captain was raising the blind, turning out the light . . . he could hear the rustling of the pages of his file . . .

He was just falling asleep with that sound in his ears when someone drove a crooked, red-hot cobbler's awl into his skull. His brain seemed to smell of burning. Yevgenia Nikolaevna had denounced him!

'Marble! Pure marble!' The words spoken to him one morning in the Znamenka, in the office of the chairman of the Revolutionary War Soviet of the Republic . . . The man with the pointed beard and sparkling pince-nez had read through Krymov's article and talked to him in a quiet, friendly voice. He remembered it all: that night he had told Zhenya how the Central Committee had recalled him from the Comintern in order to edit booklets for Politizdat. 'Once he was a human being,' he had said of Trotsky as he described how the latter had read his article 'Revolution and Reform – China and India', how he had said, 'That's pure marble.'

These words had been spoken tête-à-tête and he had never repeated them to anyone except Zhenya. The investigator must have heard them from her lips. She had denounced him.

He no longer even felt his seventy hours without sleep; he was already quite recovered. Perhaps she had been coerced? What if she had? Comrades, Mikhail Sidorovich Mostovskoy, I am dead! I've been killed. Not by a bullet from a pistol, not by someone's fist, not even by being deprived of sleep. Zhenya has killed me. I'll testify and confess to anything. But on one condition: you must confirm that it was she who denounced me.

He got out of bed and started to bang on the door with his fist. The sentry immediately looked in through the spy-hole and Krymov shouted: 'Take me to the investigator! I'll sign everything!'

The duty-officer appeared and said: 'Stop that noise. You can give your testimony when you're called.'

He couldn't just stay here alone. It was easier to be beaten up and lose consciousness. That was much better. Thanks to medical science . . .

He hobbled to his bed. Just as it seemed he was unable to endure another moment of this torment, just as his brain seemed on the point of bursting open and sending out thousands of splinters into his heart, throat and eyes, he understood: it was quite impossible that Zhenechka had denounced him. He coughed and began to shake.

'Forgive me, forgive me. I wasn't destined to be happy with you. That's my fault, not yours.'

He was gripped by a wonderful feeling, the kind of feeling that had probably never been experienced by anyone in this building since Dzerzhinsky had first set foot in it.

He woke up. Opposite him sat the vast bulk of Katsenelenbogen, crowned by his mop of dishevelled curls.

Krymov smiled and a frown appeared on his neighbour's low, fleshy forehead. Krymov understood that Katsenelenbogen had seen his smile as a symptom of madness.

'I see they gave you a hard time,' said Katsenelenbogen, pointing at Krymov's bloodstained shirt.

'They did.' Krymov grimaced. 'What about you?'

'I was having a rest in hospital. Our neighbours have left. The Special Commission has given Dreling another ten years, which makes thirty in all. And Bogoleev's been transferred to another cell.'

'I . . .'

'Go on, say what you want to say.'

'I think that under Communism the MGB will secretly gather together everything good about people, every kind word they ever say. Their agents will listen in on telephone cells, read through letters, get people to speak their minds – but only in order to elicit everything to do with faithfulness, honesty and kindness. All this will be reported to the Lubyanka and gathered into a dossier. But only good things! This will be a place where faith in humanity is strengthened, not where it is destroyed. I've already laid the first stone . . . I believe. Yes, I have conquered in spite of every denunciation and lie; I believe, I believe . . .'

Katsenelenbogen listened to him absent-mindedly.

'That's all very true. That's how it will be. All you need add is that once this radiant dossier has been gathered together, you'll be brought here, to the big house, and beaten up the same as always.'

He looked searchingly at Krymov. He couldn't understand how a man with Krymov's yellow, sallow face, a man with hollow sunken eyes and clots of black blood on his chin, could possibly be smiling so calmly and happily.

44

Paulus's adjutant, Colonel Adam, was standing in front of an open suitcase. His batman, Ritter, was squatting on the floor and sorting through piles of underwear that had been spread out on newspapers. They had spent the night burning papers in the field-marshal's office. They had even burnt Paulus's own large map, something Adam looked on as a sacred relic of the war.

Paulus hadn't slept at all that night. He had refused his morning coffee and had watched Adam's comings and goings with complete indifference. From time to time he got up and walked about the room, picking his way through the files of papers awaiting cremation. The canvas-backed maps proved hard to burn; they choked up the grate and had to be cleared out with a poker.

Each time Ritter opened the door of the stove, Paulus stretched out his hands to the fire. Adam had thrown a greatcoat over Paulus's shoulders, but he had shaken it off irritably. Adam had had to hang it up again on the peg.

Did Paulus imagine he was already in Siberia, warming his hands at the fire together with all the other soldiers, wilderness ahead of him, wilderness behind?

'I ordered Ritter to put plenty of warm underclothes in your suitcase,' said Adam. 'When we were children and we tried to imagine the Last Judgment, we were wrong. It's got nothing to do with fire and blazing coals.'

General Schmidt had called round twice during the night. The cables had all been cut and the telephones had fallen silent.

From the moment they had first been encircled, Paulus had seen very clearly that his forces would be unable to fight. All the conditions – tactical, psychological, meteorological and technical – that had determined his success during the summer were now absent; the pluses had turned into minuses. He had reported to Hitler that, in his opinion, the 6th Army should break through the encircling forces to the South-West, in liaison with Manstein, and form a corridor for the evacuation of the troops; they would have to reconcile themselves to the loss of a large part of their heavy armaments.

On 24 December Yeremenko had defeated Manstein's forces near the Myshovka River; from that moment it had been obvious to anyone that further resistance in Stalingrad was impossible. Only one man had disputed this. He had begun referring to the 6th Army as the advance post of a front that stretched from the White Sea to the Terek; he had renamed it 'Fortress Stalingrad'. Meanwhile the staff at Army Headquarters had begun referring to it as a camp for armed prisoners-of-war.

Paulus had sent another coded message to the effect that there was still some possibility of a break-out. He had expected a terrible outburst of fury: no one had ever dared contradict the Supreme Commander twice. He had heard the story of how Hitler, in a rage, had once torn the Knight's Cross from Field-Marshal Rundstedt's chest; Brauchitsch, who witnessed this scene, had apparently had a heart attack. The Führer was not someone to trifle with.

On 31 January Paulus had finally received an answer: the announcement of his promotion to the rank of Field-Marshal. He had made one more attempt to prove his point – and been awarded the highest decoration of the Reich: the Knight's Cross with oak leaves.

It gradually dawned on him that Hitler was treating him as a dead man: it had been a posthumous promotion, a posthumous award of the Knight's Cross. His existence now served only one purpose: to create a heroic image of the defender of Stalingrad. The official propaganda had made saints and martyrs of the hundreds of thousands of men under his command. They were alive, boiling their horsemeat, hunting down the last Stalingrad dogs, catching magpies in the steppes, crushing lice, smoking cigarettes made from nothing but twists of paper; meanwhile the State radio stations played solemn funeral music in honour of these still living heroes.

They were alive, blowing on their red fingers, wiping the snot from their noses, thinking about the chances of stealing something to eat, shamming illness, surrendering to the enemy or warming themselves on a Russian woman in a cellar; meanwhile, over the airwaves, choirs of little boys and girls were singing, 'They died so that Germany could live.' Only if the State should perish could these men be reborn to the sins and wonders of everyday life.

Everything had happened precisely as Paulus had predicted. This sense of his own rightness, confirmed by the absolute destruction of his army, was painful to live with. At the same time, in spite of himself, it gave him a kind of tired satisfaction, a reinforced sense of his own worth.

Thoughts he had suppressed during his days of glory now came back to him.

Keitel and Jodl had called Hitler the divine Führer. Goebbels had declared that Hitler's tragedy was that the war offered him no opponent worthy of his own genius. Zeitzler, on the other hand, had told him how Hitler had once asked him to straighten the line of the front on the grounds that its curves offended his aesthetic sensibilities. And what about his mad, neurotic, refusal to advance on Moscow? And the sudden failure of will that had led him to call a halt to the advance on Leningrad? It was only a fear of losing face that made him insist so fanatically on the defence of Stalingrad.

Now everything was as clear as daylight.

But clarity can be very terrifying. He could have refused to obey the order. Hitler would have had him executed, but he would have saved the lives of his men. Yes, he had seen many people look at him with reproach.

He could have saved his army!

But he was afraid of Hitler, afraid for his own skin!

Chalb, the chief of the SD at Headquarters, had flown to Berlin the other day. He had made some confused remark to the effect that the Führer had revealed himself to be too great even for the German people. Yes . . . Yes . . . Of course . . .

Demagogy, nothing but demagogy . . .

Adam turned on the radio. The initial crackle of interference was succeeded by music: Germany was lamenting the dead of Stalingrad. The music had a strange power. Maybe the myth created by the Führer would mean more for the people and for battles to come than the lives of the lice-ridden, frostbitten wrecks that had once been his men? Maybe the Führer's logic was not a logic that could be understood merely from reading orders, poring over maps and drawing up schedules?

Perhaps the aura of martyrdom to which Hitler had condemned the 6th Army would bestow a new existence on Paulus and his soldiers, allowing them to participate in the future of Germany?

It wasn't a matter of pencils, calculating-machines and slide-rules. This Quartermaster-General worked according to a different logic, different criteria.

Adam, dear, faithful Adam: the purest souls are constantly and inevitably a prey to doubt. The world is always dominated by limited men, men with an unshakeable conviction of their own rightness. The purest souls never take great decisions or hold sway over States.

'They're coming!' shouted Adam. He ordered Ritter to put the open suitcase out of the way and then straightened his uniform.

There were holes in the heels of the socks Ritter had just thrown into the case. What troubled Ritter was not that a careless and anxious Paulus might wear these socks, but that the holes might be glimpsed by hostile Russian eyes.

Adam adopted what he considered to be the correct pose for an adjutant to a field-marshal: he stood quite still, his hands resting on the back of a chair, his back turned to the door that any moment now would be flung open, his eyes gazing calmly, attentively and affectionately at Paulus himself.

Paulus leant back, away from the table, compressing his lips. If the Führer wanted play-acting, then he was ready to comply.

Any minute now the door would open; this room in a dark cellar would be scrutinized by men who lived on the earth's surface. The pain and bitterness had passed, what remained was fear: fear that the door would be opened, not by representatives of the Soviet High Command who had prepared their role in this solemn scene, but by wild, trigger-happy soldiers. And fear of the unknown: once this final scene had been played out, life would begin again. But what kind of life and where? Siberia, a Moscow prison, a barrack-hut in a labour camp?

45

That night the people on the left bank had seen multi-coloured flares light up the sky over Stalingrad. The German army had surrendered.

People had immediately begun crossing the Volga into the city itself. They had heard that the remaining inhabitants of Stalingrad had endured terrible hunger during these last weeks; the officers, soldiers and sailors from the Volga fleet all carried little bundles of tinned food and loaves of bread. A few of them also brought some vodka or an accordion.

These unarmed soldiers who entered Stalingrad during the night, who handed out bread and kissed and embraced the inhabitants, seemed almost sad; there was little singing or rejoicing.

The morning of 2 February, 1943, was very misty. The mist rose up from the holes pierced in the ice and from the few patches of unfrozen water. The sun rose, as harsh now in the winter winds as during the blazing heat of August. The dry snow drifted about over the level ground, forming milky spirals and columns, then suddenly lost its will and settled again. Everywhere you could see traces of the east wind: collars of snow round the stems of thorn-bushes, congealed ripples on the slopes of the gullies, small mounds and patches of bare clay . . .

From the Stalingrad bank it looked as though the people crossing the Volga were being formed out of the mist itself, as though they had been sculpted by the wind and frost. They had no mission to accomplish in Stalingrad; the war here was over and no one had sent them. They came spontaneously, of their own accord – soldiers and road-layers, drivers and gunners, army tailors, mechanics and electricians. Together with old men wrapped in shawls, old women wearing soldiers' trousers and little boys and girls dragging sledges laden with bundles and blankets, they crossed the Volga and scrambled up the slopes of the right bank.

Something very strange had happened to the city. You could hear the sound of car-horns and tractor engines; people were playing harmonicas, soldiers were shouting and laughing, dancers were stamping down the snow with their felt boots. But, for all this, the city felt dead.

The normal life of Stalingrad had come to an end several months before: schools, factories, women's dressmakers, amateur choirs and theatre groups, crèches, cinemas, the city police had all ceased to function. A new city – wartime Stalingrad – had been born out of the flames. This city had its own layout of streets and squares, its own underground buildings, its own traffic laws, its own commerce, factories and artisans, its own cemeteries, concerts and drinking parties.

Every epoch has its own capital city, a city that embodies its will and soul. For several months of the Second World War this city was Stalingrad. The thoughts and passions of humanity were centred on Stalingrad. Factories and printing presses functioned for the sake of Stalingrad. Parliamentary leaders rose to their feet to speak of Stalingrad. But when thousands of people poured in from the steppes to fill the empty streets, when the first car engines started up, this world capital ceased to exist.

On that day newspapers all over the world reported the details of the German surrender. People in Europe, America and India were able to read how Field-Marshal Paulus had left his underground headquarters, how the German generals had undergone a preliminary interrogation at the headquarters of Shumilov's 64th Army, and about what General Schmidt, Paulus's chief of staff, had been wearing.

By then Hitler, Roosevelt and Churchill were looking for new crisis points in the war. Stalin was tapping the table with his finger and asking the Chief of the General Staff if arrangements had been completed to transfer the troops from Stalingrad to other Fronts. The capital of the world war, full as it was of generals, experts in street-fighting, strategic maps, armaments and well-kept communication trenches, had ceased to exist. Or rather, it had begun a new existence, similar to that of present-day Athens or Rome. Historians, museum guides, teachers and eternally bored schoolchildren, though not yet visible, had become its new masters.

At the same time, an everyday, working city was coming into being

– with schools, factories, maternity homes, police, an opera and a prison.

A light dusting of snow had fallen on the paths along which men had carried shells, loaves of bread and pots of *kasha* to gun emplacements, along which they had dragged machine-guns, along which snipers and artillery observers had crept to their stone hiding-places.

Snow had fallen on the paths along which messengers had run between companies and battalions, the paths leading from Batyuk's division to Banniy Ovrag, to the slaughterhouse and the water-towers. Snow had fallen on the paths where the inhabitants of the wartime city had gone for a smoke, to celebrate a comrade's name-day with a few drinks, to have a wash in a cellar, to play a game of dominoes, to have a taste of a neighbour's sauerkraut. Snow had fallen on the paths leading to dear Manya and the beautiful Vera, to menders of watches and cigarette-lighters, to tailors, accordion-players and storekeepers.

A whole network of capricious, winding paths was being covered by snow; not one fresh footprint could be seen on all these thousands of kilometres. This first snowfall was soon followed by a second. The paths blurred and faded.

Meanwhile thousands of people were making new paths, ordinary paths that didn't wind about in great loops or hug the walls of ruins.

The old inhabitants of the city felt both happy and empty. After defending Stalingrad for so long, the soldiers felt strangely depressed.

The whole city was suddenly empty and everyone could feel it – from army commanders and commanders of infantry divisions to ordinary soldiers like Polyakov and Glushkov. This feeling was absurd. Why should a victorious end to the slaughter make one feel sad?

The telephone on the commanding officer's desk was silent in its yellow case. A collar of snow had settled round the housing of the machine-gun. Battery-commanders' telescopes and embrasures had clouded over. Well-thumbed maps and plans were transferred from map-cases to pouches, and sometimes to the kitbags and suitcases of commanders of platoons, companies and battalions . . .

At the same time crowds of people were wandering among the dead houses, shouting loud 'hurray's' and embracing one another. They looked at each other and thought: 'What fine brave lads you are! Just like us in your winter hats and your jackets! But what we've achieved doesn't even bear thinking about. We've lifted the heaviest burden in the world. We've raised up Truth over Lies. We've just accomplished what most people only read of in fairy-tales.'

All these people belonged to the same city: some of them came from Kuporosnaya Balka, others from Banniy Ovrag, others from the water-towers or from 'Red October', still others from Mamayev Kurgan. And the people who had lived in the centre, on the banks of the Tsaritsa, near the wharves, behind the oil-tanks, came out to meet them. The soldiers were both hosts and guests. The wind roared as they showered one another with congratulations. From time to time they fired a few shots into the air or let off a hand-grenade. They clapped each other on the back, threw their arms round each other, kissed with cold lips and then broke into light-hearted curses . . . They had all risen up from under the earth: metal-workers, turners, plough-men, carpenters, navvies . . . They had ploughed up stone, iron and clay; together they had fought off the enemy.

A world capital is unique not only because it is linked with the fields and factories of the whole world. A world capital is unique because it has a soul. The soul of wartime Stalingrad was freedom.

The capital of the war against the Fascists was now no more than the icy ruins of what had once been a provincial industrial city and port.

Here, ten years later, was constructed a vast dam, one of the largest hydro-electric power stations in the world – the product of the forced labour of thousands of prisoners.

46

The German officer had only just woken up and hadn't yet heard the news of the surrender. He had fired a shot at Sergeant Zadnyepruk and slightly wounded him. This had aroused the wrath of the Russians in charge of the operation: the German soldiers were filing out of their vast bunkers and throwing down their arms, with a loud clatter, onto the steadily growing pile of tommy-guns and rifles.

The prisoners tried to look straight ahead – as a sign that even their gaze was now captive. Private Schmidt was the only exception: he had smiled as he came out into the daylight and then looked up and down the Russian ranks as though he were sure of glimpsing a familiar face.

Colonel Filimonov, who was slightly drunk after arriving from Moscow the day before, was standing beside his interpreter and watching General Wegler's division surrender their arms. His great-coat with its new gold epaulettes, its red tabs and black edging, stood out among the filthy, scorched jackets and crumpled caps of the Russian officers and the equally filthy, scorched, crumpled clothes of the German prisoners. He had said yesterday in the Military Soviet canteen that the central commissariat in Moscow still contained supplies of gold braid that had been used for epaulettes in pre-revolutionary days; it was the done thing among his circle of friends to have one's epaulettes sewn from this fine old braid.

When he heard the shot and Zadnyepruk's wounded cry, Filimonov shouted: 'What was that? Who's shooting?'

'Some fool of a German,' several voices answered. 'They're bring-ing him along . . . he says he didn't know.'

'Didn't know?' shouted Filimonov. 'Hasn't the swine spilt enough of our blood?'

He turned to his interpreter, a tall Jewish political instructor.

'Bring me that officer straight away. I'll make him pay for that shot with his life!'

Just then Filimonov caught sight of Schmidt's large, smiling face and shouted: 'So it makes you laugh, does it, to know that another of our men's been crippled? I'll teach you, you swine!'

Schmidt was unable to understand why his well-meaning smile should have made this Russian officer scream at him with such fury. Then he heard a pistol shot, seemingly quite unconnected with these shouts. No longer understanding anything at all, he stumbled and fell beneath the feet of the soldiers behind. His body was dragged out of the way; it lay there on one side while the other soldiers marched past. After that, a group of young boys, who were certainly not afraid of a mere corpse, climbed down into the bunkers and began probing about under the plank-beds.

Colonel Filimonov, meanwhile, was inspecting the battalion com-mander's underground quarters and admiring their comfort and solidity. A soldier brought in a young German officer with calm clear eyes.

'Comrade Colonel,' said the interpreter, 'this is the man you asked to have brought to you – Lieutenant Lenard.'

'This one?' asked Filimonov in surprise. He liked the look of the officer's face and he was upset at having been involved, for the first time in his life, in a murder. 'Take him to the assembly point. And no mucking about! I want him alive and I shall hold you responsible.'

The day of judgment was drawing to an end; it was already impossible to make out the smile on the face of the dead soldier.

47

Lieutenant-Colonel Mikhailov, the chief interpreter of the 7th section of the Political Administration of the Front, was accompanying Field-Marshal Paulus to the Headquarters of the 64th Army.

Paulus had left his cellar without so much as glancing at the Soviet officers and soldiers. They had stared at him with greedy curiosity, admiring his grey rabbit-fur hat and his field-marshal's greatcoat with its band of green leather running from the shoulder to the waist. He had strode past towards the waiting jeep, head erect, not looking at the ruined city.

Mikhailov had often attended diplomatic receptions before the war and he felt confident and at ease with Paulus. He was never over-solicitous, but always cool and respectful.

He was sitting beside Paulus, watching his face and waiting for him to break the silence. He had already been present at the preliminary interrogation of the other generals; they had behaved very differently.

The chief of staff of the 6th Army had declared in a slow, lazy voice that it was the Italians and Rumanians who were to blame for the catastrophe. The hook-nosed Lieutenant-General Sixt von Armin, his medals tinkling gloomily, had added: 'And it wasn't only Garibaldi and that 8th Army of his. It was the Russian cold, the lack of supplies and munitions . . .'

Schlemmer, the grey-haired commander of a tank corps, wearing a

Knight's Cross together with a medal he had been awarded for having received five wounds, had interrupted this conversation to ask if they would look after his suitcase. After that everyone had begun talking at once: General Rinaldo, a man with a gentle smile who was head of the medical service; Colonel Ludwig, the morose commander of a tank division, whose face had been hideously scarred by a sabre cut ... Colonel Adam, Paulus's adjutant, had made the worst fuss of all. He had lost his toilet-case and he kept throwing his hands up into the air and shaking his head in despair; the flaps of his leopard-skin cap had flapped about like the ears of a pedigree dog just out of the water.

These officers had indeed become human again, but not in the most admirable manner.

The driver was wearing a smart white sheepskin coat. Mikhailov told him to drive more slowly.

'Certainly, comrade Lieutenant-Colonel,' he answered quietly.

The driver was very much looking forward to telling his comrades about Paulus, to going home at the end of the war and saying: 'Now, when I was driving Field-Marshal Paulus . . .' He was also determined to drive outstandingly well, to make Paulus say: 'So that's what a Soviet driver's like! A true professional!'

It was hard for a soldier's eye to take in this spectacle, to get used to seeing Russians and Germans in such close proximity. Cheerful squads of infantrymen were searching through cellars, climbing down into the mouths of sewers, herding the Germans up to the frozen surface.

On patches of wasteland and empty streets, with much prodding and shouting, these infantrymen then re-formed the German army, throwing men from quite different arms of the service into the same column.

The Germans trudged on, trying not to stumble, looking round now and again at the Russian soldiers and their guns. They were submissive not only because it would be so easy for the Russian soldiers to shoot them; they were submissive because of the hypnotic aura of power that surrounded them.

The field-marshal was being driven south;.the columns of prisoners were being marched in the opposite direction. A powerful loudspeaker was roaring out a well-known song:

'I left yesterday for distant lands,
My love waved her handkerchief beside the gate.'

A wounded prisoner was being carried along by two comrades; his pale, dirty arms hung round their necks. The heads of his two bearers drew closer together, his deathly pale face and burning eyes between them. Another wounded prisoner was being dragged out of a bunker on a blanket.

The snow was dotted with blue-grey stacks of weapons. They were like ricks of steel straw that had just been threshed.

A Russian soldier was being lowered into his tomb to a salute of gunfire. A few yards away lay heaps of dead Germans who had just been hauled up from the hospital cellars. A crowd of Rumanian soldiers went past, guffawing, waving their arms about, making fun of the Germans – both living and dead.

Prisoners were being herded along from the Nursery, from the Tsaritsa, from the House of Specialists . . . They walked with a very particular gait, the gait adopted by humans and animals who have lost their freedom. The lightly wounded and frostbitten were leaning on sticks or pieces of charred planks. On they marched; it seemed that all of them had the same greyish face, the same eyes, the same expression of suffering.

It was surprising how many of these men were very short, with large noses and low foreheads, with small hare-like mouths and bird-like heads. What a lot of Aryans there were whose dark skin was covered with freckles, boils and pimples.

They were weak, ugly men. None of them seemed to have strong chins, arrogant mouths, blonde hair, clear eyes or granite chests. How extraordinarily similar they were to the equally weak, ugly, unfortunate men who, in the autumn of 1941, had been prodded and beaten by the Germans towards prisoner-of-war camps in the West.

Now and then you could hear pistol-shots in the cellars and bunkers. The crowds of prisoners, still drifting along towards the Volga, understood the meaning of these shots only too well.

Lieutenant-Colonel Mikhailov continued to glance now and then at the Field-Marshal; meanwhile the driver studied his face in the mirror. Mikhailov could see a long, thin cheek; the driver could see his forehead, his eyes and his tight silent lips.

They drove past guns with barrels pointing up at the sky, past tanks painted with swastikas, past trucks whose tarpaulin covers were flapping about in the wind, past armoured troop-carriers and self-propelled guns.

The iron body, the muscles, of the 6th Army, were freezing solid, freezing into the ground. The men themselves were still marching slowly past; it seemed as if at any moment they too might come to a halt, might freeze into stillness.

Mikhailov, the driver and the armed guard were all waiting for Paulus to say something, to call out to someone or at least to look round. But he remained silent; they had no idea where his eyes were looking or what messages they were bringing him.

Was he afraid of being seen by his soldiers? Or was that the very thing he wanted? Suddenly Paulus turned to Mikhailov and asked:

'*Sagen Sie bitte, was ist es, Makhorka?*'*

This unexpected question did not help Mikhailov to understand Paulus's thoughts. In fact he was wondering anxiously whether or not he would have soup every day, whether he would have somewhere warm to sleep, whether he would be able to obtain tobacco.

48

Some German prisoners were carrying out Russian corpses from the cellar of a two-storey building that had once been the headquarters of the Gestapo.

In spite of the cold, a group of women, boys and old men were standing beside the sentry and watching the Germans lay out the corpses on the frozen earth.

Most of the prisoners wore an expression of complete indifference, they dragged their feet as they walked and breathed in the smell of death without flinching. There was just one, a young man in an officer's greatcoat, who had tied a handkerchief round his mouth and nose and was shaking his head convulsively like a horse stung by

---

* 'Tell me please, what is Makhorka?' (Makhorka is a coarse Russian tobacco.)

gadflies. The expression of torment in his eyes seemed close to madness.

Sometimes the prisoners put a stretcher down on the ground and stood over it for a while: some of the corpses were missing an arm or leg and the prisoners were wondering which of the spare limbs belonged to which corpse. Most of the corpses were half-naked or in their underclothes; a few were wearing trousers. One was quite naked: his mouth was wide open in a last cry; his stomach had sunk right into his backbone; he had reddish pubic hair and pitifully thin legs.

It was impossible to imagine that these corpses with their sunken mouths and eye-sockets had, until not long ago, been living beings with names and homes; that they had smoked cigarettes, longed for a mug of beer and said: 'My darling, my beautiful, give me a kiss – and don't forget me!'

The officer with the handkerchief round his mouth seemed to be the only person able to imagine all this. But for some reason he was the one who appeared to attract the anger of the women standing beside the entrance; they kept their eyes fixed on him and ignored the remaining prisoners – despite the fact that two of them had light patches on their overcoats where their SS insignia had once been.

'So you're trying to look away, are you?' muttered a squat woman who was holding a little boy by the hand.

The officer could sense the weight of emotion in the woman's slow, penetrating look. The air was full of a hatred that needed to be discharged; it was like the electrical energy in a storm-cloud that strikes blindly and with consuming power at one of the trees in a forest.

The officer's fellow-worker was a short soldier with a thin towel round his neck and some sacking tied with telephone cable round his legs.

The Russians standing in silence by the door looked so hostile that the prisoners felt relieved to go back down again into the dark cellar. They stayed there as long as they could, preferring the stench and darkness to the fresh air and daylight.

The prisoners were on their way back to the cellar with empty stretchers when they heard the familiar sound of Russian swear-words. They carried on at the same pace, sensing instinctively that one sudden movement would be enough to make the crowd turn on them.

The officer suddenly let out a cry and the guard said irritably: 'Hey, you brat! What's the use of throwing stones? Are you going to take over if the Fritz comes a cropper?'

Back down in the cellar the prisoners had a few words together.

'For the time being, they've only got it in for the lieutenant.'

'Did you see the way that woman looked at him?'

'You stay in the cellar this time, Lieutenant,' said a voice out of the darkness. 'If they start on you, then we'll be next.'

'No, no, it's no good hiding,' the officer murmured sleepily. 'This is the day of judgment.' He turned to his fellow-worker. 'Come on now, let's be off!'

This time their burden was lighter and they walked faster than usual as they came out of the cellar. On the stretcher lay the corpse of an adolescent girl. Her body was shrivelled and dried up; only her blonde hair still kept its warm life and colour, falling in disorder round the terrible, blackened face of a dead bird. The crowd gave a quiet gasp.

The squat woman let out a shrill cry. Her voice cut through the cold air like a blade. 'My child! My child! My golden child!'

The crowd was shaken by the way the woman had cried out for a child who wasn't even her own. The woman began tidying the girl's hair; it looked as though it had only recently been curled. She gazed at her face, at her forever twisted mouth, at her terrible features; in them she could see what only a mother could have seen – the adorable face of the baby who had once smiled at her out of its swaddling clothes.

The woman got to her feet and strode towards the officer. Everyone was struck by the way she kept her eyes fixed on him and yet at the same time managed to find a brick that wasn't part of a great frozen heap – a brick that even her poor hand could pick up, her poor weak hand that had been deformed by years of labour, that had been scalded by boiling water, icy water and lye.

The guard sensed what was about to happen and knew there was nothing he could do to stop the woman; she was stronger than his tommy-gun. The prisoners couldn't take their eyes off her; the children watched her avidly and impatiently.

The woman could no longer see anything at all except the face of the German with the handkerchief round his mouth. Not understanding what was happening to her, governed by a power she had just now seemed to control, she felt in the pocket of her jacket for a piece of bread that had been given to her the evening before by a soldier. She held it out to the German officer and said: 'There, have something to eat.'

Afterwards, she was unable to understand what had happened to her, why she had done this. Her life was to be full of moments of humiliation, helplessness and anger, full of petty cruelties that made her lie awake at night, full of brooding resentment. There was the time she quarrelled with her neighbour who had accused her of stealing a bottle of oil; the time the chairman of the district soviet, not interested in her complaints about life in a communal flat, had her thrown out of his office; the time when her son began manoeuvring to get her out of the room they shared, when his pregnant wife called her an old whore ... At one such moment, lying on her bed, full of bitterness, she was to remember that winter morning outside the cellar and think: 'I was a fool then, and I'm still a fool now.'

49

Alarming reports were reaching Novikov's headquarters from his brigade commanders. Their scouts had located German tank and artillery units that hadn't yet taken part in the fighting. The enemy was evidently bringing up his reserves.

Novikov found this information very disturbing: his forward units were advancing without securing their flanks; if the enemy should succeed in cutting the small number of passable roads, his tanks would be left with no infantry support and no fuel.

Novikov discussed the situation with Getmanov; he considered it essential to call a temporary halt to the tanks' advance and allow the forces in the rear to catch up. Getmanov was still obsessed by the idea that their corps must be the first to enter the Ukraine. In the end they agreed that Getmanov should bring up the rear while Novikov investigated the situation to the west.

Before setting off for the brigades, Novikov phoned Yeremenko's second-in-command and informed him of the situation. He knew in advance what answer he would receive; the second-in-command would never take the responsibility either of calling a halt to their advance, or of ordering them to continue.

The second-in-command said that he would alert Yeremenko and that he would request information from the intelligence service at Front HQ.

Novikov then phoned Molokov, the commander of the infantry corps next door. Molokov was a difficult, bad-tempered man who constantly suspected his neighbours of making unfavourable reports about him to Yeremenko. He and Novikov ended up arguing and even exchanging curses – not, admittedly, directed at each other, but at the widening gap opening up between the tanks and the infantry.

After that, Novikov phoned his neighbour on the left, the commander of an artillery division. He said he didn't intend to advance any further unless he received orders from Front Headquarters. Novikov could understand his point of view: he didn't want merely to play a supporting role to the tanks.

As Novikov was hanging up, Nyeudobnov came in. Novikov had never seen him looking so flustered and anxious.

'Comrade Colonel,' he said, 'I've just had a call from the chief of staff of the air army. They're about to transfer our support aircraft to the left flank.'

'What do you mean?' shouted Novikov. 'They must be out of their minds!'

'There's no mystery about it,' said Nyeudobnov. 'Some people would prefer us not to be the first to enter the Ukraine. There are more than enough men who've got their eyes on the Orders of Suvorov and Bogdan Khmelnitsky. Without air support we have no choice but to call a halt.'

'I'll phone Yeremenko straight away.'

Yeremenko, however, had left for Tolbukhin's army. His second-in-command, whom Novikov had only just phoned, again preferred not to take any decision. He merely expressed surprise that Novikov hadn't yet moved up to his brigades.

'Comrade Lieutenant-General,' said Novikov, 'I fail to understand how you can possibly, without warning, remove all air cover from the corps that has advanced furthest towards the West.'

'Your superiors are better placed than you to decide how best to make use of the support aircraft,' came the angry reply. 'Yours isn't the only corps taking part in this offensive.'

'What am I going to say to my soldiers when the Germans start pounding them?' demanded Novikov. 'How am I going to cover them? With your instructions?'

Instead of losing his temper, the second-in-command adopted a conciliatory tone.

'I'll report the situation to the commander. You set off for your brigades.'

Then Getmanov came in; he had already put on his cap and overcoat. When he saw Novikov, he threw up his hands in astonishment. 'Pyotr Pavlovich, I thought you'd already left.'

His next words were more gentle. 'You say the rear's lagging behind. Well, the officer responsible says we shouldn't be wasting trucks and precious petrol on wounded Germans.' He gave Novikov a meaningful look. 'After all, we're not a section of the Comintern. We're a fighting unit.'

'What on earth's the Comintern got to do with it?'

'Comrade Colonel,' said Nyeudobnov entreatingly, 'it's time you left. Every moment's precious. I'll do everything in my power to sort things out with Headquarters.'

Since his conversation with Darensky, Novikov had been watching Nyeudobnov constantly, following his every movement. 'Not with that very hand? I can't believe it!' he would think to himself as Nyeudobnov took hold of a spoon, speared a piece of pickled cucumber on a fork or picked up the telephone.

Now, though, Novikov had forgotten about all that. He had never seen Nyeudobnov so friendly, so concerned – so likeable even.

Getmanov and Nyeudobnov were ready to sell their souls to the devil if only they could be the first to enter the Ukraine, if only the brigades could continue their advance without delay. But there was one risk they wouldn't run: that of taking responsibility themselves for an action that might lead to a setback.

In spite of himself, Novikov had succumbed to this fever. He too wanted to be able to radio to HQ that his advance units had been the first to cross the frontier. In military terms this meant very little and certainly would not occasion the enemy any particular harm. But Novikov wanted it none the less – for the glory of it, for the Order of

Suvorov, for the rank of general it would certainly assure him. He wanted to be thanked by Yeremenko, to be praised by Vasilevsky, to hear his name over the radio on Stalin's order of the day. He even wanted his neighbours to be jealous of him. Such thoughts and feelings had never governed his acts before; it was perhaps for this very reason that they were now so intense.

There was nothing reprehensible in this ambition of his . . . Everything was the same as in Stalingrad and during 1941: the cold was just as pitiless, the soldiers were still half-dead with exhaustion, death was still as terrifying. And yet the whole spirit of the war was changing.

And Novikov, who hadn't yet understood this, was surprised to find himself in agreement for once with Getmanov and Nyeudobnov. He no longer felt irritated or resentful; he seemed quite naturally to want the same things as they did.

If his tanks advanced faster, the invaders would indeed be driven out of a few Ukrainian villages a few hours sooner. It would make him happy to see the joy on the faces of the children and old men. Some old peasant woman would fling her arms round him as though he were her own son; his eyes would fill with tears.

But, at the same time, new passions were ripening; the spirit of the war was changing. What had been crucial in Stalingrad and during 1941 was coming to be of merely secondary importance. The first person to understand this change was the man who on 3 June, 1941, had said: 'My brothers and sisters, my friends . . .'

Getmanov and Nyeudobnov were egging Novikov on; he shared their excitement, but for some strange reason kept putting off his departure. It was only as he got into his jeep that he realized it was because he was expecting Zhenya.

It was over three weeks since he had heard from her. Each time he made his way back to HQ, he hoped to find Zhenya waiting for him on the steps. She had come to share in his life. She was with him when he talked to his brigade commanders, when he was called to the telephone by Front Headquarters, when he drove up to the front line and felt his tank trembling at the shell-bursts like a young horse. Once, telling Getmanov the story of his childhood, he had felt as though he were telling it to her. He would say to himself: 'God, I really stink of vodka. Zhenya would notice in no time.' Or: 'Now, if only she could see that!'

He had wondered anxiously what she would think if she knew that he had sent a major before the military tribunal. Among the clouds of tobacco smoke and the voices of telephonists in an observation post on the front line, among the gunfire and the exploding bombs, he would be thinking of her . . .

Sometimes he felt jealous of her past. Sometimes he dreamed of her; he would wake up and be unable to get back to sleep. At times he felt sure their love would last for ever; at others he was afraid of being left on his own again.

As he got into his jeep, he glanced round at the road leading back to the Volga; it was deserted. He suddenly thought angrily that she should have arrived long ago. Perhaps she had fallen ill? Once again he remembered the day in 1939 when he had heard the news of her marriage and almost shot himself. Why did he love her? He had had other women who were just as good. Was it a joy or a kind of sickness to think so obsessively about one person? It was a good thing he hadn't got involved with any of the girls on his staff. Yes, he had a clean slate. Though there had been one night three weeks ago . . . What if she stopped on the way and spent the night in that hut? The young woman might start talking to Zhenya. She might describe him and say: 'Yes, that colonel's a splendid fellow!' What nonsense goes through one's head, what nonsense!

50

Novikov returned to his headquarters at noon on the following day. He was aching all over – in the small of his back, in his neck and spine, – after being shaken about on icy, pot-holed roads that had been ploughed up by the treads of tanks. It was as though the soldiers had infected him with their own exhaustion, with the stupefaction they felt after so many days without sleep.

As they drew up, he saw a group of people standing on the porch. There was Yevgenia Nikolaevna standing beside Getmanov, watching the approaching jeep. He felt a flame burning into him, he gasped with a mad joy that was close to pain. He was about to leap out of the still-moving jeep when Vershkov, who was sitting behind him, said:

'So the commissar's taking the air with that doctor of his. We should take a photo of them. That would make his wife happy.'

Novikov went inside. He took the letter held out to him by Getmanov, turned it over, recognized Zhenya's handwriting, and stuffed it into his pocket.

'All right,' he said to Getmanov. 'I'll tell you how I see the situation.'

'But what about the letter? Don't you love her any longer?'

'Thank you. That can wait.'

Nyeudobnov came in and Novikov began.

'The only problem is with the men themselves. They're falling asleep in their tanks during combat. They're worn out. The brigade commanders included. Karpov's not too bad, but Byelov fell asleep while he was talking to me – he hasn't stopped for five days. The drivers and mechanics are falling asleep on the move. They're too exhausted even to eat.'

'But Pyotr Pavlovich,' Getmanov broke in, 'how do you see the general situation?'

'There's no risk of a counter-offensive in our sector. The Germans have lost their nerve. They're taking to their heels as fast as they can.'

As he spoke, he could feel the envelope between his fingers. He let it go for a moment and then quickly grasped it again; he was afraid it might escape from his pocket.

'Very well,' said Getmanov. 'That seems clear enough. Now listen to what I've got to say. The general and I have been right to the top. I spoke to Nikita Sergeyevich himself. He gave his word that we would not lose our air support.'

'But Khrushchev has no direct military authority,' said Novikov.

'Yes and no,' said Getmanov. 'The general's just received confirmation from Air Army Headquarters. The aircraft are staying with us.'

'And the roads aren't bad at all,' said Nyeudobnov hurriedly. 'The forces in the rear will catch up with us in no time. The main thing, comrade Lieutenant-Colonel, is that it's your own decision.'

'Now he's demoting me,' thought Novikov. 'He really must be worried.'

'Yes, gentlemen,' said Getmanov. 'It seems more and more as

though we really will be the ones to begin the liberation of Mother Ukraine. I told Nikita Sergeyevich that our men are besieging their officers, that their greatest dream is to be called "The Ukrainian Corps".'

Novikov felt irritated by this falsehood. 'There's only one thing they're dreaming of,' he said, 'and that's having a few hours' sleep. Do you understand? They've been on the move for five days and five nights.'

'So it's been decided, has it?' said Getmanov. 'We're pressing on. Right?'

Novikov half-opened the envelope, stuck two fingers inside and felt the letter itself. His whole body ached to look again at the familiar handwriting.

'What I've decided,' said Novikov, 'is to call a halt for ten hours. The men need to recover their strength. They need a rest.'

'Ten hours!' said Nyeudobnov. 'We'll throw away everything if we lose ten hours.'

'Wait a moment,' said Getmanov. 'Let's just think about it a little.' His cheeks, his ears, even his neck were slowly turning red.

'I already have thought about it,' said Novikov with a slight laugh.

Getmanov exploded:

'To hell with them all! So what if they haven't had enough sleep! There'll be time enough for them to sleep . . . And you want to call a halt just because of that! You're dithering, Pyotr Pavlovich, and I protest! First you delay the beginning of the offensive. Now you want to put your men to bed. It's becoming quite a habit. I intend to report this to the Military Soviet. Do you think you're in charge of a kindergarten?'

'Wait a moment,' said Novikov. 'Wasn't it you who kissed me for not sending in the tanks until I'd knocked out the enemy artillery? You should put that in your report too.'

'You say I kissed you for that?' said Getmanov in astonishment. 'You must be mad! . . . Let me be quite frank. As a Communist, I feel disturbed that you, a man of the purest proletarian origin, should repeatedly allow yourself to be influenced by alien elements.'

'So it's like that, is it?' said Novikov, raising his voice. 'Very well then.'

He got to his feet, threw back his shoulders and shouted furiously:

'I'm in command here. And what I say goes. As for you, comrade Getmanov, for all I care you can write reports, stories and whole novels about me! And you can send them to whoever you please – even comrade Stalin himself.'

He went through into the adjoining room . . .

Novikov put down the letter he had just read and gave a whistle. He used to whistle like that when he was a little boy. He would stand under his friend's window and whistle to him to come out and play. It was probably a good thirty years since he had whistled like that . . .

Then he looked out through the window. No, it was still light . . . In sudden, hysterical joy he cried out: 'Thank you, thank you, thank you for everything!'

For a moment he thought he was about to fall down dead. He walked up and down the room. He looked again at the letter on his desk. It was like a white, sloughed-off skin that a viper had just crawled out of. He put his hands to his chest and his sides. The viper wasn't there. It must have crawled inside him already. It must be burning his heart with poison.

He stood for a moment by the window. The drivers were laughing as they watched Marusya the telephonist walk past to the lavatory. The driver of the staff tank was carrying a bucket from the well. Sparrows were busying themselves in the straw beside the entrance to the cow-shed. Zhenya had once said that sparrows were her favourite bird . . . And now he was on fire – just like a house. The beams had given way. The ceiling was falling in. Cups and plates were crashing to the floor. Cupboards were toppling over. Books and pillows were tumbling about, flying through the smoke and the sparks like birds . . . 'I shall be grateful all my life for everything pure and noble that you have given me. But what can I do? The past is stronger than I am. I can't kill it, I can't forget it . . . Don't blame me – not because I'm not guilty, but because neither of us know quite what I am guilty of . . . Forgive me, forgive me, I'm crying for us both.'

So she was crying, was she! Novikov felt a sudden fury. The filthy bitch! The snake! He wanted to punch her on the jaw, in the eyes. He wanted to crack that whore's nose of hers with the butt of his revolver . . .

Suddenly, unbearably suddenly, he felt helpless. There was nothing in the whole world that could help him, only Zhenya, and she had destroyed him . . .

He looked in the direction she should have been coming from and said: 'What have you done to me, Zhenechka? Can you hear me? Look at me, Zhenechka! Look what you've done to me!'

He stretched out his hands to her. Then he thought: 'All this is a waste of time.' Yes, he had waited all those years, but now she had made up her mind. She wasn't a little girl. She had dragged it out for years, but now she had made up her mind. She had made up her mind – he must try to understand that.

A few minutes later he was again trying to find refuge in hatred: 'No, no, of course you didn't want me when I was an acting major in Nikolsk-Ussuriysk. But it was another story when I was promoted. You wanted to be the wife of a general. Well, women are all the same . . .' He soon realized what nonsense this was. She had left him for a man who was on his way to a camp, to Kolyma. What would she get out of that . . . ? '"Russian women" – a poem by Nekrasov.* She doesn't love me, she loves him. No, she doesn't love him, she pities him. It's just that she pities him. But doesn't she have any pity for me? No one in the Lubyanka, no one in the camps, no one in hospital with a missing arm or leg can be more unhappy than I am. Very well, I'll go to a camp myself. Which of us will you choose then? Him! You two are the same breed, but I'm a stranger. That's what you called me – a stranger. Yes, I'll always be a peasant, a miner. Even if I become a marshal, I'll still never be an intellectual. I'll still never be able to make head or tail of all that painting of yours . . .'

In a loud hate-filled voice he asked: 'But why? Why?'

He took his pistol out of his back pocket and weighed it in the palm of his hand. 'I'm going to shoot myself. And not because I can't live without you – but to torment you with guilt. You whore!'

He put his pistol back in its place.

'She'll have forgotten me in a week.'

No, he was the one who needed to forget. He mustn't look back. He mustn't give her another thought.

He went up to the table and began to read the letter again. 'My

* A poem in celebration of the wives of the Decembrist conspirators, who followed their exiled husbands to Siberia.

dearest, my poor darling . . .' It wasn't the cruel words that hurt, it was the ones that were full of pity, full of affectionate, humiliating pity. He felt as though he could hardly breathe.

He could see her breasts, her shoulders, her knees. There she was – on her way to that wretched Krymov. 'But what can I do?' She was travelling in a crowded, airless wagon. Someone asked her a question and she answered: 'To join my husband.' She had the sad, docile eyes of a dog.

And he had looked out of this very window to see if she was on her way to him. His shoulders shook. He sniffed and gave a kind of bark; he was choking back his terrible sobs. He remembered how he'd ordered some chocolate and nougat from the Front Commissariat. 'Don't you dare touch them,' he'd said to Vershkov, 'or it'll be the end of you!'

Once again he muttered: 'See what you've done to me, my Zhenechka, my little one! You might have some pity!'

He suddenly dragged his suitcase out from under the bed. He took out Zhenya's letters and photos – the ones he'd been carrying around for years, the one she'd sent in her last letter, and the very first, cellophane-wrapped passport photo – and began tearing them to shreds with his large, powerful fingers. On tiny shreds of paper he recognized words he had read hundreds of times, words that had made his head spin. He watched her face, her neck, her eyes, her lips, all slowly disappear. He was working as fast as he could. When it was done he felt better; he felt as though he had eradicated her, as though he had stamped out the last trace of her, as though he had freed himself from a witch.

He had lived without her before. He could get over it! In a year or so he'd be able to walk straight past her without his heart so much as missing a beat. He needed her as much as a drunk needs a cork! But he understood all too quickly how vain these thoughts were. How can you tear something out of your heart? Your heart isn't made out of paper and your life isn't written down in ink. You can't erase the imprint of years.

He had allowed her to share in his thoughts, in his work, in his troubles. He had allowed her to witness his strengths and his weaknesses . . .

And the torn-up letters hadn't disappeared. The words he had read hundreds of times were still in his memory. Her eyes were still gazing at him from the photographs.

He opened the cupboard door and poured out a large glass of vodka. He drank it down and lit a cigarette. He lit it a second time – though it hadn't gone out. His head was full of clamouring grief; his insides were on fire.

'Zhenechka, my dearest, my little one, what have you done, what have you done, how could you?'

He stuffed the torn shreds of paper back into the suitcase, put the bottle back in the cupboard and thought: 'Well, that's a little better.'

Soon his tanks would reach the Donbass. He would visit the village where he had been born and the spot where his old people had been buried. His father would be proud of his Petya now; his mother would be full of pity for her unfortunate little son. When the war came to an end, he would go and live with his brother's family. His little niece would say: 'Uncle Petya, why are you so quiet?'

He suddenly remembered a moment from his childhood. The dog had gone off after a bitch on heat and had come back all chewed up. He had a torn ear, his mouth was crooked, one eye was half-closed because of a swelling, and tufts of his long hair had been torn out. He had stood there by the porch, his tail between his legs. Petya's father had looked at him and said good-naturedly: 'So you were just the best man, were you?'

Vershkov came in.

'Are you having a rest, comrade Colonel?'

'Just for a few minutes.'

He looked at his watch and thought: 'All brigades to halt until seven o'clock tomorrow morning. To be transmitted in code.'

'I'm going to visit the brigades again,' he told Vershkov.

A fast drive was a welcome distraction. They were going at eighty kilometres an hour on an appalling road. The jeep swayed wildly as it careered over the pot-holes. The driver kept looking at Novikov pathetically, begging to be allowed to drive more slowly.

They reached the headquarters of the 1st brigade. How everything had changed in only a few hours! How Makarov had changed – it was as though they hadn't seen each other for years.

Quite forgetting the usual formalities, Makarov threw up his hands in bewilderment and said: 'Comrade Colonel, Getmanov has just transmitted an order direct from Yeremenko. Your own order has been rescinded and we're to press on with the offensive immediately.'

51

Three weeks later Novikov's tank corps was withdrawn from the front line and placed in reserve. It was time to overhaul the tanks and bring the brigades up to their full strength. Both men and tanks were exhausted after covering four hundred kilometres, fighting all the way.

At the same time Novikov received a summons from Moscow. He was to report to the General Staff and to the Central Administration for Senior Field Ranks. It was uncertain whether or not he would be returning to his command.

During his absence General Nyeudobnov was to take over the command. A few days before this Getmanov heard that the Central Committee had decided to retire him from active service. He was to be appointed secretary of the *obkom* in a newly-liberated part of the Donbass; this was a post to which the Central Committee attached particular importance.

Novikov's summons provoked considerable discussion both at Front Headquarters and at the Armoured Forces Administration. Some people made out that it was of no great import, that Novikov would soon resume his command. Others argued that it had to do with Novikov's delay at the beginning of the offensive and his unfortunate decision, at the very climax of the offensive, to call a ten-hour halt in order to rest his men. Still others claimed that it was the result of his failure to establish good relations with his commissar and his chief of staff – both of whom had excellent records.

The secretary of the Front Military Soviet, a man who was usually well-informed, said it had to do with compromising ties of a personal nature. At one time he too had thought that Novikov's misfortunes stemmed from his disagreements with his commissar. But this was not the case: he had seen with his own eyes a letter of Getmanov's addressed to the very highest authorities. In this letter Getmanov protested strongly against Novikov's removal from the command. He said that Novikov was a commanding officer of outstanding abilities and a man who was both morally and politically above reproach.

The strangest thing of all was that, when he received this summons, Novikov had his first good night's sleep after weeks of painful insomnia.

52

Viktor felt as though he were being carried along at great speed by a roaring train; he found it difficult even to remember the quiet of his own house. Time had become quite dense, full of people, events and telephone calls. It already seemed ten years since Shishakov had called round. He had been attentive and friendly, full of questions about Viktor's health and all kinds of explanations. He had hinted gently that the events of the past weeks were best forgotten.

Viktor had imagined that the people who had tried to destroy him would now be too ashamed even to look at him. Instead, they greeted him joyfully on his return to the Institute, looking him straight in the eye as they expressed their heartfelt goodwill. The most extraordinary thing of all was that these people were quite sincere; now, they really did wish Viktor well.

Once again Viktor heard his work praised. Malenkov called him for an interview, looked straight at him with his quick black eyes and talked to him for the best part of an hour. Viktor was surprised at how familiar Malenkov was with his work and how easily he handled technical terms.

If this was surprising, Malenkov's last words were astonishing: 'We would be deeply regretful if anything at all were to hinder you in your work. We understand very well that there can be no practice without theory.'

Viktor really hadn't expected that.

He found it very strange, on the following day, to see the anxious, questioning look with which Shishakov greeted him and at the same time remember the anger and humiliation he had felt when Shishakov had failed to invite him to the meeting held in his house.

Markov was warm and friendly, Savostyanov as witty as ever. Gurevich came into the laboratory and embraced him, saying: 'I am glad to see you! I really am! You must be Benjamin the Fortunate!'

Yes, Viktor was still on the train.

He was asked whether he considered it necessary to expand his laboratory into an independent research institute. He was flown to the Urals by special plane, together with a Deputy People's Commissar. He was allocated a special car which Lyudmila used to go to the store, giving lifts to women who had previously pretended not to recognize her.

Everything that had once seemed impossibly complicated and confusing now happened all by itself.

Young Landesman was deeply moved. Kovchenko phoned him at home and within an hour Dubyonkov had arranged for him to be taken onto the staff of Viktor's laboratory.

On her return from Kazan, Anna Naumovna Weisspapier told Viktor that all her documentation had been arranged within two days and that Kovchenko had even arranged for a car to meet her at the station in Moscow. Anna Stepanovna had been informed by Dubyonkov in writing that she had been reinstated in her former post and that the deputy director had decided she should be paid in full for the weeks she was absent.

The new employees were constantly being fed. They said jokingly that their work was simply a matter of letting themselves be ferried, all day long, from one special canteen to another. Needless to say, this was far from the truth.

The new apparatus in Viktor's laboratory no longer seemed quite so perfect. He had the feeling that in a year's time it might seem slightly comic, like Stephenson's 'Rocket'.

What had happened in Viktor's life seemed at once both natural and unnatural. His work really was interesting and important – why shouldn't it be praised? Landesman had a talent for research – why shouldn't he work in the Institute? Anna Naumovna was indeed irreplaceable – why should she have to hang around in Kazan?

Still, Viktor knew very well that, but for Stalin's telephone call, his research – for all its excellence – would have been forgotten; and Landesman – for all his talent – would still be unemployed. But then Stalin's telephone call was no accident; it was no mere whim or caprice. Stalin was the embodiment of the State – and the State has no whims or caprices.

Viktor had been afraid that all his time would be taken up with administrative matters – plans, conferences, taking on new staff, placing orders for new equipment . . . But the cars he travelled in were fast, the meetings he attended began punctually and moved swiftly to a conclusion, and all his wishes were immediately granted. As a result, Viktor was able to spend the entire morning – the time when he did his best work – in perfect freedom in his laboratory. No one disturbed him; he was able to concentrate exclusively on his own interests. His work still belonged to him. It was all a far cry from what happened to the artist in Gogol's 'The Portrait'.

He had been even more afraid that other people might encroach on his own field. This fear also proved groundless. 'I really am absolutely free,' he said to himself in surprise.

He thought once of what Artelev had said in Kazan about military factories: how well-provided they were with raw materials, energy and machine-tools, and how free from bureaucratic interference.

'Yes,' thought Viktor. 'It is in its own absence that bureaucracy reveals itself most clearly. Whatever serves the principal aims of the State is rushed along at great speed. Bureaucracy can have two opposite effects: it can halt any movement or it can speed it up to an incredible degree – as though freeing it from the constraints of gravity.'

Not that Viktor thought often about those long conversations in that small room in Kazan. He no longer thought of Madyarov as someone remarkably intelligent and altogether exceptional. He no longer felt a constant anxiety over his fate. He was no longer obsessed by the terrible mutual suspicions harboured by him and Karimov.

Without his realizing it, everything that had happened to him began to seem quite normal, quite natural. His new life was the rule; he had begun to get used to it. It was his past life that had been the exception, and slowly he began to forget what it had been like. Was there really any truth in those reflections of Artelev's?

In the past Viktor had felt nervous and irritated as soon as he crossed the threshold of the personnel department, as soon as he felt Dubyonkov even look at him. In fact, Dubyonkov was very decent and obliging. When he phoned Viktor, he said: 'Dubyonkov speaking. I hope I'm not disturbing you, Viktor Pavlovich?'

Viktor had always regarded Kovchenko as a sinister and treacherous intriguer who would happily annihilate anyone who stood in his way; he had seemed to come from another world – a world of mysterious unwritten instructions – and to be profoundly indifferent to science itself. In fact he was not like this at all. He came round to Viktor's laboratory every day; he was a true democrat and he didn't stand on his dignity at all. He joked with Anna Naumovna, shook everyone by the hand and chatted with the technicians and metalworkers; it turned out that he had operated a lathe himself in his youth.

Shishakov was someone Viktor had disliked for years. Then one day he had lunch at his house and discovered that Shishakov was witty, hospitable, a gourmet and a fine raconteur; he enjoyed good cognac and he collected engravings. And – most important of all – he appreciated the importance of Viktor's theory.

'I've triumphed!' thought Viktor. But he knew very well that it was not an absolute victory: if the people around him now treated him differently, if they now helped rather than hindered him, it certainly wasn't because he had won their hearts with his great charm, intelligence and talent.

Nevertheless, Viktor rejoiced. He had triumphed!

There were special news bulletins on the radio nearly every evening. The Soviet offensive was still continuing. To Viktor, it seemed quite natural to link the course of his own life with that of the war, with the victory of the people and the army, the victory of the State. At the same time he knew that it wasn't really quite so simple. He was quite capable of laughing at his childish habit of always wanting to see everything in black and white: 'Stalin's done this, Stalin's done that, glory to Stalin!'

He had thought that important administrators and Party officials never talked about anything, even with their families, except the ideological purity of their cadres. He had thought they did nothing except sign papers in red pencil, read *A Short Course in the History of the Party* out loud to their wives, and dream of temporary rulings and obligatory instructions. Now he had unexpectedly discovered that they had a human side too.

Ramskov, the Secretary of the Institute Party Committee, turned out to be a keen fisherman. Before the war he had gone on a boating holiday in the Urals, together with his wife and his sons.

'What more can one ask for, Viktor Pavlovich?' he would say. 'You get up at dawn. Everything's glittering with dew, and the sand on the bank's still cold. Then you cast your lines. The water's black. It's not giving anything away, but it's full of promises . . . Wait till the war's over – then you can become one of us yourself!'

Kovchenko once talked to Viktor about childhood illnesses. Viktor was surprised how much he knew about the different treatments for rickets and tonsillitis. He had two children of his own and had also adopted a little Spanish boy. This boy was always falling ill and Kovchenko looked after him himself.

Even dry old Svechin talked to him about his collection of cacti and how he'd managed to save them from the terrible frosts during the winter of 1941.

'They're really not such bad people after all,' he thought. 'I suppose everyone has something human about them.'

Deep down, of course, Viktor understood that nothing had really changed. He was neither a fool nor a cynic; he could think for himself.

He remembered a story of Krymov's about an old comrade of his, Bagryanov, a senior investigator in the Military Prosecutor's Office. Bagryanov had been arrested in 1937 and then, during the brief spell of liberalism under Beria in 1939, had been released from the camp and allowed to return to Moscow.

Krymov had described how, one night, Bagryanov had turned up on his doorstep; he had come straight from the station and his trousers and shirt were in tatters. In his pocket was his certificate of release from the camp.

That night, Bagryanov had been full of seditious speeches and sympathy for the other prisoners; he had intended to set up as a gardener and a bee-keeper. But as he was allowed to return to his former life, his speeches gradually began to change.

Krymov had laughed as he described the slow evolution of Bagryanov's ideology. First he was given back his military uniform; at that time his views were still liberal, but he was no longer a raging Danton. Then, in exchange for his certificate of release, he was given a passport allowing him to live in Moscow. He immediately began to take up the Hegelian position: 'All that is real, is rational.' Then he was given back his flat – and began making out that most of the prisoners in the camps really were enemies of the people. Then his medals were returned to him. Finally he was reinstated in the Party without loss of seniority.

It was just then that Krymov's own difficulties had begun. Bagryanov stopped ringing him up. Krymov had met him by chance one day; he had two decorations on his tunic collar and he was getting out of a special car by the entrance to the Public Prosecutor's Office. This was only eight months after the night when a man in a torn shirt, with a certificate from a labour camp in his pocket, had sat in Krymov's room holding forth about innocent victims and blind violence.

'I thought then that he was lost to the Public Prosecutor's Office for ever,' Krymov had said with a wry smile.

It wasn't for nothing that Viktor remembered this story and recounted it to Nadya and Lyudmila. Nothing had changed in his attitude towards the victims of 1937. He was still as appalled as ever at the cruelty of Stalin. He knew very well that life hadn't changed for other people simply because he was now Fortune's pet instead of her stepson. Nothing would ever bring back to life the victims of collectivization or the people who had been shot in 1937; it made no difference to them whether or not prizes and medals were awarded to a certain Shtrum, whether he was called to see Malenkov or was pointedly not invited to a gathering at Shishakov's.

And yet something *had* changed, both in his understanding and in his actual memory of things.

[....]

Often Viktor would make little speeches to his wife.

'What a lot of nonentities there are everywhere! How afraid people are to defend their honour! How easily they give in! What miserable compromises they make!'

On one occasion he even attacked Chepyzhin: 'His passion for travelling and mountaineering conceals an unconscious fear of the complexity of life. And his resignation from the Institute reveals a conscious fear of confronting the most important question of our time.'

Yes, something was changing in him. He could feel it, but he didn't know what it was.

53

On his return to work, Viktor found Sokolov absent from the laboratory. He had caught pneumonia two days before.

Viktor learnt that before his illness he and Shishakov had agreed that he should be transferred to a different post. In the end he had been appointed director of another laboratory that was currently being reorganized. Evidently he was doing well.

Even the omniscient Markov was ignorant of the true reasons behind Sokolov's request to be transferred. Viktor felt no regret: he found it painful to think of meeting Sokolov, let alone working with him.

Who knows what Sokolov would have read in Viktor's eyes? Certainly Viktor had no right to think as he did about the wife of his friend. He had no right to be longing for her. He had no right to meet her in secret. If he'd heard a similar story about someone else, he'd have felt quite indignant. Deceiving one's wife! Deceiving a friend! But he did long for her. He did dream of meeting her.

Lyudmila and Marya Ivanovna were now seeing each other again. They had had a long telephone conversation and then met. They had both cried, each accusing herself of meanness, suspiciousness and lack of faith in their friendship.

How complicated life was! Marya Ivanovna, pure honest Marya Ivanovna, had been insincere and deceitful with Lyudmila. But only because of her love for him!

Viktor very seldom saw Marya Ivanovna now. Most of what he knew about her came from Lyudmila.

He learnt that Sokolov had been proposed for a Stalin Prize on the strength of some papers he had published before the war; that he had received an enthusiastic letter from some young physicists in England; that he might be chosen as a corresponding member of the Academy at the next elections. All this was what Marya Ivanovna told Lyudmila.

During his own brief meetings with her he never so much as mentioned Pyotr Lavrentyevich.

His work in the laboratory, his journeys and meetings were never enough to take his mind off her; he wanted to see her the whole time.

Lyudmila said several times: 'You know, I just don't understand what Sokolov's got against you now. Even Masha can't explain it.'

The explanation, of course, was simple enough, but it was impossible for Marya Ivanovna to share it with Lyudmila. It was quite enough that she had told her husband of her feelings for Viktor.

This confession had destroyed the friendship between Viktor and Sokolov for ever. She had promised her husband not to go on seeing Viktor. If she were to say one word to Lyudmila, she would be cut off from Viktor completely; he wouldn't know where she was or what she was doing. They met so seldom as it was. And their meetings were so brief. They spoke very little even when they did meet; they just walked down the street arm in arm or sat in silence on a park bench.

At the time of Viktor's troubles she had understood his feelings with a quite extraordinary sensitivity. She had been able to guess what he would think and what he would do; she had seemed able to anticipate all that was about to happen to him. The gloomier he had felt, the more passionately he had longed to see her. This perfect understanding of hers had seemed to him to be his only happiness. He had felt that with her beside him he could easily bear all his sufferings. With her he could be happy.

They had talked together one night in Kazan, they had gone for a walk in a Moscow park, they had sat together for a few moments in a square off Kaluga Street – and that was all. And then there was the present: a few telephone calls and a few brief meetings he hadn't told Lyudmila about.

Viktor knew, however, that his sin and her sin couldn't be measured by the number of minutes they had sat together on a bench. His was no mean sin: he loved her. How had she come to occupy such an important place in his life?

Every word he said to his wife was partly a lie. He couldn't help it; there was something deceitful in his every movement, in every look he gave her.

With affected indifference, he would ask her: 'Well, did your friend ring today? How is she? And is Pyotr Lavrentyevich well?'

He felt glad at Sokolov's successes, but not because he felt any goodwill towards him. No, it was because he felt it gave Marya Ivanovna the right not to feel guilty.

He found it unbearable to hear about Sokolov and Marya Ivanovna only through Lyudmila. It was humiliating for Lyudmila, for Marya Ivanovna, and for himself. He was conscious of something false even when he talked to Lyudmila about Nadya, Tolya and Alexandra Vladimirovna. There were lies everywhere. Why was this? How had it happened? His love for Marya Ivanovna was the deepest truth of his soul. How could it have given birth to so many lies?

It was only by renouncing his love that he could deliver himself, Lyudmila and Marya Ivanovna from these lies. But when he realized this was what he had to do, he was dissuaded by a treacherous fear that clouded his judgement: 'This lie isn't so very terrible. What harm does it do anyone? Suffering is more terrible than lying.'

And when he felt he was strong and ruthless enough to break with Lyudmila and ruin Sokolov's life, this same treacherous fear egged him on with a contradictory argument: 'Nothing can be worse than deceit. It would be better to break with Lyudmila altogether than to go on lying to her all the time. And making Marya Ivanovna lie to her. Deceit is more terrible than suffering.'

Viktor wasn't aware that his intelligence was now merely the obedient servant of his emotions and that there was only one way of escaping from this circle of confusion – by using the knife, by sacrificing himself rather than others.

The more he thought about it all, the less he understood. How could he unravel this tangle? How could his love for Marya Ivanovna be the truth of his life and at the same time be its greatest lie? Only last summer he had had an affair with the beautiful Nina. And they had done more than just walk round the square like schoolchildren who had fallen in love. But it was only now that he felt a sense of guilt and betrayal, a sense of having done wrong to his family.

All this consumed an incalculable amount of emotional and intellectual energy, probably as much as Planck had expended in elaborating his quantum theory.

He had once thought that his love had been born only of sorrow and tragedy . . . But now he was on the crest of the wave – and he needed Marya Ivanovna as much as ever.

She was unlike everyone else; she wasn't attracted in the least by power, riches and fame. She had wanted to share his grief, anxiety and deprivation . . . Would she turn away from him now?

He knew that Marya Ivanovna worshipped Pyotr Lavrentyevich. Sometimes this drove him almost insane.

Yevgenia was probably right. This second love, born after years of married life, must be the result of a vitamin deficiency of the soul. He was like a cow licking salt after searching for it for years in grass, hay and the leaves of trees. This hunger of the soul grew very slowly, but in the end it was irresistible. Yes, that's what it was. A hunger of the soul . . . Marya Ivanovna was indeed startlingly different from Lyudmila.

Was all this really so? Viktor didn't realize that these thoughts had nothing to do with his reason; that their truth or falsehood had nothing to do with how he acted. If he didn't see Marya Ivanovna, he was unhappy; if he knew he was going to see her, he was happy. And when he imagined a future in which they were inseparably together, he felt still more happy.

Why didn't he feel a twinge of guilt about Sokolov? Why did he feel no shame?

But what was there to be ashamed of? All they had done was walk through a park and sit down for a while on a bench.

No, it wasn't just a matter of sitting on a bench. He was ready to break with Lyudmila. He was ready to tell Sokolov that he loved his wife and wanted to take her from him.

He remembered everything that had gone wrong between him and Lyudmila: how badly she had treated his mother; how she had refused to let his cousin stay the night after his release from camp; how rude and callous, how cruel and obstinate she had sometimes been.

All this made him feel callous himself. And that was what he needed to feel, if he was to be ruthless. But Lyudmila had spent her life with him; she had shared all his troubles and difficulties. Her hair was going grey; she had suffered. Was there really nothing good in her? He had been proud of her in the past; he had loved her strength and honesty. Yes, he was simply nerving himself to be ruthless.

As he was getting ready to go out in the morning, Viktor remembered Yevgenia's visit and thought: 'All the same, it's a good thing she's back in Kuibyshev.'

Just then, as Viktor was feeling ashamed at being so mean,

Lyudmila said: 'So now Nikolay's been arrested as well. How many of our family does that make? At least Yevgenia's not in Moscow any more.'

Viktor wanted to reproach her, but stopped himself in time – that would have been too dishonest.

'Oh yes, Chepyzhin phoned,' said Lyudmila.

Viktor looked at his watch.

'I'll be back early this evening. I'll ring him then. By the way, I'm probably going to the Urals again.'

'Will you be there long?'

'No. Just two or three days.'

He was in a hurry. Today was an important day.

His work was important – even to the State – but his private thoughts were mean, petty and trivial. It was as though they were in inverse proportion.

As she was leaving, Yevgenia had asked Lyudmila to go to Kuznetsky Most and hand over two hundred roubles for Krymov.

'Lyudmila,' said Viktor. 'Don't forget the money Zhenya gave you. I think you've left it too late already.'

He didn't say this because he was worried on behalf of Krymov or Yevgenia; he said it because he was afraid that Lyudmila's negligence might bring Yevgenia back to Moscow again. Then she would start making telephone calls, sending off petitions and statements . . . In the end his flat would be nothing but a centre for agitation on behalf of political prisoners.

Viktor knew he was being both petty and cowardly. Feeling ashamed of himself, he said hurriedly: 'You must write to Zhenya. Invite her to stay in my name. Maybe she needs to come to Moscow but feels awkward about asking. Yes, Lyuda. Write to her straight away.'

He felt better after that, but then he knew it was only for his own peace of mind that he'd said it . . . How strange everything was . . . When he'd just sat in his room all day, a pariah afraid even of the house-manager and the girl at the rations desk, his head had been full of thoughts about life, truth and freedom, thoughts about God . . . That was when no one had wanted him, when the telephone had been silent for weeks on end and people had ignored him if they passed him on the street. But now, when dozens of people waited on him, phoning him up and writing to him, when a Zis-101 came to pick him up and hooted discreetly beneath the window, now he found it impossible to shed himself of petty anxieties, trivial irritations and thoughts that were emptier than the husks of sunflower seeds. He'd said the wrong thing then, he'd laughed at the wrong moment there – yes, he was obsessed by trivia.

For a while after Stalin's telephone call, he had thought that he need never know fear again. But it was still there; only its outer trappings had changed. Now it was simply a more aristocratic fear, a fear that travelled by car and was allowed to use the Kremlin telephone switchboard.

And what had once been unimaginable – an attitude of envious rivalry towards the achievements and theories of other scientists – had begun to seem quite normal. He was like an athlete – afraid of being overtaken, afraid that someone might beat his record.

He didn't really want to talk to Chepyzhin now; he didn't have the strength for what would be a long and difficult conversation. He and Chepyzhin had oversimplified when they talked about the dependence of science on the State. He himself was quite free; no one any longer thought of his theories as absurdities straight out of the Talmud. No one dared attack them now. The State needed theoretical physics; Badin and Shishakov understood that now. For Markov to show his true talent for setting up experiments, for Kochkurov to show his talent for seeing their practical applications, you needed a theoretician. Now, after Stalin's telephone call, that was generally understood. But how could he explain to Dmitry Petrovich that this telephone call had brought him freedom? Why had he suddenly become so intolerant of Lyudmila's failings? And why was he now so well-disposed towards Shishakov?

He had grown particularly fond of Markov – perhaps because he had now become genuinely interested in the personal lives of his bosses, in everything secret or half-secret, in every act of harmless cunning or outright treachery, in all the various humiliations arising from invitations or absence of invitations to the Presidium, in who figured on a special list or who merely heard the fateful words: 'You're not on the list.' Yes, he would much sooner spend a free evening chatting with Markov than be arguing with Madyarov at one of their Kazan gatherings.

Markov had an extraordinarily sharp eye for people's absurdities; he could make fun of their weaknesses lethally but without malice. His mind was very elegant and he was a first-class scientist. He was possibly the most talented experimental physicist in the country.

Viktor already had his coat on when Lyudmila said: 'Marya Ivanovna phoned yesterday.'

'Yes?' said Viktor immediately.

His face must have changed.

'What's the matter?' asked Lyudmila.

'Nothing. Nothing at all,' he said, coming back into the room.

'I didn't quite understand. Some unpleasantness at the Institute. I think Kovchenko phoned them. Anyway it's the usual story. She's worried about you. She's afraid you're going to put your foot in it again.'

'How?' asked Viktor impatiently. 'I don't understand.'

'I don't understand myself. I've already told you. She evidently didn't want to go into it at length on the phone.'

'Tell me all that again,' said Viktor. He unbuttoned his coat and sat down on a chair by the door.

Lyudmila looked at him, shaking her head from side to side. He thought her eyes seemed sad and reproachful. As though to confirm this, Lyudmila said: 'Vitya, Vitya . . . You didn't have time to phone Chepyzhin, but you're always ready to hear about dear Masha, aren't you? I thought you were late.'

Viktor gave her an odd, sideways look and said: 'Yes, I am late.'

He went up to her, took her hand and kissed it. She patted him on the head and ruffled his hair.

'You see how interesting and important Masha's become,' said Lyudmila quietly. She gave a wry smile and added: 'The same Masha who couldn't tell the difference between Balzac and Flaubert.'

Viktor looked at her: her eyes were moist, her lips almost trembling.

He shrugged his shoulders helplessly and walked out. In the doorway he turned round again.

He felt quite shaken by the look on Lyudmila's face. It was a look of utter exhaustion, touching helplessness, and shame – both on his behalf and on her own. On his way down the stairs, he thought that, if he were to break with Lyudmila and never see her again, he would remember that look until his dying day. He realized that something very important had just happened: his wife had informed him that she knew of his love for Marya Ivanovna and he had confirmed it.

All he knew for sure was that, if he saw Masha, he felt happy, and if he promised himself never to see her again, he felt he could hardly breathe.

As Viktor's car arrived at the Institute, Shishakov's drew up alongside it. The two cars stopped by the door almost simultaneously.

Viktor and Shishakov then walked side by side down the corridor. Shishakov took Viktor by the arm. 'Are you going to the Urals then?'

'I think so.'

'Soon we'll be saying goodbye for good. You'll become an independent sovereign,' said Shishakov with a smile.

'What if I ask if he's ever been in love with someone else's wife?' thought Viktor suddenly.

'Viktor Pavlovich,' said Shishakov, 'can you come round to my office about two o'clock?'

'Certainly. I'll be free by then.'

Viktor found it hard to concentrate on his work that morning.

In the laboratory Markov came up to him in his shirt-sleeves and said excitedly: 'If you'll allow me, Viktor Pavlovich, I'll come and see you a bit later. I've got something interesting to tell you.'

'I'm seeing Shishakov at two,' said Viktor. 'Come round after that. I've got something to tell you myself.'

'You're seeing Aleksey Alekseyevich,' said Markov thoughtfully. 'I think I know what about.'

54

Seeing Viktor come in, Shishakov said: 'I was just going to phone and remind you of our metting.'

Viktor looked at his watch. 'I'm not late, am I?'

Shishakov looked quite enormous as he stood there in his grey suit, his huge head covered in silvery hair. But his eyes no longer seemed cold and arrogant; they were more like the eyes of a little boy brought up on Dumas and Mayne Reid.

'My dear Viktor Pavlovich, I've got something important to discuss with you,' said Shishakov with a smile. He took Viktor by the arm and led him towards an easy chair.

'It's something very serious and rather unpleasant.'

'Well,' said Viktor, looking mournfully round the office, 'let's get down to it then.'

'What's happened,' Shishakov began, 'is that a disgusting campaign's been started up abroad, mainly in England. In spite of the fact that we're bearing nearly the whole weight of the war on our own shoulders, certain English scientists – instead of demanding the immediate opening of a Second Front – have begun an extraordinary campaign with the aim of arousing hostility towards the Soviet Union.'

He looked Viktor straight in the eye. Viktor knew this open, frank look; it was characteristic of people who were doing something dishonest.

'I see, I see,' he said. 'But what exactly is this campaign?'

'A campaign of slanders,' said Shishakov. 'They've published a list of Soviet writers and scientists they allege to have been shot. They're making out that some quite fantastic number of people have been imprisoned for political reasons. With extraordinary – and really very suspicious – vehemence, they contest the verdict – established by due process of law – on Doctors Pletnyov and Levin, the assassins of Aleksey Maximovich Gorky. All this has been published in a newspaper close to government circles.'

'I see, I see,' said Viktor. 'And is that it?'

'More or less. There's also something about the geneticist Chetverikov. A committee's been established for his defence.'

'But my dear Aleksey Alekseyevich, Chetverikov *has* been arrested.'

Shishakov shrugged his shoulders.

'As I'm sure you're aware, Viktor Pavlovich, I know nothing about the workings of the security organs. But if, as you say, he has been arrested, then it must be with good reason. You and I haven't been arrested, have we?'

Just then Badin and Kovchenko came in. Shishakov was evidently expecting them; Viktor realized they must have arranged this beforehand. Without stopping to put them in the picture, Shishakov just said: 'Sit down comrades, sit down!' and turned back to Viktor.

'So, Viktor Pavlovich, these slanders have now reached America and been published in the pages of the *New York Times*. This, naturally, has aroused indignation among the Soviet intelligentsia.'

'Of course,' said Kovchenko. 'What else could one expect?'

He looked directly at Viktor. His own brown eyes seemed so warm and friendly that Viktor was unable to come out with the thought that had immediately occurred to him: 'How can the Soviet intelligentsia be so indignant if they've never once set eyes on the *New York Times*?'

He grunted and shrugged his shoulders. This, he was aware, could be taken as a sign of agreement.

'Naturally,' Shishakov went on, 'a desire has arisen to refute these calumnies. And so we have drawn up a document.'

'You haven't done anything of the sort,' thought Viktor. 'You weren't even present when it was drawn up.'

'This document is in the form of a letter.'

'I've read it myself,' added Badin in a quiet voice. 'It's just what's needed. We want to have it signed by a small number of our most important scientists, people who are known in Europe and America.'

Viktor had known right from the beginning what all this was leading up to. What he hadn't known was the precise form Shishakov's request would take; whether he'd be asked to write an article, to make a speech at the Scientific Council, to vote . . . Now it was clear: they wanted his signature at the foot of a letter.

He began to feel sick. It was just like when they'd wanted him to make a public confession; he suddenly felt miserable, base, pathetic.

Once again, millions of tons of granite were about to come down on his shoulders . . . Professor Pletnyov! Viktor remembered an article in *Pravda*, written by some hysterical woman, full of wild accusations against the old doctor. To begin with, as so often, he had believed it all. Gogol, Tolstoy, Chekhov and Korolenko appeared to have instilled in Russians an almost religious reverence for the printed word. Finally, however, Viktor had realized that it was a calumny.

Pletnyov had then been arrested, together with Levin – another famous doctor from the Kremlin hospital. The two of them confessed to having murdered Aleksey Maximovich Gorky.

The three men were all looking at Viktor. Their eyes were warm, friendly and trusting. They accepted him as one of them. Shishakov looked on him as a brother; he understood the immense significance of Viktor's work. Kovchenko looked up to him. Badin's eyes said: 'Yes, everything you did and said seemed alien to me. But I was wrong. I didn't understand. The Party corrected me.'

Kovchenko opened a red file and handed Viktor a typewritten letter.

'Let me say one thing, Viktor Pavlovich. This Anglo-American campaign plays straight into the hands of the Fascists. It's probably the work of those swine in the Fifth Column.'

'There's no need to go on at Viktor Pavlovich,' Badin interrupted. 'He's as much a patriot as any of us. He's a Russian. A true Soviet citizen!'

'Precisely,' said Shishakov.

'No one's ever doubted it,' said Kovchenko.

'I see, I see,' said Viktor.

Only a little while ago these people had treated him with suspicion and contempt, but now these professions of trust and friendship came quite naturally to them. And Viktor, though he had not forgotten the past, accepted their friendship with the same ease and naturalness.

He felt paralysed by their trust and their kindness. He had no strength. If only they had shouted at him, kicked him, beaten him . . . Then he would have got angry and recovered his strength.

Stalin had spoken to him. They all knew this.

But the letter they wanted him to sign was terrible.

Nothing could make him believe that Doctor Levin and Professor Pletnyov had killed the great writer. His mother had seen Doctor Levin during one of her visits to Moscow. Lyudmila had been treated by him. He was a kind man, gentle and sensitive. Only a monster could slander these two doctors so appallingly.

There was something medieval about these accusations. Assassin-doctors! The murderers of a great writer, the last Russian classic! What was the purpose of such slanders? The Inquisition and its bonfires, the execution of heretics, witch-trials, boiling pitch, the stench of smoke . . . What did all this have to do with Lenin, with the construction of Socialism and the great war against Fascism?

Viktor began to read the first sheet. Shishakov asked whether he was comfortable and had enough light. Wouldn't he rather sit in the armchair? No, thank you, he was quite comfortable as he was.

Viktor read very slowly. The characters pressed against his mind without penetrating it; they were like sand on the skin of an apple.

'Your defence of Pletnyov and Levin – degenerates who are a disgrace not only to medicine, but to the human race as a whole – is grist to the mill of the anti-human ideology of Fascism . . . The Soviet nation stands alone in its struggle against Fascism, the ideology that has brought back medieval witch-trials, pogroms, torture-chambers and the bonfires of the Inquisition.'

How could one read this and not go insane?

'The blood of our sons shed at Stalingrad marks a turning-point in the war with Hitlerism; but you, in coming to the defence of these degenerates, have unwittingly . . .'

I see, I see . . . 'Nowhere in the world do scientists enjoy the affection of the people and the protective care of the State to the same degree as in the Soviet Union . . .'

'Viktor Pavlovich, will it disturb you if we go on talking?'

'No, no. Not at all,' said Viktor. At the same time he was thinking: 'Some lucky people manage to get out of this kind of thing. They fall ill, or they're at their dachas, or . . .'

'I've heard that Iosif Vissarionovich knows about this letter,' said Kovchenko. 'Apparently he approves of this initiative of our scientists.'

'That's why the signature of Viktor Pavlovich . . .' began Badin.

Viktor felt overwhelmed by disgust at his own submissiveness. The great State was breathing on him tenderly; he didn't have the strength to cast himself out into the freezing darkness . . . He had no strength today, no strength at all. He was paralysed, not by fear, but by something quite different – a strange, agonizing sense of his own passivity.

How strange man is. Viktor had found the strength to renounce life itself – and now he seemed unable to refuse candies and cookies.

But how can one just push off an omnipotent hand when it strokes your hair and pats you on the back?

Nonsense! Why was he slandering himself like this? It was nothing to do with candies and cookies. He had always been indifferent to comfort and material well-being. His thoughts, his work, all that was most precious to him, had turned out to be necessary and valuable in the struggle against Fascism. That was a true joy.

What was all this anyway? The doctors had confessed during the preliminary investigation. They had confessed during the trial itself. How could he believe in their innocence when they themselves had confessed to having murdered a great writer?

To refuse to sign the letter would be to show approval of the murder of Gorky! That was unthinkable. Did he doubt that their confessions were genuine? Had they been coerced into making them, then? But there was only one way of forcing an honourable and intelligent man to confess to being a hired assassin, thereby making himself liable to an infamous execution – and that was torture. And it would be insane even to hint at that.

But it was repugnant, quite repugnant, to think of signing this vile letter. All kinds of excuses came to mind, together with the inevitable answers ... 'Comrades, I feel ill, I'm suffering cardiac spasms.' 'Nonsense, you look fine. You're just making excuses.' 'Why do you need my signature, comrades? I'm only known to a very narrow circle of specialists. Very few people outside this country know my name.' 'Nonsense.' (How pleasant to hear that this was nonsense.) 'People abroad do know your name. In any case, it's quite unthinkable to show this letter to comrade Stalin without your signature on it. He might ask: "But why hasn't Shtrum signed?"'

'Comrades, let me say quite frankly, there are certain phrases that seem rather unfortunate. They almost bring into disrepute our whole scientific intelligentsia.' 'Please, Viktor Pavlovich, give us your suggestions. We'll be only too delighted to alter any phrases that you consider unfortunate.'

'Please understand, comrades. Here it says: "the writer Babel, an enemy of the people; the writer Pilnyak, an enemy of the people; the director Meyerhold, an enemy of the people; Academician Vavilov, an enemy of the people ..." I'm a theoretical physicist, a mathematician. Some people consider me schizophrenic, my field of study's so abstract. I'm really not competent to judge these other matters. It's best to leave people like me in peace.' 'Nonsense, Viktor Pavlovich. You have a logical mind and you understand politics extremely well. You know yourself how often you talk about politics and how apt your remarks always are.'

836

'For the love of God! Please understand that I have a conscience. I feel ill, I find all this very painful. I'm under no obligation . . . Why should I have to sign this letter? I'm exhausted. You must allow me the right to a clear conscience.'

But he couldn't get away from a sense of impotence, a sense that he had somehow been hypnotized. He was as obedient as a well-cared-for animal. And then there was fear – fear of ruining his life once again, fear of living in fear.

Could he really oppose himself to the collective again? Go back to his former solitude? It was time he took the world seriously. He had obtained things he had never even dreamed of. He could work in complete freedom; he was treated with solicitous attentiveness. And he hadn't had to beg for any of this; he hadn't repented. He had been victorious. What more could he ask for? Stalin had telephoned him.

'Comrades, this is a very serious matter. I need to think about it. Allow me to put off my decision until tomorrow.'

Viktor immediately imagined all the torment of a sleepless night: doubts, indecision, sudden decisiveness followed by terror, more doubts, another decision. All that was so exhausting. It was worse than malaria. Did he really want to prolong such torture? No, he had no strength. It was better to get it over and done with.

He took out his pen. As he did so, he saw a look of amazement on Shishakov's face. How docile this rebel had now become!

Viktor did no work that day. There were no distractions, no telephone calls. He was simply unable to work. His work seemed dull, empty, pointless.

Who else had signed the letter? Chepyzhin? Ioffe had, but Krylov? And Mandelstam? He wanted to hide behind someone's back. But it had been impossible for him to refuse. It would have been suicide. Nonsense, he could easily have refused. No, he had done the right thing. But then, no one had threatened him. It would have been all right if he had signed out of a feeling of animal fear. But he hadn't signed out of fear. He had signed out of an obscure, almost nauseous, feeling of submissiveness.

Viktor called Anna Stepanovna to his office and asked her to develop a film for tomorrow. It was a control film of experiments carried out with the new apparatus.

She finished noting everything down, but didn't move. Viktor looked at her questioningly.

'Viktor Pavlovich,' she began, 'I once thought this was impossible to put into words, but I feel I have to say it: do you realize how much you have done for me and for others? What you've done for us is more important than any great discovery. I feel better just knowing that you exist. Do you know what the mechanics, cleaners and caretakers say about you? They say that you're an upright man. I often wanted to call at your home, but I was afraid. Do you understand? Even during the most difficult days I had only to think of you and everything seemed easier. Thank you for being the man you are!'

Before Viktor had time to say anything, she had left the office.

He wanted to run down the street and scream ... Anything, anything at all rather than this shame, this torment. But this was only the beginning.

Late in the afternoon his telephone rang.

'Do you know who it is?'

He did indeed. Even his cold fingers on the receiver seemed to recognize the voice. Once again Marya Ivanovna had appeared at a critical moment.

'I'm speaking from a call-box. I can hardly hear you,' said Marya Ivanovna. 'Pyotr Lavrentyevich is feeling better. I've got more time now. If you can, come to the square at eight o'clock tomorrow.'

Suddenly her voice changed.

'My love, my dearest, my light, I'm afraid for you. Someone came round about a letter – you know the one I mean? I'm sure it was you, your strength, that helped Pyotr Lavrentyevich stand his ground. Anyway, it went all right. But I immediately began thinking how much harm you've probably done yourself. You're so awkward and angular. You always come out bleeding, while everyone else just gets a slight knock.'

Viktor put down the receiver and buried his face in his hands. He now understood the position he was in. It wasn't his enemies who were going to punish him, but his friends, the people who loved him. It was their very faith in him that would wound him.

As soon as he got home he phoned Chepyzhin; he didn't even take his coat off. As he dialled his number, he felt certain that he would be wounded yet again – by his dear friend, by his loving teacher.

Lyudmila was standing right there, but he was in too much of a hurry even to tell her what he had done. God, how quickly she was going grey! That's right, that's right, have a go at someone when their hair turns grey!

'All right, I've just heard the bulletin on the radio,' said Chepyzhin. 'But I haven't got much to say about myself. Oh yes, I quarrelled yesterday with certain prominent officials. Have you heard about this letter yet?'

Viktor's lips were quite dry. He licked them and said: 'Yes, vaguely.'

'Yes, yes, it's not something to talk about on the phone. We can discuss it when we next meet – after your trip,' said Chepyzhin.

But all this was nothing. Soon Nadya would be back. Heavens, what had he done?

55

Viktor didn't sleep that night. His heart ached. He felt weighed down by an unimaginable gloom. A conquering hero indeed!

Even when he had been afraid of the woman in the house-manager's office, he had felt stronger and freer than he did now. Now he no longer dared to take part in a discussion, to express the slightest doubt about anything. He had sacrificed his inner freedom. How could he look Chepyzhin in the eye? Or perhaps he would find it no more difficult than all the people who had greeted him so brightly and warmly on his return to the Institute?

Everything he remembered only added to the torture. There was no peace anywhere. Everything he did, even his smiles and gestures, no longer seemed a part of him; they were alien, hostile. Nadya had looked at him that evening with an expression of pitying disgust.

Only Lyudmila – who in the past had annoyed him and ticked him off more than anyone – had been of any comfort. She had simply said: 'Don't torture yourself, Viktor. To me you're the most intelligent and honourable man in the world. If that's what you did, then it's what you had to do.'

Why did he always want to approve of everything? Why had he become so accepting of things he had never been able to tolerate before? Why, whatever people were talking about, did he always have to be the optimist?

The recent military victories had corresponded to a change in his own life. He could see the power of the army, the grandeur of the State; there was light at the end of the tunnel. Why had Madyarov's thoughts come to seem so banal?

He had refused to repent when they threw him out of the Institute. How happy, how full of light he had felt. And what joy he had felt then in the people he loved! Lyudmila, Nadya, Chepyzhin, Zhenya . . . But what would he say now to Marya Ivanovna? He had always been so arrogant about Pyotr Lavrentyevich and his timid submissiveness. And now! As for his mother, he was afraid even to think of her. He had sinned against her too. He was afraid even to touch that last letter of hers. He realized with sorrow and horror how incapable he was of protecting his own soul. The power that had reduced him to slavery lay inside him.

How base he had been! Throwing stones at pitiful, defenceless people who were already spattered with blood!

All this was so painful. He could feel it in his heart. And there were beads of sweat on his forehead.

How could he have been so arrogant? Who had given him the right to boast of his purity and courage, to set himself up as a merciless judge of the weaknesses of others?

Good men and bad men alike are capable of weakness. The difference is simply that a bad man will be proud all his life of one good deed – while an honest man is hardly aware of his good acts, but remembers a single sin for years on end.

Viktor had been so proud of his courage and uprightness; he had laughed at anyone who had shown signs of weakness or fear. And now he too had betrayed people. He was ashamed of himself; he despised himself. The house he lived in, its light and warmth, had crumbled away; nothing was left but dry quicksand.

His friendship with Chepyzhin, his affection for his daughter, his devotion to his wife, his hopeless love for Marya Ivanovna, his human sins and his human happiness, his work, his beloved science, his love for his mother, his grief for her – everything had vanished.

Why had he committed this terrible sin? Everything in the world was insignificant compared to what he had lost. Everything in the world is insignificant compared to the truth and purity of one small man – even the empire stretching from the Black Sea to the Pacific Ocean, even science itself.

Then he realized that it still wasn't too late. He still had the strength to lift up his head, to remain his mother's son.

And he wasn't going to try to console himself or justify what he had done. He wanted this mean, cowardly act to stand all his life as a reproach; day and night it would be something to bring him back to himself. No, no, no! He didn't want to strive to be a hero – and then preen himself over his courage.

Every hour, every day, year in, year out, he must struggle to be a man, struggle for his right to be pure and kind. He must do this with humility. And if it came to it, he mustn't be afraid even of death; even then he must remain a man.

'Well then, we'll see,' he said to himself. 'Maybe I do have enough strength. Your strength, Mother . . .'

56

Evenings in a hut near the Lubyanka . . .

Krymov was lying on his bunk after being interrogated – groaning, thinking and talking to Katsenelenbogen.

The amazing confessions of Bukharin and Rykov, of Kamenev and Zinoviev, the trials of the Trotskyists, of the Right Opposition and the Left Opposition, the fate of Bubnov, Muralov and Shlyapnikov – all these things no longer seemed quite so hard to understand. The hide was being flayed off the still living body of the Revolution so that a new age could slip into it; as for the red, bloody meat, the steaming innards – they were being thrown onto the scrapheap. The new age needed only the hide of the Revolution – and this was being flayed off people who were still alive. Those who then slipped into it spoke the language of the Revolution and mimicked its gestures, but their brains, lungs, livers and eyes were utterly different.

Stalin! The great Stalin! Perhaps this man with the iron will had less will than any of them. He was a slave of his time and circumstances, a dutiful, submissive servant of the present day, flinging open the doors before the new age.

Yes, yes, yes . . . And those who didn't bow down before the new age were thrown on the scrapheap.

He knew now how a man could be split apart. After you've been searched, after you've had your buttons ripped off and your spectacles confiscated, you look on yourself as a physical nonentity. And then in the investigator's office you realize that the role you played in the Revolution and the Civil War means nothing, that all your work and all your knowledge is just so much rubbish. You are indeed a nonentity – and not just physically.

The unity of man's physical and spiritual being was the key to the investigators' almost uninterrupted run of successes. Soul and body are two complementary vessels; after crushing and destroying a man's physical defences, the invading party nearly always succeeded in sending its mobile detachments into the breach in time to triumph over a man's soul, to force him into unconditional capitulation.

He didn't have the strength to think about all this; neither did he have the strength not to think about it.

Who had betrayed him? Who had informed on him? Who had slandered him? Somehow these questions no longer interested him.

He had always been proud of his ability to subordinate his life to logic. But now it was different. Logic said that Yevgenia Nikolaevna had supplied the information about his conversation with Trotsky. But the whole of his present life – his struggle with the investigator, his ability to breathe and to remain himself, to remain comrade Krymov – was founded on one thing: his faith that she could not have done this. He was astonished that he could have lost this certainty for even a few minutes. Nothing on earth could have made him lose faith in Zhenya. He believed in her, even though he knew very well that no one else had known of his conversation with Trotsky, that women are weak and treacherous, and that she had abandoned him at a critical period in his life.

He described his interrogation to Katsenelenbogen, but without making any mention of this incident.

Now Katsenelenbogen no longer clowned and made jokes.

Krymov had been right about him. He was intelligent. But what he said was often both strange and terrible. Sometimes Krymov thought it quite just that the old Chekist should now himself be in a cell in the Lubyanka. He couldn't imagine it otherwise. Sometimes he thought Katsenelenbogen was mad.

Katsenelenbogen was a poet, the laureate of the State security organs.

He recounted with admiration how, during a break at the last Party Congress, Stalin had asked Yezhov why he had carried punitive measures to such extremes; Yezhov, confused, had replied that he had been obeying Stalin's own orders. Stalin had turned to the delegates around him and said, 'And he's a Party member.'

He talked about the horror Yagoda had felt . . .

He reminisced about the great Chekists, connoisseurs of Voltaire, experts on Rabelais, admirers of Verlaine, who had once directed the work of this vast, sleepless building.

He talked about a quiet, kind, old Lett who had worked for years as an executioner; how he always used to ask permission to give the clothes of the man he had just executed to an orphanage. The next moment he would start talking about another executioner who drank day and night and was miserable if he didn't have any work to do; after his dismissal he began visiting State farms around Moscow and slaughtering pigs; he used to carry bottles of pig's blood around with him, saying it had been prescribed by a doctor as a cure for anaemia.

He told of how, in 1937, they had executed people sentenced without right of correspondence every night. The chimneys of the Moscow crematoria had sent up clouds of smoke into the night, and the members of the Communist youth organization enlisted to help with the executions and subsequent disposal of the bodies had gone mad.

He told Krymov about the interrogation of Bukharin, about how obstinate Kamenev had been. Once, when he was developing a theory of his, trying to generalize, the two of them talked all through the night.

He began by telling Krymov about the extraordinary fate of Frankel, an engineer who had been a successful businessman during the NEP period.* At the very beginning of NEP, he had built a car-factory in Odessa. In the mid-twenties he had been arrested and sent to Solovki. From there, he had sent Stalin the outlines of a project that, in the words of the old Chekist, 'bore the mark of true genius'.

In considerable detail, with full economic and scientific substantiation, he had laid out the most efficient manner of exploiting the vast mass of prisoners in order to construct roads, dams, hydroelectric power stations and artificial reservoirs.

The imprisoned 'Nepman' became a lieutenant-general in the MGB – the boss appreciated the importance of his ideas.

The twentieth century finally intruded upon the sacred simplicity of penal servitude, the simplicity of spade, pick, axe, saw and gangs of convicts. The world of the camps was now able to absorb progress; electric locomotives, conveyor belts, bulldozers, electric saws, turbines, coal-cutters, and a vast car- and tractor-park, were all drawn into its orbit. It was able to assimilate cargo and passenger aircraft, radio communications, machine-tools, and the most up-to-date systems for dressing ores. The world of the camps planned and gave birth to mines, factories, reservoirs and giant power stations. The headlong pace of its development made old-fashioned penal servitude seem as touching and absurd as the toy bricks of a child.

Nevertheless, in Katsenelenbogen's view, the camp still lagged behind the world that fed it. There were still all too many scholars and scientists whose talents remained unexploited . . .

The Gulag system had yet to find a use for world-famous historians, mathematicians, astronomers, literary critics, geographers, experts on world painting, linguists with a knowledge of Sanskrit and ancient Celtic dialects. The camp had not yet matured to the stage when it could make use of these people's specialized skills. They worked as manual labourers, or as trusties in clerical jobs or in the Culture and Education Section; or else they wasted away, unable to find any practical application for their vast knowledge – knowledge that often would have been of value not only to Russia, but to the whole world.

Krymov listened. To him, Katsenelenbogen was like a scholar talking about the most important task of his life. He wasn't merely

* New Economic Policy: a period (1921–4) of relative liberalization.

glorifying the camps and singing their praises. He was a genuine researcher, constantly making comparisons, exposing shortcomings and contradictions, revealing similarities and contrasts . . .

Of course there were also shortcomings on the other side of the wire, although in an incomparably less gross form. There were many people – in universities, in publishing houses, in the research institutes of the Academy – who were neither engaged in the tasks for which they were most suited, nor working to their full capacity.

In the camps, Katsenelenbogen went on, the criminals wielded power over the political prisoners. Unruly, ignorant, lazy and corrupt, all too ready to engage in murderous fights and robberies, they were a hindrance both to the productivity of the camps and to their cultural development. But then, even on the other side of the wire, the work of scholars and important cultural figures was often supervised by people of poor education and limited vision.

Life inside the camps could be seen as an exaggerated, magnified reflection of life outside. Far from being contradictory, these two realities were symmetrical.

Now Katsenelenbogen spoke not like a poet, not like a philosopher, but like a prophet.

If one were to develop the system of camps boldly and systematically, eliminating all hindrances and shortcomings, the boundaries would finally be erased. The camp would merge with the world outside. And this fusion would signal the maturity and triumph of great principles. For all its inadequacies, the system of camps had one decisive point in its favour: only there was the principle of personal freedom subordinated, clearly and absolutely, to the higher principle of reason. This principle would raise the camp to such a degree of perfection that finally it would be able to do away with itself and merge with the life of the surrounding towns and villages.

Katsenelenbogen had himself supervised the work of a camp design office; he was convinced that, in the camps, scientists and engineers were capable of solving the most complicated problems of contemporary science or technology. All that was necessary was to provide intelligent supervision and decent living conditions. The old saying about there being no science without freedom was simply nonsense.

'When the levels become equal,' he said, 'when we can place an equals sign between life on either side of the wire, repression will become unnecessary and we shall cease to issue arrest warrants. Prisons and solitary-confinement blocks will be razed to the ground. Any anomalies will be handled by the Culture and Education Section. Mahomed and the mountain will go to meet each other.

'The abolition of the camps will be a triumph of humanitarianism, but this will in no way mean the resurgence of the chaotic, primeval, cave-man principle of personal freedom. On the contrary, that will have become completely redundant.'

After a long silence he added that after hundreds of years this system might do away with itself too, and, in doing so, give birth to democracy and personal freedom.

'There is nothing eternal under the moon,' he said, 'but I'd rather not be alive then myself.'

'You're mad,' said Krymov. 'That's not the heart of the Revolution. That's not its soul. People say that if you work for a long time in a psychiatric clinic you finally go mad yourself. Forgive me for saying this, but it's not for nothing you've been put inside. You, comrade Katsenelenbogen, ascribe to the security organs all the attributes of the deity. It really was time you were replaced.'

Katsenelenbogen nodded good-humouredly.

'Yes, I believe in God. I'm an ignorant, credulous old man. Every age creates the deity in its own image. The security organs are wise and powerful; they are what holds sway over twentieth-century man. Once this power was held by earthquakes, forest-fires, thunder and lightning – and they too were worshipped. And if I've been put inside – well, so have you. It was time to replace you too. Only the future will show which of us is right.'

'Old Dreling's going back home today, back to his camp,' said Krymov, knowing that his words would not be wasted.

'Sometimes that vile old man disturbs my faith,' Katsenelenbogen replied.

57

Krymov heard a quiet voice saying: 'It's just been announced that we've routed the German forces at Stalingrad. I think Paulus has been captured, but I couldn't quite make it out.'

He let out a scream. He was struggling, kicking at the floor. He wanted to talk to that crowd of people in padded jackets and felt boots . . . The sound of their voices was drowning the quiet conversation that was going on beside him. He was in Stalingrad . . . Grekov was making his way towards him over piles of rubble . . .

The doctor was holding him by the hand and saying: 'You must break off for a while . . . repeated injections of camphor . . .'

Krymov swallowed down a ball of salty saliva. 'No, I'm quite all right, thanks to the medicine. You can carry on. But you won't get me to sign anything.'

'You will sign, in the end,' said the investigator, with the good-natured assurance of a factory foreman. 'We've had people more difficult than you.'

This second interrogation session lasted three days. At the end of it Krymov returned to his cell.

The soldier on duty placed a parcel wrapped in white cloth beside him.

'You must sign for this parcel, citizen prisoner.'

Krymov read through the list of contents: onion, garlic, sugar, white rusks. The handwriting was familiar. At the end of the list was written: 'Your Zhenya'.

'Oh God, oh God.' He began to cry.

58

On 1 April, 1943 Stepan Fyodorovich Spiridonov received an extract from the resolution passed by the college of the People's Commissariat of Power Stations. He was to leave Stalingrad and become the director of a small, peat-burning power station in the Urals. It wasn't such a very terrible punishment; he could well have been put on trial. Spiridonov didn't say anything about this at home, preferring to wait till the bureau of the *obkom* had come to their decision. On 4 April, 1943 he received a severe reprimand from the bureau of the *obkom* for abandoning his post without leave at a critical time. This too was a lenient decision; he could well have been expelled from the Party. But to Stepan Fyodorovich it seemed cruelly unjust; his colleagues in the *obkom* knew very well that he had remained at his post until the last day of the defence of Stalingrad; that the Soviet offensive had already begun when he crossed to the left bank to see his daughter who had just given birth in a barge. He had tried to protest during the meeting, but Pryakhin had replied sternly:

'You have the right to appeal against this decision to the Central Control Commission. For my part, I think that comrade Shkiryatov will consider this decision over-lenient.'

'I am certain that the Commission will annul this decision,' Stepan Fyodorovich had insisted, but he had heard stories about Shkiryatov. In the event, he preferred not to appeal.

In any case, he was afraid that there were other reasons for Pryakhin's severity. Pryakhin knew of the family ties between Spiridonov, Yevgenia Nikolaevna Shaposhnikova and Krymov; he was hardly likely to be well-disposed towards a man who knew that he himself was an old friend of Krymov's.

Even if he had wanted to, it would have been quite impossible for Pryakhin to support Spiridonov. If he had done, his enemies – and there are always more than enough of them around a man in a position of power – would have immediately informed the appropriate authorities that, out of sympathy for Krymov, an enemy of the people, Pryakhin was supporting the cowardly deserter, Spiridonov.

It seemed, however, that Pryakhin hadn't even wanted to support Spiridonov. He evidently knew that Krymov's mother-in-law was now living in Spiridonov's flat. He probably also knew that Yevgenia Nikolaevna was in correspondence with her, that she had recently sent her a copy of her letter to Stalin.

After the meeting was over, Spiridonov had gone down to the buffet to buy some sausage and some soft cheese. There he had bumped into Voronin, the head of the *oblast* MGB. Voronin had looked him up and down and said mockingly: 'Doing your shopping just after you've incurred a severe reprimand! You are a good little housekeeper, Spiridonov.'

Spiridonov had given him a pathetic, guilty smile. 'It's for the family. I'm a grandfather now.'

Voronin had smiled back and said: 'And there was I, thinking you were preparing a food-parcel.'

'Well, thank God I'm being sent to the Urals,' Spiridonov had thought. 'I wouldn't last long if I stayed here. But what's going to become of Vera and her little boy?'

He had been driven back to the power station in the cab of a truck. He had sat there in silence, looking through the misted-over glass at the ruined city he would soon be leaving. He remembered how his wife had once gone to work along this pavement now covered in bricks. He thought how the new cables from Sverdlovsk would soon arrive at the station and he himself would no longer be there. He thought about the pimples his grandson was getting on his hands and chest from malnutrition. He thought that a reprimand really wasn't as bad as all that. And then he thought that he wouldn't be awarded the medal 'For the defenders of Stalingrad'. For some reason this last thought upset him more than everything else; more than the imminent parting from the city he was tied to by his work, by his memories of Marusya, by his whole life. He started to swear out loud.

'Who've you got it in for now, Stepan Fyodorovich?' asked the driver. 'Or did you forget something at the *obkom*?'

'Yes, yes,' said Stepan Fyodorovich. 'But it hasn't forgotten me.'

Spiridonov's flat was cold and damp. The empty windows had

been boarded over and there were large areas where the plaster had fallen from the walls. The rooms were heated only by paraffin stoves made from tin. Water had to be carried in buckets, right up to the third floor. One of the rooms had been closed off and the kitchen was used as a storeroom for wood and potatoes.

Stepan Fyodorovich, Vera and her baby, and Alexandra Vladimirovna all lived in the large room that had previously been the dining-room. The small room next to the kitchen, formerly Vera's, was now occupied by Andreyev.

Spiridonov could easily have installed some brick stoves and had the ceilings and walls replastered; he had the necessary materials and there were workmen at hand. He had always been a practical and energetic man; now, though, he seemed uninterested in such matters. As for Vera and Alexandra Vladimirovna, they seemed almost to prefer living amid this destruction. Their lives had fallen apart; if they restored the flat, it would only remind them of all they had lost.

Andreyev's daughter-in-law, Natalya, arrived from Leninsk only a few days after Alexandra Vladimirovna had arrived from Kazan. Having quarrelled with the sister of her late mother-in-law in Leninsk, she had left her son with her and come to stay for a while with her father-in-law.

Andreyev lost his temper with her and said:

'You didn't get on with my wife. And now you're not getting on with her sister. How could you leave little Volodya behind?'

Her life in Leninsk must have been very difficult indeed. As she went into Andreyev's room for the first time, she looked at the walls and ceiling and said: 'Isn't this nice?'

It was hard to see what was nice about the twisted stovepipe, the mound of plaster in the corner and the debris hanging from the ceiling.

The only light came through a small piece of glass set into the boards nailed over the window. This little porthole looked out onto a view that was far from cheerful: a buckled iron roof and some ruined inner walls that were painted blue and pink in alternate storeys.

Soon after her arrival, Alexandra Vladimirovna fell ill. Because of this she had to postpone her visit to the city centre; she had intended to go and look at the ruins of her own house. To begin with, in spite of her illness, she tried to help Vera. She lit the stove, washed nappies, hung them up to dry, and carried some of the rubble out onto the landing; she even tried to bring up the water. But her illness kept getting worse; she shivered even when it was very hot and would suddenly begin to sweat in the freezing kitchen.

She was determined not to go to bed and she didn't let on how bad she was feeling. And then one morning, going to get some wood from the kitchen, she fainted; she fell to the floor and cut her head. Vera and Spiridonov had to put her to bed.

When she had recovered a little, she called Vera into the room.

'You know, I found it harder to live with Lyudmila in Kazan than to live with you here. I came here for my own sake, not just to help you. But I'm afraid I'm going to cause you a lot of trouble before I'm back on my feet.'

'Grandma, I'm very happy to have you here,' said Vera.

But Vera's life really was very difficult. Wood, milk, water – everything was difficult to obtain. It was mild outside, but the rooms themselves were cold and damp; they needed a lot of heating.

Little Mitya had a constant stomach-ache and cried at night; he wasn't getting enough milk from his mother. Vera was busy all day – going out to get milk and bread, doing the laundry, washing the dishes, dragging up buckets of water. Her hands were red and her face was raw from the wind and covered in spots. She felt crushed by the constant work, by her constant feeling of exhaustion. She never did her hair or looked in the mirror and she seldom washed. She was always longing to sleep. By evening she was aching all over; her arms, legs and shoulders were all crying out for rest. She would lie down – and then Mitya would begin to cry. She would get up, change his nappies, feed him and walk about the room with him for a while. An hour later he would start crying again and she would have to get up. At dawn he would wake up for good; her head aching, still dazed with sleep, she would get up in the half-darkness, fetch some wood from the kitchen, light the fire, put some water on to boil for everyone's tea, and start doing the laundry. Surprisingly, she was no longer irritable; she had become meek and patient.

Everything was much easier for her after Natalya arrived.

Andreyev had gone away for a few days soon after her arrival. He wanted to see his factory and his old home in the northern part of Stalingrad. Alternatively, he may have been angry with Natalya for leaving her son in Leninsk – or perhaps he wanted to leave her his ration-card so she wouldn't eat the Spiridonovs' bread.

Natalya had got down to work almost the minute she arrived. She put her heart into the work and everything came easily to her. Sacks of coal, heavy buckets of water, tubs of washing – all this was nothing to her.

Now Vera was able to take Mitya outside for half an hour. She would sit down on a stone and gaze at the mist on the steppe, at the water sparkling in the spring sunshine.

Everything was quiet and the war was now hundreds of kilometres away. Somehow things had seemed easier when the air had been filled with the whine of German planes and the crash of shell-bursts, when life had been full of flames, full of fear and hope. Vera looked at the oozing pimples on her son's face and felt overwhelmed with pity. She felt a similar pity for Viktorov. Poor, poor Vanya! What a miserable, sickly, whining little son he had!

Then she climbed up the three flights of stairs, still covered in litter and rubbish, and returned to work. Her melancholy dissolved in the soapy water, in the smoke from the stove, in the damp that streamed down the walls.

Sometimes her grandmother would call her over and stroke her hair. Her usually calm, clear eyes would take on an expression of unbearable tenderness and sorrow.

Vera never talked to anyone – her father, her grandmother, or even five-month-old Mitya – about Viktorov.

After Natalya's arrival the flat was transformed. She scraped the mould off the walls, whitewashed the dark corners, and scrubbed off the dirt that seemed by then to have become a part of the floorboards. She even got down to the immense task of cleaning the rubbish, flight by flight, from the staircase – a job that Vera had been putting off till it got warm.

She spent half a day repairing the black, snake-like stovepipe. It was sagging horribly and a thick tarry liquid was oozing from the joints and collecting in puddles on the floor. She gave it a coat of whitewash, straightened it out, fastened it with wire and hung empty jam-jars under the dripping joints.

She and Alexandra Vladimirovna became firm friends from the first day – even though one might have expected the old woman to take a dislike to this brash young girl and her constant stream of risqué anecdotes. Natalya also made friends with dozens of other people – the electrician, the mechanic from the turbine room, the lorry-drivers.

Once, when she came back from queuing for food, Alexandra Vladimirovna said to her: 'Someone was asking for you just now – a soldier.'

'A Georgian I suppose?' said Natalya. 'Send him packing if he shows his face here again! The fool's got it into his head he wants to marry me.'

'Already?' asked Alexandra Vladimirovna in astonishment.

'They don't need long. He wants me to go to Georgia with him after the war. He probably thinks I washed the stairs just for him.'

That evening she said to Vera: 'Let's go out tonight. There's a film on in town. Misha can take us in his truck. You and the boy can go in the cab, and I'll go in the back.'

Vera shook her head.

'Go on!' said Alexandra Vladimirovna. 'I'd go myself if only I were a bit stronger.'

'No. It's the last thing I feel like.'

'We've got to go on living, you know. Here we're all widows and widowers.'

'You sit at home all day,' Natalya chided. 'You never go out. And you don't even take proper care of your father. Yesterday I did his washing myself – his socks are all in holes.'

Vera picked up her baby and went out to the kitchen. Holding her son in her arms, she said: 'Mityenka, your mama isn't a widow, is she?'

Spiridonov was always very attentive towards Alexandra Vladimirovna. He helped Vera with the cupping glasses and he twice brought a doctor from the city. Sometimes he pressed a candy into her hand, saying: 'Now don't you go giving that to Vera. That's for you – she's already had one. They're from the canteen.'

Alexandra Vladimirovna knew very well that Spiridonov was in trouble. Sometimes she asked him if he'd heard from the *obkom* yet, but he always shook his head and began talking about something else. One evening, though, after he'd been told that his affair was about to be settled, he came home, sat down on the bed beside her and said: 'What a mess I've got myself into! Marusya would be out of her mind if she knew.'

'What are they accusing you of?'

'Everything.'

Then Natalya and Vera came in and they broke off the conversation.

Looking at Natalya, Alexandra Vladimirovna realized that there is a particular type of strong, stubborn beauty that no amount of hardship can injure. Everything about Natalya was beautiful – her neck, her firm breasts, her legs, her slim arms that she bared almost up to the shoulder. 'A philosopher without philosophy,' she thought to herself. She had noticed before how women used to a life of ease began to fade, to stop taking care of themselves, as soon as they were confronted with hardship; this was what had happened to Vera. She admired women who worked as traffic-controllers for the army, women who laboured in factories or did seasonal work on the land, women who worked in filthy, dusty conditions – and still found time to look in the mirror, to curl their hair, to powder their peeling noses. Yes, she admired the obstinate birds who went on singing no matter how bad the weather.

Spiridonov was also looking at Natalya. He suddenly took Vera by the hand and pulled her towards him. As though begging forgiveness for something, he kissed her.

Apparently quite irrelevantly, Alexandra Vladimirovna said:

'Come on, Stepan! We're neither of us going to die yet. I'm an old woman – and I'm going to get better. I'm good for a few more years.'

He glanced at her and smiled. Natalya filled a basin with warm water and placed it beside the bed. Kneeling down on the floor, she said: 'Alexandra Vladimirovna! It's nice and warm in the room. I'm going to wash your feet for you.'

'You idiot – you must be out of your mind! Get up at once!' shouted Alexandra Vladimirovna.

59

During the afternoon Andreyev came back from the workers' settlement around the factory.

First he went in to see Alexandra Vladimirovna. His sullen face broke into a smile: she had got up that day for the first time. There she was, sitting at the table, her spectacles on her nose, reading a book.

He said it had taken him a long time to find the place where his house had once stood. The whole area was nothing but trenches, craters and debris. Lots of workers had already gone back to the factory, and more were appearing every day. They even had policemen there. He hadn't been able to find out anything about the men who had served in the people's militia. They were burying bodies every day, and they were still finding more in the trenches and cellars. And everywhere you looked there were pieces of twisted metal.

Alexandra Vladimirovna kept on asking questions. She wanted to know where he'd spent the night, whether it had been a difficult journey, what he'd had to eat, how badly the open-hearth furnaces were damaged, what the workers themselves were getting to eat, whether he'd seen the director . . .

That very morning Alexandra Vladimirovna had said to Vera:

'You know I've always made fun of people's superstitions and premonitions. But for once in my life I feel quite certain of something: Pavel Andreyevich is going to bring news from Seryozha.'

She was wrong, but what Andreyev did have to say was still important. The workers had told him that they were getting nothing to eat, no wages, and that the dug-outs and cellars they lived in were cold and damp. The director had become a different person. While the Germans were attacking, he had been everyone's best mate. But now he didn't so much as say hello to anyone. And he'd had a new house built for him, a new car delivered from Saratov . . .

'No one could say things are easy at the power station,' said Andreyev. 'But the workers haven't got it in for Stepan Fyodorovich. They know he's on their side.'

'That's a sad story,' said Alexandra Vladimirovna. 'But what are you going to do yourself, Pavel Andreyevich?'

'I've come back to say goodbye. I'm going home – even if I haven't got a home. I've found myself a place in a cellar with some of the other workers.'

'You're doing the right thing,' said Alexandra Vladimirovna. 'It may not be much of a life there, but it's all you have.'

'Here's something I dug up for you,' he said, taking a rusty thimble out of his pocket and handing it to her.

'I'll soon be going into town myself,' she told him. 'I want to see my own home on Gogol Street. I want to dig up bits of metal and glass too.'

'Are you sure you haven't got out of bed too soon? You look pale.'

'No. I'm just a bit upset by what you've told me. I'd like things on this earth of ours to be different.'

Andreyev gave a little cough. 'You remember Stalin's words the year before last? "My brothers and sisters . . ." But now that the Germans have been defeated, the director builds himself a villa, you can only speak to him with an appointment, and we brothers and sisters are still in our dug-outs.'

'Yes,' said Alexandra Vladimirovna, 'it's a sad story. And still no news of Seryozha — he's just vanished into thin air.'

In the evening Spiridonov came back from Stalingrad. He'd gone out in the morning without telling anyone that his case was to be settled that day.

'Is Andreyev back yet?' he asked in a brusque, authoritative tone. 'Any news of Seryozha?'

Alexandra Vladimirovna shook her head.

Vera could see at once that her father had had too much to drink. She could tell by the way he opened the door and took off his coat, by the way he put down the little presents of food he'd brought, by the tone of his questions and the strange glitter in his unhappy eyes.

He went up to Mitya, who was asleep in the laundry basket, and bent over him.

'Don't you go breathing all over him,' said Vera.

'He'll be all right,' said Spiridonov. 'He'll get used to it.'

'Sit down and have some supper! You've been drinking — and you haven't had a bite to eat with it. Do you know what? Grandmama's just got up for the first time.'

'Now that really is good news!' said Spiridonov. He dropped his spoon into the plate and splashed soup all over his jacket.

'Oh dear, you really have had a few too many,' said Alexandra Vladimirovna. 'What's happened, Stepan? Have you been celebrating?'

Spiridonov pushed away his plate of soup.

'You eat that up!' said Vera.

'Well,' said Spiridonov, 'I've got some news for you all. I've incurred a severe reprimand from the Party, and the Commissariat are transferring me to a small peat-burning generating station in the Sverdlovsk *oblast*. In a word, I'm a has-been. I get two months' salary in advance and they provide me with somewhere to live. I begin handing over tomorrow. We'll be given enough ration-cards for the journey.'

Alexandra Vladimirovna exchanged glances with Vera.

'Well that's certainly something to celebrate!'

'You can have your own room – the best room,' said Spiridonov.

'There will probably only be one room,' said Alexandra Vladimirovna.

'Well, that will be yours, Mama.'

It was the first time in his life that Spiridonov had called her Mama. There were tears in his eyes – no doubt because he'd been drinking.

Natalya came in and Spiridonov changed the subject. 'So what does the old man have to say about the factories?'

'Pavel Andreyevich was waiting for you,' said Natalya, 'but he's just gone to sleep.' She sat down at the table, resting her cheeks on her fists. 'He said the workers hardly have anything to eat at all – just a few handfuls of seeds.

'Stepan Fyodorovich,' she asked suddenly, 'is it true that you're leaving?'

'Yes,' he replied gaily. 'I've heard the news too.'

'The workers are very sorry.'

'They'll be all right. I was at college with Tishka Batrov. He'll make a splendid boss.'

'But who will you find to darn your socks with such artistry?' asked Alexandra Vladimirovna. 'Vera will never manage.'

'Now that really will be a problem,' said Spiridonov.

'It looks like we'll have to send Natalya off to the Urals too,' said Alexandra Vladimirovna.

'Sure!' said Natalya. 'I'll go any time.'

They all laughed. Then there was a strained, uncomfortable silence.

60

Alexandra Vladimirovna decided to accompany Spiridonov and Vera as far as Kuibyshev; she was intending to stay for a while with Yevgenia Nikolaevna.

The day before their departure the new director lent her a car. She set off to visit the ruins of her old home.

On the way she kept asking the driver: 'Now what's this? And what was here before?'

'Before what?' asked the driver irritably.

Three different strata of life lay exposed in the ruins: life before the war, life during the fighting, and life today. One building had started out as a tailor's and dry cleaner's; then the windows had been bricked up, leaving small loopholes where German machine-guns had been mounted; now women queued at these loopholes to receive their bread ration.

Dug-outs and bunkers had sprung up among the ruined houses. These had provided shelter for soldiers, radio-operators and command-posts. Reports had been drawn up and machine-guns had been re-loaded. And now children were playing outside them. Washing was hanging up to dry. The smoke rising up from the chimneys had nothing to do with the war.

The war had given way to peace – a poor, miserable peace that was hardly any easier than the war.

Prisoners-of-war were clearing away heaps of rubble from the main streets. Queues of people with empty milk-cans were waiting outside cellars that now housed food-stores. Rumanian prisoners were lazily digging dead bodies out of some ruins. There were groups of sailors here and there, but no soldiers at all; the driver explained that the Volga fleet was still sweeping for mines. In some places lay sacks of cement and heaps of new beams and planks. Here and there the roads had been newly asphalted.

In one empty square she saw a woman harnessed to a two-wheeled cart loaded with bundles. Two children were helping, pulling on ropes tied to the shafts.

Everybody wanted to go back into Stalingrad, back to their homes, but Alexandra Vladimirovna was about to leave.

'Are you sorry that Spiridonov's leaving?' she asked the driver.

'What does it matter to me? Spiridonov worked me hard, and so will the new man. They just sign their instructions – and off I go.'

'What's this?' she asked, pointing to a thick, blackened wall with gaping windows.

'Just various offices. What they should do is let people live here.'

'And what was it before?'

'This was the headquarters of Paulus himself. It was here he was taken prisoner.'

'And before that?'

'The department store. Don't you recognize it?'

The wartime city seemed to have overshadowed the old Stalingrad. It was all too easy to imagine the German officers coming up from the cellars, to see the German field-marshal walking past this blackened wall while the sentries all stood to attention. But was it really here that she had bought a length of material for a coat or a watch as a birthday present for Marusya? Had she really come here with Seryozha and got him a pair of skates in the sports department on the first floor?

People who visit Verdun, the battlefield of Borodino or Malakhov Kurgan at Sebastopol must find it equally strange to find children playing, women doing their washing, carts full of hay and old men carrying rakes. Columns of French soldiers and trucks covered in tarpaulins once passed over fields that are now full of vines; now there is only a hut, a few apple trees and some *kolkhoz* sheep where Murat's cavalry advanced, where Kutuzov sat in his armchair and ordered the Russian infantry to counter-attack with a wave of his tired hand. Nakhimov stood on a mound where now there are only chickens and a few goats searching for blades of grass between the stones; this is where the flash-bombs described by Tolstoy were launched, where English bullets whistled and wounded soldiers screamed.

Alexandra Vladimirovna found something equally incongruous in these queues of women, these small huts, these old men unloading planks, these shirts hanging up to dry, these patched sheets, these stockings twirling about like snakes, these notices pasted over lifeless façades.

She had realized how flat everything now seemed to Spiridonov when he had talked about the arguments in the district committee over the allocation of cement, planks and manpower. She had sensed how bored he was by the endless articles in *Stalingradskaya Pravda* about the clearing away of rubble, the cleaning up of streets, the construction of new public baths and workers' canteens. He had only come to life when he talked about the bombing, the fires, the visits of General Shumilov, the German tanks advancing from the hill-tops, the counter-fire of the Soviet artillery.

It was on these streets that the war had been decided. The outcome of this battle was to determine the map of the post-war world, to determine the greatness of Stalin or the terrible power of Adolf Hitler. For ninety days one word had filled both the Kremlin and the Berchtesgaden – Stalingrad.

Stalingrad was to determine future social systems and philosophies of history. The shadow of all this had blinded people to the provincial city that had once led a commonplace, ordered life.

Alexandra Vladimirovna asked the driver to stop, then got out of the car and picked her way with some difficulty through the debris that still littered the deserted street. She stared at the ruins, half-recognizing the remains of houses.

When she came to her own home, she found that the wall facing the street was still there. Through the gaping windows, her farsighted eyes could make out the light blue and green walls of her flat. But the rooms had no floors or ceilings and there was nothing left of the staircase. The bricks had been darkened by flames; here and there they had been scarred by splinters.

With a terrible clarity, she was aware of all that life had been for her: her daughters, her unfortunate son, Seryozha, her many irrevocable losses, her present homelessness. There she was, looking at the ruins of her home – an old, sick woman in an old coat and trodden-down shoes.

What was in store for her? Although she was seventy years old, she had no idea. What was in store for the people she loved? Again she had no idea. Through the empty windows of her house she could see the spring sky looking down at her.

The lives of those close to her were unsettled, confused, full of doubts and mistakes, full of grief. What would happen to Lyudmila? What would be the outcome of her family troubles? Where was Seryozha? Was he even alive? How hard things were for Viktor Shtrum! What would happen to Vera and Stepan Fyodorovich? Would Stepan be able to rebuild his life again and find peace? What path would Nadya follow – that clever little girl who was so difficult and so kind-hearted? And Vera? Would she be broken by the hardships and loneliness she had to endure? And Zhenya? Would she follow Krymov to Siberia? Would she end up in a camp herself and die the same death as Dmitry? Would Seryozha forgive the State for the deaths of his innocent mother and father?

Why were their destinies so confused, so obscure?

As for those who had been killed or executed, they were still alive in her memory. She could remember their smiles, their jokes, their laughter, their sad lost eyes, their hopes and despairs.

Mitya had embraced her and said: 'It doesn't matter, Mama. Please don't worry yourself about me. There are good people even in camp.' And there was young Sonya Levinton with her dark hair and the down over her upper lip. She was declaiming poems with a fierce gaiety. There was Anya Shtrum, as pale and sad as ever, as intelligent and full of mockery. And young Tolya, stuffing down his macaroni cheese – she had got quite annoyed with him for eating so noisily and for never helping Lyudmila: 'Is it too much to ask for a glass of water?' 'All right, all right, but why ask me? Why don't you ask Nadya?' And Marusya. Marusya! Zhenya always made fun of your preaching. And you tried so hard to make Stepan into a good, right-thinking Communist ... And then you drowned in the Volga with little Slava Byerozkin and old Varvara Alexandrovna ... And Mostovskoy. Please explain to me, Mikhail Sidorovich ... Heavens, what could he explain now?

All of them had been unsettled; all of them had doubts and secret griefs. All of them had hoped for happiness. Some of them had come to visit her and others had just written letters. And all the time, in spite of the closeness of her large family, she had had a deep sense of her own isolation.

And here she was, an old woman now, living and hoping, keeping faith, afraid of evil, full of anxiety for the living and an equal concern for the dead; here she was, looking at the ruins of her home, admiring the spring sky without knowing that she was admiring it, wondering why the future of those she loved was so obscure and the past so full of mistakes, not realizing that this very obscurity and unhappiness concealed a strange hope and clarity, not realizing that in the depths of her soul she already knew the meaning of both her own life and the lives of her nearest and dearest, not realizing that even though neither she herself nor any of them could tell what was in store, even though they all knew only too well that at times like these no man can forge his own happiness and that fate alone has the power to pardon and chastise, to raise up to glory and to plunge into need, to reduce a man to labour-camp dust, nevertheless neither fate, nor history, nor the anger of the State, nor the glory or infamy of battle has any power to affect those who call themselves human beings. No, whatever life holds in store – hard-won glory, poverty and despair, or death in a labour camp – they will live as human beings and die as human beings, the same as those who have already perished; and in this alone lies man's eternal and bitter victory over all the grandiose and inhuman forces that ever have been or will be . . .

Vera and Alexandra Vladimirovna were in a state of feverish anxiety during the whole of the last day. As for Spiridonov, he had been drinking since early in the morning. Workers were continually coming round and demanding to see him, but he was always out. He was sorting out his remaining affairs, calling at the *raykom*, ringing up friends, having his papers stamped at the military commissariat, talking and joking as he walked round the workshops; once, when he found himself alone for a moment in the turbine-room, he pressed his cheek against a cold fly-wheel and closed his eyes in exhaustion.

Meanwhile Vera was packing up belongings, drying nappies over the stove, preparing bottles of boiled milk for Mitya and stuffing bread into a bag. She was about to part for ever with both Viktorov and her mother. They would remain for ever alone; no one here would ask after them or spare them so much as a thought.

She was steadied by the thought that she was now the oldest in her family. She was calmer now, more reconciled to hardship than anyone else.

Looking at her granddaughter's tired, inflamed eye-lids, Alexandra Vladimirovna said: 'That's the way things are, Vera.

There's nothing more difficult than saying goodbye to a house where you've suffered.'

Natalya had promised to bake some pies for the journey. She had gone off that morning, laden with wood and provisions, to a woman she knew who still possessed a proper Russian stove. There she began preparing the filling and rolling out the dough. Her face turned bright red as she stood over the oven; it looked young and extremely beautiful. She glanced at herself in the mirror, laughed and began to powder her nose and cheeks with flour. But when her friend went out of the room, she wept into the dough.

In the end her friend noticed her tears. 'What's the matter, Natalya? Why are you crying?'

'I've grown used to them. She's a splendid old woman. And I feel sorry for Vera and her little boy.'

Her friend listened attentively and said: 'Nonsense. You're not crying because of the old woman.'

'I am,' said Natalya.

The new director promised to release Andreyev, but he wanted him to stay on for another five days. Natalya announced that she'd stay till then and then go back to her son in Leninsk. 'And then,' she said, 'we'll see how things go.'

'What will you see?' asked Andreyev.

She didn't answer. Most likely, she had been crying because she couldn't see anything at all. Andreyev didn't like his daughter-in-law to show too much concern over him; she had the feeling that he still hadn't forgiven her for the quarrels she'd had with his wife.

Spiridonov came back towards lunchtime. He told them all how the workers in the machine-room had said goodbye to him.

'Well, there's been a real pilgrimage here,' said Alexandra Vladimirovna. 'At least five or six people have come to see you.'

'Well, is everything ready, then? The truck will be here at five sharp.' He gave a little smile. 'We can thank Batrov for that.'

His affairs were all in order and his belongings were packed, but Spiridonov still felt a sense of nervous, drunken excitement. He began redoing the bundles, moving the suitcases from one place to another; it was as though he couldn't wait to be off. Then Andreyev came in from the office and asked:

'How are things? Has there been a telegram from Moscow yet about the cables?'

'There haven't been any telegrams at all.'

'The swine! They're sabotaging the whole thing. We could have had the first installations ready for May Day.'

Andreyev turned to Alexandra Vladimirovna and said: 'You really are foolish. Setting off on a journey like this at your age!'

'Don't you worry yourself! I've got nine lives. Anyway, what else can I do? Go back to my flat on Gogol Street? And the painters have already been round here. They're about to start the repairs for the new director.'

'The lout! He could have waited one more day!' said Vera.

'Why's he a lout?' asked Alexandra Vladimirovna. 'Life has to go on.'

'Well? Is lunch ready? What are we waiting for?' asked Spiridonov.

'We're waiting for Natalya and her pies.'

'We're going to miss the train waiting for those pies,' he grumbled.

He didn't feel like eating, but he'd put some vodka aside for their final meal and he did feel like a good drink. He also very much wanted just to go and sit in his office for a few minutes, but it would have been too awkward – Batrov was having a meeting with the heads of the different shops. The bitterness he felt made him still more desperate for a drink. He kept shaking his head and saying: 'We're going to be late, we're going to be late.'

There was something agreeable about this fear of being late, this anxious waiting for Natalya. He didn't realize that it was because it reminded him of times before the war when he'd gone to the theatre with his wife. Then too he had looked constantly at his watch and repeated anxiously: 'We're going to be late.'

He very much wanted to hear something nice about himself. This need made him still more depressed.

'Why should anyone pity me?' he moaned. 'I'm a coward and a deserter. Who knows? I might even have had the cheek to expect a medal "For the defenders of Stalingrad".'

'All right then, let's have lunch!' said Alexandra Vladimirovna. She could see that Spiridonov was in a bad way.

Vera brought in a saucepan of soup and Spiridonov got out the bottle of vodka. Alexandra Vladimirovna and Vera both said they didn't want any.

'So only the men are drinking,' said Spiridonov. 'But maybe we should wait for Natalya.'

At that moment Natalya came in with a large bag and began spreading her pies out on the table. Spiridonov poured out full glasses for Andreyev and himself and half a glass for Natalya.

'Last summer,' said Andreyev, 'we were all eating pies at Alexandra Vladimirovna's home on Gogol Street.'

'Well, I'm sure these will be every bit as delicious,' said Alexandra Vladimirovna.

'What a lot of us there were on that day,' said Vera. 'And now there's just you, Grandmama, and me and Papa.'

'We certainly routed the Germans,' said Andreyev.

'It was a great victory – but we paid a price for it,' said Alexandra Vladimirovna. 'Have some more soup! We'll be eating nothing but dry food on the journey. It will be days before we see anything hot.'

'No, it's not an easy journey,' said Andreyev. 'And it will be difficult getting on the train. It's a train from the Caucasus that stops here on its way to Balashov. It's always crammed with soldiers. But they will have brought some white bread with them.'

'The Germans bore down on us like a storm-cloud,' said Spiridonov. 'But where are they now? Soviet Russia has vanquished them.'

He remembered how not long ago they could hear German tanks from the power station. And now those tanks were hundreds of kilometres away. Now the main fighting was around Belgorod, Chuguyev and Kuban.

But he was unable to forget his wound for more than a moment. 'All right, so I'm a deserter,' he muttered. 'But what about the men who reprimanded me? Who are they? I demand to be judged by the soldiers of Stalingrad. I'm ready to confess all my faults before them.'

'And Mostovskoy was sitting right next to you, Pavel Andreyevich.'

But Spiridonov wouldn't be diverted. His resentment welled up again. He turned to his daughter and said: 'I phoned the first secretary of the *obkom* to say goodbye. After all, I am the only director who stayed on the right bank through the whole of the battle. But his assistant, Barulin, just said: "Comrade Pryakhin's unable to speak to you. He's engaged."'

As though she hadn't even heard her father, Vera said: 'And there was a young lieutenant, a comrade of Tolya's, sitting next to Seryozha. I wonder where he is now.'

She wanted so much to hear someone say: 'Who knows? Maybe he's alive and well, still at the front.' Even that would have consoled her a little. But Stepan Fyodorovich just went on with his own thoughts.

'So I said to him: "I'm leaving today. You know that very well." "All right then," he said, "you can address him in writing." To hell with them all! Let's have another drink! We'll never sit at this table again.'

He turned to Andreyev and raised his glass. 'Don't think badly of me when I'm gone!'

'What do you mean, Stepan Fyodorovich? We workers are on your side.'

Spiridonov downed his vodka, sat quite still for a moment – as though he'd just surfaced from under the sea – and then attacked his soup. It was very quiet; the only sound was Spiridonov munching his pie and tapping away with his spoon. Then little Mitya started screaming. Vera got to her feet, walked over to him and took him in her arms.

'You must eat your pie, Alexandra Vladimirovna!' said Natalya in a very quiet voice, as though it were a matter of life and death.

'Certainly!' said Alexandra Vladimirovna.

With drunken, joyous solemnity, Spiridonov announced:

'Natalya, let me say this is everyone's presence! There's absolutely nothing to keep you here. Go back to Leninsk for your son – and then come and join us in the Urals! It's not good to be on one's own.'

He tried to catch her eyes, but she lowered her head. All he could see was her forehead and her dark, handsome eye-brows.

'And you too, Pavel Andreyevich! Things will be easier for us if we stick together.'

'What do you mean? Do you think I'm going to begin a new life at my age?'

Spiridonov glanced at Vera. She was standing by the table with Mitya in her arms, crying. For the first time that day he saw the walls of the room he was about to leave. Everything else became suddenly of no importance: the pain of dismissal, the loss of the work he loved, his loss of standing, the burning shame and resentment that had prevented him from sharing in the joy of victory.

The old woman sitting next to him, the mother of the wife he had loved and now lost for ever, kissed him on the head and said: 'It doesn't matter, Stepan my dear. It doesn't matter. It's life.'

61

The stove had been lit the previous evening and the hut had felt stuffy all night. The tenant and her husband, a wounded soldier who'd only just come out of hospital, didn't go to sleep until it was nearly morning. They were talking in whispers — so as not to wake up the old landlady or the little girl who was sleeping on top of a trunk.

The old woman was unable to sleep. She was annoyed by all this whispering. She couldn't help but listen. She couldn't help but try to link together the odd phrases she overheard. If only they'd talk normally! Then she'd just listen to them for a little while and fall fast asleep. She wanted to bang on the wall and say: 'What's all this whispering about? Do you really think what you're saying is that interesting?'

She kept making out odd phrases here and there:

'I came straight from hospital. I couldn't get you any candies. It would have been another story if I'd been at the front.'

'And all I had to give you was potatoes fried in oil.'

Then the whispering became inaudible again. Probably the woman was crying.

Then she heard the words:

'It's my love that kept you alive.'

'I bet he's a real breaker of hearts!' thought the old woman.

She dozed off for a few minutes. She must have been snoring — when she woke up, the voices were louder.

'Pivovarov wrote to me in hospital. I'd only just been made a lieutenant-colonel. And now they're putting me forward for promotion again. It's the general's doing – he put me in command of a division. And I've been awarded the Order of Lenin. And all for that day when I was buried under the ground! When I had lost touch with my battalions and all I could do was sing stupid songs. I keep feeling as though I'm an impostor. I can't tell you how awkward I feel.'

Then they began whispering again. They must have noticed that the old woman was no longer snoring.

The old woman lived on her own. Her husband had died before the war and her one daughter lived in Sverdlovsk. She didn't have anyone at the front herself and she couldn't understand why she had been so upset by this soldier's arrival.

She didn't much like her tenant; she thought of her as a stupid, empty woman who couldn't cope on her own. She always got up late and she didn't look after her daughter – the girl went around in torn clothes and never ate proper meals. Most of the time her tenant seemed just to sit at the table, looking out of the window and not saying a word. Now and then, when the mood took her, she did get down to work – and then it turned out she could do everything. She sewed, washed the floors and made excellent soup; she knew how to milk a cow – even though she was from the city. Something was obviously wrong in her life. As for the girl, she was a strange little brat. She loved messing about with grasshoppers, cockroaches and beetles. And she didn't play with them like ordinary children – she was always kissing them and telling them stories. Then she would let them go and start crying, calling for them to come back. Last autumn the old woman had brought her a hedgehog from the forest. The girl had followed him wherever he went. He only had to give a little grunt and she was beside herself with joy. And if he went under the chest of drawers, she'd just sit there on the floor and wait for him. She'd say to her mother: 'Sh! Can't you see he's asleep?' Then the hedgehog had gone back to the forest and the little girl hadn't eaten for two whole days.

The old woman had lived in constant fear that her tenant was going to hang herself – and that she'd be left with the little girl. The last thing she wanted at her age were new anxieties.

'I don't owe anyone anything,' she would say. She couldn't rid herself of this anxiety. One morning she was going to wake up and find the woman hanging there from the ceiling. What on earth would she do with the little girl?

She'd been quite certain that the tenant's husband had abandoned her. Probably he'd found another, younger, woman at the front. That was why her tenant was always so sad. She got very few letters from him, and those she did get didn't seem to make her any happier. And she was a real clam – it was impossible to get a word out of her. Even the neighbours had noticed how peculiar she was.

The old woman had had a hard time with her husband. He was a drunkard – and a very quarrelsome one at that. And instead of just beating her like anyone else, he used to go for her with a stick or a poker. He used to beat their daughter too. And he wasn't much joy even when he was sober. He was always fussing, poking his nose into her saucepans, complaining about this and that. Everything she did was wrong – the way she milked the cow, the way she made the bed, the way she cooked. It was impossible for her to put a foot right. He was a miser, too. And he cursed and swore the whole time. In the end she'd become just as bad herself. She even swore at her beloved cow. She hadn't shed one tear over her husband when he died. He hadn't left her alone even when he was an old man, and he was quite impossible when he was drunk. He might at least have tried to behave in front of his own daughter. She felt ashamed to think of it. And how he'd snored! That had been even worse when he was drunk. And as for that cow of hers! The obstinate beast was always running away from the herd. How could an old woman ever keep up with her?

She listened to the whispering behind the partition and remembered her own difficult life with her husband. She felt pity as well as resentment. He had worked hard and earned little. They'd never have got by without the cow. And it was the dust from his mine that had killed him. But she hadn't died – she was still going strong. Once he'd brought her some beads from Yekaterinburg. She'd passed them on to her daughter . . .

Early next morning, before the little girl had woken up, the tenant and her husband set off for the next village. There they'd be able to buy some white bread with his army ration-card.

They walked along hand in hand, without saying a word. They had to go one and a half kilometres through the forest, climb down the slope and then walk along the shore of the lake.

The snow here hadn't thawed. Its large, rough crystals were filled with the blue of the lake-water. But on the sunny side of the hill the snow was just beginning to melt. The ditch beside the path was full of gurgling water. The glitter of the snow, the water and the ice on the puddles was quite blinding. There was so much light, it was so intense, that they seemed almost to have to force their way through it. It disturbed them and got in their way; when they stepped on the thin film of ice over the puddles, it seemed to be light that was crunching under their feet, breaking up into thin, splinter-like rays. And it was light that was flowing down the ditch beside the path; where the path was blocked by stones, the light swelled up, foaming and gurgling. The spring sun seemed to be closer to the earth than ever. The air was cool and warm at the same time.

The officer felt as though his throat, which had been scorched by frost and vodka, which had been blackened by tobacco, dust, fumes and swear-words, had suddenly been rinsed clean by this blue light. Then they went into the forest, into the shade of the young pine trees. Here the snow hadn't melted at all. There were squirrels hard at work in the branches above; the icy surface of the snow was littered with gnawed fir-cones and flakes of wood.

The forest seemed silent. The many layers of branches kept off the light; instead of tinkling and gurgling, it was like a soft cloak swathed round the earth.

They walked on in silence. They were together – and that was enough to make everything round about seem beautiful. And it was spring.

Still without saying anything, they came to a stop. Two fat bullfinches were sitting on the branch of a fir tree. Their red breasts seemed like flowers that had suddenly blossomed on enchanted snow. The silence was very strange.

This silence contained the memory of last year's leaves and rains, of abandoned nests, of childhood, of the joyless labour of ants, of the treachery of foxes and kites, of the war of all against all, of good and evil born together in one heart and dying with this heart, of storms and thunderbolts that had set young hares and huge tree-trunks trembling. It was the past that slept under the snow, beneath this cool half-light – the joy of lovers' meetings, the hesitant chatter of April birds, people's first meetings with neighbours who had seemed strange at first and then become a part of their lives.

Everyone was asleep – the strong and the weak, the brave and the timid, the happy and the unhappy. This was a last parting, in an empty and abandoned house, with the dead who had now left it for ever.

Somehow you could sense spring more vividly in this cool forest than on the sunlit plain. And there was a deeper sadness in this silence than in the silence of autumn. In it you could hear both a lament for the dead and the furious joy of life itself.

It was still cold and dark, but soon the doors and shutters would be flung open. Soon the house would be filled with the tears and laughter of children, with the hurried steps of a loved woman and the measured gait of the master of the house.

They stood there, holding their bags, in silence.

1960

LIST OF CHIEF CHARACTERS

The Shaposhnikov Family and their Circle

Shaposhnikova, Lyudmila Nikolaevna

Shtrum, Viktor Pavlovich — *Lyudmila's husband, a physicist, member of the Academy of Sciences*

Nadya — *daughter of Viktor and Lyudmila*

Shaposhnikova, Alexandra Vladimirovna — *Lyudmila's mother*

Shaposhnikova, Yevgenia Nikolaevna ('Zhenya') — *Lyudmila's sister*

Abarchuk — *Lyudmila's first husband, arrested in 1937*

Shaposhnikov, Anatoly ('Tolya') — *Lyudmila's son by Abarchuk, a lieutenant in the army*

Spiridinova, Marusya — *sister of Lyudmila and Yevgenia, drowned in the Volga during the evacuation of Stalingrad*

Spiridinov, Stepan Fyodorovich — *Marusya's husband, director of the Stalingrad Power Station*

Spiridinova, Vera — *daughter of Marusya and Stepan Fyodorovich*

Shaposhnikov, Dmitry ('Mitya') — *brother to Lyudmila, Yevgenia and Marusya, now in a camp as a political prisoner*

Shaposhnikov, Seryozha — *Dmitry's son, a soldier at the front, in house 6/1*

Krymov, Nikolay Grigorevich — *Yevgenia's former husband, a commissar in the Red Army*

Viktor's Colleagues

Sokolov, Pyotr Lavrentyevich	*mathematician in Viktor's laboratory*
Sokolova, Marya Ivanovna	*his wife*
Markov, Vyacheslav Ivanovich	*in charge of experimental work in Viktor's laboratory*
Savostyanov	*laboratory assistant*
Weisspapier, Anna Naumovna	*laboratory assistant*
Loshakova, Anna Stepanovna	*laboratory assistant*
Nozdrin, Stepan Stepanovich	*technician in Viktor's laboratory*
Perepelitsyn	*electrician in Viktor's laboratory*
Svechin	*head of the magnetic laboratory*
Postoev	*a doctor of physics*
Gavronov, Professor	*a specialist in the history of physics*
Gurevich, Natan Samsonovich	*a doctor of physics*
Chepyzhin, Dmitry Petrovich	*director of the Institute*
Pimenov	*administrative director of the Institute while it is in Kazan*
Shishakov, Aleksey Alekseyevich	*Academician, appointed administrative and scientific director on the Institute's return to Moscow*
Kovchenko, Kasyan Terentyevich	*appointed deputy director*
Dubyonkov	*head of the personnel department*
Ramskov	*secretary of the Institute Party Committee*
Badin	*head of the Scientific Section of the Central Committee*

Viktor's Circle in Kazan

Madyarov, Leonid Sergeyevich	*historian, Sokolov's brother-in-law*
Artelev, Vladimir Romanovich	*chemical engineer, the Sokolovs' landlord*
Karimov, Akhmet Usmanovich	*translator into Tartar*

In the German Concentration Camp

Mostovskoy, Mikhail Sidorovich	*an Old Bolshevik*
Gardi	*an Italian priest*
Ikonnikov-Morzh	*a former Tolstoyan, called 'a holy fool' by his fellow prisoners*
Chernetsov	*a former Menshevik*
Yershov, Major	*a captured Russian officer*
Nikonov, Major	*a captured Russian officer*
Osipov, Brigade Commissar	*a captured Russian officer*
Zlatokrylets, Colonel	*a captured Russian officer*
Gudz, General	*a captured Russian officer*
Kirillov, Major	*a captured Russian officer*
Kotikov	*a captured Russian officer, a Party member*
Liss, Obersturmbannführer	*SS representative on the camp administration*

In the Russian Labour Camp

Abarchuk	*Lyudmila's former husband*
Nyeumolimov	*former commander of a cavalry brigade during the Civil War*
Monidze	*former member of the Presidium of the Communist Youth International*
Rubin, Abrasha	*a medical orderly*
Barkhatov	*a criminal, Abarchuk's assistant*
Tungusov	*an old guards officer*
Ugarov, Kolka	*a criminal*
Konashevich	*a former aircraft mechanic and boxing champion*
Magar	*an Old Bolshevik, Abarchuk's former teacher*
Zakorov	*a criminal, in charge of Abarchuk's hut*
Perekrest	*leader of the coal-team*
Dolgoruky, Prince	*a mystic*
Stepanov	*former professor at the Economics Institute*

| Mishanin, Captain | *the operations officer* |
| Trufelev | *a medical orderly* |

On the Journey to the Gas Chamber

Levinton, Sofya Osipovna	*an army doctor, friend of Yevgenia*
David	*a boy*
Borisovna, Musya	*a librarian*
Bukhman, Rebekka	*a relative of David's*
Rozenberg, Naum	*an accountant*
Karasik, Natasha	*a shy girl*
Yankevich, Lazar	*a machinist*
Deborah Samuelovna	*his wife*
Vinokur, Musya	*a pretty girl*
Khmelkov, Anton	*a member of the special unit*
Zhuchenko, Trofima	*a member of the special unit*
Kaltluft, Sturmbannführer	*the commander of a Sonderkommando*

In the Lubyanka Prison

Krymov, Nikolay Grigorevich	*Yevgenia's former husband, a commissar*
Dreling	*a Menshevik*
Bogoleev	*an art historian and poet*
Katsenelenbogen	*a former Chekist and Moscow compere*

In Kuibyshev

Shaposhnikova, Yevgenia Nikolaevna	*Lyudmila's sister*
Genrikhovna, Jenny	*former governess to the Shaposhnikov family*
Shargorodsky, Vladimir Andreyevich	*an aristocrat, in exile from 1926–33*
Limonov	*a man of letters from Moscow*
Rizin, Lieutenant-Colonel	*Yevgenia's boss*
Grishin	*head of the passport department*
Glafira Dmitrievna	*senior tenant in Yevgenia's lodgings*

At Stalingrad Power Station

Spiridonov, Stepan Fyodorovich	*the director*
Spiridinova, Vera	*his daughter*
Andreyev, Pavel Andreyevich	*a guard*
Nikolayev	*the Party organizer*
Kamyshov	*the chief engineer*

Getmanov's Circle in Ufa

Getmanov, Dementiy Trifonovich	*secretary of an obkom, appointed commissar to Novikov's tank corps*
Getmanova, Galina Terentyevna	*his wife*
Nikolay Terentyevich	*Galina's brother*
Mashuk	*an official in the State security organs*
Sagaydak	*an executive in the propaganda department of the Ukrainian Central Committee*

Members of a Fighter Squadron of the Russian Air Force

Viktorov, Lieutenant	*a pilot, Vera Spiridinova's lover*
Zakabluka, Major	*the commander of the squadron*
Solomatin, Lieutenant	*a pilot*
Yeromin, Lieutenant	*a pilot*
Korol, Junior Lieutenant	*a pilot*
Martynov, Wing-Commander Vanya	*a pilot*
Golub, Political Instructor	*billeted with Viktorov*
Skotnoy, Lieutenant Vovka	*a pilot, billeted with Viktorov*
Berman	*the squadron commissar*
Velikanov, Lieutenant	*a pilot, the duty-officer*

NOVIKOV'S TANK CORPS

Novikov, Colonel Pyotr Pavlovich	*the commanding officer, Yevgenia's lover*
Nyeudobnov, General Illarion Innokyentyevich	*Novikov's chief of staff*
Getmanov, Dementiy Trifonovich	*the commissar*
Karpov, Colonel	*the commander of the 1st Brigade*
Byelov	*the commander of the 2nd Brigade*
Makarov	*the commander of the 3rd Brigade*
Fatov	*a battalion commander*
Vershkov	*Novikov's orderly*
Kharitonov	*Novikov's driver*

OFFICERS OF THE SOVIET ARMY IN STALINGRAD

Yeremenko, Lieutenant-General*	*commander-in-chief of the Stalingrad Front*
Zakharov, Lieutenant-General*	*Yeremenko's chief of staff*
Chuykov, Lieutenant-General*	*commander of the 62nd Army*
Krylov, Major-General*	*Chuykov's chief of staff*
Gurov, Divisional Commissar*	
Pozharsky*	*artillery commander of the 62nd Army*
Batyuk, Lieutenant-Colonel*	*commander of 284th Rifle Division*
Guryev, Major-General*	*commander of 39th Guards Division*
Rodimtsev*	*commander of the 13th Guards Division*
Belsky	*Rodimtsev's chief of staff*
Vavilov	*commissar of Rodimtsev's division*
Borisov, Colonel	*Rodimtsev's second-in-command*
Byerozkin, Major	*in command of a regiment*
Glushkov	*Byerozkin's orderly*
Podchufarov, Captain	*in command of a battalion*

* Historical characters.

Movshovich	in command of a battalion of sappers
Pivovarov	battalion commissar in Byerozkin's regiment
Soshkin	political instructor in Byerozkin's regiment

SOLDIERS IN HOUSE 6/1

Grekov, Captain	'house-manager'
Antsiferov, Sergeant-Major	in command of sapper detachment
Vengrova, Katya	a radio-operator
Kolomeitsev	a gunner
Batrakov, Lieutenant	in command of artillery observation post
Bunchuk	an observer
Lampasov	a plotter
Klimov	a scout
Chentsov	a member of the mortar-crew
Lyakhov	a sapper
Zubarev, Lieutenant	in command of the infantry
Shaposhnikov, Seryozha	a soldier
Perfilev	a soldier
Polyakov	a soldier

IN THE KALMYK STEPPE

Darensky, Lieutenant-Colonel	a staff officer from Front Headquarters
Alla Sergeyevna	the wife of an Army commander
Claudia	the mistress of the Member of the Military Soviet
Bova, Lieutenant-Colonel	the chief of staff of an artillery regiment

Officers of the German Army in Stalingrad

Paulus, General Friedrich* *commander of the 6th Army*
Schmidt, General* *Paulus' chief of staff*
Adam, Colonel* *Paulus' adjutant*
Bach, Lieutenant Peter *an infantry officer*
Krap *an officer in charge of a detachment of scouts, in hospital with Bach*
Gerne, Lieutenant *a staff officer in hospital with Bach*
Fresser, Lieutenant *an officer in hospital with Bach*
Lenard *an SS officer*
Chalb *the commander of the military police*
Eisenaug, Sergeant *an NCO in Bach's company*

* Historical characters.